MW00618482

Praise for *The Economics of Software Quality*

"This book provides the best treatment on the subject of economics of software quality that I've seen. Peppered with valuable industry data, in-depth analysis, empirical methods for quality improvement, and economic analysis of quality, this book is a must-read for anyone who is interested in this subject. With the many real-life and up-to-date examples and stories linking software quality to daily-life activities, readers will find this book an enjoyable read."

—*Stephen H. Kan, Senior Technical Staff Member and Program Manager, Software Quality—IBM Systems and Technology Group, and author of* Metrics and Models in Software Quality Engineering

"Finally, a book that defines the cost and economics of software quality and their relationship to business value. Facts such as the inability of testing alone to produce quality software, the value of engineering-in quality, and the positive ROI are illustrated in compelling ways. Additionally, this book is a must-read for understanding, managing, and eliminating 'technical debt' from software systems."

—*Dan Galorath, CEO, Galorath Incorporated & SEER by Galorath*

"Congrats to Capers and Olivier as they release their relevant, extensive, and timely research on the costs of defects in today's software industry. The authors don't stop with the causes of defects; they explore injection points, removal, and prevention approaches to avoid the 'technical mortgage' associated with defective software products. In today's 'quick-to-market' world, an emphasis on strengthening the *engineering* in software engineering is refreshing. If you're a software developer, manager, student, or user, this book will challenge your perspective on software quality. Many thanks!"

—*Joe Schofield, Sandia National Laboratories; Vice President, IFPUG; CQA, CFPS, CSMS, LSS BB, SEI-certified instructor*

"Whether consulting, working on projects, or teaching, whenever I need credible, detailed, relevant metrics and insights into the current capabilities and performance of the software engineering profession, I always turn to Capers Jones's work first. In this important new book, he and Olivier Bonsignour make the hard-headed, bottom-line, economic case, with facts and data, about why software quality is so important. I know I'll turn to this excellent reference again and again."

—Rex Black, President, RBCS (www.rbcs-us.com), and author of
seven books on software quality and testing, including
Managing the Testing Process, Third Edition

"This masterpiece of a book will empower those who invest in software—and the businesses and products that depend on it—to do so wisely. It is a ground-breaking work that rigorously applies principles of finance, economics, management, quality, and productivity to scrutinize holistically the value propositions and myths underlying the vast sums invested in software. A must-read if you want to get your money's worth from your software investments."

—Leon A. Kappelman, Professor of Information Systems,
College of Business, University of North Texas

"Capers Jones is the foremost leader in the software industry today for software metrics. *The Economics of Software Quality* is a comprehensive, data-rich study of challenges of quality software across the many application domains. It is an essential read for software quality professionals who wish to better understand the challenges they face and the cost and effectiveness of potential solutions. It is clear that much research and thought has been put into this."

—Maysa-Maria Peterson Lach, Senior Principal
Software Engineer, Raytheon Missile Systems

"In no other walk of life do we resist the necessity and validity of precise, rigorous measurement, as software practitioners have so vigorously resisted for more than fifty years. Capers Jones took up the challenge of bringing sanity and predictability to software production more than three decades ago, and now with Olivier Bonsignour, he brings forth his latest invaluable expression of confidence in applying standard engineering and economic discipline to what too often remains the 'Wild, Wild West' of software development."

—Douglas Brindley, President & CEO,
Software Productivity Research, LLC

The Economics of
Software Quality

The Economics of Software Quality

Capers Jones
Olivier Bonsignour

✦Addison-Wesley

Upper Saddle River, NJ • Boston • Indianapolis • San Francisco
New York • Toronto • Montreal • London • Munich • Paris • Madrid
Capetown • Sydney • Tokyo • Singapore • Mexico City

Many of the designations used by manufacturers and sellers to distinguish their products are claimed as trademarks. Where those designations appear in this book, and the publisher was aware of a trademark claim, the designations have been printed with initial capital letters or in all capitals.

The authors and publisher have taken care in the preparation of this book, but make no expressed or implied warranty of any kind and assume no responsibility for errors or omissions. No liability is assumed for incidental or consequential damages in connection with or arising out of the use of the information or programs contained herein.

The publisher offers excellent discounts on this book when ordered in quantity for bulk purchases or special sales, which may include electronic versions and/or custom covers and content particular to your business, training goals, marketing focus, and branding interests. For more information, please contact:

U.S. Corporate and Government Sales
(800) 382-3419
corpsales@pearsontechgroup.com

For sales outside the United States, please contact:

International Sales
international@pearson.com

Visit us on the Web: informit.com/aw

Library of Congress Cataloging-in-Publication Data

Jones, Capers.
    The economics of software quality / Capers Jones, Olivier Bonsignour
        p.   cm.
        ISBN 978-0-13-258220-9 (hardcover: alk. Paper) 1. Computer software—Quality control—Economic aspects. 2. Software maintenance—Economic aspects. 3. Computer software—Validation. 4. Computer software—verification. I. Subramanyam, Jitendra. II. Title.
    QA76.76.Q35J674 2012
    005.1'4—dc23

                                                                                    20110145858

Copyright © 2012 Pearson Education, Inc.

All rights reserved. Printed in the United States of America. This publication is protected by copyright, and permission must be obtained from the publisher prior to any prohibited reproduction, storage in a retrieval system, or transmission in any form or by any means, electronic, mechanical, photocopying, recording, or likewise. For information regarding permissions, write to:

Pearson Education, Inc.
Rights and Contracts Department
501 Boylston Street, Suite 900
Boston, MA 02116
Fax: (617) 671-3447

ISBN-13: 978-0-13-258220-9
ISBN-10:   0-13-258220-1

Text printed in the United States on recycled paper at Courier in Westford, Massachusetts.
First printing, July 2011

Publisher
Paul Boger

Acquisitions Editor
Bernard Goodwin

Managing Editor
John Fuller

Full-Service Production Manager
Julie B. Nahil

Copy Editor
Christal White

Indexer
Infodex Indexing Services

Proofreader
Christine Clark

Editorial Assistant
Michelle Housley

Cover Designer
Nicolas Herlem

Compositor
LaurelTech

This book is dedicated to Watts Humphrey and Allan Albrecht.
Watts was a tireless champion of software quality.
Allan developed the most effective metric for studying
software quality economics.

Contents

Foreword

As a major telecommunications company, our business consists of a complex mix of products and services. Some are decades old, and some are only emerging. In just one part of our business, customers now access sophisticated business processes via myriad mobile devices operating on multiple platforms, technologies, and standards. The mobile access revolution is only one example of the continual change we must master. In several of our new markets, some of our competitors were not even on the radar ten years ago.

The IT systems that service our customers have been built over decades of changing regulatory frameworks, intense competition, and M&A activity; these systems provide mission-critical network management, billing, and customer service infrastructure for our existing and emerging products. We simply don't have the luxury of crafting Greenfield solutions in response to pressing business needs.

Despite the complex nature of IT, our shareholders expect nothing less than continuous improvement in service quality with simultaneous cost reductions. This has been the case in our market for quite some time and a major operational focus for my organization. One area on which we have focused in addressing this challenge is measuring software development productivity and quality. As the CIO, I oversee the company's internal information technology organization and infrastructure, as well as all evolving software applications. When you get down to it, the core expertise of our business is encoded in the software that automates our mission-critical processes. It is that software layer of our IT stack that fundamentally drives our time to market, our risk profile, and our cost structure.

We measure software productivity to allocate resources and make informed tradeoffs in our investments. We measure software quality at a structural level, in addition to the functional level through testing, to make the right trade-offs between delivery speed, business risk, and technical debt—the longer-term costs of maintaining and enhancing the delivered solutions.

For several years now, we have been successfully measuring the quality of our development projects and including these metrics in some of our Service Level Agreements. We are now starting to put productivity measurements across our portfolio side-by-side with quality measurements to get a truer picture of where we are trading present delivery agility for future business agility.

The Economics of Software Quality is a landmark for three reasons. It is practical, it is data-driven, and it goes beyond the traditional treatments of quality to demonstrate how to manage structural quality—an important element of software quality for our business. Just as we invest in our enterprise architecture to actively manage the evolution of our core application software, we are putting a strong focus on the analysis and measurement of these applications at the structural level. These measures enable my organization to take a proactive stance to building a better future for our business and for me to closely manage the economic fundamentals in meeting and exceeding shareholder expectations.

As we look forward to an exciting period of rapid growth in fixed-line, mobile, data, and on-demand products and services, I can assure you that this is one book my management team and I will keep close at hand.

—Thaddeus Arroyo
Chief Information Officer, AT&T Services, Inc.

F. Thaddeus Arroyo, Chief Information Officer, is responsible for AT&T's information technology. He was appointed to his current position in January 2007, following the close of the merger between AT&T, BellSouth, and Cingular. In his role, he is responsible for directing the company's internal information technology organization and infrastructure, including Internet and intranet capabilities, developing applications systems across the consumer and mobility markets, enterprise business segments, and AT&T's corporate systems. He also oversees AT&T's enterprise data centers.

Preface

This book is aimed at software managers, executives, and quality assurance personnel who are involved in planning, estimating, executing, and maintaining software. Managers and stakeholders need to understand the economics of software quality when planning and developing new applications and enhancing or maintaining existing ones.

The goal of this book is to quantify the factors that influence software quality and provide readers with enough information for them to predict and measure quality levels of their projects and applications.

To serve this goal, we consolidate an expansive body of software quality data—data on software structural quality, software assurance processes and techniques, and the marginal costs and benefits of improving software quality. The book provides quantitative data on how high and low quality affect software project schedules, staffing, development costs, and maintenance costs. This information should enable software managers to set and track progress toward quality targets and to make the right trade-offs between speed to market and business risk.

We quantify the positive economic value of software quality and the high costs of poor software quality using software quality data from large organizations in the private and public sectors. This is not a "how to do it" book—there are many good how-to books on processes and techniques for testing, inspections, static analysis, and other quality topics. We hope to have added a substantial amount of software quality data from real-world applications to complement those how-to books and enable IT managers to quantify the relative efficacy and economic value of these techniques.

In small projects, individual human skills and experience play a major role in successful outcomes. Quality is important, but individual skill tends to be the dominant driver of high quality.

But as projects grow larger, with development teams from 20 on up to more than 1,000 personnel, individual skills tend to regress to the mean. Quality becomes progressively more important because, historically, the costs of finding and fixing bugs have been the largest known expense for large software applications. This is true of both new development as well as enhancement and maintenance.

Most discussions of software quality focus almost exclusively on *functional* quality. In this book, we expand our treatment beyond functional quality to cover *nonfunctional* and *structural* quality. Measuring structural quality requires going beyond the quality of individual components to the quality of the application as a whole. We show how to clearly define and repeatably measure nonfunctional and structural quality.

Reliable measurements of all three kinds of quality—structural, nonfunctional, and functional—are essential for a complete treatment of the economics of software quality. We use these quality metrics to compare a number of quality improvement techniques at each stage of the software development life cycle and quantify their efficacy using data from real-world applications.

To achieve high-quality levels for large systems, a synergistic set of methods is needed. These include defect prevention methods, which can reduce defect levels; pretest defect removal methods such as inspections and static analysis; and more than 40 kinds of testing.

Several newer kinds of development methods also have beneficial impacts on software quality compared to traditional "waterfall" development. These include Agile development, Crystal development, Extreme Programming (XP), Personal Software Process (PSP), the Rational Unified Process (RUP), the Team Software Process (TSP), and several others.

The generally poor measurement practices of the software industry have blurred understanding of software quality economics. Many executives and even some quality personnel tend to regard software quality as an expense. They also tend to regard quality as a topic that lengthens schedules and raises development costs.

However, from an analysis of about 13,000 software projects between 1973 and today, it is gratifying to observe that high quality levels are invariably associated with shorter-than-average development schedules and lower-than-average development costs.

The reason for this is that most projects that run late and exceed their budgets show no overt sign of distress until testing begins. When testing begins, a deluge of high-severity defects tends to stretch out testing intervals and cause massive bursts of overtime. In general, testing schedules for low-quality, large software projects are two to three times longer and more than twice as costly as testing for high-quality projects. If defects remain undetected and unremoved until testing starts, it is too late to bring a software project back under control. It is much more cost-effective to prevent defects or to remove them prior to testing.

Another poor measurement practice that has concealed the economic value of software quality is the usage of the cost-per-defect metric. It has become an urban legend that "it costs 100 times as much to fix a bug after delivery as during development." Unfortunately, the cost-per-defect metric actually penalizes quality and achieves its lowest values for the buggiest software. As quality improves, cost per defect rises until a level of zero defects is reached, where the cost-per-defect metric cannot be used at all.

The real economic value of high quality is only partially related to defect repair costs. It is true that high quality leads to fewer defects and therefore to lower defect repair costs. But its major economic benefits are due to the fact that high quality

- Reduces the odds of large-system cancellations

- Reduces the odds of litigation for outsourced projects

- Shortens development schedules

- Lowers development costs

- Lowers maintenance costs

- Reduces warranty costs

- Increases customer satisfaction

This book contains seven chapters. The Introduction in Chapter 1 discusses the fact that software has become one of the most widely used products in human history. As this book is written, a majority of all business activities are driven by software. A majority of government operations are controlled by software, such as civilian taxes, military and defense systems, and both state and local government organizations. Because software is so pervasive, high and low quality levels affect every citizen in significant ways.

Chapter 1 defines software quality, considering the topic of quality is ambiguous both for software itself and for other manufactured products. There are many diverse views of what "quality" actually means. Chapter 1 examines all of the common views and concludes that effective definitions for quality need to be predictable in advance and measurable when they occur. Because this book deals with quantification and economic topics, there is emphasis on quality factors that can be measured precisely, such as defects and defect removal efficiency. In addition to these well-defined metrics, we show how to precisely measure software structural quality. Other definitions of quality, such as fitness, use, or aesthetic factors, are important but not always relevant to economic analysis.

Chapter 2 is about estimating and measuring software quality. It is important for executives, clients, stakeholders, venture capitalists, and others with a financial interest in software to understand how quality can be predicted before projects start and measured during development and after release. Because software quality involves requirements, architecture, design, and many other noncode artifacts, the traditional lines of code metric is inadequate. This book uses function point metrics and structural quality metrics for quantifying quality. The function point metric is independent of code and therefore can deal with noncoding defects such as "toxic requirements." Structural quality metrics get to the root causes of application quality and serve as foundational measures of software costs and business risks.

Chapters 3 deals with the important topic of defect prevention. The set of methods that reduce defect potentials and minimize errors are difficult to study because they cannot be studied in isolation, but need numerous cases where a specific method was used and similar cases where the method was not used. Examples of methods that have demonstrated success in terms of defect prevention include Six Sigma, quality function deployment (QFD), test-driven development (TDD), and formal inspections. The kaizen and poka yoke inspections from Japan are also defect prevention methods. Some of these, such as inspections, happen to be effective as both defect prevention and defect removal methods.

Chapter 4 deals with pretest defect removal methods in use today. The term "pretest" refers to quality and defect removal methods that occur prior to the start of testing. Among these methods are peer reviews, formal inspections, and static analysis. Although the literature on pretest defect removal is sparse compared to the literature on testing, these methods are important and have great value. Effective pretest methods such as inspections and static analysis shorten test schedules and raise testing efficiency. Twenty-five different kinds of pretest defect removal are discussed.

Chapter 5 deals with testing, which is the traditional quality control technique for software projects. Although there is an extensive literature on testing, there is a surprising lack of quantified data on topics such as defect detection efficiency (DDE) and defect removal efficiency (DRE). If testing is performed without effective defect prevention methods and without pretest defect removal, most forms of testing are usually less than 35% efficient in finding bugs and quite expensive as well. A synergistic combination of defect prevention, pretest removal, and formal well-planned testing can raise test removal efficiency substantially. The goal of effective quality control is to approach 99% in terms of cumulative defect removal efficiency. Forty kinds of testing stages are discussed in Chapter 5.

Chapter 6 deals with post-release defect removal, which is an unfortunate fact of life for software applications. Cumulative defect removal efficiency in the United States is only about 85%, so all software applications are delivered with latent defects. As a result, customers will always find bugs, and software organizations will always need customer support and maintenance personnel available to repair the bugs. However, state-of-the-art combinations of defect prevention, pretest removal, and testing can top 96% in terms of defect removal efficiency on average and even achieve 99% in a few cases.

Chapter 7 consolidates all of the authors' data and shows side-by-side results for low-quality, average-quality, and high-quality software projects. Both the methods used to achieve high quality and the quantitative results of achieving high quality are discussed.

Using structural quality data from 295 applications from 75 organizations worldwide, we define and quantify the notion of *technical debt*—the cost of fixing problems in working software that, if left unfixed, will likely cause severe business disruption. We juxtapose this with a framework for quantifying the loss of business value due to poor quality. Together with technical debt, this business value framework provides a platform for future software economics research.

Acknowledgments

By Capers Jones

There are two authors for this book, and we each want to acknowledge those who helped in its creation.

As always, thanks to my wife Eileen for her support of the many months of time spent in writing 16 books over a 25-year period.

While this book was in process, two friends and colleagues passed away. Special thanks should go to both Al Albrecht and Watts Humphrey.

Allan J. Albrecht was one of the original creators of function point metrics, without which this book would not be possible. Al and I first met in 1978 when he gave a talk on function points at the joint IBM/SHARE/GUIDE conference in Monterey, California. Although we both worked for IBM, Al was located in White Plains, New York, and I was located in San Jose, California, so we had not met until the conference.

Al's talk and the function point metric made economic analysis of software feasible and provided insights that older metrics such as "lines of code" and "cost per defect" could not replicate.

Al Albrecht, IBM, and the conference management kindly gave permission to publish Al's paper in my second book, *Programming Productivity: Issues for the Eighties* through the IEEE Press in 1979. From this point on, all of my technical books have used function points for quantitative information about software quality, productivity, and economic topics.

After Al retired from IBM, we both worked together for about five years in the area of expanding the usage of function point metrics. Al created the first certification exam for function points and taught the metric to many of our colleagues.

Al was an electrical engineer by training and envisioned function point metrics as providing a firm basis for both quality and productivity studies for all kinds of software applications. Today, in 2011, function points are the most widely used software metric and almost the only metric that has substantial volumes of benchmark information available.

About two weeks before Al Albrecht passed away, the software industry also lost Watts Humphrey. Watts, too, was a colleague at IBM. Watts was an inventor and a prolific writer of excellent books, as well as an excellent public speaker and often keynoted software conferences.

After retiring from IBM, Watts started a second career at the Software Engineering Institute (SEI) where he pioneered the development of the original version of the capability maturity model (CMM).

Watts was one of the first software researchers to recognize that quality is the driving force for effective software development methods. It would be pointless to improve productivity unless quality improved faster and further because otherwise higher productivity would only create more defects. At both IBM and the SEI, Watts supported many quality initiatives, such as formal inspections, formal testing, and complete defect measurements, from the start of software projects through their whole useful lives.

Watts also created both the Personal Software Process (PSP) and the Team Software Process (TSP), which are among the most effective methods for combining high quality and high performance.

Watts's work in software process improvement was recognized by his receipt of the National Medal of Technology from President George Bush in 2005.

In recent years, Watts took part in a number of seminars and conferences, so we were able to meet face-to-face several times a year, usually in cities where software conferences were being held.

In this book, the importance of quality as being on the critical path to successful software development is an idea that Watts long championed. And the ability to measure quality, productivity, and other economic factors would not be possible without the function point metric developed by Al Albrecht.

Many other people contributed to this book, but the pioneering work of Al and Watts were the key factors that made the book possible.

By Olivier Bonsignour

First and foremost, I would like to thank Capers Jones. It has been a pleasure working with him on this book.

I owe a debt to my colleagues Lev Lesokhin and Bill Curtis at CAST. Lev and Bill were the first ones to suggest this project and have been exceptional sounding boards throughout. Their imprint on the ideas, organization, and content is so extensive that they should be considered coauthors of this book.

I've borrowed from the work of other colleagues at CAST. First of all, Jitendra Subramanyam, who has done a tremendous job helping me elaborate the content of this book. Also, my work with Bill Curtis and Vincent Delaroche—on the distinction between software structural quality at the application level, as opposed to quality at the component level—appears in Chapter 2. This attribute of software quality—that the whole is greater than the sum of its parts—is critical to the analysis and measurement of software quality. The definition of software structural quality metrics in that chapter is based on work I did with Bill and with Vincent. The framework in Chapter 7 for calculating the business loss caused by poor structural quality is also based on Bill's work. Jay Sappidi did the groundbreaking work of collecting and analyzing our first batch of structural quality data and crafting a definition of *Technical Debt*. Much of the structural quality analysis in Chapters 6 and 7 is based on Jay's work.

The product engineering team at CAST—Razak Ellafi, Philippe-Emmanuel Douziech, and their fellow engineers—continue to create a magnificent product that admirably serves the needs of hundreds of organizations worldwide. The CAST Application Intelligence Platform is not only a piece of fine engineering, it is also the generator of all the structural quality data in this book.

About the Authors

 **Capers Jones** is currently the President and CEO of Capers Jones & Associates LLC. He is also the founder and former chairman of Software Productivity Research LLC (SPR). He holds the title of Chief Scientist Emeritus at SPR. Capers Jones founded SPR in 1984.

Before founding SPR, Capers was Assistant Director of Programming Technology for the ITT Corporation at the Programming Technology Center in Stratford, Connecticut. He was also a manager and researcher at IBM in California.

Capers is a well-known author and international public speaker. Some of his books have been translated into six languages. All of his books have been translated into Japanese, and his newest books are available in Chinese editions as well.

Among his book titles are *Patterns of Software Systems Failure and Success* (Prentice Hall 1994), *Applied Software Measurement, Third Edition* (McGraw-Hill, 2008), *Software Quality: Analysis and Guidelines for Success* (International Thomson, 1997), *Estimating Software Costs, Second Edition* (McGraw-Hill, 2007), and *Software Assessments, Benchmarks, and Best Practices* (Addison-Wesley, 2000). The third edition of his book *Applied Software Measurement* was published in the spring of 2008. His book entitled *Software Engineering Best Practices* was published by McGraw-Hill in October 2009. His current book is *The Economics of Software Quality*, with Olivier Bonsignour as coauthor.

Capers and his colleagues have collected historical data from more than 600 corporations and more than 30 government organizations. This historical data is a key resource for judging the effectiveness of software process improvement methods. More than 13,000 projects have been reviewed.

In addition to his technical books, Mr. Jones has also received recognition as an historian after the publication of *The History and Future of Narragansett Bay* in 2006 by Universal Publishers.

His research studies include quality estimation, quality measurement, software cost and schedule estimation, software metrics, and risk analysis.

Mr. Jones has consulted at more than 150 large corporations and also at a number of government organizations such as NASA, the U.S. Air Force, the U.S. Navy, the Internal Revenue Service, and the U.S. Courts. He has also worked with several state governments.

Olivier Bonsignour is responsible for Research & Development and Product Management in a continual effort to build the world's most advanced Application Intelligence technology.

Prior to joining CAST, Mr. Bonsignour was the CIO for DGA, the advanced research division of the French Ministry of Defense. Prior to that role, also at DGA, he was in charge of application development and a project director working on IT systems that support operations. A pioneer in the development of distributed systems and object oriented development, he joined CAST after having been an early adopter of CAST technology in 1996.

Mr. Bonsignour holds a graduate degree in engineering and computer science from the National Institute of Applied Sciences (INSA), Lyon, and a master's degree in management from the executive program at IAE Aix-en-Provence. In his free time, Mr. Bonsignour enjoys swimming, cycling, and skiing, as well as sailing his boat off the coast of France.

Chapter 1

Defining Software Quality and Economic Value

Introduction

This book deals with two topics that have been ambiguous and difficult to pin down for many years: software quality and economic value.

The reason for the ambiguity, as noted in the Preface, is that there are many different points of view, and each point of view has a different interpretation of the terms. For example, software quality does not mean the same thing to a customer as it does to a developer. Economic value has a different meaning to vendors than it has to consumers. For vendors, revenue is the key element of value, and for consumers, operational factors represent primary value. Both of these are discussed later in the book.

By examining a wide spectrum of views and extracting the essential points from each view, the authors hope that workable definitions can be established that are comparatively unambiguous.

Software quality, as covered in this book, goes well beyond functional quality (the sort of thing to which customers might react to in addition to usability and reliable performance). Quality certainly covers these aspects but extends further to nonfunctional quality (how well the software does what it is meant to do) and to structural quality (how well it can continue to serve business needs as they evolve and change as business conditions do).

Why Is Software Quality Important?

Computer usage in industrial countries starts at or before age 6, and by age 16 almost 60% of young people in the United States have at least a working knowledge of computers and software. Several skilled hackers have been apprehended who were only 16 years of age.

The approximate population of the United States in 2010 was about 309,800,135 based on Census Bureau estimates. Out of the total population about 30% use computers daily either for business purposes or for recreational purposes or both; that is, about 92,940,040 Americans are daily computer users.

About 65% of the U.S. population use embedded software in the form of smart phones, digital cameras, digital watches, automobile brakes and engine controls, home appliances, and entertainment devices. Many people are not aware that embedded software controls such devices, but it does. In other words, about 201,370,087 U.S. citizens own and use devices that contain embedded software.

Almost 100% of the U.S. population has personal data stored in various online databases maintained by the Census Bureau, the Internal Revenue Service, state governments, municipal governments, banks, insurance companies, credit card companies, and credit scoring companies.

Moving on to business, data from various sources such as *Forbes*, Manta, *Business Week*, the Department of Commerce Bureau of Labor Statistics, and others reports that the United States has about 22,553,779 companies (as of the end of 2010). Of these companies about 65% use computers and software for business operations, retail sales, accounting, and other purposes—so about 14,659,956 U.S. companies use computers and software. (Corporate software usage ranges from a basic spreadsheet up to entire enterprise resource planning [ERP] packages plus hundreds of other applications.)

Based on data from the Manta website, the software deployed in the United States is provided by about 77,186 software companies and another 10,000 U.S. companies that create devices with embedded software. A great deal of embedded software and the device companies themselves have moved to China, Taiwan, Japan, India, and other offshore countries. An exception to offshore migration is the manufacture of embedded software for military equipment and weapons systems, which tends to stay in the United States for security reasons.

The U.S. military services and the Department of Defense (DoD) own and deploy more software than any other organizations in history. In fact, the DoD probably owns and deploys more software than the military organizations of all other countries combined. Our entire defense community is now dependent on software for command and control, logistics support, and the actual operation of weapons systems. Our national defense systems are highly computerized, so software quality is a critical component of the U.S. defense strategy.

Without even knowing it, we are awash in a sea of software that operates most of our manufacturing equipment, keeps records on virtually all citizens, and operates the majority of our automobiles, home appliances, and entertainment devices. Our transportation systems, medical systems, and government operations all depend on computers and software and hence also depend on high software quality levels.

While software is among the most widely used products in human history, it also has one of the highest failure rates of any product in human history due primarily to poor quality.

Based on observations among the authors' clients plus observations during expert witness assignments, the cancellation rate for applications in the 10,000 function point size range is about 31%. The average cost for these cancelled projects is about $35,000,000. By contrast, projects in the 10,000 function point size range that are successfully completed and have high quality levels only cost about $20,000,000.

When projects developed by outsource vendors are cancelled and clients sue for breach of contract, the average cost of litigation is about $5,000,000 for the plaintiff and $7,000,000 for the defendant. If the defendants lose, then awards for damages can top $25,000,000. However because most U.S. courts bar suits for consequential damages, the actual losses by the defendants can be much larger.

Of the authors' clients who are involved with outsourcing, about 5% of agreements tend to end up in court for breach of contract. The claims by the plaintiffs include outright failure, delivery of inoperable software, or delivery of software with such high defect volumes that usage is harmful rather than useful.

As of 2011, the average cost per function point in the United States is about $1,000 to build software applications and another $1,000 to maintain and support them for five years: $2,000 per function point in total. For projects that use effective combinations of defect prevention and defect removal activities and achieve high quality levels, average development costs are only about $700 per function point and maintenance, and support costs drop to about $500 per function point: $1,200 per function point in total.

Expressed another way, the software engineering population of the United States is currently around 2,400,000 when software engineers and related occupations such as systems analysis are considered. On any given day, due to poor quality control, about 1,000,000 of these workers spend the day finding and fixing bugs (and, unwittingly, injecting new bugs as part of the process).

So all of these statistics point to the fact that better software quality control in the forms of defect prevention and more effective defect removal could free up about 720,000 software personnel for more productive work than just bug repairs, easily reducing U.S. software development and maintenance costs by about 50%.

As we show later in the book, the cost savings that result from higher quality are proportional to application size. As software projects grow larger, cost savings from high quality levels increase. Table 1.1 illustrates typical software development costs for low-, average-, and high-quality software applications.

The technologies and methods associated with these three quality levels are discussed and illustrated in later sections of this chapter, as are the reasons that large software projects are so risky. Suffice it to say the "high quality" column includes effective defect prevention, effective pretest defect removal such as inspections and static analysis, and much more effective testing than the other columns.

Another major reason that software quality is important is because poor quality can and will affect each citizen personally in unpleasant ways. Every time there is a billing error, every time taxes are miscalculated, every time credit ratings change for incorrect reasons, poor software quality is part of the problem.

Early in 2010, hundreds of computers were shut down and many businesses including hospitals were disrupted when the MacAfee antivirus application mistakenly identified part of Microsoft Windows as a virus and stopped it from loading.

According to the July 25, 2010, issue of *Computerworld*, the BP drilling platform that exploded and sank had been having frequent and serious computer problems for a month prior to the final disaster. These problems prevented significant quantities of data from being analyzed that might have warned operators in time to shut down the oil pumping operation.

Table 1.1 *Software Costs by Size and Quality Level*

	(Burdened cost = $10,000 per month)		
Function Points	**Low Quality**	**Average Quality**	**High Quality**
10	$6,875	$6,250	$5,938
100	$88,561	$78,721	$74,785
1,000	$1,039,889	$920,256	$846,636
10,000	$23,925,127	$23,804,458	$18,724,012
100,000	$507,767,782	$433,989,557	$381,910,810

If your automobile braking system does not operate correctly, if a home appliance fails unexpectedly, or if a hospital makes a medical mistake, there is a good chance that poor software quality was part of the problem.

If an airline flight is delayed more than about two hours or if there is a widespread power outage that affects an entire geographic region such as New England, the odds, again, are good that poor software quality was part of the problem.

Because software is such a basic commodity as of 2011, it is useful to start by considering how much software ordinary U.S. citizens own and use. Table 1.2 shows typical software volumes associated with normal living activities.

The data in Table 1.2 comes from a combination of web sources and proprietary data provided by clients who build appliances of various kinds.

Not every citizen has all of these appliances and devices, but about half of us do. Many of us have even more than what Table 1.2 indicates, such as owning several automobiles, several cell phones, and numerous appliances. Software quality is important because it is the main operating component of almost all complex machines as of 2011.

Another reason that software quality is important is because many of us need high-quality software to go about our daily jobs. Table 1.3 shows typical software usage patterns for a sample of positions that include knowledge work, based on observations and discussions with members of various professions and from studies with the companies that provide the software.

Table 1.2 *Personal Software Circa 2011*

Products	Function Points	Lines of Code	Daily Usage Hours
Personal computer	1,000,000	50,000,000	2.00
Automobile	350,000	17,500,000	2.00
Smart appliances	100,000	5,000,000	1.00
Smart phone	25,000	1,250,000	1.50
Social networks	25,000	1,250,000	1.50
Home entertainment	10,000	500,000	2.00
Electronic book	5,000	250,000	1.00
Digital camera	2,500	125,000	0.50
Digital watch	1,500	75,000	0.50
TOTALS	1,519,000	75,950,000	12.00

As can be seen from Table 1.3, all knowledge workers in the modern world are heavily dependent on computers and software to perform their jobs. Therefore, these same workers are heavily dependent on high software quality levels. Every time there is a computer failure or a software failure, many knowledge workers will have to stop their jobs until repairs are made. Indeed, power failures can stop work in today's world.

One of the authors was once an expert witness in a software breach-of-contract lawsuit. While being deposed in Boston there was a power failure, and the court stenographer could not record the transcript. As a result, four attorneys, the stenographer, and two expert witnesses spent about two hours waiting until the deposition could continue. All of us were being paid our regular rates during the outage. We are so dependent on computers and software that work stops cold when the equipment is unavailable.

Table 1.3   *Occupation Group Software Usage Circa 2011*

Occupation Groups	Function Points	Lines of Code	Daily Usage Hours	Packages Used
Military planners	5,000,000	295,000,000	6.50	30
Physicians	3,000,000	177,000,000	3.00	20
FBI agents	1,500,000	88,500,000	3.50	15
Military officers	775,000	45,725,000	3.50	20
Attorneys	350,000	20,650,000	4.00	10
Airline pilots	350,000	20,650,000	7.00	15
Air-traffic controllers	325,000	19,175,000	8.50	3
IRS tax agents	175,000	10,325,000	5.00	10
Accountants	175,000	10,325,000	5.00	12
Pharmacists	150,000	8,850,000	4.00	6
Electrical engineers	100,000	5,900,000	5.50	20
Software engineers	75,000	4,425,000	7.00	20
Civil engineers	65,000	3,835,000	5.00	6
Police detectives	60,000	3,540,000	3.50	12
Project managers	50,000	2,950,000	2.00	7
Real estate agents	30,000	1,770,000	4.00	7
Bank tellers	25,000	1,475,000	6.00	8
School teachers	15,000	885,000	1.50	4
Retail clerks	15,000	885,000	7.00	5
AVERAGES	643,947	37,992,895	4.82	12

Similar occurrences take place after hurricanes and natural disasters that shut down power. Many retail establishments are unable to record sales information, and some stay closed even though workers and potential customers are both available. If computers and software are out of service, many businesses can no longer operate.

Software and computers are so deeply enmeshed in modern business and government operations that the global economy is at serious risk. As military planners know, nuclear explosions in the atmosphere emit an electromagnetic pulse (EMP) that damages transistors and electrical circuits. They can also cause explosions of liquid fuels such as gasoline and can detonate stored weapons.

Such "ebombs" can be designed and detonated high enough so that they don't cause injuries or death to people, but instead cause major destruction of electronic devices such as radar, electric power generation, television, computers, and the like.

As of 2011, it is thought that most major countries already have ebombs in their arsenals. CBS news reported that one or more ebombs shut down the electric capacity of Baghdad without doing physical damage to buildings or personnel during the second Iraq war. This could be one of the reasons why restoring power to Baghdad after the hostilities ended has been so difficult.

A final reason that software quality is important is because dozens of government agencies and thousands of companies have personal information about us stored in their computers. Therefore, both quality and security are critical topics in 2011.

Table 1.4 shows examples of the kinds of organizations that record personal information and the probable number of people who work in those organizations who might have access to data about our finances, our Social Security numbers, our health-care records, our dates of birth, our jobs, our families, our incomes, and many other personal topics.

Given the number of government agencies and corporations that record vital data about citizens, and the number of people who have access to that data, it is no wonder that identity theft is likely to hit about 15% of U.S. citizens within the next five years.

A Congressional report showed that the number of U.S. cyber attacks increased from about 43,000 in 2008 to more than 80,000 in 2009. As this book is being written, probably more than 10,000 U.S. hackers are actively engaged in attempting to steal credit card and financial information. Computers, networks, and smart phones are all at considerable risk. Security vulnerabilities are linked closely to poor quality, and many attacks are based on known quality flaws.

Table 1.4   *Estimated Applications with Personal Data*

Organizations	Function Points	Lines of Code	Personnel with Access	Packages Used
Internal Revenue Service	150,000	7,500,000	10,000	10
Banks	125,000	6,250,000	90,000	12
Insurance companies	125,000	6,250,000	75,000	15
Credit card companies	125,000	6,250,000	3,000	10
Credit bureaus	120,000	6,000,000	1,500	9
Census Bureau	100,000	5,000,000	1,000	5
State tax boards	90,000	4,500,000	200	5
Airlines	75,000	3,750,000	250	12
Police organizations	75,000	3,750,000	10,000	5
Hospitals	75,000	3,750,000	1,000	5
Web-based stores	75,000	3,750,000	1,500	12
Municipal tax boards	50,000	2,500,000	20	3
Motor vehicle department	50,000	2,500,000	200	3
Physicians offices	30,000	1,500,000	50	6
Dental offices	30,000	1,500,000	50	6
Schools/universities	25,000	1,250,000	125	8
Clubs and associations	20,000	1,000,000	250	3
Retail stores	20,000	1,000,000	100	4
TOTALS	1,360,000	68,000,000	194,245	133

Because computers and software are now the main tools that operate industry and government, software quality and software security are among the most important topics of the modern world. Indeed, the importance of both quality and security will increase over the next decade.

From an economic standpoint, higher software quality levels can shorten development schedules, lower development and maintenance costs, improve customer satisfaction, improve team morale, and improve the status of the software engineering profession all at the same time.

Defining Software Quality

Quality has always been a difficult topic to define, and software quality has been exceptionally difficult. The reason is that perceptions of quality vary from person to person and from object to object.

For software quality for a specific application, the perceptions of quality differ among clients, developers, users, managers, software quality personnel, testers, senior executives, and other stakeholders. The perceptions of quality also differ among quality consultants, academics, and litigation attorneys. Many definitions have been suggested over the years, but none have been totally satisfactory or totally adopted by the software industry, including those embodied in international standards.

The reason that quality in general and software quality in particular have been elusive and hard to pin down is because the word "quality" has many nuances and overtones. For example, among the attributes of quality can be found these ten:

1. *Elegance or beauty* in the eye of the beholder

2. *Fitness of use* for various purposes

3. *Satisfaction of user requirements*, both explicit and implicit

4. *Freedom from defects*, perhaps to Six Sigma levels

5. *High efficiency of defect removal* activities

6. *High reliability* when operating

7. *Ease of learning* and *ease of use*

8. *Clarity of user guides* and HELP materials

9. *Ease of access* to customer support

10. *Rapid repairs* of reported defects

To further complicate the definition, quality often depends on the context in which a software component or feature operates. The quality of a software component is not an intrinsic property—the exact same component can be of excellent quality or highly dangerous depending on the environment in which it operates or the intent of the user.

This contextual nature of software quality is a fundamental challenge and applies to each of the ten attributes just listed. What is elegant in one situation might be downright unworkable in another; what is highly reliable under certain conditions can quickly break down in others.

A closely related complication is what Brooks calls "changeability" of software. "In short, the software product is embedded in a cultural matrix of applications, users, laws, and machine vehicles. These all change continually, and their changes force change upon the software product." (Brooks 1995, p.185)

This brings us to the distinction between testing and software quality. Software quality is often loosely equated with the activities of testing or quality assurance. However, contextuality and Brooks' notion of changeability of software are the reasons why software quality *cannot be equated with testing or quality assurance*.

Testing can only tackle known unknowns. If you don't know what you're testing for, you are not, by definition, conducting tests. But software, by its very nature is subject to unknown unknowns. No amount of functional or nonfunctional testing can be designed to detect and correct these problems. For example, the behavior of the application can change when

- One or more application components are switched out for new components

- Components change for technology reasons (such as version upgrades)

- Components change for business reasons (such as for new features or a change in workflow)

- Or the application's environment (perhaps the technology stack, for example) changes

It is impossible to devise tests for these conditions in advance. However, from experience we know that some applications are more robust, reliable, and dependable than others when the environment around them changes. Some applications are much easier to modify or extend in response to pressing business needs. These attributes of an application—robustness, dependability, modifiability, and so on—are reliable indicators of application quality that go beyond the defects identified during testing or the process inefficiencies or compliance lapses indentified in quality assurance. Therefore, the quality of an application can and must be defined in such a way as to accommodate these indicators of quality that outrun those identified in testing and quality assurance. How the concepts of contextuality and changeability can be accounted for in defining and measuring software quality is addressed at length in Chapter 2.

There are seven criteria that should be applied to definitions of software quality in order to use the definition in a business environment for economic analysis:

1. The quality definition should be *predictable* before projects start.

2. The quality definition should be *measurable* during and after projects are finished.

3. The quality definition should be *provable* if litigation occurs.

4. The quality definition should be *improvable* over time.

5. The quality definition should be *flexible* and encompass all deliverables.

6. The quality definition should be *extensible* and cover all phases and activities.

7. The quality definition should be *expandable* to meet new technologies such as cloud computing.

In addition, the various nuances of quality can be categorized into seven major focus areas or quality types:

1. *Technical or Structural quality*, which includes reliability, defects, and defect repairs

2. *Process quality*, which includes development methods that elevate quality

3. *Usage quality*, which includes ease of use and ease of learning

4. *Service quality*, which includes access to support personnel

5. *Aesthetic quality*, which includes user satisfaction and subjective topics

6. *Standards quality*, which includes factors from various international standards

7. *Legal quality*, which includes claims made in lawsuits for poor quality

The reason that taxonomy of quality types is needed is because the full set of all possible quality attributes encompasses more than 100 different topics. Table 1.5 lists a total of 121 software quality attributes and ranks them in order of importance.

The ranking scheme ranges from +10 for topics that have proven to be extremely valuable to a low of −10 for topics that have demonstrated extreme harm to software projects.

Table 1.5 *Seven Types of Software Quality Factors*

	Quality Factors	Value
	Technical Quality Factors	
1	Few requirements defects	10.00
2	No toxic requirements	10.00
3	Zero error-prone modules	10.00

(Continued)

Table 1.5   *(Continued)*

	Quality Factors	Value
	Technical Quality Factors	
4	Low defect potentials	10.00
5	Use of certified reusable code	10.00
6	Low rates of severity 1 and 2 defects	10.00
7	High reliability	9.90
8	Strong security features	9.90
9	Few design defects	9.50
10	Few coding defects	9.50
11	Low bad-fix injection rate	9.50
12	Low rates of invalid defect reports	9.50
13	Low rates of legacy defects	9.50
14	Easy conversion to SaaS format	9.00
15	Easy conversion to Cloud format	9.00
16	Fault tolerance	8.00
17	Few defects in test cases	8.00
18	Low cyclomatic complexity	7.50
19	Low entropy	7.00
	Process Quality Factors	
20	Customer support of high quality	10.00
21	High defect detection efficiency (DDE)	10.00
22	High defect removal efficiency (DRE)	10.00
23	Accurate defect measurements	10.00
24	Use of formal defect tracking	10.00
25	Accurate defect estimates	10.00
26	Low total cost of ownership (TCO)	10.00
27	Executive support of quality	10.00
28	Team support of quality	10.00
29	Management support of quality	10.00
30	Accurate quality benchmarks	10.00
31	Effective quality metrics	10.00
32	Minimizing hazards of poor quality	10.00
33	Use of formal quality improvement plan	10.00
34	COQ: appraisal	10.00

	Quality Factors	Value
	Process Quality Factors	
35	COQ: prevention	10.00
36	COQ: internal failure	10.00
37	COQ: external failure	10.00
38	Cost of learning (COL)	10.00
39	Quality improvement baselines	9.90
40	Function point quality measures	9.80
41	Quality and schedules	9.00
42	Quality and costs	9.00
43	Use of formal inspections	9.00
44	Use of automated static analysis	9.00
45	Use of formal test case design	9.00
46	Use of reusable test data	9.00
47	Use of formal SQA team	9.00
48	Use of trained test personnel	9.00
49	Use of formal test library controls	9.00
50	Use of formal change management	9.00
51	Use of Six Sigma for software	9.00
52	Use of Team Software Process (TSP)	9.00
53	Use of Agile methods	9.00
54	Use of Rational methods (RUP)	9.00
55	Use of hybrid methods	9.00
56	Use of Quality Function Deployment (QFD)	9.00
57	Use of trained inspection teams	9.00
58	Use of CMMI levels = > 3	9.00
59	Use of legacy renovation tools	9.00
60	Low rates of false-positive defects	9.00
61	Low rates of duplicate defect reports	8.75
62	Use of refactoring and restructuring	8.50
63	Six-Sigma quality measures	8.50
64	High test coverage	8.00
65	Low Cost of Quality (COQ)	8.00
66	Use of automated test tools	8.00

(Continued)

Table 1.5   *(Continued)*

	Quality Factors	Value
	Process Quality Factors	
67	Use of story point quality metrics	2.00
68	Use of Use Case point quality metrics	2.00
69	Use of waterfall methods	1.00
70	Lines of code quality measures	−5.00
71	Use of CMMI levels = < 2	−5.00
72	Cost-per-defect quality measures	−7.00
73	Executive indifference to high quality	−10.00
74	Management indifference to high quality	−10.00
75	Team indifference to high quality	−10.00
76	Customer indifference to high quality	−10.00
	Usage Quality Factors	
77	Ease of use	10.00
78	Useful features	10.00
79	Ease of learning	10.00
80	Good tutorial manuals	10.00
81	Good training courses	10.00
82	Good on-line HELP	10.00
83	Useful HELP information	9.75
84	Defect repair costs	9.25
85	Low cost of learning (COL)	9.25
86	User error handling	9.00
87	Speed of loading	9.00
88	Speed of usage	9.00
89	Good nationalization for global products	9.00
90	Documentation defects	9.00
91	Easy export of data to other software	9.00
92	Easy import of data from other software	9.00
93	Useful manuals and training	8.50
94	Good assistance from live experts	
	Service Quality Factors	
95	Good customer service	9.50
96	Rapid defect repair speed	9.25
97	Good technical support	9.00

	Quality Factors	Value
	Service Quality Factors	
98	Good HELP desk support	9.00
99	Use of formal incident management	8.00
100	Use of ITIL policies	8.00
	Aesthetic Quality Factors	
101	High user satisfaction	10.00
102	Superior to competitive applications	10.00
103	Superior to legacy applications	10.00
104	Quick start-up and shut-down times	9.00
105	No feature bloat	7.00
	Standards Quality Factors	
106	ISO/IEEE standards compliance	10.00
107	Certification of reusable materials	10.00
108	Corporation standards compliance	10.00
109	Certification of test personnel	8.00
110	Certification of SQA personnel	8.00
111	Portability	7.00
112	Maintainability	6.00
113	Scalability	5.00
	Legal Quality Factors	
114	Good warranty	10.00
115	Partial warranty: replacement only	4.00
116	Litigation for poor quality—consequential	−10.00
117	Litigation for poor quality—contractual	−10.00
118	Litigation for poor quality—financial loss	−10.00
119	Litigation for poor quality—safety	−10.00
120	Litigation for poor quality—medical	−10.00
121	No warranty expressed or implied	−10.00

A total of 121 quality factors is far too cumbersome to be useful for day-to-day quality analysis. Table 1.6 lists the top 12 quality factors if you select only the most significant factors in achieving quality based on measurements of several thousand applications.

As of 2011, 11 of these 12 quality factors are technically achievable. Item 114 on the list, Good warranty, is not yet practiced by the software industry. This situation needs to change, and the software industry needs to stand behind software applications with effective warranty coverage.

Table 1.6 *The 12 Most Effective Software Quality Factors*

1. Low defect potentials
2. Effective defect prevention methods
3. High defect detection efficiency (DDE)
4. High defect removal efficiency (DRE)
5. Use of pretest inspections
6. Use of pretest static analysis
7. Use of formal test case design
8. Good ease of learning
9. Good ease of use
10. Good technical support
11. High user satisfaction
12. Good warranty

Though all 121 of the quality factors are important, in order to deal with the economic value of quality, it is obvious that the factors have to be capable of quantitative expression. It is also obvious that the factors have to influence these seven topics:

1. The costs of development, maintenance, enhancement, and support.

2. The schedules for development, maintenance, enhancement, and support.

3. The direct revenue that the application will accrue if it is marketed.

4. The indirect revenue that might accrue from services or related products.

5. The learning curve for users of the application.

6. The operational cost savings that the application will provide to users.

7. The new kinds of business opportunities that the application will provide to users.

This book concentrates on software quality factors that have a tangible impact on costs and revenue. And to deal with the economic value of these quality factors, the book addresses three critical topics:

- What are the results of "average quality" in terms of costs, schedules, revenue, and other financial topics? Once defined, average quality will provide the baseline against which economic value can be measured.

- What are the results of "high quality" in terms of cost reduction, schedule reduction, higher revenues, new market opportunities, and other financial topics?

- What are the consequences of "low quality" in terms of cost increases, schedule increases, reduced revenue, loss of customers, and other financial topics?

Usually, more insights result from polar opposites than from average values. Therefore the book concentrates on the economic value from high quality and the economic losses from low quality.

While average quality is important, it is not very good, nor has it ever been very good for software. Therefore, it is important to know that only better-than-average software quality has tangible economic values associated with it.

Conversely, low software quality brings with it some serious economic consequences, including the threat of class-action litigation, the threat of breach of contract litigation, and, for embedded software in medical devices, even the potential threat of criminal charges.

Defining Economic Value and Defining the Value of Software Quality

Not only is "quality" an ambiguous term because of multiple viewpoints, but the term "value" is also ambiguous for the same reason. Indeed the concept of economic value has been a difficult one for every industry and for all forms of economic theory for more than 150 years.

Some economic theories link value to cost of production and to the price of various commodities. Other economic theories link value to usage of the same commodities. John Ruskin even assigned a moral element to value that dealt with whether wealth or various commodities were used for beneficial or harmful purposes. All of these theoretical economic views about value are interesting but somewhat outside the scope of this book.

For software, the perception of economic value can vary between enterprises that produce software and enterprises that consume or use software. These two views correspond to classic economic theories that assign value based on either production or on usage—both are discussed.

But software has another view of value that is not dealt with very often in standard economic theories. In modern businesses and governments, the people who pay for internal software application development are neither the producers nor the consumers.

Many software projects are commissioned and funded by executives or senior managers who will probably never actually use the software itself. These senior executives have a perception of value that needs to be considered—at the executive level, value of software can be delineated in a few different ways:

1. Software that can lower current operational costs

2. Software that can increase revenue by selling more current products

3. Software that can increase revenue by creating innovative new lines of business or by producing novel new products

For the first 20 years of the software industry between about 1950 and 1970, operating cost reduction was the primary economic reason for building software applications. Many clerical and paper-pushing jobs were converted from manual labor to computers.

From about 1970 to 1990, computers and software started to be aimed at improving manufacturing and marketing capabilities so that companies could build and sell more of their current products. Robotic manufacturing and sophisticated customer support and inventory management systems made significant changes in industrial production, marketing, and sales methodologies.

From about 1990 through today, computers and software have been rapidly creating new kinds of businesses that never existed before in all of human history. Consider the products and business models that are now based on the Internet and the World Wide Web.

Modern companies such as Amazon, Google, and eBay are doing forms of business that could not be done at all without software and the Web. At a lower level, computer gaming is now a multi-billion dollar industry that is selling immersive 3D products that could not exist without software. In other words, the third dimension of economic value is "innovation" and the creation of entirely new kinds of products and new business models.

In sum, when considering the economics of software and also of software quality, we need to balance three distinct threads of analysis:

1. Operating cost reductions

2. Revenue from increasing market share of current products or services

3. Revenue from inventing entirely new kinds of products and services

To come to grips with both the value of software itself and economic value of software quality, it is useful to explore a sample of these disparate views, including both the value of high quality levels and the economic harm from poor quality levels. In Chapter 7 we present quantitative frameworks for measuring the operating costs and the business impact of software quality.

The Economic Value of Software and Quality to Enterprises That Build Internal Software for Their Own Use

Building software internally for corporate or government operations was the first application for computers in a business setting. The reason this was the first response is because there were no other alternatives in the late 1950s and early 1960s due to the lack of other sources for software.

In the 1960s when computers first began to be widely used for business purposes, there were few COTS companies and no enterprise-resource planning companies (ERP) at all. The outsource business was in its infancy, and offshore outsourcing was almost 20 years in the future. The initial use of computers was to replace labor-intensive paper operations with faster computerized applications. For example, insurance claims handling, accounting, billing, taxation, and inventory management were all early examples of computerization of business operations.

The software for these business applications were built by the companies or government groups that needed them. This began an interesting new economic phenomenon of large companies accumulating large software staffs for building custom software even though software had nothing to do with their primary business operations.

By the 1990s, many banks, insurance companies, and manufacturing companies had as many as 10% of their total employment engaged in the development, maintenance, and support of custom internal software.

The same phenomenon occurred for the federal government, for all 50 of the state governments, and for about the 125 largest municipal governments.

In 2011, the 1,000 largest U.S. companies employed more than 1,000,000 software engineers and other software occupations. Some of these companies are very sophisticated and build software well, but many are not sophisticated and have major problems with cost overruns, schedule slippage, and outright cancellation of critical software projects.

The same statement is true of government software development. Some agencies are capable and build software well. But many are not capable and experience cancellations, overruns, and poor quality after deployment.

Examples of enterprises that build their own custom software include Aetna, Citizens, Proctor and Gamble, Ford and General Motors, Exxon Oil, the federal government, the state of California, the city of New York, and thousands of others.

Most internal software development groups operate as cost centers and are not expected to be profitable. However, they may charge other operating units for their services. Some software groups are funded by corporations as overhead functions, in which case they work for free. Very few operate as profit centers and sell their services to other companies as well as to internal business units.

Between about 1965 and 1985 these internal development groups were building applications for two main purposes:

1. To reduce operational costs by automating labor-intensive manual activities

2. To allow companies to offer new and improved services to customers

By the end of the last century and continuing through 2011, the work patterns have shifted. About 75% of "new" applications in 2011 were replacements for aging legacy applications built more than 15 years ago. These aging legacy applications require so much work to keep them running and up to date that more than 50% of internal software staffs now work on modifying existing software.

And, of course, the software personnel spend a high percentage of every working day finding and fixing bugs.

Since the early 1990s outsource vendors, COTS vendors, and open source vendors have entered the picture. As a result, the roles of internal software groups are evolving. Due to the recession of 2008 through 2010, many internal software groups have been downsized, and many others are being transferred to outsourcing companies.

As of 2011 only about 20% of the work of internal software groups involves innovation and new forms of software. The new forms of innovative software center on web applications, cloud computing, and business intelligence. However, numerous software projects are still being built by internal software groups even if the majority of these "new" projects are replacements or consolidations of aging legacy applications.

The economic value of software quality for internal software projects centers on these topics:

- Reduced cancellation rates for large applications

- Earlier delivery dates for new applications

- Reduced resistance from operating units for accepting new software

- Faster learning curves for bringing users up to speed for new software

- More and better services and products for clients

- Reduced development costs for new applications

- Reduced maintenance costs for released applications

- Reduced customer support costs for released applications

- Reduced executive dissatisfaction with the IT function

The economic consequences of low quality for in-house development include

- Protracted delays in delivering new applications

- Major cost overruns for new applications

- High probability of outright cancellation for large new applications

- Damages to business operations from poor quality

- Damages to customer records from poor quality

- Executive outrage over poor performance of IT group

- High odds of replacing in-house development with outsourcing

- Long learning curves for new applications due to poor quality

- Poor customer satisfaction

- High maintenance costs due to poor quality

- High customer support costs due to poor quality

The internal software development community does not do a very good job on software quality compared to the embedded software community, the systems software community, the defense software community, or even the commercial software community. One of the reasons why many companies are moving to outsource vendors is because internal software quality has not been effective.

Among the gaps in software quality control for the internal software community can be found poor quality measurements, failure to use effective defect prevention techniques, failure to use pretest inspections and static analysis tools, and failure to have adequately staffed Software Quality Assurance (SQA) teams. In general, the internal software community tests software applications but does not perform other necessary quality activities.

Poor quality control tends to increase executive dissatisfaction with the IT community, lower user satisfaction, and raise the odds that enterprises will want to shift to outsourcing vendors.

The Economic Value of Software and Quality to Internal Software Users

As of mid-2010 the Bureau of Labor Statistics reported that employment for the United States is about 139,000,000. (Unfortunately, this number is down about 7,000,000 from the 2007 peak before the "Great Recession" when U.S. employment topped 146,000,000.)

Of these U.S. workers, about 20% are daily software and computer users, roughly 27,800,000. Some of these people who work for small companies use only a few commercial software packages such as spreadsheets and word processors. However, about 40% of these workers are employed by either companies or government agencies that are large enough to build internal software. In other words, there are about 11,120,000 workers who use internally developed software applications as part of their daily jobs.

Note that these users of computers and software are not "customers" in the sense that they personally pay for the software that they use. The software is provided by corporations and government agencies so that the workers can carry out their daily jobs.

Examples of common kinds of internal software used by companies circa 2011 include retail sales, order entry, accounts payable and receivable, airline and train reservations, hotel reservations, insurance claims handling, vehicle fleet control, automobile renting and leasing, shipping, and cruise line bookings. Other examples include hospital administration, Medicare and Medicaid, and software used by the Internal Revenue Service (IRS) for taxation.

In today's world, internal development of software is primarily focused on applications that are specific to a certain business and hence not available from COTS vendors. Of course, the large enterprise-resource planning (ERP) companies such as SAP, Oracle, PeopleSoft, and the like have attempted to reduce the need for in-house development. Even the most complete ERP implementations still cover less than 50% of corporate software uses.

In the future, Software as a Service (SaaS), Service-oriented Architecture (SOA), and cloud computing will no doubt displace many in-house applications with equivalent Web-based services, but that time is still in the future.

The economic value of high-quality internal software to users and stakeholders has these factors:

- Reduction in cancelled projects

- Reduction in schedule delays

- Reduction in cost overruns

- Reduction in user resistance to new applications
- Rapid deployment of new applications
- Short learning curves to get up to speed in new applications
- Higher user satisfaction
- Higher reliability
- Better and more reliable customer service
- Reduced maintenance costs for released applications
- Reduced customer support costs for released applications

The economic consequences of low quality for internal users and stakeholders include

- Risk of cancelled projects
- Schedule delays for large applications
- Cost overruns for large applications
- Business transaction errors that damage customers or clients
- Business transaction errors that damage financial data
- Possible class-action litigation from disgruntled customers
- Possible litigation from customers suffering business losses
- Possible litigation from shareholders about poor quality
- Protracted delays in delivering new services
- Poor customer satisfaction
- High maintenance costs due to poor quality
- High customer support costs due to poor quality

For more than 50 years, internal software has been a mainstay of many corporations. However, due in large part to poor quality levels, a number of corporations and some government agencies are re-evaluating the costs and value of internal development. Outsourcing is increasing, and international outsourcing is increasing even more quickly.

Process improvements are also popular among internal software development groups. These range from being moderately successful to being extremely successful. As is discussed throughout this book, success tends to correlate with improved quality levels.

The Economic Value of Software and Quality to Commercial Software Vendors

Because there are now thousands of commercial software companies and many thousands of commercial software applications, it is interesting to realize that this entire multibillion dollar industry is younger than many readers of this book.

The commercial software business is a by-product of the development of electronic computers and only began to emerge in the 1960s. Word processing only entered the commercial market in about 1969 as an evolution of electric typewriters augmented by storage for repetitive text such as forms and questionnaires.

Spreadsheets first became commercial products circa 1978 with VisiCalc, although there were earlier implementations of computerized spreadsheets by IBM and other computer and software companies.

A spreadsheet patent was filed in 1971 by Reny Pardo and Remy Landau. This patent became famous because it was originally rejected by the U.S. patent office as being pure mathematics. It was only in 1983 that the Patent Office was overruled by the courts and software implementations of mathematical algorithms were deemed to be patentable.

As this book is written, there are more than 77,000 software companies in the United States. The software industry has generated enormous revenue and enormous personal wealth for many founders such as Bill Gates of Microsoft, Steve Jobs of Apple, Larry Ellison of Oracle, Larry Page and Sergey Brin of Google, Jeff Bezos of Amazon, and quite a few more.

As of 2011, about 75% of the revenue of software companies comes from selling more and more copies of existing applications such as Windows and Microsoft Office. About 25% of the revenue of software companies comes from innovation or the creation of new kinds of products and services, as demonstrated by Google, Amazon, and hundreds of others.

This is an important distinction because in the long run innovation is the factor that generates the greatest economic value. Companies and industries that stop innovating will eventually lose revenues and market share due to saturation of the markets with existing products.

One other interesting issue about innovation is that of "copy cats." After a new kind of software application hits the market, fast-followers often sweep right into the same market with products that copy the original features but include new features as well. In the commercial software business these fast followers tend to be more successful than the original products, as can be seen by looking at the sales history of VisiCalc and Microsoft Excel.

A number of software companies are now among the largest and wealthiest companies in the world. There are also thousands of medium and small software companies as well as giants. Examples of software companies include CAST, Microsoft, Symantec, IBM, Google, Oracle, SAP, Iolo, Quicken, Computer Aid Inc. and hundreds of others.

The primary value topic for commercial software itself is direct revenue, with secondary value deriving from maintenance contracts, consulting services, and related applications.

For example, most companies that lease large enterprise resource-planning (ERP) packages such as Oracle also bring in consulting teams to help deploy the packages and train users. They almost always have maintenance contracts that can last for many years.

As to the economic value of software quality in a commercial context, the value of quality to the commercial vendors themselves stems from these topics:

- Reduced cancellation rates for large applications

- Earlier delivery dates for new applications

- Favorable reviews by the press and user groups

- Reduced development costs for new applications

- Reduced maintenance costs for released applications

- Reduced customer support costs for released applications

- Increased market share if quality is better than competitors

- Fewer security flaws in released applications

The economic consequences of low quality for commercial vendors include

- Possible class-action litigation from disgruntled customers

- Possible litigation from customers suffering business losses

- Protracted delays in delivering new applications

- Unfavorable reviews by the press and user associations

- Poor customer satisfaction

- Loss of customers if competitive quality is better

- High maintenance costs due to poor quality

- High customer support costs due to poor quality

- Elevated numbers of security flaws in released applications

The commercial software world has only a marginal reputation for software quality. Some companies such as IBM do a good job overall. Others such as Symantec, Oracle, and Microsoft might try to do good jobs but tend to release software with quite a few bugs still latent.

If the commercial software vendors were really at state-of-the art levels of quality control, then software warranties would be both common and effective. Today, the bulk of commercial software "warranties" include only replacement of media. There are no guarantees that software will work effectively on the part of commercial software vendors.

The Economic Value of Software and Quality to COTS Users and Customers

As of 2011 there are about 14,659,956 U.S. companies that use computers and software. But the largest 1,000 companies probably use 50% of the total quantity of COTS packages.

There are more than 150,000 government organizations that use computers and COTS software when federal, state, and municipal agencies are considered as a set (roughly 100,000 federal and military sites; 5,000 state sites; and 50,000 municipal sites).

The main economic reason that companies, government agencies, and individuals purchase or lease commercial software packages is that packaged software is the least expensive way of gaining access to the features and functions that the package offers.

If we need an accounting system, an inventory system, and billing system, or even something as fundamental as a word processor or a spreadsheet, then acquiring a package has been the most cost-effective method for more than 50 years.

For a company or user to attempt to develop applications with features that match those in commercial packages, it would take months or even years. We buy software for the same reason we buy washing machines and automobiles: they are available right now; they can be put to use immediately; and if we are lucky, they will not have too many bugs or defects.

In the future, SaaS, SOA, and cloud computing will no doubt displace many applications with equivalent Web-based services. However, this trend is only just beginning and will probably take another ten years or more to reach maturity.

The open source companies such as Mozilla and the availability of Web-based packages such as Google Applications and Open Office are starting to offer alternatives to commercial packages that are free in many cases. As of 2011 usage of commercial software is still more common than usage of open source or Web-based alternatives, but when the two compete head-to-head, the open source versions seem to be adding new customers at a faster rate.

Examples of companies that use COTS packages include manufacturing companies, law firms, medical offices, small hospitals, small banks, retail stores, and thousands of other companies. All government units at the federal, state, and municipal levels use COTS packages in large numbers, as do the military services. These enterprises use the software to either raise their own profitability or to lower operating costs, or both.

The economic value of high software quality to corporate and government consumers of commercial software has these factors:

- Rapid deployment of COTS applications

- Quicker deployment of new services and functions

- Short learning curves to get up to speed in COTS applications

- Minimizing the risks of in-house development

- Minimizing the risks of outsource development

- Reduced maintenance costs for released applications

- Reduced customer support costs for released applications

The economic consequences of low quality for COTS users include

- Business transaction errors that damage customers or clients

- Business transaction errors that damage financial data

- Possible class-action litigation from disgruntled customers

- Possible litigation from customers suffering business losses

- Possible litigation from shareholders about poor quality

- Protracted delays in delivering new services

- Poor customer satisfaction

- High maintenance costs due to poor quality

- High customer support costs due to poor quality

As an example of the hazards of poor quality from COTS packages, one of the authors lives in Narragansett, Rhode Island. When the town acquired a new property tax software package, tax bills were about a month late in being sent to homeowners, and there were many errors in the calculations. The system also lagged in producing financial reports for the town council. Eventually, the package was withdrawn, and an alternate package from another vendor was used in its place.

A study by one of the authors of the corporate software portfolio for a large manufacturing company in the Fortune 500 class found that out of 3,200 applications in the portfolio, 1,120 were COTS packages acquired from about 75 different vendors.

The total initial cost for these COTS applications was about $168,000,000. Annual leases amounted to about $42,000,000.

Approximately 149 people were devoted exclusively to the operation and maintenance of the COTS packages. In a single year, about 18,072 high-severity bugs were reported against the COTS applications in the portfolio.

Indeed, bugs in COTS packages are so common that one large commercial software vendor was sued by its own shareholders, who claimed that poor quality was lowering the value of their investments. The case was settled, but the fact that such a case was even filed illustrates that the COTS vendors need better quality control.

COTS packages are valuable and useful to be sure. But due to the marginal to poor software quality practices of the commercial vendors, customers and users need to expect and prepare for significant quantities of bugs or defects and significant staffing and effort to keep COTS packages up and running.

The Economic Value of Software and Quality to Embedded Software Companies

Embedded software is present in thousands of products in 2011. For consumer products such as digital watches, digital cameras, smart phones, and similar devices, high quality is fairly common; bugs or low quality is fairly rare.

For more complex devices that might affect human life or safety, the quality levels are still quite good, but bugs or errors can have serious consequences for both those who use the software and for the companies that produce the devices. Bugs or errors in medical devices, automobile brake systems, aircraft navigation devices, and weapons systems can lead to death, injuries, and enormous recall and recovery costs.

The economic value of software for embedded software producers derives primarily from sales of physical equipment rather than the software itself. Examples of companies that create devices with embedded software include Boeing, Motorola, AT&T, Nokia, medical equipment companies such as Advanced Bionics, and many others. In total probably 10,000 companies produce embedded devices and the software within them.

As of 2011, about 45% of the revenue of embedded software companies has come from selling more and more copies of existing products such as digital watches, digital hearing aids, and digital cameras.

About 55% of the revenue of embedded software companies has come from innovation or the creation of new kinds of products and services that did not exist before, such as cochlear implants, the Amazon Kindle and other eBook readers, and the control systems of modern automobiles and aircraft.

The economic value of software quality inside embedded software devices stems from these topics:

- Reduced cancellation rates for complex devices

- Creating new kinds of devices never marketed before

- Earlier delivery of new devices

- Rapid approvals by government oversight organizations

- Rapid customer acceptance of new devices

- Reduced development costs for new devices

- Reduced maintenance costs for released devices

- Reduced customer support costs for released devices

- Increased market share if quality is better than competitors

The economic consequences of low quality for embedded vendors include

- Possible criminal charges if devices causes death or injury

- Possible class-action litigation from disgruntled customers

- Possible litigation from customers suffering business losses

- Possible government action against medical devices for poor quality

- Possible shareholder litigation for poor quality

- Protracted or negative approvals by government oversight groups

- Poor customer satisfaction

- Loss of customers if competitor's quality is better

- High maintenance costs for devices with poor-quality software

- High customer support costs for devices with poor-quality software

Because complex devices won't operate without high-quality software, the embedded software world has one of the best reputations for software quality and also for customer support. Some companies such as Advanced Bionics, Motorola, Apple, and Garmin do a good job overall.

A sign of better-than-average quality control in the embedded domain is the fact that many embedded device companies have product warranties. In general, warranties are more common and more complete for embedded software than for other forms of software.

The Economic Value of Software and Quality to Embedded Equipment Users

The economic value of software to users of equipment controlled by embedded software is the ability to operate complex devices that would not exist without the embedded software. Examples of such devices include robotic manufacturing, undersea oil exploration, medical equipment such as MRI devices and cochlear implants, navigation packages on board ships and aircraft, and all forms of modern communication including television, radio, and wireless.

The major difference between embedded software and other kinds of software is that users are operating physical devices and might not even be aware that the devices are controlled by software. Even if users know that embedded software is in a device, they have no direct control over the software other than the controls on the devices themselves. For example, users can make many adjustments to digital cameras but only by means of using the knobs, buttons, and screens that the cameras have and not by direct changes to the embedded software itself.

The main economic reason that companies, government agencies, and individuals acquire embedded devices is because there are no other alternatives available. You either have a computerized magnetic resonance imaging device (MRI) or you can't perform that kind of diagnosis. There are no other choices.

Embedded devices have also lowered the costs and expanded features in many consumer products. For example, a number of modern digital watches integrate standard time keeping with stop watches, elapsed time keeping, and even tide calculations and the phases of the moon.

Modern digital cameras have a host of functions that were not available on normal film cameras, such as electronic zooming in addition to optical zooming; red-eye correction; and the ability to switch between still and animated photography at will.

Usage of embedded devices has been growing exponentially for about 25 years. As of 2011 at least 150,000,000 U.S. citizens own digital watches, digital cameras, or other personal embedded devices.

Approximately 1,500,000 U.S. patients have digital pacemakers, and the rate of increase is more than 5% per year. There are more than 5,000 installed MRI devices, and more than 1,000,000 U.S. patients undergo MRI diagnoses per year.

According to Wikipedia about 30,000 U.S. citizens now hear as a result of having cochlear implant surgery. (Cochlear implants use a combination of an external microphone and an internal computer surgically implanted under the skin. Small wires from the processor replace the damaged cilia in the inner ear. Cochlear implant devices are fully software controlled, and the software can be upgraded as necessary.)

Most modern factories for complex devices such as automobiles are now either fully or partly equipped with robotic machine tools.

Almost all modern automobiles now use embedded devices for controlling anti-lock brakes (which would otherwise be impossible); fuel injection; navigation packages; and in some cases controlling suspension and steering. Automobile entertainment devices such as satellite radios, standard radios, DVD players, and the like are also controlled by embedded devices and software.

The economic value of high embedded software quality to corporate and government consumers involves these factors:

- New features and functions only available from embedded devices

- Onsite upgrades to new embedded software versions

- Reduced maintenance due to reduction in mechanical parts

- Rapid deployment of new equipment

- Fewer product malfunctions

- Quicker deployment of new services and functions

The economic consequences of low quality for embedded device users include

- Possible death or injury from software bugs in medical devices

- Possible death or injury from software bugs in automobiles

- Possible death or injury from software bugs in aircraft

- Disruption of robotic manufacturing due to bugs or errors

- Inability to make repairs without replacing embedded devices

- Possible class-action litigation from disgruntled customers

- Possible litigation from customers suffering business losses

- Protracted delays in delivering new services

- Poor customer satisfaction

- High customer support costs due to poor quality

Modern devices controlled by embedded software are one of the greatest machine revolutions in all of history. There are now dozens of complicated devices such as drone aircraft, remotely controlled submarines, MRI medical devices, cochlear implants, and robotic manufacturing that would be impossible without embedded devices and the software that controls them.

Embedded software and embedded devices are advancing medical diagnosis and medical treatments for conditions such as deafness and heart conditions. Today, there are thousands of embedded devices carrying out functions that were totally impossible before about 1975.

The Economic Value of Software and Software Quality to Other Business Sectors

There are a number of other business sectors that might be discussed in the context of the value of software and the value of software quality. Among these can be found

- Outsource software vendors and outsource software clients and users

- Defense software vendors and defense software clients and users

- Systems software vendors and systems software clients and users

- Open source software vendors and open source software clients and users

- Gaming software vendors and gaming software clients and users

- Smart phone software vendors and smart phone software clients and users

The views of both value and the value of software quality in these business sectors, however, are similar to the sectors already discussed. High quality benefits costs, schedules, and customer satisfaction. Low quality leads to cost and schedule overruns and dissatisfied customers.

Multiple Roles Occurring Simultaneously

Many large enterprises have multiple roles going on simultaneously. For example, a major corporation such as AT&T performs all of these roles at the same time:

- They build internal IT software for their own use.
- They build web applications for marketing and customer support.
- They build embedded software for sale or lease to clients.
- They build systems software for sale or lease to clients.
- They commission domestic outsource groups to build software under contract.
- They commission offshore outsource groups to build software under contract.
- They purchase and lease COTS packages.
- They acquire and utilize open source software.
- They offer business services that depend upon software.

This is a very common pattern. Many large corporations build and consume software of multiple types. However, regardless of the pattern, software quality is a critical success factor on both the development and the consumption sides of the equation.

Summary and Conclusions

The topic of software quality has been difficult to define for more than 50 years. The topic of economic value has been difficult to define for more than 150 years. When the two topics are combined into a single book, it is necessary to start by considering all of the alternatives that surround both terms.

The economic value of software needs to be analyzed from both the production and consumption sides of the equation.

The value of software quality needs to be analyzed in terms of the benefits of high quality and the harmful consequences of poor quality. And here, too, both the production and consumption of software need to be considered:

High quality	Value to producers
	Value to stakeholders and financial backers
	Value to users and consumers
Low quality	Risks and hazards to producers
	Risks and hazards to stakeholders and financiers
	Risks and hazards to users and consumers

The essential message that will be demonstrated later in the book is that a high level of software quality will raise the economic value of software for the producers, financiers, and the consumers of software applications.

Conversely, low software quality levels will degrade the economic value of software for both the producers and consumers of software applications.

But achieving high levels of software quality needs effective defect prevention, effective pretest defect removal, effective testing, effective quality estimation, effective quality measurements, effective teams, and effective management. Testing alone has never been sufficient to achieve high-quality software.

Chapter 2

Estimating and Measuring Software Quality

Introduction

To predict the future of a software project with acceptable accuracy, it is necessary to measure past projects and also to keep track of the activities of current and ongoing projects. Estimation and measurement are closely aligned, and good historical data is of great value in estimating the outcomes of future software projects.

Productivity and schedule predictions can often be made from observations and benchmarks from similar projects. But quality benchmarks are rare, and therefore most managers and software engineers are not able to predict quality with anything that approaches accuracy. Indeed, a common reason for both cancelled projects and litigation is that of excessive bugs that surface during testing and stretch out schedules until the project's value turns negative. Often the number of bugs that occur surprises development personnel, managers, and clients. Few people know how many bugs or defects are likely to occur in software projects.

Local history from within your own enterprise is the most valuable if it is complete and accurate. But acquiring benchmark data from external sources such as the nonprofit International Software Benchmark Standards Group (ISBSG) is also of value. ISBG has more than 5,000 projects with productivity, but only a few hundred of these also have quality data. This indicates how rare quality measurements are in the software industry.

The correlation between estimation and measurement is particularly strong for quality predictions. If there are gaps in historical cost and productivity data, they can be repaired by interviewing team members. But if there are gaps and errors in quality data, such as failing to record defects found prior to function testing, there is no easy way to repair the missing data because no one can remember the numbers of bugs and defects found earlier.

As of 2011 some commercial software estimation tools predict quality levels with good accuracy. Indeed, commercial tools such as COCOMO II, KnowledgePlan, SEER, SLIM, and Software Risk Master are probably the most accurate methods for quality estimation, due to having data from thousands of historical projects. But based on the author's interviews with client companies, less than 25% of software engineering groups utilize automated cost and quality estimation tools.

In 2011 the majority of U.S. software project managers, software engineers, and software quality assurance (SQA) personnel are not well trained in software quality estimation. Based on interviews during assessment studies, an alarming number of the same personnel are not well trained in quality measurement methods either.

Indeed, a major "knowledge gap" of the entire software engineering community is a lack of understanding of the combined results of software defect prevention methods, pretest defect removal methods such as inspections and static analysis, and effective software testing methods. Testing alone has never been sufficient to achieve high quality levels, nor is testing alone cost effective.

Every effective definition of software quality must meet three key criteria:

1. It should be predictable before projects start.

2. It should be measurable while projects are underway.

3. It should be measurable after deployment during maintenance.

These criteria raise important questions about what exactly should be predicted and measured to understand software quality economics. The ten key topics that need to be both measured and estimated include

1. Software defect potentials

2. Software defect prevention methods

3. Software pretest defect removal methods

4. Software testing defect removal methods

5. Pre-release defect removal costs and schedules

6. Post-release defects found by customers

7. Post-release defect removal costs and schedules

8. Bad fixes or secondary defects found in defect repairs themselves

9. Defect detection efficiency or the percentage of defects identified before release

10. Defect removal efficiency, or the percentage of defects removed prior to delivery of the application to its customers and users

The phrase *software defect potentials* originated at IBM circa 1973. This phrase defines the sum total of all classes of software defects that might occur in requirements, design, code, user documents, and other deliverables. IBM's knowledge of defect potentials was the result of many years of careful measurement. Five major sources comprised IBM's original measures of defect potentials starting in the early 1970s at IBM San Jose: 1) requirements defects, 2) design defects, 3) coding defects, 4) document defects, and 5) bad fixes or secondary defects introduced from bug repairs themselves. This book uses the original five but adds database defects, test case defects, and website defects because they are significant in volume and impact.

The phrase *defect prevention* also originated at IBM. This phrase defines the effectiveness of methods that lower defect potentials such as Joint Application Design (JAD), prototyping, Six-Sigma for software, and Quality Function Deployment (QFD). As it happens some methods of defect removal such as inspections and static analysis are also quite effective in preventing defects. Here, too, careful measurement was what enabled IBM to judge defect prevention effectiveness.

The phrase *pretest defect removal* refers to traditional desk checking, to informal peer reviews, to formal inspections of design and code, and to the modern tools that perform static analysis of source code. Pretest defect removal is an important part of an effective software quality control approach. Pretest removal is efficient in finding bugs and is also cost-effective. Pretest defect removal also shortens test cycles and raises testing efficiency.

The phrase *testing defect removal* refers to the entire gamut of test stages used on software applications. The many forms of software testing that may be utilized include subroutine test, unit test, new function test, regression test, performance test, security test, usability test, component test, platform test, independent test, system test, external Beta test, and acceptance test. Testing in all its forms seldom tops 85% in total defect removal efficiency. A combination of pretest removal and testing removal is necessary to top 95% in defect removal efficiency. As it happens, 95% is a good demarcation line between good quality and mediocre quality.

The phrase *pre-release defect removal costs* refers to the sum total of costs for both pretest removal activities such as inspections and static analysis combined with the costs of all testing stages.

The phrase *post-release defects* refers to defects that are still present and latent when software applications are delivered to users. Obviously, the phrase does not refer to defects that might be present during an external Beta test or customer acceptance test. This phrase means defects that are still present after all forms of internal defect removal have been completed. Software applications are routinely delivered to customers with hundreds or even thousands of latent defects still present. Customer-reported defects for commercial and information system software usually total between 15% and 35% of latent defects in the first year. Users of embedded applications and weapons systems usually find more than 75% in the first year due to the nature of the devices that contain the software.

The phrase *post-release defect removal costs* refers to the combined costs of customer support and the repair costs for customer-reported defects after formal release.

The phrase *bad fixes* refers to a troubling phenomenon first noted within IBM in the early 1970s. It often happens that attempts to fix bugs include new bugs or defects in the fixes themselves. Indeed, the U.S. average for bad-fix injections is about 7%. However, in some cases such as software with high complexity and poor structures, bad-fix injections have topped 25%. In one lawsuit in which one of the authors worked as an expert witness, the vendor attempted to fix a bug four times. Each fix failed to repair the original bug, and each fix contained new bugs. Finally, a fifth attempt did repair the original bug and seemed free of secondary bugs as well. But nine calendar months had passed between the date that the original bug was first reported and the date of the fifth and final defect repair.

The phrase *defect detection efficiency* (DDE) refers to the percentage of defects that are found and identified by software developers prior to the release of the software to clients. Note that there is a sharp distinction between "defect detection" and "defect removal." In today's world of lax quality control, some companies do not repair all defects found via inspection, static analysis, and testing. In order to meet delivery schedules, the software may be shipped with known defects still latent within it. The current U.S. average for defect detection efficiency circa 2011 seems to be about 92%, with a range that runs from 80% up to 99%.

The phrase *defect removal efficiency* (DRE) refers to the percentage of defects that are found, identified, and removed by software developers prior to the release of the software to clients. The current U.S. average for defect removal efficiency circa 2011 is about 85%, with a range that runs from below 75% up to 99% in very rare cases. To calculate defect removal efficiency, the calculations are based on total defects repaired prior to release plus customer-reported defects for the first 90 days after release. For example, if the developers found 90 bugs before release and the clients reported ten bugs in the first three months, then defect removal efficiency for this example is 90%. This is a very important quality metric because applications that top 95% in defect removal efficiency tend to have shorter schedules and lower costs than similar applications with lower levels of defect removal efficiency. The applications also have happier customers and lower maintenance costs.

The ten topics discussed on the previous pages expand into hundreds of subtopics. For the purposes of quality estimation and quality measurement, it is necessary to understand the details of three of the ten topics: 1) defect potentials, 2) defect prevention, and 3) defect removal.

Using Function Point Metrics for Defect Potentials

This book uses function point metrics for quantifying defect potentials. The specific form of function point is version 4.2 as defined by the International Function Point Users Group (IFPUG).

The reason that function points are the best choice for measuring defect potentials is that the older "lines of code" or LOC metric can only be used to quantify coding defects. When all sources and kinds of software defects are considered as a set, coding defects only comprise about 17% of the total defect volume. The LOC metric cannot be used to measure requirements defects, architecture defects, design defects, or any other of the noncoding defects.

There are deeper and more serious issues with lines of code metrics that are discussed later in this chapter.

There are many other function point metrics in existence. Some of these include COSMIC function points, NESMA function points, Finnish function points, the older Mark II function points, and engineering function points.

In addition, there are other metrics that are somewhat analogous to function points but use different factors and adjustment ratios. Use-case points, story points, and web-object points are examples of these quasi-functional metrics.

Software Defect Potentials

Software bugs or defects stem from many sources and have many causes. To predict future volumes of bugs, it is necessary to have accurate measurements of bugs from all sources in current and historical projects.

Because most companies lack good historical data for quality and bugs, they must of necessity depend on synthetic data derived from similar companies or on the predictions of quality estimation tools. Information provided in this chapter can be used to predict defects, but so many variables are involved that the commercial software estimation tools that include quality estimates are the best choice.

Table 2.1 attempts to show the approximate average values for all of the sources of defects that affect software applications. These average values have wide ranges of more than 3 to 1 based on application size, team skills, CMMI levels, methodologies, certified reusable materials, and other factors as well.

Some of the averages have a significant margin of error because of the lack of standard size metrics for database volumes, websites, and test libraries. As a surrogate, all of the size data is based on the assumed size of the software application that is being developed or maintained. This is not a perfect assumption, but it has the convenience of allowing all forms of defects to be expressed using a single metric and to show the relative proportions of each source.

The technology assumptions underlying Table 2.1 assume CMMI level 1 and a traditional waterfall development method. Later in the book alternate assumptions such as higher CMMI levels and alternative development methods such as Agile, RUP, and TSP are discussed and illustrated. The data in Table 2.1 is derived from more than 13,000 projects examined between 1973 and 2010.

Table 2.1 differs from similar tables in prior books by one of the authors such as *Software Assessments, Benchmarks, and Best Practices* (Jones 2000), *Estimating Software Costs* (Jones 2007), *Applied Software Measurement* (Jones 2008), and *Software Engineering Best Practices* (Jones 2010). These prior books only discussed defects from five sources: requirements, design, code, documents, and bad fixes. This book discusses defects from eight sources. In addition, bad fix defects are not shown as a separate category in this book but rather are included in the eight defect sources; however, bad-fix injections still average about 7% of defect repair attempts.

Table 2.1 illustrates all of the possible sources of software defects that aggregated together comprise the "defect potentials" of modern software applications.

Table 2.1 *Software Defect Potentials*

	Defects per Function Point	Percent of Total Defects
Requirement Defects	1.15	9.58%
Legacy requirement defects		
Toxic requirement defects		
Impossible requirements		
Omitted requirements		
Defects in new requirements		
Defects in changed requirements		
Bad-fix injection for requirement defects		

	Defects per Function Point	Percent of Total Defects
Architectural Defects	0.25	2.08%
Legacy architectural defects		
Enterprise architectural defects		
Structural architectural defects		
Security architectural defects		
Supply-chain architectural defects		
Platform architectural defects		
Cloud-related architectural defects		
Bad-fix injection for requirement defects		
Design Defects	1.50	12.50%
Legacy design defects		
Omitted design features		
External design defects (usability, interfaces)		
Internal design defects (performance, extensibility)		
Supply-chain design defects		
Platform design defects		
Cloud-related design defects		
Security design defects		
Bad-fix injection for design defects		
Coding Defects	2.00	16.67%
Legacy code defects		
Reusable code defects		
Violations of SANS coding principles:		
Insecure interactions		
Risky resource management		
Porous security defenses		
Performance-related code defects		
Structural and complexity code defects		
Error-handling code defects		
Memory management code defects		
Defects in comments and headers		
Defects in error-messages		
Bad-fix injection for coding defects		

(Continued)

Table 2.1   *(Continued)*

	Defects per Function Point	Percent of Total Defects
Test Plan and Test Case Defects	1.85	15.42%
Legacy test case defects		
Reusable test case defects		
Omitted test plan features		
Omitted test cases and low coverage		
Test case design defects		
Test case structural defects		
Test case platform defects		
Duplicate test cases		
Bad-fix injection for testing defects		
User Documentation Defects	0.75	6.25%
Legacy documentation defects		
Omissions from user documents		
Errors or omissions in installation instructions		
Errors or omissions in operating instructions		
Errors or omissions in application removal		
Errors of fact in user documents		
Errors of clarity and understandability		
Errors in HELP text and instructions		
Errors or omissions in translations		
Bad-fix injection for documentation defects		
Database Defects	2.75	22.92%
Legacy database defects		
Reusable database defects		
Third-party database defects		
Structural database defects		
Performance database defects		
Security database defects		
Omitted data		
Factual errors in data		
Bad-fix injections for database defects		

	Defects per Function Point	Percent of Total Defects
Website Defects	1.75	14.58%
Legacy website defects		
Broken or missing website links		
Third-party website defects		
Structural website defects		
Performance website defects		
Security website defects		
Navigation website defects		
User instruction website defects		
Bad-fix injections for website defects		
TOTAL	12.00	100.00%

As can be seen from Table 2.1, modern applications can and do contain defects from a wide variety of sources and causes. Indeed, coding defects are less than 20% of the total volume of defects for all applications larger than about 100 function points or 5,000 source code statements in size.

Defect potentials go up with application size. This fact has been known since the 1950s and has been verified by measurements of thousands of applications ranging from 10 function points to more than 300,000 function points. However, defects in requirements and design increase at a faster rate than coding defects. Table 2.2 illustrates average defect potentials for applications between 10 and 100,000 function points in size.

Table 2.2 *Defect Potentials by Application Size*

Defect Source	Application Size in Function Points				
	10	100	1,000	10,000	100,000
Requirements	0.25	0.75	1.00	1.25	1.50
Architecture	0.05	0.10	0.25	0.50	0.75
Design	0.50	1.00	1.25	1.50	1.75
Source Code	1.65	1.70	1.75	2.00	2.10
Test Materials	1.25	1.50	1.85	2.00	2.10
Documents	0.60	0.65	0.70	0.75	0.80
Database	1.50	2.00	2.75	3.00	3.20
Websites	1.25	1.50	1.75	2.00	2.25
TOTAL	7.05	9.20	11.30	13.00	14.45

Testing primarily concentrates on coding defects. But for large systems and large applications, coding defects are not the main source of trouble. Coding defects are also the easiest to eliminate. For large systems, requirements defects, architectural defects, and design defects are the main sources of quality problems. Of course, large databases and large websites have serious quality problems, too.

Modern business applications have become so complex that they have been decomposed into several different subsystems, or tiers, built on different software platforms using different programming languages. Not surprisingly, a National Research Council study on "dependable software" concluded that testing is no longer sufficient to ensure an application will be reliable, efficient, secure, and maintainable (Jackson, 2009). To reduce the business risk of these multi-tier applications, it is essential to supplement testing with static analysis for measuring and controlling application quality and dependability.

The majority of defects that cause system outages, performance degradation, security breaches, and exorbitant maintenance costs are no longer isolated in a single file or piece of code (Hamill, 2009). The most catastrophic problems occur in interactions among the various tiers of an application. Even more challenging, these defects are not failures to satisfy the functional requirements provided by the customer but rather are nonfunctional defects in the engineering of the application's architecture or source code (Spinellis, 2007). Test cases are usually designed to detect functional defects. To find the defects that cause the most severe damage during operations, one needs to analyze the structural quality of an application—the integrity of its internal structural and engineering characteristics.

One of the problems with printed books, as opposed to dynamic estimates, is that books have trouble dealing with multiple concurrent factors. Predicting software defect potentials is a highly complex task that includes

- Client understanding of their own requirements

- Team skills in similar applications

- Methodologies used for defect prevention

- Pretest defect removal methods

- Cyclomatic complexity of code

- Test case design methods

- Test coverage percent

- Test library control methods

Each of the factors cited here can have about a 20% impact one way or the other on software defect potentials, and all of them can be in play at the same time.

The Special Case of Software Requirements

One of the traditional definitions of software quality for more than 50 years has been "conformance to requirements." This is an unfortunate definition, however, because requirements themselves are filled with defects that generate about 20% of the total volume of software defects. The current U.S. average for requirements defects is about 1.00 per function point. It is obvious that conformance to a major source of error is not a safe definition for software quality.

Not only are software requirements defects numerous, but they are also very resistant to removal via standard methods such as static analysis and testing. After a requirement defect is actually in an approved requirements document, then test cases written using those requirements will tend to confirm the defect rather than challenge it.

A prime example of a "toxic requirement" that could not be removed via normal testing was the famous Y2K problem. The use of two digits for calendar dates originated as an explicit user requirement in the 1960s when storage was expensive and limited. Of course, at the end of 1999 when the year changed to 2000, all sorting operations based on dates would have been thrown off. This explains why so many millions of dollars were spent on Y2K repairs.

Another requirement error with possibly serious consequences is the omission of a paper trail in electronic voting machines, which makes it difficult to detect errors, hacking, and deliberate falsification.

The software engineering community has an ethical and professional obligation to assist clients in understanding and eliminating toxic requirements. The clients themselves cannot be expected to understand the intricacies of putting business applications onto computers, so it is up to the software engineering community to keep their clients from implementing harmful requirements. This community should have a kind of Hippocratic Oath that includes the concept of "first, do no harm."

By fortunate coincidence the structure of the function point metric is a good match to the fundamental issues that should be included in software requirements. In chronological order these seven fundamental topics should be explored as part of the requirements gathering process:

1. The *outputs* that should be produced by the application

2. The *inputs* that will enter the software application

3. The *logical files* that must be maintained by the application

4. The *entities and relationships* that will be in the logical files of the application

5. The *inquiry types* that can be made against the application

6. The *interfaces* between the application, other systems, and users

7. Key *algorithms* and *business rules* that must be present in the application

Note that the first and most important requirement to be analyzed is that of *outputs*. Companies that do polls and opinion surveys such as Gallup and Nielsen discovered many years ago that when a new survey is needed, the initial step is to produce a mock report that will show the clients what kinds of information will be produced by the survey.

The reason for this is that if *inputs* are attempted before *outputs* are clearly understood, there is a tendency to gather far more data than is really needed. Therefore, the requirements analysis process needs to start with the outputs and deliverables of software applications.

Five of these seven topics are the basic elements of the International Function Point Users Group (IFPUG) function point metric: that is, outputs, inputs, logical files, inquiries, and interfaces.

The fourth topic, "entities and relationships," is part of the British Mark II function point metric and the newer COSMIC function point.

The seventh topic, "algorithms," was a standard factor of the feature point metric, which added a count of algorithms to the five basic function point elements used by IFPUG.

There is such a strong synergy between requirements and function point analysis that it would be possible to construct a combined requirements analysis tool with full function point sizing support as a natural adjunct. Indeed, a working version of such a tool was developed, but the company that commissioned it unfortunately went out of business before the tool could be deployed.

If full automation of both requirements and function points is to be possible, the requirements themselves must be fairly well structured and complete. Toward that end, in addition to the 7 fundamental requirement topics, there are also 13 other ancillary topics that should be resolved during the requirements gathering phase:

1. The *size* of the application in function points and source code

2. The *schedule* of the application from requirements to delivery

3. The *cost* of the application by activity and also in terms of cost per function point

4. The *quality levels* in terms of defects, reliability, and ease-of-use criteria

5. The *hardware platform(s)* on which the application will operate

6. The *software platform(s)* such as operating systems and databases

7. The *security criteria* for the application and its companion databases

8. The *performance criteria*, if any, for the application

9. The *training requirements* or form of tutorial materials that may be needed

10. The *installation requirements* for putting the application onto the host platforms

11. The *reuse criteria* for the application in terms of both reused materials going into the application and also whether features of the application may be aimed at subsequent reuse by downstream applications

12. The *use cases* or *major tasks* users are expected to be able to perform via the application

13. The *control flow* or sequence of information moving through the application.

These 13 supplemental topics are not the only items that can be included in requirements, but none of these 13 should be omitted by accident given that they can all have a significant effect on software projects.

The synergy between function points and software requirements is good enough so that it is now technically possible to merge the requirements gathering process and the development of function point metrics and improve both tasks simultaneously.

Indeed, a modern requirements generation and analysis tool would include these features and functions:

1. **A method for extracting algorithms and business rules from legacy application source code:** A majority of "new" applications are in fact replacements for legacy applications. Unfortunately, most legacy applications have not updated their requirements and design documents, so the source code is the sole repository for missing algorithms and business rules. A tool that can perform forensic analysis of legacy code would be a significant advance in dealing with legacy requirements.

2. **A method of identifying and displaying common generic features used by many similar applications:** About 75% of the features of most software applications are also used by other applications and could be embodied in a set of reusable objects that would include source code, test cases, requirements specifications, and user information. By starting requirements analysis with a list of standard reusable components, the work of requirements analysis would be greatly simplified. This topic and the previous topic are synergistic because forensic analysis of legacy applications should be able to identify common and generic features.

3. **A method of automatically sizing the application as a natural byproduct of requirements analysis:** Because function point metrics are closely related to application requirements, size could be generated automatically from requirements lists. Indeed, manual function point analysis is based on requirements, and that process lends itself to full automation. It is already possible to perform size approximations of applications via pattern matching. Extending that capability to specific features rather than the overall application would add value to the requirements analysis process. In addition to sizing, related features that could perform risk analysis, solution modeling, and total cost of ownership (TCO) predictions would add a dose of reality to requirements analysis.

4. **A method of automatically defining test cases as a natural byproduct of requirements analysis:** It is a logical necessity that "testable requirements" be identified and test plans and test cases prepared. For requirements that are derived from legacy applications, the test cases and other materials should be part of the package of reusable material. If not, then the data mining tool that extracts missing algorithms and business rules should define test cases at the same time. For new and unique applications, testable requirements should automatically couple the requirements themselves with test cases and test scripts.

5. **A method of dealing with the dynamic aspects of software applications:** When software is executing, it has more moving parts and they move more rapidly than any other known product. This fact indicates that software requirements and design tools should not be based exclusively on static representations such as text, tables, diagrams, and screen images. Software requirements tools should facilitate modeling of the application when it is operating, and that implies a need for animation—probably full-color, three-dimensional animation.

6. **A method for dealing with the growth of requirements over time:** The measured rate at which requirements grow during development is about 1% per calendar month. After the software is deployed, the measured

rate at which it continues to be enhanced or changed averages about 8% per calendar year for as long as the software continues to be used. These percentages are based on the predicted size of the application at the end of the requirements phase. The initial requirements should envision a multiyear, multirelease strategy and facilitate subsets of applications too large to be designed in a single release.

7. **A method for dealing with applications that will operate on a variety of platforms, such as Windows, Linux, Leopard, Android, and the like:** In addition, the requirements analysis process also needs to consider newer topics such as cloud computing and SOA. In today's world, many applications will operate on multiple platforms and be available as both installed applications and web-enabled applications. All potential variations of hosting and deployment need to be included in requirements.

8. **A method for dealing with applications that will operate in multiple countries:** Nationalization and regionalization are so common that a robust requirements analysis tool would include built-in navigation for handling topics such as language translations, currency exchange rates, local laws and policies, and even topics such as dealing with frequent power outages, which are not uncommon and will become more common. Also needed is information about local laws and security restrictions in various countries. The recent flap about prohibiting Blackberry cell phones in Bahrain illustrates why nationalization is a critical topic for software requirements...although the Bahrain incident may be more political than technical.

9. **A method for reviewing and analyzing examples of similar applications that have been developed in the past or are widely deployed within the same industry:** This kind of data would include benchmarks of cost and schedule information, architectural and design features, and surveys of user associations. Instead of jumping into the dark using only local requirements, it would be very effective to gather data from perhaps 10 to 50 similar applications. Indeed, some of the features of these applications might be useful for requirements analysis of the local application. At the time this book is being written, one of the authors is working on software risk assessment for a state government. One of the applications being assessed has already been attempted and failed in several others states. This kind of survey of similar applications can provide valuable information during requirements analysis.

10. **A method for dealing with security flaws and possible security attacks:** In the modern world, all software applications are at risk. Applications that deal with financial data, medical records, national security, tax

information, and other valuable kinds of data are at extreme risk. A modern requirements generation tool should include expert advice on dealing with security flaws before development begins, and the tool should suggest the most effective strategies for minimizing the risks of denial-of-service attacks, viruses, worms, bot nets, and other modern security problems. Indeed, in today's world not only conventional security problems need to be considered, but also possible disruption of electronic devices and computers due to electro-magnetic pulses (EMP).

In summary form, a modern requirements generation tool would probably support 3D, full-color, animated graphical representations; include a full inventory of generic features that are available in reusable form; and include features for sizing, generating test cases, and generating security prevention methods. It would also support multiple platforms and multiple countries as well as link to benchmark sources such as the International Software Benchmark Standards Group (ISBSG) to seek out applications of the same size, type, and class.

The Origins of Software Requirements

The software industry has been extremely successful in generating revenue and creating wealth. Many of the wealthiest citizens in the United States and other countries are software entrepreneurs such as Bill Gates, Larry Ellison, Steve Jobs, and the like.

That fact is relevant to understanding the origins of software requirements. Although some requirements are based on market studies and user requests, the really valuable requirements that have generated billions of dollars in revenue stemmed from inventors of new forms of software.

Table 2.3 shows the approximate distribution of current software features and also of software revenue that is derived from those features.

Although software stakeholders and software users generate the largest numbers of features and create the largest volumes of requirements, the major software revenue producers are original inventions of new kinds of software and derivatives of those inventions by fast followers and later competitors.

If you look at the most successful software products such as the first spreadsheets, the Google search engine, the first estimation tool based on function points, and GPS navigation systems, they did not result from gathering requirements from stakeholders but rather from original inventions by knowledge workers who were trying to solve problems that affected them personally. However, because inventors are not always successful business people, it often happens that fast followers and competitors generate more revenue than the original inventors.

Table 2.3 *Requirements Origins and Value*

	Percent of Features	Percent of Revenue
Inventors	5.00%	15.00%
Fast followers	15.00%	25.00%
Competitors	10.00%	20.00%
Stakeholders	20.00%	10.00%
Users	20.00%	5.00%
Market studies	15.00%	5.00%
Hardware needs	10.00%	15.00%
Developers	2.50%	2.50%
Others	2.50%	2.50%
TOTALS	100.00%	100.00%

There are many complicated hardware devices that require software to operate. For example, cochlear implants that restore hearing to the deaf include a small computer that is surgically attached to the skull, small wires that substitute for damaged cilia, and an external microphone and power supply. But it is the onboard software that handles features such as noise cancellation, frequency adjustments, automatic volume control, and the like.

For physical devices the majority of requirements are based on the needs and characteristics of the devices themselves. Because high quality and reliability are mandatory for embedded devices, the requirements methods and quality methods are unusually rigorous.

Another area where requirements are based on external issues is that of commercial software packages such as spreadsheets, enterprise-resource planning (ERP) packages, and hundreds of others. For many commercial packages, requirements do not come from users directly, but rather from studies of the features that competitors are offering. Of course, there are marketing studies and focus groups, but when a competitor brings out something innovative and new, all other companies in the same space will attempt to replicate it. The commercial anti-virus market has dozens of companies whose products are not quite identical but probably have more than 95% common feature sets.

The most ambiguous requirements and the ones that have the greatest volume of changes and the most defects are for software applications that companies design and build to support business operations. Business rules are often ambiguous and may change unexpectedly due to government regulations, mergers with other companies, or unanticipated factors such as offerings by competitors.

Also, the stakeholders who pay for business applications are usually executives and managers, but they do not use the software themselves. Therefore, the funding sources for business software and the actual users of the software may have differing views about what is needed.

When business applications are turned over to outsource contractors for development, yet another layer of complexity is introduced. The outsource vendors may or may not have any familiarity with the business domain the software supports. They may also be geographically separated from both the funding stakeholders and the users themselves.

One surprising source of "requirements" was discovered by IBM in the 1970s. When analyzing the features of IBM's commercial software packages, it was discovered that almost 10% of the features in the deployed applications were not in the requirements at all!

What was happening was that the IBM developers were spontaneously adding new features that seemed useful to them, even though the features were not in the original requirements. This same phenomenon has since been observed in many other companies. Indeed, some companies such as Google actually encourage the practice.

In general, these developer-originated features are benign, and some are valuable. But from time to time these undocumented features may be used for malicious purposes such as back doors for malware.

What is probably the best solution is a method of formally promoting these developer-originated features into the formal requirements and including them in security inspections, testing, static analysis, and the like. They should also be documented in user manuals.

The Size, Structure, and Completeness of Software Requirements

Anyone who has tried to read the software requirements for a large application will know that it is slow going through material that is often difficult to understand. This should not be a surprise.

Software applications themselves usually consist of about 20% input screens; 50% invisible processing logic; and 30% output displays and reporting.

Software requirements, on the other hand, consist of about 75% text; 15% graphs and tables; 5% screen images; and 5% diagrams. Text is the most widely used representation method for requirements, but it is not very effective for that purpose. If the unified modeling language (UML) is used for requirements, the graphics contents would be higher. Even with use cases and some graphical representations such as those offered by the UML, going through and understanding requirements tends to be a daunting task.

Table 2.4 shows the approximate sizes and completeness for software requirements for applications between 10 and 100,000 function points in size.

Table 2.4 is based on normal information systems applications. Requirements for original inventions and for embedded software have different attributes.

The primary reason that completeness declines as application size increases is that if the number of pages in the requirements actually matched the overall size of software applications, at about 50,000 function points the requirements would go beyond the lifetime reading speed of a typical college graduate!

The gaps and omissions in normal requirements are one of the reasons why requirements grow and change during software development. Table 2.5 shows the approximate monthly growth rate in requirements, and then the cumulative growth from the end of the requirements phase until deployment.

As can be seen from Table 2.5 for applications of 1,000 function points,m less than 10% of delivered features are due to requirements changes. But for applications of 10,000 function points, requirements changes after the initial requirements phase constitute about 27% of delivered features. For massive systems in the 100,000 function point size range, the total growth due to requirements changes tops 50%. The longer the project's schedule, the greater the growth rate of changing requirements.

Table 2.4 *Software Requirements Size and Completeness*

Application Size in Function Points	Requirements Pages per Function Point	Total Pages in Requirements	Requirements Completeness
10	1.35	14	97.00%
100	1.15	115	95.00%
1,000	0.75	750	80.00%
10,000	0.60	6,000	60.00%
100,000	0.15	15,000	20.00%
AVERAGE	0.50	5,005	39.00%

Table 2.5 *Software Schedules and Requirements Growth*

Application Size in Function Points	Application Schedule in Calendar Months	Monthly Rate of Requirements Growth	Monthly Growth in Function Points	Total Growth of Application in Function Points
10	0.50	1.00%	0.10	0.03
100	4.50	1.00%	1.00	2.25
1,000	15.00	1.25%	12.50	93.75
10,000	44.00	1.25%	125.00	2,750.00
100,000	68.00	1.50%	1,500.00	51,000.00
AVERAGE	26.40	1.20%	327.72	10,769.21

Some changes in requirements are due to poor requirements analysis. Other changes are due to external events such as changes in tax laws, new mandates, mergers and acquisitions, and other business topics outside the control of the software development teams.

Software requirements grow most rapidly through the design and coding phases. At some point in time it is necessary to freeze all new requirements for the current release and defer them to future releases. This point in time is usually near the end of the coding phase and prior to the start of formal testing by test specialists. Therefore, the time period of requirements growth in Table 2.5 is artificially set to be 50% of the total schedule in calendar months. Of course this is an arbitrary simplification that varies in real life.

It is not widely known or discussed in the software literature, but software requirements changes tend to have a higher defect potential than original requirements (due to rushing them) and a lower defect removal efficiency rate (due to skimping on quality control). Therefore, requirements changes contribute more than their fair share to overall defects in software applications. A 10% growth in application size due to changing requirements will result in about a 12% increase in delivered defects. A 30% growth in application size due to changing requirements can result in more than a 40% increase in delivered defects.

Table 2.6 shows the approximate volumes of software requirements defects and average rates of defect removal efficiency prior to deployment. Table 2.6 is based on ordinary information systems where the requirements derive from users and stakeholders.

Table 2.6 assumes average but inadequate quality control for requirements defects. In other words, testing is the primary defect removal method, and formal requirements inspections, quality function deployment (QFD), and joint application design (JAD) are not assumed in Table 2.6.

Table 2.6 *Software Defects and Requirements Growth*

Application Size in Function Points	Requirements Defect Potentials in Function Points	Total Requirements Defects	Average Defect Removal Efficiency	Average Number of Delivered Requirements Defects
10	0.50	5	95.00%	0
100	0.75	75	90.00%	8
1,000	1.00	1,000	85.00%	150
10,000	1.05	10,500	80.00%	2,100
100,000	1.10	110,000	75.00%	27,500
AVERAGE	0.88	24,316	85.00%	5,952

When the analysis turns to requirements created by inventors or for embedded applications and commercial packages, both the sources of requirements and defect potentials are quite different than they are for ordinary information systems.

For software applications that are created out of the mind of individual inventors to solve problems that are important to them personally, it is fair to claim that there are zero requirements defects. Of course, fast followers will soon improve the initial concepts, but when something unique and novel is added to the software world, there are no other users besides the original inventor.

For embedded applications that control physical devices, the bulk of the software requirements are derived from the hardware requirements. There may be defects in these hardware requirements, but they are more or less outside the control of the software development groups. In any case, embedded applications seem to have only about 20% of the numbers of software requirements defects as do information systems.

Commercial software such as operating systems, office suites, and enterprise-resource planning (ERP) packages have a lot of bugs and defects in their design and source code but not a great many requirements defects. The reason for this is that requirements tend to be based on what features competitors have in the market, rather than features derived from users or stakeholders.

In fact, many commercial software packages suffer more from "feature bloat" than from requirements defects. As an example, one of the authors of this book has written 15 previous books and more than 200 journal articles using Microsoft Word. Yet he has used hardly more than 5% of the total feature set of this massive product. In 2011 Microsoft Word is probably approaching 5,000 function points in size, but to simply write ordinary formatted text and edit with spell checking only takes about 250 function points.

Of course, Microsoft Word has millions of users, and each one probably needs a slightly different set of features. Some users need to include mathematical formulae, some need many different fonts, some need multiple columns, and so forth.

What seems to happen is that some commercial software products in competitive fields tend to get into "feature races" where each new release brings out something that, hopefully, the competitors don't have. Because commercial packages have to be updated often due to competitive pressures, their features tend to get larger and more baroque each year.

Minimizing Software Requirements Defects

Software requirements for information systems are large but incomplete; difficult to understand; omit needed topics such as quality; and contain numerous defects, some of which may be "toxic" and should not be included in the software application at all. What can be done to improve the chronic problems with software requirements?

In the long term, a complete evaluation of current requirements analysis methods plus experiments with advanced topics such as certified reuse and 3D animation might make significant improvements in requirements and also improvements in software development practices.

In the near term, we have to deal with requirements methods, tools, and techniques that are currently available and easily acquired. Following are discussions of current techniques that are available for minimizing chronic requirement problems for software applications.

Standard Requirements Outline

There are a number of suggested outlines for software requirements specifications. The outline shown here depicts both the features of the application itself and also a set of logistical topics that need to be analyzed and resolved while the requirements are being developed. There are 25 topics that describe the software application and 20 logistical topics, as shown in Table 2.7.

Table 2.7   *Software Requirements Contents*

	Application Features
1	Application outputs
2	Application inputs
3	Certified reusable material
4	Uncertified reusable material
5	Logical files inherited
6	Logical files created
7	Logical files maintained (legacy)
8	Logical files in other applications
9	Logical files from external sources
10	Entities and relationships
11	Inquiry types
12	Interfaces—other internal software
13	Interfaces—COTS software
14	Interfaces—hardware
15	Interfaces—users
16	Business rules—new
17	Business rules—legacy

	Application Features
18	Algorithms—new
19	Algorithms—legacy
20	Hardware platforms
21	Software platforms
22	Security criteria
23	Performance criteria
24	Installation criteria
25	Sample use cases
	Application Logistics
1	Legacy applications being replaced
2	Competitive applications
3	Application value—financial
4	Application value—intangible
5	Application risks—tangible
6	Application risks—intangible
7	Planned release intervals
8	Application size for each release
9	Rate of requirements changes
10	Application schedule
11	Application staffing
12	Application costs
13	Application quality
14	Application training
15	Number of application users
16	Number of countries
17	Application distribution channels
18	Application warranty provisions
19	Application intellectual property
20	Application contract clauses

Table 2.7 is intended to be a generalized table of contents that would work for information systems, web applications, embedded applications, and systems software. Military and government software would need to include special topics such as independent verification and validation (IV&V) and independent testing that are seldom used in the civilian sector.

A standard outline for requirements is synergistic with many other approaches and could be used in conjunction with Joint Application Design (JAD), Quality Function Deployment (QFD), use cases, and many others.

Joint Application Design (JAD)

For gathering information system requirements, a technique called Joint Application Design (JAD) was developed by IBM Toronto in the mid-1970s and now has more than 30 years of empirical data that demonstrates its value.

Joint application design involves a group of four to eight stakeholders and users who work with a group of four to eight software architects and designers to hammer out the requirements for a new application.

The JAD sessions are often held in offsite locations to minimize interruptions. The participants are asked to free up their calendars for the duration of the JAD session, which can run from a few days to as long as two weeks. Because everyone has other kinds of business responsibilities, the JAD sessions normally are restricted to perhaps six hours per day so that the participants can handle urgent duties that are part of their regular jobs.

The JAD method of software requirements gathering has been used for many years and has demonstrated success for fairly large applications in the 10,000 function point size range. The JAD approach tends to collect at least 90% of application requirements for the initial release. JAD requirements tend to have low levels of defects, usually below 0.25 per function point. Requirements changes with JAD are usually below 0.5% per calendar month or less than half of average change rates.

If an application is larger than 100,000 function points or has more than 100,000 users, even JAD may not be sufficient. If the application has hardware components as well as software, then hardware representatives must be present, too.

Embedded Users

A recent variation on the JAD approach is part of the Agile method of software development. Instead of a limited period of cooperation between developers and the user community, one or more user representatives are "embedded" in the development team and work with the team throughout the development cycle.

The user representative(s) and the developers jointly create the requirements for critical features that normally can be developed in a period of two weeks, more or less. These are called *sprints*. The idea is to construct software applications by building specific features that can be put to use as quickly as possible, rather than designing and building the application as a continuous stream.

The embedded user method has proven to be useful for hundreds of smaller applications below about 2,500 function points in size. As applications grow beyond 10,000 function points in size or have more than about 1,000 users, no single user representative can deal with all of the possible features that might be needed.

Agile has developed some approaches for combining teams of users, but for really large applications (>10,000 function points and more than 1,000 users), alternate methods such as the Rational Unified Process (RUP) and the Team Software Process (TSP) seem to yield better results than Agile.

When used for smaller projects in the 1,000 function point size range, the embedded user method seems to be effective, and requirements defects are usually below 0.25 per function point.

The concept of requirements creep is difficult to measure in an Agile environment because the basic idea of Agile is to design and build applications as a series of "sprints," each of which contains one or more critical features. Because the sprints are so short, there is not really time enough for many unplanned requirements changes.

Use Cases

Software use cases were probably first formulated by Ivar Jacobsen, who also was a key player in the Unified Modeling Language (UML) and also the Rational Unified Process (RUP). Use cases have been utilized since about 1986 and are commonly associated with Agile development and its many variations.

Use cases describe scenarios of what transpires when users (termed "actors") carry out specific functional tasks using a software application. Use cases come in several flavors and have several levels of detail, all of which are outside the scope of this book.

Use cases and function point metrics are somewhat congruent in theory because they both deal with aspects of software applications that have value to users. From a practical point of view, the use case community has not been a widespread adopter of standard function point metrics such as those of the International Function Point Users Group (IFPUG). Instead, there is a separate "use case point" that was developed to provide a somewhat similar kind of quantification.

While standard function points can be applied to applications that utilize use cases, the reverse is not true. Use case points cannot be used to measure projects unless use cases are themselves utilized. Therefore, side-by-side comparisons between projects utilizing use cases and projects utilizing other notations such as user stories, Nassi-Shneiderman charts, decision tables, and so on are not feasible with use-case points although easy to accomplish with standard function points.

Use cases are somewhat prolix and average around 1.5 pages per function point for applications between 100 and about 1,500 function points in size.

Above that size range, the volume of use cases per function point declines because there would be too many use cases to keep track of. Use cases cannot cover 100% of software operations and activities, so additional methods are needed to express mathematical algorithms and some kinds of business rules.

For any given size of application, use cases have about the same defect potentials as textual representation—that is, between about 0.5 and 1.15 defects per function point. Use cases can be inspected, and indeed this is a recommended quality step for use cases in complex systems.

When use cases are constructed using the graphical representations of the Unified Modeling Language (UML) they are fairly easy to comprehend and fairly easy to inspect.

User Stories

The Agile methods collectively have correctly identified excessive paperwork as a chronic software problem, as indeed it is. User stories are an attempt to create a fairly concise and relatively informal method of describing user requirements in short sentences and few paragraphs.

A typical user story might start with something like, "When I start a session with the application, I would like to choose between a new session or restoring my most recent session."

For small projects below 1,000 function points in size and with fewer than 100 total users, the user story method seems to be concise and fairly trouble-free. User stories average below 0.5 pages per function point and seem to contain fewer than 0.5 defects per function point.

However for applications at or above 10,000 function points that have as many or more than 1,000 users who may not utilize the software in exactly the same way, the user story method begins to run past its comfort zone. For such large applications, the number of user stories would probably go up to more than 1.25 pages per function point while defects in the stories might top 0.75 defects per function point.

Unless the user stories are inspected, there is no other effective approach for eliminating requirement defects in the stories. It is possible to create test cases from user stories, and that is recommended, but the essential goal of requirements quality is to get rid of requirements defects before they migrate into source code.

Prototyping

Prototyping of software applications prior to formal construction has a long and generally successful history with a reasonable quantity of empirical data. However, prototypes have some limits and boundary conditions that need to be considered, as follows.

Prototypes are often written in higher-level programming languages than the applications themselves. For example, a prototype might be constructed in Visual Basic, and the application itself might be written in Java or Objective C. Prototypes average about 10% of the functionality of the application that is being prototyped. This fact has some implications.

Prototypes are seldom used for applications below 100 function points in size because the entire application can be developed fairly easily and quickly, so it probably does not need a prototype.

Applications with more than 10,000 function points prototypes are seldom used because prototyping 10% of the features would amount to 1,000 function points, which is a significant piece of work in its own right. Because the most common sizes of software applications are between about 500 and 1,500 function points, prototypes are valuable adjuncts to mid-sized development projects.

Prototypes come in three distinct flavors: disposable, evolutionary, and time box. As the name implies, a "disposable" prototype can be discarded after it has served its purpose of trying out features and interfaces for a proposed application. Evolutionary prototypes, on the other hand, are intended to gradually grow and evolve until they become the proposed application. Time-box prototypes are created in a specific time window such as one week or two weeks. The short time limits mean that most time-box prototypes are disposable.

On the whole, disposable prototypes and time-box prototypes are cheaper and more cost-effective than evolutionary prototypes. The reason for this is that prototypes are often developed quickly and somewhat carelessly. They are seldom given formal inspections, nor are formal test cases and test scripts always prepared for prototypes. The Software Quality Assurance (SQA) groups are seldom involved in validating prototypes. Of course, static analysis tools can and should be used for prototypes. But the bottom line is that quality control for evolutionary prototypes is so lax that they tend to have significant defect potentials of more than about 1.25 bugs or defects per function point. Defect removal efficiency against prototypes is usually below 80% unless static analysis tools are used.

Disposable prototypes no doubt have the same or even higher defect potentials, but the defects in disposable prototypes are transient and disappear when the prototype is discarded. Most of them do not end up in the final application.

On the whole, disposable prototypes that illustrate user interfaces and critical calculations are quicker, cheaper, and potentially safer than evolutionary prototypes. By definition, prototypes are "quick," and that quickness does not lend itself to evolving into completed applications.

Quality Function Deployment (QFD)

Quality Function Deployment (QFD) is one of a number of sophisticated quality methods that are more widely used in Japan than in the United States. The early work on QFD in the 1970s was carried out by Dr. Shigeru Mizuno and Yoji Akao in a manufacturing context. QFD proved to be successful in a number of complex product designs and gradually made its way across the Pacific to the United States and then into software projects.

QFD has an extensive literature base and numerous books and articles. QFD also has a large association of users called The Quality Function Deployment Institute. Several aspects of QFD have become catch phrases and are widely cited: "The voice of the customer" and "The house of quality." The first phrase refers to formal QFD methods for analyzing customer quality needs. The second phrase refers to a special graphical representation that in fact resembles a house with a pitched roof. This graphical technique combines quality requirements from the user with quality responses from the engineering community.

Empirical data on QFD has shown that it does in fact benefit software quality and minimize requirements defects. Further, the benefits are most pronounced for large and complex applications where other methods seem to run out of steam.

From limited data available in the United States, QFD seems to reduce requirements and design defects by about 75% compared to other requirements methods. However, QFD is not a 100% solution for software requirements and design, so it can be combined with UML diagrams, use cases, and other forms of representation.

Formal Requirements Inspections

The last of the methods discussed in this section are among the oldest methods available: formal inspections of software requirements using methods developed by IBM in the late 1960s and early 1970s.

Formal inspections have extensive literature and a number of books and articles available. There is also a nonprofit Software Inspection User Association on the Web.

To utilize formal inspections there must be a team of trained individuals that include a moderator and a recorder. In addition, there may be other inspectors, plus, of course, the person whose work products are being inspected. Inspection teams have a minimum size of three (moderator, recorder, and principal); an average size of five (moderator, recorder, principal, and two other inspectors); and a maximum size of eight.

For the larger inspection groups, the additional inspectors normally are part of the overall quality team but work in Software Quality Assurance (SQA), testing, or sometimes technical writing.

Formal inspections have demonstrated about the highest levels of defect removal efficiency ever recorded. They average about 85% efficiency in finding defects and have occasionally topped 97%. Further, inspections are equally effective against all software deliverables including but not limited to

- Requirements

- Design

- Project plans

- Source code

- Test plans

- Test cases

- User manuals

- Training materials

- HELP text

Inspections can either cover 100% of specific deliverables, or they can be used only for the most critical features. Obviously, 100% inspections are more thorough but also more costly.

The protocols for formal inspections call for delivering the materials to be inspected one week early so that the team can go over them ahead of time. The first inspection session starts by having the recorder collect the defect reports noted during the week of lead time.

Because the inspection teams have other work, inspections are limited to two-hour sessions and a maximum of two sessions per work day. Usually inspections are held in the form of face-to-face meetings in private conference rooms. But it is possible to hold inspections remotely via Skype or webinar tools. Usually a given inspection session will not cover more than about 25 pages of text material, about 150 source code statements, or about ten test cases.

An important point about inspections is that their main goal is to find defects, not to repair them on the spot. Every defect is recorded, but the repair efforts take place after the inspection sessions are done.

From time to time, so many defects may be found that the inspection team decides that another inspection will be needed for the same material after the repairs are made.

For large corporations such as IBM there is usually an inspection coordinator who handles the reservations for inspection room; the distribution of materials to be inspected; and the data on inspection hours, costs, and discovered defects that are reported after every inspection.

While this description of the inspection process might make it sound time-consuming and expensive, empirical data demonstrates that applications that use formal inspections have shorter schedules and lower costs than similar applications that use only testing. A prime example was the IBM IMS database product in the 1970s. Prior to inspections, IMS testing took about 90 days of three-shift testing. After inspections had been deployed, the same testing cycle was reduced to 30 days of one-shift testing.

Inspections are not only one of the top-ranked methods of defect removal, but they are surprisingly one of the top-ranked methods of defect prevention. The reason that inspections are so effective as a defect prevention method is that the participants in inspections will spontaneously avoid making the same kinds of defects that the inspections discover. Thus, within about a year of deploying inspections, defect potentials tend to drop by about 50% for all deliverables that were inspected.

Conclusions about Software Requirements Defects

The topic of software requirements defects is not covered thoroughly in either the software engineering literature or the software quality literature. There are a number of anecdotal reports about specific requirement failures, but there is a shortage of large-scale analysis that includes statistically valid samples.

Table 2.8 summarizes the approximate results of a number of software requirements methods and approaches. The table shows both the approximate completeness of the requirements based on using the approach and also the approximate defect potentials in terms of defects per function point.

Of the requirements methods that are available in 2011, the most effective combinations would be to use Joint Application Design (JAD), Quality Function Deployment (QFD), requirements inspections, and prototypes.

The least effective combinations would be to use informal requirements gathering and normal text documents. This combination ranks low in completeness and high in requirement defect potentials.

In the future, the combination of dynamic modeling of requirements, data mining of legacy applications, and certified reusable requirements would be superior to any combination available in 2011.

Table 2.8 *Overview of Software Requirements Methods*

	Requirements Completeness	Requirements Defects per Function Point
Dynamic modeling	97.00%	0.10
Novel new inventions	97.00%	0.01
Quality Function Deployment (QFD)	96.00%	0.25
Requirement inspections	95.00%	0.10
Certified reusable requirements	90.00%	0.10
Joint Application Design (JAD)	85.00%	0.50
Embedded users	83.00%	0.65
Use cases	80.00%	0.80
User stories	75.00%	0.90
Mining legacy applications	70.00%	0.20
Hardware requirements (embedded)	70.00%	0.40
Competitive analysis	70.00%	0.15
Prototyping	62.00%	0.55
User focus groups	60.00%	0.30
Informal requirements gathering	57.00%	1.00
Market surveys	55.00%	0.30
Normal text documents	50.00%	1.10
AVERAGES	76.00%	0.44

The Special Case of Coding Defects

There are at least 2,500 programming languages in existence as of 2011. Of these languages about 1,000 are "dead" and no longer used. Another 1,000 are used for special purposes and do not show up in normal software. But around 500 programming languages are used for software applications.

Languages have long been defined as having "levels." The general concept of a language "level" is that high-level languages can create more functionality with fewer code statements than low-level languages.

In the early 1970s IBM decided to quantify language levels so that their relative performance could be evaluated. The initial way of quantifying language levels was to start with basic assembly language. This was defined as a "level 1 language" with the meaning that it was the lowest-level programming language. (Machine language is even lower, but it is not a programming language in the normal sense of the phrase.)

Other languages were defined relative to assembly using the formula that measured the number of assembly-language statements that would be required to produce the functionality of one statement in a higher-level language. For example, COBOL was analyzed and determined to be a "level 3 language." The meaning of this definition is that it requires three statements in basic assembly language to perform functions that could be performed by a single COBOL statement. If you wrote an application that required 1,000 COBOL statements, it would take about 3,000 basic assembly statements.

In 1975 when IBM first developed function point metrics, as part of the calibration process both function point totals and code volumes were measured for hundreds of applications and dozens of programming languages. As a result, the language level concept was expanded to include not only code statements relative to basic assembly language, but also the number of code statements normally required to produce one function point.

When the idea of language levels was placed on a quantitative basis, it was possible to create tables of languages that showed the levels of hundreds of them. As of 2011, conversion tables between logical source code statements and IFPUG function point metrics are available from multiple sources for more than 1,000 programming languages.

Companies such as the David Consulting Group, Gartner Group, and Software Productivity Research (SPR) publish and market such tables. Because new programming languages appear at a rate of more than one per month, these tables need constant updates.

By the early 1980s, conversion between logical code statements and function point metrics had been measured for hundreds of programming languages. Mathematical conversion between logical code statements and function point metrics is termed *backfiring*. Since about 1984, backfiring has been the most widely used method for quantifying the function point totals of aging legacy applications where the code exists but where written requirements and specifications may no longer be available. Backfiring is popular but not very accurate due to wide variations in individual programming styles.

Backfiring is based on average values for code statements per function point. But individual programmers can and do vary by at least two to one on either side of these average values.

Starting in about 2008 more sophisticated methods were developed. Several companies such as CAST Software and Relativity Technologies developed automated parsing tools that could extract business logic from source code and synthesize function point totals using the actual IFPUG counting rules. In other words, these automated tools mined legacy code and created synthetic specifications that could then be used for function point analysis.

Table 2.9 *Language Level Examples*

Language Level	Sample Languages	Source Code per Function Point
1	Basic Assembly	320
2	C	160
3	COBOL	107
4	PL/I	80
5	Ada95	64
6	Java	53
7	Ruby	46
8	Oracle	40
9	Pearl	36
10	C++	32
11	Delphi	29
12	Visual Basic	27
13	ASP NET	25
14	Eiffel	23
15	Smalltalk	21
16	IBM ADF	20
17	MUMPS	19
18	Forte	18
19	APS	17
20	TELON	16
10	AVERAGE	58

Conversion between function points and logical code statements for thousands of different programming languages is outside the scope of this book. But to illustrate the fairly simple mathematics involved, Table 2.9 shows a sample of the language levels of 20 different programming languages:

Although Table 2.9 treats language levels as constants, the levels can vary due to new language features or to dialects of languages that have the same name but different syntaxes. The levels also vary by programming styles of individual programmers. Languages with many users such as Java tend to have the widest ranges of language levels.

Table 2.9 also is based on "logical source code statements." Counting source code using logical code statements is a distinct method and produces different results from counting physical lines of code. Many programming languages allow multiple instructions to be placed on the same physical line. The following example shows five logical code statements but only one physical line:

Instruction 1: Instruction 2: Instruction 3: Instruction 4: Instruction 5

Conversely, some programming languages allow segmenting a logical statement across a number of physical lines. The following example shows one logical code statement but six physical lines of code:

If A equals value N then

Branch to routine X1 if N = 1

Branch to routine X2 if N = 2

Branch to routine X3 if N = 3

Branch to routine X4 if N = 4

Otherwise branch to routine X5

These large differences in apparent code size based on counts of physical lines can produce code volume variances of about an order of magnitude when all common programming languages are considered.

Adding to the difficulty of code counting, quite a few languages such as Visual Basic can produce executable code without using lines of source code at all. Such languages produce code from buttons, pull-down menus, and other visual techniques that access prebuilt functions that the language provides.

It is astonishing that a field called "software engineering" would use a metric with such a huge range of variations for more than 50 years without creating effective counting standards.

There are many tools available that count physical lines, but some of these tools include blank lines between paragraphs, comments, and headers as well as actual source code statements.

Needless to say, backfiring based on counts of physical lines and backfiring based on counts of logical statements would produce very different results. Unfortunately, code counting methods have never been standardized.

A survey by one of the authors of major software journals such as *IEEE Software*, *The IBM Systems Journal*, and several others found that about one-third of the articles that cited code volumes used logical statements; one-third used physical lines of code; and the remaining third provided code volume numbers but did not state whether the numbers meant physical or logical code counts.

One other complicating factor is that a majority of software applications use as least two programming languages simultaneously, and some may use as many as 15 different languages. For example, COBOL and SQL were a common pair of languages in the 1980s, and JAVA and HTML are common today.

When the mathematics of backfiring was first developed in IBM circa 1975, the counts were based on logical code statements. This is because programmers tend to think in terms of logical code statements and not in terms of physical lines. Therefore, logical code counts provide a better approximation for programming's mental efforts.

These variations in counting source code combined with thousands of programming languages and an almost unlimited combination of languages among applications make the prediction and measurement of coding bugs or defects much more complicated than it should be.

To illustrate some of the complexity of determining source code size volumes, Table 2.10 shows examples of two common languages, C and Visual Basic. The starting assumption of Table 2.10 is that 1,000 logical code statements are produced in both languages. As can be seen, this constant value of 1,000 logical code statements produces very different counts for physical lines of code and also for function points.

Table 2.10 illustrates how variations in language levels and variations in code counting rules make it very tricky to achieve useful data about application size.

Let us now consider how to deal with defect potentials across variations in language levels and code counting levels. Table 2.11 makes a starting assumption that both the C and Visual Basic examples from Table 2.10 contained ten defects.

However, in Table 2.11 the coding defects are expressed in terms of "KLOC." In this term, "K" is the abbreviation for 1,000, and "LOC" is the abbreviations for "lines of code." Thus, 1 KLOC is 1,000 lines of code. (Note: Electrical engineering uses K to mean a value of 1,028, but software engineering uses K for an even 1,000.)

Table 2.10 *Examples of Size Variances by Counting Method*

Language Level	Language	Logical Code Statements	Physical Lines of Code	Logical Code per Function Point	Function Points	Physical Code per Function Point
2.50	C	1,000	3,000	128	8	384
8.00	Visual Basic	1,000	750	40	25	30

Table 2.11 *Examples of Defect Variance by Counting Method*

Language Level	Language	Coding Defects	Defects per Logical KLOC	Defects per Physical KLOC	Defects per Function Point
2.50	C	10	10.00	10.00	1.28
8.00	Visual Basic	10	10.00	13.30	0.39

As shown, the same ten defects are normalized to very different results based on code counting rules and function points.

Thus far, we have held defect values constant. But in fact there usually are many more coding bugs in low-level languages such as basic assembly, C, and macro-assembly than there are in higher-level languages such as Java, Perl, and Ruby. Table 2.12 illustrates the approximate range in coding defect potentials for language levels 1 (basic assembly) through level 20, which is where some of the program generator and object-oriented languages can be found.

Note that for most language levels there may be as many as 50 different languages at the same level. The total number of known programming languages tops 2,500 as of 2011. Therefore, Table 2.12 uses language levels as an abstract value rather than trying to deal with thousands of individual languages.

Table 2.12   *Code Defects for 20 Levels of Programming Languages*

Language Level	Code Defects per KLOC (Logical Statements)	Source Code per Function Point	Function Points	Defects Per Function Point	Bad Fix Injection Percent
1	40	320	3	12.80	12.00%
2	36	160	6	5.76	10.00%
3	33	107	9	3.52	10.00%
4	32	80	13	2.56	9.00%
5	30	64	16	1.92	9.00%
6	27	53	19	1.44	8.00%
7	26	46	22	1.19	8.00%
8	24	40	25	0.96	8.00%
9	23	36	28	0.82	7.00%
10	22	32	31	0.70	7.00%
11	21	29	34	0.61	7.00%
12	20	27	38	0.53	6.00%
13	18	25	41	0.44	6.00%
14	17	23	44	0.39	6.00%
15	15	21	47	0.32	5.00%
16	14	20	50	0.28	5.00%
17	13	19	53	0.24	5.00%
18	12	18	56	0.21	5.00%
19	11	17	59	0.19	4.00%
20	10	16	63	0.16	3.00%
AVERAGES	22.20	57.56	32.81	1.75	7.00%

Note that Table 2.12 shows "code defect potentials" or the probable number of coding defects in the original code. But as these defects are found and repairs are attempted, it must be understood that bad fixes or new defects will be accidentally included in the defect repairs themselves. Older low-level programming languages tend to have higher percentages of bad-fix injections than do modern high-level languages.

As can be seen, coding defect potentials vary with language levels. Coding defects also vary with individual programming skills, with language familiarity, and with volumes of certified reusable code.

In the absence of firm knowledge about what languages will be used and the capabilities of the programming team, a starting point for predicting code defect levels is to use average values of about 22 defects per KLOC (logical code statements) or 1.75 code defects per function point.

If you happen to count code using physical lines instead of logical statements, then you need to know the actual syntax of the languages that will be used. You also need to know whether or not the code counting tools (if any) count blank lines and comments as well as true code. As a general rule, physical lines of code are too variable and unreliable to yield effective defect potentials for coding defects.

Estimating Software Defect Prevention

Software defect prevention is discussed in some detail in Chapter 3. The discussion here in Chapter 2 provides only some approximate guidelines for factoring defect prevention into quality estimates and quality measurements.

For measurement purposes it is necessary to have at least two data points for every defect prevention method: 1) One or more applications that used a specific defect prevention method; and 2) A similar set of application that did not use the defect prevention method.

In other words, to understand a defect prevention method such as Quality Function Deployment (QFD) you need samples of applications that used the method and samples of similar applications that did not use it. And, of course, you need a very good quality and defect measurement program.

Defect prevention is measured as the difference between the two applications in total defects and in defects by origin point such as requirements, design, code, documents, or bad-fix injections.

Because two data points are not statistically valid, analyzing defect prevention is of necessity a long-term project that requires several years of data collection and probably several hundred projects. This is why most of the reports on defect prevention come from large companies such as IBM that have sophisticated quality measurement programs and many years of accumulated historical data. Indeed, IBM has data on some applications with more than 25 years of continuous history. Universities are seldom equipped or funded to carry out long-range, multiyear studies that involve hundreds of projects.

One way of integrating defect prevention into quality estimates is to show how various methodologies affect defect totals. In the absence of any solid historical data, a useful way of predicting defect potentials is to raise application size in function points to a specific power. A default value for this is to raise application size in function points to the 1.2 power. The result will be the approximate total number of defects found in requirements, design, code, user documents, and bad fixes. But to factor in defect prevention, a range of powers is suggested. Table 2.13 provides approximate but useful power ranges associated with various defect prevention methodologies and some that are harmful as well.

Table 2.13   *Estimating Defect Potentials with Defect Prevention Methods*

(Power levels for 1,000 function point applications)			
	Power Level	Defect Potential	Defects per Function Point
Optimal Methods	1.18	3,467	3.47
Change control automation			
CMMI 5			
Formal inspections			
Mathematical test case design			
Quality Function Deployment (QFD)			
Risk and quality analysis			
Team Software Process (TSP)			
Effective Methods	1.19	3,715	3.72
Agile			
CMMI 3			
Formal change control			
Joint Application Design (JAD)			
Rational Unified Process (RUP)			
SCRUM sessions			
SQA team			
Static analysis			

	Power Level	Defect Potential	Defects per Function Point
Test-driven development			
XP (Extreme programming)			
Neutral Methods	1.20	3,981	3.98
Agile development			
CMMI 1			
CMMI 2			
Informal change control			
Normal requirements gathering			
Requirements changes (average)			
Below Average Methods	1.22	4,571	4.57
No quality planning			
No SQA team			
Normal test case design			
Requirements changes (many)			
Schedule pressure			
Waterfall development			
Harmful Methods	1.24	5,248	5.25
Ad hoc change control			
Ambiguous requirements			
CMMI 0 (not used)			
Excessive schedule pressure			
Informal requirements gathering			
No formal methodology			
No inspections			
Requirements changes (numerous)			

Although Table 2.13 has a high margin of error, some of the topics do have fairly good supporting evidence. For example, formal inspections of requirements, design, and code have been in use for more than 40 years. Many similar projects can be compared with those that used inspections and those that did not. Static analysis is a newer technology, but here, too, there are hundreds of similar applications that either used or did not use modern static analysis tools.

Estimating Software Defect Detection and Defect Removal

In the 1970s when IBM first studied defect detection efficiency (DDE) and defect removal efficiency (DRE), the two topics were close to being synonymous. Various methods such as inspections and testing discovered defects. The discovered defects were repaired before the applications were delivered to clients. In those days, average software applications were below 1,000 function points in size.

As applications grew in size and complexity, defect detection efficiency and defect removal efficiency gradually moved apart. For massive applications in the 100,000 function point size range, there were many more defects. Defect repairs and regression testing became more time-consuming.

To achieve announced delivery dates, a number of bugs that had been detected late in the testing cycle were not repaired or at least not fully regression tested by the day of the application's release. Out of the last 100 bugs detected, probably 25 were not fully repaired by delivery day. As a result, software vendors such as IBM almost immediately followed up the initial release with a second release that contained repairs for these unrepaired bugs

In fact, IBM and some other companies developed a release numbering approach that showed whether a release was primarily for new features or primarily for defect repairs. Releases that were integer values such as 1.0, 2.0, 3.0, and the like were primarily for new features. Releases that were decimal values such as 1.1, 2.1, or 3.1 were primarily releases for bug repairs. This rule was not fixed, and both numbers might contain both forms of updates, but the essential idea became known to customers.

Although IBM had a good track record for quality and repaired defects promptly, not all vendors followed suit. As a result, the initial releases of software applications became highly suspect by clients and consumers due to their known tendency to have large numbers of latent defects.

Indeed, some clients would not lease or purchase Release 1.0 of software packages because of suspected latent defects. A few vendors tried to get around this reluctance by identifying their very first releases of software as "Release 2.0." But this did not really fool anybody.

To use software effectively for business purposes, most of the latent defects need to be fixed. Many large companies have fairly sophisticated maintenance teams available for installing commercial-off-the-shelf (COTS) applications. These client maintenance teams can and do fix serious defects that are encountered during installation and acceptance testing.

Table 2.14 *Defect Detection versus Defect Removal Efficiency by Size*

	Defect Potential per Function Point	Total Defect Potential	Defect Detection Efficiency	Defect Removal Efficiency	Delivered Defects	Difference between DDE and DRE
1	3.50	4	99.00%	98.00%	0	1.00%
10	4.00	40	97.00%	95.00%	1	2.00%
100	4.50	450	94.00%	90.00%	27	4.00%
1,000	5.00	5,000	90.00%	85.00%	500	5.00%
10,000	5.50	55,000	88.00%	82.00%	6,600	6.00%
100,000	6.50	650,000	85.00%	78.00%	97,500	7.00%
AVERAGE	4.83	118,416	92.17%	88.00%	17,438	4.17%

As a result, some commercial software vendors became lax in repairing defects detected during about the last three months of application testing and integration. The idea was that leaving some bugs latent in the application would speed up delivery. Further, having the bugs repaired by client maintenance groups would be cheaper than repairing the same bugs with internal personnel.

As a result, in 2011 there is sometimes a very large difference between defect detection efficiency (DDE) and defect removal efficiency (DRE). Table 2.14 illustrates the modern differences between defect detection and defect removal by application size.

As can be seen in Table 2.14, the gap between defect detection efficiency and defect removal efficiency grows steadily wider as software applications increase in overall size.

The result of this disconnect between detection and removal is that large applications will not be very reliable for several months until most of the latent defects present at delivery are fixed by either customers or by developers, or both.

One important topic for both quality estimation and quality measurement is to know the defect removal efficiency levels of both pretest removal activities and testing. Testing has never been very efficient in finding bugs nor has testing been cost effective when used by itself. Pretest inspections and static analysis are about 25% more efficient than testing. Further inspections and static analysis can raise testing efficiency levels by about 5%. Table 2.15 shows the ranges of defect removal efficiency for a sample of pretest and testing activities.

All combinations of testing alone seldom top 85% in cumulative defect removal efficiency. To achieve cumulative levels of defect removal efficiency that exceed 95%, it is necessary to use both pretest defect removal activities and also at least eight kinds of formal testing. The good news is that topping 95% in defect removal efficiency levels has lower costs and shorter schedules than testing alone. In other words, not only is quality "free," but it also speeds up development.

Table 2.15 *Pretest and Test Defect Removal Efficiency Ranges*

Pretest Defect Removal	Minimum	Average	Maximum
Formal design inspections	65.00%	87.00%	97.00%
Formal code inspections	60.00%	85.00%	96.00%
Static analysis	65.00%	85.00%	95.00%
Formal requirement inspections	50.00%	78.00%	90.00%
Pair programming	40.00%	55.00%	65.00%
Informal peer reviews	35.00%	50.00%	60.00%
Desk checking	25.00%	45.00%	55.00%
Average	48.57%	69.29%	79.71%
Test Defect Removal	**Minimum**	**Average**	**Maximum**
Experiment-based testing	60.00%	75.00%	85.00%
Risk-based testing	55.00%	70.00%	80.00%
Security testing	50.00%	65.00%	80.00%
Subroutine testing	27.00%	45.00%	60.00%
System testing	27.00%	42.00%	55.00%
External Beta testing	30.00%	40.00%	50.00%
Performance testing	30.00%	40.00%	45.00%
Supply-chain testing	20.00%	40.00%	47.00%
Cloud testing	25.00%	40.00%	55.00%
Function testing	33.00%	40.00%	55.00%
Unit testing (automated)	20.00%	40.00%	50.00%
Unit testing (manual)	15.00%	38.00%	50.00%
Regression testing	35.00%	35.00%	45.00%
Independent verification	20.00%	35.00%	47.00%
Clean-room testing	20.00%	35.00%	50.00%
Acceptance testing	15.00%	35.00%	40.00%
Independent testing	15.00%	35.00%	42.00%
AVERAGE	29.24%	44.12%	55.06%

Measuring Application Structural Quality

Unlike the quality of the *process*, by which software is built, enhanced, and maintained; functional, nonfunctional, and structural quality have to do with the software *product* itself—the thing that generates business value. Managing software quality by managing delivery risk alone only addresses a part of the problem. It's like addressing the symptoms of a disease rather than taking aim at curing its cause. To get to the root causes, we have to define, analyze, and measure software *product* quality.

The structural quality of software is affected by attributes at numerous levels of abstraction. The layered approach to calculating characteristic measures displayed in Figure 2.1 was first proposed by Boehm and his colleagues at TRW (Boehm, 1978) and is the approach taken in the ISO 9126 and 25000 series standards. These attributes can be measured from the parsed results of a static analysis of the application source code. Even dynamic characteristics of applications such as reliability and performance efficiency have their causal roots in the static structure of the application.

We discuss the attributes underlying each critical application characteristic in the following sections.

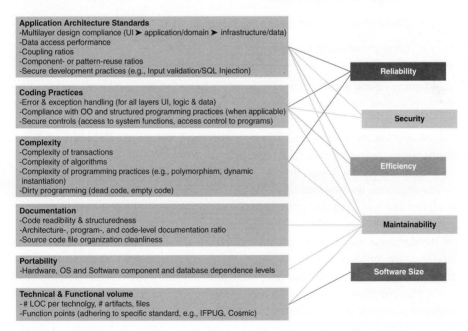

Figure 2.1 *Measurable software attributes based on application characteristics*

Measuring Reliability

Assessing reliability requires checks of at least the following software engineering practices and technical attributes:

- Application Architecture Practices
  - Multilayer design compliance
  - Coupling ratio
  - Components or patterns reuse ratio
- Coding Practices
  - Error and exception handling (for all layers GUI, Logic, and Data)
  - Compliance with OO and structured best programming practices (when applicable)
- Complexity
  - Transaction's complexity level
  - Complexity of algorithms
  - Complexity of programming practices
  - Dirty programming

Whenever good practices are violated, it becomes more difficult to stabilize the application and to ensure it will perform effectively when encountering unexpected events in its computing environment. Poor reliability increases the risk of application failure and resulting loss to the business. Reliable, resilient applications must guarantee that exceptional situations such as external failures or incorrect inputs will not, in turn, produce unpredictable results or outages.

For instance, the absence or misuse of a layered architecture leads to a more complex and less reliable application. Layers ensure the separation of concerns (http://en.wikipedia.org/wiki/Separation_of_concerns) as, for example, when all the database access paths are centralized in a component so that data integrity is easily enforced. Interactions between layers should also be carefully checked to make sure only the necessary ones are allowed.

At the component level, reducing the level of dependency and coupling between components contributes to the robustness of an application. Indeed, if a component in the application is used by too many other components, a defect in its implementation or modification will affect a much larger portion of the application, increasing the likelihood it can cause an outage. In addition, having more highly coupled components dramatically increases the testing required, and with limited time and resources, testing may not be able to detect complicated failure modes in the application. The correlation between complexity and error-prone components has been demonstrated many times (Curtis, 1979).

To be reliable, applications need to be coded defensively to protect against problems that are known to have caused catastrophic failures. A state-of-art error and exception handling process should make an application resilient to unexpected, erroneous, or uncommon but legitimate events by taking corrective action or at least by providing meaningful information that enables support teams to identify and remediate the problem. Other forms of defensive coding should provide time-outs, circuit-breakers, and bulkheads to ensure problems among components of the system do not propagate until they cause a failure (Nygard, 2008).

A full assessment of reliability requires analysis that is sensitive to known problems in specific programming paradigms. For example, the misuse or heavy use of some object-oriented features such as inheritance or polymorphism, as well as the use of powerful programming techniques such as Dynamic Instantiation, creates situations where the technical teams cannot fully assess the behavior of the application before it goes into production. This has made object-oriented techniques difficult to use in safety-critical applications. Indeed, as the predictability of the system declines, its testability is compromised. This is the reason why some of these coding techniques are forbidden by standards boards in some industries that produce life critical software (see The Motor Industry Software Reliability Association [MISRA] at http://www.misra.org.uk).

Measuring Performance Efficiency

Assessing performance efficiency requires checking at least the following software engineering practices and technical attributes:

- Application Architecture Practices
  - Data access performance
- Coding Practices
  - Compliance with OO and structured best programming practices

Experience has shown that major performance or scalability problems often stem from not following the recommended architecture or industry best practices, notably regarding data access and data handling (see High-Performance Client/Server at http://www.amazon.com/High-Performance-Client-Server-Chris-Loosley/dp/0471162698). For instance, setting an incorrect indexing strategy or generating a huge flow of data between the data layer and the business layer can lead to severe scalability issues. All these practices are called *Performance by Design*.

Many quality assurance managers complain that they lack the resources required to fully simulate the operational environment when performing stress and load testing. However, many causes of performance degradation are well known weaknesses in the source code that can be detected during structural analysis prior to deploying the code into the operational environment. Many of these problems are difficult to write test cases for, but their characteristic patterns can be detected from the parsed elements of the application. These weaknesses can sit harmlessly in the code until dramatic increases in the amount of data being handled or the frequency of transactions that inevitably occur during operations expose their effects in severely degraded performance.

Measuring Security

Assessing security requires at least checking the following software engineering practices and technical attributes:

- Application Architecture Practices
  - Multilayer design compliance
  - Security good practices (Input Validation / SQL Injection / Cross-Site Scripting [see CERT's Top 25: http://www.sans.org/top25-programming-errors/])
- Programming Practices (code level)
  - Error and exception handling
  - Security good practices (system functions access, access control to programs)

Computing the level of compliance of an application's source code to secure programming best practices as well as in-house security rules will give some insight about the level of security, and will serve as an early alert within the development cycle, reducing both costs of remediation and risks of releasing vulnerabilities.

Security can be measured by evaluating compliance with architecture rules, especially those regarding interactions within a layered architecture (see Dept. of Homeland Security's Defense in Depth, https://buildsecurityin.us-cert.gov/bsi/articles/knowledge/principles/347-BSI.html) as well as organizational security rules. As an example, the use of custom tags (method calls) from each dynamic web page may require specific parameters and access to the Framework's security functionalities (validation methods in the presentation layer as well as specific authentication methods on the business logic side).

Uncaught exceptions that are not properly handled can provide opportunities to hackers for breaching the application. For example, if a client receives an uncaught runtime exception that is thrown several layers in the call stack before it is handled, the handling code might expose some functionality that should remain hidden. Additionally, investigations should be carried out to prevent the creation of logic bombs. A *logic bomb* is usually defined as a program that has been deliberately written or modified in order to wreck an information system and its content when certain conditions (unexpected and unauthorized by legitimate users or owners of the software) are met (see http://en.wikipedia.org/wiki/Logic_bomb).

Measuring Maintainability

Assessing maintainability requires checking the following software engineering practices and technical attributes:

- Application Architecture Practices
  - Multilayer design compliance
  - Coupling ratio
  - Components or pattern reuse ratio
- Programming Practices (code level)
  - Compliance with OO and structured best programming practices (when applicable)
- Complexity
  - Complexity level of transactions
  - Complexity of algorithms
  - Complexity of programming practices
- Dirty programming
- Documentation
  - Code readability
  - Architecture, programs, and code documentation embedded in source code
  - Source code files' organization and cleanliness

- Portability

  - Hardware, OS, middleware, software components, and database independence

- Technical and Functional Volume

  - #LOC per technology, #artifacts, #files, #function points ...

Whenever architectural practices in a multi-tier application are not enforced, developers spend excessive time locating the point for implementing a change, as well as tracing its potential side effects across different tiers. Ignoring architectural rules and OO design principles (inheritance misuse, for example) makes application features extremely difficult to identify and trace. High coupling between components can also result in a higher time spent on a given maintenance task as the developer and the tester will have to ensure that the modification made has no side impacts on all the components using the modified one. Not surprisingly, studies have reported that approximately 50% of a maintenance programmer's time is spent trying to understand what is happening in the code before attempting its modification. When an overly complex application is transferred to a new team, they struggle to understand its organization and may take a year or more to become productive. These violations and degradations of the software quality over time are often referred as *design erosion* (see Design Erosion in Evolving Software Products at http://soft.vub.ac.be/FFSE/Workshops/ELISA-submissions/06-VanGurpEtAl-position.pdf).

Specific programming techniques such as dynamic instantiation or dynamic programming in general require high levels of expertise, very careful coding, as well as more time to identify where and how to make the changes (see "Use of Inheritance and Polymorphism in a Reliable Software System" http://www.aicas.com/papers/DA_Scharnberg.pdf). Maintainability of an application also depends very much on complexity. Code, Algorithmic and Control Flow Complexity, and specific programming techniques such as dynamic coding, although elegant, can increase the time and cost of maintenance.

Compliance with naming and coding conventions results in precise, readable, and unambiguous source code that accelerates code understanding and makes code discovery more intuitive. Finally, the volume of the software has an impact on its maintainability. Growth in size implies an increase in complexity of the software (more artifacts, more dependencies between the artifacts, hence more impact in case of modifications).

Measuring Size

The size of the application source code can impact the quality of the application because as it grows, complexity usually increases and testability becomes more difficult. Different size class applications require different approaches and planning assumptions to quality assurance. Also, application size serves as a normalizing measure to compare defect and software weakness rates by project, application, and/or team.

Measuring application size requires that the whole source code has been correctly gathered, including database structure script, data manipulation source code, components headers, configurations files, and so on. There are several software sizing methods, including

- # LOC

- # of artifacts

- Full inventory metrics: #files, #functions, #classes, #tables

- Function points (specific standards can apply: IFPUG, COSMIC, and so on)

Functional weight metrics or functional size measurement (Garmus & Herron, 2001) pertain to the estimation of the functional weight of the application. The function point metric (see http://en.wikipedia.org/wiki/Function_point) is the primary measure used for that purpose. Invented by Allan J. Albrecht (1979) of IBM in the mid-1970s, it is derived from a weighted formula that includes five elements: inputs, outputs, logical files, inquiries, and interfaces.

The International Function Points User Group (IFPUG) (http://en.wikipedia .org/wiki/IFPUG) proposes the most widely used method to count function points documented in the IFPUG CPM (Counting Practices Manual). There are other methods such as COSMIC (see http://en.wikipedia.org/wiki/COSMIC_ Software_Sizing) or Backfired Function Points developed by Caper Jones and SPR (see http://www.spr.com/programming-languages-table.html).

Summary of Application Structural Quality Measurement Attributes

Table 2.16 summarizes the elements of an application to be measured in assessing each of the application characteristics. Note that some attributes of source code affect several application characteristics. Each characteristic predicts a different set of problems that create cost for IT or risk to the business.

Without thorough measurement of these characteristics, neither IT nor the business can assess the risk or cost of ownership of its application portfolio.

Table 2.16 *Relations Between Measureable Attributes and Structural Quality Characteristics*

Attributes of the Source Code	Reliability	Efficiency	Security	Maintainability	Size
Application Architecture Practices					
Multilayer design compliance	✔		✔	✔	
Data access performance		✔			
Coupling ratio	✔			✔	
Components or pattern reuse ratio	✔			✔	
Security good practices			✔		
Coding Practices					
Error and exception handling	✔		✔		
Compliance with OO and structured best programming practices	✔	✔		✔	
Security good practices			✔		
Complexity					
Complexity level of transactions	✔			✔	
Complexity of algorithms	✔			✔	
Complexity of programming practices	✔			✔	
Dirty programming	✔			✔	
Documentation					
Code readability				✔	

Attributes of the Source Code	Reliability	Efficiency	Security	Maintainability	Size
Architecture, programs, and code documentation embedded in source code				✔	
Source code files organization cleanliness				✔	
Portability					
Hardware, OS and software component, and database dependence level				✔	
Technical & Functional Volume					
# LOC per technology, # artifact files...				✔	✔
Function points				✔	✔

The definition and measurement of structural quality is theoretically rich and taps into the considerable body of software engineering expertise. To ensure that the theory applies in the real world, it is important to validate structural quality problems with the occurrence of problems that are known to be caused by lapses in structural quality.

In this regard, the best independent validation of structural quality lapses is to compare them with business-disruption defects that are logged in an IT organization's defect tracking system.

Over the course of the last five years, CAST has studied this very connection. The data is from CAST customers around the world and covers a variety of technologies and operating environments.

The correlation between the structural quality problems identified and the severe defects logged is consistently high. This is strong validation for the way in which CAST defines and measures structural quality—the basis upon which structural quality lapses, or "critical violations" are identified. Figures 2.2 to 2.4 display the results of validating structural quality metrics in real-world IT business applications.

Figure 2.2 tracks multiple releases of a business-critical order management application in a large telecom company. Over multiple major releases of the order management system shown on the X axis, structural quality defects were tracked (left-hand Y axis) in terms of number of critical violations per back-fired

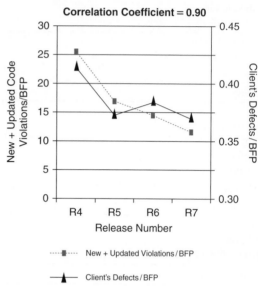

Figure 2.2   *Telecom order management application—comparison of structural quality lapses to severe defects*

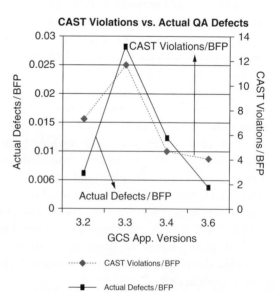

Figure 2.3   *Credit management application in an IT service provider—comparison of structural quality lapses to severe defects*

function point (BFP). The right-hand Y axis measures the number of defects per BFP logged in the defect tracking system for the order management application. The correlation between structural quality problems highlighted and the defects logged is 0.90.

Similarly, Figure 2.3 shows a credit management application that was tracked through multiple versions. A comparison of the structural quality lapses detected (CAST Violations/BFP) versus the actual defects per BFP shows similar tight correlation.

Figure 2.4 shows the structural quality of a handful of high-transaction order routing applications in an investment bank. Two kinds of measurements were made. First, Application A was measured at each major version (top chart). Second, the structural quality of Application A was compared at a point in time with Applications C and B (lower chart). In both comparisons, the structural quality lapses highlighted closely track the defects logged.

Validating the structural quality lapses found by an automated system such as CAST across multiple technologies and under different operating environments and conditions is a necessary step in the measurement of structural quality.

▪ **Client:**
Large Investment Bank

▪ **Industry:**
Financial Services

▪ **Applications Analyzed:**
Order routing system, institutional trading system (more than 50 million transactions/day), trader centralized customer repository

▪ **Technologies:** C++, PL/SQL, .NET, Oracle

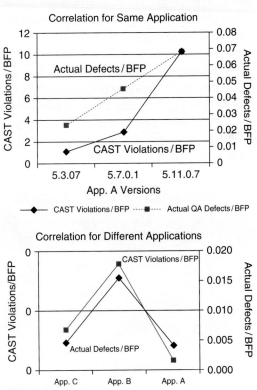

Figure 2.4 *Trading order routing applications in an investment bank—comparison of structural quality lapses to severe defects*

Examples of Structural Quality Assessments

This section describes several examples of application quality problems to help clarify why they are different from code quality problems and why they often escape detection by traditional quality practices such as testing and static analysis inside an Integrated Development Environment (IDE).

Bypassing the Architecture

One of the biggest sources of problems in multi-tier applications is when a component in one tier directly accesses a component in another tier and bypasses a required architectural component that plays a critical role in managing the flow to the accessed component. Two such instances that impact the robustness of an application are displayed in Figure 2.5.

For instance, the logic tier may be architected to separate the components that manage the business logic from those that manage access to the data. In path 1, a developer in the interface tier has directly accessed a component that makes queries to the data tier, bypassing one or more components in the logic tier that were designed to be the only components that could access the data query components.

The problem with this violation of the architecture is that developers working on the data access components only know how their components are being accessed within the logic tier because the architecture did not provide access from components in other tiers. If they make a change to the data access components, they may only communicate it to those working in the logic tier and test it against components within their tier, given that it is consistent with the

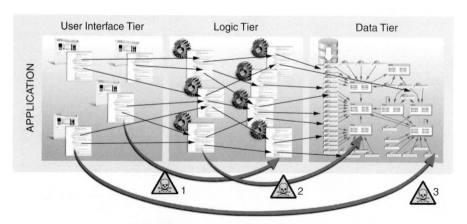

Figure 2.5 *Bypassing the architecture*

architecture. These changes may cause failures because direct calls from the user interface tier have not been modified to become consistent with changes to the data access components and were not part of testing.

In path 2, a developer of a component that manages the business logic has directly accessed a table of data without going through the data access components provided in the architecture. Similar to the problem in path 1, if a change is made to the structure of the table, information regarding the change may only be propagated to the data access components, given they are the approved access mechanisms. Unless the person changing the data table explicitly tests for many possible paths through the data beyond those approved in the architecture, this violation will not be detected. Consequently, path 2 will begin experiencing failures or erroneous output because it is unaware of the changes to the table it is accessing.

Another instance of the path 2 problem occurs when a developer implements a procedure that bypasses the approved data access components and alters or manipulates data. For sensitive or complex information, a data update is often a complicated mix of technical and business logic issues. Consequently, architects and database administrators usually define a set of components (SQL stored update procedures or components in a so-called persistence layer) whose use is mandatory for developers writing code that modifies existing data.

Bypassing these data access components leads to erratic application behavior. Indeed, the data access components are often carefully designed to retrieve high volumes of data. When bypassed, what was meant to be an efficient process can now become a performance drag or failure. Developers often do not know the full context in which the query operates—for example, they may not know how the database table indexes are set up. The same SQL query can perform drastically differently depending on the nature of these details. The result is inordinate response lags, unpredictable behavior, wasted hardware resources, and business loss.

Bypassing these data access components also undermines the control and coordination required to ensure data integrity. The result is data corruption that can go undetected until discovered in inconsistent reports. Unapproved data access can pass undetected through functional testing and is best discovered by tracing data flows against well-defined data access rules.

A particularly serious form of architectural bypass provides hackers unauthorized access to sensitive or confidential data. Normally, users are required to be authorized for the level of access they are allowed in the system. If an entry from the user interface is allowed to access functions or data by a path that bypasses user authentication processes as in path 3, then security can be easily breached. Functions and databases are usually designed to assume that user requests have been vetted by authentication procedures that protect the data from unauthorized access. Consequently, these types of security weaknesses should be detected by tracing the data flows from the user interface to ensure that all entry paths are properly authenticated when accessing other tiers of the application.

Failure to Control Processing Volumes

Applications can behave erratically when they fail to control the amount of data or processing they allow. This problem often results from a failure to incorporate controls at several different architectural tiers, as depicted in Figure 2.6.

A user enters a query requesting a large range of data, not knowing the extensive size of the data covered by this request. In the logic tier, no paging or cache mechanism is provided to manage the results of excessively large data volumes. The data access method has been set to an eager fetch, thereby getting all relevant data from the table accessed and all dependent tables, regardless of volume. The table being accessed has grown dramatically through extended use and consequently pours forth more data than the application can effectively manage. As a result, the application behaves erratically—normally for queries yielding small amounts of data but inconsistently when the application becomes overwhelmed by large data volumes.

The potential for this erratic behavior cannot be detected within the confines of a single tier of the application. It can only be detected when inputs in the user interface tier are compared to tables in the data tier and the logic tier is inspected for mechanisms to control the volume of data returned. Consequently, we must analyze whether the application has adequate mechanisms for controlling its processing volumes embedded across its interacting tiers.

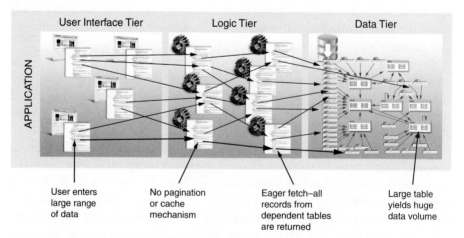

Figure 2.6 *Failure to set processing limits*

Application Resource Imbalances

Modern application platforms use resource pooling and database connection pooling (.NET, Java application servers, and so on) to manage the load of multiple transactions. Consequently, software vendors typically recommend the use of an "open late, close early" approach so that connections to the database from other application tiers are held open for the shortest time possible. Developers not closing a connection soon enough or forgetting to close it defeat the purpose of connection pools by tying up the available connections, causing the application to degrade until it is unusable. One way to enforce the open late, close early rule is to force all developers to write the open and the close connection code within the same method to prevent connection creep. This nonfunctional problem is difficult to test for and is best detected by analyzing the structure of how connections are managed in the application.

When database resources in a connection pool are mismatched with the number of request threads from an application, resource contention will block the threads until a resource becomes available, tying up CPU resources with the waiting threads and slowing application response times (Figure 2.7). If the database begins throwing exception conditions, the application code must be designed to handle them appropriately or risk locking up the application. Resource imbalances are difficult to detect in functional test and may elude stress testing if the environment is not sufficient to simulate heavy load conditions. It should be detected through evaluating the application architecture for potential load imbalances between requesting threads and size of connection pools.

Communication between tiers or components of an application can become overloaded when using a point-to-point communication scheme between servers running the application because every server must maintain a communication link with every other server hosting the application. When only two servers

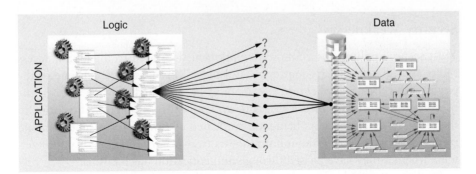

Figure 2.7 *Imbalance between application resources*

are communicating the load is low. However, if there are multiple servers hosting the application, the number of open communication links goes up exponentially, slowing and perhaps even locking the application. Under such circumstances, a multicast or publish-subscribe model may be more appropriate. Such application communication problems are difficult to test for and are best identified by evaluating the architecture of the application and how it manages communication among servers.

Applications that work well in one environment may exhibit performance or stability problems in other environments for which their architectures or code were not designed. For instance, consider a user interface on an application in a local area network environment that makes separate calls to the database to fill each field on the screen. Because local area networks are fast, there may be little performance penalty for the many database calls. However, if this application is expanded across geographically separated units, the application will respond poorly as these many database accesses crawl across the slower communication lines outside the local area network. Developers who are not experienced in distributed applications often fail to understand the performance implications of how their components interact with other application tiers, harming their scalability and performance.

Interactions between the data tier and either the user interface or logic tier that performed well under initial loads may slow dramatically with rapid increases in the volume of data or frequency of transactions. For instance, if a developer instantiates an object in a loop that accesses a table in the data layer that has grown substantially larger, the repeated calls as the loop iterates will slow performance. In SQL programming, functions embedded in WHERE clauses or queries without indexes can cause substantial performance penalties as the data or frequency of processing grows. The performance penalties for these violations of good practice can often increase processing times by an order of magnitude or more.

Security Weaknesses

Most secure applications contain a component dedicated to managing access rights and related security matters. As displayed in Figure 2.8 (1), one of the easiest ways for an application's security to be breached is when code in the user interface provides direct access to an application's functionality prior to the requester's access rights being authenticated as valid. This problem should be detected by analyzing the input requests from secure functionality to determine whether they have passed through authentication mechanisms.

Hackers frequently take advantage of gaps in security between the different tiers of an application through cross-site scripting and SQL injection. Cross-site

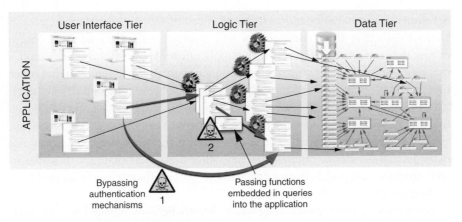

Figure 2.8   *Enabling security lapses*

scripting involves embedding Javascript into an otherwise innocent user input. Similarly, SQL injection involves embedding an SQL query into a user input. In both cases the hacker is hoping that the application will not recognize a harmful input to the user interface tier and allow it to execute in either the logic or database tier where it can return results such as confidential customer or financial information as in Figure 2.8. These types of security attacks can be successful when the application lacks appropriate sanitization checks across the tiers on the user's input, its processing request, or the contents to be returned. These types of security holes between application tiers can be detected by evaluating the application to ensure that appropriate checks on input values, processing requests, and output content have been implemented in the appropriate tiers of the application architecture.

Hackers can also gain access to corporate networks from error messages delivered to the end users that contain server names, IP addresses, application server versions, and other information that could be misused to leverage the vulnerabilities of the server and penetrate the application to get personal customer data. The presence of Java code in a web page can generate exceptions that occasionally reveal information hackers can use to penetrate other application tiers. This sensitive information can also be revealed by comments in web pages that are visible to end users. This problem can be minimized by detecting the use of Java code in web-based user interfaces and the use of components outside the user interface tier to forward calls to the application server.

Lack of Defensive Mechanisms

Many of the problems described here that cause damaging consequences in operations result from misunderstood interactions among systems. Because developers cannot understand all the nuances of the different languages and technologies that their components will interact with, they need to design robust defenses into their tiers of the application. Application quality implies that a tier or its component parts are designed with an understanding that other tiers may fail, may respond in ways that had not been anticipated, may overload the available resources or connections, or may behave erratically. Given that the developers implementing one tier cannot anticipate every situation, they must implement defensive code that sustains the application's performance in the face of stresses or failures affecting other tiers. Tiers that lack these defensive structures are fragile because they fail to protect themselves from problems in their interaction with other tiers.

For instance, applications hang when threads become blocked and are unable to terminate. A firewall may terminate a connection it assumes to be inactive without providing a notice of termination to the connection points of the application tiers involved. Because TCP does not provide timeout mechanisms, the tiers may assume they are connected and continue waiting for responses that will never come. Similarly, when multiple threads need to synchronize on multiple resources spread across an application, they can deadlock when different threads lock up resources needed by other threads and the various threads cannot gain access to all the resources needed to complete their processing.

Solutions to problems such as these involve defensive code such as timeout mechanisms or circuit breakers in the requesting tier that terminate requests and free threads from their blocked states. However, the absence of such defensive mechanisms will often not be detected during functional testing and may not appear unless load testing stresses a tier to the point of blocking requests from threads in other tiers. These problems can be detected dynamically by simulating the appropriate stress conditions, or statically when searching for appropriate defensive code to handle the possible stresses a tier's design can encounter.

Each of these application structural quality problems result in unpredictable application performance, business disruption, and data corruption and make it difficult to alter the application in response to pressing business needs. Reliably detecting these problems requires an analysis of each application component in the context of the entire application as a whole and evaluation of the structural quality of individual components *in the context of the application as a whole.*

Desiderata for Systems Evaluating Structural Quality

Evaluating the structural quality of modern business applications in the context of the numerous interconnections with other systems, databases, middleware, and APIs can only be accomplished by a system that satisfies the following conditions.

A system for evaluating structural quality must

- **Handle numerous technologies:** Comprehensive coverage of the entire system from end to end. In modern systems, this means it has to cover multiple languages, technologies, and frameworks all the way from the GUI front end to the middleware to the database.

- **Generate detailed logical views:** A detailed architectural/logical view of the entire system from end to end. The quality measurement system must be able to create detailed architectural maps of the entire system—views of all the components and how they are interconnected. It must be able to capture the logical aspects of the system, not simply the physical representation of it. It must be able to use this detailed logical view to evaluate the product quality of the system in the context of the entire system.

- **Make software engineering knowledge explicit:** It must be able to check the entire application against hundreds of implementation patterns that encode software engineering best practices.

- **Generate actionable metrics:** The quality metrics must not just inform, but they also must guide the improvement of software quality by showing what to do first, how to do it, what to next, and so on (that is, both prioritize and guide practical action). It must be able to do this in a way that teaches developers best practices and changes their behavior without disrupting their normal work habits.

- **Be automated:** Finally, it must be able to do all this in an automated way. No human or team of humans can be expected to have visibility into the entire application end to end, hold this in their heads at all time, and check the structural quality of this large-scale system against thousands of software engineering best practices. Only an automated system for evaluating structural quality can do this.

Three Problems That Distort Software Economic Analysis

Software is a manufactured product, and therefore software projects should be analyzed using the basic methods of manufacturing economics. For more than 150 years the standard economic definition of productivity has been

"Good or services produced per unit of labor or expense."

Economic theorists define quality differently, but a workable software quality definition that supports manufacturing economic studies is

> "Software quality is defined as freedom from defects that will either cause an application to stop completely or will cause it to produce inaccurate and unreliable results."

There are, of course, many aesthetic aspects of quality that might be considered, but aesthetic views are outside the scope of manufacturing economics. Poor aesthetics might lower sales revenue compared to excellent aesthetics, but poor aesthetics do not affect software's manufacturing costs. Defects, on the other hand, raise both production costs and lengthen schedules and are therefore a proper study under the canons of manufacturing economics.

Unfortunately, software has lagged in terms of economic understanding for more than 50 years. There are three main reasons why even in 2010 software economic studies are poorly performed and filled with errors and false assumptions. In fact, the term "professional malpractice" can be applied to some of these errors.

The three key problems that have distorted software economic understanding (and software quality economic understanding) are

1. Software cost and resource data "leak" and omit almost 50% of the real effort that goes into software projects. This leakage causes productivity rates to seem higher than they really are. The leakage is partly due to excessive concentration on coding and not enough attention on even more expensive noncoding cost drivers such as requirements, design, and business analysis. For economic purposes, software project measures should use a standard taxonomy of project activities to ensure that no key cost drivers are omitted by mistake.

2. The traditional "lines of code" (LOC) metric has no standard definition. Physical lines of code and logical code statements can differ by more than 1,000%, but both are used interchangeably. Either form of the LOC metric can only be applied to coding. The other major cost drivers such as requirements, design, business analysis, architecture, and many others are invisible when using lines of code metrics. Worse, LOC metrics penalize high-level languages and make low-level languages look much better than they are. This problem is so severe that LOC metrics should be classed as "professional malpractice" when used for studies that involve more than one language.

3. The widely-cited "cost-per-defect" metric actually penalizes quality and achieves its lowest values for the buggiest applications. This problem is

due to ignoring fixed costs. The oft-repeated aphorism that "it costs 100 times as much to fix a bug after release as during design" is based on a flawed analysis that ignores fixed costs. Due to fixed costs, the following rule applies: "Cost per defect is always cheapest where the number of defects found is highest." This is why front-end defects are always cheaper than tail-end defects. Worse, the cost-per-defect metric focuses too much attention on defect repairs and ignores the greater economic advantages of high quality in shortening schedules and lowering costs.

To understand the economics of software quality, it is necessary to understand the economics of software itself. And to understand the economics of software, it is necessary to understand the economic distortions caused by the three problems just cited.

Leakage from Software Historical Data

As the developer of a family of software cost estimating tools, one of the authors of this book is often asked what seems to be a straight-forward question: "How accurate are the estimates compared to historical data?"

The answer to this question is surprising. Usually the estimates are far more accurate than the historical data because the "historical data" is incomplete and omits most of the actual costs and work effort that were accrued. In some cases, "historical data" only captures 30% or less of the full amount of effort that was expended.

Thus, when the outputs from an accurate software cost estimating tool are compared to what is called "historical data," the results tend to be alarming. The outputs from the estimating tool often indicate higher costs, more effort, and longer schedules than the historical data indicates. It is seldom realized that the difference is because of major gaps and omissions in the historical data itself, rather than because of errors in the estimates.

It is fair to ask if historical data is incomplete, how is it possible to know the true amounts and judge the quantity of missing data that was omitted from a project's historical data collections?

To correct the gaps and omissions that are normal in cost tracking systems, it is necessary to interview the development team members and the project managers. During these interview sessions, the contents of the historical data collected for the project are compared to a complete work breakdown structure derived from similar projects. For each activity and task that occurs in the work breakdown structure, but which is missing from the historical data, the developers are asked whether or not the activity occurred. If it did occur, the developers are asked to reconstruct from memory or their informal records the number of hours that the missing activity accrued.

Problems with errors and "leakage" from software cost tracking systems are as old as the software industry itself. The first edition of one of the author's books, *Applied Software Measurement*, was published in 1991. The third edition was published in 2008. Yet the magnitude of errors in cost tracking systems is essentially the same today in 2011 as it was in 1991. The most common omissions from historical data, ranked in order of significance, include the following:

Sources of Historical Cost Errors	Magnitude of Cost Errors
1) Unpaid overtime by exempt staff	(up to 25% of reported effort)
2) Charging time to the wrong project	(up to 20% of reported effort)
3) User effort on software projects	(up to 20% of reported effort)
4) Management effort on software projects	(up to 15% of reported effort)
5) Specialist effort on software projects 　　Human factors specialists 　　Data base administration specialists 　　Integration specialists 　　Quality assurance specialists 　　Technical writing specialists 　　Education specialists 　　Hardware or engineering specialists 　　Marketing specialists 　　Metrics and function point specialists	(up to 15% of reported effort)
6) Effort spent prior to cost tracking start up	(up to 10% of reported effort)
7) Inclusion/exclusion of non-project tasks 　　Departmental meetings 　　Courses and education 　　Travel	(up to 25% of reported effort)
Overall Error Magnitude	(up to 125% of reported effort)

Not all of these errors are likely to occur on the same project, but enough of them occur so frequently that ordinary cost data from project tracking systems is essentially useless for serious economic study, for benchmark comparisons between companies, or for baseline analysis to judge rates of improvement.

A more fundamental problem is that most enterprises simply do not record data for anything but a small subset of the activities actually performed. In carrying out interviews with project managers and project teams to validate and correct historical data, this author observed the following patterns of incomplete and missing data, using the 40 activities of the author's chart of accounts as the reference model as shown in Table 2.17.

Table 2.17 *Incompleteness of Software Project Historical Data*

	Activities	Historical Data Completeness	Percent of Total
1	Business analysis	Missing or incomplete	0.03%
2	Risk analysis/sizing	Missing or incomplete	0.00%
3	Risk solution planning	Missing or incomplete	0.01%
4	Requirements	Missing or incomplete	3.84%
5	Requirement inspection	Missing or incomplete	0.96%
6	Prototyping	Missing or incomplete	2.30%
7	Architecture	Missing or incomplete	0.31%
8	Architecture inspection	Missing or incomplete	0.09%
9	Project plans/estimates	Missing or incomplete	0.15%
10	Initial design	Missing or incomplete	3.07%
11	Detail design	Incomplete	4.60%
12	Design inspections	Missing or incomplete	1.53%
13	Coding	Complete	23.02%
14	Code inspections	Missing or incomplete	7.67%
15	Reuse acquisition	Missing or incomplete	0.05%
16	Static analysis	Missing or incomplete	0.02%
17	COTS package purchase	Missing or incomplete	0.09%
18	Open source acquisition	Missing or incomplete	0.02%
19	Code security audit	Missing or incomplete	0.12%
20	Independent Verif. & Valid.	Missing or incomplete	0.02%
21	Configuration control	Missing or incomplete	0.15%
22	Integration	Missing or incomplete	0.15%
23	User documentation	Missing or incomplete	0.92%
24	Unit testing	Complete	4.60%
25	Function testing	Missing or incomplete	9.21%
26	Regression testing	Missing or incomplete	3.07%
27	Integration testing	Missing or incomplete	9.21%
28	Performance testing	Missing or incomplete	0.77%
29	Security testing	Missing or incomplete	0.92%
30	Usability testing	Missing or incomplete	0.46%
31	System testing	Missing or incomplete	4.60%

(Continued)

Table 2.17   *(Continued)*

	Activities	Historical Data Completeness	Percent of Total
32	Cloud testing	Missing or incomplete	0.31%
33	Field (Beta) testing	Missing or incomplete	0.23%
34	Acceptance testing	Missing or incomplete	0.23%
35	Independent testing	Missing or incomplete	0.15%
36	Quality assurance	Missing or incomplete	0.92%
37	Installation/training	Missing or incomplete	0.09%
38	Project measurement	Missing or incomplete	0.03%
39	Project office	Missing or incomplete	0.77%
40	Project management	Missing or incomplete	15.34%
		Complete = 27.62%	100.00%
		Missing or incomplete = 72.38%	

Because of Department of Defense rules for contracts, DoD software projects keep more accurate data than 90% of civilian projects. And as a result, DoD projects all seem to be much lower in productivity than civilian projects of the same size and type. When specific activities are measured such as coding, DoD projects are actually equal and sometimes superior to civilian projects.

However, DoD projects create about twice as many documents than similar civilian projects, and the documents are almost twice as large as their civilian counterparts. To understand these issues, activity-level measurements are needed.

When the authors and their colleagues collect data, they ask the managers and personnel to try and reconstruct any missing cost elements. Reconstruction of data from memory is plainly inaccurate, but it is better than omitting the missing data entirely.

Unfortunately, the bulk of the software literature and many historical studies only report information to the level of complete projects, rather than to the level of specific activities. Such gross "bottom-line" data cannot readily be validated and is almost useless for serious economic purposes."

To illustrate the effect of "leakage" from software tracking systems, consider what the complete development cycle would look like for a sample project. The sample is for a PBX switching system written in the C programming language. Table 2.18 illustrates a full set of activities and a full set of costs.

Table 2.18 *Example of Complete Costs for Software Development*

Average monthly salary =	$5,000
Burden rate =	50%
Fully burdened monthly rate =	$7,500
Work hours per calendar month =	132
Application size in FP =	1,500
Application type =	Systems
CMM level =	1
Programming lang. =	C
LOC per FP =	128

Activities	Staff Funct. Pt. Assignment Scope	Monthly Funct. Pt. Production Rate	Work Hours per Funct. Pt.	Burdened Cost per Funct. Pt.	Schedule Months	Staff	Effort Months
01 Requirements	500	200	0.66	$37.50	2.50	3.00	7.50
02 Prototyping	500	150	0.88	$50.00	3.33	3.00	10.00
03 Architecture	1,000	300	0.44	$25.00	3.33	1.50	5.00
04 Project Plans	1,000	500	0.26	$15.00	2.00	1.50	3.00
05 Initial Design	250	175	0.75	$42.86	2.86	3.00	8.57
06 Detail Design	250	150	0.88	$50.00	1.67	6.00	10.00
07 Design Reviews	200	225	0.59	$33.33	0.89	7.50	6.67
08 Coding	150	25	5.28	$300.00	6.00	10.00	60.00
09 Reuse acquisition	500	1,000	0.13	$7.50	0.50	3.00	1.50

(Continued)

Table 2.18   (Continued)

Activities	Staff Funct. Pt. Assignment Scope	Monthly Funct. Pt. Production Rate	Work Hours per Funct. Pt.	Burdened Cost per Funct. Pt.	Schedule Months	Staff	Effort Months
10 Package purchase	2,000	2,000	0.07	$3.75	1.00	0.75	0.75
11 Code inspections	150	75	1.76	$100.00	2.00	10.00	20.00
12 Ind. Verif.& Valid.	1,000	250	0.53	$30.00	4.00	1.50	6.00
13 Configuration mgt.	1,500	1,750	0.08	$4.29	0.86	1.00	0.86
14 Integration	750	350	0.38	$21.43	2.14	2.00	4.29
15 User documentation	1,000	75	1.76	$100.00	13.33	1.50	20.00
16 Unit testing	200	150	0.88	$50.00	1.33	7.50	10.00
17 Function testing	250	150	0.88	$50.00	1.67	6.00	10.00
18 Integration testing	250	175	0.75	$42.86	1.43	6.00	8.57
19 System testing	250	200	0.66	$37.50	1.25	6.00	7.50
20 Field (Beta) testing	1,000	250	0.53	$30.00	4.00	1.50	6.00
21 Acceptance testing	1,000	350	0.38	$21.43	2.86	1.50	4.29
22 Independent testing	750	200	0.66	$37.50	3.75	2.00	7.50
23 Quality assurance	1,500	250	0.53	$30.00	6.00	1.00	6.00
24 Installation/training	1,500	250	0.53	$30.00	6.00	1.00	6.00
25 Project management	1,000	75	1.76	$100.00	13.33	1.50	20.00
Cumulative Results	420	6	22	$1,249.94	24.65	3.57	249.99

Table 2.19 *Example of Partial Costs for Software Development*

Average monthly salary =	$5,000
Burden rate =	50%
Fully burdened monthly rate =	$7,500
Work hours per calendar month =	132
Application size in FP =	1,500
Application type =	Systems
CMM level =	1
Programming lang. =	C
LOC per FP =	128

Activities	Staff Funct. Pt. Assignment Scope	Monthly Funct. Pt. Production Rate	Work Hours per Funct. Pt.	Burdened Cost per Funct. Pt.	Schedule Months	Staff	Effort Months
01 Coding	150	25	5.28	$300.00	6.00	10.00	60.00
02 Unit testing	200	150	0.88	$50.00	1.33	7.50	10.00
Cumulative Results	171	21	6.16	$350.00	6.60	8.75	70.00

Now consider what the same project would look like if only coding and unit testing were recorded by the company's tracking system. Table 2.19 illustrates the results.

Instead of a productivity rate of 6 function points per staff month, Table 2.18 indicates a productivity rate of 21 function points per staff month. Instead of a schedule of almost 25 calendar months, Table 2.19 indicates a schedule of less than 7 calendar months. And instead of a cost of $1,874,910, the reported cost is only $525,000.

Errors of this magnitude should not occur, but regrettably not only do they occur, but they occur in almost 90% of all software productivity measurement reports!

Yet both Tables 2.18 and 2.19 are for exactly the same project. What passes for "historical data" unfortunately more often matches the partial results shown in Table 2.19 than the complete results shown in Table 2.18.

Internal software projects where the development organization is defined as a cost center are the most incomplete and inaccurate in collecting software data. Many in-house projects by both corporations and government agencies lack useful historical data. Thus such organizations tend to very optimistic in their internal estimates because they have no solid basis for comparison. If they switch to a commercial estimating tool, they tend to be surprised at how much more costly the results might be.

External projects that are being built under contract and projects where the development organization is a profit center have stronger incentives to capture costs with accuracy. Thus contractors and outsource vendors are likely to keep better records than internal software groups.

Table 2.20 shows the approximate distribution of tracking methods noted at more than 150 companies visited by one of the authors.

Leakage from cost tracking systems and the wide divergence in what activities are included presents a major problem to the software industry. It is very difficult to perform statistical analysis or create accurate benchmarks when so much of the reported data is incomplete and there are so many variations in what gets recorded.

The gaps and variations in "historical data" explain why the authors and their colleagues find it necessary to go on site and interview project managers and technical staff before accepting historical data. Unverified historical data is often so incomplete as to negate the value of using it for benchmarks and industry studies.

The problems illustrated by these tables are just the surface manifestation of a deeper issue. After more than 50 years, the software industry lacks anything that resembles a standard chart of accounts for collecting historical data. This lack is made more difficult by the fact that in real life, there are many variations of activities that are actually performed. There are variations due to application size, application type, and methodologies.

As we all know, a waterfall project and an Agile project do not perform the same sets of activities. But both waterfall and Agile projects tend to omit more effort than they record, and neither tracks costs and effort down to activity levels.

Table 2.20 *Distribution of Cost Tracking Methods*

Activities	Percent of Projects
Coding only	25.00%
Coding, Unit test	25.00%
Design, Coding, and Unit test	15.00%
Requirements, Design, Coding, and Unit Test	10.00%
All development, but not Project Management	10.00%
All development and Project Management	15.00%
	100.00%

Economic Problems with Lines of Code (LOC) Metrics

When multiple programming languages are included in productivity studies that use the lines of code or LOC metric, the results violate standard economic methods so severely that LOC metrics should be classified as professional malpractice.

The statement that LOC metrics constitute professional malpractice is a serious charge and should not be taken lightly. The reason is because LOC metrics violate the basic principles of manufacturing economics and indeed show the highest productivity rates for the lowest-level languages. The following case study demonstrates why LOC metrics are flawed (it's from an actual consulting engagement commissioned by a European telecommunications company).

One of the authors and his colleagues were commissioned by a European telecommunications company to explore an interesting problem. Many of this company's products were written in the CHILL programming language. CHILL is a fairly powerful third-generation procedural language developed specifically for telecommunications applications by the CCITT, an international telecommunications association.

Software engineers and managers within the company were interested in moving to object-oriented programming using C++ as the primary language. Studies had been carried out by the company to compare the productivity rates of CHILL and C++ for similar kinds of applications. These studies concluded that CHILL projects had higher productivity rates than C++ when measured with the productivity metric, "Lines of Code per staff month" or LOC per staff month.

The author was asked to explore the results of these experiments and either confirm or challenge the finding that CHILL was superior to C++.

Because many other programming languages are used for PBX switching systems, the study included a total of ten languages. Data was available from several companies that produced similar PBX switches. Although the actual PBX software sizes ranged from about 1350 to 1700 function points, all were mathematically adjusted to the same size—1500 function points.

To ensure consistent results, all versions were compared using the same sets of activities, and any activities that were unique for a particular project were removed. The data was normalized using the CHECKPOINT measurement and estimation tool. This tool facilitates comparisons between different programming languages and different sets of activities, given that it can convert applications to the same size and highlight and mask activities that are not common among all projects included in the comparison. For example, if one project collected data on unpaid overtime but a similar project did not, CHECKPOINT could provide synthetic values for unpaid overtime.

The full set of activities studied numbered more than twenty, but a final presentation to the client used consolidated data based on six major activities:

1. Requirements

2. Design

3. Coding

4. Integration and Testing

5. Customer Documentation

6. Management

The consolidation of data to six major activities was done primarily to simplify presenting the results. The more granular data utilized included activity and task-level information. For example, the cost bucket labeled "Integration and Testing" really comprised information derived from integration, unit testing, new function testing, regression testing, stress and performance testing, and field testing.

The first topic of interest is the wide range in the volume of source code required to implement essentially the same application. Note that the function point total of the PBX project used for analysis was artificially held constant at 1500 across all ten versions in this example.

In real life, of course, the functionality varied among the projects utilized. Table 2.21 gives the volumes of source code and the number of source code statements needed to encode one function point for the ten examples.

Table 2.21   *Function Point and Source Code Sizes for Ten Versions*

Language	Size in Function Pt.	Language. Level	LOC per Function Pt.	Size in LOC
Assembly	1,500	1	250	375,000
C	1,500	3	127	190,500
CHILL	1,500	3	105	157,500
PASCAL	1,500	4	91	136,500
PL/I	1,500	4	80	120,000
Ada83	1,500	5	71	106,500
C++	1,500	6	55	82,500
Ada95	1,500	7	49	73,500
Objective C	1,500	11	29	43,500
Smalltalk	1,500	15	21	31,500
AVERAGE	1,500	6	88	131,700

The next topic of interest was the amount of effort required to develop the ten examples of the project. Table 2.22 gives the effort for the six major activities and the overall quantity of effort expressed in terms "staff months." Note that the term "staff month" is defined as a typical working month of about 22 business days and includes the assumption that project work occurs roughly 6 hours per day, or 132 work-hours per month.

Note that because the data came from four companies, each of which had varying accounting assumptions, different salary rates, different work month definitions and work patterns, and other complicating factors, the separate projects were run through the CHECKPOINT tool and converted into standard work periods of 132 hours per month, at costs of $10,000 per month.

None of the projects were exactly 1,500 function points in size, and the original sizes ranged from about 1,300 to 1,750 function points in size. Here, too, the data normalization feature was used to make all 10 versions identical in factors that would conceal the underlying similarities of the examples.

It can readily be seen that the overall effort associated with coding and testing are much less significant for high-level and object-oriented languages than for procedural and low-level languages. However, the effort associated with initial requirements, design, and user documentation are comparatively inelastic and do not fluctuate in direct proportion to the volume of code required.

The most interesting results are associated with measuring the productivity rates of the ten versions. Note how apparent productivity expressed using the metric Lines of Code per Staff Month moves in the opposite direction from productivity expressed terms of Function Points per Staff Month.

Table 2.22 *Staff Months of Effort for Ten Versions of the Same Software Project*

Language	Req. (Months)	Design (Months)	Code (Months)	Test (Months)	Doc. (Months)	Mgt. (Months)	TOTAL (Months)
Assembly	13.64	60.00	300.00	277.78	40.54	89.95	781.91
C	13.64	60.00	152.40	141.11	40.54	53.00	460.69
CHILL	13.64	60.00	116.67	116.67	40.54	45.18	392.69
PASCAL	13.64	60.00	101.11	101.11	40.54	41.13	357.53
PL/I	13.64	60.00	88.89	88.89	40.54	37.95	329.91
Ada83	13.64	60.00	76.07	78.89	40.54	34.99	304.13
C++	13.64	68.18	66.00	71.74	40.54	33.81	293.91
Ada95	13.64	68.18	52.50	63.91	40.54	31.04	269.81
Objective C	13.64	68.18	31.07	37.83	40.54	24.86	216.12
Smalltalk	13.64	68.18	22.50	27.39	40.54	22.39	194.64
AVERAGE	13.64	63.27	100.72	100.53	40.54	41.43	360.13

The data in Table 2.23 is derived from the last column of Table 2.24, or the total amount of effort devoted to the ten projects. Table 2.24 gives the overall results using both LOC and function point metrics:

As can easily be seen, the LOC data does not match the assumptions of standard manufacturing economics and indeed moves in the opposite direction from real economic productivity.

Table 2.23   *Productivity Rates for 10 PBX Software Projects*

Language	Effort (Months)	Function Pt. per Staff Month	Work Hours per Function Pt	LOC per Staff Month	LOC per Staff Hour
Assembly	781.91	1.92	68.81	480	3.38
C	460.69	3.26	40.54	414	3.13
CHILL	392.69	3.82	34.56	401	3.04
PASCAL	357.53	4.20	31.46	382	2.89
PL/I	329.91	4.55	29.03	364	2.76
Ada83	304.13	4.93	26.76	350	2.65
C++	293.91	5.10	25.86	281	2.13
Ada95	269.81	5.56	23.74	272	2.06
Objective C	216.12	6.94	19.02	201	1.52
Smalltalk	194.64	7.71	17.13	162	1.23
AVERAGE	360.13	4.17	31.69	366	2.77

Table 2.24   *Rankings of Productivity Levels Using Function Point Metrics*

Productivity Ranking Using Function Point Metrics	Productivity Ranking Using LOC Metrics
1 Smalltalk	1 Assembly
2 Objective C	2 C
3 Ada95	3 CHILL
4 C++	4 PASCAL
5 Ada83	5 PL/I
6 PL/I	6 Ada83
7 PASCAL	7 C++
8 CHILL	8 Ada95
9 C	9 Objective C
10 Assembly	10 Smalltalk

It has been known for many hundreds of years that when manufacturing costs have a high proportion of fixed costs and there is a reduction in the number of units produced, the cost per unit will go up. This is a basic rule of manufacturing economics.

The same logic is true for software. When a line of code, or LOC, is defined as the unit of production and there is a migration from low-level procedural languages to high-level and object-oriented languages, the number of "units" that must be constructed declines.

The costs of paper documents such as requirements and user manuals do not decline and tend to act like fixed costs. This inevitably leads to an increase in the Cost per LOC for object-oriented projects and a reduction in LOC per staff month when the paper-related activities are included in the measurements.

On the other hand, the function point metric is a synthetic metric totally divorced from the amount of code needed by the application. Therefore, function point metrics can be used for economic studies involving multiple programming languages and object-oriented programming languages without bias or distorted results. The function point metric can also be applied to noncoding activities such as requirements, design, user documentation, integration, testing, and even project management.

To illustrate the hazards of LOC metrics without any ambiguity, Table 2.24 simply ranks the ten versions in descending order of productivity. As can be seen, the rankings are completely reversed between the function point list and the LOC list.

When using the standard economic definition of productivity, which is *goods or services produced per unit of labor or expense*, the function point ranking matches economic productivity assumptions.

The function point ranking matches economic assumptions because the versions with the lowest amounts of both effort and costs have the highest function point productivity rates and the lowest costs per function point rates.

The LOC rankings, on the other hand, are the exact reverse of real economic productivity rates. This is the key reason why usage of the LOC metric is viewed as "professional malpractice" when it is used for cross-language productivity or quality comparisons involving both high-level and low-level programming languages.

The LOC metric is so hazardous for cross-language comparisons that a strong case can be made that using lines of code for normalization of data involving multiple or different languages should be considered an example of professional malpractice.

The phrase *professional malpractice* implies that a trained knowledge worker did something that was hazardous and unsafe and that the level of training and prudence required to be in the profession should have prevented the unsafe practice. Because it is obvious that the LOC metric does not move in the same direction as economic productivity and indeed moves in the opposite direction, it is a reasonable assertion that misuse of Lines of Code metrics should be viewed as professional malpractice if a report or published data caused some damage or harm.

Indeed, the whole case study was based on the fact that the client measured productivity using LOC metrics and mistakenly concluded that a low-level procedural language had higher productivity than a high-level OO language.

One of the severe problems of the software industry has been the inability to perform economic analysis of the impact of various tools, methods, or programming languages. It can be stated that the LOC metric has been a significant barrier that has slowed down the evolution of software engineering because it has blinded researchers and prevented proper exploration of software engineering factors.

Economic Problems with Cost-per-Defect Metrics

The oldest metric for software quality economic study is that of *cost per defect*. Though there may be earlier uses, the metric was certainly used within IBM by the late 1960s for software and probably as early as the 1950s for hardware.

As commonly calculated, the cost-per-defect metric measures the hours associated with defect repairs and the numbers of defects repaired and then multiplies the results by burdened costs per hour.

The cost-per-defect metric has developed into an urban legend, with hundreds of assertions in the literature that early defect detection and removal is cheaper than late defect detection and removal by more than 10 to 1.

This urban legend is true mathematically, but there is a problem with the cost-per-defect calculations. Due to fixed costs, cost per defect is *always* cheapest where the greatest numbers of defects are found. As quality improves, cost per defect gets higher and higher until zero defects are encountered, where the cost-per-defect metric goes to infinity.

More important, the cost-per-defect metric tends to ignore the major economic value of improved quality: shorter development schedules and reduced development costs outside of explicit defect repairs.

Typical data for cost per defect varies from study to study but resembles the following pattern that occurs in numerous articles and books:

Defects found during requirements = $250

Defects found during design = $500

Defects found during coding and testing = $1,250

Defects found after release = $5,000

Although such claims are often true mathematically, there are three hidden problems with cost per defect that are usually not discussed in the software literature:

1. Cost per defect penalizes quality and is always cheapest where the greatest numbers of bugs are found.

2. Because more bugs are found at the beginning of development than at the end, the increase in cost per defect is artificial. Actual time and motion studies of defect repairs show little variance from end to end.

3. Even if calculated correctly, cost per defect does not measure the true economic value of improved software quality. Over and above the costs of finding and fixing bugs, high quality leads to shorter development schedules and overall reductions in development costs. These savings are not included in cost-per-defect calculations, so the metric understates the true value of quality by several hundred percent.

Let us consider these problem areas using three case studies that illustrate the main points.

In all three cases, A, B, and C, assume that test personnel work 40 hours per week and are compensated at a rate of $2,500 per week or $75.75 per hour using fully burdened costs. Assume that all three software features being tested are 100 function points in size.

Case A: Poor Quality

Assume that a software engineer spent 15 hours writing test cases, 10 hours running them, and 15 hours fixing ten bugs: 40 hours in all. The total hours spent was 40, and the total cost was $2,500. Because ten bugs were found, the cost per defect was $250. The cost per function point for the week of testing would be $25.00.

Case B: Good Quality

In this second case, assume that a software engineer spent 15 hours writing test cases, 10 hours running them, and 5 hours fixing one bug, which was the only bug discovered: 30 hours in all.

Because no other assignments were waiting and the software engineer worked a full week, 40 hours were charged to the project. The total cost for the week was still $2,500, so the cost per defect has jumped to $2,500. This is because the costs for writing test cases and running them are inelastic and act like fixed costs.

Table 2.25   *Cost per Defect for Six Forms of Testing*

	Writing Test Cases	Running Test Cases	Repairing Defects	TOTAL COSTS	Number of Defects	$ per Defect
(Assumes $75.75 per staff hour for costs)						
Unit test	$1,250.00	$750.00	$18,937.50	$20,937.50	50	$418.75
Function test	$1,250.00	$750.00	$7,575.00	$9,575.00	20	$478.75
Regression test	$1,250.00	$750.00	$3,787.50	$5,787.50	10	$578.75
Performance test	$1,250.00	$750.00	$1,893.75	$3,893.75	5	$778.75
System test	$1,250.00	$750.00	$1,136.25	$3,136.25	3	$1,045.42
Acceptance test	$1,250.00	$750.00	$378.75	$2,378.75	1	$2,378.75

If the 10 hours of slack time are backed out, leaving 30 hours for actual testing and bug repairs, the cost per defect would be $2,273.50 for the single bug.

Based on thousands of projects in hundreds of companies, it can be stated as a general rule that when quality improves, cost per defect rises sharply. The reason is that writing test cases and running them act like fixed costs. It is a well-known law of manufacturing economics that

> "If a manufacturing cycle includes a high proportion of fixed costs and there is a reduction in the number of units produced, the cost per unit will go up."

As an application moves through a full test cycle that includes unit testing, function testing, regression testing, performance testing, system testing, and acceptance testing, the time required to write test cases and the time required to run test cases stays almost constant; but the number of defects found steadily decreases.

Table 2.25 shows the approximate costs for the three cost elements of preparation, execution, and repair for the test cycles just cited using the same rate of $75.75 per hour for all activities.

Note that while cost per defect steadily gets higher as defect volumes decline, testing cost per function point matches manufacturing economic assumptions and gets steadily lower. Note also that testing cost per function point can be added to show the grand total of testing costs. Cost-per-defect data cannot be added across multiple test stages, although it can be averaged.

Test Stage	Test Cost per Function Point
Unit test	$209.37
Function test	$95.75
Regression test	$57.88
Performance test	$38.94
System test	$31.36
Acceptance test	$23.79
TOTAL	$457.09

What is most interesting about Table 2.25 is that cost per defect rises steadily as defect volumes come down, even though Table 2.25 uses a constant value of five hours to repair defects for every single test stage! In other words, every defect identified throughout Table 2.25 had a constant cost of $378.25 when only repairs are considered.

In fact, all three columns use constant values, and the only true variable in the example is the number of defects found. In real life, of course, preparation, execution, and repairs would all be variables. But by making them constant, it is easier to illustrate the main point: *Cost per defect rises as numbers of defects decline.*

Because the main reason that cost per defect goes up as defects decline is due to the fixed costs associated with test-case preparation and execution, it might be thought that those costs could be backed out and leave only defect repairs. Doing this would change the apparent results and minimize the errors, but it would introduce three new problems:

1. Removing quality cost elements that may total more than 50% of total cost of quality (COQ) would make it impossible to study quality economics with precision and accuracy.

2. Removing preparation and execution costs would make it impossible to calculate cost of quality (COQ) because the calculations for COQ demand all quality cost elements.

3. Removing preparation and execution costs would make it impossible to compare testing against formal inspections because inspections do record preparation and execution as well as defect repairs.

The third case study deals with zero defects. Although no bugs or defects were found, that does not mean that no costs were expended.

Case C: Zero Defects

In this third case, assume that a tester spent 15 hours writing test cases and 10 hours running them: 25 hours in total. No bugs or defects were discovered, so the actual cost for defect repairs was $0.00.

Because no defects were found, the cost-per-defect metric cannot be used at all. But 25 hours of actual effort were expended writing and running test cases. If the software engineer had no other assignments, he or she would still have worked a 40-hour week, and the costs would have been $2,500.

If the 15 hours of slack time are backed out, leaving 25 hours for actual testing, the costs would have been $1,893.75. With slack time removed, the cost per function point would be $18.38. But cost per defect cannot be calculated due to having zero defects.

Time and motion studies of defect repairs do not support the aphorism that "it costs 100 times as much to fix a bug after release as before." Bugs typically require between 15 minutes and 6 hours for repairs regardless of where they are found.

(There are some bugs that are expensive and may takes several days or more to repair. These are called *abeyant defects* by IBM. Abeyant defects are customer-reported defects the repair center cannot re-create due to some special combination of hardware and software at the client site. Abeyant defects comprise less than 5% of customer-reported defects.)

Considering that cost per defect has been among the most widely used quality metrics for more than 50 years, the literature is surprisingly ambiguous about what activities go into cost-per-defect metrics. More than 75% of the articles and books that use cost-per-defect metrics do not state explicitly whether preparation and executions costs are included or excluded. In fact, a majority of articles do not explain anything at all but merely show numbers without discussing what activities are included.

Another major gap is that the literature is silent on variations about cost per defect by severity level. A study done by the author at IBM showed these variations in defect repair intervals associated with severity levels.

Table 2.26 shows the results of the study. Because these are customer-reported defects, "preparation and execution" would have been carried out by customers, and the amounts were not reported to IBM.

As can be seen, the overall average would be close to perhaps five hours, although the range is quite wide.

Table 2.26 *Defect Repair Hours by Severity Levels for Field Defects*

	Severity 1	Severity 2	Severity 3	Severity 4	Invalid	Average
> 40 hours	1.00%	3.00%	0.00%	0.00%	0.00%	0.80%
30–39 hours	3.00%	12.00%	1.00%	0.00%	1.00%	3.40%
20–29 hours	12.00%	20.00%	8.00%	0.00%	4.00%	8.80%
10–19 hours	22.00%	32.00%	10.00%	0.00%	12.00%	15.20%
1–9 hours	48.00%	22.00%	56.00%	40.00%	25.00%	38.20%
> 1 hour	14.00%	11.00%	25.00%	60.00%	58.00%	33.60%
TOTAL	100.00%	100.00%	100.00%	100.00%	100.00%	100.00%

In Table 2.26, severity 1 defects mean that the software has stopped working. Severity 2 means that major features are disabled. Severity 3 refers to minor defects. Severity 4 defects are cosmetic in nature and do not affect operations. Invalid defects are hardware problems or customer errors inadvertently reported as software defects. A surprisingly large amount of time and effort goes into dealing with invalid defects, although this topic is seldom discussed in the quality literature. It sometimes takes several hours of research to discover that a specific defect report was not caused by software but by other factors such as hardware, competitive software, or perhaps an electrical surge.

Useful Rules of Thumb for Predicting Software Defect Potentials

From collecting defect data on hundreds of applications whose function point totals were known, it was possible to develop useful rules of thumb that can predict approximate defect potentials. The rule of thumb operates reasonably well for applications between 10 function points in size and 10,000 function points in size. For massive applications in the 100,000 function point plateau, the rule of thumb predicts a larger quantity of defects than will probably occur by about 30%.

The defect potentials that are predicted are found in these five categories:

- Requirements defects

- Design defects

- Code defects

- Document defects

- Bad fixes

The rule of thumb works by using a calculator or spreadsheet and raising the applications size in function points to the specified power. For example, a TSP project of 1,000 function points raised to the 1.15 power would predict 2,818 potential defects.

Table 2.27 shows how the rule of thumb operated for a sample of software development methods plus various CMMI levels. This rule of thumb is not, of course, extremely accurate, but it gives results that are much better than most managers or software engineers would achieve by guessing.

Note that the defect potentials for massive applications of 100,000 function points are 30% below those predicted by the specified power due to exceeding the useful limit of the power. Power curves are useful within certain ranges, and the most effective range for these defect prediction rules of thumb is between 100 and 10,000 function points. The rules of thumb are not completely accurate at any range, but they are closer to reality than guessing and much better than no quality estimates at all.

Table 2.27   *Rule of Thumb for Predicting Software Defect Potentials*

| | | (Raise application size in function points to the powers shown) | | | | |
Methods	Power Level	10 Function Points	100 Function Points	1,000 Function Points	10,000 Function Points	100,000 Function Points
CMMI 5	1.18	15	229	3,467	52,481	556,030
TSP	1.18	15	229	3,467	52,481	556,030
PSP	1.18	15	229	3,467	52,481	556,030
QFD	1.18	15	229	3,467	52,481	556,030
CMMI 4	1.19	15	240	3,715	57,544	623,876
XP	1.19	15	240	3,715	57,544	623,876
CMMI 3	1.19	15	240	3,715	57,544	623,876
RUP	1.19	15	240	3,715	57,544	623,876
SCRUM	1.19	15	240	3,715	57,544	623,876
JAD	1.19	15	240	3,715	57,544	623,876
CMMI 2	1.20	16	251	3,981	63,096	700,000
Agile	1.20	16	251	3,981	63,096	700,000
CMMI 1	1.20	16	251	3,981	63,096	700,000
Waterfall	1.22	17	275	4,571	75,858	881,248
CMMI 0	1.24	17	302	5,248	91,201	1,109,425

Summary and Conclusions on Software Quality Estimation and Measurement

For more than 50 years, the most expensive activity in all of software has been that of finding and fixing bugs. For many large systems, testing and defect repairs cost more than coding. And, of course, after the software is released, there are user-reported bugs to be fixed, too. Over the complete life of a software application from early requirements through final retirement many years later, defect repairs are usually the largest annual cost.

Because so much time, energy, and money are expended on software defect repairs, it is urgent for all managers and all software engineers to be able to predict how many defects are likely to occur.

To gain such knowledge, both measurement of quality and estimation of quality are mission-critical activities for software applications and the teams that build and maintain them.

But the real value of software quality measurement and software defect estimation is not just to accumulate knowledge, but to use that knowledge to plan effective strategies for both defect prevention and defect removal.

As is discussed in Chapter 7, a well-designed combination of defect prevention and defect removal activities can lower software total costs of ownership by about 50% and can shorten software development schedules by between 10% and 20%. For software, high quality has a higher return on investment (ROI) than any other known factor.

Chapter 3

Software Defect Prevention

Introduction

Software defect prevention is the most difficult quality topic to discuss, to measure, to improve, and to prove that it has economic value. The reason for this difficulty is because defect prevention is a negative factor that reduces defect potentials. Therefore, it is necessary to have at least two data points for every defect prevention method:

1. Results of applications that did *not* use the defect prevention method.

2. Results of similar applications that *did* use the defect prevention method.

Of course, two data points are not statistically reliable. As a result of this difficulty, hundreds of applications need to be measured and evaluated to express the probable effects of defect prevention methods. Even then the true effectiveness of defect prevention methods remains somewhat uncertain because other methods and factors may also be present or because several prevention methods were deployed simultaneously. The first studies on defect prevention at IBM in the 1970s included hundreds of applications and took place over a period of more than three years.

IBM's early and complete quality measurements created one of the key metrics for software quality analysis: defect potentials. Because the IBM quality measures started early during requirements and continued all the way through development and then into the field to record defects found by customers, IBM had a complete inventory of defects found in requirements, design, source code, documents, and bad fixes or secondary defects.

After several hundred applications had been measured, the IBM historical data on defects could be used to predict future defects in new applications. The sum total of all defects found during development and by customers was termed the "defect potential" of an application. IBM's first software cost-estimating tool in 1973 was probably the first predictive tool to estimate software defect potentials or the total number of defects found in all major deliverables.

Defects are an important indicator of software quality, but they are by no means the only such indicator. As we saw in Chapter 2, the root causes of non-functional defects are to be found in the structural quality of an application. Defects are the most visible indicators of software quality problems, while structural quality factors remain buried in the way the application's design and architecture are implemented in the source code. In this chapter we restrict our attention to defects; structural quality is covered in detail in various other places in the book, namely, Chapters 2, 4, 6, and 7.

The Early History of Defect Prevention Studies in the 1970s at IBM

In the early 1970s IBM software teams noted that software applications were growing larger and more complex. Defects tend to increase with application size, and application sizes were rapidly growing. IBM's excellent quality measurement program also noted that testing was inadequate to achieve high quality levels for applications larger than about 1,000 function points.

For larger applications, test coverage tended to drop below 80%, and defect removal efficiency levels were usually below 85%. Most forms of testing individually were below 35% in defect removal efficiency. Even six to eight different kinds of testing stayed below 85% in defect removal efficiency.

One thread of IBM research to improve software quality was the development of formal inspections of requirements, design documents, source code, and other deliverables. Inspections were measured for the numbers of defects removed and also for the amount of time and effort that the inspections required. The inspection process originated at IBM Kingston as part of the work of Michael Fagan, Lew Priven, Ron Radice, Roger Stewart, and other colleagues.

In a very short time, about six months, it was discovered that formal inspections of design documents and source code were achieving defect removal efficiency levels in excess of 85%, which was much higher than any form of testing then available. Within about a year it was also discovered that the applications that had been inspected had higher levels of test defect removal efficiency by about 5% than similar uninspected applications using the same test stages. The inspections were providing the test personnel with more complete and accurate requirements and specification documents, so better and more complete test cases were created due to the pretest inspections.

The combination of formal inspections with formal testing was achieving defect removal efficiency levels as high as 97%, which was a very significant improvement. Even better, the cumulative effort and the combined schedule for the inspected projects were both about 15% below those of similar applications that had been tested but not inspected. The reason for this was because the inspections removed so many bugs prior to the start of testing that test schedules were cut in half and sometimes even more than half.

As inspections began to spread from IBM Kingston to other IBM development labs, data continued to be gathered both for projects where inspections were used and also for projects that did not use the inspection methodology.

After about three years of data collection and analysis it was discovered that the IBM development teams who participated in the inspection process were spontaneously avoiding making the kinds of errors that the inspections found. In other words, it was discovered that inspections *prevented* defects from occurring, as well as *removed* defects that did occur. So far as the author knows, the IBM discovery that formal inspections reduced defect potentials circa 1973 was the first study of software defect prevention.

Table 3.1 illustrates the approximate defect prevention and defect removal data from the early studies by IBM in the 1970s. The table reflects data gathered after about 18 months of inspection usage, when defect prevention was starting to become a visible phenomenon.

Table 3.1 *Defect Prevention and Defect Removal Results of Formal Inspections*

	(Application example is 1,000 function points in size)		
	No Use of Inspections	Inspections Used	Difference
Defect Potential per Function Point	5.5	4.2	1.3
Defect Potential	5,500	4,200	1,300
Inspection Efficiency	0	85.00%	85.00%
Defects Removed	0	3,570	3,570
Defects Remaining	5,500	630	4,870
Testing Efficiency	79%	84%	5%
Removed via Testing	4,345	536	3,810
Defects Delivered	1,155	95	1,061
Defects Delivered per Function Point	1.16	0.09	1.06
Inspection Schedule (months)	0.00	2.00	−2.00
Testing Schedule (months)	6.50	3.50	3.00
Total Defect Removal Schedule (months)	6.50	5.50	1.00

It's easy to see why test schedules are significantly reduced when using pretest inspections before testing starts. The number of defects still present at the start of testing are only a small fraction of those present in projects that do not use pretest inspections. (Incidentally, this same effect also occurs when modern pretest methods such as static analysis tools are used before testing begins.)

From this start, IBM and other major companies continued to collect data that could be used to study both defect prevention and defect removal. Defect removal studies can normally show quantitative results in 6 months to 12 months from samples of about 50 projects or fewer.

Defect prevention, on the other hand, normally requires between 24 months and 48 months and several hundred projects. Defect prevention needs many more data points to show a convincing correlation between a specific method and defect potentials because both usage and nonusage need to be compared.

It is hard to do defect prevention analysis across multiple companies. The best sources of data are large corporations such as IBM, Microsoft, Motorola, Raytheon, and the like that have good and consistent measurement programs and many different software development labs that use different combinations of methods and tools.

(One of the authors has worked with about 600 companies, including some 150 Fortune 500 companies and 30 government agencies. Only about 20 of these have enough long-range data to be useful for judging defect prevention effectiveness. Many of the others actually use some of the methods that improve prevention, but they don't have measurements that are capable of showing their impact.)

Some of the other methodologies that were examined by IBM during the 1970s included joint application design (JAD), higher-level programming languages such as PL/I and APL, clean-room development, software quality assurance teams, and use of reusable design and code.

While the idea of defect prevention is to find methods that lower defect potentials, it was also discovered by IBM that a small number of practices raised defect potentials higher than corporate average values. Some of the negative practices included requirements changes in excess of 1% per calendar month and excessive schedule pressure that arbitrarily shortened the time available for key tasks such as design inspections.

Although defect prevention is still a difficult and complicated topic to explore, as of 2011 enough data has been collected to show the approximate results for a fairly large number of methods and practices.

Table 3.2 has a high margin of error, but it shows a sample of 65 methods that either lower defect potentials (at the top of the table) or make defect potentials worse (at the bottom of the table). Table 3.2 is based on an application size of a nominal 1,000 function points, where average defect potentials are about

5.0 per function point. Given that defects go up with increasing application size, this table should not be used for larger applications in the 10,000 function point size range.

Table 3.2 *Effectiveness of Software Defect Prevention Methods*

	(Reductions in defects per function point for 1,000 function points)			
	Defect Prevention Methods (In Order of Effectiveness)	**Defect Prevention Efficiency**	**Defects Potentials without Prevention**	**Defect Potentials with Prevention**
1	Reuse (certified sources)	85.00%	5.00	0.75
2	Inspections (formal)	60.00%	5.00	2.00
3	Quality Function Deployment (QFD)	57.50%	5.00	2.13
4	Prototyping—functional	52.00%	5.00	2.40
5	Risk analysis (automated)	48.00%	5.00	2.60
6	PSP/TSP	44.00%	5.00	2.80
7	Static analysis of source code	44.00%	5.00	2.80
8	Root cause analysis	41.00%	5.00	2.95
9	Quality in all status reports	40.00%	5.00	3.00
10	Joint Application Design (JAD)	40.00%	5.00	3.00
11	Test-driven development	37.00%	5.00	3.15
12	CMMI 5	37.00%	5.00	3.15
13	Defect measurements (complete)	36.00%	5.00	3.20
14	Test case design (mathematical)	34.00%	5.00	3.30
15	Patterns (design)	34.00%	5.00	3.30
16	Automated quality predictions	33.00%	5.00	3.35
17	Patterns (code)	33.00%	5.00	3.35
18	Agile embedded users	33.00%	5.00	3.35
19	Six Sigma for software	32.00%	5.00	3.40
20	Patterns (requirements)	28.00%	5.00	3.60
21	Patterns (defect removal sequence)	27.00%	5.00	3.65
22	CMMI 4	27.00%	5.00	3.65
23	Security reviews (formal)	25.00%	5.00	3.75
24	Inspections (informal)	24.00%	5.00	3.80
25	Poka-yoke	23.00%	5.00	3.85
26	Cost of Quality (COQ) data	23.00%	5.00	3.85

(Continued)

Table 3.2   *(Continued)*

Defect Prevention Methods (In Order of Effectiveness)	Defect Prevention Efficiency	Defects Potentials without Prevention	Defect Potentials with Prevention
27 CMMI 3	23.00%	5.00	3.85
28 Risk analysis (manual)	22.00%	5.00	3.90
29 Kaizen	22.00%	5.00	3.90
30 XP (Extreme programming)	21.00%	5.00	3.95
31 Patterns (risks and security)	20.00%	5.00	4.00
32 Scrum sessions (daily)	20.00%	5.00	4.00
33 Rational Unified Process (RUP)—original	20.00%	5.00	4.00
34 Rational Unified Process (RUP)—customized	19.00%	5.00	4.05
35 Cyclomatic complexity measures	19.00%	5.00	4.05
36 Peer reviews (informal)	16.00%	5.00	4.20
37 Test coverage analysis	16.00%	5.00	4.20
38 Extended use cases	16.00%	5.00	4.20
39 Software Quality Assurance (SQA)	15.00%	5.00	4.25
40 Patterns (test materials)	15.00%	5.00	4.25
41 Six Sigma (lean)	13.00%	5.00	4.35
42 Decision-logic tables	12.50%	5.00	4.38
43 Function point quality measures	12.50%	5.00	4.38
44 Reuse (uncertified sources)	12.00%	5.00	4.40
45 CMMI 2	12.00%	5.00	4.40
46 Six Sigma (generic)	12.00%	5.00	4.40
47 Clean-room development	11.00%	5.00	4.45
48 Certified SQA, test personnel	11.00%	5.00	4.45
49 Basic use cases	10.00%	5.00	4.50
50 Patterns (architecture)	10.00%	5.00	4.50
51 ISO quality standards	10.00%	5.00	4.50
52 Data-flow diagrams	10.00%	5.00	4.50
53 Total Quality Management (TQM)	9.00%	5.00	4.55
54 Patterns (user documents/HELP)	8.00%	5.00	4.60
55 Pair programming	8.00%	5.00	4.60
56 CMMI 1	3.00%	5.00	4.85

	Defect Prevention Methods (In order of effectiveness)	Defect Prevention Efficiency	Defects Potentials without Prevention	Defect Potentials with Prevention
57	LOC quality measures	−2.00%	5.00	5.10
58	CMMI 0 (CMMI not used at all)	−4.50%	5.00	5.23
59	No quality predictions	−6.00%	5.00	5.30
60	Inexperienced software developers	−7.00%	5.00	5.35
61	Inexperienced software managers	−8.00%	5.00	5.40
62	"Good enough" quality fallacy	−9.00%	5.00	5.45
63	No defect or quality measures	−12.50%	5.00	5.63
64	Excessive schedule pressure	−15.00%	5.00	5.75
65	Excessive requirements changes	−20.00%	5.00	6.00
	Average	*20.64%*	*5.00*	*3.97*

Table 3.2 has a high margin of error, but the fact that defect prevention can be studied at all is due to many years of continuous measurements. Most of the measurements associated with defect prevention come from large companies such as IBM, Motorola, and AT&T, which have had sophisticated quality measurements for more than 35 years.

Defect prevention analysis requires much more data than defect removal. The defect prevention data has to reflect similar applications that either used or did not use specific methods. A minimum sample for evaluating defect prevention is about ten projects that used a specific approach such as formal inspections compared to ten similar projects that did not.

Synergistic Combinations of Defect Prevention Methods

Table 3.2 shows results for various methodologies in isolation. However, in real life many of these defect prevention methods are synergistic and work together. Others are somewhat antagonistic and do not work well together. Some of the combinations of defect prevention methods that illustrate synergy or antagonism include the following.

Certified reuse combined with patterns: Certified reusable components can be combined with reusable "patterns" for requirements, architecture, design, user documents, and some but not all code segments. This combination is quite rare in 2011 but has the theoretical capability of lowering defect potentials by as much as 95%. Pattern matching combined with certified reusable components is potentially an entirely new mode of software engineering that promises to replace today's manual effort and line-by-line coding with construction based on catalogs of certified materials and patterns derived from the most successful applications. In theory, pattern matching and certified reusable components can approach zero defects. This field is gaining attention, but a great deal more work is needed.

Small business applications: For small business applications in the 1,000 function point size range, an effective combination would be embedded users and the Agile development method and test-driven development; automated risk analysis, and static analysis on all code segments. This combination should lower defect potentials by about 45% and ensure that defect removal efficiency is in the range of 95%.

Large business applications: For fairly large business applications in the 10,000 function point size range, an effective synergistic combination using today's methods would combine Joint Application Design (JAD) with automated risk analysis, inspections of requirements, design, and critical code segments plus static analysis of 100% of the code. A formal development method such as the Rational Unified Process (RUP) or Team Software Process (TSP) would be utilized. Quality should be estimated and should also be the #1 topic discussed in all status reports. This combination can lower defect potentials by about 55% and raise defect removal efficiency levels to more than 95%.

Technical and embedded software: For technical and embedded applications a synergistic combination would include Quality Function Deployment (QFD); the Team Software Process (TSP); inspections of critical requirements, architecture, and design documents; and static analysis of all code segments. Tests cases would be designed using formal mathematical methods that would ensure high coverage. Cyclomatic complexity would be measured and kept below values of around 10. Quality would be the #1 topic in all status reports. This combination can lower defect potentials by more than 60% and raise defect removal efficiency up to perhaps 97%.

Military and defense software: For military and defense applications an effective combination would include higher CMMI levels of 3 and above; Quality Function Deployment (QFD); formal inspections of key deliverable such as requirements and design; and static analysis of all code. Robust development methods such as the Rational Unified Process (RUP) or the Team Software Process (TSP) would be utilized. Formal test case design using mathematical methods; quality predictions; quality measurements; and quality status tracking would also be part of the combination. This combination can lower defect potentials by perhaps 50% and raise defect removal efficiency levels about 96%.

Antagonistic methods that may not work well together: Not all defect prevention methods fit comfortably with other defect prevention methods. One example is that the Agile methods are somewhat antagonistic to the rigor of the higher CMMI levels. For another example, code inspections and static analysis cover similar kinds of defects, and probably both are not needed. If both inspections and static analysis are used, then inspections should examine critical code segments and look for topics such as security flaws where static analysis may not be as effective. Development methods such as Agile development, the Rational Unified Process (RUP), and the Team Software Process (TSP) are not exactly antagonistic, but usually one or the other of these will be selected, and they won't all be used concurrently. It is possible to hybridize methods and select useful features from each, but hybrid methods require considerable sophistication to be successful. That being said, some of the hybrids are successful. There are so many combinations of possible methods that not all of them have been analyzed. Even though individual methods have demonstrated success, combinations of several methods that seem antagonistic or weakly synergistic do not have enough data to judge the final results.

Combinations of helpful and harmful methods used concurrently: It sometimes happens that helpful and harmful methods are used at the same time on the same projects. For example, a project might set out to use Quality Function Deployment (QFD) but is suddenly hit by excessive schedule pressure by clients or executives so that the QFD work is abbreviated. Unfortunately, in situations where helpful and harmful defect prevention approaches are used concurrently, the harmful methods seem to end up on top. That is, defect potentials will go up instead of coming down. As a general rule, it is much easier to harm a software project than it is to make it better.

Harmful combinations that raise defect potentials: Looking at the harmful end of the spectrum, some combinations of methods raise defect potentials and make applications risky with a high chance of failure. Harmful combinations include but are not limited to: informal requirements gathering; no risk analysis; no sizing; no quality predictions; no quality in status reports; no inspections of deliverables; poor requirements change control process combined with >2% requirements growth per calendar month; excessive schedule pressure from clients and management; a "good enough" quality attitude; and casual test case design methods. The development method would be either informal or at best a traditional "waterfall" approach. Applications using this combination will have defect potentials at least 50% higher than normal, combined with defect removal efficiency levels that may drop down below 80%. Applications developed using this unfortunate combination have more than a 30% chance of cancellation and more than a 75% chance of major cost and schedule overruns.

Defect Potentials and Defect Origins

Until this point the discussion of defect potentials has dealt with complete applications. However, defects stem from a variety of origin points, and not every defect prevention method is equally effective against all sources of defects.

Table 3.3 shows defect potentials by origin for applications of 1,000 function points. The table also shows the methods of defect prevention associated with each origin point. Note that not every defect prevention method is used at the same time. Usually between one and four defect preventions might be applied concurrently. However, Table 3.3 lists all of the defect prevention methods that have demonstrated success against defect origin points.

Table 3.3 indicates only approximate results. Ranges of defect prevention effectiveness can and do vary based on team experience and the rigor with which the methods are utilized.

In Table 3.3 the defect prevention methods are shown alphabetically under each defect origin point. In other words, the sequence does not reflect the effectiveness of the prevention methods.

Table 3.3   *Software Defect Prevention by Defect Origins*

	Former Defect Potential	Percent Change	New Defect Potential
Requirement Defect Prevention	1.15	−25.00%	0.86
Agile embedded users			
Business analysts			
Data mining of legacy code			
Defect measurements (requirements)			
Function-point sizing			
Inspections (requirements)			
Joint Application Design (JAD)			
Patterns (requirements)			
Quality Function Deployment (QFD)			
Requirement change control board			
Requirement change estimation			
Reusable requirements (certified)			
Root-cause analysis			
Static analysis of legacy code			
Test-based development (XP)			
Architectural Defect Prevention	0.25	−35.00%	0.16
Architects (application)			
Architects (enterprise)			
Defect measurements (architecture)			
Experience in similar applications			

	Former Defect Potential	Percent Change	New Defect Potential
Formal architecture methods			
Function point sizing			
Inspections (architecture)			
Patterns (architecture)			
Reusable architecture (certified)			
Root-cause analysis			
Design Defect Prevention	1.50	−50.00%	0.75
Data mining of legacy code			
Defect measurements (design)			
Experience in similar applications (clients)			
Experience in similar applications (team)			
Formal design methods such as UML			
Formal development methods such as TSP			
Function point sizing			
Inspections (design)			
Patterns (designs)			
Performance models or prototypes			
Reusable designs (certified)			
Root-cause analysis			
Static analysis of legacy code			
Three-dimensional, animated design models			
Coding Defect Prevention	2.00	−60.00%	0.80
Adherence to SANS coding principles:			
Secure interactions			
Secure resource management			
Effective security defenses			
Cyclomatic complexity measures			
Defect measurements (bad fixes)			
Defect measurements (source code)			
Error-prone module analysis/removal			
Experience (in programming languages)			
Experience (in similar applications)			

(Continued)

Table 3.3   *(Continued)*

	Former Defect Potential	Percent Change	New Defect Potential
Formal methods such as PSP, TSP, and XP			
Function point sizing			
Inspections (legacy source code)			
Inspections (major code changes)			
Inspections (new source code)			
Lines of code sizing (logical statements)			
Patterns (coding)			
Reusable code (certified)			
Root-cause analysis			
Static analysis of legacy code			
Static analysis of new code			
Static analysis of reused code			
Static analysis of third-party code			
Test Plan and Test Case Defect Prevention	1.85	−50.00%	0.93
Automated testing			
Defect removal efficiency measures			
Formal mathematical test case design			
Formal test library controls			
Inspections (test cases)			
Inspections (test plans)			
Inspections (test scripts)			
Measuring, eliminating duplicate test cases			
Measuring, eliminating test coverage gaps			
Patterns (testing)			
Reusable test cases (certified)			
Risk-based test case design			
Static analysis of code defect repairs			
Test coverage analysis (legacy code)			
Test coverage analysis (new code)			
Test coverage analysis (updated code)			
Test plan and test case measurements			

	Former Defect Potential	Percent Change	New Defect Potential
User Documentation Defect Prevention	0.75	–20.00%	0.60
Documentation measurements			
Editing legacy documents			
Inspections (document updates)			
Inspections (user documents)			
Patterns (documentation)			
Professional translators (international)			
Reusable documents from similar applications			
Standard reader-comment forms			
Standard tables of contents			
Technical writers			
Use of automated text analysis (FOG index)			
Using documents during formal testing			
Database Defect Prevention	2.75	–60.00%	1.10
Automated migration (legacy data)			
Data analysts			
Database security inspections			
Database structural modeling			
Developing a "data point" metric for sizing			
Inspections (database)			
Measuring database quality			
Measuring data defect removal efficiency (DRE)			
Patterns (databases)			
Quality Function Deployment (QFD)			
Six Sigma for data errors			
Website Defect Prevention	1.75	–45.00%	0.96
Developing a "web content point" metric for sizing			
Formal inspections of websites			

(Continued)

Table 3.3 *(Continued)*

	Former Defect Potential	Percent Change	New Defect Potential
Measuring website defect removal efficiency (DRE)			
Measuring website quality			
Patterns (websites)			
Reusable content (certified)			
Root-cause analysis of website errors			
Six Sigma for website errors			
Static analysis of website code			
Website customer opinion surveys			
Website modeling with active links			
TOTALS	12.00	51.35%	6.16

Although Table 3.3 has a high margin of error, some of the topics do have fairly good supporting evidence. For example, formal inspections of requirements, design, and code have been in use for more than 40 years and have very good data from hundreds of projects. Hundreds of similar projects can be compared between those that used inspections and projects that did not. Static analysis is a newer technology, but here, too, there are hundreds of similar applications that either used or did not use modern static analysis tools.

Defect Prevention, Patterns, and Certified Reusable Materials

Informal software reuse has been common since the industry began. Programmers and software engineers use code from their own past applications or borrow code from colleagues.

However, the potential value of reusable materials includes much more than source code. It is possible to reuse requirements, architecture, design, code, test cases, segments of user documents, data, and portions of websites.

But casual reuse of multiple artifacts is potentially hazardous because all of the reused materials probably contain bugs and latent defects. For software reuse to achieve its full potential as a defect prevention method, the reused materials need to be certified to approximate zero-defect levels.

A certification process for reusable materials would include formal inspections of documents, code, and test materials; static analysis of all code; formal testing of all code; and trial usage in real applications for a 12-month period.

Table 3.4 *Defect Prevention from Certified Reuse*

Defect Sources	Former Defect Potential	Percent Change	New Defect Potential
Requirements	1.15	–80.00%	0.23
Architecture	0.25	–95.00%	0.01
Design	1.50	–90.00%	0.15
Source Code	2.00	–85.00%	0.30
Test Materials	1.85	–75.00%	0.46
Documents	0.75	–75.00%	0.19
Database	2.75	–50.00%	1.38
Websites	1.75	–65.00%	0.61
TOTAL	12.00	–72.25%	3.33

Certification would need to be performed by an independent group such as Software Quality Assurance (SQA) with its own management chain. Indeed possible, a nonprofit certification organization would be useful for the industry.

As of 2011 formally certified reusable materials are rare. Therefore, Table 3.4 is partly hypothetical. But it is based on empirical observations from companies such as IBM that used very sophisticated quality control and also kept very detailed records of bugs and defects.

A formal certification program for reusable software materials would cost about $150 per function point in total. But certified reusable materials would generate development savings of about $750 per function point and mainte-nance and support savings over a five-year period of about $1,250 per function point: application savings of $2,000 per function point.

When other factors are included, such as lower odds of litigation, faster learning curves, fewer outages and business interruptions, the full value of certi-fied reusable materials would probably top $10,000 per function point over typical application life cycles of development plus 15 years of usage.

Software Defect Prevention and Application Size

As application size increases, defect potentials go up significantly. While the value of effective defect prevention goes up with application size, it becomes progressively more difficult to apply methods such as Quality Function Deploy-ment (QFD), Joint Application Design (JAD), and many others because team sizes become large enough to be unwieldy. Also, large applications tend to have thousand if not millions of users, so requirements defect prevention is difficult due to the fact that large numbers of users will have large numbers of needs for software applications.

Table 3.5 shows the approximate results of the defect prevention methods applied to applications of five different size plateaus from 10 function points up to 100,000 function points:

Table 3.5 *Defect Prevention by Application Size*

Defect Source	Application Size in Function Points				
	10	100	1,000	10,000	100,000
Requirements	0.25	0.75	1.00	1.25	1.50
Architecture	0.05	0.10	0.25	0.50	0.75
Design	0.50	1.00	1.25	1.50	1.75
Source Code	1.65	1.70	1.75	2.00	2.10
Test Materials	1.25	1.50	1.85	2.00	2.10
Documents	0.60	0.65	0.70	0.75	0.80
Database	1.50	2.00	2.75	3.00	3.20
Websites	1.25	1.50	1.75	2.00	2.25
Defect Potentials	7.05	9.20	11.30	13.00	14.45
Prevention %	−25%	−33%	−43%	−45%	−47%
New Defect Potentials	5.29	6.16	6.44	7.15	7.66

As is evident, the effectiveness of most forms of defect prevention begins to slow down for large applications in the 10,000 and 100,000 function point size range.

However, patterns and certified reusable materials are much more effective than ordinary forms of defect prevention. As a result, they continue to be very effective across all size ranges from 10 to 100,000 function points. Table 3.6 illustrates the potential reduction in total defects via certified reuse of all major software deliverables.

Given the overall effectiveness of certified reusable materials, it would be great if this method became more widely deployed in the future.

In addition to certification, a successful reuse program would also include a taxonomy of reusable features and a catalog that includes and describes their functions and purposes.

Reusing source code is comparatively straightforward. But reusing requirements, architecture, design, and other noncoding artifacts requires rethinking software engineering in a fairly major fashion. The emergence of pattern-based design and development are examples of reuse at higher levels of abstraction.

Table 3.6 *Defect Prevention from Certified Reuse by Application Size*

Defect Source	Application Size in Function Points				
	10	100	1,000	10,000	100,000
Requirements	0.25	0.75	1.00	1.25	1.50
Architecture	0.05	0.10	0.25	0.50	0.75
Design	0.50	1.00	1.25	1.50	1.75
Source Code	1.65	1.70	1.75	2.00	2.10
Test Materials	1.25	1.50	1.85	2.00	2.10
Documents	0.60	0.65	0.70	0.75	0.80
Database	1.50	2.00	2.75	3.00	3.20
Websites	1.25	1.50	1.75	2.00	2.25
Defect Potentials	7.05	9.20	11.30	13.00	14.45
Reuse prevention %	−70.00%	−70.00%	−72.50%	−75.00%	−77.00%
New Defect Potentials	2.12	2.76	3.11	3.25	3.32

Analysis of Defect Prevention Results

The software industry develops new methodologies several times a year. New programming languages are developed more than once a month. New tools are put on the market almost every week. As a result, any discussion of software methods for defect prevention will need to be updated fairly often to stay current with new methods and practices.

Following are discussions of representative samples of development methods and practices that have been shown to reduce defect potentials when used carefully by trained personnel. The sample list is only a small subset of the full list of 65 methods. Also included are samples of a few methods that raise defect potentials.

New methods will probably be developed even before the list is published and will certainly come out at frequent intervals after publication. However, the list provides a good sample of defect prevention methods and some observations on synergies and antagonisms among the methods. Note that some methods are effective in raising defect removal efficiency as well as in lowering defect potentials. The list is in alphabetical order.

The primary purpose of most of the methods discussed is not defect prevention, but some other business or technical purpose such as requirements gathering or design creation. Defect prevention is a secondary and sometimes fortuitous benefit.

Agile Embedded Users

Primary purpose:	Requirements definition
Application Size Ranges:	< 1,000 function points
Application Types:	Primarily information technology (IT) applications
Prevention Effectiveness:	–25%
Removal Effectiveness:	+ 05%
Synergies:	Scrum sessions; test-driven development; XP
Antagonisms:	CMMI, RUP, TSP, inspections
Current usage:	> 35% of IT applications below 1,000 function points
	< 5% of embedded, commercial, and defense projects

The Agile development methods (of which there are many) are attempts to streamline software development by dividing software applications into small portions that can be developed in short time spans called *iterations* or *sprints*. The Agile methods also minimize paperwork volume by using abbreviated methods such as user stories in place of formal requirements documents.

One novel aspect of the Agile method is to embed one or more user representatives into the team itself to provide user requirements and to assist in reviewing and using the segments as they are finished. This method has been proven effective for applications below 1,000 function points in size, where the total number of users is below 100.

For large applications in the 10,000 function point size range or with more than 1,000 users, no single individual can provide enough requirements to be effective. The Agile approach can be scaled upward to deal with multiple user representatives, but large systems are not the Agile forte.

The Agile embedded-user approach is congruent with daily Scrum status sessions. The Agile approach is antagonistic to formal methods such as the Rational Unified Process (RUP), the Team Software Process (TSP), the Capability Maturity Model Integrated (CMMI), and formal inspections. Some attempts at hybridizing Agile with other methods have been developed with mixed results.

Automated Quality Predictions

Primary purpose:	Early warning of quality issues; risk avoidance
Application Size Ranges:	100 to more than 100,000 function points
Application Types:	Commercial, embedded, systems, IT, and web software
Prevention Effectiveness:	–35%
Removal Effectiveness:	+ 05%

Synergies:	CMMI, QFD, RUP, Six-Sigma, TSP
Antagonisms:	Agile
Current usage:	< 20% of IT applications
	> 25% of embedded, systems, and defense projects

Automated software quality predictions are standard features of several commercial software estimation tools such as KnowledgePlan, SEER, and SLIM. In general, these tools are more accurate than manual estimates because their predictions are based on hundreds or even thousands of historical projects.

If these quality estimation tools are used early during requirements, as they should be, they can be used to select an optimal series of defect prevention and defect removal activities. Indeed, projects and companies that utilize automated estimation tools tend to have fewer cancelled projects and better quality than those using manual estimation methods.

Estimation support of Agile applications is more complex than other methods because of the segmentation of projects into sprints and because of embedded users. There are tools that can predict defects in Agile projects, but the Agile community is not as strong on software quality predictions as it might be.

Early knowledge of defect potentials and probable defect removal efficiency levels allow managers and software engineers to make better choices of defect prevention and defect removal methods. This is why automated quality estimation tools benefit both prevention and removal simultaneously.

Benchmarks of Software Quality Data

Primary purpose:	Historical data collection
Application Size Ranges:	100 to 10,000 function points
Application Types:	Primarily information technology (IT) applications
Prevention Effectiveness:	–15%
Removal Effectiveness:	+10%
Synergies:	CMMI, JAD, RUP, TSP, Waterfall, Function points
Antagonisms:	Agile, lines of code (LOC)
Current usage:	< 20% of IT applications < 10,000 function points
	< 0.1% of IT applications > 10,000 function points
	< 5% of embedded, commercial, and defense projects

Any attempt to introduce process improvements, and especially quality improvements, is likely to be rejected by higher management due to the mistaken belief that higher quality means higher costs. The best method of countering this fallacy is to show management a sample of historical benchmarks gathered from the industry that prove that high quality lowers costs.

One of the largest and most accessible collections of benchmark data comes from the International Software Benchmark Standards Group (ISBSG). This is a nonprofit organization with headquarters in Australia, but they collect data from the United States, Europe, and from some countries in Asia.

There are other sources of benchmark data besides ISBSG, but theirs is the data that is probably the best known. It is interesting that ISBSG and most other benchmark organizations only support function point metrics. There are no effective collections of benchmark databased on lines of code for reasons discussed earlier.

A data repository that goes beyond function point data is the *Appmarq* repository, which currently contains around 300 applications from over 75 companies worldwide. Appmarq contains application structural quality metrics as defined in Chapter 2. These structural quality metrics are further discussed in Chapters 4, 6, and 7.

The costs of function point analysis, however, average about $6.00 per counted function point. These high costs limit function point analysis to small and medium projects. Applications larger than 10,000 function points are almost never counted because the costs and schedules are too high.

In 2011 and beyond, the newer high-speed, low-cost functional sizing methods will expand the number and size range of function point data, but 99.9% of all historical data using function points comes from applications < 10,000 function points. The average size of applications counted and benchmarked using function points is only about 750 function points.

ISBSG and the other benchmark groups support several kinds of function point measurements: COSMIC function points, FISMA function points, IFPUG function points, and NESMA function points are the most common variants. However, as of 2011 about 80% of all benchmark data were expressed in terms of IFPUG function points. IFPUG function points are used almost exclusively in the United States. COSMIC function points are seldom used in the United States but are fairly common in the United Kingdom and Western Europe, although both the Netherlands and Finland have developed local function point metrics.

Capability Maturity Model Integrated (CMMI)

Primary purpose:	Software process improvement
Application Size Ranges:	1,000 to more than 100,000 function points
Application Types:	Military, defense, embedded, and systems software
Prevention Effectiveness:	Varies from < 10% to > 45% by CMMI level
Removal Effectiveness:	Varies from < 05% to > 15% by CMMI level

Synergies:	QFD, RUP, ISO standards, Six Sigma, TSP
Antagonisms:	Agile
Current usage:	> 85% of defense and military software applications
	< 10% of IT, commercial, web, embedded projects

The Software Engineering Institute (SEI) was incorporated in 1984. Under the guidance of Watts Humphrey and later of Dr. Bill Curtis and other colleagues, the SEI developed an assessment method for software development practices called the "capability maturity model" or CMM for short. This model was first published in 1987.

In 1996 the model was expanded to include acquisition as well as development. The newer version was called the Capability Maturity Model Integration or CMMI. There is also a "people" capability maturity model for dealing with various personnel issues.

Because early funding for the SEI and the CMM came from the Defense Analysis Research Projects Agency (DARPA), the CMM quickly became a standard for military software applications. Indeed, achieving level 3 on the older CMM was a military standard for software contracts.

One of the authors of this book worked at the SEI and guided the CMMI development practice for several years. The other author was contracted by the U.S. Air Force to measure the results of ascending the CMM from level 1 up to level 5.

Data from both authors indicate that the older CMM and the newer CMMI have dual benefits in reducing defect potentials and raising defect removal efficiency levels. The benefits increase with higher CMMI levels.

That is to say, if you measure a sample of 50 software projects at CMMI level 3 and compare their results to a sample of 50 projects of about the same size and type at CMMI level 1, the defect potentials of most (but not all) of the CMMI 3 projects will be lower than the CMMI 1 projects and also lower than non-CMMI projects.

In spite of the demonstrated success of the CMM and CMMI, the methods are still concentrated in military and defense software applications. In studies involving state government software organizations and various industry organizations, not only is the CMMI sparsely utilized, but a significant number of CIO and software personnel have never even heard of the Software Engineering Institute.

Studies were done in 2009 and 2010 that noted only about a 5% usage of CMMI among several state governments and industry groups. More than 75% of some 200 participants in these studies did not know what "CMMI" meant and had not heard of the SEI. This is a sign that the SEI needs to expand its marketing outside of the traditional defense sector.

Certification Programs

Primary purpose:	Improving technical skills
Application Size Ranges:	1,000 to more than 100,000 function points
Application Types:	Commercial, embedded, systems, IT, and defense software
Prevention Effectiveness:	–10%
Removal Effectiveness:	+ 10%
Synergies:	CMMI, QFD, RUP, Six Sigma, TSP
Antagonisms:	Agile
Current usage:	> 10% of test and quality personnel in systems software
	< 5% of test personnel in other forms of software

Software engineering is not a recognized profession by the Department of Commerce. Instead, it is viewed as a craft performed by skilled workmen. This is because software lacks any kind of licensing or government-sanctioned certification as do other forms of engineering such as electrical engineering, civil engineering, mechanical engineering, and the like. This lack of "official" licensing and certification has caused some state governments such as Texas to prohibit the title "software engineer" on the grounds that legally software personnel are not licensed engineers and therefore have no right to call themselves engineers.

In spite of the lack of official licensing and certification, there are more than a dozen forms of certification available for software personnel, test personnel, and software quality personnel. The people who seek certification, as a general rule, are people who are fairly serious about their work and want to improve. Although the actual results of certification are hard to pin down (given that certification is not recorded during normal benchmarks), there is enough evidence to suggest that certification benefits both defect prevention and defect removal.

Because certification is not backed by government agencies, the certification groups are usually nonprofits such as the Software Engineering Institute (SEI), the Project Management Institute (PMI), the International Function Point Users Group (IFPUG), the American Society of Quality (ASQ), and many others. Some commercial companies such as the Quality Assurance Institute (QAI) Microsoft offer certification. Some of the many forms of certification that exist in 2011 include

1. Certified function point counter (COSMIC)

2. Certified function point counter (IFPUG)

3. Certified function point counter (NESMA)

4. Certified function point counter (FISMA)

5. Certified CMMI SCAMPI appraiser

6. Certified computing professional (CCP)

7. Certified quality analyst (CQA)

8. Certified software project manager (CSPM)

9. Certified software quality engineer (CSQE)

10. Certified software test manager (CSTM)

11. Certified software tester (CSTE)

12. Certified scope manager (CSM)

13. Certified Six Sigma green belt

14. Certified Six Sigma black belt

15. Certification by Microsoft (various products)

In addition to personal certifications, there are also organizational certifications. The two that are best known in the software world are certification by the SEI to demonstrate various levels on the CMMI and certification by the International Standards Organization (ISO) for compliance with software-related standards such as those dealing with quality, such as ISO 9000–9004.

Some of these organizational certifications have business and contract significance. Here are three examples:

1. ISO quality certification may be needed to sell software products in Europe.

2. SEI certification to level 3 or higher may be needed for defense software contracts.

3. Function point certification may be needed for government software contracts in Brazil and South Korea.

Because the empirical results of certification are both scarce and ambiguous, this area needs additional research. But until certification is included in software benchmarks, it will remain difficult to gather sufficient data to understand the impact of various certification programs.

Cost-per-Defect Measures

Primary purposes:	Measure quality costs (CAUTION: UNRELIABLE)
Application Size Ranges:	1,000 to more than 100,000 function points
Application Types:	Military, defense, embedded, and systems software
Prevention Effectiveness:	–10%
Removal Effectiveness:	+05%
Synergies:	CMMI
Antagonisms:	Function point quality measures
Current usage:	> 75% of defense and military software applications
	> 35% of IT, commercial, web, embedded projects

As noted earlier in the book, cost per defect penalizes quality because it achieves its lowest results for the buggiest software. As quality improves and defects decline, cost per defect goes up and up until zero defects are reached, where cost per defect becomes infinite.

In spite of wide use for more than 50 years, the cost-per-defect metric is highly unreliable and is economically invalid under a number of conditions. The popular software anecdote that "it costs 100 times to fix a bug in the field as in development" and its many variations have become commonplace but are not accurate in many cases. More precisely, the cost-per-defect metric is valid mathematically, but is not valid economically. That seems to be a paradox, so explanations and examples are needed.

One of the problems with the cost-per-defect metric is that it tends to ignore fixed costs and hence can fluctuate in counter-intuitive ways. Here are two simplified examples to illustrate the problem:

> **Case 1**: Suppose a poorly developed Java program of 25,000 LOC is being tested, and a total of 500 bugs are found during testing. Assume that test case preparation cost $5,000, executing the tests cost $20,000, and fixing the bugs cost $25,000. The entire testing cycle cost $50,000, so the cost per defect of the 500 bugs is exactly $100.

> **Case 2**: Assume that the application used modern defect prevention and pretest static analysis approaches, so that the number of bugs found during testing was only 50 instead of 500, which is an order of magnitude improvement. In this scenario, test case preparation cost $5,000; executing the test cases cost $17,500; and fixing the bugs cost only $2,500. Now the total testing cost has declined to $25,000. However, the cost per defect for the 50 bugs has risen to $500, or five times greater than the low-quality example!

Obviously, test case preparation is a fixed cost, and test case execution is comparatively inelastic and only partly dependent on the number of defects encountered.

As can be seen, the cost-per-defect metric tends to escalate as quality improves and does not capture the real economic advantages of higher quality.

The basic reason why cost per defect ascends as defect volumes decline is due to fixed costs. You must still create test cases and run them even if few or no defects are found.

A larger example can illustrate the impact of fixed costs and how both cost per defect and defect repairs per function point respond to the same numbers of defects and the same repairs.

Assume that you have a software project of 100 function points in size, and it contains exactly 100 defects. Assume that you will put this project through a series of six consecutive test steps, each of which is 50% efficient and will find half of the defects that are present.

Assume that for each of the six testing steps, preparation of test cases costs $500, and execution or running of the test cases also costs $500. These are fixed costs and do not vary in this case-study example.

Now assume that for each defect encountered, it will cost exactly $100 to repair. This is also a fixed cost in this example. Let us examine the six-stage test series when preparation and execution costs are part of the picture. So, here you can easily see the origin of the software legend that "it costs ten times as much to fix a defect at the end of the development cycle than at the beginning."

What happens is that the fixed costs for preparation and execution gradually overshadow the variable repair costs. This means that as the number of defects found declines, the cost per defect will go up. On the other hand, both total costs and cost per function point match the real economic observation that costs go down as defect volumes go down.

Table 3.7 *Comparison of Cost per Defect and Cost per Function Point for Six Consecutive Testing Stages*

Defect Potential		100
Test 1	*Defects found*	50
	Preparation	$500
	Execution	$500
	Repairs	$5,000
	TOTAL	$6,000
	Cost per defect	$120
	Cost per function point	$60

(Continued)

Table 3.7   *(Continued)*

Test 2	*Defects found*	25
	Preparation	$500
	Execution	$500
	Repairs	$2,500
	TOTAL	$3,500
	Cost per defect	$140
	Cost per function point	$35
Test 3	*Defects found*	12
	Preparation	$500
	Execution	$500
	Repairs	$1,200
	TOTAL	$2,200
	Cost per defect	$183
	Cost per function point	$22
Test 4	*Defects found*	6
	Preparation	$500
	Execution	$500
	Repairs	$600
	TOTAL	$1,600
	Cost per defect	$267
	Cost per function point	$16
Test 5	*Defects found*	3
	Preparation	$500
	Execution	$500
	Repairs	$300
	TOTAL	$1,300
	Cost per defect	$433
	Cost per function point	$13
Test 6	*Defects found*	1
	Preparation	$500
	Execution	$500
	Repairs	$100
	TOTAL	$1,100
	Cost per defect	$1,100
	Cost per function point	$5

When the project is released to customers and maintenance begins, the cost-per-defect metric will grow even larger because it is necessary to train at least one person to maintain the software. Further, that person must spend at least some time answering client questions and assisting clients during the installation and start-up period.

The following data assumes that only a single bug or defect was reported in the first year of use but that the customers were provided with a trained support person who assisted in installation and answered start-up questions during the first year.

Year 1	Defects found	1
	Preparation	$2,000
	Execution	$1,500
	Repairs	$100
	TOTAL	$3,600
	Cost per defect	$3,600
	Cost per function point	$36

As can be seen from the flow of data through the series, the cost-per-defect metric rises steadily as defect volumes decline. However, this phenomenon is decoupled from the real economic situation where overall defect repair costs decline but are affected by fixed costs.

The data just presented used a constant $100 for each defect repaired. However, by including fixed and inelastic costs, the apparent cost per defect ranged from $120 early in the removal cycle to $3,600 after delivery, which is a 30 to 1 difference. Had the project in question been commercial software with field service as part of the picture, a range of 100 to 1 could easily occur.

By contrast, analyzing the economics of a testing and maintenance series using "defect repair costs per function point" gives a much better picture of the real value of quality and how fixed and variable costs interact.

In spite of the economic flaws associated with the cost-per-defect metric, the reports of steadily increasing defect repair costs downstream often lead to use of pretest inspections, static analysis, and improved test case design and testing methods. This is an interesting example of a flawed approach that nonetheless has generated some beneficial results.

Cost of Quality (COQ)

Primary purpose:	Quantify economics of quality
Application Size Ranges:	100 to more than 100,000 function points
Application Types:	All types of software
Prevention Effectiveness:	−25%
Removal Effectiveness:	< 20%
Synergies:	CMMI, RUP, TSP, QFD, JAD
Antagonisms:	Agile due to low usage of metrics; earned-value metrics
Current usage:	> 50% of defense and military software applications
	< 20% of IT, commercial, web, embedded projects

The Cost of Quality (COQ) method is older than the software industry. The phrase "cost of quality" is unfortunate because it is the lack of quality that really drives up costs. While the basic cost of quality approach generates useful information for manufactured products, it is not totally adequate for software.

However, a number of software companies utilize the cost-of-quality concept, which originated with Joseph Juran and was made popular by Phil Crosby's well-known book, *Quality Is Free*. Among the author's clients, about 155 companies out of roughly 600 have at least partial cost of quality data.

The original cost-of-quality concept utilized three general cost buckets for exploring software quality economics:

1. Prevention costs

2. Appraisal costs

3. Failure costs

The cost-of-quality concept originated in the manufacturing sector and is not necessarily an optimal concept for software quality. From both an economic and a psychological point of view, some of the concepts need to be expanded and tailored to the needs of software quality. Further, the value factors and return on investment figures associated with software quality also need expansion.

A cost structure of quality more suited to the nature of software work would expand on the three cost buckets of the original cost-of-quality concept and resemble the following:

1. Defect prevention costs

2. User satisfaction optimization costs

3. Data quality defect prevention costs

4. Data quality defect removal costs

5. Quality awareness/training costs

6. Non-test defect removal costs (inspections, static analysis, and so on)

7. Testing defect removal costs (all forms of testing)

8. Post-release customer support costs

9. Warranty support and product recall costs

10. Litigation and damage award costs

11. Quality savings from reduced scrap/rework

12. Quality savings from reduced user downtime

13. Quality value from reduced time-to-market intervals

14. Quality value from enhanced competitiveness

15. Quality value from enhanced employee morale

16. Quality return on investment (ROI)

The purpose of this expanded set of quality cost buckets is to allow accurate economic measurement of the impact of various levels and severities of software defect rates. Economic measurement also includes the value of quality and the return on investment for quality-related activities.

A short hypothetical example can illustrate some of the basic premises involved. Assume a commercial software house is building two products at the same time. Both are 1,000 function points in size. One achieves high quality levels, and the other is of low quality. The burdened compensation rates are the same for both, $7,500 per staff month.

Assume that the high-quality product uses a synergistic combination of defect prevention, inspections, and formal testing. It has a defect potential of three bugs per function point and an overall removal efficiency of 96%, so the number of delivered defects was 0.12 per function point.

Assume the low-quality product invested nothing into defect prevention or inspections but did have formal testing. It has a defect potential of five bugs per function point and an overall removal efficiency of 90%, so that 0.5 bugs per function point were delivered. (This is more than four times the quantity of the high-quality product.)

Table 3.8   *Comparison of Low and High Quality*

	Low	High	
(Data expressed in terms of cost per function point)			
Activity	Quality	Quality	Difference
Pre-Release			
Prevention	$0	$62.50	$62.50
Inspection	$0	$156.25	$156.25
Testing	$468.75	$218.75	–$250.00
Subtotal	$468.75	$437.50	–$31.25
Post-Release			
Support	$312.50	$250.00	–$62.50
Maintenance	$312.50	$150.00	–$162.50
Subtotal	$625.00	$400.00	–$225.00
TOTAL	$1093.75	$837.50	–$256.25
Revenue	$1062.50	$1,375,00	$312.50
Profit	–$31.25	$537.50	$568.75

Table 3.8 shows development costs and the expenses for the first 12 months of customer use. The revenue and profit figures also reflect one year of sales. All of the data is expressed in terms of costs per function point.

As can be seen, the investment in defect prevention and pretest inspections generate a small saving of $31.25 per function point during development. However, both customer support costs and post-release maintenance costs are substantially reduced, so the tangible cost savings are significant.

Even more significant, the sales volumes of the high-quality product ramped up very quickly while the sales volumes of the low-quality product lagged due to the fact that the first customers were dissatisfied and "flamed" the product via Internet forums. Thus, the high-quality product made a profit in its first year on the market, while the low-quality product lost money.

This hypothetical example merely indicates the kind of information that can demonstrate the comparative value of high versus low quality levels in terms of both direct cost reduction and higher levels of sales volumes and profitability.

Although the data is hypothetical, it is not unrealistic. High quality for commercial software usually pays off with both direct cost reductions and higher sales volumes. Vendors should be sensitive to the fact that not only do customer associations exist, they share information about software quality. The Internet has opened up a whole new way of transmitting information anywhere in the world instantly.

Cyclomatic Complexity Measures (and Related Complexity Measures)

Primary purposes:	Improving test coverage
Application Size Ranges:	1 to more than 100,000 function points
Application Types:	All types of software
Prevention Effectiveness:	–05%
Removal Effectiveness:	+25%
Synergies:	CMMI, RUP, TSP, Agile
Antagonisms:	None
Current usage:	> 75% of defense and military software applications
	< 50% of IT, commercial, web, embedded projects

Cyclomatic and essential complexity were both made famous by the mathematician Tom McCabe in 1975. Both measure control flows of software applications. Cyclomatic complexity measures all paths; essential complexity eliminates redundant paths.

Cyclomatic complexity is based on graph theory, and the general formula is "edges minus nodes plus unconnected parts times two." Figure 3.1 illustrates a simple graph of software control flow. In this graph there are no branches, so the cyclomatic complexity level is 1. Obviously, branches raise cyclomatic complexity levels.

Empirical evidence for more than 35 years indicates that software with cyclomatic complexity levels of less than 10 are generally perceived by software engineers as being fairly simple and easy to follow.

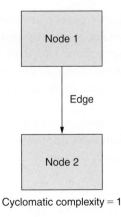

Cyclomatic complexity = 1

Figure 3.1 *The minimum cyclomatic complexity with no branching*

As cyclomatic complexity levels go up above 20, perceptions of complexity ramp up sharply. Defect potentials go up, and defect removal efficiency comes down. Test coverage comes down sharply. There are many practical and economic reasons for keeping cyclomatic complexity levels below 10, ideally below 5. This may not always be possible, but among the software community, it is common knowledge that high levels of cyclomatic complexity are harmful.

That being said, the topic of complexity remains an ambiguous topic that has no exact definition to which all researchers agree. While cyclomatic and essential complexity have clear meanings, there are numerous other kinds of complexity that affect software but are neither measured nor factored in to quality predictions.

When we speak of complexity in a software context, we can be discussing the difficulty of the problems that the software application will attempt to implement, the structure of the code, or the relationships among the data items that will be used by the application. In other words, the term complexity can be used in a general way to discuss problem complexity, code complexity, and data complexity. Cyclomatic complexity only measures code complexity.

Among one of the author's clients, about 450 enterprises out of 600 utilize some form of complexity measurement tools for their software projects that measure cyclomatic complexity levels. Many commercial tools are available that perform such calculations.

The use of complexity measurement tools is common among systems and military software (> 75% of projects), and slightly less common among management information systems, outsourced software, web, and commercial software (< 60% of projects).

What is interesting about the usage of complexity measurement tools is the seemingly random patterns with which usage occurs. We often see two nearly identical projects in the same company where one may have utilized complexity analysis tools and the other, for no particular reason, did not.

The scientific and engineering literature encompasses no fewer than 30 different flavors of complexity, some or all of which may be found to be relevant for software applications. Some of the varieties of complexity encountered in the scientific literature that show up in a software context include the following.

Algorithmic complexity concerns the length and structure of the algorithms for computable problems. Software applications with long and convoluted algorithms are difficult to design, to inspect, to code, to prove, to debug, and to test.

Code complexity concerns the subjective view of development and maintenance personnel about whether the code they are responsible for is complex or not. Interviewing software personnel and collecting their subjective opinions is an important step in calibrating more formal complexity metrics such as cyclomatic and essential complexity. Unless real software people who have to work with the code assert that a cyclomatic complexity of 20 is tougher than a cyclomatic complexity of 10, it might not matter. However, subjective views of code complexity do seem to correlate with cyclomatic complexity.

Combinatorial complexity concerns the numbers of subsets and sets that can be constructed out of *N* components. This concept sometimes shows up in the way modules and components of software applications might be structured.

Computational complexity concerns the amount of machine time and the number of iterations required to execute an algorithm. Some problems are so computationally complex that they are considered noncomputable. Other problems are solvable but require enormous quantities of machine time, such as cryptanalysis or meteorological analysis of weather patterns.

Cyclomatic complexity is derived from graph theory and was made popular for software by Dr. Tom McCabe. Cyclomatic complexity is a measure of the control flow of a graph of the structure of a piece of software. The general formula for calculating cyclomatic complexity of a control flow graph is "edges minus nodes plus unconnected parts times two." Cyclomatic complexity is often used as a warning indicator for potential quality problems.

Data complexity deals with the number of attributes associated with entities. For example, some of the attributes that might be associated with a human being in a typical medical office database of patient records could include date of birth, sex, marital status, children, brothers and sisters, height, weight, missing limbs, and many others. Data complexity is a key factor in dealing with data quality.

Diagnostic complexity is derived from medical practice, where it deals with the combinations of symptoms (temperature, blood pressure, lesions, and so on) needed to identify an illness unambiguously. For example, for many years it was not easy to tell whether a patient had tuberculosis or histoplasmosis given that the superficial symptoms were essentially the same. For software, diagnostic complexity comes in to play when customers report defects, and the vendor tries to isolate the relevant symptoms and figure out what is really wrong.

Entropic complexity is the state of disorder of the component parts of a system. Entropy is an important concept because all known systems have an increase in entropy over time. That is, disorder gradually increases. This phenomenon has been observed to occur with software projects, considering that many small changes over time gradually erode the original structure. Long-range studies of software projects in maintenance mode attempt to measure the rate at which entropy increases and whether it can be reversed by approaches such as code restructuring.

Essential complexity is also derived from graph theory and was made popular by Dr. Tom McCabe. The essential complexity of a piece of software is derived from cyclomatic complexity after the graph of the application has been simplified by removing redundant paths. Essential complexity is often used as a warning indicator for potential quality problems. As with cyclomatic complexity, a module with no branches at all has an essential complexity level of 1. As unique branching sequences increase in number, both cyclomatic and essential complexity levels rise.

Fan complexity refers to the number of times a software module is called (termed "fan in") or the number of modules which it calls (termed "fan out"). Modules with a large fan in number are obviously critical in terms of software quality because they are called by many other modules. However, modules with a large fan out number are also important and are hard to debug because they depend on so many extraneous modules. Fan complexity is relevant to exploration of reuse potentials.

Flow complexity is a major topic in the studies of fluid dynamics and meteorology. It deals with turbulence of fluids moving through channels and across obstacles. A new subdomain of mathematical physics called "chaos theory" has elevated the importance of flow complexity for dealing with physical problems. Many of the concepts, including chaos theory itself, appear relevant to software and should be explored. For example, control flows through software with high levels of cyclomatic complexity seems to resemble the flows of turbulent liquids, which are difficult to predict.

Function point complexity refers to the set of adjustment factors needed to calculate the final adjusted function point total of a software project. Standard U.S. function points as defined by the International Function Point Users Group (IFPUG) have 14 complexity adjustment factors. The British Mark II function point uses 19 complexity adjustment factors. The SPR function point and feature point metrics use 3 complexity adjustment factors.

Graph complexity is derived from graph theory and deals with the numbers of edges and nodes on a graphs created for various purposes. The concept is significant for software because it is part of the analysis of cyclomatic and essential complexity and also part of the operation of several source code restructuring tools.

Halstead complexity is derived from the "software science" research carried out by the late Dr. Maurice Halstead and his colleagues and students at Purdue University. The Halstead software science treatment of complexity is based on four units: 1) number of unique operators (for example, verbs); 2) number of unique operands (nouns); 3) instances of operator occurrences; and 4) instances of operand occurrences. The Halstead work overlaps linguistic research in that it seeks to enumerate concepts such as the vocabulary of a software project.

Information complexity is concerned with the numbers of entities and the relationships between them that might be found in a database, repository, or data warehouse. Informational complexity is also associated with research on data quality.

Logical complexity is important for both software and circuit designs. It is based on the combinations of AND, OR, NOR, and NAND logic conditions that are concatenated. This form of complexity is significant for expressing algorithms and for proofs of correctness.

Mnemonic complexity is derived from cognitive psychology and deals with the ease or difficulty of memorization. It is well known that the human mind has both a temporary and permanent memory. Some kinds of information (such as names or telephone numbers) are held in temporary memory and require conscious effort to move them into permanent memory. Other kinds of information (smells or faces, for example) go directly to permanent memory. This topic is important for software debugging and during design and code inspections. Many procedural programming languages have symbolic conventions that are very difficult to either scan or debug because they oversaturate human temporary memory. Things such as nested loops that use multiple levels of parentheses, "(((...)))," tend to swamp human temporary memory capacity.

Organizational complexity deals with the way human beings in corporations arrange themselves into hierarchical groups or matrix organizations. This topic might be assumed to have only an indirect bearing on software, except for the fact that many large software projects are decomposed into components that fit the current organization structure. For example, many large projects are decomposed into segments that can be handled by eight-person departments whether or not that approach meets the needs of the system's architecture.

Perceptional complexity is derived from cognitive psychology and deals with the arrangements of edges and surfaces that appear simple or complex to human observers. For example, regular patterns appear simple, but random arrangements appear complex. This topic is important for studies of visualization, software design methods, and evaluation of screen readability. As an example, when chess pieces are set up in patterns derived from actual chess games, it is easy for experienced chess players to remember the locations of the pieces. But when chess pieces are placed randomly on a chessboard, even experienced chess players have trouble remembering their locations.

Problem complexity concerns the subjective views of people regarding the difficulty of various kinds of problems they have been asked to solve. Psychologists know that increasing the numbers of variables and the length of the chain of deductive reasoning usually brings about an increase in the subjective view that the problem is complex. Inductive reasoning also adds to the perception of complexity. In a software context, problem complexity is concerned with the algorithms that will become part of a program or system. Determining the subjective opinions of real people is a necessary step in calibrating more objective complexity measures.

Process complexity is mathematically related to flow complexity, but in day-to-day software work it is concerned with the flow of materials through a software development cycle. This aspect of complexity is often dealt with in a practical way by project management tools that can calculate critical paths and PERT diagrams (Program Evaluation and Review Technique) of software development processes.

Semantic complexity is derived from the study of linguistics and is concerned with ambiguities in the definitions of terms. Already cited in this book are the ambiguous terms "quality," "data," and "complexity." This topic is relevant to software for a surprising reason: Many law suits between software developers and their clients can be traced back to the semantic complexity of the contract, where both sides claim different interpretations of the same clauses.

Syntactic complexity is also derived from linguistics and deals with the grammatical structure and lengths of prose sections such as sentences and paragraphs. A variety of commercial software tools are available for measuring syntactic complexity using metrics such as the FOG index. (Unfortunately, these tools are seldom applied to software specifications, although they would appear valuable for that purpose.)

Topologic complexity deals with rotations and folding patterns. This topic is often explored by mathematicians, but it also has relevance for software. For example, topological complexity is a factor in some of the commercial source code restructuring tools.

As can be seen from the variety of subjects included under the blanket term "complexity," this is not an easy topic to deal with. From the standpoint of software quality, six flavors of complexity stand out as being particularly significant:

1. Subjective code complexity (determined by interviews)

2. Cyclomatic complexity

3. Data complexity

4. Information complexity

5. Process complexity

6. Problem complexity (determined by interviews)

If these six aspects of complexity are high, based on either the subjective opinions of the technical staff who are building the software or on objective metrics, then quality, schedules, and costs are all likely to be troublesome for the project in question. Conversely, if these six aspects of complexity are low, then the software project is not likely to prove troublesome.

High complexity tends to raise defect potentials. Low complexity tends to lower defect potentials. But the various forms of complexity that impact software projects remains largely unexplored and therefore ambiguous.

Unfortunately, complexity and size usually go hand-in-hand for software, so the low-complexity projects tend to be those of less than 100 function points in size, while many of the projects larger than 1,000 function points in size, and almost all software projects above 10,000 function points in size, rank rather high in terms of the six complexity factors that are most troublesome for software.

Most forms of complexity have two independent root causes for why they occur in software projects:

1. Software development is a very difficult and challenging intellectual exercise, and some of the problems are just plain hard no matter what kind of complexity you consider.

2. Software development practices are lax enough so that sometimes complexity in terms of poor code structure or questionable design practices appears to be an accidental byproduct of poor training, inexperience, or excessive haste.

Although the two root causes are independent variables, they can and often do occur together. When very hard problems are coupled with lax, careless, or poorly trained developers, the projects seldom have a happy ending and may not get finished at all.

Another aspect of an increase in cyclomatic complexity is a need for more and more test cases to cover all paths and permutations of paths. Indeed, full coverage testing is difficult for cyclomatic complexities above 10 and probably impossible for cyclomatic complexities higher than 20.

Much of the literature on software complexity concentrates only on code and sometimes only on the control flow or branching sequences. While code complexity is an important subject and well worthy of research, it is far from the only topic that needs to be explored.

A great deal more research is needed on all forms of software complexity and particularly on complexity associated with algorithms, visualization, software requirements, specifications, test cases, and data complexity.

Defect Measurements and Defect Tracking

Primary purposes:	Improving quality by quantifying defects and sources
Application Size Ranges:	1 to more than 100,000 function points
Application Types:	All types of software
Prevention Effectiveness:	–35%
Removal Effectiveness:	+25%
Synergies:	CMMI, RUP, TSP, Agile, QFD, JAD, earned value
Antagonisms:	None
Current usage:	> 55% of defense and military software applications
	< 15% of IT, commercial, web, embedded projects

Given the relatively high effectiveness of defect measurement programs for both defect prevention and defect removal, it is distressing to see the low penetration of such a powerful quality weapon.

Defect tracking, or keeping tabs on defects from when they first occur until they are repaired and the fixes distributed, is more common. However, defect tracking is concerned with mechanics such as speed of repair and not with fundamental topics such as defect origins and root causes.

Until recently accurate and automated defect tracking was a capability that few companies had because it was necessary to build custom defect tracking systems. Therefore, only major companies such as AT&T, Boeing, Hewlett-Packard, IBM, Microsoft, Motorola, Northrup-Grumman, Raytheon, Siemens-Nixdorf, and the like had fully automated defect tracking systems.

Starting in the 1990s, continuing through today, many new commercial defect tracking tools have entered the U.S. commercial market on various platforms such as Windows, Linux, Leopard, and more recently Android. Accurate and automated software defect tracking is now within the grasp of any company that chooses to do it.

The overall functions of modern commercial defect tracking tools include tracking defects by severity level and by origin and routing the defect to the appropriate repair facility. Some have even more advanced functions such as keeping records of duplicate defects, invalid defects submitted by mistake, and the like.

It is an interesting observation that some of these new commercial defect tracking tools were created by former employees of the companies that had built internal defect tracking systems. Having used such systems and seen their capabilities, it is obvious that a fast-growing commercial market existed. A Google search of the phrase "software defect tracking tools" turned up more than 25 companies and 50 tools in the summer of 2010. Most defect tracking tools were commercial, but a few were open source.

For those interested in defect tracking tools and defect measurement tools, the following capabilities should be included:

- Defects from all major sources should be capable of being recorded, that is, defects in requirements, design, source code, user documents, and bad fixes or secondary defects. It would also be useful to be able to add other sources of defects, such as errors in test cases or data errors.

- Defect causes should be included, that is, errors of omission, errors of commission, errors of ambiguity, and errors of capacity or performance.

- Duplicate reports of the same defect should be recorded and noted, although for quality analysis purposes most statistics are based on valid unique defects. However, a large number of duplicate defect reports for a high-severity defect is an important topic that should be noted.

- In addition to real bugs or defects, it will often happen that invalid defect reports are received. (One of the authors once received a bug report against a direct competitor's software product that was mailed to us by mistake.) Examples of invalid defect reports include hardware problems misdiagnosed as software problems, user errors, and problems with things like the operating system misdiagnosed as being an error in an application running under the operating system. Because invalid defect reports are both numerous and expensive, they should be recorded as a standard feature of defect tracking systems.

- Although not critical to the repairs of defects, it is helpful to record the method through which the defect report was received. The major channels for reporting defects to vendors include websites, text messages, voice telephone calls, faxes (declining), e-mail (common when supported by vendors), and some via face-to-face discussions in situations where there is on-site service such as during the deployment of ERP packages. This kind of data is useful in planning staffing resources for things like hot lines and customer support desks.

- Defect severity levels should be recorded, ranging from critical down to minor. However, assigning defect severity is a very subjective field, so provisions are needed to allow the severity levels to change if needed.

- A small but significant number of defects are eventually turned in to suggestions for future enhancements. Therefore, capability is needed to convert defect reports into possible new features.

- The date that defects are first reported should be recorded, as should the date when other key events occur, such as turning the defect over to the repair team, and the date of the final defect resolution, plus the date when the repaired software was released back to clients.

- The defect tracking tool should have a built-in warning system so that defects that have aged beyond user-specified boundary points are highlighted. For example, a critical severity 1 defect that is more than one week old without being repaired is in need of some kind of alarm signal.

- Some defect tracking systems also record the effort needed to repair the defect. If this feature is included, it should be granular enough to capture all relevant activities such as defect analysis, design changes, code changes, creation of new test cases, testing, and so on.

- A significant number of defects cannot be replicated by the vendor's repair team. This situation is usually because of some special or unique combination of hardware and software used by the customer. The term used by IBM for these difficult problems was *abeyant defects*. The term meant that repairs had to be postponed until additional information could be elicited about the special conditions that caused the problem to occur. Abeyant defects are usually the longest to repair and often the most expensive, so defect tracking systems need to be able to highlight them when they occur.

- Some kind of statistical summarization capabilities (either built-in or external) are needed that can produce reports for executives about total defects reported by time period, defects by application, defects reported by customer, defects by severity level, and defects by origin. In addition, topics such as average defect repair times, maximum and minimum defect repair times, and other productivity topics need to be reported. A final statistical capability is normalizing the data to show defects reported by function point, by KLOC, and by other size metrics. Ideally, the statistical engine should be able to report on defect potentials (total defects from all sources) and on cumulative defect removal efficiency (percent of defects removed prior to release). Some companies are also able to calculate the specific defect removal efficiency levels of various kinds of inspection, of static analysis, and of many kinds of testing.

Companies that have sophisticated defect measurement and tracking tools, such as IBM and Motorola, for example, tend to note reductions over time in defect potentials and increases over time in defect removal efficiency levels.

The overall cumulative costs of finding and fixing bugs are usually the most expensive cost element for building large software systems. Therefore, an effective defect tracking tool is very useful for both quality and productivity improvements.

Formal Inspections

Primary purposes:	Improving quality by removing defects before testing
Application Size Ranges:	1 to more than 100,000 function points
Application Types:	All types of software
Prevention Effectiveness:	–55%
Removal Effectiveness:	+85%
Synergies:	CMMI, RUP, TSP, Agile, QFD, JAD, earned value
Antagonisms:	Agile
Current usage:	> 35% of defense, systems, and embedded applications
	< 10% of IT, commercial, and web applications

Formal inspections were developed at IBM during the 1970s. For more than 35 years formal inspections have been measured to have the highest defect removal efficiency levels of any form of defect removal. Because participants in inspections spontaneously avoid making the kinds of errors that inspections find, formal inspections are also one of the top-ranked defect prevention methods.

Given 35 years of solid empirical data about the technical success of inspections, an important question is why inspections have such low usage rates even in 2011. Ideally, formal inspections would be used on 100% of mission-critical software projects and on all of the critical sections of other software projects. But even in 2011 inspection usage is fairly sparse.

The answer to this question is discouraging social commentary on how the software engineering community learns new skills. Formal inspections are not owned by any company, and the method is in the public domain. Therefore, no one except a few consultants who teach inspections makes any money from using the technique.

Although there are many books and articles about inspections that are available upon demand, there is no active marketing push for inspections. To discover the value of inspections it is necessary to seek out information about effective quality methods, and very few people take the time to do this.

Instead, most methods are adopted either because of well-funded marketing programs by vendors or because of sociological reasons. When methods such as Agile, RUP, and TSP achieve a critical mass of usage (often due to marketing), other companies will adopt the same methods without much analysis because the methods have become popular.

Inspections have not yet achieved the critical mass necessary to become self-sustaining or to expand rapidly, primarily due to a lack of marketing dollars. Because no one owns inspections, no one can make much money from them. By contrast, the newer method of static analysis has many more users than inspections because more than a dozen tool vendors such as CAST, Coverity, Instantiations, KLOCwork, and the like all have effective marketing programs.

Although formal design and code inspections originated more than 35 years ago, they still are the top-ranked methodologies in terms of defect removal efficiency. (Michael Fagan, formerly of IBM Kingston, first published the inspection method.) Further, inspections have a synergistic relationship with other forms of defect removal such as testing and also are quite successful as defect prevention methods.

Recent work on software inspections by Tom Gilb and his colleagues continues to support the earlier finding that the human mind remains the tool of choice for finding and eliminating complex problems that originate in requirements, design, and other noncode deliverables. Indeed, for finding the deeper problems in source code, formal code inspections still outrank testing in defect removal efficiency levels.

Among one of the authors' clients, about 100 enterprises out of 600 are using formal inspections more or less the way the method was designed and intended. However, another 125 are using semi-formal inspections, design reviews, structured walkthroughs, or one of a number of local variations on the inspection process.

The most effective usage of formal inspections among the author's clients occurs among large corporations that produce systems and embedded software such as computer manufacturers, telecommunication manufacturers, aerospace manufacturers, medical equipment manufacturers, and the like. These companies have learned that if software is going to control complex physical devices, it has to have state-of-the-art quality levels, and only inspections can achieve the necessary quality.

Most forms of testing are less than 30% efficient in finding errors or bugs. The measured defect removal efficiency of both formal design inspections and formal code inspections is sometimes more than 85% efficient, or almost three times as efficient as most forms of testing.

Tom Gilb, one of the more prominent authors dealing with inspections, reports that some recorded inspection efficiencies have been as high as 90%. Other authors such as Lew Priven and Roger Steward report inspection defect removal rates topping 95%. So as far as can be determined, this level of efficiency would be a "world record" that is never even approached by testing with the possible exception of high-volume Beta testing involving more than 10,000 simultaneous Beta test sites.

A combination of formal inspections, static analysis, formal testing by test specialists, and a formal (and active) quality assurance group are the methods that are most often associated with projects achieving a cumulative defect removal efficiency higher than 99%.

Formal inspections are manual activities in which from four to six colleagues go over requirement and design specifications page by page using a specific protocol. Code inspections are the same idea but go over listings or screens line by line. To term this activity an "inspection," certain criteria must be met, including but not limited to the following:

1. A moderator should be appointed to keep the session moving.

2. A recorder must be present to keep notes.

3. Adequate preparation time is needed before each session.

4. Records of discovered defects must be kept.

5. Defect data should not be used for appraisals or punitive purposes.

The original concept of inspections was based on actual meetings with live participants. The advent of effective online communications and collaborative tools over the Web for supporting remote inspections now means that inspections can be performed electronically, which saves on travel costs for teams that are geographically dispersed.

Any software deliverable can be subject to a formal inspection, and the following deliverables have now developed enough empirical data to indicate that the inspection process is generally beneficial:

- Architecture inspections

- Requirements inspections

- Project plan inspections

- Software cost estimate inspections

- Software marketing plan inspections

- Software governance plan inspections

- Software security plan inspections

- Design inspections

- Database design inspections

- Code inspections

- Test plan inspections

- Test case inspections

- User documentation inspections

- Plaintiff complaints in breach of contract litigation

- Defendant responses in breach of contract litigation

Formal inspections for software artifacts have a defect removal efficiency rate that ranges from just under 50% to more than 85% and an average efficiency level of roughly 65%. This is overall the best defect removal efficiency level of any known form of error elimination. Static analysis tools have about the same level of defect removal efficiency but, of course, only tackle a narrow band of code-related defects.

Thanks to the flexibility of the human mind and its ability to handle inductive logic as well as deductive logic, inspections are the most versatile form of defect removal and can be applied to essentially any software artifact. Indeed, inspections have even been applied recursively to themselves to fine-tune the inspection process and eliminate bottle necks and obstacles.

Most software development organizations don't actually do research or collect data on effective tools and technologies. They base their technology decisions and adoptions to a large degree on how persuasive tool and methodology vendors' sales personnel are.

It is even easier if the sales personnel make the tool or method sound like a "silver bullet" that will give miraculous results immediately upon deployment with little or no training, preparation, or additional effort. Given that inspections are not sold by tool vendors and do require several days of upfront training, they are not a "glamorous" technology. Hence many software organizations don't even know about inspections and have no idea of their versatility and effectiveness.

The companies that are most likely to use inspections are those that for historical or business reasons have some kind of research capability that looks for "best practices" and tries to adopt them.

It is a telling point that all of the "top gun" software quality houses and even industries in the United States tend to utilize pretest inspections. For example, formal inspections are very common among computer manufacturers, telecommunication manufacturers, aerospace manufacturers, defense manufacturers, medical instrument manufacturers, and systems software and operating systems developers. All of these need high-quality software to market their main products, and given that inspections top the list of effective defect removal methods, they're the way to go.

One of the most effective ways of illustrating the effectiveness of formal inspections is to produce graphs that connect the point where software defects are *discovered* with the point in software development where the defects *originate*.

Whenever there is an acute angle in the line connecting defect discovery and origin points, there is a serious problem with software quality control because the gap between making an error and finding it can amount to many months.

The goal of defect removal is to have the angle connecting defect origins and discoveries approach 90 degrees. Although a 90-degree angle is unlikely, formal inspections can at least bring the angle up from perhaps 30 degrees to more than 60 degrees.

As is shown in Figure 3.2, software projects that do not utilize formal inspections enter a "zone of chaos" during the test cycle. This is because problems with requirements and specifications that are deep in the process suddenly emerge that require extensive and expensive repair and rework.

Note in Figure 3.3 how the lines connecting the discovery points of defects with their origins have obtuse angles. Also note how defects that originate

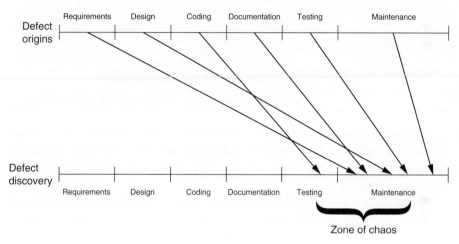

Figure 3.2 *Defect origins and discovery points without usage of formal inspections*

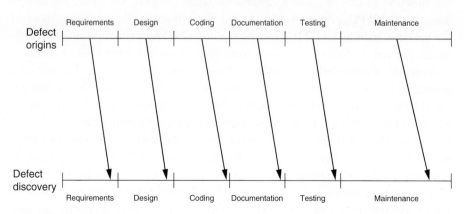

Figure 3.3 *Defect origins and discovery points with usage of formal inspections*

within a phase tend to be eliminated during that phase. One value of inspections is that most defects are contained within a phase, and do not pass on to downstream phases.

Function Point Quality Measures

Primary purposes:	Improving quality by normalizing defect volumes;
	Improving quality economics
Application Size Ranges:	1 to more than 100,000 function points
Application Types:	All types of software
Prevention Effectiveness:	−25%
Removal Effectiveness:	+25%
Synergies:	CMMI, RUP, TSP, Agile, QFD, JAD, earned value
Antagonisms:	Lines of code (LOC); cost per defect; story points
Current usage:	< 5% of defense and military software projects
	< 15% of embedded, systems, and commercial projects
	> 25% of small IT and web projects
	< 1% of IT projects larger than 10,000 function points

Because this book utilizes function point metrics, it is appropriate to include a short discussion of what function points are and why they have become so common for normalizing both quality and productivity data for software projects.

As this book is written, the function point community seems to know quite a bit about software quality; however, the software quality community does not always know much about function points.

Among the one of the author's clients, about 500 out of 600 companies now use function points in some locations for some projects. Of these, about 450 use standard IFPUG function points, and the remaining 50 use one or more of the variants such as COSMIC function points; NESMA function points; *backfiring*, defined as direct conversion from lines of code counts based on logical statements; or some other alternative. Quite a few clients also utilize use-case points, story points, or newer metrics that have the flavor of function points but use different factors and adjustments. Of course, military and defense clients still use LOC metrics, but even here some use function points as well.

The number of function point users among the author's clients is so large because of a bias in the data. This author has been well known for his work in function point metrics since 1985 when his first estimating tool based on function points was released. Also in 1986, Allan Albrecht, the inventor of function points, retired from IBM and collaborated with the author to create the first course in function points counting. Therefore, companies using function points tend to seek them out more than companies that don't use function points.

Interestingly, about 400 of these clients use lines of code and function point metrics concurrently. For these corporations, backfiring (which can also be defined as direct conversion of older lines of code data into function point form) is the most common motivation for using both metrics. A strong secondary motivation is because some of the clients' own clients (such as the U.S. military services) may require lines of code under some situations.

The function point metric was invented in the mid-1970s by Allan J. Albrecht of IBM White Plains in association with several colleagues. The function point metric was put into the public domain by IBM at a joint IBM/SHARE/GUIDE conference in Monterey, California, in October of 1978. At that conference Allan Albrecht gave the first public speech on the function point metric. From that beginning, the usage of the function point metric has spread rapidly throughout the world.

In 1984 a nonprofit organization was created in Toronto, Canada, made up of companies that were using function points. This organization was originally staffed only by part-time volunteers but quickly grew to such a size that formal incorporation and a permanent staff appeared desirable. In 1986, the nonprofit International Function Point Users Group (IFPUG), as it became known, was incorporated in Westerville, Ohio, and hired a small permanent office staff to handle administration.

This group in 2011 is now the largest software measurement association in the United States. Affiliated function point users groups are the largest software measurement associations in perhaps 25 countries.

The function point metric is a way of determining the size of a software application by enumerating and adjusting five visible aspects that are of significance to both users and developers. Standard IFPUG function points consist of five key external factors:

1. **Inputs** that enter the application (for example, input screens, forms, commands, and so on)

2. **Outputs** that leave the application (output screens, reports)

3. **Inquiries** that can be made to the application (queries for information)

4. **Logical files** maintained by the application (tables, text files)

5. **Interfaces** between the application and others (shared data, messages)

When the raw total of these five factors has been enumerated, then an additional set of 14 influential factors are evaluated in order to adjust for complexity.

These adjustment factors are evaluated for impact using a scale that runs from 0 (no impact) to 5 (major impact).

The 14 adjustment factors are outside the scope of this book but include topics such as whether the application requires distributed functions, uses data communications, will have high transaction volumes, and a number of similar topics.

The adjustment factors are converted into a weighting scale that can modify the initial raw total by a range that runs from about 65% of the initial value for rather simple applications to 135% of the initial value for highly complex applications. After complexity adjustment, the final value is termed the "adjusted function point total" of the application and is the value used when discussing quality or productivity in terms of function points.

From the standpoint of quality, function points can be used for a number of useful purposes, including but not limited to

- Normalizing defect data across requirements, design, coding, documentation, and bad fix defect categories.

- Estimating the numbers of test cases and test runs that may be required.

By interesting coincidence the five standard IFPUG factors for counting function points plus the inclusion of algorithms (from feature points) and the inclusion of entities and relationships (from Mark II function points) provides a useful set of the key software features for which test cases are normally constructed:

- Algorithms

- Inputs

- Outputs

- Entities and relationships

- Logical files

- Inquiries

This means that companies that utilize function point metrics are in a very good position to predict the number of test cases and test runs that will be needed as early as the requirements phase. Further, rather accurate defect estimates can also be made, as can opportunities for applying defect prevention methods.

Although function point metrics were not invented for quality assurance purposes, they have been found to be very synergistic with the goals and approaches of software quality. Indeed, they open up some new forms of quality research such as exploration of front-end requirements defects and the rate at which requirements changes "creep" that could not easily be studied before function points were developed.

Counting and adjusting function points for an application is not trivial, nor is it overwhelmingly difficult. The normal training course for those who set out to learn function point counting runs for two days and includes several hands-on counting exercises. To ensure precision and consistent application of the counting rules, the International Function Point Users Group (IFPUG) offers periodic certification examinations.

IFPUG also codifies and maintains the formal counting rules, which are revised as needed. For example, this book assumes Version 4.2 of the IFPUG counting rules.

The normal raw materials used to determine function point totals are the requirements and functional specifications for the software application. Because function points are independent of the code, the counts need not be delayed until coding is underway or complete.

For existing or legacy applications it is also possible to derive approximate function point totals using backfiring. (Backfiring from counts of physical lines is too ambiguous and uncertain to be recommended.)

It is also possible to use *data mining* on legacy applications and extract hidden business rules and algorithms from the code itself. These can be assembled into a synthetic specification that permits normal function point analysis. Several companies have developed high-speed counting tools for legacy applications based on this method. These tools approach normal function point analysis in accuracy and are much more accurate than backfiring.

To understand why anyone would bother to use function points, it is necessary to consider the limitations of the LOC metric, which function points replace or augment. The function point metric is normally used in place of or in addition to the older software metric based on the number of *source lines of code (SLOC)* in a software application.

When software began to be used for business purposes, there was significant interest in measuring the productivity of creating new programs. It was natural to measure software productivity using SLOC because most programs were small and coding absorbed more than 90% of the total effort needed to make a computer perform work.

Software researchers began to develop more and more powerful programming languages that did not have a 1 to 1 correspondence with computer machine language. These languages were called "higher-level" languages because one statement in such a language could cause the execution of several machine languages.

Table 3.9 *Evolution of Programming Languages and Software Effort at 10-Year Intervals*

Year	Coding Percent	Non-Coding Percent	Most Common Programming Languages/Techniques
1950	90%	10%	Machine language
1960	80%	20%	Assembly
1970	70%	30%	COBOL, FORTRAN, Assembly, + 200 others
1980	60%	40%	COBOL, BASIC, + 300 others
1990	50%	50%	Visual Basic, COBOL, 4GLs, +400 others
2000	30%	70%	Visual Basic, Object-Oriented, C, + 600 others
2010	20%	80%	Visual Basic, OO, C#, Ruby, Java, +2,000 others

These higher-level compiled or interpreted languages were often created for special purposes. For example, the language FORTRAN was created for mathematics and scientific work (FORTRAN stands for Formula Translator.) The COBOL language was created for business applications (COBOL stands for Common Business Oriented Language.)

As more and more programming languages and special-purpose languages were created, the concept of a line of code became less useful for measuring the productivity of software development. Indeed, for many modern languages such as Visual Basic, some parts of application development are derived from using controls, buttons, or manipulating graphic symbols, so the entire concept of a line of code is losing relevance.

As fourth-generation languages, application and program generators, "visual" languages, object-oriented languages, database languages, and specialized languages began to multiply, pure coding steadily declined in both absolute effort and as a percentage of the total effort needed to build software applications. Table 3.9 oversimplifies the situation but shows the general trend over time.

Because bugs or defect levels increase with size, larger systems had much more expensive inspection and testing activities associated with them than did the smaller applications of an earlier day. For large applications written in higher-level languages, coding became only a minority cost element. In descending order, the four major cost drivers of the initial release of large software applications include but are not limited to

1. Testing and defect removal

2. Production of paper planning and specification documents

3. Meetings and communication among team and with clients

4. Coding

Unfortunately, the LOC metric is not a good choice for normalizing the three top cost elements of software—defect removal costs, paperwork costs, and meeting and communication costs. This means that economic studies of full software life cycles were difficult to perform using LOC metrics, and major research topics tend to be under-reported, or worse, reported incorrectly.

As these simple examples show, the function point metric matches the standard economic definition of productivity: *Productivity is the amount of goods or services produced per unit of labor or expense.*

In this case, a function point is a very practical, workable surrogate for the "goods or services" that a software program provides to users.

By contrast, a line of code is not an effective surrogate for software goods or services because there is no advantage to the users in having a lot of code in a language such as Assembly, when they could have identical features with much less code in other programming languages such as Java, Ruby, ASP Net, and the like.

The ability of the function point metric to perform very accurate software economic studies explains why this metric has become the most widely used metric in the software industry for economic analysis. It also explains why function points are used for economic analysis in this book. They are the only available metric that matches the assumptions of standard economics. Some of the common measures for which function points are used include

- Function points produced per staff month

- Work hours required to produce one function point

- Work hours required to support one function point

- Work hours required to maintain (fix bugs) per function point

- Cost per function point for development

- Cost per function point for maintenance

- Defects per function point during development

- Defects per function point for released software

The use of function points is now so common that the U.S. Internal Revenue Service and the revenue services of many other countries are now using function points to determine the tax value of software. At least two countries, Brazil and South Korea, require the use of function points for government software contracts.

Function point metrics can be used to predict not only coding defects, but also defects in noncode items such as requirements and specifications (as shown in Table 3.10).

Table 3.10 *U.S. Averages for Software Defect Levels circa 2011*

Defect Origin	Defects per Function Point
Requirements	1.00
Design	1.25
Code	1.75
User documents	0.60
Bad fixes	0.40
TOTAL	5.00

Thus, function points open up quality research for exploring both front-end defect levels and also peripheral defect levels such as user manuals and screens, as well as continuing to support research in coding defect levels. However, as previously discussed, coding defects require special calculations when using function point metrics.

It is an interesting sociological phenomenon that because of the usefulness of function points as a quality metric, the international function point user community may have more quality data available than any of the major quality associations. In any case, there is a need for coordination and communication between the function point organizations and the software quality organizations, considering both share common goals of better measurement and better quality.

There is a dogma among many developers of real-time, systems, and embedded software that asserts, "Function points are only for management information systems." This is nonsense. Allan Albrecht, who invented function points, is an electrical engineer and had always designed function points to work on engineering projects. It is only a historical accident that IBM first used function points for management information systems.

Function points can and are being used for real-time and embedded software such as fuel injection systems, operating systems, telephone switching systems, ship-board gun control systems, the embedded software in the Tomahawk cruise missile, aircraft flight control software, and many other kinds.

Function point metrics are not perfect. But for economic analysis of software itself and of software quality, function points are the best available metric. Neither lines of code nor cost per defect are valid for economic analysis.

Some of the newer and specialized metrics such as story points and use-case points are too specialized: They only measure projects that utilize use cases or story points and can't be used to analyze other projects that use methods such as Nassi-Shneiderman charts, data-flow diagrams, or decision logic tables.

Function points are neutral and can therefore be used across all forms of software such as embedded and web projects; across all development methods such as Agile and RUP; and across all programming languages ranging from Assembly language through Ruby and Perl.

ISO Quality Standards, IEEE Quality Standards, and Other Industry Standards

Primary purposes:	Standardizing quality definitions
	Standardizing quality documentation
Application Size Ranges:	1 to more than 100,000 function points
Application Types:	All types of software
Prevention Effectiveness:	–10%
Removal Effectiveness:	+10%
Synergies:	CMMI, RUP, TSP, QFD, Six Sigma
Antagonisms:	Agile
Current usage:	> 70% of defense and military software projects
	> 35% of embedded and systems projects
	< 10% of IT and web projects

As this book is being written (in 2011) there are many national and international standards organizations that create standards for software and for software quality. Some of these organizations include but are not limited to

- AIAA—The American Institute of Aeronautics and Astronautics

- ANSI—The American National Standards Institute

- BSI—The British Standards Institution

- COPANT—The Pan-American Standards Commission

- DIN—The Deutsches Institut fur Normung

- DOD—The Department of Defense (for military standards)

- ESO—The European Standards Organization

- EIA—The Electronic Industries Association

- IEC—The International Electrotechnical Commission

- IEEE—The Institute of Electrical and Electronics Engineers

- ISACA—The Information Systems Audit and Control Association

- ISO—The International Organization for Standardization

- ITU—The International Telecommunications Union

- JISC—The Japanese Industrial Standards Committee

- NIST—The National Institute for Standards and Technology

- PASC—The Pacific Area Standards Congress

- SAC—The Standards Administration of China

- SEI—The Software Engineering Institute

- SIS—The Swedish Standards Institute

The global total of standards organizations probably exceeds 300. The global total of actual standards probably exceeds 25,000. For software and software quality in the United States, the major standards organizations are the DOD, ANSI, ISO, SEI, the IEEE, and NIST. The total number of standards for software probably exceeds 150 and for quality probably exceeds 20.

The large number of standards organizations and the even larger number of standards indicate a strong global interest in standardization. In spite of the obvious interest in standards and the efforts devoted to creating them, there is a shortage of empirical data about the actual effectiveness of standards in the software quality domain. This is true for both defect removal efficiency and defect prevention.

One of the authors has visited dozens of companies and collected quality data from hundreds of projects that used various standards such as ISO 9001–9004, DOD 2167A, ISO/IEC 12207, and the like. Data has also been gathered from about the same number of similar projects that did not use any international of software standards at all.

The studies by the author were not commissioned specifically to study standards, but rather to collect data on productivity and quality. The presence or absence of standards was noted, but so were many other topics such as methodologies, defect removal methods, organization structures, and so forth.

Table 3.11 shows the overall results for projects that used any of the international software and quality standards compared to those that used none. However, the table has a high level of uncertainty because too many other factors were also part of the data. The projects in both samples ranged from 1,000 to about 50,000 function points because the author is almost never commissioned to study small projects below 1,000 function points.

The preliminary conclusion reached by the author is that international standards are not very effective in raising quality levels because there is almost no difference between the standards and nonstandards groups with the very best quality levels.

Table 3.11 *Software Quality Standards and Software Defect Potentials*

	(Data Expressed in terms of defects per function point)		
Percent of Projects by Quality Levels	Standards Utilized	Standards not Utilized	Difference
Excellent quality: Defect potentials < 4.00	5.55%	5.25%	0.30%
Good quality: Defect potentials 4.00 to 5.00	20.50%	18.00%	2.50%
Average quality: Defect potentials 5.00 to 6.00	56.45%	46.50%	9.95%
Poor quality: Defect potentials > 6.00	17.50%	30.25%	–12.75%
TOTALS	100.00%	100.00%	0.00%

However, there is a fairly large difference at the bottom of the table for the applications with poor quality. It would appear, and this is only a hypothesis, that international software standards are effective in minimizing the projects with really bad quality.

The conclusion that standards are more effective in warding off poor quality than in actually raising quality levels is a topic that needs additional study and confirmation. If the results are confirmed by other studies, it would still indicate that international standards are valuable in a software context because poor quality has been an endemic problem for the industry for more than 50 years.

Other quality factors had similar patterns. High levels of defect removal efficiency were about equal between the standard and nonstandard groups. However, defect removal efficiency below 85% was about twice as common among the nonstandard projects.

What the data suggests is that a small number of managers and personnel know enough and care enough about quality to do a very good job. These outstanding personnel are about equally divided among projects that use international standards and those that don't. This explains the similar grouping at the high-quality end of the spectrum.

At the low end of the spectrum for poor quality, applying international standards provides the benefits of both measuring quality and paying attention to defect removal and defect prevention. In other words, quality standards are somewhat similar in their effects to vaccinations. Getting a vaccination does not make people healthier, but it lowers the odds of getting sick. Quality standards may not make projects healthier, but they lower the odds of becoming unhealthy.

Some specific topics that would be useful for future research on standards are these:

- Do quality standards reduce software defect potentials below 5 per function point?

- Do quality standards raise defect removal efficiency levels above 95%?

- Do quality standards lower the number of bad test cases below 15%?

- Do quality standards lower the rate of bad fix injections below 7%?

- Do quality standards increase reliability under field conditions?

- Do quality standards increase customer satisfaction levels?

- Do quality standards reduce the number of canceled or delayed projects?

- Do quality standards reduce the incidence of litigation for breach of contract?

- Do quality standards reduce the incidence of litigation for poor quality control?

When projects using standards are compared to similar projects that use "best practices" but do not use any standards, the results are pretty close together.

Software standards groups such as ISO, the IEEE, DOD, ANSI, and so on should consider the methods through which medical and pharmaceutical standards are set. Although medical standards are not perfect, their concept that a therapy should be proven to be effective and its side effects understood before it becomes a standard is missing from many software standards.

It would be a strong statement that software is approaching the status of a real profession if software standards included information similar to medical and pharmaceutical standards on efficacy, counter-indications, known hazards, and potential side effects.

Quality Function Deployment (QFD)

Primary purposes:	Identifying customer quality requirements
	Identifying engineering responses to quality requirements
Application Size Ranges:	1,000 to more than 100,000 function points
Application Types:	All types of software

Prevention Effectiveness:	−55%
Removal Effectiveness:	+30%
Synergies:	CMMI, RUP, TSP, Six Sigma
Antagonisms:	Agile
Current usage:	< 15% of defense and military software projects
	< 20% of embedded, commercial, and systems projects
	< 01% of IT and web projects

As of 2011 Quality Function Deployment (QFD) is simultaneously one of the most effective defect prevention methods developed and one of the least utilized in the United States. Like many quality control approaches, QFD originated in Japan for manufactured products. Also like many Japanese quality methods, QFD was applied to software and migrated to other countries.

Quality Function Deployment originated in Japan in the 1970s for dealing with the quality of complex manufactured devices, such as automobiles. (Toyota was one of the pioneers of QFD, for example.)

Like several other Japanese quality approaches, QFD moved to the United States as a manufacturing approach and was then later deployed for software projects. Only about a dozen of the author's clients utilize QFD for software, and they are all high-technology manufacturing companies (AT&T, Ford, General Motors, Hewlett-Packard, and Motorola are a few examples).

Further, these same organizations had used QFD for software only once or at most twice, so they were still in startup mode. Therefore, the total sample of uses of QFD for software projects in the United States as this book is written is fewer than 30.

Because the companies using QFD are already fairly sophisticated in their approaches to quality control, the apparent success of QFD as a software quality approach may be misleading.

QFD is a very formal, structured group activity involving clients and product development personnel. QFD is sometimes called "the house of quality" because one of the main kinds of planning matrices resembles the peaked roof of a house.

In the course of the QFD sessions, the users' quality criteria are exhaustively enumerated and defined. Then the product's quality response to those requirements is carefully planned so that all of the quality criteria are implemented or accommodated.

For the kinds of software where client quality concerns can be enumerated and where developers can meet and have serious discussions about quality, QFD appears to work very well: embedded applications, medical devices, switching systems, manufacturing support systems, fuel-injection software controls, weapons systems, and the like.

Also, QFD requires development and QA personnel who know a lot about quality and its implications. QFD is not a "quick and dirty" approach that works well using short-cuts and a careless manner. This is why QFD and Agile are cited as being "antagonistic."

The QFD software projects that we have examined have significantly lower rates of creeping requirements and also much lower than average volumes of both requirements and design defects than U.S. norms. However, the kinds of software projects that use QFD typically do not have highly volatile requirements.

Requirements errors identified after QFD is completed have only amounted to approximately 0.2 problems per function point versus about 0.75 for the United States as a whole. Design problems as found using formal inspections have also been lower than average and run only to about 0.5 defect per function point rather than 1.0. Coding defects have been lower than U.S. norms but not lower than typical for high-technology software projects using formal structured coding approaches; that is, about 1.1 coding defects per function point versus U.S. norms of roughly 1.75.

Expressed another way, raising the function point total of an application to the 1.2 power will give a useful approximation of overall defect potentials for "average" software projects in the United States. For projects using QFD, raising application size to the 1.15 power gives a better approximation. This indicates a significant impact in terms of defect prevention.

Interestingly, for defect removal efficiency, the QFD projects and similar projects are running about the same: Roughly 96% of defects are eliminated prior to deployment. However, it is obvious that any project with a 96% defect removal efficiency level used pretest inspections and formal testing by testing specialists. These approaches are common among the kinds of high-technology corporations that are also likely to use quality function deployment. They are congruent with QFD.

The initial results are favorable enough to recommend at least substantial experiments with the QFD approach. The only caveat is that for certain kinds of software, such as financial applications and web applications with thousands of users, each of whom might have different quality criteria, it is not possible to gather all of the users together or explore their quality needs completely.

QFD is now finding its way through many of the "high-tech" companies such as AT&T, Intel, Motorola, and Hewlett-Packard. The more recent experiences with QFD for software are favorable enough so that this methodology can now be added to the lists of approaches with good to excellent empirical results, although the sample size is small enough so that caution is indicated.

From observations among clients who are QFD users, it is uncertain that the QFD approach would give the same level of results in companies that lack QA organizations, formal testing, and a tendency to use careful specification and design methods. And because most companies in this class have not yet experimented with QFD and many have not yet even heard of it, there is no empirical data to back up this observation.

Risk Analysis

Primary purposes:	Identifying risks early enough to eliminate them
	Identifying application size prior to funding
Application Size Ranges:	1,000 to more than 100,000 function points
Application Types:	All types of software
Prevention Effectiveness:	–35%
Removal Effectiveness:	+25%
Synergies:	CMMI, RUP, TSP, QFD, JAD, Six Sigma
Antagonisms:	Agile
Current usage:	> 50% of defense and military software projects
	> 70% of embedded, commercial, and systems projects
	< 10% of IT and web projects

Software development is a high-risk undertaking. The risk of outright failure, cost overruns, schedule delays, and poor quality are endemic in the software industry. Empirical data has proven that risks increase as application size goes up. In a software context, the value of risk analysis correlates directly with size, as shown in Table 3.12.

Because of the strong correlation between application size and serious risk, it is urgent that application size should be estimated during risk studies. Further, because deploying effective solutions could take weeks or months, it is important that both sizing and risk analysis take place during early requirements.

Table 3.12 *Software Risk Probabilities and Application Size*

Application Size in Function Points	Project Failure %	Project Delay %	Poor Project Quality %
1	0.10%	0.20%	1.00%
10	1.00%	2.00%	5.00%
100	3.00%	7.00%	10.00%
1,000	10.00%	15.00%	25.00%
10,000	30.00%	40.00%	75.00%
100,000	50.00%	85.00%	95.00%

If risk analysis is not performed until after the requirements are complete, it may well be too late to deploy some of the effective risk solutions such as requirement inspections and quality function deployment (QFD). Fortunately, several methods of early sizing are now available, including pattern matching using size data from historical projects whose sizes are already known.

Software risks are numerous and varied. Table 3.13 shows a sample of 160 software risks used by one of the authors for software risk analysis. The risks in Table 3.13 are ordered by risk type and by risk severity within each type.

Table 3.13 *Software Risks by Category and Severity*

	(Minimum severity = 1; Maximum severity = 10)	
		Severity
	Health and Safety Risks	
1	Risk of application failure causing death	10.00
2	Risk of application failure causing serious illness or injury	9.99
3	Risk of application failure damaging medical activities	9.90
4	Risk of application causing environmental damages	9.80
5	Risk of team fatigue due to excessive overtime	8.00
	Security Risks	
6	Risk of loss or theft of proprietary source code	10.00
7	Risk of electromagnetic pulse shutting down software	10.00
8	Risk of application failure degrading national security	10.00
9	Risk of poor security flaw removal	9.90
10	Risk of security flaws in application	9.75
11	Risk of poor security flaw prevention	9.60
12	Risk of violating the 25 SANS coding problems	9.50
13	Risk of security flaws in uncertified reused code	9.50
14	Risk of data theft from application	9.00
15	Risk of deliberate "back door" traps placed by developers	9.00
16	Risk of theft of intellectual property	8.50
	Quality Risks	
17	Risk of defect removal efficiency < 85%	9.90
18	Risk of excessive defect levels: > 6.0 per function point	9.85
19	Risk of poor estimation of bugs, defect removal efficiency	9.50
20	Risk of premature application release with excessive bugs	9.50
21	Risk of poor test case and test script design methods	9.40
22	Risk of poor test library controls	9.40

	Quality Risks	
23	Risk of testing with amateurs rather than professionals	9.40
24	Risk of high code complexity that raises "bad fixes" > 10%	9.25
25	Risk of error-prone modules in application	9.25
26	Risk of claiming to use inspections, but only partially	9.00
27	Risk of inadequate defect removal methods, low efficiency	9.00
28	Risk of late and inadequate defect tracking	9.00
29	Risk of poor data quality with serious errors	9.00
30	Risk of poor test coverage	8.75
31	Risk of poor quality in COTS packages	8.75
32	Risk of insufficient Quality Assurance (QA) reviews	8.75
33	Risk of poor quality in reused components	8.50
34	Risk of not using pretest inspections: requirements, design	8.50
35	Risk of not using pretest static analysis of source code	8.50
36	Risk of understaffing Quality Assurance	8.25
37	Risk of poor quality in outsourced projects	8.25
38	Risk or errors or bugs in test cases	8.00
39	Risk of low operational reliability	7.50
40	Risk of poor quality by open source providers	7.50
41	Risk of duplicate test cases	7.00
	Legal Risks	
42	Risk of inadequate warranties for quality and security	9.75
43	Risk of incurring contract penalties	9.50
44	Risk of former employees violating noncompete agreements	9.25
45	Risk of breach of contract litigation on outsourced projects	9.00
46	Risk of application failure causing violations of laws	9.00
47	Risk of poorly constructed contracts that leave out risks	8.40
48	Risk of poorly constructed contracts that leave out quality	8.25
49	Risk of application being charged with patent violations	8.25
50	Risk of Sarbanes-Oxley litigation	7.50
	Traditional Software Risks	
51	Risk of inadequate progress tracking	9.70
52	Risk that designs are not kept updated after release	9.25
53	Risk of unstable user requirements	9.25
54	Risk that requirements are not kept updated after release	9.25

(Continued)

Table 3.13   *(Continued)*

	Traditional Software Risks	
55	Risk of clients forcing arbitrary schedules on team	9.10
56	Risk of omitting formal architecture for large systems	9.10
57	Risk of inadequate change control	9.00
58	Risk of executives forcing arbitrary schedules on team	8.80
59	Risk of not using a project office for large applications	8.75
60	Risk of missing requirements from legacy applications	8.50
61	Risk of missing user requirements due to user uncertainty	8.00
62	Risk of slow application response times	8.00
63	Risk of inadequate maintenance tools and workbenches	8.00
64	Risk of application performance problems	8.00
65	Risk of poor support by open source providers	7.75
66	Risk of reusing code without test cases or related materials	7.00
67	Risk of excessive feature "bloat"	7.00
68	Risk of inadequate development tools	6.50
69	Risk of poor help screens and poor user manuals	6.00
70	Risk of slow customer support	6.00
71	Risk of inadequate functionality	6.00
	Financial Risks	
72	Risk of application failure causing major financial loss	9.95
73	Risk of consequential damages > $1,000,000,000	9.90
74	Risk of features slipping from planned release	9.50
75	Risk of project termination due to poor quality, overruns	9.50
76	Risk of "leakage" from software cost and historical data	9.00
77	Risk of bankruptcy by vendor	9.00
78	Risk of significant project cost overruns	8.90
79	Risk of significant project schedule overruns	8.90
80	Risk of application failure causing moderate financial loss	8.75
81	Risk of cost overruns on outsourced projects	8.50
82	Risk of schedule delays on outsourced projects	8.50
83	Risk of project value dipping below project costs	8.25
84	Risk of inadequate cost accounting	8.00
85	Risk of bankruptcy by client	8.00
86	Risk of application violating standard accounting practices	7.00
87	Risk of negative earned value for project	6.00

	Business Risks	
88	Risk of toxic or harmful requirements	9.95
89	Risk of application failure damaging business data	9.90
90	Risk of application failure damaging distribution	9.85
91	Risk of application failure damaging transportation	9.80
92	Risk of application failure affecting operation of equipment	9.80
93	Risk of application failure damaging retail activities	9.75
94	Risk of application obsolescence before completion	9.70
95	Risk of application failure damaging law enforcement	9.70
96	Risk of application failure damaging government activities	9.60
97	Risk of application failure damaging communications	9.50
98	Risk of poor governance by executives	9.50
100	Risk of application failure damaging manufacturing	9.50
101	Risk of application failure damaging stock values	9.50
102	Risk of application failure shutting down vital equipment	9.25
103	Risk of rubber-stamp phase reviews without real oversight	9.20
104	Risk of missing critical market window	9.00
105	Risk of competitive applications with better features	9.00
106	Risk of poor or missing project historical data	8.50
107	Risk of executive and client dissatisfaction with project	8.50
108	Risk of poor support by COTS vendors	8.25
	Social Risks	
109	Risk of poor managers driving out top technical staff	10.00
110	Risk of ignoring learning curve for new methodologies	10.00
111	Risk of poor organization structures	8.80
112	Risk of low team morale from excessive schedule pressure	8.00
113	Risk of poor communication among supply chain members	8.00
114	Risk of stakeholder disputes that change requirements	7.75
115	Risk of poor communications among team members	7.70
116	Risk of low user satisfaction levels	7.00
117	Risk of poor communications with stakeholders	7.00
118	Risk of major management disagreements	6.50
	External Risks	
119	Risk of natural disaster affecting projects	8.00
120	Risk of loss of stakeholders or clients during development	7.00
121	Risk of loss of key personnel during development	5.75

(Continued)

Table 3.13   *(Continued)*

	Ethical Risks	
122	Risk of fraudulent progress/status reports	10.00
123	Risk of project managers ignoring risks	9.50
124	Risk of project managers concealing risks from clients	9.50
125	Risk of noncompete violations by former employees	9.50
126	Risk of false claims by methodology enthusiasts	9.15
127	Risk of false claims of high CMMI levels	9.00
128	Risk of claiming to use a methodology, but not really doing so	8.50
129	Risk of false claims by outsource vendors	8.00
130	Risk of false claims by COTS vendors	8.00
	Knowledge Risks	
131	Risk of users not fully understanding their own requirements	10.00
132	Risk of inadequate requirements analysis for large systems	10.00
133	Risk of effective solutions not being known by managers	9.75
134	Risk of effective solutions not being known by team	9.75
135	Risk of inadequate schedule planning	9.60
136	Risk of late start in deploying risk solutions	9.50
137	Risk of estimates being rejected due to lack of benchmarks	9.45
138	Risk of using unsuitable development methodology	9.40
139	Risk of manual estimates for large applications	9.25
140	Risk of poor project oversight by clients	9.25
141	Risk of "good enough" fallacy applied to application	9.00
142	Risk of inadequate sizing prior to funding project	9.00
143	Risk of insufficient project management skills	9.00
144	Risk of excessive optimism in initial plans, estimates	9.00
145	Risk of poorly trained management personnel	9.00
146	Risk of inadequate user-error prevention	9.00
147	Risk of team size not matching project needs	9.00
148	Risk of poorly trained maintenance personnel	8.60
149	Risk of inadequate defect prevention	8.50
150	Risk of poorly trained development personnel	8.50
151	Risk of poorly trained support personnel	8.40
152	Risk of poorly trained test personnel	8.25
153	Risk of application architectural flaws	8.25
154	Risk of inadequate user guides and HELP screens	8.00

	Knowledge Risks	
155	Risk of poor usability and poor interfaces	8.00
156	Risk of poorly trained QA personnel	8.00
157	Risk of international misunderstandings for global projects	8.00
158	Risk of inadequate programming languages	7.75
159	Risk of insufficient technical skills	7.25
160	Risk of application violating international standards	5.50

Among one of the author's total of about 600 clients, roughly 175 of them tend to utilize formal or semi-formal risk-analysis phases when attempting major software development projects. These clients primarily build embedded, systems, and defense applications (although some build commercial and IT applications).

Some of the other 425 enterprises may do informal risk analysis or utilize project management tools that have risk-analysis capabilities, but "risk analysis" is not a formally identifiable activity in their software development chart of accounts.

The general topic of risk analysis overlaps a number of other topics that are discussed in this book. In fact, there are so many overlaps that it is good to highlight them by pointing out in alphabetic order what other topics have risk analysis overtones:

- Active quality assurance

- Assessments and software quality

- Formal design and code inspections

- Joint application design (JAD)

- Methodologies such as RUP and TSP

- Outsource and contract quality levels

- Project management and software quality

- Prototyping

- Quality assurance tool capacities

- Quality function deployment (QFD)

- Risk-based testing

- Six Sigma

When doing assessment and baseline studies in companies that do perform formal risk analysis, the quality results seem to be significantly better than similar companies without risk analysis in terms of both defect prevention and defect removal.

The problem with this statement is that the companies that include formal risk analysis are usually in the industries that have much better than average quality results anyway, such as aerospace, computer manufacturing, defense weapons systems, embedded devices, telecommunication manufacturing, medical instruments, and commercial software houses that build operating systems or systems software.

By identifying risks early, it is possible to deploy effective risk solutions. It is also possible to use methods such as Quality Function Deployment (QFD), inspections, static analysis, and risk-based testing that both prevent risks from turning into real problems and raise the efficiency of finding risks.

Six Sigma

Primary purposes:	Identifying causes of risks
	Keeping risks or bugs < 3.4 opportunities per million
Application Size Ranges:	1,000 to more than 100,000 function points
Application Types:	All types of software
Prevention Effectiveness:	–15%
Removal Effectiveness:	+10%
Synergies:	CMMI, RUP, TSP, QFD, JAD, Six Sigma
Antagonisms:	Agile
Current usage:	> 40% of defense and military software projects
	> 40% of embedded, commercial, and systems projects
	< 10% of IT and web projects

The phrase Six Sigma, which originated at Motorola, refers to defect densities of 3.4 "opportunities" for defects per million chances. The approach was originally used for complex manufactured devices such as cell phones but has expanded to scores of manufactured products and software, too.

The original Six Sigma approach was formal and somewhat expensive to deploy. In recent years subsets and alternatives have been developed such as "lean Six Sigma" and "Six Sigma for software" and "design for Six Sigma."

Because the Six Sigma definition is hard to visualize for software, an alternative approach would be to achieve a cumulative defect removal efficiency rate of 99.999999% prior to delivery of a product. This method is not what

Motorola uses, but it helps to clarify what would have to be done to achieve Six Sigma results for software projects.

Given that the current U.S. average for software defect removal efficiency is only about 85%, and quite a few software products are even below 70%, it could be interpreted that software producers have some serious catching up to do. Even top-ranked software projects in the best companies do not go beyond about 98% in cumulative defect removal efficiency.

As it happens, there are a few software products that appear to have achieved Six Sigma quality levels. In the past 30 years, the author has observed four projects that achieved Six Sigma results in their first year of deployment out of a total of almost 13,000 thousand projects.

Surprisingly, the prognosis for achieving Six Sigma quality levels for software is fairly good. The best of the available technologies today can approach this level if a full suite of defect prevention and defect removal operations are carried out synergistically. Indeed, for software projects where reuse of certified materials tops 75% by volume, and where formal inspections are used to augment testing, Six Sigma quality levels should be achieved routinely.

Because the technology for achieving Six Sigma quality levels exists, that does not mean that the software industry is now ready to try. There are both sociological and technical reasons that hold quality back, such as the widespread lack of appreciation of the correlation between high quality and short schedules and the shortage of commercial reusable materials certified to zero-defect levels.

Static Analysis

Primary purposes:	Identifying structural defects in source code
	Defining rules for software code defect identification
Application Size Ranges:	1 to more than 100,000 function points
Application Types:	All types of software
Prevention Effectiveness:	–45%
Removal Effectiveness:	+85%
Synergies:	Agile, CMMI, RUP, TSP, QFD, JAD, Six Sigma
Antagonisms:	None
Current usage:	> 65% of open source software projects
	> 50% of defense and military software projects
	> 50% of embedded, commercial, and systems projects
	> 25% of IT and web projects

Commercial static analysis tools are comparatively new and had a great increase in numbers and features just before the turn of the century, which allowed some of them to be used to find Y2K problems. However, the original concept of static analysis is much older and stems from early features added to compilers to perform syntax checking. In the 1970s a tool called Lint contained many of the features now standard in static analysis tools—no need to compile or execute the code—finding syntactic and structural errors.

Over time, basic syntax checking was expanded to include linking and calls; system-level structural analysis (many static analysis tools provide cyclomatic complexity metrics); and to find security vulnerabilities.

Static analysis tools in 2011 are numerous and quite effective. They find many difficult bugs in a very short time. Indeed, removal efficiency tops 85%. However, static analysis tools have been troubled by an issue called "false positives." That is, some of the reported defects are not in fact defects but coding features that the tool mistakenly identified as an error. Early static analysis tools topped 10% in false positives; the best of today's tools seem to be below about 3%.

Another issue with static analysis tools is that they do not support all 2,500 programming languages that are known to exist. Only about 25 languages are supported by static analysis tools, including

1. ActionScript

2. Ada95

3. ASP NET

4. C

5. C++

6. C#

7. COBOL

8. Fortran

9. HTML

10. Java

11. Javascript

12. JCL

13. Perl

14. PL/I

15. Python

16. Objective C

17. SQL

18. VB Net

19. Visual Basic

20. XML

There may be specialized static analysis tools that are custom-built for other languages, but as of 2011 the C dialects and Java have dozens of commercial static analysis tools available.

The engines that make static analysis tools effective are libraries of rules that define the conditions to be examined. Early static analysis tools contained perhaps 50 rules. Some of today's commercial static analysis tools contain more than 1,500. Indeed, some of these tools allow user-defined rules to be added to the rule library to look for special or unique conditions.

It is obvious why static analysis tools are effective in terms of defect removal. The rule-based engines methodically seek out and eliminate numerous syntactic and structural defects, as well as defects in logic.

It is not so obvious why static analysis tools are also useful for defect prevention. There are two main reasons:

1. The rule libraries that come with static analysis tools are useful for defect prevention.

2. Some of the static analysis tools also suggest corrections for defects and present these suggestions to the developers. Therefore, scores of problems are not only found, but programmers get to see effective solutions while examining the static analysis results.

Given the low cost and high effectiveness of static analysis tools, both the numbers of vendors and the effectiveness of the tools should continue to grow for perhaps four more years. By about 2015 the number of static analysis vendors will be so large that the weaker players will start to drop out. No doubt, if static analysis follows the precedence of other kinds of tools, by 2020 there will probably be fewer than half a dozen very large companies that have absorbed dozens of small static analysis companies. No doubt some of these large companies will also offer tools for testing and dynamic analysis as well as for static analysis.

Because the current market for quality tools circa 2011 is fragmented into a number of discrete niches, it would probably benefit quality as a technology if large companies could integrate defect prevention, inspections, static analysis, testing, security analysis, data quality analysis, code restructuring, code conversion, and migration of legacy applications.

Because of the low cost and high speed of static analysis tools, they are used very widely for open source applications. Indeed, static analysis tools are one of the reasons why open source quality compares well to commercial software.

Static analysis tools are also important in the certification process for reusable code modules.

It is theoretically possible to elevate the logic and Boolean logic of static analysis above the code itself and apply the same principles to use cases or at least to the meta-languages that underlie use cases. Even English text in requirements and design, data flow diagrams, decision tables, quality function deployment "house of quality" diagrams, and other forms of representation could be examined by future generations of static analysis tools.

Summary and Conclusions of Software Defect Prevention

As of 2011 there are at least 65 software design, development, and predictive methods that benefit defect prevention (or make it worse in some cases). Many of these methods benefit defect removal as well.

To use a medical analogy, defect removal tools and methods operate in the same fashion as antibiotics. That is, defect removal methods such as testing target specific kinds of software defects and eliminate them. As with antibiotics, the effectiveness of defect removal is always less than 100%, so many bugs or defects will escape and be found in delivered applications.

Defect prevention methods operate in the same fashion as vaccinations. Defect prevention methods do not kill active defects, but they raise the software immunity levels so that fewer defects are created. Here, too, as with vaccinations, effectiveness is less than 100%.

Effective quality control needs a combination of defect prevention methods and defect removal methods. As this book is written (in 2011) the U.S. average for software defect potentials is about 5.0 per function point, defect removal efficiency is about 85%, and delivered defects total around 0.75 per function point.

Using state-of-the-art defect prevention and defect removal methods, it is possible to cut defect potentials down to 2.5 defects (or 1.5 with certified reuse); defect removal efficiency can approach 99%; and delivered defects can drop down to only 0.025 defects per function point.

Today, a typical application of 1,000 function points will contain 5,000 defects and deliver about 750 defects to customers using the normal waterfall approach. It is theoretically possible therefore to cut the defect potentials down to 2,500 and deliver only 25 defects to customers using state of the art defect prevention and removal methods. This is not Six Sigma in terms of delivered defects, but it is about as close as contemporary software methods and tools could achieve.

Chapter 4

Pretest Defect Removal

Introduction

Testing is the traditional form of software defect removal. Indeed, testing is the only form of defect removal for many software applications. But after more than 50 years of software history, data on testing costs and testing effectiveness demonstrate that both testing efficiency and testing expenses are directly related to pretest activities.

If test cases are designed using requirements and specification documents that contain serious errors, then test cases tend to confirm these upstream errors rather than weed them out. This explains why testing did not find the Y2K defect for many years. Because two-digit dates were not thought of as defects, no methods found them. Far-sighted quality analysts and software engineers warned that they would eventually cause trouble, but when the trouble is more than ten years away, it is seldom taken seriously. The hazardous two-digit Y2K format originated as a requirement in the 1960s and hence test cases did not look for the problem up until about 1995. Upstream defects originating in requirements and design tend to be invisible to testing.

Another reason for pretest defect removal is cost and schedule reduction. If software is riddled with high-severity defects when testing starts, then test schedules will stretch out almost to infinity, and testing costs can be astronomical.

The point at which most failing projects first show signs of serious trouble is when testing starts. Many projects that are cancelled or have major delays for delivery showed no signs of overt distress until testing started. Carelessness and lax pretest defect removal activities tend to be invisible before testing starts.

If software contains large numbers of defects at the start of testing, then test schedules and test effort become unpredictable and always exceed their planned durations and costs. What occurs is a lengthy cycle of running test cases, finding and fixing bugs, and then rerunning test cases. Ideally, software applications will require fewer than half a dozen builds during testing. But if large numbers of defects are present, sometimes more than 25 or even 50 builds are needed, which add to overall schedules and costs.

Although pretest defect removal activities have been utilized since the software industry began, the literature on software quality is sparse for pretest defect removal compared to testing. A quick scan of books on Amazon and other Internet bookstores indicates about a 20 to 1 ratio between books on testing and books on pretest removal activities.

This disparity in books is unfortunate because pretest defect removal is just as important as testing. Indeed, from an economic viewpoint it is even more important than testing because effective pretest defect removal raises testing efficiency, lowers testing costs, shortens testing schedules, and generates a very solid return on investment.

From both an economic and quality assurance standpoint, defect prevention, pretest defect removal, and formal testing are all necessary to achieve a combination of low costs, short schedules, and low levels of defects present in the software when it is delivered to customers.

This chapter discusses the economic and defect removal efficiency data for a sample of 25 pretest removal activities:

1. Personal desk checking

2. Informal peer reviews

3. Automated text analysis

4. Proofs of correctness

5. Scrum sessions

6. Poka yoke

7. Kaizen

8. Pair programming

9. Client reviews of specifications

10. Independent verification and validation (IV&V)

11. Software Quality Assurance (SQA) reviews

12. Phase reviews

13. Formal requirements inspections: original

14. Formal requirements inspections: changes

15. Formal architecture inspections

16. Formal design inspections: original

17. Formal design inspections: changes

18. Formal code inspections: original

19. Formal code inspections: changes

20. Formal test plan inspections

21. Formal test case inspections

22. Formal document inspections

23. Reinspection of materials that fail inspections

24. Document editing: user manuals

25. Static analysis of source code

These 25 activities are not the only known forms of pretest defect removal, but the set of 25 provides a good sample of methods that can find and eliminate defects prior to testing. Some of these methods also work for defect prevention, and many of them have been shown to improve testing effectiveness.

As of 2011 the most effective forms of pretest defect removal are formal inspections and static analysis. Of these two, static analysis has almost a 50% penetration or usage on software projects among the authors' clients. By contrast, inspections are only used on 10% of projects or less. The sociological reason for this is that inspections are in the public domain, so there are no marketing campaigns of sales efforts. Static analysis, on the other hand, is a fast-growing and competitive sub-industry with numerous vendors all marketing products at the same time.

The most widely used forms of pretest defect removal are personal desk checking, client reviews, Scrum sessions, and peer reviews. Desk checking has almost 100% usage among software engineers. Of the other methods, Scrum is currently on a fast growth path but still is used only by 35% or so of projects, based on samples from among the authors' clients.

Note one important attribute of pretest defect removal activities. Some of these are used for both original work and also for changes and updates to the original work. For example, formal inspections can be used for initial design and also for major changes to the initial design.

This factor makes planning and estimating tricky. For example, if the original design is for 900 function points, it is likely that changes and updates will add another 100 function points during development. Both the inspections of the original work and the inspections of the changed materials need to be dealt with for cost studies and for defect removal efficiency studies.

No software project will use all 25 of the pretest defect removal activities cited in this book. However, various combinations of pretest defect removal have demonstrated simultaneous improvements in quality combined with schedule and cost reductions. The combinations vary between small applications below 1,000 function points in size and large systems above 10,000 function points.

Small Project Pretest Defect Removal

1. Personal desk checking

2. Scrum sessions

3. Client reviews of specifications

4. Informal peer reviews

5. Static analysis of source code

Large Project Pretest Defect Removal

1. Personal desk checking

2. Client reviews of specifications

3. Independent verification and validation (IV&V)

4. Software Quality Assurance (SQA) reviews

5. Phase reviews

6. Formal requirements inspections: original

7. Formal requirements inspections: changes

8. Formal architecture inspections

9. Formal design inspections: original

10. Formal design inspections: changes

11. Formal code inspections: original

12. Formal code inspections: changes

13. Formal test plan inspections

14. Formal test case inspections

15. Formal document inspections

16. Reinspection of materials that fail inspections

17. Document editing: user manuals

18. Static analysis of source code

Some of the pretest defect removal methods in this chapter are either experimental or have not been used widely enough to have solid data on their effectiveness. They are included in this book because preliminary data indicates potential benefits.

Experimental and rarely used forms of pretest defect removal

1. Automated text analysis

2. Proofs of correctness

3. Poka yoke

4. Kaizen

5. Pair programming

Poka yoke and Kaizen are Japanese methods that originated for manufacturing. They are now migrating to other countries and to software projects. They are promising but still under investigation in a software context.

Pair programming and proofs of correctness are academic creations that seldom if ever occur in commercial software organizations. The data for these methods is sparse and somewhat negative. Pair programming is expensive and seems to add little value considering that it doubles the effort to program. Pair programming is almost exclusively used on small projects with teams of fewer than a dozen software engineers. It has not been encountered among the authors' clients for large teams on large projects where 500 software engineers are working concurrently. Due to the recession that started in 2008, more of the authors' clients are laying off personnel rather than hiring.

The available data on pair programming is ambiguous. If 100 examples are noted, pair programming may be effective for 10 of them, neutral for 25, more expensive than regular one-person development for 40, much more expensive for about 15, and abandoned due to personnel or other reasons for 10. A Google search using the phrase "problems of pair programming" turned up more than a dozen reports with conclusions similar to those in this book. Pair programming is not a panacea; it is sometimes a success, sometimes a failure.

Proofs of correctness sound useful, but errors in the proofs themselves seem to be common failings not covered by the literature. Further, large applications may have thousands of provable algorithms, and the time required to prove them all might take many years.

Automated text analysis has been used successfully for other fields outside of software and may be beneficial in a software context. Two interesting measures of textual complexity, the Fog index and the Flesch-Kincaid index, would seem to be suitable for software requirements and specification documents. (The Fog index was developed by Robert Gunning in 1952. The Flesch-Kincaid index was developed by Rudolph Flesch and extended by J. Peter Kincaid. Both measure text complexity and readability. The Flesch-Kinkaid index was funded by the Department of Defense and later became a standard for military training manuals. These indexes are discussed in more detail later in the chapter.) As software reuse becomes more common, these tools could be expanded to generate application models based on historical data.

Small Project Pretest Defect Removal

In this book a "small software project" is defined as a software application that is below 1,000 function points in size or 50,000 source code statements in a language such as Java. The team size for such small applications is normally fewer than six software engineers.

Specialists such as software quality assurance (SQA), software architects, and even testing specialists seldom are present on small projects. By and large, small projects are handled by generalists who deal with requirements, design, coding, and testing.

One exception to the use of generalists may be a professional technical writer to handle user documents. This is because good writing about software is a rare skill in the software engineering domain. For small Agile projects a user's representative may be embedded in the team to provide requirements in real time.

The defect potentials for small software projects are usually fairly low, as seen in Table 4.1, and comprise the following kinds of defects in approximately these totals.

Table 4.1 *Defect Potentials for 1,000 Function Points*

Defect Origins	Defects per Function Point	Defects in Application
Requirements	0.75	750
Design	1.00	1,000
Source code	1.75	1,750
Documents	0.65	650
Bad fixes	0.27	270
Total Defects	4.42	4,420

Note that there are wide ranges of defect potentials and defect removal efficiency levels. The data in Table 4.1 approximates average values, but the range can be as much as 25% higher or lower for every defect source.

Table 4.2 is complex and attempts to show a full sequence of pretest defect removal activities for a small application of 1,000 function points. Some explanations are needed about what Table 4.2 actually shows.

The top row shows the approximate *defect potential*, or total numbers of defects anticipated in requirements, design, code, and user documents. Defect potentials are predicted values based on historical data from similar projects.

There are five forms of defect removal illustrated in Table 4.2:

1. Personal desk checking

2. Scrum sessions

3. Client reviews of specifications

4. Informal peer reviews

5. Static analysis of source code

For each of these five removal activities, Table 4.2 shows five rows of data:

1. The approximate removal efficiency against each defect source

2. The number of defects found and removed

3. The number of defects remaining after the removal activity

4. The number of "bad fixes" or new bugs included in defect repairs

5. The total number of bugs remaining for the next removal step

It should be noted that tables such as 4.2 can only be created by companies that have careful and complete defect measurement programs that include origin codes for software defects.

Each form of defect removal is aimed at a specific type of defects, but that does not mean that other types won't be found during the removal activities. For example, code inspections are obviously aimed at coding defects, but code inspections can and do find a few defects in design documents and even defects in user manuals.

At the end, Table 4.2 summarizes the cumulative defect removal efficiency of all five activities against all sources of defects.

Table 4.2   *Pretest Defect Removal Stages for 1,000 Function Points*

	Requirements Defects	Design Defects	Code Defects	Document Defects	TOTAL DEFECTS
Potentials	750	1,000	1,750	650	4,150
Desk Check	5.00%	12.50%	20.00%	7.50%	13.52%
Defects found	38	125	350	49	561
Defects left	713	875	1,400	601	3,589
Bad fixes	2	6	18	2	28
Remainder	715	881	1,418	603	3,617
Scrum	15.00%	20.00%	2.50%	17.50%	11.74%
Defects found	107	176	35	106	424
Defects left	607	705	1,382	498	3,192
Bad fixes	5	9	2	5	21
Remainder	613	714	1,384	503	3,214
Client Reviews	40.00%	20.00%	1.00%	15.00%	14.85%
Defects found	245	143	14	75	477
Defects left	368	571	1,370	428	2,736
Bad fixes	12	7	1	4	24
Remainder	380	578	1,371	432	2,760
Peer Reviews	25.00%	25.00%	22.00%	12.50%	21.56%
Defects found	95	145	302	54	595
Defects left	285	434	1,069	378	2,165
Bad fixes	5	7	15	3	30
Remainder	290	441	1,084	380	2,195
Static Analysis	5.00%	25.00%	85.00%	0.00%	47.67%
Defects found	14	110	922	0	1,046
Defects left	275	331	163	380	1,149
Bad fixes	1	6	46	0	52
Remainder	276	336	209	380	1,201
TOTAL REMOVED	499	699	1,622	284	3,104
TOTAL BAD FIXES	25	35	81	14	155
TOTAL REMAINING	276	336	209	380	1,201
REMOVAL EFFICIENCY	66.55%	69.88%	92.71%	43.67%	74.80%

Table 4.2 illustrates two chronic problems of the software industry:

1. Most forms of defect removal have comparatively low removal efficiency levels. This is why so many different kinds of defect removal are necessary.

2. It is much harder to remove defects from requirements and design than it is from source code. But if those defects are not removed prior to testing, testing itself cannot find them. Static analysis cannot find them, either because they tend to be errors of logic and omissions of features rather than concise coding bugs.

If front-end defects are not removed via pretest removal activities, the front-end defects in requirements and design will find their way into the code and get released. These defects usually do not cause severity 1 bugs that stop applications from running, but they do cause a great many severity 2 bugs such as miscalculations or incorrect reports. They also cause many severity 3 bugs or minor inconveniences. (The IBM 4-level severity scale is used in this book because it is widely used by the authors' clients.)

The effort and costs of pretest defect removal activities are not well covered in the literature, with the exceptions of formal inspections and static analysis. An integral part of the inspection process is to record hours spent on preparation, on holding the inspection sessions, and on defect repairs after the inspection sessions. Several of the static analysis tool vendors have performed cost-benefit studies with published results.

However, desk checking, scrum sessions, client reviews of materials, and informal peer reviews have only sparse data available. Data on scrum session effort and costs can be derived from knowing their average duration, number of participants, and frequency of occurrence.

Table 4.3 shows the approximate effort and costs for the set of small-project, pretest defect removal activities discussed here. A word of explanation is needed about the table. The table shows an application of 1,000 function points or about 50,000 Java statements. The schedule for this project was derived by raising 1,000 function points to the 0.38 power and rounding the result to 14, which is the number of calendar months from start of requirements to delivery. The number of software engineers is assumed to be six, and they are assumed to be of average experience. The methodology is standard waterfall and CMMI level 1.5, which indicates a level-1 group that is advancing towards level 2. (While the Software Engineering Institute does not endorse decimal values, they do occur and are intended to show progress toward higher levels. Among the authors' clients, most use some form of fractional CMMI level in discussions about where their status.)

The number of work hours per month is assumed to be 132. The burdened monthly cost is assumed to be $7,500, which is equivalent to $51.82 per hour.

The table shows three work activities: preparation, execution, and defect repairs. Preparation is the up-front work carried out prior to the defect removal activity itself. Execution is performing the defect removal activity. Defect repair, as the name implies, is the effort for fixing bugs after the activity has been performed.

Because static analysis tools usually suggest defect repairs as part of their fundamental operation, the human part of defect repairs is fairly low when static analysis tools are used. However, due to false positives and a need to examine the implications of the suggested repairs, static analysis tools do require manual effort for defect repairs.

The various defect repair activities are assumed to take place in "sessions" for portions of the 1,000 function point application. For example, desk checking is assumed to take place over a set of 50 sessions during the coding phase. In Table 4.3 scrum sessions are assumed to occur once a week, but other intervals such as twice a week or daily often occur.

Table 4.3   *Effort and Costs for Small Project Pretest Defect Removal*

(Application size is 1,000 function points with 6 software engineers)						
Pretest Removal Activities	Team Size	Work hours per session	Number of sessions	Staff Hours	Costs	$ per Function Point
Desk check						
Preparation	6.00	0.10	50	30.00	$1,585	$1.58
Execution	6.00	1.00	50	300.00	$15,846	$15.85
Repairs	6.00	4.15	50	1,245.00	$65,761	$65.76
Total	6.00	5.25	50	1,575.00	$83,192	$83.19
Scrum						
Preparation	8.00	0.10	56	44.80	$2,366	$2.37
Execution	8.00	0.50	56	224.00	$11,832	$11.83
Repairs	8.00	1.85	56	828.80	$43,777	$43.78
Total	8.00	2.45	56	1,097.60	$57,975	$57.98
Client review						
Preparation	1.00	0.20	10	2.00	$106	$0.11
Execution	1.00	1.50	10	15.00	$792	$0.79
Repairs	6.00	9.00	10	540.00	$28,523	$28.52
Total	6.00	10.70	10	642.00	$33,910	$33.91

Pretest Removal Activities	Team Size	Work hours per session	Number of sessions	Staff Hours	Costs	$ per Function Point
Peer review						
Preparation	6.00	0.50	25	75.00	$3,962	$3.96
Execution	6.00	2.50	25	375.00	$19,808	$19.81
Repairs	6.00	4.50	25	675.00	$35,654	$35.65
Total	6.00	7.50	25	1,125.00	$59,423	$59.42
Static analysis						
Preparation	6.00	0.50	28	84.00	$4,437	$4.44
Execution	6.00	0.50	28	84.00	$4,437	$4.44
Repairs	6.00	4.50	28	756.00	$39,932	$39.93
Total	6.00	5.50	28	924.00	$48,806	$48.81
TOTALS						
Preparation	5.40	1.40	34	235.80	$12,455	$12.45
Execution	5.40	6.00	34	998.00	$52,714	$52.71
Repairs	6.40	24.00	34	4,044.80	$213,646	$213.65
Total	6.40	31.40	34	5,363.60	$283,305	$283.31

Table 4.3 shows only the direct effort and direct costs associated with performing the set of pretest defect removal activities. There are other costs such as acquiring static analysis tools and providing training in methods such as formal inspections. However, these costs are usually treated as overhead costs rather than being charged to specific projects.

For small projects, generalists are the norm, and they may not be fully trained in defect removal activities. It is fortunate that small projects have low defect potentials because high-efficiency defect removal requires training and technical knowledge outside of the usual software engineering curricula.

Large System Pretest Defect Removal

When the focus changes from small projects of 1,000 function points or less to large systems of 10,000 function points or more, there are six critical changes that usually occur:

1. Software defect potentials increase significantly with application size. For large applications, defect potentials are closer to 6.0 per function point rather than the 4.0 per function point that is normal for small programs.

2. Front-end defects in requirements, architecture, and design are much more numerous for large systems than for small applications.

3. Test coverage drops for large systems and seldom tops about 80%.

4. Defect removal efficiency drops down for large systems and is usually below 85% unless pretest defect removal activities are carried out with professional skill levels.

5. Large systems usually employ specialists for software quality assurance (SQA) and testing instead of the general software developers used on small projects.

6. Large systems utilize more forms of pretest defect removal and more forms of testing than do small applications.

Table 4.4 shows the approximate defect potentials for a large system in the 10,000 function point size range:

A comparison of large-system defects in Table 4.4 with small application defects in Table 4.1 shows several alarming changes:

- Defect potentials for all sources of defects have increased.

- Requirement and design defects have increased faster than code defects.

- Architecture defects occur for large systems but not for small programs.

These increases in defect potentials explain why serious defect prevention, serious pretest removal, and professional-grade testing are needed to be

Table 4.4   *Defect potentials for 10,000 Function Points*

Defect Origins	Defects per Function Point	Defects in Application
Requirements	1.10	11,000
Architecture	0.30	3,000
Design	1.30	13,000
Source code	1.77	17,700
Documents	0.75	7,500
Bad fixes	0.42	4,176
Total Defects	5.64	56,376

successful for large systems. Small projects can sometimes get by with informal defect removal methods if the teams are fairly competent. But for large systems the higher defect potentials and the increased difficulty of testing necessitate very thorough pretest defect removal activities.

(The software quality literature does not often discuss errors in test cases themselves. In fact, this topic is seldom studied at all except by a few large companies such as IBM. Assuming about 2.5 test cases per function point, a 10,000 function point application would have about 25,000 test cases.

Out of these 25,000 test cases, there would probably be errors in about 6%, or 1,500 defects in test cases themselves. This is one of the reasons why formal inspections are used for test plans and test cases, although not as often as the situation warrants.

Table 4.5 illustrates the rather elaborate set of pretest software defect removal methods that are utilized on a large system of 10,000 function points, assuming that very high quality levels are needed.

Comparatively few large systems would utilize all nine of the pretest methods shown in Table 4.5. The most likely applications for such intensive pretest removal activities would be large systems software applications that control complex physical devices such as mainframe telephone switching systems, large operating systems, and process controls systems. Weapons systems and applications with severe failure consequences such as medical devices would also deploy a wide variety of intense pretest defect removal activities.

Some of the pretest removal methods are used for both large projects and smaller applications, but three of the methods in Table 4.5 are used almost exclusively for larger systems: architecture inspections, independent verification and validation (IV&V), and Software Quality Assurance (SQA) reviews.

Small software projects seldom have a formal architecture and therefore don't utilize architecture inspections. Small projects are normally not required to have independent verification by a third party (although some military or government projects might require IV&V). Software Quality Assurance (SQA) teams are often understaffed, so their services are usually reserved for large and/or mission-critical applications.

Table 4.5 shows an unusually sophisticated combination of pretest removal activities that are only used by very sophisticated companies primarily for systems and embedded applications, military software, and important commercial products. A series with so many stages would seldom be utilized for information technology applications or for web projects.

Table 4.6 shows a more typical pattern with only three kinds of pretest removal activity: desk checking, client reviews, and a review by a Software Quality Assurance (SQA) group.

Table 4.5 *Pretest Defect Removal for 10,000 Function Points*

(Note: This table represents high-quality defect removal operations.)

Pretest Defect Removal Methods	Architecture Defects per Function Point	Requirements Defects per Function Point	Design Defects per Function Point	Code Defects per Function Point	Document Defects per Function Point	TOTALS
Defect Potentials per FP	0.30	1.10	1.30	1.80	0.75	5.25
Defect Potentials	3,000	11,000	13,000	18,000	7,500	52,500
Desk checking	10.00%	5.00%	12.50%	20.00%	7.50%	12.64%
Defects discovered	300	550	1,625	3,600	563	6,638
Bad-fix injection	9	17	49	108	17	199
Defects remaining	2,691	10,434	11,326	14,292	6,921	45,663
Client reviews	10.00%	30.00%	12.50%	1.00%	15.00%	13.13%
Defects discovered	269	3,130	1,416	143	1,038	5,996
Bad-fix injection	8	94	42	4	31	180
Defects remaining	2,414	7,210	9,868	14,145	5,851	39,488
Requirement inspection	5.00%	82.50%	10.00%	5.00%	8.50%	15.73%
Defects discovered	121	5,948	987	707	497	8,260
Bad-fix injection	4	178	30	21	15	248
Defects remaining	2,290	1,083	8,852	13,416	5,339	30,980
Architecture inspection	80.00%	10.00%	10.00%	2.50%	12.00%	12.27%
Defects discovered	1,832	108	885	335	641	3,801

Bad-fix injection	55	3	27	10	19	114
Defects remaining	403	972	7,940	13,071	4,679	27,065
Design inspection	10.00%	14.00%	80.00%	7.00%	16.00%	30.27%
Defects discovered	40	136	6,352	915	749	8,192
Bad-fix injection	1	4	191	27	22	410
Defects remaining	361	832	1,397	12,128	3,908	18,627
Static analysis	12.50%	15.00%	20.00%	85.00%	10.00%	59.86%
Defects discovered	45	125	279	10,309	391	11,149
Bad-fix injection	1	4	8	309	12	334
Defects remaining	315	703	1,110	1,510	3,506	7,143
Code inspection	2.00%	2.00%	7.00%	85.00%	3.00%	20.81%
Defects discovered	6	14	78	1,283	105	1,487
Bad-fix injection	0	0	2	39	3	45
Defects remaining	308	689	1,030	188	3,397	5,612
IV & V	10.00%	12.00%	18.00%	7.00%	18.00%	16.46%
Defects discovered	31	83	185	13	611	923
Bad-fix injection	1	2	6	0	18	28
Defects remaining	277	603	839	174	2,767	4,661
SQA review	10.00%	17.00%	22.00%	12.00%	25.00%	22.05%
Defects discovered	28	103	185	21	692	1,028
Bad-fix injection	1	3	6	1	21	51
Defects remaining	248	498	649	153	2,055	3,582
Pretest defects removed	2,752	10,502	12,351	17,847	5,445	48,898
Pretest efficiency %	91.73%	95.47%	95.01%	99.15%	72.60%	93.14%

Table 4.6 *Pretest Defect Removal for 10,000 Function Points*

(Note: This table represents low-quality defect removal operations.)

Pretest Defect Removal Methods	Architecture Defects per Function Point	Requirements Defects per Function Point	Design Defects per Function Point	Code Defects per Function Point	Document Defects per Function Point	TOTALS
Defect Potentials per FP	0.40	1.15	1.40	1.85	0.80	5.60
Defect potentials	4,000	11,500	14,000	18,500	8,000	56,000
Desk checking	10.00%	5.00%	12.50%	20.00%	7.50%	12.54%
Defects discovered	400	575	1,750	3,700	600	7,025
Bad-fix injection	12	17	53	111	18	211
Defects remaining	3,588	10,908	12,198	14,689	7,382	48,764
Client reviews	10.00%	30.00%	12.50%	1.00%	15.00%	13.14%
Defects discovered	359	3,272	1,525	147	1,107	6,410
Bad-fix injection	11	98	46	4	33	192
Defects remaining	3,218	7,537	10,627	14,538	6,241	42,162
SQA review	10.00%	17.00%	22.00%	12.00%	25.00%	17.19%
Defects discovered	322	1,281	2,338	1,745	1,560	7,246
Bad-fix injection	10	38	70	52	47	362
Defects remaining	2,887	6,217	8,219	12,741	4,634	34,554
Pretest defects removed	1,113	5,283	5,781	5,759	3,366	21,301
Pretest efficiency %	27.83%	45.93%	41.29%	31.13%	42.07%	38.04%

Table 4.6 illustrates why software testing costs can go out of control in the absence of professional levels of pretest defect removal. The failure to utilize either inspections or static analysis prior to testing leaves applications with thousands of latent defects. These latent defects slow down test activities and stretch out test schedules far beyond expectations. Numbers of software builds also increase when large numbers of defects are present at the start of testing.

Organizations that use such a sparse sequence of pretest defect removal activities usually have higher defect potentials as well. A side-by-side comparison of the high-quality and low-quality results shows why pretest defect removal is an important topic.

A 10,000 function point application will have a team of about 65 people at its peak. The personnel involved normally include architects, business analysts, database administrators, designers, developers, configuration control specialists, managers, metrics specialists, project office personnel, quality assurance personnel, technical writers, testers, and perhaps more. Unfortunately, some companies only count developers and test personnel and therefore seem to have much smaller staffs.

A 10,000 function point application will also have a development schedule of more than 36 calendar months. The total of 56,000 bugs or defects is equivalent to about 861 bugs or defects per staff member, or roughly 24 bugs or defects per staff month over the full development cycle. Looking at the defect potentials another way, if each staff member or software engineer creates only one bug per day, the total would approximate 56,000 when all staff days are accumulated.

Readers may be surprised by the large numbers of software bugs or defects, but software development is a complex activity, and making mistakes or defects is all too easy. The ultimate solution would be to construct software applications from certified reusable materials that approach zero defects, but that solution is still some years in the future.

Table 4.7 *Comparison of High-Quality and Low-Quality Pretest Defect Removal*

	High-Quality Projects	Low-Quality Projects	Difference
Defect potentials per function point	5.25	5.60	0.35
Defects in Application	52,500	56,000	3,500
Pretest removal stages	7	3	−4
Defects removed	48,898	21,301	−27,597
Defects remaining	3,582	34,554	30,972
Defects remaining per function point	0.36	3.46	3.10
Pretest defect removal efficiency	93.14%	38.04%	−55.10%

Another possibility might be to adopt the principle of redundancy, which is widely used in critical physical devices. However, the architecture for software redundancy circa 2011 is not yet advanced enough to make redundancy widespread.

There are also questions about the comparative costs of zero-defect reusable materials compared to double or triple redundancy. Unfortunately, neither side of this interesting question has enough reliable data to do more than speculate. There is data for reuse but little available data on redundancy.

As long as the majority of software applications are custom-designed and hand-coded, defect volumes will remain higher than desirable. To control high volumes of defects, defect prevention, pretest defect removal, and more than a dozen forms of testing are all necessary.

Analysis of Pretest Defect Removal Activities

In this section the major forms of pretest defect removal cited earlier will be discussed in terms of efficiency and the effort required for performing the methods. The information in this section comes from observations of clients in the United States, Europe, and Japan. Some data also comes from depositions and discovery documents from software litigation. Because samples for some of the methods are small, results may vary from what is discussed in this section.

Personal Desk Checking

Usage:	> 75% of low-level code; < 30% of high-level code
	> 75% of text documents such as requirements
Defect removal efficiency range:	
Minimum =	< 25%
Average =	35%
Maximum =	> 50%
Preparation time:	None
Execution time:	80% of normal reading speed for text (< 200 words per minute)
	About 5 logical code statements per minute for source code
Synergies:	Agile, RUP, TSP, and CMMI
Counter indications:	None

Personal desk checking is the oldest form of software defect removal. It has been used continuously since the start of the computer era circa 1950. Between about 1950 and perhaps 1975, desk checking was far more common than testing.

In the early days of computing between about 1950 and 1975, access to computers for testing was severely limited. Computers were used to run production work during daylight hours. Normally, programmers had only one test opportunity per day, and often testing had to take place at night and sometimes well after midnight. Therefore, desk checking was the standard method for removing defects from requirements, design, and source code defects.

In those days of limited test time and fairly primitive test case design, testing was less than 70% efficient in finding bugs, so personal desk checking was a necessary adjunct to testing in order to reduce testing costs and raise the chance of the software working successfully.

The reason that personal desk checking rates fairly low in defect removal efficiency is because of the natural human tendency to be blind to our own mistakes. If we make an error we usually do so because we think the action was correct. We don't realize that an error occurred. Therefore, some other method such as peer review or testing is needed to find most errors.

This phenomenon occurs in many other fields besides software development. For example, it is easier for chess kibitzers to see bad moves than it is for the players themselves.

This tendency for people to be blind to their own mistakes explains why newspapers and magazines have utilized proofreaders and copy editors for hundreds of years. Although seldom utilized for software projects, proofreading and copyediting of requirements, specifications, and source code would probably be effective for software projects. Trained proofreaders and copy editors top 95% in defect removal efficiency levels for journal articles, books, and newspapers. Proofreading and copy editors might not find factual errors, but they are extremely efficient in finding syntactic errors, grammar errors, and structural errors.

Personal desk checking is still a common method of pretest defect removal. Desk checking in 2011 can be augmented by static analysis for coding defects and by spell checkers and complexity tools for text documents.

Informal Peer Reviews

Usage:	< 50% of software applications
Defect removal efficiency range:	
Minimum =	< 35%
Average =	45%
Maximum =	> 65%
Preparation time:	< 30 minutes
Execution time:	70% of normal reading speed for text (< 200 words per minute)
	About 3 logical code statements per minute for source code
Synergies:	Agile, waterfall, and small projects < 5 team members
Counter indications:	Large systems > 10,000 function points need inspections

Because of the well-known problems associated with finding our own errors in both text documents and source code, peer reviews by colleagues have been used almost as long as personal desk checking.

Obviously, for peer reviews to be used, the application needs to be larger than a one-person project. Therefore, peer reviews are widely used among team members who are working on the same project and are seldom used for small bug repairs and minor updates that involve only one person. Also, peer reviews are seldom used for the thousands of small one-person "applets" that are marketed for smart phones and hand-held devices.

Although peer reviews are used for larger systems, the higher defect removal efficiency levels of formal inspections makes peer reviews only a secondary form of pretest removal for applications larger than about 1,000 function points in size. Of course, for Agile projects that don't use formal inspections, peer reviews may still be utilized.

The technical reviews for books such as this one comprise a form of peer review. Publishers ask three to five experts in related topics to review manuscripts and suggest useful changes, which indeed has occurred for this very book.

Peer reviews are not the same as proofreading and copyediting, however. Peer reviews are concerned with finding technical, structural, and logical problems. Proofreading and copyediting are concerned with finding syntactical and grammatical errors. However, copy editors may note errors of fact, and peer reviewers may note syntactical problems. But the emphasis for peer reviews is validity of data, logic, structure, and technical issues.

Even in 2011 with methods such as static analysis and text analysis available, peer reviews are still useful defect removal methods for small projects with team sizes of two to four people and for Agile projects.

Peer reviews also have some value for defect prevention given that after reviewing code and documents, participants tend to spontaneously avoid the mistakes that are noted.

Peer reviews are useful for learning also. When novice personnel review the work of experts, they can learn useful information about effective design and coding practices. Conversely, when experts review the work of novices, they point out problems that novices need to understand.

Of course, novice-to-novice reviews are not very effective, but they are still better than nothing. Expert-to-expert reviews can be highly effective but sometimes encounter the sociological problem that experts may have big egos and don't like to have their mistakes pointed out.

Automated Text Checking for Documents

Usage:	< 10% of civilian software applications
	> 85% of military software applications
Defect removal efficiency range:	
Minimum =	< 05%
Average =	10%
Maximum =	> 12%
Preparation time:	< 30 minutes
Execution time:	> 2,000 words per minute
Synergies:	Software projects > 1,000 function points
Counter indications:	None

The phrase *automated text checking* refers to the usage of computerized tools that evaluate the readability of text documents. There are several forms of automated text analysis that could be and sometimes are applied to software requirements, architecture, design, and user documentation.

These tools are somewhat more sophisticated than the spelling and grammar checkers that are now standard features for word processors. However, some word processors also include readability scoring such as Google Docs and even Microsoft Word.

An educator named Rudolf Flesch designed a readability index for text materials (later extended by J. Peter Kinkaid). The formula for the Flesch index is

- *(total words / total sentences) – (total syllables / total words)*

For the Flesch index, high scores indicate easier readability levels. The overall results would be

- 90 to 100: Easy to read, even by children

- 70 to 90: Easy to read by literate high school students

- 50 to 70: Easy to read by the majority of adults

- 30 to 50: Difficult to read, even by college graduates

- 10 to 30: Difficult to read, even by graduate students

Popular journals usually have Flesch readability scores of 65 or higher. Journals such as the *Harvard Law Journal* usually have readability scores of 35 or lower. Technical journals such as *IEEE Software* often have readability scores of 30 or lower. Software requirements and specifications usually have readability scores below 25, which indicate very difficult comprehension for most readers.

An example of the Flesch readability index is in order. The first paragraph of this section contains 42 words and two sentences. There are 83 syllables. Using the Flesch formula cited above, the Flesch index would be

- *19 derived from:*
- *21 (42 words/2 sentences) – 1.976 (83 syllables/42 words)*

The reason for the low readability score is because the first paragraph of this section has two very long sentences and uses a great many multisyllabic words.

Although civilian software projects don't use Flesch readability indexes often, the Department of Defense requires that readability scores be used for military software documents.

Surprisingly, the state of Florida also requires the use of the Flesch readability index on legal documents such as insurance contracts. Indeed, widespread usage of the Flesch index on legal documents such as mortgages and credit card applications should be encouraged and possibly even required by law. This would be especially useful for sections in legal documents that discuss penalties and fees. The Flesch readability method would also benefit end-user license agreements (EULA) for commercial software applications.

A variation of the Flesch index called the Flesch-Kincaid index converts the readability scores into approximate grade levels. These grade-level scores are widely used in primary and secondary schools to evaluate texts and reading materials.

Another readability index is called the Gunning Fog Index. (Fog is apparently not an acronym but is used in the normal way to indicate haze and poor visibility.) It was developed by Robert Gunning in 1952. The Gunning formula shows the approximate grade level the reader would need to have achieved to understand a given text passage. The resulting score is based on the following data gleaned from the text:

1. Count the number of words in a given text passage.

2. Count the average sentence length.

3. Count words with three or more syllables (excluding proper names and some others).

4. Add the average sentence length and the number of compound words.

5. Multiply by 0.4.

Using the Gunning formula on the first paragraph of this section produces the following results.

- There are 42 words.

- The average sentence length is 21 words.

- The number of words with three or more syllables is 11.

- The resulting Fog index is 12.8, which indicates that the text passage should be understandable by a high school senior.

There is more subjectivity with the Gunning Fog index than with the Flesch index because some multisyllabic words are not counted because they are so common. For example, the word "mechanical" has four syllables but is common enough that it would seldom be viewed as difficult. This subjectivity means that two different people might not get identical Gunning Fog indices if they evaluated the same text passage.

These automated text readability analysis methods do not find defects, per se, but by simplifying the text and making it more readable and understandable, they lead to much higher removal efficiency levels for inspections, peer reviews, and client reviews of textual materials.

The various text analysis tools are useful for ordinary text documents but have no impact on graphical materials such as use cases, data flow diagrams, flow charts, Nassi-Shneiderman charts, and the many other kinds of graphical representations used for software applications. It is technically possible to construct a graphical readability index, but thus far none have been commercially deployed.

As software reuse evolves into a mature discipline, it is possible to envision software requirements, architecture, and design tools that would include standard outlines, links to descriptions of standard reusable functions, and integrated complexity analysis of both text and graphics.

The first sequence of using such an automated requirements and design tool would be to place the application on a standard taxonomy in order to provide an unambiguous basis for further analysis. The taxonomy would show the nature, scope, class, and type of the software application to be developed.

PROJECT NATURE: _____

1. New program development

2. Enhancement (new functions added to existing software)

3. Maintenance (defect repair to existing software)

4. Conversion or adaptation (migration to new platform)

5. Reengineering (reimplementing a legacy application)

6. Package modification (revising purchased software)

PROJECT SCOPE: _____

1. Algorithm

2. Subroutine

3. Module

4. Reusable module

5. Disposable prototype

6. Evolutionary prototype

7. Subprogram

8. Standalone program

9. Component of a system

10. Release of a system (other than the initial release)

11. New departmental system (initial release)

12. New corporate system (initial release)

13. New enterprise system (initial release)

14. New national system (initial release)

15. New global system (initial release)

PROJECT CLASS: _____

1. Personal program for private use

2. Personal program to be used by others

3. Academic program developed in an academic environment

4. Internal program for use at a single location

5. Internal program for use at a multiple locations

6. Internal program for use on an intranet

7. Internal program developed by external contractor

8. Internal program with functions used via time sharing

9. Internal program using military specifications

10. External program to be put in public domain

11. External program to be placed on the Internet

12. External program to be placed in a cloud

13. External program leased to users

14. External program bundled with hardware

15. External program unbundled and marketed commercially

16. External program developed under commercial contract

17. External program developed under government contract

18. External program developed under military contract

PROJECT TYPE: _____

1. Nonprocedural (generated, query, spreadsheet)

2. Applet for smart phone or hand-held devices

3. Batch application

4. Web application

5. Interactive application

6. Interactive graphical user interface (GUI) application program

7. Batch database applications program

8. Interactive database application program

9. Client/server application program

10. Computer game

11. Scientific or mathematical program

12. Expert system

13. Systems or support program, including "middleware"

14. Service-oriented architecture (SOA)

15. Communications or telecommunications program

16. Process-control program

17. Trusted system

18. Embedded or real-time program

19. Graphics, animation, or image-processing program

20. Multimedia program

21. Robotics or mechanical automation program

22. Artificial intelligence program

23. Neural net program

24. Hybrid project (multiple types)

After the application is placed on a standard taxonomy, the requirements, architecture, and design tool would then show the probable sets of functions and features that will be included, and identify those features that exist in the form of reusable components. Analysis of hundreds of applications using this taxonomy shows surprising similarities among projects that share the same taxonomy patterns even though they might be developed by totally different companies. Applications with the same pattern have these characteristics:

- About 90% common features among all applications with the same pattern

- Application sizes in function points within 12% of one another

- Development schedules within 30% of one another in duration

These similarities do not appear to be coincidences. It happens that applications that share a common pattern using the taxonomy usually are performing similar functions and have similar business cases.

Of course, the applications do vary in terms of programming languages and sometimes in terms of architecture, but the similarities are very common, which makes taxonomy analysis a useful adjunct for requirements and design. Applications sharing the same taxonomy are also candidates for construction from certified reusable materials.

What could be an interesting study but outside the scope of this book, would be to enumerate the numbers of applications that comprise the most common taxonomy patterns. It is probably the fact that taxonomy patterns have shared requirements that makes commercial software and enterprise resource planning (ERP) tools profitable industries. In other words, these commercial software packages are aimed at the markets where taxonomy patterns are most prevalent.

As a minor example, there are millions of users of word processing applications and spreadsheets. It would be a waste of money and time for companies to develop these generic applications when they can be acquired as either open-source software or fairly low-cost commercial packages.

It is obvious that taxonomy analysis could be used to study software usage patterns as well as providing background information for common requirements and design features.

Rather than starting requirements, architecture, and design with a clean slate, the tool would provide information on the features and functions that are associated with the specific taxonomy for the application to be developed.

For the features that are available in the form of standard reusable components, the tool would then construct a set of general requirements, architecture, and design topics based on analysis of historical projects that share the same taxonomy placement. Ideally, these descriptions of standard features would have high readability indexes.

The basic idea is to minimize custom design and hand-coding by capturing the essential features of similar applications and using an automated tool to construct the basic requirements, architecture, and design documents. Assuming that most applications consist of about 85% generic features that are widely used, the effort for requirements and design would focus on the 15% unique features that would be needed.

The value of this approach is that if the reusable components have been certified and approach zero defects, then the defect potentials even for large applications would drop below 1.0 per function point. By including reusable test materials and utilizing static analysis tools, defect removal efficiency levels should top 98% on average and more than 99.9% for critical features and functions.

By fortunate coincidence, the structure of function point metrics is a good match to the fundamental issues that should be included in software requirements, architecture, and designs and also eventually become available in the form of reusable components.

In chronological order, these seven fundamental topics should be explored as part of the requirements gathering process:

1. The *outputs* that should be produced by the application

2. The *inputs* that will enter the software application

3. The *logical files* that must be maintained by the application

4. The *entities and relationships* that will be in the logical files of the application

5. The *inquiry types* that can be made to the application

6. The *interfaces* between the application and other systems

7. Key *algorithms* that must be present in the application

Five of these seven topics are the basic elements of the International Function Point Users Group (IFPUG) function point metric.

The fourth topic, "entities and relationships," is part of the British Mark II function point metric and the newer COSMIC function point.

The seventh topic, "algorithms" is a standard factor of the feature point metric, which added a count of algorithms to the five basic function point elements used by IFPUG.

(The similarity between the topics that need to be examined when gathering requirements and those used by the functional metrics makes the derivation of function point totals during requirements a fairly straightforward task.)

There is such a strong synergy between requirements and function point analysis that it would be possible to construct a combined requirements analysis tool with full function point sizing support as a natural adjunct, although the current generation of automated requirements tools are not quite at that point.

If full automation of requirements, design, architecture, and function points is to be possible, the requirements themselves must be fairly well structured and complete. Toward that end, in addition to the 7 fundamental requirement topics, there are also 13 other ancillary topics that should be resolved during the requirements gathering phase:

1. The *size* of the application in function points and source code

2. The *schedule* of the application from requirements to delivery

3. The *development cost* of the application in terms of cost per function point

4. The *quality levels* in terms of defects, reliability, and ease of use criteria

5. The *hardware platform(s)* on which the application will operate

6. The *software platform(s)* such as operating systems and databases

7. The *security criteria* for the application and its companion databases

8. The *performance criteria*, if any, for the application

9. The *training requirements* or form of tutorial materials that may be needed

10. The *installation requirements* for putting the application onto the host platforms

11. The *reuse criteria* for the application in terms of both reused materials going into the application and also whether features of the application may be aimed at subsequent reuse by downstream applications

12. The *use cases or major tasks* users are expected to be able to perform via the application

13. The *control flow* or sequence of information moving through the application

These 13 supplemental topics are not the only items that can be included in requirements, but none of these 13 should be omitted by accident because they can all have a significant effect on software projects.

There are also seven critical business topics that should be studied during the requirements gathering and analysis phase:

1. The *work value* of the application to end users

2. The *financial value* of the application to the company that develops it

3. The *financial value* of the application to clients and customers

4. The *return on investment* for building the application

5. The *risks* that might occur during development

6. The anticipated *total cost of ownership (TCO)* for the application

7. The anticipated *cost of quality (COQ)* for the application

The synergy between function points and software requirements is good enough so that it is now technically possible to merge the requirements gathering process and the development of function point metrics and improve both tasks simultaneously.

In the future, automated tools that support requirements gathering, design, construction from reusable materials, complexity of text, and function point analysis could add rigor and improve the speed of critical development activities. Because requirements gathering has been notoriously difficult and error-prone, this synergy could benefit the entire software engineering domain.

Proofs of Correctness

Usage:	Experimental: < 5% of software applications
	< 10% of academic software applications
	< 1% of commercial software
Defect removal efficiency range:	
Minimum =	< 05%
Average =	15%
Maximum =	> 20%
Preparation time:	> 30 minutes per proof
Execution time:	> 90 minutes per proof (4 proofs per day in total)
Synergies:	Academic projects < 100 function points
Counter indications:	Applications > 1,000 function points

The idea of using mathematical proofs for validating software algorithms is intellectually appealing and especially so among academics. However, there is very little empirical data on several topics that need to be well understood if proofs of correctness are to become useful tools for professional software development as opposed to academic experiments:

1. How many algorithms need to be proved in applications of specific sizes?

2. Are there upper limits on the size of applications where proofs can be used?

3. How many errors will be in the correctness proofs themselves?

4. What are the measured costs of correctness proofs compared to other methods?

5. What percentage of software engineers are qualified to perform proofs?

6. What effect will correctness proofs have on schedules?

7. What effect will correctness proofs have on creeping requirements?

In a language such as Java, one function point is roughly equivalent to 50 source code statements. Not every function point contains provable algorithms, but for an application of 1,000 function points in size or 50,000 Java statements, there will probably be at least 200 algorithms that might require proofs of correctness.

Most of the data published on proofs of correctness deal with either academic exercises or very small applications below 100 function points in size.

Whether or not correctness proofs might be useful for applications the size of Windows 7 (160,000 function points or 8,000,000 source code statements) is unknown but doubtful.

Assuming the same ratio shown here of one provable algorithm for every five function points, Windows 7 would have about 32,000 provable algorithms. For a single mathematician or qualified software engineer, performing 32,000 proofs would of necessity be an undertaking that would last perhaps 36 calendar years, assuming no other work was performed other than performing four proofs during an eight-hour day. For such a large system at least 35 people would be needed to carry out the correctness proofs, and the time might still take more than one calendar year.

There is very little data on errors in correctness proofs themselves, but a speaker at a conference once cited an example of 13 proofs, all of which contained errors. The measured rate of errors in ordinary bug repairs is about 7%. If correctness proofs had roughly the same incidence, then there would be errors in at least a significant percentage of proofs.

From software demographic studies carried out by one of the authors, there are about 70 different occupations associated with the software engineering field. Software engineers themselves are usually less than one-third of the total team size. Other team members include architects, business analysts, systems analysts, database analysts, quality assurance personnel, technical writers, test personnel, and many others. Correctness proofs require a fairly high level of mathematical training, which implies that only a small percentage of software engineers and other personnel are qualified.

For a large system of 10,000 function points and a staff of 65 total personnel, probably only about 5 would be qualified to perform mathematical proofs of correctness. For a 10,000 function point application there would probably be about 2,000 provable algorithms, which would require that 400 proofs be performed by each qualified person.

At a rate of four proofs per day, it would take 80 consecutive days to perform the proofs. In other words, correctness proofs would add 80 days to the development schedule and absorb the full-time efforts of five key personnel who would have no time left over for other tasks.

Outside of software engineers, the percentage would no doubt be lower for business analysts, architects, technical writers, database analysts, testers, quality assurance personnel, and other specialists. The bottom line is that attempting correctness proofs for large systems would probably require more skilled practitioners than are readily available. Proofs would also require a significant amount of schedule time and also saturate the work of key team members.

Assuming that correctness proofs require active participation by the most qualified software engineers working on software projects, it is an unanswered question as to whether the proofs add value commensurate with the increased schedule and increased costs that will occur.

Almost all of the literature on software correctness proofs assumes a static set of requirements that do not change while the proofs are being performed, or afterwards for that matter. But the measured rate at which real-world software applications change their requirements is more than 1% per calendar month. There is no data and not even much in the way of anecdotal evidence that discusses the effectiveness of correctness proofs for applications that have rapidly changing requirements. Suppose you are half-way through the proof of a complex algorithm. Suddenly a business problem requires the addition of four more parameters to the algorithm. Correctness proofs and dynamic requirements are not a good combination.

Correctness proofs circa 2011 are primarily an experimental method used on very small projects. Correctness proofs are unproven for large software applications, and a surface analysis indicates that they would probably be expensive and ineffective for applications larger than a few hundred function points in size.

For larger applications a few proofs might be useful for critical algorithms, but the method of correctness proofs does not seem to be suitable for general deployment on applications larger than 1,000 function points in size or for applications with hundreds of provable but unstable algorithms that might change during development.

Scrum Sessions

Usage:	> 90% of Agile applications
	< 20% of non-Agile applications
Defect removal efficiency range:	
Minimum =	< 35%
Average =	55%
Maximum =	> 70%
Preparation time:	< 15 minutes per participant
Execution time:	< 30 minutes per participant (sessions limited to 15 minutes)
Synergies:	Agile projects < 2,000 function points in size
Counter indications:	Large systems > 50 personnel and > 1,000 customers

The word *scrum* comes from the field sport of rugby. The idea of scrum is that the whole team moves downfield at the same time. The word scrum was first applied to software by Hirotaka Takeuichi and Ikuro Nonaka in about 1986. Other researchers such as Ken Sutherland and Jeff Schwaber also used the analogy of rugby and the word scrum when discussing the principles of Agile development.

Because rugby is a team sport, software applications developed using the scrum approach also feature teams. The members of these teams include a "scrum master" who is a de facto project manager or coach, although the teams are self-organized; an embedded user representative or stakeholder; and a variable number of team members that can range from three to ten, but probably averages around five software engineers plus one or more specialists as needed. Among the specialists might be technical writers, business analysts, or database analysts, based on the nature of the application. For embedded software applications, one or more of the specialists might be an electrical or mechanical engineer.

In theory Agile and scrum teams are self-organized and consist of generalists. But it is not possible to develop specialized applications such as embedded software or financial software without some specialization.

Projects that use Agile and scrum principles are decomposed into small work units called "sprints" that can be developed in a two-week period (more or less). The embedded user provides the requirements for each sprint. At the completion of a sprint, the source code and supporting documentation should be ready to go into production.

A feature of scrum that has an impact on pretest defect removal is the use of daily scrum meetings or "stand ups." These are normally limited to 15 minutes, and during these meetings each member describes what he or she has done since the day before, what they plan to do next, and any problems, bugs, or issues that might slow them down. It is this last segment or the description of problems that might slow things down that is relevant to pretest defect removal.

Another feature of the scrum development method that benefits defect removal is test-based development, which consists of writing test cases before writing the code itself. The effectiveness of test-based development will also be discussed in the next chapter on testing, but early concentration on test cases prior to coding serves as both a defect prevention mechanism and a pretest defect removal mechanism. Test-driven development (TDD) is a useful byproduct of the scrum and Agile methods.

Although the concept of scrum originated in an Agile context, the usefulness of the daily scrum meetings has expanded outside of Agile, and scrum meetings are now used by other methods such as the Rational Unified Process (RUP) from time to time. Indeed, one of the reviewers of this book works for an organization using scrum and RUP concurrently.

For software applications up to about 2,000 function points in size, the Agile and scrum methods have proven to be both popular and successful. For larger applications in the 10,000 to 100,000 function point size range, team sizes go up to 65 personnel for 10,000 function points and around 700 personnel for applications of 100,000 function points.

The larger sizes obviously require numerous teams and also makes the two-week sprints difficult to accomplish. Further, for large applications there may be more than 100,000 users, and therefore no single embedded user can possibly identify requirements for major applications above 10,000 function points in size.

Agile does include methods for scaling up to larger projects. However, for these larger projects, alternative approaches such as the Team Software Process (TSP) seem to be more effective in terms of quality levels.

As with any methodology, Agile and scrum have failures as well as successes. A Google search on the phrase "Agile failures" and "scrum failures" turns up about as many reports as the opposite phrase "Agile successes" and "scrum successes."

There are methods under the Agile umbrella for dealing with larger applications, but they are not used often enough to judge their effectiveness. Also, the sparse data typically collected under the Agile method has resulted in a shortage of empirical data on actual effort, costs, and delivered defect rates.

The overall defect removal efficiency levels associated with scrum might be higher than those shown here, but the Agile and scrum development teams are not very rigorous on capturing defect removal data, so not much gets published.

Poka Yoke

Usage:	< 1% of U.S software applications
	> 25% of Japanese software applications
Defect removal efficiency range:	
Minimum =	< 25%
Average =	40%
Maximum =	> 50%
Preparation time:	< 3 minutes per participant
Execution time:	> 5 minutes per participant
Synergies:	Higher CMMI levels, RUP, TSP, Agile
Counter indications:	None

The phrase *poka yoke* is Japanese. The term poka means error or mistake, and the term yoke means prevent or eliminate. In other words, poka yoke refers to methods that can eliminate common errors.

The poka yoke concept was created by Shigeo Shingo and was originally utilized by Toyota for correcting errors in manufacturing stages. More recently, the concepts of poka yoke have been applied to some Japanese software projects and also to some European and American software projects. For example, Hewlett-Packard uses poka yoke for software applications that are intended to operate in multiple countries and use multiple national languages.

The original poka yoke method identified three kinds of corrective procedures:

1. Contact

2. Fixed-value

3. Motion sequence

The contact method uses physical attributes such as shape or surface texture and ensures that parts are properly aligned. For software projects the logical equivalent of the contact method would be to ensure that critical topics such as security are included in all major deliverables such as requirements, design, code, and test cases.

The fixed-value method uses counts of occurrences such as spot welds and ensures that the correct numbers of steps have been used. For software projects the logical equivalent of the fixed value method would be check lists of topics that are to be included in requirements and design documents, plus check lists for code that ensures that topics such as comments have been included in standard volumes.

The motion sequence method takes the flow of actions during an assembly phase into consideration and makes sure that they are performed in proper sequence. There are several logical equivalents for the motion sequence method. At the highest level this approach would ensure that a full set of pretest defect removal activities and test stages are utilized based on the size, type, and class of software. At lower levels this approach would ensure that a specific pretest removal operation such as a design inspection followed the normal protocols of preparation lead times, number of hours per inspection session, time for post inspection defect repairs, and accumulation of quantitative data on defects found and hours spent.

An important recent set of findings that could be melded into the poka yoke approach would be a checklist of the 25 common coding defects identified by MITRE and the SANS Institute. Every software engineer should receive this checklist and also receive training in how to avoid these 25 problems.

The first example of poka yoke in manufacturing in the 1960s solved a problem for assembling a switch with two buttons that had springs to restore the buttons to their original positions after being pushed. Sometimes the assembly workers would accidentally fail to install one of the springs, so when the defective switches reached customers, they had to be disassembled and reassembled, at considerable cost.

The original manufacturing sequence called for the worker to take two springs from a parts bin and then assemble the switch. Because the springs were taken from the parts bin one at a time, sometimes the worker would forget a spring.

The poka yoke solution was to place a small bowl next to the switch. The first action performed by the assembly workers was to place two springs in the bowl. By using the bowl prior to starting assembly, it became almost impossible for the worker to forget to install both springs.

This rather simple solution illustrates the philosophy of poka yoke. Look for simple and inexpensive solutions that will either prevent defects or eliminate them quickly and easily. In other words, poka yoke is about simplifying complex processes, not developing elaborate schemes.

The poka yoke method and philosophy seem to be a good fit for software applications, and it is hoped that poka yoke will attract wider attention as its successes become more widely known.

Kaizen

Usage:	< 10% of U.S software applications
	> 75% of Japanese software applications
Defect removal efficiency range:	
Minimum =	< 50%
Average =	75%
Maximum =	> 85%
Preparation time:	> 16 hours per participant
Execution time:	> 10 hours per participant
Synergies:	Higher CMMI levels, RUP, TSP, Agile, XP
Counter indications:	Waterfall

Considering that Japan is an island country with minimal natural resources used by modern industry, the fact that it has developed one of the strongest economies in world history is largely intertwined with the fact that Japanese products have also achieved the highest quality levels in world history for manufactured products.

Although Toyota's recent problems with braking systems have damaged the reputation of Japan and Toyota itself, a great many quality methods either originated in Japan or were first deployed in Japan. Among these can be found Kaizen, poka yoke, Quality Circles, and Quality Function Deployment (QFD).

The success of modern Japanese products in electronics, automobiles, motorcycles, shipbuilding, optics, and other complex devices may lead to the conclusion that the quality of Japanese manufacturing is a recent phenomenon. However, Japan has a history of quality and craftsmanship that is several thousand years old.

In a number of technologies such as lacquer ware, silk production, ceramics, steel and sword making, fine carpentry, and jewelry making, Japanese quality levels have been high for as long as such artifacts have been created. For example, the steel itself and the quality of Japanese swords produced more than a thousand years ago rank among the best in human history.

In the United States it is common to take some credit for the quality of Japanese manufactured goods considering the work of the Americans W. Edwards Deming and Joseph Juran was so influential among Japanese manufacturers in the late 1940s and early 1950s.

However, neither Deming nor Juran would even have been listened to if there had not already been a strong interest in quality on the part of their Japanese students. (This explains why Deming and Juran were initially ignored in the United States until after their methods had been demonstrated in Japan.) What Deming and Juran accomplished was essentially showing how a strong personal drive to achieve quality could be channeled toward large-scale production where products were created by huge teams of workers rather than by individual craftsmen working alone.

Deming and Juran facilitated the industrialization of Japanese quality in large-scale manufacturing enterprises, but they did not have to awaken a basic interest in achieving high quality levels. That was already present in Japan.

The Kaizen approach is based on the view that improvements in final results can only be derived from continuous examination of both product quality and the process of development, followed by the steady chipping away of things that cause problems or obstacles to progress. In other words, careful measurement of quality, careful analysis of problems and their causes, followed by the elimination of those causes, can gradually lead to excellence.

The Kaizen concept is the exact opposite of the "silver bullet" approach that is so common in the United States. (The phrase "silver bullet" is based on a famous horror movie called *The Werewolf* where bullets made out of silver were the only thing that could kill werewolves. The phrase was applied to software development by Fred Brooks in his famous book, *The Mythical Man-Month*.)

One of the reviewers, Tom Poppendieck, made an interesting statement about the difference between Japanese and American methods: "The Western approach is to define an ideal process and then attempt to get everyone to comply. The Eastern approach is to start where you are, and then relentlessly improve, paying attention to and fixing even small problems because big problems result from the unfortunate alignment of small problems."

In the United States, there is a tendency to focus on one thing and assume that something like buying a new CASE tool, adopting the object-oriented paradigm, achieving ISO-9001 certification, or adopting Agile will trigger a miraculous improvement in software productivity, quality, schedules, or all three at once.

The Kaizen approach leads to a different method of progress in Japan compared to that in the United States. Kaizen is based on solid empirical data, statistical analysis, root cause analysis, and other methods that are neither trivial nor inexpensive. A substantial amount of time on the part of both management and technical workers in Japan is devoted to analysis of the way things are done and to evaluating possible improvements.

In the United States, by contrast, changes often occur almost like religious conversions based on faith. A topic will become popular and then sweep through companies and even industries whether there is tangible evidence of improvement or not.

In a software context, the onsite work that one of the authors has done in Japan indicates a tendency toward careful gathering of requirements and somewhat more careful design of software applications than U.S. norms, with a corresponding reduction in front-end defect levels.

For programming itself, Japanese programmers, U.S. programmers, and European programmers are roughly equivalent in making errors, although obviously there are huge personal differences in every country. However, Japanese programmers tend to be somewhat more industrious at desk checking and unit testing than is typical in the United States, with a corresponding elevation in defect removal efficiency. Very noticeable is the fact that "bad fix" injection rates tend to be lower in Japan than in the United States. Only in the case of documentation errors does the balance of software defects favor the United States.

Most Japanese programmers would be quite embarrassed if they turned over source code to a test or quality assurance group that would not even compile properly and had obvious bugs still present in it on the day of turnover. However, the phenomenon of programmers throwing buggy code "over the wall" to a test or QA group is distressingly common in the United States.

Table 4.8 gives rough differences between the United States and Japan, although the margin of error is high. It should be noted that much of one of the author's work with Japanese companies has been in the area of high-technology products and software and not so much with information systems, so there is a visible bias.

Of the six industries that stand out globally as having the best quality levels, one of the author's data from companies in Japan includes five: 1) Computer manufacturing; 2) High-end audio and television manufacturing; 3) Telecommunication manufacturing; 4) Aerospace manufacturing; and 5) Medical instrument manufacturing.

The authors have not been commissioned to explore Japanese defense and military software, although there is no reason to suspect that it would not also be part of the top six, given that military software has rather good quality levels in every country where studies are performed.

We also have sparse data from the Japanese commercial software houses. Another domain where we have no data is the Japanese computer and software game industry, although observations at a distance indicates that the game industry has better tool capacities than almost any other. Software game development is an interesting industry that has been on a fast track and has become extremely profitable. Studies of game software development would be useful, but, unfortunately, the authors have no clients in the game business.

Like every country, Japan is heterogeneous in terms of software practices and results. In general the large high-technology corporations do a creditable job on software quality (for example, Nippon Telegraph, Sony, Mitsubishi, Hitachi, Kozo Keikaku, or NEC) Even within this set, not every lab nor every project is identical.

When smaller companies are examined, the results vary widely, just as they do in the United States and Europe. However, the tendency to deal with requirements and design somewhat more formally than is common in the United States does tend to occur rather often, as can be seen by the following rough comparison in Table 4.8.

Table 4.8 *Comparison of U.S. and Japanese Software Defect Potentials and Defect Removal Efficiency Levels*

(Defects expressed in terms of defects per function point)			
	U.S. Software Averages	Japanese Software Averages	Difference
Requirements	1.00	0.60	−0.40
Design	1.25	1.15	−0.25
Code	1.75	1.75	0.00
User documentation	0.60	0.75	0.15
Bad Fixes	0.40	0.25	−0.15
TOTAL DEFECTS	5.00	4.50	−0.50
Defect Removal Efficiency	85%	93%	7.0%
Delivered Defects	0.75	0.32	−0.43

The average software quality results in Japan are somewhat superior to average software quality results in the United States or anywhere else for that matter. However, the best-in-class U.S. companies such as AT&T or Microsoft and the best-in-class Japanese companies such as Hitachi, Sony, or Nippon Telegraph are virtually indistinguishable in final software quality results, even if they approach quality in slightly different ways.

It is a significant observation that for high-technology products at least, the Japanese attention to software quality tends to minimize time-to-market intervals and allows Japanese products to enter new markets slightly faster than any country from which we've collected data.

There is a tendency in the United States to be pejorative toward successful competitors. Many U.S. analysts have asserted that Japanese industries tends to be "fast followers" rather than leaders of innovation. This is a dangerous fallacy. The per capita rate of inventions and major patents (including U.S. patents) in Japan is approximately equal to that of the United States. In a number of high-technology arenas Japanese innovation has been world-class and outpaced other countries such as the United States.

One of the precursor methods for examining quality is that of "quality circles." It is interesting that quality circles have been successful and widely used in Japan but have not been as successful in the United States. No doubt there are sociological differences that explain this phenomenon, but one obvious reason is that U.S. workers are not trained as well as their Japanese colleagues in basic quality control methods.

The concept of quality circles originated in the manufacturing and high-technology sectors where it has proven to be valuable not only in Japan but also in the United States and Europe. The early quality circle approach surfaced in the 1950s as Japan began to rebuild major industries that were damaged during World War II.

The fundamental concept of quality circles is that of a group of employees who work in the same general area and share data and ideas on improving the quality of their areas' products and processes.

Quality circles are not just casual social groups, but are actually registered by a national organization in Japan. The quality circle concept is supported by the Japanese government and the executives of all major corporations.

The number of Japanese companies with quality circles tops 80%, and perhaps one Japanese worker out of every three is a member of a quality circle. Although there is some ambiguity in the data, it appears that quality circles in Japan are perhaps an order of magnitude more common than in the United States.

In Japan quality circle members receive formal training in statistics, graphing methods, and root cause analysis, and they also receive useful tools such as statistical packages, chalk boards, graphic templates, and the like. U.S. workers, and especially U.S. software workers, have nothing like this kind of training in quality analysis.

In Japan quality circles have also been applied to software and have been generally successful. In the United States quality circles have been attempted for software, but most U.S. software quality circles have been short-lived and have faded out in fewer than six months.

Psychological studies of U.S. programmers and software engineers such as those by Dr. Bill Curtis and Dr. Gerald Weinberg have found a very low need for social interaction. Because quality circles are built upon social interaction, this could explain why quality circles have not been visibly successful for U.S. software.

During his visits to Japan and to Japanese software factories and labs, one of the authors observed a somewhat more extensive set of social interactions among the Japanese programming community than is common among domestic U.S. consulting clients.

Pair Programming

Usage:	< 10% of U.S academic applications
Defect removal efficiency range:	
Minimum =	< 05%
Average =	10%
Maximum =	> 15%
Preparation time:	> 8 hours per participant
Execution time:	> 8 hours per participant
Synergies:	Small academic applications < 100 function points
Counter indications:	All applications > 1,000 function points or teams > 100 people

The idea of pair programming is for two software engineers or programmers to share one workstation. They take turns coding, and the other member of the pair observes the code and makes comments and suggestions as the coding takes place. The pair also has discussions on alternatives prior to actually doing the code for any module or segment.

Pair programming originated as an academic experiment and is used primarily for small test applications or for experiments sponsored by universities. There is little if any use of pair programming among commercial and industrial software groups, although some XP and Agile teams have used it. To date, almost all of the data for pair programming comes from experiments where the software is less than 100 function points in size. Among the authors' clients, the largest use of pair programming involved only about a dozen people. Although there may be large-scale uses of pair programming, the authors have not encountered this method on large systems with teams of several hundred mixed personnel. Since 2008 and the recession, a majority of clients are downsizing rather than hiring.

The method of pair programming has some experimental data that suggests it may be effective in terms of both defect removal and also defect prevention. However, the pair programming method has so little usage on actual software projects that it is not possible to evaluate these claims as of 2011 on large-scale applications in the 10,000 function point size range.

Google search phrases such as "success of pair programming" and "problems with pair programming" turn up about equal numbers of studies and citations. However, pair programming does tend to attract interest and perhaps should be examined more carefully, assuming that the recession eases and personnel increases start up again.

What the literature on pair programming lacks is specific information on topics such as

1. The largest numbers of pairs used on a single project

2. The number of pairs where results were better than single programmers

3. The number of pairs where results were equal to single programmers

4. The number of pairs where results were worse than single programmers

5. The number of pairs that were dissolved due to personal disputes

6. The use of the pair concept for other deliverables such as design or test cases

7. The impact of ancillary methods such as inspections and static analysis

8. The use of other groupings such as three or four concurrent workers

University-sponsored studies have found that pair programming develops code segments with about 15% fewer defects than individual programmers. Coding time is also shorter for pairs, although total effort is higher.

However, the experiments that showed improvements for pair programming used only a single variable—that is, pairs of programmers versus individual programmers. There was no attempt to include other methods such as static analysis, peer reviews, or formal code inspections, all of which reduce defects and are widely used to support the work of individual programmers.

Individual programmers whose work is examined via peer reviews or formal inspections tend to have lower defect levels than those reported for pair programming. Peer reviews also yield shorter schedules and lower costs than pair programming. Inspections result in many fewer defects than pair programming and have approximately the same amount of effort and the same schedule.

Individual programmers who use static analysis tools also have many fewer bugs than pair programmers and also much shorter schedules and much lower costs.

Single-variable experiments are not really adequate to judge the effectiveness of pair programming or any other software methodology.

On the surface, pair programming comes close to doubling the effort required to complete any given code segment. Indeed, due to normal human tendencies to chat and discuss social topics, there is some reason to suspect that pair programming would be more than twice as expensive as individual programming.

Pair programming has only been applied to coding and not to other software development activities. It is difficult to imagine how large development teams would react to having pairs develop the code when all other work products are developed individually or by working teams.

In other words, the "pair" concept has not been utilized for requirements, architecture, software design, database design, and user documentation. Because these activities have larger staffs and are more expensive than the code itself, the use of pair programming would probably not be effective for large systems in the 10,000 function point size range in which programmers are normally less than 50% of the total team.

A study commissioned by AT&T and performed by one of the authors together with colleagues was to identify the number of technical occupation groups employed by major software organizations. The study found more than 75 distinct occupation groups. Examples of the various occupation groups include the following 25:

1. Architects (Software/Systems)

2. Business analysts

3. Capability Maturity Model (CMMI) Specialists

4. Configuration Control Specialists

5. Cost Estimating Specialists

6. Database Administration Specialists

7. Education Specialists

8. Embedded Systems Specialists

9. Function Point Specialists (certified)

10. Graphical User Interface (GUI) Specialists

11. Integration Specialists

12. ISO Certification Specialists

13. Maintenance Specialists

14. Customer support Specialists

15. Microcode Specialists

16. Network maintenance Specialists

17. Performance Specialists

18. Project librarians

19. Software engineers

20. Software Quality Assurance (SQA) Specialists

21. Security Specialists

22. Systems Analysis Specialists

23. Technical Writing Specialists

24. Testing Specialists

25. Web Development Specialists

An unanswered question from the literature on pair programming is whether or not the same concept would be relevant to the many other occupation groups that participate in software projects.

Until additional information becomes available from actual projects rather than from small academic experiments, there is not enough data to judge the impact of pair programming in terms of defect removal or defect prevention. Given that alternatives exist with better data and better results (peer reviews, static analysis, and formal inspections), the pair programming method looks like a method that costs more than it returns value.

Client Reviews of Specifications

Usage:	< 50% of U.S software applications
Defect removal efficiency range:	
Minimum =	< 15%
Average =	25%
Maximum =	> 45%
Preparation time:	> 2 hours per participant
Execution time:	> 4 hours per participant
Synergies:	Agile, CMMI, RUP, TSP when clients are available
Counter indications:	Applications such as embedded where clients are indirect

One of the authors often works as an expert witness in lawsuits for software projects that were cancelled and never finished or for projects that never worked successfully after they were deployed.

It is an interesting phenomenon that in almost all of these lawsuits the defendants (who were software outsource vendors) charged that the plaintiffs (that is, the customers) failed to review designs and other documents in a timely manner or did not point out any problems during those reviews. Indeed, in a few cases the defendants claimed that the plaintiffs actually approved the very materials that were cited when the litigation was filed.

The software quality literature is essentially silent on client reviews, even though client reviews are fairly important for applications that clients commission and pay for. Further, client reviews are among the very oldest forms of pretest defect removal and have been used since the earliest known computer programs in the 1950s.

Not every software project has reviews by clients or end users. Such reviews are common for information technology applications, which are funded by clients or by client executives. However, for commercial applications and for embedded applications, there may not be any clients during development. Some of these applications are built on "spec" in the hope that they will create new markets, rather than being developed in response to explicit client requests.

For applications that are original inventions (such as the first spread sheet, the first search engine, or the first software cost estimation tool), the "client" was the inventor personally. End users did not even know about the inventions until the applications were released to the outside world. As it happens, some of these original inventions went on to attract millions of users and become very successful commercial applications.

The major items that clients review during software development projects that are directly funded by clients include these 12 items:

1. Requirements

2. Requirements changes

3. Architecture

4. High-level design, user stories, use cases

5. Data flow and data structure design

6. Development plans

7. Development cost estimates

8. Development quality estimates

9. Training materials

10. HELP text and help screens

11. Features of COTS packages

12. High-severity bug or defect repairs

Clients are not usually asked to review the inner workings of software applications such as

1. Detailed designs

2. Legacy source code

3. Reused source code

4. New source code

5. Test scripts

6. Test cases

7. Low-severity bug reports

Client reviews of software artifacts vary widely, and there are no "standard" methods that describe how these reviews take place. Indeed, there are no international standards for client reviews and also no formal training or certification.

There are also no benchmarks for client reviews given that most companies do not record either numbers or the costs of the defects that are found by clients or the effort expended in finding them. In fact, the data used in this section comes primarily from depositions and discovery documents produced during software breach-of-contract lawsuits.

For financial applications in large U.S. companies, there are some regulations associated with Sarbanes-Oxley law that requires active governance of software projects by client executives and management. But "governance" is not a single method and varies from company to company. Overall, Sarbanes-Oxley seems to have resulted in more oversight and more careful reviews from software executives than previously occurred but only for financial software in major corporations. Sarbanes-Oxley is not used for small companies or government software.

Because clients pay for the software they are outside of the control of software project managers and software quality assurance. While many clients pay serious attention to software and are active and effective participants during reviews, others tend to assume (often incorrectly) that the software teams know what they are doing. Unfortunately, passive or partial reviews by clients is a feature in a distressing number of software lawsuits.

The bottom line for software client reviews is that they range from almost totally ineffective to fairly good. But the average seems to hover around a level that might be called "marginally adequate."

Independent Verification and Validation (IV&V)

Usage:	> 85% of U.S military and government applications
	> 5% of civilian software applications
Defect removal efficiency range:	
Minimum =	< 10%
Average =	20%
Maximum =	> 35%
Preparation time:	> 16 hours per participant
Execution time:	> 40 hours per participant
Synergies:	Military and government software applications
Counter indications:	Commercial software and nongovernmental projects

Independent verification and validation (IV&V) have been standard requirements for military and government applications for more than 25 years. Verification is also included in various international standards such as ISO-9000 and many newer standards as well. There is also a related requirement to perform independent testing.

The operative word "independent" usually means that an external company or third party is hired to review the work of a software contractor. The reason that the verification work is assigned to an independent company is to ensure objectivity. There is an assumption that internal verification might be less effective if the verification group and the development group are part of the same company, considering there would be a vested interest in giving favorable reviews.

While IV&V is often carried out remotely at the vendor's offices, some activities are carried out on site. NASA, for example, has an IV&V facility where all such studies are centralized.

The IV&V process depends heavily on checklists of various documents and items that should be produced, such as project plans, cost estimates, quality estimates, test plans, test scripts, and more than 100 others. The preliminary portion of an IV&V study is to ensure that all required deliverable items have in fact been produced by the vendor or contractor. This portion of IV&V work is usually done well. Because the checklists are thorough, the contractors are encouraged to be complete in producing deliverable items.

However, checklists are only part of the IV&V activities. It is also necessary for the IV&V team to read or review at least a significant sample of the delivered items—sometimes a 100% sample. This portion of the IV&V work is where defects are found.

While some of the IV&V reviewers may be experts in the kinds of applications they review, others are not. Indeed, a substantial number of IV&V reviews may be carried out by subcontractors whose knowledge of the application area is sparse. This is one of the reasons why IV&V defect removal efficiency levels are lower than some other forms of defect removal such as formal inspections.

If independent testing is part of the IV&V contract, then the IV&V company will also create and execute test cases. These independent tests are roughly equivalent to system testing, given they are intended to test the full application. From limited samples, IV&V testing is somewhat lower in defect removal efficiency than internal system testing and is usually in the 30% range.

IV&V is primarily a government-sponsored activity that originated because the government lacked internal skills to be sure that projects were adequate in quality assurance. There is a shortage of empirical data that compares the costs and defect removal efficiency levels of IV&V and independent testing against corporate internal reviews and internal testing.

It is interesting that corporations such as IBM that do not utilize IV&V usually have higher levels of defect removal efficiency than civilian government projects of the same size and type that do utilize IV&V. This is not a criticism of IV&V, which probably raises the defect removal efficiency of government software projects. It is a general observation that corporations are often more effective than government agencies in building large software projects. On the other hand, military software projects are usually equal to leading companies such as IBM in defect removal efficiency and better than civilian government agencies.

As might be expected, Agile projects are not a good match for IV&V. For one thing, Agile projects produce very few documents, so the IV&V checklists would not be effective. Another point is that the bureaucracy associated with IV&V is counter to the lean Agile philosophy. If government agencies make a shift toward Agile development, it will be interesting to see if an Agile IV&V method might be created, too.

Agile enthusiasts claim that the Agile approach creates all of the really important documents. This may be true, but government contracts and military contracts often require production of many more documents than are truly necessary.

Historically, government and military software projects have created about three times the total volume of documents as have civilian projects of the same size. Although document volumes have been reduced for the military as they attempt to follow civilian best practices, anyone who works for state governments or the federal government on a software project will no doubt be tasked with significant document demands that are counter to the Agile approach and perhaps technically unnecessary as well.

The software industry has been one of the most paper-intensive industries of the past two hundred years. Agile correctly identified much of paper as being irrelevant and possibly harmful. However, government regulations and mandates tend to lag behind technology itself.

Software Quality Assurance (SQA) Reviews

Usage:	> 85% of systems and embedded applications
	> 50% of large commercial applications
	< 15% of web and information technology applications
	< 5% of small applications below 1,000 function points
	< 3% of Agile projects
Defect removal efficiency range:	
Minimum =	< 35%
Average =	55%
Maximum =	> 65%
Preparation time:	> 16 hours per SQA participant
Execution time:	> 40 hours per SQA participant
Synergies:	Embedded, systems, IT, and military software
Counter indications:	Small projects < 500 function points in size

The phrase "software quality assurance" is ambiguous in common usage. The original meaning in companies such as AT&T, IBM, Boeing, Raytheon, and other large corporations is a separate group that reports to its own management chain and is responsible for measuring and ensuring the quality of products (including software) prior to release to customers. These SQA groups are tasked with measuring quality, teaching, participating as moderators in inspections, and reviewing test and quality plans. The only do limited and specialized testing.

In these companies the SQA group is separate from the testing organization. SQA reports to a vice president of quality, while testing reports to project management. The reason for separate reporting is to ensure that SQA personnel cannot be coerced into giving favorable reviews to projects with low quality due to threats by their own managers.

A more recent definition that is common among smaller companies is to use "software quality assurance" as a synonym for testing. In this situation SQA refers to an ordinary test group that reports to project management. In this situation there will probably not be a VP of quality.

Among the 600 or so enterprises comprising the authors' client bases, fewer than about 250 have any kind of formal quality assurance departments, and more than 350 either have no SQA function or assign SQA duties to development personnel.

Even the companies with SQA departments do not utilize their services on every project or even on every class of project. While most external projects that go to customers have some kind of SQA analysis applied, internal web projects, information technology projects, building local internal tools, and some incoming software from contractors or vendors may have no visible SQA activity. Even for products that go to customers, SQA involvement may be limited to larger projects or those viewed as mission-critical. This is due to a chronic shortage of SQA personnel, made worse by the recession of 2008–2010.

In general, the projects that have formal SQA groups assigned report to a vice president whose title is probably Chief Technology Officer, CTO. The information system and web projects that usually lack formal SQA usually report to a vice president whose title is probably Chief Information Officer, or CIO.

This is a statement based on observations, but of course there are exceptions. There are some CIOs who have SQA organizations. There are a few CTOs in small companies that lack a formal SQA organization. But for companies with more than 1,000 total software personnel and that build both product and internal software, the product side is at least five times more likely to have a formal SQA group than the internal information technology side.

The empirical results of having formal quality assurance departments range from very good to negligible. The very good results come from well-staffed and well-funded software quality assurance groups that report directly to a VP of quality and are able to take a proactive role in quality matters.

The negligible results come from understaffed "token" SQA groups, some of which have only one or two employees, even for software organizations with more than 500 total software personnel.

In between are SQA groups whose staffing levels range from less than 1% of total software employment to about 3% of software employment. At the low end of SQA staffing, only a few reviews of critical projects can be accomplished. At the high end of SQA staffing, SQA reviews, participation in inspections, and limited or special testing can occur for important projects but not for 100% of all projects.

Three important issues regarding software quality assurance groups are: 1) Where should they be placed organizationally? 2) How big should they be for optimal results? and 3) Should there even be a separate QA group, or should quality be an overall team responsibility?

There is some excellent software produced by small companies that lack quality assurance but have capable teams and know quality best practices. However, from studies performed in large companies, the size and roles of the software quality assurance groups tend to correlate with actual product quality, using defect detection efficiency (DDE) and defect removal efficiency (DRE) as the benchmarks.

The most effective quality assurance groups typically average about 5% of the total software staff in size. The top executive is usually a director or VP of Quality, who is a peer to other senior operational executives.

The following Figure 4.1 shows how an effective and active QA fits with other operating groups in high-technology companies such as computer manufacturers.

This diagram assumes a large high-technology corporation that will have at least 5,000 total software personnel. The software engineering and product side will have about 1,250 technical personnel building and enhancing software products, 750 personnel maintaining existing software products; 500 personnel in testing roles; 250 in customer support; 200 building in-house tools and internal applications; 150 in quality assurance roles; and 500 in specialist roles such as technical writing, database administration, measurements, network management, system administration, and the like. Thus, the product software personnel total to about 3,600 (of whom management and administrative personnel are assumed to comprise about 15%).

The information systems community would total about 1,000 personnel who are building and maintaining internal management information systems and web applications. This side usually lacks a formal SQA group, but between 250 and 500 of the IT personnel will be involved in testing.

Note that unlike the product side, the IT community often assigns development and maintenance work to the same teams, even though this approach optimizes neither development nor maintenance.

(The reason for this is that high-severity defects occur at random intervals and take precedence over planned development work. The need to return to planned development work sometimes makes defect repairs less thorough than needed. Of course, for high-quality software with few defects this is not usually a major problem. But for low-quality software, maintenance tasks will delay development.

A possible alternative might be to replace the teams that produce low-quality software with outsource vendors. In fact, this is a common reason for outsourcing.

The remaining 400 software personnel would comprise the staffs of the top executives and the VP level (roughly 100) and also various liaison and specialist personnel such as those responsible for training and education, standards, process improvements, productivity measurements, and the like.

The usual practice in the high-tech world is for the product software groups to report to their own VPs of software or Chief Technology Officers (CTO), while the information technology software groups report to a chief information officer (CIO).

Figure 4.1 highlights the overall top levels of executives and management observed in large high-technology companies.

Note that the QA organization would have its own chain of command up to the VP level and that the top Quality VP reports directly to the CEO. This is necessary to prevent coercion. It is an unwise practice to have the QA group subordinate to the executives whose products they are ensuring. You do not

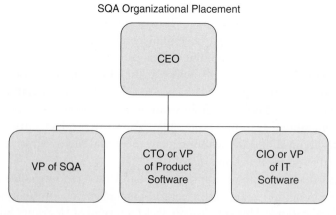

SQA Organizational Placement

Figure 4.1   *Software quality assurance placement within large enterprises*

want to have SQA appraisals and salary levels in the hands of the managers whose products are being assessed, for obvious reasons.

The SQA VP is responsible for more than software quality, of course, and may hold the title of "Vice President of Quality" if hardware quality is also included. The vice presidential position in Figure 4.1 is similar to the position Phil Crosby occupied when he worked for Harold Geneen, the Chairman of ITT, prior to founding his own company. It is worthwhile to read Phil's famous book *Quality Is Free* (Mentor Books, 1979) to get an idea of how a VP of quality operates in a large multi-national corporation.

Underneath the corporate VP of quality who handles both hardware and software would also be found a VP or director of software quality, depending on the overall size of the company.

An interesting anomaly in SQA placement is based on real-life experience that the SQA function is usually focused externally on the software products that reach customers. For reasons of corporate culture and historical accident, the SQA groups are seldom utilized on three key classes of software projects:

1. Information technology systems built for internal use by the company itself

2. COTS packages such as ERP packages acquired from vendors

3. Tools and testing software built for internal use by the company itself

When performing assessments and benchmark studies in large corporations, it is an interesting phenomenon that software reaching customers usually has much more rigorous quality control and much better testing than in-house software.

In high-technology organizations such as IBM, SQA executives have the authority to stop products from being shipped or even announced if the quality levels are below satisfactory corporate targets. While the development side can appeal, the appeal usually goes directly to the president or CEO (or a divisional president in really large companies).

Note that quality assurance is not just testing. Indeed, testing should normally be carried out in combination by the development teams themselves for unit testing, by testing specialists in a formal test organization for stress, regression, and system testing.

Although the SQA group does not handle the main stream of testing, the SQA group may have an independent test library and serve as an in-house independent test team. The SQA group might also handle usability testing and in large corporations might even run a special usability lab.

One important topic not often stressed in the literature, but interesting and significant, is the fact that the independent SQA organizations in really large companies (AT&T, IBM, Hitachi, Siemens-Nixdorf, and so on) actually do research and may even have formal quality research laboratories.

In fact, most of the "best practices" for software quality tend to originate within the SQA research labs of large multinational corporations. Just to cite a few examples of quality innovations coming out of SQA research labs, consider design and code inspections, joint application design (JAD), quality estimation tools, quality reliability models, quality function deployment (QFD), software defect severity levels, and the orthogonal defect measurement approach. Both the measurement of defect potentials and defect removal efficiency levels originated in IBM's SQA research labs in the early 1970s.

The SQA research labs are not usually large in number and seldom exceed more than 10 to 25 personnel. However, the researchers are usually free from day-to-day SQA tasks and concentrate most of their time on quality exploration and advanced technology development.

At IBM there was a very fruitful collaboration between the SQA research lab and the software development labs. Many joint studies and combined reports were produced. For example, the SQA research lab at IBM Palo Alto in conjunction with the development lab built IBM's first quality estimation model in the 1970s.

Another "best practice" in the software SQA domain is that of a quality measurement department. Here, too, the sizes are not large, and from about 5 to 15 personnel would handle the formal analysis and reporting.

One reason for assigning quality measurement to SQA instead of to developers is because having the SQA team collect the data ensures objectivity and lack of coercion. Someone collecting quality data who reports to a development manager may well be subjected to pressure if defect levels are embarrassingly bad.

Some of the kinds of measurement data collected by SQA measurement teams include but are not limited to

1. Software defects by origin

2. Software defects by calendar time period

3. Software defects by geographic region

4. Software defects by customer

5. Software defects by specific application

6. Pretest defect removal methods used

7. Pretest defect removal efficiency levels

8. Testing methods used

9. Testing defect removal efficiency levels

10. Defect prevention methods used

11. Defect prevention effectiveness

12. Reliability of software after release

13. Defect repair intervals for internal defects

14. Defect repair intervals for external defects

15. Cost of quality (COQ) and defect repair costs

It might be thought that such measures would be taken by development groups themselves, but this seldom happens in the United States. Even worse, in most of the litigation for breach of contract, not only are measures sparse and inadequate, but harmful data is often concealed from both clients and higher management until it is too late to fix the problems. Project management is the weak link in collecting useful data and also the primary source of concealed problems.

Normally, SQA groups are not involved with customer satisfaction measurements nor with team morale measurements. However, both customer satisfaction and team morale have good correlations with low defect levels and high levels of defect removal efficiency. SQA personnel assigned to specific projects, plus the software development, maintenance, and testing managers and team members provide the raw data for the SQA measurements.

The SQA measurement department analyzes the results, performs various statistical studies and correlation analyses and produces monthly executive reports and the quality portions of annual software progress reports.

Monthly quality reports show both current month and at least a 12-month rolling average of open and closed defects, severity levels, defects by product, by country, ages of defects, and a number of other basic statistical facts.

User satisfaction data is measured, too, but the data is usually collected by the sales and marketing organizations who are in direct daily contact with customers. Eventually, the user satisfaction and defect data come together for correlation analysis and special studies.

The quality measurement data and the user satisfaction data is consolidated with productivity, cost, and schedule data to put together an overall annual picture of software operations.

Quality data itself is reported monthly to the top executives of the company (including the CEO), but in addition there is an annual software report that shows all important aspects of software within the company—that is, portfolio size, software personnel on board, personnel turnover rates, quality, defect removal efficiency, user satisfaction, project failures versus successes, schedules, costs, and so on.

The recession of 2008 through 2011 has led to an unfortunate reduction in overall SQA staffing in the United States and in other countries, too. It is an unfortunate fact of life that specialists such as SQA, training specialists, technical writers, measurement specialists, and administrative personnel are usually the first to be let go during times of economic hardship. The bottom line is that an effective SQA team is a valuable asset that pays for itself by improving both defect prevention and defect removal.

Phase Reviews

Usage:	> 50% of large systems above 10,000 function points
	< 5% of small applications below 1,000 function points
Defect removal efficiency range:	
Minimum =	< 15%
Average =	20%
Maximum =	> 25%
Preparation time:	> 16 hours per participant
Execution time:	> 8 hours per participant
Synergies:	CMMI, RUP, and military software
Counter indications:	Agile and small projects < 1,000 function points in size

In the 1960s and 1970s when software applications began to grow larger than 100,000 code statements, the development efforts were divided into a number of discrete "phases," each of which produced deliverable items. Phase reviews were an integral part of *waterfall* development for large applications.

The numbers and definitions of phases varied from company to company, but a typical phase pattern would resemble the following:

Software Development Phases

1. Requirements

2. High-level design

3. Detailed design

4. Coding

5. Integration and testing

6. Installation and training

7. Maintenance and enhancement

A long-standing problem with the phase concept is that many critical activities span multiple phases. For example, software quality assurance spans at least five of the seven phases, project management spans all seven, and technical writing of user manuals spans at least four of the seven.

For companies building large applications such as IBM and AT&T, the end of each phase was finalized by a *phase review*, which covered business issues, technical issues, and quality issues.

The nominal purpose of phase reviews was to ensure that applications under development were more or less on time and within budget and would meet corporate quality goals when released.

The participants in phase reviews in companies such as IBM included development management, quality assurance management, divisional executives who were funding the project, and sometimes executives from marketing or sales if the application were a commercial product. If the application were an operating system component or involved hardware, then phase reviews would also include engineering management from the hardware side.

Because executives are quite busy, phase reviews were normally kept to a single business day. However, preparations for the phase review started several weeks or even a month prior to the date of the actual phase review.

The "voting members" of phase reviews who were responsible for determining if the project should continue on to the next phase or be terminated were all fairly senior executives. Technical personnel would, of course, give presentations and be available to answer questions, but the phase review decision makers were normally directors, vice presidents, and senior management.

Because quality and defects were part of the phase review process, the preparations for phase reviews included fairly careful analysis of all defects discovered during the phase that was being reviewed, plus projections of potential future defects. This is why phase reviews are included under the heading of pretest defect removal. The phase reviews themselves did not find very many defects, but the preparation leading up to the phase reviews often found and eliminated a significant number of defects.

Unfortunately, over time phase reviews began to lose effectiveness and became somewhat perfunctory rather than rigorous. Because development executives had a vested interest in passing the phase reviews and moving to the next phase, there was a gradual tendency by development management to whitewash problems or at least push the problems forward to the next phase by asserting that they were under control and could be fixed downstream.

Dr. Fred Brooks' classic book, *The Mythical Man-Month*, provides an excellent overview of what life was like in IBM during the period when phase reviews were a major activity for large applications.

Having participated in a number of IBM phase reviews, the effectiveness of the reviews in terms of defect removal was largely dependent on the energy of the software quality assurance (SQA) team prior to the phase review. If SQA groups were energetic and effective, then the phase reviews would be effective in terms of defect prevention and removal.

Part of the SQA role would be to convince project managers that methods such as formal inspections should be utilized and that truncating test schedules because of delivery date pressure was a bad idea.

From time to time, the phase reviews would uncover serious quality issues. These might be disclosed during phase reviews, but they could not be resolved during them. What would occur is that the quality issue would be examined in depth by an audit team who would report back to the phase review members with recommendations.

One of the authors was part of such an audit team for an interesting quality problem. A project manager asserted that due to tight delivery schedules, formal inspections would not be held. The manager's assertion was that inspections would delay the start of testing, which was true. The local SQA manager objected to the elimination of inspections on the grounds that testing was not efficient enough to achieve corporate quality goals.

What the audit team found out was that components that were inspected prior to the start of testing did indeed start testing late, but they exited testing early with very few bugs or defects being found. Conversely, components that bypassed inspections started testing early, but they exited testing late due to excessive defects.

The conclusion and recommendation of the audit team to the phase review executives was that testing should be delayed until inspections were held and completed. Although this would delay the start date for testing of a number of components, the audit team provided data that the final end date for testing would not slip but would probably be a week shorter than originally planned. At the time, this was a counter-intuitive recommendation. It had been tacitly assumed by project management that test schedules were inelastic, and any delay in starting testing would automatically result in a delay in completing testing.

But based on the evidence presented, the phase review executives endorsed the proposal to delay testing until after pretest inspections were complete. The story had a happy ending because inspections were used and because test completion was indeed a week earlier than originally planned. Even better, post-release defect reports from customers were well below corporate averages.

Phase reviews can be effective methods of pretest defect removal if quality is included in the phase review and if the company has a good quality measurement program and a software quality assurance (SQA) group in place.

Phase reviews are not as likely to be effective for projects that do not measure quality or that lack SQA involvement.

Inspections (Requirements, Architecture, Design, Code, and Other Deliverables)

Usage:	> 75% of systems and embedded applications
	> 35% of large commercial applications
	< 5% of web and information technology applications
	< 5% of small applications below 1,000 function points
Defect removal efficiency range:	
Minimum =	< 65%
Average =	85%
Maximum =	> 97%
Preparation time:	> 3 hours per inspection participant
Execution time:	> 4 hours per inspection session per participant
Synergies:	Embedded, systems, and military software
Counter indications:	Agile projects; small projects < 500 function points in size

Formal inspections were developed by IBM in the early 1970s when it was noted that testing was not sufficient to achieve high quality levels for large applications in excess of 10,000 function points.

Inspections soon demonstrated very high levels of defect removal efficiency, plus added value in defect prevention and raising testing defect removal efficiency levels. Overall, formal software inspections have achieved the highest levels of defect removal efficiency of any known methodology.

A useful way of showing the combined impacts of various defect removal operations is to show the permutations that result from using various methods singly or in combination.

Because 4 factors generate 16 permutations, the results show that high quality levels need a multifaceted approach. Table 4.9 shows the cumulative defect removal efficiency levels of all 16 permutations of four factors:

- The phrases *design inspections* and *code inspections* refer to formal inspections following the protocols defined by Michael Fagan: that is, training of participants, careful selection of participants, materials delivered well prior to the inspection day, both a moderator and recorder present, adequate time and facilities provided, and defect statistics kept for subsequent analysis.

- The phrase *quality assurance* refers to an active software quality assurance group, as defined earlier in this chapter. That is, the SQA staff will be in the range of about 3% to 5% of the software development population so that each QA analyst will support no more than 20 to 30 developers.

- *Formal testing* refers to testing specialists under these conditions: 1) A test plan was created for the application; 2) The specifications were complete enough so that test cases can be created without notable gaps; 3) Test library control tools are utilized; and 4) Test coverage analysis tools are utilized.

The data shown in Table 4.9 is derived from empirical studies carried out in corporations whose quality data is precise enough for this kind of analysis. Examples of such companies include AT&T, Bellcore, Hewlett-Packard, IBM, Microsoft, Motorola, and Raytheon.

Table 4.9 *Defect Removal Efficiency Levels and Permutations of Four Factors*

		Worst	Median	Best
1	**No design inspections**	30%	40%	50%
	No code inspections			
	No quality assurance			
	No formal testing			
2	No design inspections	32%	45%	55%
	No code inspections			
	Formal quality assurance			
	No formal testing			
3	No design inspections	37%	53%	60%
	No code inspections			
	No quality assurance			
	Formal testing			
4	No design inspections	43%	57%	66%
	Formal code inspections			
	No quality assurance			
	No formal testing			
5	**Formal design inspections**	45%	60%	68%
	No code inspections			
	No quality assurance			
	No formal testing			
6	No design inspections	50%	65%	75%
	No code inspections			
	Formal quality assurance			
	Formal testing			
7	No design inspections	53%	68%	78%
	Formal code inspections			

		Worst	Median	Best
	Formal quality assurance			
	No formal testing			
8	No design inspections	55%	70%	80%
	Formal code inspections			
	No quality assurance			
	Formal testing			
9	Formal design inspections	60%	75%	85%
	No code inspections			
	Formal quality assurance			
	No formal testing			
10	Formal design inspections	65%	80%	87%
	No code inspections			
	No quality assurance			
	Formal testing			
11	Formal design inspections	70%	85%	90%
	Formal code inspection			
	No quality assurance			
	No formal testing			
12	No design inspections	75%	87%	93%
	Formal code inspections			
	Formal quality assurance			
	Formal testing			
13	Formal design inspections	77%	90%	95%
	No code inspections			
	Formal quality assurance			
	Formal testing			
14	Formal design inspections	83%	95%	97%
	Formal code inspections			
	Formal quality assurance			
	No formal testing			
15	Formal design inspections	85%	97%	99%
	Formal code inspections			
	No quality assurance			
	Formal testing			

(Continued)

Table 4.9   *(Continued)*

		Worst	Median	Best
16	Formal design inspections	95%	99%	99.99%
	Formal code inspections			
	Formal quality assurance			
	Formal testing			

As can be seen from the progression through the 16 permutations, achieving high levels of software quality requires a multi-faceted approach. No single method is adequate. In particular, testing alone is not sufficient; quality assurance alone is not sufficient; inspections alone are not sufficient. Although not shown in the table, static analysis alone is not sufficient, either.

However, if static analysis were used to replace code inspections in Table 4.9, the cumulative results would be almost identical. Inspections and static analysis are both highly effective methods for code defect removal. Because static analysis is about five times faster than formal code inspections, there is some debate about whether or not code inspections should be used if static analysis is being used.

In a situation where static analysis being used, it should be used first before inspections. The code inspections can be applied to the most critical modules or code segments. In other words, static analysis negates the need for 100% code inspections, but inspections are still valuable for perhaps 10% of the most critical code segments.

Because the ranges of defect removal efficiency levels are rather broad, it is of interest to discuss how many projects have achieved various levels of removal efficiency. Using sample data from 1,500 projects, Table 4.10 gives approximate distributions of defect removal efficiency. (Note that this data has a bias toward systems software and military projects because more companies in these domains keep defect removal efficiency data than for information technology, commercial, or outsource groups.)

The picture this data presents is interesting. Obviously, achieving high defect removal efficiency levels is a technical possibility since it has been done. Also obviously, quite a few companies do not know how to go about achieving high levels of defect removal efficiency because low levels of defect removal efficiency are far more common than high levels.

Although the results have nothing to do with software, a plot of the time 1,500 army recruits would need to run a mile would have a similar distribution. One or two of the recruits might be able to approach a four-minute mile, and maybe 25 or so in fewer than five minutes, but hundreds would have trouble running a mile in fewer than ten minutes. Probably close to 200 would fall out and not be able to complete a one-mile run at all. In both track and software, if you want to be really good, you have to work at it.

Table 4.10 *Distribution of 1500 Software Projects by Defect Removal Efficiency Level*

Defect Removal Efficiency Level (Percent)	Number of Projects	Percent of Projects
=> 99%	6	0.40%
95–99%	104	6.93%
90–95%	263	17.53%
85–90%	559	37.26%
80–85%	408	27.20%
< 80%	161	10.73%
TOTAL	1,500	100.00%

Although formal design and code inspections originated more than 35 years ago, they still are ranked among the best methodologies in terms of defect removal efficiency. (Michael Fagan, formerly of IBM Kingston, first published the inspection method together with colleagues Bob Kohli, Lew Priven, Ron Radice, and Roger Stewart.) Further, inspections have a synergistic relationship with other forms of defect removal such as static analysis and testing and also are quite successful as defect prevention methods.

Recent work on software inspections by researchers such as Roger Stewart, Lew Priven, Ron Radice, Karl Wiegers, Jerry Weinberg, and Gary Gack in the United States and Tom Gilb and his colleagues in Europe and the United Kingdom continue to support the early finding that the human mind remains the tool of choice for finding and eliminating complex problems that originate in requirements, design, and other noncode deliverables. Indeed, for finding the deeper problems in source code, formal code inspections still outrank testing in defect removal efficiency levels although static analysis achieves results that are comparable to inspections.

That being said, the experience and expertise of the inspection team plays a large part in the defect removal efficiency of the inspections. Top personnel with long experience outperform novices or those with less stellar abilities. Also, formal training of inspection personnel is a critical precursor to successful inspections.

Among our clients, about 125 enterprises out of 600 are using formal inspections more or less the way the method was designed and intended. However, another 200 are using semi-formal inspections, design reviews, peer reviews, structured walkthroughs, or one of a number of local variations on the inspection process.

The most effective use of formal inspections among our clients occurs in large corporations that produce systems software, such as computer manufacturers, telecommunication manufacturers, aerospace manufacturers, and the like. These companies have learned that if software is going to control complex physical devices, it has to have state-of-the-art quality levels, and only inspections can achieve the necessary quality.

Inspections originated as live meetings held in small conferences rooms with between three and eight participants, with five being the average number. In today's world of easy web access and tools such as Skype and webinar tools, remote inspections are possible. Lew Privin and Roger Stewart report that remote inspections do not match the defect removal efficiency of live inspections, but they are a great deal cheaper if any form of travel would be required. It is not yet clear if the reduction in efficiency for remote inspections is due to limits in the technology or because human group interactions tend to raise the efficiency levels.

Most forms of testing are less than 35% efficient in finding errors or bugs. The measured defect removal efficiency of both formal design inspections and formal code inspections is usually more than 65% efficient, or twice as efficient as most forms of testing. Tom Gilb, one of the more prominent authors dealing with inspections, reports that some design and code inspection efficiencies have been recorded that are as high as 88%. For some deliverables, inspections have even topped 97%, which no other method has achieved. So far as can be determined, this level of efficiency would be a "world record" that is never even approached by testing (with the possible exception of high-volume Beta testing involving more than 10,000 simultaneous Beta test sites).

A combination of static analysis, formal inspections, formal testing by test specialists, and a formal (and active) quality assurance group are the methods that are most often associated with those projects achieving a cumulative defect removal efficiency approaching or even higher than 99%.

Formal inspections are manual activities in which from as few as three to as many as eight colleagues go over design specifications page by page, using a formal protocol. Code inspections are the same idea but go over listings or screens line by line. To term this activity an "inspection," certain criteria must be met, including but not limited to

1. A moderator must be in place to keep the session moving.

2. A recorder needs to be present to keep notes.

3. Adequate preparation time must be allowed before each session.

4. Inspection sessions are limited to a maximum of four hours.

5. Records must be kept of defects discovered.

6. Records must be kept of preparation, execution, and defect repair times.

7. Defect data should not be used for appraisals or punitive purposes.

The minimum number of participants in a formal inspection is three: the moderator, the recorder, and the person whose work is being inspected.

The average number of participants is five: the moderator and recorder, the person whose work is being inspected, and two inspectors.

Due to the normal sociology of group dynamics, inspections with more than seven or eight participants tend to decline in effectiveness and also chew up resources at a faster rate than value is returned. Large group meetings are notoriously prone to getting off the track and moving into irrelevant topics. Therefore, the inspection moderator must be energetic and keep the sessions focused on the work at hand.

Although experts are better at finding defects than novices, inspections are such a powerful learning tool that if both experts and novices are part of the same inspection team, the novices will learn important information faster than in ordinary class-room training because they are learning about real-life problems in real time.

Any software deliverable can be subject to a formal inspection, and the following deliverables have now developed enough empirical data to indicate that the inspection process is generally beneficial:

- Architecture inspections

- Project development plan inspections

- Project cost estimate inspections

- Requirements inspections

- Design inspections

- Database design inspections

- Code inspections: new code

- Code inspections: legacy code

- Code inspections: COTS code

- Test plan inspections

- Test script inspections

- Test case inspections

- User documentation inspections

For every software artifact where formal inspections are used, they range from just under 50% to more than 85% in defect removal efficiency and have an average efficiency level of roughly 65%. A very small number of inspections have topped 95%, but these happened to include top performers and very experienced personnel.

Overall, inspections provide the best defect removal efficiency level of any known form of error elimination and cover the broadest range of deliverables. Static analysis achieves similar results for code defects, but only for about 25 programming languages out of more than 2,500.

For unknown reasons the life expectancy of programming languages is shorter than the life expectancy of many applications written in the languages. For example, in 2011 there are still extant applications written in mumps, chill, bliss, jovial, and coral. But hardly any programmers know these languages, and apparently no new work is being created using them.

The existence of so many programming languages makes maintenance much more difficult than it should be and does not improve development as much as the language designers claim.

What comes to mind in thinking about programming languages is that each language is aimed at a narrow class of problems. Because the software industry faces a wide range of problems, many languages are used.

Of the software applications analyzed, more than 50% used at least two languages (such as COBOL and SQL or Java and HTML). A few applications have used more than 12 languages concurrently.

An analogy to programming languages is perhaps pharmaceuticals. There are thousands of prescription drugs, but each one is approved only for a narrow range of medical conditions.

To continue, thanks to the flexibility of the human mind and its ability to handle inductive logic as well as deductive logic, inspections are also the most versatile form of defect removal and can be applied to essentially any software artifact. Indeed, inspections have even been applied recursively to themselves in order to fine-tune the inspection process and eliminate bottle necks and obstacles.

It is sometimes asked, "If inspections are so good, why doesn't everyone use them?" This is an important question, and its answer reveals a basic weakness of the software industry. Inspections have been in the public domain for more than 35 years. Therefore, no companies except a few training companies try to "sell" inspections. On the other hand, there are many vendors with elaborate marketing programs selling testing tools. If you want to use inspections, you have to seek them out and adopt them. There are few web advertisements, and no live salesmen will appear given that the inspection methodology is in the public domain.

Most software development organizations don't actually do research or collect data on effective tools and technologies. They make their technology decisions to a large degree by means of two methods: 1) adopting the current methods used by other companies, or 2) listening to tool and methodology vendors and adopting those where the sales personnel are most persuasive.

It is even easier if the sales personnel make the tool or method sound like a "silver bullet" that will give miraculous results immediately upon deployment with little or no training, preparation, or additional effort. Given that inspections are not sold by tool vendors and do require training and effort, they are not a "glamorous" technology. Hence, many software organizations don't even know about inspections and have no idea of their versatility and effectiveness.

Another reason for adopting technologies is because many other companies have adopted the same technology. The software industry tends to be somewhat "cultish" about software technologies, and new ones surface about every five years and sometimes become very popular for a few years. In the past we have seen methods such as Rapid Application Development (RAD), computer-aided software engineering (CASE), object-oriented development (OO), and more recently Agile development.

Because the software industry is very lax and seldom collects empirical data on the effectiveness of methods and practices, it usually takes a few years before methods either prove themselves to be useful or fall by the wayside and stop being used.

Over the past 20 years or so, the methods that were transient and quickly disappeared after a burst of initial usage and claims of success included RAD and CASE. Methods whose values have gradually been proven include the higher levels of the CMMI, the Rational Unified Process (RUP), the personal software process (PSP), and the Team Software Process (TSP). As of 2011 Agile and Scrum are both on a rapid growth path, but empirical data is still somewhat sparse.

While the rapid expansion of Agile is interesting, the increase in usage of Agile by larger and larger companies brings with it an increase in variations. As large companies such as IBM move toward Agile, the politics of the individual development labs will no doubt lead to local variations. Really large companies seldom do anything consistently in every location, and this may lead to progress by means of a kind of drunkard's walk. Effective variations will prosper while ineffective variations will fade away. The Agile literature is already divided into subcamps who have introduced variations into the earlier Agile concepts.

Both inspections and static analysis belong to the set of methods and practices that appear valuable over the long range. But as of 2011 formal inspections have a very slow growth path, and static analysis appears to be growing very rapidly in terms of both vendors and usage of static analysis tools.

The reason why static analysis is growing much faster than inspections is due to the marketing dollars being spent by the 30 or so companies that market static analysis tools. Both methods are effective, but static analysis exists in the form of commercial tools with active marketing and sales, while inspections exist as a public-domain methodology with little or no active marketing.

For mission-critical applications, both code inspections and static analysis are recommended prior to testing. In cases where both are used, static analysis should be used first, and then inspections would follow. It does not make sense to use human participants to find the kinds of mistakes static analysis tools can find in a few minutes.

When static analysis is used in conjunction with code inspections, the inspections tend to be used for critical modules and components that might comprise less than 10% of the total code volume in the application. In other words, static analysis will handle the entire application, and inspections will look for defects in key algorithms and critical features.

The companies that are most likely to use inspections are those that, for historical or business reasons, have some kind of research capability that looks for "best practices" and tries to adopt them. Another attribute of companies that use inspections is that they also build very complex physical devices that depend on software to operate: medical devices, aircraft flight controls, weapon systems, process control systems, automotive braking systems, and the like. If the need for quality is high and the risks or liabilities for low quality are severe, then inspections are the tool of choice.

It is a telling point that all of the "top gun" software quality houses and even industries in the United States tend to utilize pretest inspections. For example, formal inspections are very common among computer manufacturers, telecommunication manufacturers, aerospace manufacturers, defense manufacturers, medical instrument manufacturers, and systems software and operating systems developers. All of these need high-quality software to market their main products, and inspections top the list of effective defect removal methods.

One reason why inspections have proven themselves to be a success in terms of defect removal efficiency is because inspections include the collection of data on both defects and effort, and this has been true since the early 1970s. Table 4.11 shows 25 of the kinds of data items that are collected when using formal inspections.

The data collected when using formal inspections is probably better than the quality data collected by 90% of U.S. companies. Indeed, inspection data is a useful model for other kinds of defect removal activities.

Formal inspections collect a very large volume of useful information. One important rule is associated with inspection data. Because inspections are peer reviews and require candor and honesty, the data on defects found during inspections cannot be used by management for appraisals, evaluations, or personnel actions.

Table 4.11 *Software Inspection Data Collection*

1. Inspection team size (average)
2. Inspection team size (maximum)
3. Inspection team size (minimum)
4. Quantity of material inspected per session
5. Preparation lead time (days prior to inspections)
6. Number of inspections per team
7. Number of inspections per week
8. Number of inspections (total)
9. Number of security flaws found by inspection
10. Number of defects found by inspection
11. Number of defects fixed after discovery
12. Number of defects not fixed after discovery
13. Defect removal efficiency by inspection type
14. Defect origins (requirements, design, etc.)
15. Defect latency (time from discovery to repair)
16. Defect severity levels by inspection type
17. Root causes of defects by inspection type
18. Inspection preparation effort by inspection type
19. Inspection execution effort by inspection type
20. Defect repair effort by test inspection type
21. Defects repaired per time period
22. Defects found per team member
23. Defects repaired per team member
24. Bad-fix injections by inspection type
25. Invalid defects or false positives

Normally, someone from Software Quality Assurance (SQA) serves as the recorder, and the data is not made available to the managers of the participants, other than in aggregate or sanitized form. Managers are also not commonly invited to inspections and do not participate. One exception to this rule are managers or technical leaders who are also developers. In this case a manager's own work can be inspected. However, if the manager also participates in an inspection of someone else's work, care must be taken not to misuse the findings for appraisals or personnel actions.

Because inspections are so effective, most managers do not object to the fact that the data is not available for personnel issues. If the data were turned over to managers for personnel purposes, the inspection team would not be motivated to find defects, and the effectiveness and efficiency of formal inspections would be severely degraded.

Inspections are both efficient in finding defects and also cost effective. They should be added to the set of standard defect removal activities for all large or significant software projects.

Defects in Text Documents and Graphics

Errors of omission

Missing requirements

Missing security features

Errors of commission

Inconsistencies between components

Logic and control flow errors

Security flaws

Performance problems

Interface problems

Usability problems

Defects in Source Code

Errors of omission

Missing security checks

Missing calculations and algorithms

Missing comments

Missing checks for user errors

Errors of commission

Failure to validate user inputs for correctness

Control flow and branching errors

Memory management errors

User error-handling errors

Security flaws and vulnerabilities

Careless initiation or shut-down routines

Hard-coding of variables that should be in tables

As can be seen, formal inspections are quite versatile and can find almost any kind of problem that affects software applications. When companies start using formal inspections, there are some logistical issues that need to be dealt with:

- Inspections work best if participants receive formal training and have access to books and reference materials that describe the inspection process. The training should occur before the inspections start. Books and training materials should probably be ordered at least two weeks prior to holding the first inspection. This is true for ebooks as well as paper books. Formal training for inspections varies by instructor but is available in one-day, two-day, and three-day courses. Inspection training is also available online in the form of recorded webinars.

- Because multiple inspections will be taking place concurrently, there is a need for an inspection logistics coordinator who will control the rooms that are set aside for inspections.

- Because senior personnel and top experts will be in great demand for inspection participation, the logistics control coordinator needs to ensure that team members are not swamped by so many inspections that they interfere with regular work.

- Data collected about defects discovered, preparation time, and inspection effort hours needs to be turned in to the inspection logistics control point so that statistical analysis can occur.

- After inspections have been used for a period of time such as six to nine months, their effectiveness as defect prevention mechanisms will cut down on the numbers of defects that inspections find. Some inspections will find zero defects due to increased defect prevention.

- When inspection defects drop down significantly, there is a tendency by top managers to want to eliminate inspections on the grounds that they are no longer needed. This is a logistical error because within a few months defects will climb back up again.

- When inspection defects drop down significantly, it is possible to switch from 100% inspections to critical feature inspections and concentrate only on the 15% to 20% of the materials that are vital to the success of the applications being inspected.

- Inspection preparation and the inspection sessions will find defects, but they are not intended to repair the defects on the fly. Defect repairs are carried out by the developers after the inspection sessions and not during the inspection sessions. This is a logistical factor that keeps the inspections focused and concise.

- For source code inspections, the code to be inspected should already have been subjected to static analysis. Unit testing is normally a post-inspection activity, although sometimes the sequence is reversed. However, unit testing before inspections or before static analysis will be more costly than necessary.

- From time to time so many defects will be found that the inspection team will decide that the entire deliverable may need to be redeveloped. This does not occur often, but it can occur. When this does happen the inspection team will ask for a follow-on inspection of the revised materials.

- Because software requirements grow and change at measured rates of more than 1% per calendar month, inspections will be needed for significant new features based on new requirements. In the course of a complete software development cycle, about 10% of the formal inspections will be on new features that were added after the original inspection of the deliverable items. Sometimes the new features will require reinspection of older materials.

- After defects are identified during inspections, the developer agrees to repair the defects. At the end of each inspection the developer should project repair times. The moderator is tasked with following up to be sure that repairs have taken place. If the repairs are significant, reinspections might be needed.

It is useful to know the approximate amount of time needed for inspection preparations, inspections sessions themselves, and for defect repairs after the inspections are over. Table 4.12 provides approximate time interval ranges for a sample of inspection materials.

Note that the information in Table 4.12 is for each inspection participant. If there are five participants, the data applies to each of them individually. However, defect repairs only apply to the authors or developers of the materials. The other inspection participants do not repair the defects that are discovered via inspections, although no doubt they may offer useful suggestions to the developers.

Table 4.12 *Inspection Preparation and Execution Guidelines*

Deliverables	Preparation Units per hour	Execution Units per hour	Repairs per Defect
Requirements	3–10 pages	3–10 pages	1–3 hours
Requirement changes	4–15 pages	4–15 pages	1–3 hours
Architecture	3–10 pages	3–10 pages	2–4 hours
Architecture changes	4–12 pages	4–12 pages	2–4 hours
Initial design	4–12 pages	4–12 pages	1–3 hours
Detailed design	3 -10 pages	3 -10 pages	1–4 hours
Design changes	5–15 pages	5–15 pages	1–4 hours
UML diagrams	6–20 pages	5–12 pages	0.5–2 hours
Flowcharts	5–10 pages	5–10 pages	0.5–1 hours
Data flow diagrams	5–10 pages	5–10 pages	0.5–1 hours
Decision tables	2–6 tables	2–5 tables	0.5–1 hours
QFD diagrams	3–7 diagrams	3–7 diagrams	0.5–2 hours
Project plans	7–20 pages	7–20 pages	0.5–2 hours
Legacy code	75–125 LOC	75–125 LOC	1–6 hours
COTS code	60–100 LOC	60–100 LOC	1–5 hours
Low-level source code	50–125 LOC	50–125 LOC	1–6 hours
High-level source code	100–200 LOC	100–250 LOC	1–2.5 hours
Test plans	7–15 pages	7–15 pages	0.5–1.5 hours
Test scripts	4–12 pages	4–12 pages	0.5–2 hours
Test cases	100–150 LOC	100–150 LOC	0.5–2 hours
HELP screens	10–25 screens	10–20 screens	0.5–1.5 hours
Training materials	10–20 pages	10–20 pages	1–3 hours
Reference manuals	5–15 pages	5–15 pages	0.5–2 hours

To summarize what 35 years of empirical observations have shown, formal inspections rank as the one of the most effective known forms of defect removal. Inspections also cover the widest range of software deliverables. The human mind is more flexible and better able to detect defects and omissions than any other technique.

Formal inspections should be a standard part of software defect removal for all applications that handle important information or for all software applications that control embedded devices and have possible significance for human life and safety.

Inspections combine high levels of defect removal efficiency with a very favorable return on investment because inspections raise testing efficiency while lowering testing costs and shortening testing schedules. Inspected requirements and design documents also allow the creation of more complete test suites that will have better test coverage.

In the 1990s a method of studying defect densities was borrowed from biology and is known as the *capture-recapture method*. To estimate an animal population, researchers capture and tag a sample of animals in a specific area and then release them. Later, after the animals have had a chance to resume their normal dispersal patterns, another sample is caught. If the second sample captures 90% of animals already tagged, then it is safe to assume that the population is only slightly larger than the tagged sample. However, if the second sample only captures 1% of animals already tagged, it can be assumed that a large wild population exists.

The same method can be applied to software by tagging defects and then releasing them to be found again, either by other teams of inspectors or by down-stream testing. This method does yield useful results for predicting undiscovered or latent defects.

However, the kinds of data collected during inspections and testing also resembles another method used in biology. For migrating species that travel the same routes every year, counting a sample that moves past a fixed point at the same time each year can be used to predict the overall population growth or decline.

Thus, companies that have 10 or more years of reliable inspection and test data already know the approximate numbers of defects in various software deliverables. They can use the capture-recapture method too, if desired, but the accumulation of historical data over time yields similar results.

As early as 1970 a variation on the capture-recapture method was used at IBM. This method was based on creating deliberate defects and inserting them into software prior to inspections and prior to testing. If 100 artificial defects were inserted into a large code sample and function testing found 35 of them, it was probable that function testing was about 35% efficient.

However, a problem with artificial defect insertion is that "wild" defects may not resemble the "tame" defects that were injected. The capture-recapture method, on the other hand, deals with 100% wild defects, so there is no reason to doubt that marked and unmarked defects might be so different as to throw off the results.

Book and journal publishers have known for hundreds of years that authors have trouble finding their own mistakes. They also know that mistakes or defects irritate readers. As a result major journals such as *Fortune*, *Forbes*, *Scientific American*, and the *Journal of the American Medical Association* always use both copy editors and proofreaders. Obviously, they also use spell checkers and text analysis tools that evaluate readability such as those that produce Flesch readability scores or FOG index readability scores. These tools are used first prior to actual copyediting.

User Documentation Editing and Proofreading

Usage:	< 50% of large commercial applications
	> 50% of embedded and systems software
	< 5% of information technology or web applications
Defect removal efficiency range:	
Minimum =	< 55%
Average =	80%
Maximum =	> 95%
Preparation time:	> 0.5 hours per editor per document
Execution time:	> 2.5 hours per session per editor
Synergies:	Embedded, systems, and miltary software
Counter indications:	Agile projects; applications with few users

Copy editors are the first line of defense. They read manuscripts submitted by authors and look for errors of grammar, structure, or usage. These editors also question the origins of factual statements and ensure that mathematical errors are not present in tables or calculations or formulae.

Experienced copy editors are valuable assets to publishers and authors, and they can be more than 90% efficient in finding many kinds of defects. For example, during the production of this book copy editors went over every page and every table. From past experience with other books written by the same authors, copy editors make significant improvements in readability and also find an embarrassing number of technical problems, such as errors in tables or inconsistent data for the same topic discussed in different chapters.

Copyediting is somewhat slower than ordinary reading and usually is below a rate of about 100 words per minute. This is because the copy editor is constantly checking for consistency and errors.

Proofreaders are the final line of defense. They usually work in pairs with one proofreader reading aloud and the other checking the manuscript word by word. The use of pairs has been shown to be more than 90% efficient in finding accidental problems such as using "their" in place of "there" or other problems that elude automated spell checkers.

Proofreading takes place at the rate of spoken English (or other national languages) and therefore proceeds at a rate of only about 30 words per minute. Because proofreading involves two people, it is evident that proofreading is a relatively expensive operation.

Due to the recession and the reduced profitability of many newspapers and magazines, proofreading is becoming a dying art. Most papers have substituted automated tools for live proofreading, and this is true of many journals with financial problems. Top-ranked journals such as *Fortune* and *Scientific*

American still use copy editors and proofreaders, but many other journals can no longer afford to have both.

In a software context only a small percentage of companies employ professional technical writers, copy editors, and proofreaders. For the most part, the companies with fully staffed technical publication departments are large companies such as IBM, Raytheon, Hewlett-Packard, Oracle, and Microsoft. These companies produce large and complex software packages that require training materials prior to use reference materials during use, and active HELP facilities to deal with usage problems.

If a software user manual explains how to operate medical equipment or control complex financial applications, errors in the text or accompanying illustrations can have dangerous consequences.

Unfortunately, good technical writing is a fairly scarce skill. Probably less than 5% of the population can write really well. No more than 20% of the population can write well enough to create effective reference manuals. As a result, there is a fairly large market for technical writing consultants who can create good user manuals.

Smaller companies often use subcontract technical writing or bring in consultants to handle creation of user guides, training materials, and HELP screens.

One interesting business problem was noted by IBM in the 1970s. At the time technical writers were paid somewhat less than software engineers. But technical writers needed to understand programming, so all IBM technical writers received training in programming. It was soon noted that a significant percentage of these writers requested transfers into programming jobs due to the inequity in pay. The obvious solution was to pay technical writers and programmers the same amounts.

It should be noted that text reusability and internal plagiarism are not harmful within companies. IBM performed a survey of user opinions about various technical manuals for all of their software applications. After the results had been tabulated, IBM then collected copies of the ten technical manuals with the most favorable user comments and provided them to all technical publication departments in the company. IBM technical writers did not have to imitate the structure and format of these ten manuals, but they were encouraged to read them and emulate the features that made the manuals popular with customers.

The surveys found that manuals that matched customer usage patterns tended to get favorable reviews. In other words, the manuals started with installation of the software, then discussed initialization for first use, and then discussed the features that were most likely to be used. Shutting down the application and saving unfinished work were also discussed. While this sounds obvious, a surprising number of software and computer manuals tend to put installation and initialization information somewhere in the back as an appendix. Shut-down information is often not discussed at all!

For internal software built within companies for their own use, and for many web applications, manuals are created by software engineers or by amateurs who are not professional writers. Editing, if it happens at all, tends to be informal peer reviews. While this approach can be successful, it usually is not. However, due to economic forces augmented by the recession that started in 2008, informal technical writing by amateur software engineers is the norm and is likely to stay that way.

The bottom line on copyediting and proofreading is that several hundred years of empirical data show that they are both successful and top 90% in defect removal efficiency levels for text documents. Removal efficiency is only about 80% of UML and graphics due to the ambiguity of nontext materials.

Unfortunately, due to economic pressures made worse by the recession, copyediting and proofreading are seldom used in 2011 for software technical manuals and HELP text other than by major corporations that create large and complex software applications.

Automated Static Analysis of Source Code

Usage:	> 75% of systems and embedded applications
	> 75% of open source applications
	> 75% of games and entertainment applications
	> 75% of large commercial applications
	> 75% of web applications
	> 70% of Agile applications
	< 35% of information technology applications
	< 15% of legacy applications
Defect removal efficiency range:	
Minimum =	< 60%
Average =	85%
Maximum =	> 95%
Preparation time:	< 0.25 hours per code segment or application
Execution time:	< 0.25 hours per 10K of source code
Synergies:	All applications in languages supported by static analysis
Counter indications:	Applications in languages not supported by static analysis

Automated static analysis has become one of the leading methods for software defect removal from source code. The first citations about automated static analysis for source code seem to be from 1979 when a tool called "Lint" that analyzed C code was first released. From that point on, more and more static analysis tools became available. Not only were more static analysis tools developed, but more and more features were added to the tools.

The early static analysis tools analyzed code structure and syntax. However, many additional kinds of features have been added. Today's static analysis tools are rule driven and can check for security vulnerabilities, generate complexity metrics, and identify some potential performance bottlenecks. Some static analysis tools have more than 1,500 rules and allow users to add additional rules if needed.

Static analysis tools can also look at large-scale structural problems that are not easily detected by testing because they involve multiple layers and sometimes even supply chains.

Let's consider static analysis in the context of three basic types of software product quality.

1. **Functional Quality**: A measure of *what* the software does versus what it's supposed to do

2. **Nonfunctional Quality**: A measure of *how well* it does it versus how well it's supposed to do it

3. **Structural Quality**: A measure of how well it will continue to perform as it is meant to in the future

When it comes to the quality of the software product, functional quality alone is not enough. If all that matters is having the right functionality, then every car that lines up on the NASCAR starting grid would win the race! But of course, winning the race takes more than satisfying the functional specification—it takes superior performance in the real world.

Similarly, nonfunctional quality is not enough. Nonfunctional quality focuses on the visible behavior of the software, the availability and latency of critical transactions. While this is important (in addition to the software's usability), these performance indicators are skin deep. To equate them with product quality would be to equate, for example, the destruction left in the wake of an uncontrolled skid with the quality of the suspension system that was the root cause of this destruction.

Availability and latency are classic examples of "visible" or "above-the-waterline" metrics. They are rear-view mirror metrics with little or no predictive power. They tell you how the system is doing (symptoms) but not *why* things are going well (or badly).

On the other hand, structural quality measures how well the application is *designed* and how well it is *implemented* (the quality of the coding practices and the degree of compliance with the best practices of software engineering that promote security, reliability, and maintainability). Structural quality metrics track the root causes of application latency and availability. They are forward-looking metrics that enable us to control how an application performs, how readily it can be enhanced in response to urgent business requests, and how much it will cost to maintain.

Let's consider what structural quality would be for a house. In this analogy, structural quality would *not* be about the number of rooms or the way in which the rooms are furnished. Rather, structural quality would be about the engineering design (for example, where the load-bearing walls are placed, the strength and pliability of materials used) and how well the materials come together (the soundness of joints, the organization of the electrical and plumbing lines). A house with high structural quality is typically easy to maintain and extend.

In addition to traditional functional and stress or load testing, multi-tier IT business applications should also be subjected to an analysis of their critical structural quality characteristics. Participants in recent Executive Forums conducted by the Consortium for IT Software Quality (www.it-cisq.org) prioritized the structural characteristics of business applications they felt were most critical to measure and control. These characteristics were selected from among the static characteristics of software quality described in ISO-25010 (which updates ISO-9126). The five structural characteristics they prioritized are described as follows.

1. **Reliability:** Measures the degree to which an application performs its required functions under stated conditions for a specified period of time. Reliability also describes the robustness and resiliency of the application's architecture under conditions that would ordinarily cause an application to fail. Reliability is typically evaluated by operational measures such as the mean-time-to-failure. However, the causes of poor reliability are to be found in violations of good architectural and coding practice, which can be detected as static quality attributes of an application. Assessing the static attributes underlying an application's reliability provide an estimate of the level of business risk and the likelihood of potential application failures and defects the application will experience when placed in operation. Reliability prevents application outages, operational downtime, and errors that directly affect users, thus enhancing a company's business performance.

2. **Performance Efficiency:** Relates application performance to the amount of resources used under stated conditions, especially during operations. Performance efficiency is frequently measured by application response time or the amount of computing resources or bandwidth consumed

during execution. As was the case with reliability, the causes of performance inefficiency are often to be found in violations of good architectural and coding practice that can be detected as static quality attributes of an application. These static attributes predict potential operational performance bottlenecks and future scalability problems, particularly for applications requiring high execution speed for handling complex algorithms or huge volumes of data. Analyzing and remediating the causes of poor performance efficiency avoids loss of customer satisfaction from slow responses and the degraded performance of mission-critical business processes.

3. **Security**: Measures the degree of protection of information and data from unauthorized access or manipulation. Measures of security predict the likelihood an application can be penetrated by unauthorized people or systems. Many security vulnerabilities result from poor coding and architectural practices such as SQL injection or cross-site scripting. Analysis of these vulnerabilities in the source code can lead to prioritizing actions that optimize an application's security and the customer's confidence in the protection of their confidential information.

4. **Maintainability**: Measures the effort, cost, and accuracy of correcting, altering, or enhancing a business application. Maintainability includes concepts of modularity, understandability, changeability, testability, reusability, and transferability from one development team to another. Given that 50% of application maintenance activity is spent trying to figure out the structure and inter-relationships within the source code (Ben-Menachem, 1997), maintainability is a critical cost and time-to-delivery driver for IT. Improving maintainability is crucial for mission-critical applications where competitiveness is driven by tight time-to-market schedules. The more easily maintained an application, the less likely new defects will be injected into it during modification or enhancement, thus improving other quality attributes such as reliability and security.

5. **Size**: The volume or amount of intellectual property in a business application. Although size is not typically considered a quality issue, it is a critical attribute of software that figures into many calculations related to quality and productivity. Size has traditionally been reported as the number of lines of source code, which was challenged in Chapter 2. However, IT often prefers to report size as a measure that is more related to amount of value provided to the business. Function points were first

released in 1979 (Albrecht, 1979) as a measure of the functionality an application delivered to the business. Other metrics are also used for size, including but not limited to COSMIC function points (and a dozen other variations), use-case points, and the new RICE object points for very large ERP applications.

Many of the existing software measures count structural elements of the application that result from parsing the source code such as individual instructions (Park, 1992), tokens (Halstead, 1977), control structures (McCabe, 1976), and objects (Chidamber and Kemerer, 1994). However, measuring software characteristics such as performance efficiency, security, and maintainability also requires the ability to measure violations of good architectural and coding practice, which we will call "weaknesses." These weaknesses may not fail a test case, but they represent bad practices that under specific circumstances can lead to outages, performance degradations, security breaches, corrupted data, and myriad other problems (Nygard, 2007). A well-known example of weaknesses is the Common Weakness Enumeration (CWE.Mitre.org; Martin, 2001), a repository of weaknesses in the source code that makes applications vulnerable to security breaches.

The measurement of critical application characteristics involves measuring a blend of both weaknesses and structural elements in the architecture, coding, inline documentation, and other aspects of the application.

Because static analysis tools are fairly inexpensive (many are available from open source providers), very fast, and quite effective, they have become a mainstream method for code defect removal.

As of 2011 there are about 50 open source static analysis tools and 50 commercial static analysis tool vendors. Assuming that each static analysis tool has 100 companies for clients, and each company has 100 users of static analysis, the total would be about 1,000,000 users of static analysis tools in the United States. Because the total software population of the United States is about 2,400,000, that would indicate a significant market penetration.

An obvious question that might be asked by readers is, "If static analysis is so good, why isn't the market penetration 100%?" The answer to this is because of natural human resistance to new ideas even though they turn out to be extremely valuable.

A quick survey of inventions and discoveries shows that even world-changing technologies were sometimes rejected at the outset. For example, John Ericssonn, who was an early developer of screw propellers for boat propulsion had his prototype rejected by the British Admiralty. An earlier invention by Ericssonn, a steam-powered fire engine, was rejected by British fire brigades. So many of Ericsson's inventions were originally rejected that he went bankrupt and spent time in debtors' prison even though all of the rejected inventions later became successful. (Ericsson's most famous invention was the famous iron-clad gunboat, the *USS Monitor*, which fought the equally famous *USS Merrimac* in the first naval battle between ironclads.) Other inventions that had slow starts include the self-leveling naval canon, tank treads, vaccination, sterile surgical procedures, and the theories of evolution and continental drift.

Because of the low cost and high efficiency of static analysis tools, they have become the quality tool of choice for open source applications, which are often developed on a shoe string with very little discretionary funding.

There are four issues with static analysis tools that should be considered because they have an impact on tool usage:

1. Out of about 2,500 programming languages, the whole industry of static analysis tools supports fewer than 50. Many legacy languages such as APL, CORAL, CHILL, Bliss and the like are not supported or at least do not show up in web searches.

2. Static analysis tools have a tendency to report "false positives." That is to say, some of the reported defects found by static analysis tools are not defects but have been misidentified as defects. Currently, false positives seem to range between about 3% and 7%. Some of the tools can be adjusted for thoroughness, and false positives go up with defect removal efficiency.

3. In spite of being helpful in finding security flaws and vulnerabilities, there is a need for more rules and better analysis of security issues in source code.

4. Many applications are written in multiple programming languages. Some applications have more than 12 languages concurrently. An example of multiple languages for legacy applications would be COBOL and SQL. An example of multiple languages for modern applications would be Java and HTML. The point is that for static analysis tools, which examine source code, multiple languages add to the effort and reduce efficiency somewhat.

Table 4.13 shows a sample of 30 languages that cited static analysis support from surveying the Web for programming languages supported by static analysis tools.

The opposite case is shown in Table 4.14. This is a list of 30 languages for which web searches did not turn up any static analysis tool support. This does not mean that no static analysis tools exist that support these languages, but that the tools are probably fairly obscure or they would have turned up near the top of the search list.

Table 4.13 *Languages Supported by Static Analysis*

1	.NET
2	ActionScript
3	Ada 83
4	Ada 95
5	Apex
6	ASC
7	Basic
8	C
9	C#
10	C++
11	COBOL
12	Eiffel
13	Erlang
14	Fortran
15	Java
16	JavaScript
17	Jython
18	Links
19	Objective-C
20	Pascal
21	Perl
22	PHP
23	PL/I
24	Python
25	Ruby
26	Smalltalk
27	SQL
28	Visual Basic
29	XML
30	Xquery

Table 4.14   *Languages Not Supported by Static Analysis*

1	APL
2	Assembly
3	Awk
4	Bliss
5	CHILL
6	Clarion
7	Clipper
8	ColdFusion
9	CORAL
10	D
11	Dylan
12	Forth
13	Haskell
14	Hermes
15	Jovial
16	Lisp
17	Logo
18	Lua
19	Modula
20	Mumps
21	Oberon
22	Pop
23	Postscript
24	Prolog
25	QBE
26	Rexx
27	Sather
28	Scheme
29	Scheme
30	Verilog

Both Tables 4.13 and 4.14 are subject to rapid changes for these reasons:

1. New static analysis tools appear to be coming out monthly.

2. New features are being added to static analysis tools monthly.

3. New languages are being supported by static analysis tools monthly.

4. New programming languages appear to be coming out monthly.

It is an unanswered question why the software industry has developed about 2,500 programming languages to date and keeps creating new languages almost every month. In theory, the industry should be able to code any known application using fewer than ten programming languages optimized for critical tasks such as performance, security, data manipulation, and several others.

A corollary question is whether the 2,500 different programming languages indicate a success for software engineering or a failure for software engineering. One hypothesis is that having so many languages is closer to a failure than to a success.

Having so many languages increases the learning curves for software developers and degrades the performance of software maintainers. Software maintenance is especially damaged by aging legacy languages, which may lack compilers or interpreters, to say nothing of lacking static analysis tools.

An economic analysis of software programming languages would probably indicate a negative return on investment for about 2,300 out of 2,500 languages. About 150 would have marginally positive ROI, and only about 50 would have strongly positive ROI.

Returning now to static analysis, because the tools are cheap, fast, and effective, they can be run as often as needed. Some suggested usage patterns for static analysis include

1. Immediately after clean compiles for software modules

2. Immediately after making changes to software modules

3. Immediately after merging code from other sources into applications

4. Immediately prior to performing manual code inspections

5. Immediately prior to performing unit testing

6. Immediately prior to every build

7. Immediately after final build and integration

8. Immediately after completion of external Beta test

9. Immediately prior to renovating legacy applications

10. Immediately after renovating legacy applications

11. Immediately prior to installing COTS applications

12. Immediately after modifying COTS applications

13. As an adjunct to external Beta tests by customers

14. As an adjunct to acceptance test by customers

15. As a method of discovery during software litigation for poor quality and breach of contract

In the course of developing a complete software application, programmers might run static analysis tools from between 25 to 50 times based on code changes and numbers of application builds.

Static analysis tools themselves are not "static" and indeed are evolving at a fairly rapid rate. Some future additions to static analysis capabilities might include the following:

- Better analysis and detection of security vulnerabilities

- Elevation of the methodology to analyze UML or meta-languages

- Inclusion of logic to detect possible theft of source code

- Automatic generation of equivalent function points via "backfiring"

- Suggestions for improving common routines such as error handling

- Identification of potential "back door" threats

Given the history and evolution of static analysis tools, three statements can be made with a high degree of certainty:

1. Static analysis tool capabilities will continue to improve.

2. New static analysis tools will continue to enter the market.

3. New programming languages will continue to come out, whether the new languages are needed or not.

As of 2011 static analysis has become the most widely used automated defect detection method after testing. Static analysis benefits defect removal and also benefits defect prevention. Static analysis is inexpensive itself and also lowers testing costs, so the ROI for using static analysis is higher than for almost any other defect detection method.

Summary and Conclusions about Pretest Defect Removal

The software quality literature on testing outnumbers the quality literature on pretest defect removal by at least 20 to 1 based on a survey of software book titles on Amazon, Borders, and other web-based book dealers. Pretest software defect removal deserves to be studied in its own right. It also deserves a significant increase in publication as the main topic of books and articles and research. What happens to software before testing is an important factor that determines testing speed and testing costs.

The literature needs to expand for topics such as inspections, static analysis, and client reviews of software artifacts. Indeed, as of 2011 the literature is almost completely silent on customer or client reviews, even though they have been among the most widely used forms of defect removal for more than 50 years.

Many kinds of pretest defect removal activities are highly efficient and also cost-effective. Several of these, such as formal inspections and static analysis, are efficient in finding bugs and also raise the defect removal efficiency of various kinds of testing. These methods can lower testing costs and schedules by more than 30%. They also speed up development and reduce maintenance and customer support costs. As is discussed in Chapter 7, the ROI of the better forms of pretest software defect removal is more than $10 for every $1.00 that is spent.

Chapter 5

Software Testing

Introduction

Testing has been the primary form of defect removal since the software industry began. For many software projects, it is the *only* form of defect removal utilized. Because testing is among the oldest forms of software defect removal, there is substantial literature about testing itself, about test case design, about test library control, and there are also many other "how to do it" books for various kinds of testing. Testing also is a field in which several companies and nonprofit groups offer certification. There are ISO, IEEE, and other standards on testing as well.

Yet considering the importance of testing and its universal penetration of the software industry and the large number of books published about testing, it is surprising that so little quantitative data is available on testing and test results. The phrase *quantitative data* in a testing context includes the following kinds of information that should be widely available:

1. Numbers of test cases created for all major forms of testing

2. Normalized number of test cases per function point or per KLOC

3. Total sizes of test libraries for various kinds of software

4. Distribution of effort among test planning, test case design, and testing

5. Test team size ranges for applications > 1,000 function points

6. Numbers of test stages used for applications > 1,000 function points

7. Differences in testing for web projects, embedded projects, and other types

8. Ranges of defect removal efficiency of each major form of testing

9. Ranges of defect removal efficiency by defect severity level

10. Ranges of "false positives" or erroneous defect reports during testing

11. Numbers of defects or bugs in test cases and test scripts themselves

12. Numbers of duplicate or redundant test cases in test libraries

13. Numbers of builds performed during various test cycles

14. Schedule ranges observed for various kinds of testing

15. Bad-fix injection rates noted for each major form of testing

16. Statistical studies of professional testers versus development testing

17. Statistical studies of effectiveness of certification of test personnel

18. Statistical studies of effectiveness of international test standards

19. Combined statistical studies of pretest removal and testing together

20. Combined statistical studies of prevention methods and testing together

21. Test coverage or percentage of application code executed

22. Impact of cyclomatic and essential complexity on test coverage

Of these 22 topics of interest, only numbers 21 and 22 seem to have substantial data available in the testing and quality literature circa 2011. However, number 21, on coverage, is ambiguous because there are so many kinds of "coverage" to consider, such as total branches, total lines of code, total requirements, and so on.

There are numerous books on testing, but very few include data on numbers of test cases needed for applications of various sizes and types, numbers of application builds, defect removal efficiency levels, or even the distribution of costs among test case preparation, test execution, and defect repairs. The quantitative data that is most often discussed is that of test coverage, or the percentage of an application's source code that test cases actually execute.

This lack of quantitative data does not speak well for the professionalism of the software industry. For more than 50 years finding and fixing bugs has been the most expensive identifiable software cost driver. High defect levels are the primary reason for software schedule and cost overruns. High defect levels also trigger cancelled projects and are frequently cited in litigation that occurs in the aftermath of cancelled projects.

Knowing the impact of defects on software projects and the impact of test cases and test effort on project performance is critical information. The lack of this data goes far in explaining the endemic problems of large applications such as high cancellation rates and frequent schedule delays.

In the absence of data and the presence of the serious problems of building large software projects, some companies attempt to arbitrarily limit projects to a maximum size or to a maximum schedule duration. This is not a true solution to software quality problems.

In fact, the companies with such arbitrary limits routinely use applications such as operating systems and ERP packages, which are much larger and took more time than their own internal arbitrary limits. Arbitrary limits tend to bring on unanticipated consequences. In fact, some of the companies that use arbitrary limits still have quality problems.

Somewhat surprisingly, the largest amount of quantitative data about testing does not come from the test and quality assurance literature, but from the companies that design and market commercial software estimation tools such as KnowledgePlan, SEER, SLIM, COCOMO II, Software Risk Master, and the like.

These estimation tools predict numbers of test cases, numbers of bugs, defect removal efficiency, and testing effort. The data itself comes from onsite data collection by the estimation companies. However, the penetration of commercial estimation tools is much lower than that of testing tools. Only about 20% of U.S. companies and 15% of European companies use commercial estimation tools, but 100% of all companies perform testing.

Some of these tools also predict defects by severity level. The most common form of severity level for software was developed by IBM in the late 1960s and includes four severity levels plus several additional categories:

Severity 1 = total application failure

Severity 2 = major software defects

Severity 3 = minor software defects

Severity 4 = cosmetic defects that do not affect operation of the software

Invalid = defects that turn out to be hardware, user, or other problems

Duplicate = reports of the same defect from multiple clients

Abeyant = defects that are so unique the change team cannot duplicate them

Incident = a momentary software failure that disappears upon reboot

Typically, severity 1 defects in released software are a very small number, ranging from a fraction of 1% up to perhaps 3%. Severity 2 defects are more common and range up to 25% of customer-reported defects. Severity 3 defects typically comprise about 30%, and severity 4 defects comprise about 42%.

Invalid defects can amount to 15% of customer defect reports. Many of these are hardware errors, but some are user errors. Some invalid defects are true defects but reported to the wrong software location. As an example, one of the authors received a client defect report that was for a competitive software application. Some defects reported against applications turn out to be true defects but are defects in the operating system or some other layer.

Some of the benchmark groups such as the International Software Benchmark Standards Group (ISBSG), David Consulting Group (DCG), Quantitative Software Management (QSM), Process Fusion, and Software Productivity Research (SPR) collect at least some information on test case volumes and testing costs. However, ISBSG only recently added quality benchmarks in 2009. Considering all available sources, there is still a significant shortage of quantitative data on testing costs, efficiency, and how pretest defect removal impacts test results.

Recording basic information such as numbers of test cases created, numbers of builds, methods of test case design, forms of testing utilized, numbers of defects found by those test cases, and errors in the test cases themselves might add valuable information that could raise testing efficiency levels higher than they are today.

This book and some of the authors' prior books contain quantitative data on some of the 22 topics derived from client studies and from litigation, but additional data from multiple sources would be beneficial. Indeed, it would be useful to include such data as part of standard benchmarks collected for all software projects.

Among our approximately 600 client organizations, testing is the only quality control method used by all 100% of them. However, the variety and forms of testing vary considerably. The range of testing activities performed by our clients runs from a single perfunctory unit test by the programmer who wrote the program to a coordinated series of 16 discrete testing activities, with at least 10 of them performed by professional testers or quality assurance personnel. (Such extensive testing tends to occur primarily for large systems software or military applications.)

The information in this chapter is derived from observations and internal data collected by the authors' client companies. Some of these include IBM, AT&T, Motorola, Hewlett-Packard, ITT, Siemens Nixdorf, Nokia, Nippon Telephone and Telegraph, Sony, Boeing, General Electric, Exxon, Raytheon, Lockheed, Oracle, Aetna Insurance, American Commerce Insurance, Hartford Insurance, Sun Life Insurance, several Blue Cross companies, NASA, the U.S. Air Force, the U.S. Navy, the states of South Carolina, California, New York, and Oklahoma, the Internal Revenue Service (IRS), General Motors, Ford, EDS, Accenture, Nielsen, and another 125 or so.

There is a bias in the data in this book because most of the authors' client companies are large corporations or large government groups. The reason for this bias is that small companies seldom commission assessment and benchmark studies, while large organizations do so quite frequently. One of the reasons for this situation is that such studies are performed by consultants on a fee basis and hence cost more money than small companies might wish to spend.

This also explains a bias in the industries from which the data is derived. Systems, defense, and embedded software companies often use external consultants for benchmarks and assessments. Information technology and web companies do so less often; state governments are the same. Companies that build computer games and entertainment software seldom do external benchmarks. Open source companies almost never commission external benchmarks or assessments. (The reason for this in an open source context is probably the high costs of such studies and the small budgets of open-source companies.) These biases mean that large companies and large projects provide the bulk of the information used in this book.

The total number of kinds of testing used among the authors' clients is shown in Table 5.1. Table 5.1 assumes a nominal application size of 10,000 function points or 500,000 logical source code statements in a language such as Java. Components are assumed to be 1,000 function points or about 50,000 source code statements. Modules are assumed to be 100 function points or 5,000 code statements. Subroutines are assumed to be 1 function point or 50 source code statements.

Table 5.1 *Summary Overview of Major Software Testing Stages*

			(Data sorted in descending order of defect removal efficiency)		
	Testing Stages	Assignment Scope in Function Points	Number of Test Cases per Function Point	Defect Removal Efficiency Percent	Bad fix Injection Percent
	General Testing				
1	Subroutine testing	5	0.25	60.00%	2.00%
2	System testing	2,000	1.50	55.00%	7.00%
3	PSP/TSP Unit testing	50	3.50	50.00%	2.00%
4	Integration testing	2,000	1.50	50.00%	5.00%
5	Agile and XP testing	100	2.00	50.00%	3.00%
6	Component testing	1,250	1.75	40.00%	3.00%

(Continued)

Table 5.1   *(Continued)*

	Testing Stages	Assignment Scope in Function Points	Number of Test Cases per Function Point	Defect Removal Efficiency Percent	Bad fix Injection Percent
	General Testing				
7	New function testing	125	2.50	40.00%	5.00%
8	Regression testing	150	2.00	35.00%	7.00%
9	Unit testing	50	3.00	35.00%	4.00%
	AVERAGE	637	2.00	46.11%	4.22%
	SUM		18.00		
	Automatic Testing				
10	Virus/spyware test	15,000	3.50	80.00%	4.00%
11	System test	3,500	2.00	40.00%	8.00%
12	Regression test	3,500	2.00	37.00%	7.00%
13	Unit test	150	0.05	35.00%	4.00%
14	New function test	500	3.00	35.00%	5.00%
	AVERAGE	4,530	2.11	45.40%	5.60%
	SUM		10.55		
	Specialized Testing (Special defects)				
15	Virus testing	5,000	0.70	98.00%	2.00%
16	Spyware testing	5,000	1.00	98.00%	2.00%
17	Limits/capacity testing	7,500	0.50	90.00%	5.00%
18	General security testing	5,000	0.40	90.00%	4.00%
19	Penetration testing	5,000	4.00	90.00%	4.00%
20	Reusability testing	2,500	4.00	88.00%	0.25%
21	Firewall testing	25,000	2.00	87.00%	3.00%
22	Litigation testing (code theft)	5,000	3.00	85.00%	1.00%
23	Performance testing	10,000	0.50	80.00%	7.00%
24	Litigation testing (quality)	5,000	2.00	80.00%	1.00%
25	Nationalization testing	3,500	0.30	75.00%	10.00%
26	Scalability testing	10,000	0.40	65.00%	6.00%
27	Platform testing	10,000	0.20	55.00%	5.00%
28	Clean room testing	1,000	3.00	45.00%	7.00%
29	Patent testing	10,000	0.15	40.00%	3.00%
30	Independent testing	15,000	0.20	37.00%	12.00%
31	Supply chain testing	75,000	0.30	35.00%	10.00%

	Testing Stages	Assignment Scope in Function Points	Number of Test Cases per Function Point	Defect Removal Efficiency Percent	Bad fix Injection Percent
	Specialized Testing (Special defects)				
32	Cloud testing	15,000	0.25	35.00%	5.00%
33	SOA orchestration	15,000	0.20	30.00%	5.00%
	AVERAGE	12,079	1.22	68.58%	4.86%
	SUM		23.10		
	User Testing				
34	Usability testing	5,000	0.25	65.00%	4.00%
35	Case study testing	5,000	0.10	65.00%	2.50%
36	Local nationalization	4,000	0.40	60.00%	3.00%
37	Lab testing	15,000	1.25	45.00%	5.00%
38	External Beta testing	5,000	1.00	40.00%	7.00%
39	Acceptance testing	15,000	0.30	30.00%	8.00%
40	Prepurchase testing	30,000	0.10	25.00%	8.00%
	AVERAGE	11,286	0.49	47.14%	5.36%
	SUM		3.40		
	TOTAL TEST CASES		55.05		

Table 5.1 will probably be controversial for several reasons. One of the reasons for controversy is the fairly low level of defect removal efficiency for many kinds of testing listed—there are, of course, ranges above and below the data shown in Table 5.1.

Another reason for controversy is that Table 5.1 is not complete, and at least ten other kinds of testing are occasionally used (the authors lack data for these additional forms of testing).

A third reason is that testing nomenclature varies from company to company and also changes over time. For example, the term *system test* as used in Table 5.1 was originally defined by IBM in the 1970s as the final internal test stage for large systems after all components had been tested separately and the final system integration had taken place. Normally, "systems" were fairly large and ranged between 10,000 and 100,000 function points in size. In today's world the *system test* can mean the last internal test stage regardless of whether the application is a true multicomponent system larger than 10,000 function points or merely a small stand-alone program fewer than 100 function points in size.

More recently the Agile methods have started to use *unit test* in a fashion that differs from older uses. In older paradigms unit testing came after coding, but in Agile test-driven development (TDD), the test case comes before the code.

It is an interesting question that if test-driven development had existed in 1985, would it have prevented the Y2K problem from occurring? The most probable answer is that TDD would not have eliminated Y2K if the embedded users insisted on a two-digit date format. TDD does not eliminate toxic user requirements, which can still find their way into code if users insist on doing something harmful.

Some additional forms of testing not shown in Table 5.1 were pointed out by Rex Black, a testing consultant and author: accessibility testing, interoperability testing, sociability testing, data migration testing, and data quality testing. The last two forms of testing dealing with data are important, but there is no available size metric for data volumes, so it is not possible to show numbers of data defects in a normalized form. (The industry needs a "data point" metric similar to function points for software.)

As stated previously, Table 5.1 assumes a nominal size of 10,000 function points or 500,000 logical code statements in a language such as Java. Test defect removal efficiency goes down as application size goes up, as does test coverage. Table 5.1 is intended to show only approximate results derived from a number of companies, but results can and do vary widely.

The columns of Table 5.1 have the following meanings:

The column labeled **Assignment Scope in Function Points** refers to the approximate number of function points that will normally be tested by one person— either a professional tester or a software developer. The ranges in assignment scopes are about 25% in either direction from the nominal values presented.

The column labeled **Test Cases per Function Point** shows the average values from among the authors' clients. However, there are wide ranges of perhaps −25% to +50% from the nominal values in the table.

The column labeled **Defect Removal Efficiency Percent** shows the approximate percentage of defects present that the testing will discover. It would actually be more proper to label the column Defect Detection Efficiency because not every defect found by testing is fixed prior to release. Here, too, there are ranges of results of perhaps −15% and +20%. Also the efficiency levels shown for specialized tests such as virus tests are for specific kinds of defects such as viruses and not for general defects. The specialized forms of testing are fairly efficient against a narrow range of defect types.

The column labeled **Bad-Fix Injection Percent** shows the approximate percentage of defect repairs that contain a new defect accidentally included in the repairs themselves. Bad-fix injections need additional study because the test and quality literature does not cover this problem well. Bad fixes have the mathematical effect of lowering defect removal efficiency levels because the new defects need to be added to the total numbers of defects.

One of the authors worked as an expert witness in a lawsuit where a software vendor attempted to fix a defect in a financial package. Each of the first four attempts failed to repair the original defect, and all four "fixes" contained new defects embedded in the repairs themselves.

From the initial attempt until the fifth and finally successful attempt to repair the defect, more than nine calendar months had elapsed. (During this nine-month period the plaintiff was forced to restate prior year financial results due to the original bug and also lost a long-term banking relationship and a favorable line of credit.)

Bad fixes are endemic problems but are usually only measured by companies such as IBM, Raytheon, Northrup Grumman, Motorola, and Hewlett-Packard, which perform root cause analysis or which include defect origin codes in their quality measurement systems. The availability of data on bad-fix injections combined with root-cause analysis can be used to lower bad-fix injection rates. In fact, among the companies with the best quality measures, including bad-fix injections, the rates of bad fixes are usually less than 2% as opposed to more than 7%. Also data on bad-fix injections provides an incentive to identify and eliminate error-prone modules, given that bad fixes for these modules can top 20%.

The general forms of testing are concerned with every kind of software and seek to eliminate common kinds of bugs such as branching errors, looping errors, incorrect outputs, and the like.

The specialized forms of testing are narrow in focus and seek specific kinds of errors such as security flaws or problems that only occur under full load conditions or problems that might slow performance. These specialized forms of testing are usually quite efficient against narrow classes of defects.

The automated forms of testing are similar in purpose to the manual forms but are set up to run test cases under software control. The forms of testing involving users are aimed primarily at usability problems and ensuring that all requirements have in fact been implemented.

There are obviously ranges for every column in Table 5.1. The table merely shows the wide variety of forms of testing and the approximate results for each form for a fairly large system.

As discussed in Chapter 4, testing is strongly influenced by pretest defect removal activities such as static analysis and formal inspections. These pretest activities lower the numbers of bugs or defects that will be present when testing begins and therefore reduce testing costs and help testing schedules.

The pretest activities of inspections and static analysis also have been shown to raise testing efficiency levels by providing more complete requirements and specifications from which to construct test cases.

Surprisingly for so common an activity as testing, the exact definition of what the word "testing" means is somewhat ambiguous. In this book testing means "the dynamic execution of software and the comparison of that execution against a set of known, predetermined criteria."

Under the definition of testing used here, static defect removal methods such as formal design and code inspections are not viewed as testing. Testing involves execution of the code itself, which allows testing to discover dynamic errors in control flow logic and performance. Chapter 4 dealt with static defect removal and pretest defect removal activities such as client reviews and formal inspections.

The term *software* in a testing context, then, can mean any of the following:

- An individual instruction (about .001 function points).

- A small subroutine of perhaps 10 instructions in length (about .01 function points).

- A module of perhaps 100 instructions in length (about 1 function point).

- A complete program of perhaps 1,000 instructions in length (10 function points).

- A component of a system of perhaps 10,000 instructions in length (100 function points).

- An entire software system that can range from 100,000 statements (1,000 function points) to more than 10,000,000 instructions in length (100,000 function points). Large enterprise resource planning (ERP) packages approach 300,000 function points in size, as do some large military applications.

- Applications developed under service oriented architecture (SOA) or assemblages of components that were developed separately but are loosely coupled to address common problems and share common data. These range between about 10,000 and 100,000 function points.

- A linked chain of applications that are intended to operate concurrently and pass data back and forth among organizations that are part of a common supply chain. Such chains can be as small as two applications totaling fewer than 1,000 function points to larger than 25 applications totaling to more than 1,000,000 function points.

Any one of these software groupings can be tested, and often tested many times, in the course of software development activities. The smaller units such as individual code statements, subroutines, and modules are usually tested by means of individual test cases created by the programmers themselves. The larger units such as programs, components, and systems are usually tested by suites of test cases operating under test scripts kept in formal test libraries. Often these large-scale tests are performed by test specialists rather than by developers.

The term *execution* means running the software on a computer with or without any form of instrumentation or test control software being present.

The phrase *predetermined criteria* means that what the software is supposed to do is known prior to its execution so that what the software actually does can be compared against the anticipated results to judge whether or not the software is behaving correctly.

It is interesting to consider the forms of testing our clients utilize and the approximate percent of projects in our knowledge base (out of about 13,000 projects) that have been exposed to various kinds of testing.

Table 5.2 uses the same taxonomy as Table 5.1 but shows the approximate percentage of client projects that used each method. The test methods are sorted into observed frequency of usage.

Table 5.2   *Frequency of Test Stage Usage*

	Testing Stages	Percent of Projects Using
	General Testing	
1	Subroutine testing	100%
2	Unit testing	100%
3	Regression testing	90%
4	New function testing	90%
5	Integration testing	60%
6	System testing	40%
7	XP testing	30%
8	Component testing	20%
9	PSP/TSP Unit testing	15%
	AVERAGE	61%
	Automatic Testing	
10	Regression test	70%
11	Unit test	70%
12	New function test	50%
13	Virus/spyware test	25%
14	System test	20%
	AVERAGE	47%
	Specialized Testing (Special defects)	
15	Limits/capacity testing	60%
16	General security testing	50%
17	Virus testing	40%
18	Spyware testing	40%

(Continued)

Table 5.2   *(Continued)*

	Testing Stages	Percent of Projects Using
	Specialized Testing (Special defects)	
19	Performance testing	40%
20	Nationalization testing	12%
21	Independent testing	12%
22	SOA orchestration	10%
23	Scalability testing	10%
24	Reusability testing	10%
25	Cloud testing	9%
26	Penetration testing	8%
27	Supply chain testing	7%
28	Firewall testing	4%
29	Litigation testing (quality)	3%
30	Platform testing	3%
31	Litigation testing (code theft)	2%
32	Patent testing	2%
33	Clean room testing	1%
	AVERAGE	17%
	User Testing	
34	External Beta testing	70%
35	Acceptance testing	55%
36	Prepurchase testing	40%
37	Usability testing	35%
38	Local nationalization	15%
39	Case study testing	3%
40	Lab testing	3%
	AVERAGE	31%

No company or project studied by the authors uses all 40 forms of testing shown in Table 5.2. The table merely shows the full variety of testing observed. (There may also be other kinds of testing in addition to the 40 shown here.) The average number of test stages among the author's clients is about six:

1. Subroutine test

2. Unit test

3. Function test

4. Regression test

5. System test

6. Beta test

The cumulative defect removal efficiency for these six kinds of testing usually runs from about 75% through 85%. For small applications below 1,000 function points, test defect removal efficiency can sometimes top 90%, but this has not been noted for large systems above 10,000 function points.

Among our clients, it is interesting to note that the only forms of testing that are truly universal are testing of individual subroutines as they are created and then unit testing of entire modules. Testing of the entire application upon completion is also very common, but not every company uses the term "system testing" for small applications. Tables 5.1 and 5.2 assume that the term system refers to larger assemblages in the range of 10,000 function points or larger.

Small programs developed by one person don't have structures called *components* and don't perform some of the kinds of tests associated with large systems such as integration tests. As a general rule, the larger the application, the more kinds of testing stages are likely to be performed.

Function points	Test Stages
1	1
10	3
100	6
1,000	6
10,000	10
100,000	15

For the more specialized forms of testing, such as performance testing or security testing, only a minority of projects among our clients perform such testing. Sometimes the specialized forms of testing are not needed, but sometimes they are needed and are skipped over due to schedule pressures or poor decision making by project managers.

Black Box and White Box Testing

The software testing literature often divides testing into major forms termed *black box testing* and *white box testing* (also known as *glass box testing*). The distinction between the two concerns the knowledge that the test case developers have.

For black box testing, the inner structure or control flow of the application is not known or viewed as irrelevant for constructing test cases. The application is tested against the external specifications and/or requirements to ensure that a specific set of input parameters will in fact yield the correct set of output values.

For white box testing, the test case developer is privy to the inner structure of the application and knows the control flow through the application or at least knows the control flow if the software works correctly. This form is also sometimes known as "glass box" testing because the inner structure and control flow of the application are known and utilized for test case construction.

Black-box testing is useful for ensuring that the software more or less is in accordance with the written specifications and written requirements.

White box, or glass box, testing is useful for ensuring that all or at least most paths through the application have been executed in the course of testing. This form is also useful for nonfunctional testing dealing with performance, load, and security issues.

Some forms of testing are mixed and include both black and white box test cases simultaneously.

Of the 40 forms of testing discussed in this section, almost half are black box, and almost half are white box. Samples of black box, white box, and mixed box testing are shown here:

Subroutine testing	White box
Unit testing	White box
Viral protection testing	White box
Stress or capacity testing	White box
Performance testing	White box
Security testing	White box
System testing of full application	Black box
New function testing	Black box
Lab testing	Black box
Usability testing	Black box
Customer acceptance testing	Black box
Field (Beta) testing	Black box
Clean room statistical testing	Black box
Independent testing	Mixed
Regression testing	Mixed
Integration testing	Mixed
Platform testing	Mixed

Both white and black box testing methods are useful, so there is no serious debate or argument in the software testing literature that one form is superior to the other. The testing literature usually agrees that both forms are desirable and necessary. However, there is some debate as to whether black box testing in the form of clean room or statistical testing is adequate.

Functional and Nonfunctional Testing

Another division of testing into two separate forms is that of functional testing and nonfunctional testing. The phrase *functional testing* refers to tests that examine the features that users have requested the application to perform. Functional test cases are derived from requirements and ensure that the requirements have all been implanted and the software is executing them correctly.

The phrase *nonfunctional testing* refers to tests that evaluate attributes of software such as its speed of execution, the time the software needs to start up and shut down, security, and sometimes the memory space needed when the application is executing.

The main distinction between functional and nonfunctional testing is that functional testing concerns the features that are specifically spelled out in user requirements. The nonfunctional kinds of testing are concerned with the mechanics of putting a software application onto a computer and ensuring that it operates with acceptable levels of performance.

Among the authors' clients, both functional and nonfunctional testing are routinely carried out. Typically, out of every 100 test cases, about 70 would test functional issues, and 30 would test nonfunctional issues, although there are of course wide variations between functional and nonfunctional testing.

The major forms of testing that cover nonfunctional issues are performance tests, limits tests, and various kinds of security testing.

The major forms of testing that cover functional issues are new function testing, case-study testing, and system testing. The other forms of testing would typically include both functional and nonfunctional test cases.

Automated and Manual Testing

In the early days of the software industry, applications were small, and manual testing was the norm. Soon applications began to grow larger, and application usage stretched out over many years, so it became necessary to keep libraries of test cases that could be used for regression testing to ensure that updates did not damage existing features.

Companies such as IBM, AT&T, and later Microsoft began to build proprietary test case library tools that could keep track of test cases and also run collections of test cases. The value of these tools led to a market for test case automation and eventually to open source test case automation.

Today as this book is written, test automation of various forms is ubiquitous and used for a majority of applications larger than about 500 function points. Test library automation and support for regression tests, performance tests, and other kinds of testing that use test cases more than once are the most common uses.

There are dozens of test tool vendors that provide a wide spectrum of automated test capabilities. The most common uses for test automation are test library control, regression testing, and testing for situations where many different combinations of factors are being tested such as graphical user inputs (GUI) and load testing.

As of 2011 both manual and automated testing are used by the authors' clients, but about 85% have some form of test automation. As a rule, large companies that build large software applications are more extensively automated than small companies that build small applications.

Discussion of the General Forms of Software Testing

The general forms of software testing occur for almost any kind of software: systems software, commercial software, military software, information systems, or anything else.

While the general forms of software testing are common and usually well understood, not all companies use the same vocabulary to describe them. The following brief definitions explain the common meanings of the general forms of testing discussed here.

Subroutine Testing

Usage:	> 99% of custom-coded software
	> 90% of defect repairs
Defect removal efficiency range:	
Minimum =	< 25%
Average =	55%
Maximum =	> 75%
Synergies:	All applications and all languages
Counter indications:	None

Subroutine testing is the lowest-level form of testing noted among our clients. Recall that a *subroutine* is a small collection of code that may constitute fewer than ten statements or perhaps one-tenth of a function point.

Subroutine testing is performed almost spontaneously by developers and is very informal. Essentially this form of testing consists of executing a just-completed subroutine to see if it compiles properly and performs as expected. Subroutine testing is a key line of defense against errors in algorithms in spite of its being informal and under-reported in the testing literature. Subroutine testing is a white box form of testing.

Subroutine testing is also common for defect repairs and for enhancements to legacy applications. Essentially subroutine testing is used on every small block of code as it is created.

Due to the very small quantity of code tested in this fashion, subroutine testing does not attack large-scale structural errors nor flow of data or control across entire systems. Its main purpose is to ensure correctness of small pieces of code before they are aggregated into larger modules, components, or applications.

PSP/TSP Unit Testing

Usage:	> 100% of PSP/TSP projects
	< 1% of non-PSP/TSP projects
Defect removal efficiency range:	
Minimum =	< 25%
Average =	65%
Maximum =	> 95%
Synergies:	Formal development, RUP, higher CMMI levels
Counter indications:	Agile

PSP/TSP Unit testing is part of the Personal Software Process (PSP) and Team Software Process (TSP). These methods were developed by Watts Humphrey, who was IBM's director of software engineering and also one of the developers of the capability maturity model (CMM) at the Software Engineering Institute (SEI).

Because Watts knew from IBM data that poor quality degraded productivity and stretched out schedules, his PSP and TSP methods are both quality-centric. The salient feature of PSP and TSP is that all software developers are trained to understand defect origins, defect prevention, defect removal, and defect measurement.

The PSP/TSP test stages are embedded in a process that uses pretest inspection, defect measurements, and formal test case designs. As a result, requirements and specifications are low in defects and fairly clear, so it is possible to create effective test cases. Due to the low numbers of defects when testing starts, PSP/TSP testing is comparatively fast. From samples noted by the authors, PSP/TSP applications always top 95% in cumulative defect removal efficiency and keep high levels of removal efficiency even for large systems above 10,000 function points in size.

PSP/TSP methods are synergistic with static analysis, which would normally be carried out prior to unit testing.

Extreme Programming (XP) Unit Testing

Usage:	> 100% of XP projects
	> 60% of Agile projects
	Defect removal efficiency range:
Minimum =	< 35%
Average =	50%
Maximum =	> 85%
Synergies:	Agile and all forms of test-driven development; static analysis
Counter indications:	None, but this method and PSP/TSP testing overlap

XP Unit testing is found in "extreme programming," which is one of the popular Agile development methodology variants created by Kent Beck and several colleagues. With XP unit testing the test scripts and test cases for modules and components are created before the code itself is created.

This method of concentrating on test case design before testing leads to better-than-average test coverage and higher-than-average test defect removal efficiency levels. Up to about 1,000 function points, XP testing and PSP/TSP testing seem to have similar results, and both are better than many forms of informal traditional testing. As applications grow into large systems and top 10,000 function points, the PSP/TSP methods seem to pull ahead of XP and most other forms of development.

XP testing is synergistic with static analysis. However, the Agile and XP projects seldom utilize formal inspections, in part because their requirements and specifications are not structured with inspections in mind.

Unit Testing

Usage:	> 85% of waterfall projects
	> 80% of defect repairs
Defect removal efficiency range:	
Minimum =	< 25%
Average =	35%
Maximum =	> 55%
Synergies:	Static analysis
Counter indications:	High levels of cyclomatic complexity

Unit testing is the lowest-level form of testing normally discussed in the testing literature. It is the execution of a complete module or small program that will normally range from perhaps 100 to 1,000 source code statements, or roughly from 1 to perhaps 10 function points. Unit testing is used for new development and also for defect repairs.

When unit testing is performed for enhancements to legacy applications or for defect repairs, it may be necessary to test surrounding modules in addition to the new code that is being added.

Although unit testing may often be performed informally, it is also the stage at which actual test planning and test case construction begins. Unit testing is usually performed by the programmers who write the module, and hence seldom has available data on defect levels or removal efficiency. This is because defects would be self-reported. (Note that for testing under clean room concepts, unit testing is *not* performed by the developers, so data on defect removal may be recorded in this situation.)

Even in the normal situation of unit testing being performed by developers, enough companies have used volunteers who record defects found during unit testing to have at least an idea of how efficient this form of testing is. Unit testing is a white box form of testing. Unit testing is also often plagued by "bad test cases," which themselves contain errors. In addition, unit testing has a significant number of bad fixes or bugs accidentally included in defect repairs themselves.

Unit testing is the level at which cyclomatic complexity becomes a barrier to high test coverage and high levels of defect removal efficiency. Modules below 10 in cyclomatic complexity can usually be tested thoroughly, but the paths through modules with cyclomatic complexity levels of 20 or higher cause test coverage and defect removal efficiency to decline abruptly.

Unit testing can be performed manually or with the support of various kinds of test automation tools. Automated unit testing is increasing in frequency of use. It is synergistic with static analysis, which would normally be performed prior to unit testing. Unit testing is also synergistic with code inspections among large corporations that produce systems software or military software.

New Function Testing

Usage:	> 99% of new software projects
	> 99% of enhancements to legacy applications
Defect removal efficiency range:	
Minimum =	< 30%
Average =	40%
Maximum =	> 55%
Synergies:	Regression testing; static analysis; inspections
Counter indications:	None

New function testing is often teamed with regression testing, and both forms are commonly found when existing applications are being updated or modified. As the name implies, new function testing is aimed at validating new features that are being added to a software package.

For entirely new projects, as opposed to enhancements, this form of testing is sometimes known as "component testing" because it tests the combined work of multiple programmers whose programs in aggregate may comprise a component of a larger system.

Often new function testing is performed by testing specialists since it covers the work of a number of programmers. For example, typical size ranges of major new functions added to existing software packages can exceed 10,000 source code statements or 100 function points.

New function testing is normally supported by formal test plans, planned test cases, and occurs on software that is under full configuration control. Also defect reporting for new function testing is both common and reasonably accurate. Both white box and black box forms of new function testing have been noted, although black box testing is more common.

New function testing is a key line of defense against errors in intermodule interfaces and the movement of data from place to place through an application. New function testing is also intended to verify that the new or added features work correctly.

New function testing is strongly synergistic with both static analysis and with formal code inspections. Normally, static analysis would be performed first, followed by code inspections of critical modules, followed by new function testing. This three-way combination can top 99% in code defect removal efficiency, although of course requirements errors might still be present and undetected.

New function testing is strongly impacted by combinatorial complexity. As a result formal test case design using mathematical models such as those based on design of experiments can yield high test efficiency levels without generating an infinite number of test cases.

New function testing is also strongly impacted by cyclomatic complexity. Both test coverage and defect removal efficiency levels tend to decline as cyclomatic complexity goes up.

(Curiously, IBM data on defects found that for some enhancement projects low cyclomatic complexity modules had more defects than high cyclomatic complexity modules. Investigation of this data found that the high complexity modules were being assigned to top experts because they were so complex, while the simple modules were being assigned to novices.)

From observations among the authors' clients, new function testing efficiency is higher for CMMI levels 3 through 5 than for lower levels.

Regression Testing

Usage:	> 95% of new applications
	> 97% of legacy enhancements
	> 85% of software defect repairs
Defect removal efficiency range:	
Minimum =	< 25%
Average =	35%
Maximum =	> 45%
Synergies:	Static analysis; formal test libraries
Counter indications:	None

Regression testing is the opposite of new function testing. The word *regression* means to slip back, and in the context of testing, regression means accidentally damaging an existing feature as an unintended byproduct of adding a new feature. Regression testing also checks to ensure that prior known bugs have not inadvertently stayed in the software after they should have been removed.

Regression testing starts during development after a majority of modules have been coded. It continues throughout development and indeed continues for many years of application usage.

After a few years of software evolution, regression testing became one of the most extensive forms of testing because the library of available test cases from prior releases tends to grow continuously. Also regression testing involves the entire base code of the application, which for major systems can exceed 10,000,000 lines of code or 100,000 function points.

Regression testing can be performed by developers, professional test personnel, or software quality assurance. Regardless of who performs regression tests, the application is usually under full configuration control. Both white box and black box forms of regression testing have been noted.

Regression test libraries, though often extensive, are sometimes troublesome and have both redundant test cases and test cases which themselves contain errors. An IBM study of a regression test library found both duplicate test cases and test cases with errors. Such studies are rare but should be more common because duplicate and erroneous test cases add to testing costs but degrade defect removal efficiency.

In today's world regression testing can be augmented by static analysis of legacy code prior to making changes or major renovations.

Regression testing is strongly impacted by high cyclomatic complexity levels of 20 or higher, which lowers test coverage and defect removal efficiency.

Integration Testing

Usage:	> 99% of applications > 10,000 function points
	> 85% of applications > 1,000 function points
	< 10% of applications < 100 function points
Defect removal efficiency range:	
Minimum =	< 35%
Average =	50%
Maximum =	> 65%
Synergies:	Formal development, static analysis, inspections
Counter indications:	None

Integration testing, as the name implies, is testing of a number of modules or programs that have come together to comprise an integrated software package. Since integration testing may cover the work of dozens or even hundreds of programmers, it also deals with rather large numbers of test cases. Normally, integration testing occurs with fairly large applications > 1,000 function points in size.

Integration testing often occurs in "waves" as new builds of an evolving application are created. Microsoft, for example, performs daily integration of developing software projects and hence also performs daily integration testing. Other companies may have longer intervals between builds, such as weekly or even monthly.

Applications undergoing integration testing are usually under formal configuration control. Integration testing normally makes use of formal test plans, planned suites of test cases, test library support tools, and formal defect reporting procedures. Both black box and white box forms of integration testing have been noted. Integration testing can be performed by developers themselves, by professional test personnel, or by software quality assurance. However, professional test personnel performance is usually more effective than that of developers.

Integration testing is synergistic with and benefits from static analysis and formal inspections. Integration testing is made less effective by high levels of cyclomatic complexity of 20 or more.

Because of the large number of test cases that might be produced for integration testing, formal mathematical test case design methods such as those based on the design of experiments approach can yield high test coverage and high defect removal efficiency levels with a comparatively small number of test cases.

System Testing

Usage:	> 99% of applications > 10,000 function points
	> 75% of applications > 1,000 function points
	> 50% of applications > 100 function points
Defect removal efficiency range:	
Minimum =	< 25%
Average =	55%
Maximum =	> 95%
Synergies:	Static analysis; inspections; formal test case design
Counter indications:	None

System testing of full applications is usually the last form of internal testing before customers get involved with field testing (Beta testing). For large systems, a formal system test can take many months and can involve large teams of test personnel. Also the entire set of development programmers may be needed in order to fix bugs that are found during this critical test stage.

The phrase system testing originated for large applications in the 10,000 function point size range. Today the term is ambiguous and is applied to the final stage of testing for applications of almost any size. Also system testing is sometimes an umbrella term that includes specialized testing such as performance or security. These ambiguities make it hard to pin down true results.

System testing demands formal configuration control and also deserves formal defect tracking support. System testing is normally based on black box principles, although sometimes the white box testing form is used. System testing can be performed by developers, professional test personnel, or by quality assurance personnel. However, for large companies and large applications > 10,000 function points in size, professional test personnel are the most common system test groups.

For software that controls physical devices (such as telephone switching systems, medical devices, weapons systems, automotive controls, and so on), the phrase system test may include concurrent testing of hardware components. In this case, other forms of engineers and quality assurance may also be involved such as electrical or aeronautical engineers dealing with the hardware. Microcode may also be part of system test. For complex hybrid products, system testing is a key event.

System testing may sometimes overlap a specialized form of testing termed *lab testing*, where special laboratories are used to house complex new hardware/software products that will be tested by prospective clients under controlled conditions. Usually, this occurs only for hardware that is so large or so delicate that it cannot easily be moved.

System testing is benefited by pretest static analysis and code inspections and is degraded by high levels of cyclomatic complexity. Also, system testing is severely degraded for applications that contain error-prone modules.

In the 1970s IBM did a frequency distribution of customer-reported defects. For several large applications such as the MVS operating system and the IMS database product, there was a highly skewed distribution of defects. In the case of IMS there were 425 modules in the application, and 57% of all reported defects were found in only 35 of these modules. About 300 modules were zero-defect modules with no defect reports at all. Alarmingly, bad-fix injections for error-prone modules topped 35%, so one bug repair out of every three added a new bug!

Other companies, such as AT&T, Motorola, and Raytheon, performed similar analyses and found that error-prone modules were distressingly common in large applications. These modules are typically high in cyclomatic complexity (> 50) and hence have low test coverage and low levels of test defect removal efficiency.

Often it is necessary to surgically remove the error-prone modules and redevelop them using better techniques than originally deployed. (In the case of the 35 error-prone modules in IMS, none had been inspected and all had experienced truncation of testing due to schedule pressure.)

Existing error-prone modules are difficult and expensive to repair, but a combination of formal inspections plus pretest static analysis is effective in immunizing against error-prone module creation. Indeed, from the IBM studies of error-prone modules, inspections were 100% effective in prevention.

When inspections and removal of error-prone modules occurred for IMS, testing costs and schedules declined by 65%. Customer satisfaction based on IBM market surveys increased by 75%, and development schedules for IMS releases were shortened by 15%.

Error-prone modules can cause significant harm to large systems, and there is a need for constant analysis of this common problem. A formal defect tracking and measurement program that can identify defects to the level of individual modules is a good tool that can identify such modules in existing legacy software. Inspections and static analysis can immunize new modules and prevent them from becoming error-prone.

The Specialized Forms of Software Testing

These specialized forms of software testing occur with less frequency than the general forms and are most common for systems software, military software, commercial software, contract software, and software with unusually tight criteria for things like high performance or ease of use.

Stress or Capacity Testing

Usage:	> 90% of applications with high transaction rates
	< 50% of applications with large volumes of data
Defect removal efficiency range:	
Minimum =	< 45%
Average =	65%
Maximum =	> 90%
Synergies:	Inspections, static analysis
Counter indications:	None

Stress or capacity testing is a specialized form of testing aimed at judging the ability of an application to function when nearing the boundaries of its capabilities in terms of the volume of information used. For example, capacity testing of the word processor used to create this book (Microsoft Word for Windows Version 7) might entail tests against individual large documents of perhaps 200 to 300 pages to judge the upper limits that can be handled before MS Word becomes cumbersome or storage is exceeded. It might also entail dealing with even larger documents, say 2,000 pages, segmented into master documents and various sections. For a database application, capacity testing might entail loading the database with 10,000 or 100,000 or 1,000,000 records to judge how it operates when fully populated with information.

Capacity testing is usually a black box form of testing, often performed by testing specialists rather than by developers. And it may either be a separate testing stage or performed as a subset of integration or system test. Usually, it cannot be performed earlier because the full application is necessary.

This form of testing is common among applications that support millions of users such as online sales applications for companies such as Amazon and eBay. It is also common for applications such as insurance claims processing or banking where huge volumes of data are recorded and accessed.

Performance Testing

Usage:	> 95% of weapons systems
	> 90% of applications with high transaction rates
	> 50% of embedded and systems applications
	> 50% of games (anecdotally)
Defect removal efficiency range:	
Minimum =	< 70%
Average =	80%
Maximum =	> 95%
Synergies:	Static analysis, inspections
Counter indications:	None

Performance testing is a specialized form of testing aimed at judging whether or not an application can meet the performance goals set out for it. For many applications, performance is only a minor issue, but for some kinds of applications, it is critical. For example, weapons systems, aircraft flight control systems, fuel injection systems, access methods, and telephone switching systems must meet stringent performance goals, or the devices the software is controlling might not work.

Performance testing is a white-box form of testing, often performed by professional testers and sometimes supported by performance or tuning specialists. Some aspects of performance testing can be done at the unit test level, but the bulk of performance testing is associated with integration and system testing since interfaces among the full product affect performance.

Performance testing is also a factor in the computer gaming industry and especially for online games with many concurrent players.

The specialized forms of testing tend to have high levels of defect removal efficiency against narrow classes of defects. The test cases themselves are often prepared by specialists rather than general developers or even professional testers. For embedded applications and those that control hardware devices, other forms of engineering such as electrical or mechanical may be involved.

Viral Protection Testing

Usage:	> 90% of financial and banking applications
	> 90% of defense and law-enforcement applications
	> 70% of web applications that collect personal data
	< 50% of general information technology applications

Defect removal efficiency range:	
Minimum =	< 90%
Average =	95%
Maximum =	> 98%
Synergies:	Inspections; static analysis
Counter indications:	None

Viral protection testing, a white box form, is rapidly moving from a specialized form of testing to a general one, although it still has been noted on less than half of our client's projects. The introduction of software viruses by malicious hackers has been a very interesting sociological phenomenon in the software world. The number of viruses number in the thousands, and more are being created daily.

Virus protection has now become a minor but growing sub-industry of the software domain with dozens of vendors such as Norton, Microsoft, Kaspersky, Panda, AVG, Avira, and many more. Although commercial virus protection software can be run by anybody, major commercial developers of software also use special proprietary tools to ensure that master copies of software packages do not contain viruses.

The antivirus applications need almost daily updates of definitions due to the fact that new viruses occur daily. Some viruses are polymorphic and change structures and signatures in an effort to avoid detection.

A problem of growing significance is the increase in viruses and other forms of malware that seek out and disable antivirus software or block access to antivirus definitions. Essentially a major economic battle is taking place between malware developers and antivirus companies and government organizations. To combat the increasing threats, both government agencies such as the FBI and Homeland Security and large corporations such as IBM, Google, and Microsoft have major cyber security research programs underway.

Most of the antivirus programs and antivirus testing is an attempt to destroy existing viruses. Some interesting research and results are taking place with new methods of raising the immunity of software to viral attacks.

The FBI started a partnership organization, called InfraGuard, with businesses that is intended to share data on software and computer security issues. According to the InfraGuard website, about 350 of the Fortune 500 companies are members. This organization has local branches affiliated with FBI field offices in most major cities such as Boston, Chicago, San Francisco, and the like. However, smaller companies have not been as proactive as large corporations in dealing with security matters. Membership in InfraGuard would be a good first step.

The Department of Homeland Security also has a joint government-business group for Software Assurance (SwA). This group has published a Software Security State of the Art Report (SOAR) that summarizes current best practices for prevention, defense, and recovery of security flaws. Participation in this group and following the principles discussed in the SOAR report would be valuable as well. A 2009 Congressional security report chaired by Representative James Langevin of Rhode Island dealt with the growing number of software security threats.

The need to address security as a fundamental principle of architecture, design, and development needs additional coverage. Software security consultant Ken Hamer-Hodges pointed out that security cannot be truly solved by after-market testing and add-on antivirus applications. His goal is automating computer security to move the problem from the user to the system itself. The way to do this, he asserts, is through detailed boundary management and tighter controls on authorization and access. Also security frames such as Google Caja, which prevents redirection to phishing sites, are emerging as are the new eprogramming languages designed to ensure optimum code security.

The training of business analysts, systems analysts, and architects in security topics has not been keeping pace with the changes in malware, and this gap needs to be corrected quickly because threats are becoming more numerous and more serious.

It is useful to compare security infections with medical infections. Some defenses against infections such as firewalls are like biohazard suits, except the software biohazard suits tend to leak.

Other defenses such as antivirus and antispyware applications are like antibiotics that stop some infections from spreading and also kill some existing infections. However, as with medical antibiotics, some infections are resistant and are not killed or stopped. Over time the resistant infections tend to evolve more rapidly than the infections that are killed, which explains why polymorphic viruses are now the virus of choice.

What might be the best long-term strategy for software would be to change the DNA of software applications and increase their natural immunity to infections via better architecture, better design, more secure programming languages, and better boundary controls.

One way to solve security problems is to consider the very foundations of the science and to build boundary control in physical terms based on "Principle of Least Authority," where each and every subroutine call is to an instance of a protected class of object. There should be no global items, no global name space, and no global path names such as C:/directory/file. Every subroutine should be a protected call with boundary checking, and all program references should be dynamically bound from a local name at runtime with access control checks, included at all times.

Some general security topics that need to be addressed by means of virus testing, static analysis, or inspection (or all three) include

- Password structures and security (often outdated by today's technology)
- Email links that can redirect access to harmful sites
- The preview panes in all inboxes
- What happens when opening email attachments
- Attacks via Java, JavaScript, or ActiveX
- Not displaying your email address on your website
- Not following links without knowing what they link to
- Not letting computers save passwords
- Distrusting the "From" line in email messages
- Upgrading to latest security levels, particularly for Internet Explorer
- Never running a program unless it is trusted
- Reading the User Agreement on downloads (they may sell your personal data)
- Expecting email to carry worms and viruses
- Just saying no to pop-ups
- Saying no if an application asks for additional or different authorities
- Saying no if it asks to read or edit anything more than a Desktop folder
- Saying no if it asks for edit authority
- Saying no if it asks for read authority with a connection to the Web
- During an application install, supplying a new name, new icon, and a new folder path
- Saying no when anything asks for web access, beyond a specific site

Security is so hazardous as of 2011 that some sophisticated organizations prefer that computer users have two computers. One of these would used for web surfing and Internet access; the second would not be connected to the Internet and would accept only trusted inputs on physical media that are, of course, checked for viruses and spyware.

It is quite alarming that hackers are now organized and have journals, websites, and classes available for teaching hacking skills. In fact, a review of the literature indicates that there is almost as much information available about how to hack as on how to defend against hacking.

Viral testing and the use of firewalls, antivirus packages, antispyware packages, and careful physical security are important in today's world. However, as the race between hackers and security companies escalates, it is also necessary to use constant vigilance. Virus definitions should be updated daily, for example. Recent advances include biological defenses such as using finger prints or retina patterns to gain access to software and computers.

Information stored in computers, such as Social Security numbers, credit card numbers, and bank account numbers, is among the most valuable commodities in human history. Valuable commodities always attract thieves, and computer data is no exception. Until recently, computer security was far less sophisticated than physical security at banks, so computerized data was the target of choice for modern high technology thieves.

Penetration Testing

Usage:	> 50% of classified defense applications
	> 50% of law-enforcement applications
	< 10% of financial or medical applications
Defect removal efficiency range:	
Minimum =	< 80%
Average =	95%
Maximum =	> 98%
Synergies:	Inspections; static analysis
Counter indications:	None

Penetration testing is a special form of testing that originated for classified military software applications. In recent years due to the increase in cybercrime and hacking, penetration testing has begun to be used for a few critical financial applications and other kinds of software that contain highly valuable data. The term *penetration testing* refers to deliberate attempts by "white hat" ethical hackers or security specialists to break into and seize control of software. Organizations that utilize penetration testing include the military, the FBI, CIA, Homeland Security, the DIA, and other security organizations, and the Internal Revenue Service (IRS). Overseas security organizations probably also perform penetration testing.

In certain conditions the phrase penetration testing goes beyond software hacking and can include breaking and entering, breaches of physical security, and even attempted bribery of employees by the penetration team. Needless to say, penetration testing is an expensive form of testing that requires considerable expertise on the part of the penetration test personnel.

Software penetration testing looks for and utilizes security vulnerabilities. A less expensive form of penetration testing involves large companies offering rewards to hackers and programmers who find security vulnerabilities and report them to the company rather than putting the information on the Web or making it available to black hat hackers for malicious purposes. Paying fees for reports of security flaws is becoming a common practice in 2011.

Security Testing

Usage:	> 85% of financial and banking applications
	> 85% of web and online commercial software
	> 75% of web applications that collect personal data
Defect removal efficiency range:	
Minimum =	< 75%
Average =	90%
Maximum =	> 95%
Synergies:	Inspections; static analysis
Counter indications:	None

General security testing is most common and most sophisticated for military software, followed by software that deals with very confidential information such as bank records, medical records, tax records, and the like.

The organizations most likely to utilize security testing include the military, National Security Agency (NSA), Central Intelligence Agency (CIA), Federal Bureau of Investigation (FBI), and other organizations who utilize computers and software for highly sensitive purposes. These use both general security testing and for really critical applications and critical data, penetration testing.

Security testing is a white box form of testing usually performed by highly trained specialized personnel. Indeed, as just noted in the previous section, some military projects use *penetration teams* who attempt to break the security of applications by various covert means.

It has been noted that one of the easiest ways to break into secure systems involves finding disgruntled employees, so security testing may have psychological and sociological manifestations.

Platform Testing

Usage:	> 90% of high-volume commercial software
	> 90% of high-volume computer games
	< 20% of general information technology applications
Defect removal efficiency range:	
Minimum =	< 40%
Average =	55%
Maximum =	> 75%
Synergies:	Inspections; static analysis
Counter indications:	None

Platform testing is a specialized form of testing found among companies whose software operates on different hardware platforms under different operating systems. Many commercial software vendors market the same applications for Windows XP, Windows Vista, Windows 7, Mack Leopard, Linux, UNIX, Android, Symbian, and sometimes for other platforms as well.

While the features and functions of the application might be identical on every platform, the mechanics of getting the software to work on various platforms requires separate versions and separate test stages for each platform. Platform testing is usually white box.

In today's world where multi-platform software is the new normal, methods and languages such as Java facilitate cross-platform operability.

Another aspect of platform testing is to ensure that the software package correctly interfaces with any other software packages that might be related to it. For example, when testing software cost-estimating tools, this stage of testing would verify that data can be passed both ways between the estimating tool and various project management tools. For example, suppose a cost-estimating tool such as KnowledgePlan is intended to share data with Microsoft Project under Windows 7 and also under Windows XP and Vista and then under Mac Leopard as well. It is necessary to test the data-sharing features for all of the operating systems so the interfaces would be verified.

Platform testing is also termed compatibility testing by some companies. Regardless of the nomenclature used, the essential purpose remains the same: to ensure software that operates on multiple hardware platforms, under multiple operating systems, and interfaces with multiple applications can handle all varieties of interconnection.

Supply Chain Testing

Usage:	> 30% of multicompany manufacturing applications
	< 10% of general information technology applications
Defect removal efficiency range:	
Minimum =	<30%
Average =	35%
Maximum =	> 50%
Synergies:	Inspections; static analysis
Counter indications:	None

Supply chain testing is a recent form of specialized testing noted among our clients. This form of testing involves multiple companies who use software packages that pass data back and forth along the supply chain. Needless to say, the companies involved in supply chain testing need to cooperate and establish an overall test coordination function.

Supply chain testing is most commonly performed by manufacturers whose products are developed using components produced by scores or even hundreds of subcontractors. Often part of the contractual obligations of the subcontractors is to utilize specific software packages and to cooperate in supply chain testing. This form of testing is found among defense contractors, aerospace contractors, automobile contractors, and manufacturers of specialized equipment.

Clean Room Testing

Usage:	> 90% of clean room applications
	> 0% of non-clean room applications
Defect removal efficiency range:	
Minimum =	< 30%
Average =	45%
Maximum =	> 55%
Synergies:	Static analysis
Counter indications:	Agile projects

Clean room statistical testing is found only in the context of clean room development methods. The clean room approach is unusual in that the developers do not perform unit tests, and the test cases themselves are based on statistical assertions of usage patterns.

Clean room testing is inextricably joined with formal specification methods and proofs of correctness. Clean room testing is a black box form of testing and is always performed by testing specialists or quality assurance personnel rather than developers themselves.

The clean room method was developed by IBM and was designed by the late Dr. Harlan Mills. Because the clean room method works best for small applications with very stable requirements, it has not become a widespread approach. For large and complex applications with many requirements changes, the clean room method would be expensive and probably ineffective.

Litigation Testing

Usage:	> 90% of intellectual property lawsuits
	> 50% of breach-of-contract lawsuits
	> 50% of lawsuits alleging poor quality
	< 10% of lawsuits involving theft of computer data
Defect removal efficiency range:	
Minimum =	< 70%
Average =	85%
Maximum =	> 95%
Synergies:	Inspections; static analysis
Counter indications:	None

Litigation testing often occurs during lawsuits that allege poor software quality on the part of the defendant. While discovery documents and depositions gather quite a bit of historical data on the quality and test methods used, sometimes expert witnesses working for the plaintiff and/or the defendant prepare special tests to find out how many bugs might still be present that are similar to the bugs that triggered the litigation.

Other forms of litigation such as intellectual property cases may also perform special kinds of testing. In the case of charges of theft of intellectual property from source code, several tools have been developed to analyze source code and compare the structure and features of two different applications to ascertain if code might have been illegally copied from one application to another. These tools are special variations of static analysis tools.

Sometimes testing also occurs. Testing may occur to prove that a particular bug in one version of the program was also present in the other version of the program. As it happens, bugs or defects tend to be fairly unique, so having identical bugs in two separate applications is supporting evidence of copied code.

Indeed, some developers deliberately insert "harmless" bugs, such as small segments of dead code, specifically to prove later theft if it should occur. Other such theft-prevention techniques include inserting coded messages in comments.

Cloud Testing

Usage:	> 90% of applications intended for cloud execution
Defect removal efficiency range:	
Minimum =	< 25%
Average =	35%
Maximum =	> 45%
Synergies:	Inspections; static analysis
Counter indications:	None

Cloud testing is one of the newest forms of testing with barely more than five years of accumulated history as this book is written. Applications designed for cloud usage run remotely from the Internet. Many cloud applications will have large numbers of users, so performance testing and load testing are particularly important for cloud applications. However, cloud applications are also subject to normal quality problems, security problems, and usability problems. As a general rule the applications intended to operate in the cloud will have a normal set of "ground" tests prior to "cloud" testing, which usually occur at about the same time as integration or system testing.

Although cloud testing is new, it is on a fast growth track. New tools and new methods for cloud development and cloud testing are occurring almost every month. Cloud testing and testing applications designed to operate as Software as a Service (SaaS) are equivalent and for practical purposes identical.

Service Oriented Architecture (SOA) Testing

Usage:	> 99% of applications intended for service-based execution
Defect removal efficiency range:	
Minimum =	< 25%
Average =	30%
Maximum =	> 40%
Synergies:	Inspections; static analysis; cloud testing
Counter indications:	None

Service Oriented Architecture (SOA) testing is another new form of testing with only a few years of empirical data available. The concept of SOA is to develop useful application features by sharing software and data that might have been developed independently. SOA is an approach to software reuse but elevates the concept from reusable modules up to reusable applications or at least to fairly large reusable components. Further, SOA components may have been developed at different times using different programming languages and sometimes by different companies.

As this book is written in 2011, SOA is still somewhat experimental. The individual SOA components all need normal pretest inspections, static analysis, and conventional testing. But special kinds of testing will be needed to carry out the equivalent of system testing due to the loose coupling of the components and the data that passes back and forth among the components. Performance testing, load testing, security testing, and usability testing are also important for SOA applications.

Based on the SOA concept of construction from reusable components or applications, there is some question as to who "owns" SOA applications and is responsible for their overall quality. No doubt if there are significant quality flaws that end up in court under litigation, there will be complex legal questions as to where liability resides. As this book is written, there seem to be more questions than answers for SOA testing.

There is little or no empirical data on overall SOA test coverage (although individual components may have this) and also little empirical data on other quality topics such as cyclomatic and essential complexity of SOA applications, test coverage, and whether or not pretest inspections are even possible for SOA applications given the heterogeneity of SOA components.

Independent Testing

Usage:	> 90% of military and defense applications
	< 20% of civilian applications
Defect removal efficiency range:	
Minimum =	< 25%
Average =	37%
Maximum =	> 45%
Synergies:	Higher CMMI levels; inspections; static analysis
Counter indications:	Agile; small applications < 500 function points

Independent testing is very common for military software because it was required by Department of Defense standards. It can also occur for commercial software, and indeed there are several commercial testing companies who do testing on a fee basis. However, independent testing is comparatively rare for management information systems, civilian systems software projects, web applications, and outsource or contract software.

Independent testing, as the name implies, is performed by a separate company or at least a separate organization from the one that built the application. Both white box and black box forms of independent testing are noted.

A special form of independent testing may occur from time to time as part of litigation when a client charges that a contractor did not achieve acceptable levels of quality. The plaintiff or defendant, or both, may commission a third party to test the software.

Another form of independent testing is found among some commercial software vendors who market software developed by subcontractors or other commercial vendors. The primary marketing company usually tests the subcontracted software to ensure that it meets their quality criteria.

Nationalization Testing

Usage:	> 90% of applications intended for cloud execution
Defect removal efficiency range:	
Minimum =	< 65%
Average =	75%
Maximum =	> 90%
Synergies:	Inspections; static analysis; international client reviews
Counter indications:	None

Nationalization testing occurs when software is intended to operate in several countries and be understood in several national languages. This kind of testing involves translations of user instructions and HELP text plus translation of some or all comments in the source code.

The phrase *nationalization testing* is not adequate because a number of countries such as Canada and Belgium have several official languages within the national boundaries. Although "localization testing" is perhaps a better term, nationalization testing has been in use since about 1970.

Most of the code will be identical for all countries and regions, but some will require modification such as date formats and the use of commas and periods for large numbers. Some table-driven values also require changes such as numbers of public holidays.

Among the trickiest topics that may need change are sorting sequences, considering traditional sorting in Japan is not based on an alphabet but on a famous poem that uses every syllable once. Almost all of the text and user information for commercial software will require translation.

Nationalization testing attempts to validate that use of the software can be performed by customers whose languages are Korean, Japanese, German, Arabic, or any other language where the software is to be marketed.

In today's world automatic translation by means of software is widely available and inexpensive, but not elegant in results. Therefore, nationalization testing may be augmented by inspections or reviews by prolific speakers of the languages in question.

Case Study Testing

Usage:	> 25% of novel applications with patentable features
Defect removal efficiency range:	
Minimum =	< 35%
Average =	65%
Maximum =	> 75%
Synergies:	Static analysis
Counter indications:	Inspections or white box testing

Case study testing is a special kind of testing usually performed for novel software that is under development and contains valuable trade secret information or patentable algorithms. For case study testing, clients do not have the software itself but only have access to the input parameters. The inputs are answered by clients and returned to the software development locations where the software is executed, and then the results are sent back to the client.

This form of testing is extremely black-box and even "blind" because no one but a few developers have access to the algorithms, source code, specifications, or other proprietary materials. Clients who do have access to prerelease versions of the software will have to sign nondisclosure agreements.

A recent example of case study testing involved testing a patentable high-speed function point sizing method. Clients who had applications that had already been sized using normal function point analysis answered the questions used as inputs to the high-speed method. The developer then sized the application with the client's inputs and reported the resulting size back to the clients for comparison to manual size methods.

In one of the case-study tests, the measured size was 1803 function points, and the predicted size by the high-speed method was 1787 function points. However, in another trial the predicted value was 1260 function points, and the application had been measured at 785 function points. This kind of testing is used to preserve intellectual property prior to patenting it and is used only for novel applications that contain valuable trade secrets.

The Forms of Testing Involving Users or Clients

For many software projects, the clients or users are active participants at various stages along the way, including but not limited to: requirements gathering via JAD and other methods, examining quality requirements via QFD, prototyping specific features, requirements and design (but not code) inspections, and several forms of testing. The testing stages in which users actively participate include the following.

Agile Testing

Usage:	> 90% of Agile applications
Defect removal efficiency range:	
Minimum =	< 40%
Average =	50%
Maximum =	> 65%
Synergies:	Static analysis; XP testing
Counter indications:	CMMI, RUP, PSP/TSP

Agile testing is one of the newer forms of testing. Because Agile projects have "embedded" users, these users provide the requirements for each sprint or iteration. Users also assist developers in defining the appropriate test cases for each sprint or iteration—primarily black-box test cases.

Of course, for larger applications that might have thousands of users, no single user can provide either requirements or sufficient data for test case development. However, for normal Agile projects, < 1,000 function points, the embedded users provide effective assistance in test case design and development, as well as validation of test results.

Agile test cases in the extreme programming (XP) form are developed prior to writing the code, but this practice occurs on less than 100% of Agile projects, and sometimes coding precedes test case development.

Usability Testing

Usage:	< 50% of applications with complex human interfaces
Defect removal efficiency range:	
Minimum =	< 55%
Average =	65%
Maximum =	> 85%
Synergies:	Inspections; static analysis; nationalization testing
Counter indications:	None

Usability testing is a specialized form of testing sometimes performed in usability laboratories. In such cases usability testing involves actual volunteer clients who utilize the software under controlled and sometimes instrumented conditions so that their actions can be observed by psychologists and ergonomic specialists.

The author has visited several usability labs, and they are well instrumented. IBM's lab is used not only to test software use features but also hardware components. For example, a minor hardware modification discovered via a usability lab was to put a scuff-resistant finish on the bottom foot of hardware such as large disk drives and mainframe cases that stand directly on the floor.

Usability testing of this fashion is common for commercial software produced by large companies such as IBM and Microsoft and also for military software involving complex weapons systems. It may also be used for complex heavy equipment and medical devices. The usability labs cost several million dollars, and the staffing of such labs includes cognitive psychologists, graphics artists, and other fairly uncommon specialists.

Simpler forms of usability testing can occur with any kind of software, however. Usability testing is a black box form of testing and usually occurs at about the same time as system test. Sometimes usability testing and Beta testing are concurrent, but it is more common for usability testing to precede Beta testing.

In the simpler forms of usability testing, a sample of volunteer clients utilize the software and then report their experiences to the vendor or developer. These simple methods are fairly effective but, of course, not as effective as the kind that involves usability laboratories.

Field Beta Testing

Usage:	> 90% of commercial applications from large vendors
	> 50% of commercial applications from small vendors
Defect removal efficiency range:	
Minimum =	< 35%
Average =	40%
Maximum =	> 85%
Synergies:	Inspections; static analysis; nationalization testing
Counter indications:	None

Field (Beta) testing is a common testing technique for commercial software. The word *Beta* is the second letter in the Greek alphabet. Its use in testing stems from a testing sequence used by hardware engineers that included Alpha, Beta, and Gamma testing. For software, Alpha testing more or less dropped out of the lexicon circa 1985, and Gamma testing was almost never part of the software test cycle. Thus the word Beta is the only one still commonly used for software and is used to mean an external test involving customers. Sometimes the phrase Alpha testing still is used for various kinds of prerelease internal testing. Among the authors' clients Alpha testing is most widely used for embedded devices with both software and hardware components.

Microsoft has become famous by conducting the most massive external Beta tests in software history with occasionally more than 100,000 customers participating. High-volume Beta testing with thousands of customers is very efficient in terms of defect removal efficiency levels and can exceed 85% removal efficiency if there are more than 1,000 Beta test participants.

However, for small companies with fewer than a dozen clients whose applications have few Beta test participants, defect removal efficiency is usually around 35% to 50%. Needless to say, Beta test efficiency goes up with numbers of clients. That being said, there is a curious distribution of Beta test results. Usually less than 20% of the Beta test clients report 80% of all bugs. As many as 50% of Beta test clients report no bugs at all. Companies keep records of such things and usually seek out the clients that have been most effective in finding bugs during Beta testing.

Beta tests usually occur after system testing and is a black box form of testing. External Beta testing and internal usability testing can occur concurrently, however, Beta testing may involve special agreements with clients to avoid the risk of lawsuits should the software manifest serious problems.

Lab Testing

Usage:	< 40% of applications controlling complex hardware
Defect removal efficiency range:	
Minimum =	< 35%
Average =	45%
Maximum =	> 65%
Synergies:	Inspections; static analysis; nationalization testing
Counter indications:	None

Lab testing is done primarily on hybrid products that consist of complex physical devices that are controlled by software, such as central office telephone switching systems, complex weapons systems, process control applications, and large medical instruments.

It is obvious that conventional field testing or Beta testing of something like a PBX telephone switch, a cruise missile, a CAT scan machine, or an MRI machine is infeasible due to the need for possible structural modifications to buildings, special electrical wiring, heating and cooling requirements, to say nothing of zoning permits and authorization by various boards and control bodies.

Therefore, the companies that build such complex devices often have laboratories where clients can test out both the hardware and the software prior to having the equipment installed on their own premises.

Lab testing with the users present is normally a black box form of testing, although if certain kinds of problems are noted such as performance or capacity problems, white box testing can be part of the process, too.

Lab testing is normally found only in large companies that construct large hybrid devices with complex hardware and software components.

Customer Acceptance Testing

Usage:	> 90% of applications intended for client execution
Defect removal efficiency range:	
Minimum =	< 25%
Average =	30%
Maximum =	> 45%
Synergies:	Inspections; static analysis; nationalization testing
Counter indications:	None

Customer acceptance testing is commonly found for contract software developed by outsourcing vendors. It is often found for management information systems, systems software, and military software. The only form of software where acceptance testing is rare or does not occur is that of high-volume commercial "shrink-wrapped" software. Even here, some vendors and retail stores provide a money-back guarantee that permits a form of acceptance testing. How the customers go about acceptance testing varies considerably, but usually acceptance testing is a black box form of testing.

For outsourced projects, acceptance testing is a fairly critical step, and failure during acceptance testing can lead to litigation for breach of contract. Because acceptance testing is performed at the client site by the client's personnel, the vendors might not have access to the test plans, test scripts, or test cases. Data on such topics is available from discovery and deposition documents if litigation occurs but is not usually available if acceptance testing is successful and the application is delivered as planned.

Test Planning

For applications that are to be tested by professional test personnel separate from the development personnel, the creation of a formal test plan is a standard precursor to test case design. As a general rule test plans are created for applications that are larger than about 250 function points in size. The larger the application, the larger and more complex the test plan.

With more than 50 years of testing history, there are numerous models for test plans that are generic and can be modified slightly for any kind of software.

In practice, test plan models are most effective when they are derived from similar kinds of software applications—embedded software models, military models, web application models, and client-server models, for example.

The normal content of a formal test plan includes testing objectives, test personnel, test schedules, test resources, defect tracking, input criteria, exit criteria, and test library controls. If there are reusable test cases for purposes such as regression testing, they will be cited.

It is possible to include test plan generation features in tools that are used to collect and analyze requirements. Because the major components of function point metrics (inputs, outputs, inquiries, logical files, and interfaces) are congruent with topics that need to be tested, it would also be possible to include automatic sizing of software applications and probably automatic generation of some test cases as well.

The widely used IEEE 829–2008 standard for Software Test Documentation is a good generic description of test plan contents. A related standard is IEEE 1012–2004 for software verification and validation. ISO standard 9001–2008 is also relevant to test planning because it deals with quality and control of quality.

Test Case Design Methods

For all software applications larger than about 50 function points in size, test case designers immediately encounter the daunting problems of combinatorial complexity. Because many factors need to be tested such as inputs, outputs, inquiries, control flow, performance, security, data flow, and a host of others, the numbers of test cases needed to achieve high levels of test coverage and high levels of defect removal efficiency approaches infinity.

A theoretical study at IBM about testing the MVS operating system noted that millions of test cases and around-the-clock execution for more than ten years would be needed to approach 100% test coverage. At the time MVS was roughly 100,000 function points in size and continuing to grow at around 8% per year. When normal growth was included the study found that 100% coverage was impossible under real-world conditions.

As a result of combinatorial complexity, test case design has always been a balance between test coverage and test economics. Although not exactly a pure form of combinatorial complexity, Tom McCabe's cyclomatic complexity measure also affects test case designs. Modules and code segments with cyclomatic complexity levels higher than 10 would require so many test cases that test coverage cannot approach 100%.

A study by IBM found that the majority of situations where high cyclomatic complexity occurrence was due to poor training, excessive haste, or carelessness. In general, high complexity is an avoidable situation.

More recent work on test-driven development (TDD) asserts that creating test cases prior to the code will minimize cyclomatic complexity. This might be true for individual code segments by one developer or a pair, but it is not yet demonstrated that high complexity levels are minimized for large structures involving large teams of developers.

Because functional test cases are derived from requirements and design, the better the front-end documents are, the better the test cases are. This is why formal inspections of requirements and design benefit testing. It is also why automated readability tools such as the Fog index and the Flesch readability index can have an indirect benefit on test coverage and completeness.

The representation methods used as source documents for test cases and test scripts can be in many forms such as text, use-case diagrams, user stories, decision table, HIPO diagrams, flowcharts, data flow diagrams, and a number of others.

Many books on testing have sample test cases, outlines for test cases and test scripts, and other kinds of information that need not be repeated in this book. There are also numerous courses available from both universities and commercial education groups that teach testing methods and test case design methods.

However, one new test case design method is significant because it has been demonstrated in numerous trials to create a minimum number of test cases combined with maximum test coverage. This method is based on the logic of the design of experiments and was developed by a researcher named Justin Hunter (whose father did pioneering work in the design of experiments).

Gary Gack, a colleague of Hunter, points out that if there are 60 parameters and each parameter has from 2 to 5 values, the total number of test cases to check every combination would be: 1,746,756,896,558,880,852,541,440.

By using the design of experiment approach, all of the two-way combinations can be tested using only 36 test cases.

The design of experiment method is fairly new and somewhat experimental, but the results are promising to date.

There are other methods for minimizing test case volumes while maintaining reasonable test coverage. However, testing software does encounter very serious problems with combinatorial complexity, so brute force methods will not be successful for large systems. Some form of mathematical derivation of test cases is needed.

When test cases are designed and created, many of them have residual value for regression testing. That said, test libraries need automated support because they tend to grow continuously for as long as software applications are being used and hence changing and adding new features.

Test case design is an intellectually challenging discipline. Fortunately, training is readily available. Preparing a new test case can take from a low of 10 minutes to a high of about 75 minutes. Many test cases are reusable both for later regression testing and sometimes for similar applications. For this reason, careful preparation of original test cases is time well spent.

The new form of test case design based on design of experiments has a learning curve initially. When the method is mastered, test case design and development seems to be more rapid than many other methods of test case development. Individual test case construction may run from about 15 minutes to perhaps 25 minutes. However, there is some overall preliminary work to identify all of the parameters that need to be tested. This work is done at the application level rather than the level of specific test cases and may require several hours. However, the results are then relevant to all subsequent test cases, which may be more than 50.

Modifying existing test cases to deal with functional updates is fairly efficient and probably takes between 3 and 20 minutes per test case.

More study is needed on the ranges of effort needed to prepare test cases based on the methodologies used in preparation.

Errors or Bugs in Test Cases

A study performed by IBM on test libraries for several IBM commercial applications found two troubling phenomena: 1) about one-third of the total test cases were duplicates, which added costs but not value to testing, and 2) there were errors in many test cases themselves. Running a defective test case adds costs but lowers testing efficiency because the defective test cases usually don't find defects or may report false positives.

These phenomena were also noted during internal assessments at several other companies. However, the general literature on testing does not have much information available on either numbers of defects in test cases themselves or on duplicate test cases. Both problems seem to be common enough to be termed endemic.

The reason that there are defects in test cases is because they are almost as hard to write as the code itself. The reason there are duplicate test cases is because for large systems multiple test personnel create test cases, and sometimes they end up creating duplicates without realizing it.

It is asserted that test-driven development (TDD), which creates the test cases prior to creating the code, will reduce both test case errors and also cyclomatic complexity of the code. This may be true, but the sparse measures associated with Agile development makes it hard to validate the assertion.

Among the methodologies that capture extensive data, such as the personal software process (PSP) and the team software process (TSP), there is evidence that defective tests cases are reduced and that cyclomatic complexity is lower than that noted on similar applications of the same size and type using less formal methods.

In theory, a test library should control how test cases are added and weed out duplicates and defective test cases. In practice, many test libraries accept new test case as they are submitted with little or no verification or validation.

Although the data is incomplete, the design of experiments method of test case development seems to have fewer bad or defective test cases than any other method noted to date.

Numbers of Testing Stages for Software Projects

Looking at the data from another vantage point, if each specific kind of testing is deemed a "testing stage," it is interesting to see how many discrete testing stages occur for software projects. The overall range of testing stages among the authors' clients and their software projects runs from a low of 1 to a high of 16 out of the total number of testing stages of 40 discussed here at the beginning of this chapter.

Table 5.3   *Approximate Distribution of Testing Stages for U.S. Software Projects*

Number of Testing Stages	Percent of Projects Utilizing Test Stages
1 testing stage	2%
2 testing stages	8%
3 testing stages	10%
4 testing stages	12%
5 testing stages	13%
6 testing stages	21%
7 testing stages	10%
8 testing stages	7%
9 testing stages	5%
10 testing stages	4%
11 testing stages	3%
12 testing stages	1%
13 testing stages	1%
14 testing stages	1%
15 testing stages	1%
16 testing stages	1%
17 testing stages	0%
18 testing stages	0%
19 testing stages	0%
20 testing stages	0%
TOTAL	100%

As can be seen from the distribution of results in Table 5.3, the majority of software projects in the United States (70%) use six or fewer discrete testing stages, and the most common pattern of testing observed includes the following:

- Subroutine testing
- Unit testing
- New function testing
- Regression testing
- Integration testing
- System testing

These six forms of testing are very common on applications of 1,000 function points or larger. These six also happen to be generalized forms of testing that deal with broad categories of errors and issues.

Below 100 function points sometimes only three testing stages are found, assuming the project in question is new and not an enhancement:

- Subroutine testing
- Unit testing
- New function testing

The other forms of testing that are less common are more specialized, such as performance testing or capacity testing, and deal with a narrow band of problems that not every application is concerned with.

This information is derived from several hundred companies, but the sample is not as large as it should be for statistical certainty. More study of testing patterns and numbers of test stages would be useful and provide additional data for analyzing testing efficiency and testing economics.

Testing Pattern Variations by Industry and Type of Software

There are, of course, very significant variations between industries and various kinds of software in terms of typical testing patterns utilized, as follows:

End-user software is the sparsest in terms of testing, and the usual pattern includes only two test stages: subroutine testing and unit testing. Of course, end-user software is almost all less than 100 function points in size and may have only the creator as the sole user.

In today's world a large number of professionals such as accountants, marketing specialists, and other knowledge workers are computer literate and can produce computer programs if they want to. Indeed, there are some suggestions in the literature that end-user development may be a cost-effective method because such applications require little except compilers and debugging tools.

However, end-user applications have some substantial legal liability issues associated with them. If the end user changes jobs, does the software belong to the company or to the developer? If an end-user application damages company data or has serious defects, should the developer be liable for damages?

If the end user quits, will his or her replacement be required to use the software? Because end-user software has little or no documentation, it is not usually capable of being handed on to successors in the same position. The bottom line is that end-user software in a corporate or government context has many hazards that require careful analysis and also legal opinions by corporate attorneys.

Information technology (IT) or *management information systems (MIS)* software projects use from three up to perhaps eight forms of testing. A typical MIS testing stage pattern would include 1) subroutine testing, 2) unit testing, 3) new function testing, 4) regression testing, 5) system testing, and 6) user acceptance testing. MIS testing is usually performed by the developers themselves, so that testing by professional test personnel or by quality assurance personnel is a rarity in this domain. As a result, formal performance testing, security testing, and other kinds of specialized testing may not occur.

Web applications tend to have performance and load issues and often use pretest static analysis. A common pattern of testing for web applications would include 1) subroutine testing, 2) unit testing, 3) new function testing, 4) regression testing, and 5) performance testing. If the web application deals with financial information or other confidential data, then 6) security testing would also be needed. Larger web applications might also use 7) integration and/or 8) system testing. If the web application is built under contract or by an outsource vendor, then 9) acceptance testing would occur.

External Beta testing is not too common because of the need to get the web application running effectively before turning it over to actual clients. However, some web applications such as Firefox and Open Office do utilize Beta testing. High-volume Beta testing with several thousand participants is effective in terms of defect removal efficiency and also fairly inexpensive for vendors.

Smart-phone applets are almost all small. The typical sizes of smart phone applets run from 25 to 250 function points, although some larger applications such as Office to Go top 1,000 function points in size. Many smart-phone applets are developed in their entirety by a single person. Small one-person applications normally use static analysis prior to testing, and then subroutine testing and unit testing comprise the most common test stages.

Open source software development is difficult to characterize because there are so many different methods deployed, and open source is so widely distributed. Open source applications often use static analysis prior to testing because it is efficient and inexpensive, especially if open source static analysis tools are used. The individual programmers who work on open source software normally use subroutine testing and unit testing. Some of the open source packages such as Open Office and Firefox also use higher-level forms of testing including performance testing, security testing, and external Beta testing.

Computer gaming is a field where the authors have no direct clients and therefore no direct data. However, from discussions with colleagues who do work in the computer game field, quality is a rather important topic that tends to differentiate the top games from the lower-tier games.

Modern interactive computer games have extraordinary timing and performance constraints, so obviously performance testing is common for game development. A typical pattern for games, from second-hand information, would be 1) static analysis prior to testing followed by 2) subroutine testing, 3) unit testing, 4) new function testing, 5) regression testing, and of course, 6) performance testing, and 7) system testing. Because games often have fairly large teams of a dozen or more developers, integration testing and/or system testing would usually occur. External Beta testing can occur for games, too, although usually special permission or nondisclosure agreements may be needed.

Outsource vendors doing information systems are similar to their clients in terms of testing patterns. MIS outsource vendors use typical MIS patterns; systems software vendors use typical systems software patterns; and military outsource vendors use typical military test patterns. This means that the overall range of outsource testing can run from as few as 3 kinds of testing up to a high of 16. Usually, the outsource vendors utilize at least one more stage of testing than their clients.

For business reasons outsource vendors tend to be fairly sophisticated and many have developed good quality control practices. Indeed, a significant percentage of outsource companies tend to be at CMMI levels 3 through 5.

This does not guarantee that outsource vendors will always produce high-quality software, and litigation does occur for perhaps 5% of outsource projects. However, from performing assessment and benchmark data collection among both outsource vendors and their clients, the outsource vendors are usually somewhat better in quality control.

Commercial software developed by major vendors such as Microsoft, IBM, Sun, Oracle, SAP, Google, and Computer Associates (CA) will typically use a 14-stage testing series: 1) subroutine testing, 2) unit testing, 3) new function testing, 4) regression testing, 5) performance testing, 6) stress or load testing, 7) integration testing, 9) usability testing, 10) platform testing,

11) nationalization testing; 12) system testing, 13) viral testing, and 14) field testing, which is often called external or Beta testing.

Small software vendors, however, who develop small applications of fewer than 1,000 function points may only use six testing stages: 1) subroutine testing, 2) unit testing, 3) new function testing, 4) regression testing, 5) system testing, and 6) Beta testing.

Major software vendors such as Microsoft, Oracle, Google, Computer Associates (CA), and IBM have large departments of professional testers who take over after unit testing and perform the major testing work at the higher levels such as integration, system, and specialized testing such as performance or stress testing.

Systems software is often extensively tested and may use as many as 13 different testing stages. A typical testing pattern for a software system in the 10,000 function point range would include 1) subroutine testing, 2) unit testing, 3) new function testing, 4) regression testing, 5) performance testing, 6) stress/capacity testing, 7) integration testing, 8) usability testing, 9) system testing, 10) viral testing, 11) security testing, 12) nationalization testing, 13) lab testing and/or field testing, which is often called external or Beta testing. Pretest static analysis and pretest inspections are widely used for systems software. Indeed, among the author's clients, systems software developers use formal inspections more frequently than any other class of software group.

The larger systems software companies such as AT&T, Siemens-Nixdorf, IBM, and so on typically utilize professional testing personnel after unit testing. Also the systems software domain typically has the largest and best equipped software quality assurance groups and the only quality assurance research labs.

For systems software testing, various engineers other than software engineers may be involved in testing because the hardware needs to be tested at the same time as the software.

Medical devices that require government certification must pass through a series of special kinds of testing culminating with tests on patients.

Some of the large systems software organizations may have three different kinds of quality-related laboratories:

1. Quality research labs

2. Usability labs

3. Hardware/software product test labs

Indeed, the larger systems software groups are among the few kinds of organizations that actually perform research on software quality, in the classical definition of "research" as formal experiments using trial and error methods to develop improved tools and practices.

Military software uses the most extensive suite of test stages, and large weapons or logistics systems may include 16 discrete testing stages: 1) subroutine testing, 2) unit testing, 3) new function testing, 4) regression testing, 5) performance testing, 5)stress testing, 7) integration testing, 8) independent testing, 9) usability testing, 10) nationalization testing, 11) lab testing, system testing, 12) viral testing, 13) security testing, 14) penetration testing, 15) field/Beta testing, and 16) customer acceptance testing.

Only military projects routinely utilize "independent testing" or testing by a separate company external to the developing or contracting organization. Military projects often utilize the services of professional testing personnel and also quality assurance personnel.

However, there are several companies that perform independent testing for commercial software organizations. Often smaller software companies that lack full in-house testing capabilities will utilize such external testing organizations.

Military software projects also use an extensive suite of pretest defect removal activities including but not limited to formal inspections, independent verification and validation (IV&V), static analysis, and audits. In some cases, there may also be oversight committees and even Congressional oversight groups, although the latter is quite rare.

Testing Pattern Variations by Size of Application

Another interesting way of looking at the distribution of testing stages is to look at the ranges and numbers of test stages associated with the various sizes of software applications, as shown in Table 5.4.

Table 5.4 *Ranges of Test Stages Associated with the Size of Software Applications*

Size of Application in Function Points	Number of Test Stages Performed		
	Minimum	Average	Maximum
1	1	3	4
10	1	4	5
100	2	5	8
1,000	3	9	11
10,000	4	10	13
100,000	6	12	16

As is evident from the data, the larger applications tend to utilize a much more extensive set of testing stages than do the smaller applications, which is not unexpected.

It is interesting to consolidate testing variations by industry and testing variations by size of application. Table 5.5 shows the typical number of test stages observed for six size plateaus and eight software classes.

Table 5.5 *Numbers of Test Stages by Application Size and Class*

	(Size of Application in IFPUG Function Points)						
Class	1	10	100	1,000	10,000	100,000	Average
End-user	1	2	2				1.67
Applet	1	2	3				2.00
Web	2	3	3	6	7		4.20
IT	2	3	4	6	7	8	5.00
Outsource	2	3	5	7	8	10	5.83
Systems	3	4	7	11	12	14	8.50
Embedded	3	4	7	12	13	16	9.17
Military	4	5	8	12	14	16	9.83
AVERAGE	2.25	3.25	4.88	9.00	10.17	12.80	7.06

If a cell in Table 5.5 is blank, that means that no applications of that size have data available. Essentially it means that no applications of such sizes seem to exist.

Table 5.5 makes it clear that large systems use many more kinds of testing than small applications. It also makes it clear that the more complex technical forms of software such as embedded and military software use more kinds of testing than information technology and web applications.

There are wide variations in testing patterns, so this table has a significant margin of error. However, the data is interesting and explains why the commercial, systems, and military software domains often have higher reliability levels than other forms.

This table also illustrates that there is no single pattern of testing that is universally appropriate for all sizes and all classes of software. The optimal pattern of defect removal and testing stages must be matched to the nature of the application.

Using the permutation of topics shown in the software taxonomy (nature, scope, class, type, problem complexity, code complexity, and data complexity) there are 35,190,000 kinds of applications. These range from small one-person end-user spreadsheets of about 1 function point up to massive enterprise resource planning (ERP) applications of about 300,000 function points.

Even if project type is the sole variable, there are still 23 general types of software. Because one of these types is "hybrid," which involves more than one type in the same application (such as client-server), it can be seen that an optimal set of defect removal methods can vary widely.

Because of the variables involved, the selection of an optimal defect removal series is difficult to do by untrained amateurs. It is also difficult to do without data on defect removal efficiency levels. However, several commercial estimating tools do have a feature the uses pattern matching to show the sequence of defect removal methods used on similar benchmark applications with the best quality results, for applications of the same size, type, and class as the one being estimated.

Testing Stages Noted in Lawsuits Alleging Poor Quality

It is an interesting observation that for outsource, military, and systems software that ends up in court for litigation that involves assertions of unacceptable or inadequate quality, the number of testing stages is much smaller, while formal design and code inspections were not utilized at all.

Table 5.6 shows the typical patterns of defect removal activities for software projects larger than 1,000 function points in size where the client sued the developing organization for producing software with inadequate quality levels.

The table simply compares the pattern of defect removal operations observed for reliable software packages with high quality levels to the pattern noted during lawsuits where poor quality and low reliability was part of the litigation.

Table 5.6 *Defect Removal and Testing Stages Noted During Litigation for Poor Quality*

	Reliable Software	Software Involved in Litigation for Poor Quality
Formal design inspections	Used	Not used
Formal code inspections	Used	Not used
Subroutine testing	Used	Used
Unit testing	Used	Used
New function testing	Used	Rushed or omitted
Regression testing	Used	Rushed or omitted
Integration testing	Used	Used
Security testing	Used	Rushed or omitted
Performance testing	Used	Rushed or omitted
Usability testing	Used	Rushed or omitted
System testing	Used	Rushed or omitted
Capacity testing	Used	Rushed or omitted
Acceptance testing	Used	Used and failed

The phrase "rushed or omitted" indicates that the vendor departed from best standard practices by eliminating a stage of defect removal or by rushing it in order to meet an arbitrary finish date or commitment to the client.

It is interesting that during the depositions and testimony of the litigation, the vendor often counter-charges that the shortcuts were made at the direct request of the client. Sometimes the vendors assert that the client ordered the shortcuts even in the face of warnings that the results might be hazardous.

As can be seen, then, software developed under contractual obligations is at some peril if quality control and testing approaches are not carefully performed.

Using Function Points to Estimate Test Case Volumes

Function point and the related feature point metrics are starting to provide some preliminary but interesting insights into test case volumes. This is not unexpected given the fundamental parameters of both function points and feature points all represent topics that need test coverage:

- Inputs

- Outputs

- Inquires

- Logical files

- Interfaces

- Algorithms (feature points only)

Because function points and feature points can both be derived during requirements and early design stages, this approach offers a method of predicting test case numbers fairly early. The method is still somewhat experimental, but the approach is leading to interesting results, and usage is expanding.

Table 5.7 shows preliminary data on the number of test cases that have been noted among our clients, using "test cases per function point" as the normalizing metric. This table has a high margin of error, but as with any other set of preliminary data points, it is better to publish the results in the hope of future refinements and corrections than to wait until the data is truly complete.

Table 5.7 *Ranges of Test Cases per IFPUG Function Point*

	(Data expressed in terms of test cases per IFPUG function point)			
	Testing Stages	Minimum Number of Test Cases	Average Number of Test Cases	Maximum Number of Test Cases
	General Testing			
1	Subroutine testing	0.18	0.25	0.33
2	PSP/TSP Unit testing	2.45	3.50	4.55
3	XP testing	1.40	2.00	2.60
4	Component testing	1.23	1.75	2.28
5	Integration testing	1.05	1.50	1.95
6	System testing	1.05	1.50	1.95
7	New function testing	1.75	2.50	3.25
8	Regression testing	1.40	2.00	2.60
9	Unit testing	2.10	3.00	3.90
	AVERAGE	1.40	2.00	2.60
	SUM	12.60	18.00	23.40
	Automatic Testing			
10	Virus/spyware test	2.45	3.50	4.55
11	System test	1.40	2.00	2.60
12	Regression test	1.40	2.00	2.60
13	Unit test	0.04	0.05	0.07
14	New function test	2.10	3.00	3.90
	AVERAGE	1.48	2.11	2.74
	SUM	7.39	10.55	13.72
	Specialized Testing (Special defects)			
15	Virus testing	0.49	0.70	0.91
16	Spyware testing	0.70	1.00	1.30
17	Limits/capacity testing	0.35	0.50	0.65
18	General security testing	0.28	0.40	0.52
19	Penetration testing	2.80	4.00	5.20
20	Reusability testing	2.80	4.00	5.20
21	Firewall testing	1.40	2.00	2.60
22	Litigation testing (code theft)	2.10	3.00	3.90
23	Performance testing	0.35	0.50	0.65

(Continued)

Table 5.7   *(Continued)*

	Testing Stages	Minimum Number of Test Cases	Average Number of Test Cases	Maximum Number of Test Cases
	Specialized Testing (Special defects)			
24	Litigation testing (quality)	1.40	2.00	2.60
25	Nationalization testing	0.21	0.30	0.39
26	Scalability testing	0.28	0.40	0.52
27	Platform testing	0.14	0.20	0.26
28	Clean room testing	2.10	3.00	3.90
29	Patent testing	0.11	0.15	0.20
30	Supply chain testing	0.21	0.30	0.39
31	Cloud testing	0.18	0.25	0.33
32	SOA orchestration	0.14	0.20	0.26
33	Independent testing	0.14	0.20	0.26
	AVERAGE	0.85	1.22	1.58
	SUM	16.17	23.10	30.03
	User Testing			
34	Usability testing	0.18	0.25	0.33
35	Case study testing	0.07	0.10	0.13
36	Local nationalization	0.28	0.40	0.52
37	Lab testing	0.88	1.25	1.63
38	External Beta testing	0.70	1.00	1.30
39	Acceptance testing	0.21	0.30	0.39
40	Prepurchase testing	0.07	0.10	0.13
	AVERAGE	0.34	0.49	0.63
	SUM	2.38	3.40	4.42
	TOTAL TEST CASES PER FUNCTION POINT	38.54	55.05	71.57

The usage of function point metrics also provides some rough rules of thumb for predicting the overall volumes of test cases that are likely to be created for software projects.

- Using the design of experiment method, raising the application to the 1.025 power will give an approximation of the numbers of test cases created by that method.

- Raising the function point total of the application to the 1.05 power will give an approximation of the minimum number of test cases using normal ad hoc test case development methods.

- Raising the function point total to the 1.2 power gives an approximation of the average number of test cases.

- Raising the function point total to the 1.3 power gives an approximation of the maximum number of test cases.

These rules of thumb are based on observations of software projects whose sizes range between about 100 function points and 100,000 function points. Rules of thumb are not accurate enough for serious business purposes such as contracts but are useful in providing estimating "sanity checks."

Because of combinatorial complexity, it is usually impossible to write and run enough test cases to fully exercise a software project larger than about 100 function points in size. The number of permutations of inputs, outputs, and control flow paths quickly becomes astronomical. However, the design of experiment testing approach does cut back on total test cases without any apparent reduction of defect removal efficiency.

For really large systems that approach 100,000 function points in size, the total number of test cases needed to fully test every condition can be regarded, for practical purposes, as an infinite number. Also the amount of computing time needed to run such a test suite would also be an infinite number, or at least a number so large that there are not enough computers in any single company to approach the capacity needed.

Therefore, the volumes of test cases shown here are based on empirical observations, and the numbers assume standard reduction techniques such as testing boundary conditions rather than all intermediate values and compressing related topics into equivalency classes.

Using Function Points to Estimate the Numbers of Test Personnel

One of the newest but most interesting uses of function point metrics in a testing context is to use function points for predicting the probable number of test personnel that might be needed for each test stage and then for the overall product.

Table 5.8 has a high margin of error, but the potential value of using function points for test staffing prediction is high enough to make publication of preliminary data useful.

As an example of how to use the data in this table, if integration testing has an average assignment scope of 2,000 function points and the application to be tested is 10,000 function points in size, then a test team of five people would be indicated.

Table 5.8   *Ranges of Testing Assignment Scopes per Tester or Developer*

	Testing Stages	Minimum Assignment Scope (Function Points)	Average Assignment Scope (Function Points)	Maximum Assignment Scope (Function Points)
	(Data expressed in IFPUG function points per tester or developer)			
	General Testing			
1	Subroutine testing	3	5	9
2	PSP/TSP Unit testing	33	50	88
3	XP testing	65	100	175
4	Component testing	813	1,250	2,188
5	Integration testing	1,300	2,000	3,500
6	System testing	1,300	2,000	3,500
7	New function testing	81	125	219
8	Regression testing	98	150	263
9	Unit testing	33	50	88
	AVERAGE	414	637	1,114
	Automatic Testing			
10	Virus/spyware test	9,750	15,000	26,250
11	System test	2,275	3,500	6,125
12	Regression test	2,275	3,500	6,125
13	Unit test	98	150	263
14	New function test	325	500	875
	AVERAGE	2,945	4,530	7,928
	Specialized Testing (Special defects)			
15	Virus testing	3,250	5,000	8,750
16	Spyware testing	3,250	5,000	8,750
17	Limits/capacity testing	4,875	7,500	13,125
18	General security testing	3,250	5,000	8,750
19	Penetration testing	3,250	5,000	8,750
20	Reusability testing	1,625	2,500	4,375
21	Firewall testing	16,250	25,000	43,750
22	Litigation testing (code theft)	3,250	5,000	8,750
23	Performance testing	6,500	10,000	17,500
24	Litigation testing (quality)	3,250	5,000	8,750
25	Nationalization testing	2,275	3,500	6,125

Testing Stages	Minimum Assignment Scope (Function Points)	Average Assignment Scope (Function Points)	Maximum Assignment Scope (Function Points)
Specialized Testing (Special defects)			
26 Scalability testing	6,500	10,000	17,500
27 Platform testing	6,500	10,000	17,500
28 Clean room testing	650	1,000	1,750
29 Patent testing	6,500	10,000	17,500
30 Supply chain testing	48,750	75,000	131,250
31 Cloud testing	9,750	15,000	26,250
32 SOA orchestration	9,750	15,000	26,250
33 Independent testing	9,750	15,000	26,250
AVERAGE	7,851	12,079	21,138
User Testing			
34 Usability testing	3,250	5,000	8,750
35 Case study testing	3,250	5,000	8,750
36 Local nationalization	2,600	4,000	7,000
37 Lab testing	9,750	15,000	26,250
38 External Beta testing	3,250	5,000	8,750
39 Acceptance testing	9,750	15,000	26,250
40 Prepurchase testing	19,500	30,000	52,500
AVERAGE	7,336	11,286	19,750

For some of the test stages such as subroutine testing and unit testing, the normal practice is for the testing to be performed by developers. In this case, the data simply indicates the "average" sizes of subroutines and stand-alone programs tested by an individual developer.

Using Function Points to Estimate Testing Effort and Costs

Another use of the function point metric in a testing context is to estimate and later measure testing effort (and costs). A full and formal evaluation of testing requires analysis of three discrete activities:

1. Test preparation

2. Test execution

3. Defect repairs

Test preparation involves creating test cases, validating them, and putting them into a test library.

Test execution involves running the test cases against the software and recording the results. Note that testing is an iterative process, and the same test cases can be run several times if needed, or even more. Typically high-quality software will use many fewer build and test cycles than low-quality software. High-quality software usually requires fewer than five build and test cycles, while low-quality software may require more than ten.

Defect repairs concerns fixing any bugs that are found via testing, validating the fixes, and then rerunning the test cases that found the bugs to ensure that the bugs have been repaired and no "bad fixes" have inadvertently been introduced.

With a total of 40 different kinds of testing to consider, the actual prediction of testing effort is too complex for simplistic rules of thumb. Several commercial estimating tools such as CHECKPOINT, COCOMO II, PRICE-S, SEER, and SLIM can predict testing costs for each test stage and then aggregate overall testing effort and expenses for any size or kind of software project. These same tools and others within this class can also predict testing defect removal efficiency levels.

Table 5.9 shows the approximate average values for preparation, execution, and defect repairs noted among the authors' clients.

Table 5.9 *Test Effort for Preparation, Execution, and Defect Repairs*

	(Data expressed in minutes per test case)		
Testing Stages	Test Case Design and Preparation Minutes per Test Case	Test Case Execution Minutes per Test Case	Defect Repair Minutes per Test Case
General Testing			
1 Subroutine testing	5.00	1.00	10.00
2 PSP/TSP Unit testing	6.00	1.00	15.00
3 XP testing	5.00	1.00	15.00
4 Component testing	40.00	5.00	90.00
5 Integration testing	40.00	5.00	90.00
6 System testing	30.00	7.00	120.00
7 New function testing	30.00	2.00	90.00
8 Regression testing	10.00	2.00	90.00
9 Unit testing	10.00	1.00	30.00
AVERAGE	19.56	2.78	61.11
SUM	176.00	25.00	550.00
Automatic Testing			
10 Virus/spyware test	35.00	1.00	75.00

	Testing Stages	Test Case Design and Preparation Minutes per Test Case	Test Case Execution Minutes per Test Case	Defect Repair Minutes per Test Case
	Automatic Testing			
11	System test	30.00	1.00	120.00
12	Regression test	5.00	1.00	90.00
13	Unit test	10.00	1.00	30.00
14	New function test	30.00	1.00	90.00
	AVERAGE	43.65	1.00	81.00
	SUM	110.00	5.00	405.00
	Specialized Testing (Special defects)			
15	Virus testing	35.00	10.00	120.00
16	Spyware testing	60.00	45.00	300.00
17	Limits/capacity testing	30.00	3.00	180.00
18	General security testing	45.00	30.00	300.00
19	Penetration testing	120.00	320.00	360.00
20	Reusability testing	30.00	3.00	30.00
21	Firewall testing	15.00	2.00	30.00
22	Litigation testing (code theft)	180.00	15.00	60.00
23	Performance testing	25.00	5.00	120.00
24	Litigation testing (quality)	60.00	15.00	90.00
25	Nationalization testing	20.00	10.00	90.00
26	Scalability testing	20.00	3.00	60.00
27	Platform testing	20.00	10.00	90.00
28	Clean room testing	120.00	10.00	90.00
29	Patent testing	50.00	30.00	240.00
30	Supply chain testing	60.00	60.00	300.00
31	Cloud testing	45.00	60.00	240.00
32	SOA orchestration	45.00	60.00	240.00
33	Independent testing	35.00	25.00	75.00
	AVERAGE	53.42	37.68	65.95
	SUM	1,015.00	716.00	3,015.00
	User Testing			
34	Usability testing	15.00	5.00	120.00
35	Case study testing	25.00	10.00	90.00
36	Local nationalization	20.00	7.00	90.00

(Continued)

Table 5.9   *(Continued)*

Testing Stages	Test Case Design and Preparation Minutes per Test Case	Test Case Execution Minutes per Test Case	Defect Repair Minutes per Test Case
User Testing			
37 Lab testing	90.00	75.00	240.00
38 External Beta testing	10.00	15.00	120.00
User Testing			
39 Acceptance testing	10.00	10.00	120.00
40 Prepurchase testing	7.00	5.00	120.00
AVERAGE	25.29	18.14	128.57
SUM	177.00	127.00	900.00
Overall Average	35.48	14.90	84.16
Cumulative Sum	1,478.00	873.00	4,870.00
Percent of Total	20.47%	12.09%	67.44%

A few words of caution are needed about the data in Table 5.9. First the Average numbers listed are based on the mode rather than the mean. The reason for this is that range of effort is so wide that means would distort the results. A few defects require many months to resolve rather than minutes or hours.

(Readers are probably accustomed to the urban legend that asserts that "it costs 100 times as much to fix a bug after release as during development." Unfortunately, this is not true. The legend is based on ignoring the fixed costs of writing and running test cases.)

Second, individual skills and experience levels can cause variations of about −50% and plus 75% for the nominal results shown in Table 5.9.

Third, only about 10% of test cases actually find any bugs. The rest find nothing at all. Though Table 5.1 seems to indicate that every test case will have defect repairs, this is not realistic. Indeed, if formal pretest inspections and static analysis tools are run prior to testing, more than 97% of all test cases will find no bugs because so few are left to find.

Fourth, test cases are run more than once. Some are reused during unit, new function, regression, and system testing, to name a few. Others are run many times during individual test stages. For example, an application might go through 15 builds, and each build will have both new function and regression test cases run against it. This means a specific test case, which might take 60 minutes to build, can be run 25 times, and during those 25 runs it might find perhaps one or two bugs.

Fifth, some test cases are duplicated, and some have defects of their own. Running duplicate or defective test cases adds costs to testing but does not add value. In fact, defective test cases lower defect removal efficiency and have negative value.

Too many variables are involved for a static representation in a table or graph to be really accurate for publication in a book. Therefore, for the purposes of this book, a major simplifying assumption is used. The assumption is that the proportion of total software effort devoted to testing correlates exactly with the number of test stages that are involved. This assumption has a few exceptions but seems to work well enough to have practical value.

The percentages shown in Table 5.10 for testing are based on the total development budget for the software project in question.

The same table also shows the approximate defect removal efficiency correlated with number of test stages for coding defects. Here, too, as the number of test stages grows larger, defect removal efficiency levels increase. The essential message is that if you want to approach zero-defect levels using testing as the primary defect removal method, be prepared to perform quite a few testing stages.

Table 5.10   *Number of Testing Stages, Testing Effort, and Defect Removal Efficiency*

Number of Testing Stages	Percent of Effort Devoted to Testing	Cumulative Defect Removal Efficiency
1 testing stage	10%	50%
2 testing stages	15%	60%
3 testing stages	20%	70%
4 testing stages	25%	75%
5 testing stages	30%	80%
6 testing stages*	33%*	85%*
7 testing stages	36%	87%
8 testing stages	39%	90%
9 testing stages	42%	92%
10 testing stages	45%	94%
11 testing stages	48%	96%
12 testing stages	52%	98%
13 testing stages	55%	99%
14 testing stages	58%	99.9%
15 testing stages	61%	99.99%
16 testing stages	64%	99.999%
17 testing stages	67%	99.9999%
18 testing stages	70%	99.99999%

*Note: Six test stages, 33% costs, and 85% removal efficiency are approximate U.S. averages for software projects => 1,000 function points in size.

This simplified approach is not accurate enough for serious project planning or for contracts, but it shows overall trends well enough to make the economic picture understandable.

This table also explains why large systems have higher testing costs than small applications and why systems and military software have higher testing costs than information systems: More testing stages are utilized.

Note, however, that the table does not show the whole picture (which is why commercial estimating tools are recommended). For example, if formal pretesting design and code inspections are also utilized, they alone can approach 80% in defect removal efficiency and also raise the efficiency of testing.

Thus projects that utilize formal inspections plus testing can top 99% in cumulative defect removal efficiency with fewer stages than shown here, given the table illustrates only testing.

Testing by Developers or by Professional Test Personnel

One of the major questions concerning software testing is who should do it. The possible answers to this question include: A) the developers themselves; B) professional test personnel; C) professional quality assurance personnel; C) some combination of A, B, and C.

Note that several forms of testing such as external Beta testing and customer acceptance testing are performed by clients themselves or by consultants that the clients hire to do the work.

There is no definitive answer to this question, but some empirical observations may be helpful:

- The defect removal efficiency of black box testing is higher when performed by test personnel or by quality assurance personnel rather than by developers themselves.

- Black box testing performed by clients (such as Beta and acceptance testing) varies widely, but efficiency rises with the numbers of clients involved.

- For usability problems, testing by clients themselves outranks all other forms of testing.

- The defect removal efficiency of the white box subroutine and unit testing stages is highest when performed by developers themselves.

- The defect removal efficiency of specialized kinds of white box testing such as security or viral protection testing is highest when performed by professional test personnel rather than by the developers themselves.

Table 5.11 shows the authors' observations of who typically performs various test stages from among our client organizations. Note that because our clients include quite a few systems software, military software, and commercial software vendors, we probably have a bias in our data given that these domains are much more likely to utilize the services of professional test and quality assurance personnel than are the MIS and outsource domains.

The table is sorted in descending order of the development column. Note that this order illustrates that early testing is most often performed by development personnel, but the later stages of testing are most often performed by testing or quality assurance specialists.

Table 5.11 *Observations on Performance of Test Stages by Occupation Group*

Testing Stage	Developers	Testers	Qual. Assur.	Clients
Subroutine testing	100%	0%	0%	0%
Unit testing	90%	10%	0%	0%
New function testing	50%	30%	20%	0%
Integration testing	50%	30%	20%	0%
Viral testing	50%	30%	20%	0%
System testing	40%	40%	20%	0%
Regression testing	30%	50%	20%	0%
Performance testing	30%	60%	10%	0%
Platform testing	30%	50%	20%	0%
Stress testing	30%	50%	20%	0%
Security testing	30%	40%	30%	0%
Supply chain testing	20%	50%	30%	0%
Usability testing	10%	10%	30%	50%
Acceptance testing	0%	0%	0%	100%
Lab testing	0%	0%	0%	100%
Field (Beta) testing	0%	0%	0%	100%
Clean room testing	0%	50%	40%	10%
Independent testing	0%	60%	40%	0%
AVERAGE	31%	31%	18%	20%

As Table 5.11 shows, among our clients, testing by developers and testing by professional test personnel are equal in frequency, and are followed by testing involving software quality assurance (SQA) and finally testing by customers or their designated testers.

Testing by development personnel is much more common for the smaller forms of testing such as subroutine and unit testing and Agile testing. For the larger forms (such as system testing) and for the specialized forms (performance or security testing, for example), testing by professional test personnel or by quality assurance personnel become more common.

Testing should be part of a synergistic and integrated suite of defect prevention and defect removal operations that may include prototyping, quality assurance reviews, pretest inspections, formal test planning, multistage testing, and measurement of defect levels and severities.

For those who have no empirical data on quality, the low average defect removal efficiency levels of most forms of testing will be something of a surprise. However, it is because each testing step is less than 100% efficient that multiple test stages are necessary in the first place.

Testing is an important technology for software. For many years, progress in testing primarily occurred within the laboratories of major corporations that built systems software. However, in recent years a new sub-industry has appeared of commercial test tool and support companies. This new sub-industry is gradually improving software test capabilities as the commercial vendors of testing tools and methodologies compete within a fast-growing market for test-support products and services.

Summary and Conclusions on Software Testing

Testing is one of the oldest forms of software defect removal and has provided more than 50 years of accumulated information. This is why there are so many books on testing compared to other forms of quality and defect removal.

In spite of the plenitude of published books, there is a significant shortage of reliable quantitative data on testing efficiency, testing costs, and how testing relates to pretest defect removal methods such as inspections and static analysis.

Unfortunately, the software industry has concentrated on testing to the exclusion of other and sometimes more cost-effective methods of defect removal. If testing is the only form of software defect removal used, costs will be high, and defect removal efficiency levels will seldom if ever top 80% for large systems in the 10,000 function point size range.

To achieve high levels of defect removal efficiency levels and to do so with fairly short schedules and low costs, a synergistic combination of defect prevention methods, pretest defect removal methods, and formal testing all need to be utilized. Testing alone is too expensive and too low in defect removal efficiency to be the only method used for quality control of software applications. Testing is important and can be valuable, but it needs to be used in conjunction with other methods such as inspections and static analysis.

Another shortage of empirical data in the software quality literature is longitudinal studies that measure the full sequence of defect removal activities starting with early requirements inspections and continuing through customer acceptance testing. This sequence can include more than 25 discrete defect removal activities, and it would be useful to know the cumulative results of common sequences.

A final observation is that testing is a skill-based activity that requires training and experience to be effective. As a result certified professional test personnel tend to outperform developers in testing defect removal efficiency. This is not to say that developers should stop testing, but after unit testing is finished, professional testing personnel will generate better results for function, regression, and system testing, as well as all of the specialized forms of testing.

For an activity with more than 50 years of usage, testing data is still less complete than it should be for both defect removal effectiveness and cost distribution among the activities of test preparation, test execution, and defect repairs.

Chapter 6

Post-Release Defect Removal

Introduction

Because software defect removal efficiency averages only about 85% and essentially never equals 100%, there will always be latent defects present in software at the time of delivery. IBM called these defects in delivered software *latent defects* because until the software is released, these defects have yet to manifest as problems experienced by users.

Some of these latent defects were discovered during testing but were not repaired by the time the software was released. Other defects were not discovered and were unknown to the developers and test personnel at the time of release.

Still other defects will be in the form of "bad fixes" or new defects accidentally included in prior defect repairs. From about 1% to as many as 5% of delivered defects may be embedded in defect repairs created during the last two weeks prior to delivery.

For some enhancements to legacy applications, defects in the older code may have persisted for a number of years. This fact is especially true if the legacy application contains error-prone modules, which are unusually high in complexity and hence also high in latent defects.

The essential point is that software applications are delivered to clients with latent defects present in the code. This statement seems to be true for 100% of new applications at their first release, but it remains true for subsequent releases. Sometimes software does not stabilize or approach zero-defect status for more than five years after the initial release. Even then, enhancements and new features will contain additional latent defects.

Latent defects also occur with applications running online or available from the Web. The difference in distribution channels does not reduce the odds of latent defects being present in released software applications.

A portion of latent defects remains even after functional and nonfunctional testing. These latent defects are caused by *lapses in the structural quality of the software*—the quality of the architectural design and its implementation. As we saw in Chapters 2 and 4, functional and nonfunctional testing are insufficient for detecting these lapses in structural quality. This chapter discusses how these structural quality lapses alone can result in a significant amount of technical debt—over $1 million for a typical business application of around 374,000 lines of code (KLOC).

In the early days of commercial software, most (usually more than 98%) of the latent defects at the point of delivery were those that had escaped detection via testing and other forms of defect removal. Only defects found during the last week prior to release were repaired, plus bad fixes in defects repaired during the last two weeks prior to release.

More recently, some commercial vendors have begun to deliver software with a significant number of detected but unrepaired defects. For small applications below 1,000 function points there may be dozens of latent defects. For larger systems in the range of 10,000 function points, perhaps several hundred known defects are present at the time of release. For massive applications in excess of 100,000 function points, such as Microsoft Windows 7 or SAP or Oracle, there may be thousands of latent defects. The delivery of software with known defects seems to be motivated by three factors:

1. The desire to achieve earlier delivery dates

2. The questionable assumption that a rapid follow-on release will fix the defects

3. The intent to use the skills of customers themselves for at least some defect repairs

For some kinds of commercial software such as operating systems, enterprise resource planning systems (ERP), financial applications, and other kinds of "mission-critical" software packages, the clients often have experienced and skilled personnel available to perform installations. These skilled personnel also find, report, and sometimes repair critical defects as they occur. Essentially the first few months of deployment of a complex software application are a kind of continuation of the Beta test. A few vendors even compensate users for repairing defects or identifying security flaws.

This situation has become common enough that many customers prefer not to install the first release of new software packages but wait several months for a second release or at least until many latent defects have been repaired via a "service pack."

Commercial software is not alone in this. Embedded applications, internal applications, systems software, and military software also contain latent defects at the time of delivery. This is true for both the initial releases of new applications and also for every subsequent release with new features.

Post-Release Defect Severity Levels

Software defects vary widely in how much harm they might cause. To keep tabs on the seriousness of software defects, it is a standard practice to assign severity levels to defects reported by customers. The IBM severity scale, one of the oldest methods of assigning severity levels to defects, dates back to the late 1950s and is still in use today.

Because IBM dominated mainframe computing for many years, the IBM severity levels were used by many other companies. There are four plateaus of severity using the IBM scale, plus some additional categories:

IBM Severity Scale	Definition
Severity 1	Software does not operate at all.
Severity 2	Disruption or errors in a major feature.
Severity 3	Minor disruption; software still usable.
Severity 4	Cosmetic error that does not impact operation.
Invalid defect	**Problem caused by hardware or other software**
Duplicate defect	Additional reports of a known defect.
Abeyant defect	Unique defect that cannot be duplicated.
Improvement	A defect report is actually a suggested improvement.

The IBM method is not the only way of dealing with severity levels. Some companies use a scale with only three severity plateaus; some use five. Other methods such as *orthogonal defect reporting*, attempt to provide a more descriptive method than the original severity code. However, the IBM severity scale is still the most widely used as of 2011.

The high-severity defects are, of course, more important to customers than the low-severity defects. As a result, software development groups and maintenance groups exert considerable effort to repair high-severity defects as fast as possible. Table 6.1 shows the approximate distribution of defect reports by severity level for the first 90 days of software usage.

Note that changing the size of the application or changing the numbers of customers would lead to different results. Table 6.1 shows approximate results for 1,000 function points and 1,000 customers.

The final row of Table 6.1 shows that a small number of defect reports are viewed as *possible enhancements* rather than defects. This controversial topic can lead to arguments between clients and software development groups. However, if the report is accepted as valid and the software development group agrees to make changes based on the report, the situation is usually acceptable to both parties.

High-severity defects usually get temporary repairs within a few days. A quick service release may accumulate defect repairs at the end of the first three months, although sometimes these releases are earlier. Because high-severity defects are repaired faster than low-severity defects, clients tend to assign level 2 severity codes to many more defects than probably deserve this level.

Within IBM and many other companies, the initial severity level is assigned by the customers who report the software defect, or it is assigned by customers in conjunction with their IBM account representatives. But the final severity level is assigned by the maintenance team that actually repairs the defects.

Table 6.1 *Software Defects by Severity Level for First 90 Days of Use*

	(Assumes 1,000 function points and 1,000 customers)				
	Number Reported	Percent Reported	Temporary Repair Days	Permanent Repair Days	Per Function Point
Severity 1	7	1.87%	2	60	0.01
Severity 2	119	31.73%	5	60	0.12
Severity 3	151	40.27%	20	60	0.15
Severity 4	98	26.13%	None	60	0.10
TOTAL	375	100.00%	9	60	0.38
Invalid	47	12.53%	None	None	0.05
Duplicate	305	81.33%	9	60	0.31
Abeyant	2	0.53%	7	60	0.00
Improvement	10	2.67%	None	120	0.01

As a general rule, the final assignments of severity 2 volumes by the maintenance personnel seldom tops 20% of the total, whereas the initial customer-assigned severity levels are often 35% or more at severity 2. The clients tend to use severity 2 as a catch-all level for any bugs they want to get fixed in a hurry regardless of the intrinsic severity of the problems.

Software defects themselves are not usually measured in terms of function points nor in terms of lines of code. However, defects tend to be fairly small:

- Severity 1 defects range from a single line of code up to perhaps 25, so the range in function points would be from about 0.01 up to 0.5 if backfiring is applied.

- Severity 2 defects range from a single line of code up to perhaps 100, so the range would be from 0.01 to 2.0 function points. However, if requirements errors get into code, such as the Y2K problem, they can be scattered across thousands of locations in larger applications, and some of these can top 100 function points.

- Severity 3 defects range from a single line of code up to perhaps 50, so the range would be from 0.01 to 1.0 function points.

- Severity 4 defects often have zero function points because they often don't involve errors in code or the execution of software. For example, a spelling error in a HELP screen would be an example of a severity 4 defect with a size of 0 function points and 0 lines of code. Even if severity 4 defects involve code, they are usually only a few lines or a fraction of a function point.

Severity Levels from a Structural Quality Perspective

Defect levels serve as "above the water line" measures of software quality. Another approach to measuring quality has its focus at the structural level—the quality of the design and the quality of the implementation of the software and how the entire software product hangs together.

Structural quality assessments are based on the degree to which the software being assessed accords with the body of software engineering rules. These rules are codified in industry standards such as ISO-9126, the emerging ISO-25000 standard, by standards bodies such as the Software Engineering Institute (SEI) and the Object Management Group (OMG), and companies that have developed the various languages and technologies (Java and .NET, for example) that are in use today. Developers and architects are explicitly or implicitly aware of many of these rules. However, it is humanly impossible to store the whole set in one's head and apply it as code is being designed, developed, enhanced, or maintained. Rule checkers in Integrated Development Environments (IDEs) go part way to managing this task, but they are deficient in two ways:

- First, they are specific to a particular language or technology, which becomes a disadvantage when dealing with most applications, which are a mix of technologies.

- Second, IDE rule checkers lack the full context of the application—they are local and real-time, while many of the significant and hard-to-catch defects in software are those that lurk at the boundaries of languages, technologies, and tiers. This limitation is due to the contextual nature of structural quality as described in Chapters 1 and 2, which discussed how the quality of a local component can depend on the environment in which it operates.

Static analysis reveals quality flaws that are known as "violations." Violations are instances where an application fails to satisfy one or more rules of software engineering. Violations can be grouped according to their potential customer impact in terms of the problems or the defects they can create if left unresolved. The higher the potential customer impact, the higher the severity of the violation. The most severe violations are categorized as "critical violations."

One of the authors has analyzed a set of about 300 applications worldwide from 75 organizations in a number of industry sectors. The data on the density of critical violations (number of critical violations per KLOC) is presented in Figure 6.1. This approach supplements the data on defect severity levels. Moreover, because it is obtained from an automated analysis and measurement system it is immune to the problems of subjectivity that creep into reporting, categorizing, and evaluating the severity of defects.

In the analysis method that was used, Critical Violations are triggered when the software under analysis fails to satisfy a set of rules or patterns of software engineering. Field studies have revealed that Critical Violations triggered by structural quality lapses are very closely correlated with high-severity defects recorded in defect logs (see Figures 2.2, 2.3, and 2.4 in Chapter 2 for additional detail). Hence, *Critical Violations are reliable indicators of severe business disruption.*

Figure 6.1 shows that values roughly between 60 and 160 Critical Violations per KLOC are the most frequent across the entire data set of roughly 300 applications. The distribution mean without outliers included is 112 Critical Violations per KLOC with a very large standard deviation of approximately 64. It is

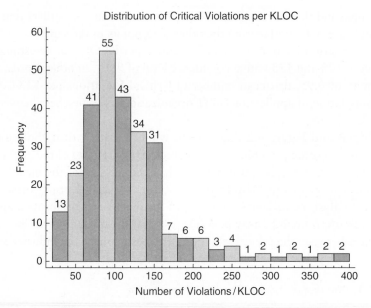

Figure 6.1   *Distribution of critical violation density*

quite obvious that the Critical Violations per KLOC are not distributed normally, as can be seen from high Kurtowsis and Skewness values: 7.5 and 1.8, respectively. These statistics are captured in Table 6.2.

The trimmed mean here refers to the mean of the sample with outliers removed. There's a small difference between the mean calculated over the entire

Table 6.2   *Critical Violation Density Statistics*

Mean with Outliers	137.106
Mean without Outliers	115.498
Trimmed Mean with Outliers	111.921
Trimmed Mean without Outliers	109.386
Standard Deviation with Outliers	165.998
Standard Deviation without Outliers	63.5238
Kurtosis	7.53224
Skewness	1.81568
Estimate of Population Mean at 95% Confidence (without Outliers)	{107.985, 123.012}
Estimate of Population Mean at 99% Confidence (without Outliers)	{105.598, 125.398}

data sample and the trimmed mean. This illustrates that the outliers that are in the sample are not very far from the other data points in the sample.

The population mean of Critical Violations per KLOC can be estimated to be between 108 and 123 with a confidence level of 95%. In other words, with a probability of 0.95, the mean number of Critical Violations per KLOC in the entire population of applications in IT organizations is somewhere between 108 and 123.

Table 6.3 and Figure 6.2 illustrate to what extent Critical Violations per KLOC vary according to industry sector, region, age, or size of the application.

The Financial Services sector has less than a one-third of the mean Critical Violation density of the Manufacturing sector. To further study these differences, an analysis of variance (ANOVA) of the means was performed, applying both the Bonferroni and Tukey post-hoc tests to statistically test for meaningful differences between the critical violation densities between the industry sectors.

Table 6.3   *Number of Applications by Industry Sector*

Energy & Utilities	32
Financial Services	54
Insurance	29
IT and Business Consulting	9
Manufacturing	15
Other	23
Public Administration	75
Software ISV	12
Telecommunications	47

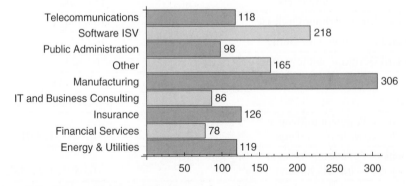

Mean Number of Critical Violations per KLOC by Industry Sector

Figure 6.2   *Mean critical violation density by industry sector*

The statistical analysis shows that there is a difference in mean Critical Violation densities between the Manufacturing sector on the one hand and the Energy & Utilities, Financial Services, Insurance, IT Business Consulting, and Telecommunications sectors on the other. None of the other differences between mean Critical Violation densities are meaningful. For example, in Figure 6.2 we cannot distinguish if the difference in means between the Public Administration and Energy & Utilities sectors is real or simply due to the random variation of Critical Violation densities within these sectors.

Strictly speaking, this type of statistical analysis of variance between means requires equal size samples in each industry sector—a condition that is obviously violated by the data. Hence it is best to be conservative about claims about the differences between Critical Violation densities until we have studied this further. As will be evident, this caveat holds for all subsequent cuts of the data covered in the following sections.

Table 6.4 shows the number of applications by technology. Statistical analysis of the variation of mean Critical Violation densities between technologies reveals a meaningful difference in the mean Critical Violation densities between .NET applications on the one hand and COBOL, Java EE, and Mixed Technologies applications on the other. COBOL and Mixed Technology applications are also significantly different from Oracle 4GL applications. None of the other differences in means illustrated in Figure 6.3 are significant, that is, distinguishable from random variation of Critical Violation densities in applications.

Table 6.5 shows the number of applications by region. Although there is some variation in the mean Critical Violation density by region (Figure 6.4), statistical analysis reveals that these differences are not significant—in other words, they cannot be distinguished from differences due to random variation of these densities in each region. Hence we can conclude (with a grain of salt due to the caveat about equal sample sizes stated above) that mean Critical

Table 6.4 *Number of Applications by Technology*

ABAP	1
C/C++	10
COBOL	30
Java EE	139
Mixed Technologies	43
.NET	16
Oracle 4GL	50
Other	7

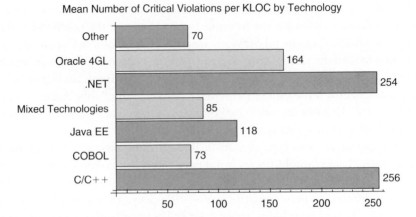

Figure 6.3   *Mean critical violation density by technology*

Table 6.5   *Number of Applications by Region*

Asia	56
Europe	158
North America	59
Other	23

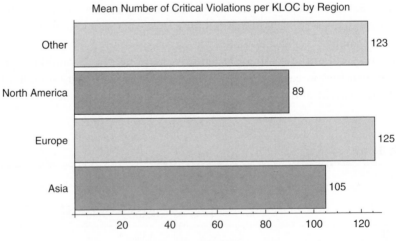

Figure 6.4   *Mean critical violation density by region*

Violation density is not related to the region in which the application is developed; all regions are about the same.

The Age of Application Dropdown segment displayed in Figure 6.5 is used in data collection to give application owners an easy way to submit the age of

Table 6.6 *Number of Applications by Age*

Age of Application Dropdown	12
Between 5 and 10 years	199
Less than 5 years	54
Older than 10 years	31

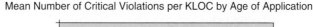

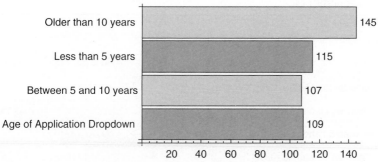

Figure 6.5 *Mean critical violation density by application age*

their applications. For our purposes here, we can ignore that segment of the data because no further information about application age can be determined from that segment.

Table 6.6 shows the number of applications by age. Statistical analysis reveals that the differences in mean Critical Violation density are not significant. In other words, they cannot be distinguished from differences caused by random variation of mean densities within each age group.

A similar conclusion holds for the final segment we consider here: applications segmented by their size in KLOCs, as reflected in Table 6.7 and Figure 6.6.

Once again, statistical analysis reveals no real differences in mean Critical Violation density for different application sizes.

To summarize, a study of 288 applications from 75 organizations worldwide shows that variations in mean Critical Violation density are significant across industry sectors and application technology but are not significant across development region, application age, or application size.

Critical Violation density is a key measure of software structural quality. Critical Violations are reliable indicators of high-severity defects. In this regard they can be used to identify the root causes of these defects post-release. Critical Violations are also central to the quantification of *Technical Debt*: the cost to fix the problems in an application post-release that will, if left unaddressed, lead to severe business disruption. Technical Debt is covered in some detail in Chapter 7.

Table 6.7   *Number of Applications by Size*

Between 0 and 5 KLOC	13
Between 1,000 and 5,000 KLOC	21
Between 100 and 1,000 KLOC	120
Between 10 and 50 KLOC	70
Between 50 and 100 KLOC	50
Between 5 and 10 KLOC	17
Greater then 5,000 KLOC	5

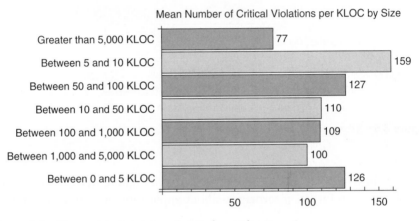

Figure 6.6   *Mean critical violation density by application size*

Maintainability of Software

The topic of software maintainability is widely discussed but poorly understood. IBM performed an extensive series of interviews with maintenance programmers in order to get first-hand information from practitioners regarding what makes maintainability better or worse.

Software maintainability can be measured using several metrics in combination. The three that are most useful are

1. **Maintenance assignment scope:** This is the volume of an application that one programmer can sustain for one year. The measured range of maintenance assignment scopes runs from a low of 300 function points to a high of about 3,000 function points. Somewhere close to 1,000 function points is the norm. Expressed using logical code statements for a language such as Java, the equivalent results would be from a low

15,000 code statements up to a high 150,000 code statements. This data is collected by dividing application sizes by maintenance team sizes. It works well for maintenance programming. However, there are also call center personnel, test personnel, integration personnel, and other specialists that are not included in the basic calculation for maintenance assignment scope. The same idea works for these specialists, but of course the actual values can be quite different.

2. **Cyclomatic complexity of the source code:** The measurement of code complexity is fully automated and available from both commercial companies and open source providers. Cyclomatic complexity levels below 10 are associated with easier maintenance, while levels above 25 become progressively harder to maintain. High complexity is seldom if ever necessary, so high levels of Cyclomatic complexity usually indicate careless programming practices.

3. **Entropy or rate of structural decay:** Numerous small changes to software applications over time tend to degrade the original structure and raise cyclomatic complexity levels. If complexity analysis tools are run frequently, the rate of change can be derived.

Entropy or structural complexity seems to increase at just over 1% per year, which means that applications with long periods of use of more than 10 years become steadily more difficult to maintain or change safely. It is possible to refactor or restructure code that is high in cyclomatic complexity. Manual refactoring is difficult and expensive, but automated restructuring is fairly inexpensive. The caveat is that automated restructuring tools only work for about a dozen programming languages out of some 2,500.

From the IBM interviews with maintenance programmers, here are the topics that were cited by dedicated maintenance personnel as having a positive impact on their work:

• **Training:** Many maintenance personnel are not properly trained in the application prior to being assigned maintenance responsibility. For large systems the training should include overall application functions and then the specifics of the components assigned to individual maintenance personnel.

About one day of overall training per 100,000 function points is a good start. For specific components, about one day of training per 1,000 function points is useful. A very effective way of handling training at little cost is to engage maintenance personnel in formal inspections.

- **Structural diagrams**: Because large volumes of code are difficult to understand, large systems need to be supported by structural diagrams that show control flow, branches, and other paths through the application. Such diagrams may be produced before development (and if so, should be kept current), or they can be produced after release using a variety of commercial tools that analyze code and generate structural diagrams and other kinds of useful data.

- **Comments clarity and completeness**: Comments are widely used by maintenance personnel. They should be clear and complete and should be accurate. Surprisingly, too many comments degrade understanding and are almost as bad as too few. Every module should have header comments that explain its purpose. Calls or branches should be explained. Error messages also need explanation.

- **No error-prone modules**: Error-prone modules are a maintenance nightmare. They are unusually high in complexity, difficult to understand, and may perform arcane calls to other code segments. When they come into existence, error-prone modules usually can't be fixed in place. Therefore, code inspections and static analysis are the methods of choice to keep error-prone modules from being created in the first place.

- **Maintenance tools and workbenches**: A fairly wide variety of tools and workbenches can assist in software maintenance. These include actual maintenance workbenches that assist in analyzing code structure; static analysis tools that can be used frequently; code restructuring tools; automated test tools; and tools that can analyze source code and create readable structure diagrams.

- **Maintenance workloads**: At IBM the number of software bugs fixed per month was on average about 10. For very buggy applications this number sometimes topped 20, but with increased speed came increased numbers of bad fixes. The gist of the comments by maintenance personnel was to try and keep the volume of defects per month at or below 10 at least for severity 1 and severity 2 defect levels. Invalid defects, duplicate defects, and other topics require adjustments to maintenance workloads.

- **Programming languages**: Some programming languages are hard to understand and therefore hard to maintain; Assembly language and APL are examples. Other languages are fairly straightforward and can facilitate maintenance, such as Ada, COBOL, Java, Objective-C, and PL/I. However, with 2,500 known programming languages it is not easy to sort them all out into "easy" and "difficult" categories. Also choice of programming languages may be made for business or technical reasons in which ease of understanding has only a small part.

- In today's world most applications use at least two languages (such as Java and HTML), and some may use a dozen or more. A new language is released monthly, and this rate of creation has been sustained for almost 50 years. As of 2011 there are more than 2,500 languages in use, although only about 50 have substantial numbers of programmers that actually use them.

- A common and increasing maintenance problem is how to deal with legacy applications written in "dead" languages such as mumps or Coral where there are few programmers who know the language, few tools, and perhaps only limited availability of compilers or interpreters. For whatever reason, languages only stay active for about ten years and then drop out of use.

- The plethora of languages makes maintenance very difficult, and there are no signs that this problem will ease up in the foreseeable future. It might be useful to establish a kind of museum of ancient programming languages that would preserve at least workable compilers, assemblers, or interpreters.

- It is possible to convert some older languages such as COBOL into more recent languages such as Java. However, there are only a few languages where this kind of automated conversion is available. From discussing the results with programmers, automatic conversion is often somewhat difficult to read. Comments from the original version may be missing or no longer relevant.

To return to the main theme, the best combination of maintainability factors would be low cyclomatic complexity levels in a well-commented and easy language such as Java that is being maintained by well-trained personnel with sophisticated tools available. In this case, maintenance assignment scopes would probably top 3,000 function points or 150,000 logical statements assigned to each maintenance programmer.

The worst combination of maintainability factors would be to throw untrained novice maintenance personnel at an aging application written in either assembly language or a "dead" language that has no comments or documentation, combined with high cyclomatic complexity, and several messy error-prone modules. In this case, maintenance assignment scopes would probably drop below 300 function points or 15,000 logical statements assigned to each maintenance programmer.

The IBM study is not recent and should probably be performed again. Also many new topics should be included such as maintenance outsourcing (not covered in the IBM study), maintenance by developers rather than full-time maintenance programmers, maintenance by clients, and open source maintenance. For a topic as important as maintainability, the current literature seems to have many gaps and omissions.

Defect Discovery Rates by Software Application Users

Clients will discover a majority of latent defects as the software goes into production and begins to accumulate usage hours. The rate at which latent defects are discovered is surprisingly variable. The three major factors that influence the discovery of latent defects are

1. Defect discovery goes up with numbers of users.

2. Defect discovery goes up with numbers of usage hours.

3. Defect discovery goes down with increasing application size.

In other words, software that is used by 10,000 people will uncover latent defects at a faster rate than software used by 10 people. Software that executes 24 hours a day, every day of the week will uncover latent defects at a faster rate than software that operates only an hour a day or only once or twice a month. A software application of 100 function points will uncover a higher percentage of latent defects than an application of 10,000 function points mainly because more of the features are used for small applications than large.

However, there are some interesting exceptions and also some special situations:

1. Released software with defects in the install procedure delays usage.

2. Released software with many severity 1 and 2 defects will delay usage.

3. Released software with long learning curves delays usage.

4. Defects in financial software tend to spike at the end of quarters and fiscal years.

5. Not all reported defects are valid; some are false positives or invalid.

6. Some defects only occur for one customer, and no one else experiences them.

7. About 70% of reported defects will be reported by multiple customers.

The first four topics are reasonably self-explanatory. Software that is difficult to install or that exhibits high-severity defects early on will not uncover latent defects rapidly because users don't trust the application or because the high-severity defects delay usage for actual production runs.

Financial applications use more features at the end of each quarter and fiscal year than for ordinary daily transactions, so when usage goes up, more latent defects are found and reported.

Calendar events or external events can cause spikes in reported defects. Obviously, the former Y2K problem triggered a very large spike. The roll out of the Euro also caused a large spike in defect repairs, as did the starting date for Sarbanes-Oxley legislation. In today's world, the Obama Health Care reforms are on the verge of requiring many large-scale updates to health care applications. Significant changes in government regulations, state or federal tax regulations, or changes in the structure of widely used data items such as telephone numbers or Social Security numbers will always trigger software changes, and spikes in defect reports as well.

Invalid Defect Reports

The fifth topic of invalid defect reports refers to defects that were thought to be true software defects but upon investigation turned out to be something else. Some invalid defects may be hardware problems; some may be operating system problems misidentified as application defects; some may be true defects reported against the wrong application; some may be user errors; and some may be inexplicable issues that disappear spontaneously.

These transient defects of unknown origins may be due to momentary power surges or voltage changes that affect computers briefly. They may also be due to random combinations of software middleware and other applications that occasionally combine in a unique pattern that causes a transient problem.

For in-house software with few users, invalid defects are not a serious issue. But for commercial software with numerous users, about 15% of customer-reported defects are eventually classed as invalid. However, just because defect reports are "invalid" does not mean they are inexpensive. Indeed, due to the difficulty of diagnosing invalid defects, some of these take longer to identify than valid defects.

Invalid defects are not well covered in the quality literature, but they are very common and surprisingly expensive. Incidentally, the "cost per defect" metric has little reported data on invalid defects. Simple invalid defects such as reporting a bug against the wrong application or obvious user errors can be identified in a few minutes. Subtle invalid defects such as hardware errors, operating system errors, or errors in other applications that are misidentified can take hours or days to identify. Note that for "invalid" defects, actual repairs may not be necessary, but diagnostic analysis can be time-consuming.

One surprising statistic about invalid defect reports is that the number of invalid defect reports goes up at a higher rate than valid defect reports. Users do not trust unreliable software that contains true bugs that cause them frequent problems; therefore, they report bugs without bothering to do much analysis.

Because of the frequency of invalid defects, it is important for economic studies of software quality to distinguish between "defect analysis" and "defect repairs." Invalid defects often require protracted defect analysis but, of course, result in a zero dollar value for defect repairs.

The statement of no repairs being needed for invalid defects is not quite true because some misidentified defects such as operating system problems will need to be repaired by someone but usually not by the application maintenance team that is handling the diagnosis. Thus these defect repairs should not be charged to the application that handled the initial diagnosis, but to the application or system that contained the actual defect, which is often some other company.

As an example of an invalid defect, a defect report was sent to one of the author's company by surface mail that was for a competitor's software product. The defect was rerouted by the author's company to the correct location. Although this only took a few minutes and did not require either repairs or analysis, it did take about 15 minutes to log the defect report, read it, and then reroute the defect to the other company. A short courtesy response was sent back to the customer with the competitor's correct address in case there were any more defect reports against the same product. Even obvious invalid defect reports such as this still have some logistical costs associated with them.

Invalid defects or false positives can occur during testing and with static analysis as well as after release, although prerelease invalid defects seldom top 6%. Even formal inspections can have a few invalid defects, but here the percentage is less than 1%. The most common form of invalid defects with inspections has to do with issues that upon investigation are deemed to be potentially useful features that were not included in the current release. In other words, a defect report is converted into a proposed enhancement or new feature.

A corollary factor with software is that of *undocumented features*. For a variety of reasons, software applications have features that are not discussed in user manuals and may be deliberately concealed. For example, sometimes games or riddles are deliberately inserted in applications by programmers. Sometimes more sinister features are hidden in software such as "back doors" and other security vulnerabilities.

These undocumented features are not necessarily "defects" in the sense that they don't always stop operation of software applications or cause serious problems. However, some of these undocumented features can be used by hackers, and others may be accidentally misused by customers if they become aware of their existence. Microsoft's operating systems have a long history of undocumented features.

Invalid defects are an ambiguous topic when it comes to calculating cost of quality (COQ). Because most of these invalid defect reports are not due to actual errors in the software against which they were reported, it would seem logical to exclude invalid defect logistics costs from COQ calculations.

On the other hand, because processing invalid defect reports is actually part of the customer support group's expenses, the costs cannot be ignored. The authors' solution to this problem is to use a separate line item in COQ reporting for invalid defects.

Abeyant Defects That Occur Under Unique Conditions

The sixth topic also presents a difficult challenge for maintenance and support personnel. A very small percentage of defects only occur for a single client or for a single computer system and do not occur for other customers. Indeed, the application maintenance team often cannot replicate the problem on their versions of the application.

The term used by IBM for these unique defects is *abeyant*, which means the defect repairs cannot be performed without gathering additional data about the specific applications and hardware configuration that triggered the defect report.

Needless to say, abeyant defects are among the most difficult and expensive form of defects to repair. An "average" abeyant defect can take more than a week from the initial report to the maintenance team before the causes are known and sometimes an additional week or two for a remedy to be found. A great many phone calls, some computer-to-computer connections, and possible onsite visits may be needed to find out about the true cause of an abeyant defect. Fortunately, abeyant defects are fairly rare and may only occur once or twice a year.

It is interesting that most of these abeyant defects are of the severity 2 category, although a few are of the severity 1 category. It often happens that some unique combination of hardware and software operating on the client's computer caused the defect to occur. Therefore, a great deal of additional information about the client configuration is needed.

The cost-per-defect metric is actually close to being correct in asserting that abeyant defects cost about 100 times as much as simple defects. However, this is not a comparison between early and late defect removal. It is a comparison of post-release abeyant defects compared to normal defects that have fairly obvious causes. Abeyant defects almost always cost between five and ten times more to repair than defects that occur in many installations.

Because abeyant defects occur due to unique and unusual combinations of hardware and software that operate concurrently, it is difficult to find and eliminate such problems prior to release. Neither internal test organizations nor development groups have exactly the same configurations deployed as customers do, so abeyant defects are extremely difficult to prevent or remove. Static analysis seems to have the best record of elimination abeyant defects, but even that method is not 100% effective.

Duplicate Defects Reported by Many Customers

The seventh topic, duplicate defect reports, is primarily an issue for commercial software with many users. For commercial software with many customers about 70% of reported defects will be reported more than once. More than 10,000 customers reported a bug in the install procedure of a Word Perfect release in the 1990s on the first day the software was released. This fact was reported in newspapers and news magazines because all of the simultaneous phone calls temporarily saturated the local phone system.

One of the authors of this book happened to be in the offices of a company that marketed a mainframe security device that included a random number generator that was synchronized with hand-held devices that created new passwords every minute. Accidently, leap year was excluded from the devices.

At 12:01 a.m. on February 29, customers suddenly found themselves locked out of their computers. Urgent phone calls began from the international timeline and steadily moved around the world—this problem affected every single user in every time zone as soon as the calendar switched to February 29.

As the timeline moved around the world, hundreds of calls came in to the company. As it happened, the leap-year problem was diagnosed within about 3 hours, and a work-around was available within about 12 hours. Even so, a released defect that impacted every customer in every time zone was a potentially catastrophic situation for the company.

Duplicate defects can occur for in-house software, but because the clients and maintenance personnel often know each other and may be colocated, word quickly spreads, so duplicate reports are not numerous.

Because defect reports normally include symptoms and descriptive materials, the maintenance teams quickly discover duplicates and usually inform users that the bug has already been reported and repairs are underway. In fact, companies such as Microsoft and IBM may send the repair to clients as soon as their reports have been found to be duplicates, assuming a repair is available.

Actual software quality levels are usually measured on the basis of *valid unique defects*, which means that both duplicate defects and invalid defects are excluded from quality calculations such as defect discovery efficiency (DDE) and defect removal efficiency (DRE).

However, for quality economic analysis, the costs of handling duplicate defects needs to be included because if there are thousands of duplicate reports from thousands of customers, the total costs can be significant. Indeed, duplicate defect reports are numerically the most common reason for calling customer support.

As might be expected, duplicate defects go up with numbers of users. For applications with only a few users, duplicates are not very expensive. But for companies like Microsoft, Google, Sony, and Motorola that might have a million users the first week of a new release, duplicates are expensive.

In fact, sometimes duplicates occur in such large volumes that they overload phone lines or slow down email responses. This is one of the reasons why there are often very long waits to contact technical support personnel by phone. The computer gaming industry also has large volumes of duplicate defects given that some games can top 100,000 users the first week of release.

Duplicate defects should be part of cost of quality (COQ) calculations, but the author suggests a separate line for recording their costs. Even if there are 10,000 duplicate reports of the same defect, it only needs to be fixed once. However the logistics costs for recording these defects and responding to customer calls and emails can be huge. For economic understanding, quality cost data collection should be able to distinguish between valid unique defect reports, duplicate defect reports, and invalid defect reports.

First-Year Defect Discovery Rates

IBM has kept defect data on applications for as long as 25 years of usage. It is interesting that defects introduced in the very first release might not surface until three to five years later.

The general trend for defect discovery during the first year of usage resembles the patterns shown in Table 6.8, although there are wide variations.

Embedded software and systems software that operate physical devices have a higher first-year discovery rate than information systems. Embedded and systems software users also find more defects in the first three months. The reason is that physical devices tend to execute software rather intensely, and so many latent defects are noted quickly.

Table 6.8   *Discovery Patterns of Latent Defects During the First Year of Usage*

Month	Embedded Software	Commercial Software	Information Software	Web Software	Military Software	AVERAGE
1	12.00%	5.00%	7.00%	13.00%	15.00%	10.40%
2	13.00%	7.00%	8.00%	15.00%	16.00%	11.80%
3	14.00%	8.00%	8.00%	16.00%	14.00%	12.00%
4	9.00%	9.00%	9.00%	9.00%	10.00%	9.20%
5	8.00%	11.00%	9.00%	8.00%	9.00%	9.00%
6	7.00%	12.00%	8.00%	6.00%	9.00%	8.40%
7	6.00%	9.00%	7.00%	5.00%	6.00%	6.60%
8	6.00%	7.00%	6.00%	5.00%	6.00%	6.00%
9	6.00%	7.00%	6.00%	5.00%	6.00%	6.00%
10	5.00%	5.00%	6.00%	4.00%	4.00%	4.80%
11	4.00%	5.00%	5.00%	4.00%	3.00%	4.20%
12	3.00%	5.00%	5.00%	4.00%	1.00%	3.60%
TOTAL	93.00%	90.00%	84.00%	94.00%	99.00%	92.00%

Because only about 35% of latent defects are discovered in the first three months of software deployment, it is obvious that calculations of defect detection efficiency (DDE) and defect removal efficiency (DRE) using only 90 days of data will overstate true efficiency levels. Indeed, when defect removal efficiency was first calculated circa 1973, annual defect results were used.

However, it soon became obvious that multiple releases would occur in the first year. Therefore, to measure efficiency against initial defects, a shorter interval was needed. The switch to 90 days was to show approximate results against the initial release before enhancements, new features, and bug repairs made the calculations excessively complex.

Measuring Defect Detection Efficiency (DDE) and Defect Removal Efficiency (DRE)

The normal calculations for measuring defect detection efficiency (DDE) and defect removal efficiency (DRE) are simple in principle but can be tricky in real life. The development and test teams keep records of all defects found prior to release. When the software is released to customers, all customer-reported defects are counted for a specific time period such as 90 days. After the time period has expired, internal defects and customer-reported defects are summed together to calculate DDE and DRE. A simple example follows:

Assume that 200 defects were found via inspections.

Assume that all 200 defects were repaired.

Assume that 400 defects were found via static analysis.

Assume that all 400 defects were repaired.

Assume that 300 defects were found via testing.

Assume that 200 of these defects were repaired prior to release.

Assume that 100 of these defects were released to customers.

Assume that customers reported 100 defects in the first 90 days of usage.

The total number of defects discovered prior to release was 900 out of 1,000, so defect detection efficiency (DDE) is 90%. The total number of defects repaired prior to release was 800 out of 1,000, so defect removal efficiency (DRE) was 80%.

Of course, all latent defects certainly cannot be found in a 90-day period. But because several years might pass before all latent defects surface, having a standard cut-off date provides a useful point for comparison even if the true percentages are low because many latent defects still remain undetected until after the 90-day period.

Although the calculations are simple on the surface, some complicating factors need to be discussed and included in the calculations. One obvious question is whether defects found by customers during an external Beta test should be classified as internal or external defects.

In this situation, the application has not been formally released, so the customer-reported Beta test defects would be considered to be internal defects found via testing.

Consider also that about 5% to 8% of defect repairs will probably contain new defects in the repairs themselves. These bad fixes may not be detected for several weeks or more, so some will be released to customers. But bad-fix injections need to be included in the DDE and DRE calculations. Assume that 10 defects were released to customers in the form of bad fixes to the 200 defects repaired after testing. These 10 defects should be added in to the grand total.

Another complicating factor is that after the release date of the software to customers, internal test and quality assurance personnel may continue to find and repair defects. This raises the obvious question as to whether defects found by in-house personnel after software is released to customers should be counted on the client side or the internal side of the DDE and DRE equations. Although there are valid arguments for both sides of the question, for consistency with the way Beta test defects are counted, it is best to use the formal delivery date as the dividing line between internal and external defect reports. (Counting post-release defects on the client side, even if they are found by internal personnel, also discourages releasing software with known defects).

Thus if an application is formally delivered to customers on June 15, 2011, all defects prior to that date would be classified "internal," and all defects after that date would be classified "external." Defects found on June 15 would also be classified as external.

The calculation for defect detection efficiency (DDE) and defect removal efficiency (DRE) is based on *valid unique defects*. This means that invalid defects and duplicate defects are excluded from the calculations. However, numbers of such defect reports and the effort and costs to process them should be collected.

In the simple example just shown, customers probably reported an additional 5 defects that were invalid. Probably 60 of the 100 defects found by customers were reported by more than one customer.

A complicating factor not included in the example, but that can happen in real life, is to issue another release of the software package before the 90-day period for calculating DDE and DRE. Unless every defect report is identified against every release, separating defects across multiple releases is a tricky task. In fact, this is the main reason for a 90-day wait. If longer intervals were used there would be multiple releases.

The International Software Benchmark Standard Group (ISBSG) uses a 30-day wait to ensure no new releases interfere with the calculations. But such a low percentage of total defects arrives in the first 30 days that this method leads to significant undercounts and gives a possibly false impression of better quality than really exists.

A final complicating factor is that some customer-reported defects are judged to be suggestions for improvement rather than defects in the current release. If this situation occurs and the software developer agrees to include the suggested improvement in a later release, then it should not be counted as a defect against the current release. In this example, assume about five reports that came in as defect reports were converted into suggestions for improvement.

Variations in Post-Release Defect Reports

Post-release bug reporting by users is surprisingly ambiguous given the more than 60 years of bug reporting practice. The oldest form of bug reporting noted by the authors is that of IBM's well-known "authorized program analysis report," or APAR, which dates back to the early 1960s.

IBM also had a form for reporting internal defects during testing. This was called a *program trouble memorandum* or PTM. The two forms were similar, but the APAR captured additional information on the client and the industry in which the clients resided, plus information about the hardware and software platforms in use when the defect was first noted.

As of 2011 there are at least 50 commercial bug tracking tools on the commercial market and a similar number of open source tools. There are also proprietary bug reporting methods developed and used by hundreds of companies. Some nonprofit user organizations also have samples of bug reports.

Regardless of the company or group that provides bug reporting methods and tools, it is important that the initial bug report contain enough information so that development and/or maintenance personnel can duplicate the bug, analyze the causes of the bug, and be sure that the same bug was not already reported.

Some companies use separate forms or questionnaires for internal bug reports during inspections, static analysis, and testing, and then for external bugs reported by clients after release. However, it is better to develop a single bug-report form or questionnaire that can serve consistently throughout both software development and maintenance.

Note that bug or defect reports need several kinds of information, some of which is returned to clients while other information may be proprietary or used only inside the organization that owns the software. The primary categories of information available to the public would be

1. The symptoms of the bug ranging from total failure to specific errors

2. The identity of specific bugs in mnemonic form

3. The serial number assigned to the bug

4. The apparent severity level of the bug when first reported

5. The revisions to severity levels after analysis

6. The date the initial bug report was made

7. The dates the bug was assigned to repair personnel

8. The date final repairs were made

9. The hardware platform in use when the bug was reported

10. The software platform in use when the bug was reported

11. The component that was being executed when the bug was noted (if known)

12. What actions the user was performing when the bug occurred

If a single bug-report form is going to be used throughout development and maintenance, then it is important to identify during which activity the defect was detected and related information:

1. The bug was detected during inspection preparation.

2. The bug was detected during an inspection session.

3. The bug was detected during quality assurance review.

4. The bug was detected during static analysis.

5. The bug was detected during independent verification and validation.

6. The bug was detected during a specific test run for a specific build.

7. The bug was detected during execution of the software at an internal site.

8. The bug was detected during execution of the software at a customer site.

9. The version or release number of the software application containing the bug.

10. The operating system in use when the bug was detected.

11. The hardware platform in use when the bug was detected.

For post-release bugs this information is usually provided by customers or by a customer support representative based on conversation with customers. For bugs found during development, the development, quality assurance, or test personnel provide the information.

When bugs are reported, additional information is added by the maintenance personnel. Some of the additional topics would be

1. Whether the bug is a real bug, invalid, or a possible enhancement

2. Whether the bug is the initial report or a duplicate

3. The severity level of the bug after analysis by the software maintainers

4. Whether or not the bug impacts other applications

5. Whether or not the bug impacts reusable components

Clients have no way of knowing about duplicate bug reports, nor do they know about invalid defect reports unless someone in the maintenance group tells them.

For sophisticated companies such as IBM, bugs are analyzed for root causes. This allows interesting studies of the time spans between the origin point of bugs and their points of detection. For example, if a bug originates in user requirements but escapes detection until after release, it is obvious that pretest inspections should be used.

If a bug is due to a "bad fix" of a previous bug, that fact should be recorded. If a bug was not detected due to errors in a test case, that fact should be recorded. Defect root-cause analysis is an important activity that can lead to long-range reductions in defects and long-range improvements in defect removal efficiency levels.

The proprietary information that would probably not be reported back to the clients (unless contractual obligations required it) would be the hours spent analyzing and repairing the bug, along the lines of the following:

1. Name(s) of the bug repair personnel

2. Names of customer support personnel

3. Number of duplicate reports of the same bug

4. Names of specific clients that report bugs

5. Names of companies or individuals reporting duplicates

6. Root cause or origin of the bug

7. Cyclomatic complexity of the software module containing the bug

8. Number of bad fixes while attempting repairs

9. Number of times the same bug has been reopened due to bad fixes

10. Errors in test cases or test libraries

11. Error-prone modules in software applications

12. Call center time spent answering questions about the same bug

13. Time span from bug origin point to discovery point

14. Preparation effort for inspections, static analysis, or testing

15. Preparation schedules for inspections, static analysis, or testing

16. Preparation effort for duplication external bug reports

17. Execution effort for inspections, static analysis, or testing

18. Execution schedules for inspections, static analysis, or testing

19. Analysis schedule time for identifying the bug

20. Analysis effort for identifying the bug

21. Defect repair hours for preliminary work-around (if any)

22. Defect repair hours for final bug repairs

23. Build and integration hours to integrate bug repairs

24. Regression test hours to ensure no harm occurs from bug repairs

25. Hours for inspection of defect repairs (if any)

26. Hours for static analysis of defect repairs

27. Hours for testing defect repairs

28. Litigation filed by disgruntled clients due to poor quality

The information that is normally deemed "proprietary" is that associated with defect repair effort and costs. The information that is public is that associated with defect repairs and severity levels.

However, if there is litigation between a client and an outsource vendor, then almost all information about defect repair effort and costs will probably be disclosed during the discovery and deposition phases of the lawsuit. In fact, one of the decisions in an antitrust suit against IBM was an order by the judge for IBM to provide maintenance information on defect repairs to competitors.

Variations in Methods of Reporting Software Defects

The software literature on the topics of customer support or planning is not clear about how many support personnel may be needed when software applications are released. Some useful rules of thumb for planning software support and maintenance are

- One software support person is needed for about every 10,000 function points.

- One software support person is needed for about every 250 users or clients.

- One software support person is needed for about every 400 monthly emails.

- One maintenance programmer is needed for about every 1,500 function points.

- One maintenance programmer can repair about 10 defects per month.

These rules of thumb provide short wait periods for reaching support personnel and quick turnarounds of reported defects. Telephone wait periods would be less than five minutes, and temporary repairs would be developed in two days or less. Responses to email would probably occur a day after receipt.

Unfortunately, due to economic pressure, most companies do not support software with enough personnel for quick access or rapid turnaround. Therefore, the most likely ratios of support will be in the vicinity of

- One software support person assigned for about every 50,000 function points

- One software support person assigned for about every 1,500 users or clients

- One software support person assigned for about every 2,000 monthly emails

- One maintenance programmer assigned for about every 3,500 function points

- One maintenance programmer needed to repair about 20 defects per month

Under these assumptions, waits in excess of 30 minutes will occur before gaining access to support personnel. Defect repairs may take more than 15 days from initial report to at least a temporary fix. Responses to emails might not occur until the week following receipt. Unfortunately, due to pressures to fix many defects, bad-fix injection rates tend to be higher than 8%.

It should be noted that many software vendors have decided to make a profit out of released defects and therefore charge customers for telephone calls or other methods of access to support and maintenance personnel. Sometimes there are annual maintenance contracts, and sometimes there are specific charges for each call.

Given the volume of released software defects and the rate at which they are discovered after release, at least one year of free customer support and maintenance should probably be provided for all commercial software applications.

Another bad habit by software vendors is deliberate withdrawal of support and maintenance for specific releases after new releases become available. For example, some antivirus applications stop upgrading virus definitions unless a new service agreement and payments are received.

The bottom line is that the software industry releases many more bugs or defects than it should release given the state of the art of software quality control. The software industry has also been attempting to generate additional revenues for fixing released defects and for providing customer support. This situation is endemic and will probably continue in the future.

One possible approach to changing this unpleasant situation would be for at least one major software company to embrace state of the art software quality control methods and to also offer an effective warranty against defects that included free repairs and free customer support for at least a year after every release. This does happen from time to time, but the practice should be common and not an exception.

There are significant variances in how customer-reported defects are submitted among various classes of software:

- **Cloud software or software as a service:** For software that is located on a remote server such as the Google Office Applications, defects are normally reported via email, although some telephone support may be available. Once reported, the client should be notified of status by the vendor. However, there will be no repairs or installation of new versions on the part of clients because these actions occur on the vendor's server. In the long run these remote applications can save clients quite a bit of money by reducing the logistics effort of installing new versions. At some point it will be interesting to compare long-range customer costs for remote software versus locally installed software.

- **Internal software:** Normally, defects are reported by email or phone call to a service desk, or even by face-to-face meetings if clients and service personnel are in the same building. In larger companies there may be some kind of service-level agreement between the client organization and the software organization. In very large companies the concepts of the information technology infrastructure library (ITIL) may be used. Normally, internal support and maintenance groups are funded as cost centers and provide services to clients without charge.

- **Outsource software:** Normally, the contract between the client and the outsource vendor will include clauses for defect reporting, defect repair intervals, levels of customer support, and sometimes service-level agreements in terms of reliability or numbers of bugs without some kind of penalty being invoked. There may also be clauses with special benefits for the vendor in the case of very low defect levels. Defect reporting methods are started during requirements, and formal records are kept by both parties due to contractual obligations.

- **Open source software:** Normally, defect reports against open source software are by email to a service location or URL. In a few cases there may be access to live support personnel, perhaps on a fee basis.

- **Embedded software:** Defect reports against embedded software may not be able to distinguish between true software defects and hardware defects. Some repairs may require replacement of embedded devices themselves. In other cases, such as cochlear implants, field updates to software can be performed by audiologists. Some embedded manufacturers of medical devices have round-the-clock customer support desks.

- In recent months serious problems with embedded devices such as Toyota braking systems have focused attention on serious defects in embedded products. The most alarming thing about the situation is the pattern of initial denial and deception by vendors before finally admitting to problems.

- For inexpensive devices such as watches there may not be any repairs, and the devices are merely discarded and replaced by newer models or by similar products from other manufacturers.

- **Military software:** Due to the need to keep combat equipment at a high state of readiness, military software repairs tend to be quite sophisticated, and some aspects are often classified. There are usually multiple repair facilities, and some of these are located close to the areas where the devices are being used. In situations where proximity is not possible, such as devices onboard surface ships, submarines, and aircraft, then double or triple redundancy of critical components is the norm. Automatic monitoring of device performance and automatic reporting of failures or deviations is common for military software.

- For military logistics software or applications that handle mundane topics such as payroll and inventory management, there will be defect reporting channels between software maintenance teams and software users or their designated support officers. Normally, these channels are specified in contracts.

- **Commercial software:** The lack of effective warranties for commercial software and the difficulties of gaining access to customer support are well-known problems for the larger commercial software vendors. Telephone waits of more than 30 minutes to reach a live customer support representative are common. When one is finally reached, often the advice provided often does not solve the problem and may even make it worse. These statements tend to be true for large companies whose software applications have more than 100,000 users. Such large organizations typically have a multi-tier customer support organization with the first tier consisting of personnel who only know basic information and deal primarily with very simple problems. For more complex problems, clients are routed to a second or third tier, in which the reps have greater expertise.

Commercial software websites have sections on known bugs and also frequently asked questions (FAQ), which summarize the most common questions asked by clients of call-center personnel. These FAQ lists are moderately beneficial and can reduce actual calls by perhaps 12% by providing information about common issues.

For really massive commercial applications such as mainframe operating systems in the 150,000 function point size range and enterprise resource planning (ERP) packages in the 250,000 function point size range, there may be permanent onsite support personnel at least for major customers. Whether or not the vendor has onsite support, the clients will have permanent support teams available because these large applications are mission-critical and cannot be taken offline without serious disruptions of business activities. Incidentally, large commercial software packages such as operating systems and ERP packages may have several thousand latent defects when they are delivered, and quite a few of these will be detected during the installation and customization of the packages. This is why both vendor personnel and in-house personnel may require weeks or months to successfully deploy and customize really large software packages.

For smaller applications released by smaller companies with perhaps only a few hundred users, customer support is often fairly quick and surprisingly effective. In fact, for some small software companies the developers themselves handle customer support, so bug reports may be given to the actual programmer who created the code.

For large applications developed by big companies such as Microsoft or IRM and whose customers work in large companies, defect reporting may involve both client support personnel and vendor support personnel. Sometimes as many as four people on the client side and six people on the vendor side are involved with a single defect report.

Who Repairs Defects after They Are Reported?

The software industry is divided into two major camps when it comes to post-release defect repairs. In about 70% of companies visited by the authors, defects are repaired by development personnel who also work on enhancements and perhaps new development projects too. For the other 30% of companies, primarily large enterprises with thousands of software personnel, maintenance specialists are employed who work primarily on defect repairs but are not tasked with enhancements or new development work. (Some maintenance specialists may be assigned very small enhancements that require a day or less to complete. These are usually trivial changes such as modifying a report or screen format.)

Another fairly recent trend that has been accelerating over the past 15 years is to outsource software maintenance tasks while keeping new projects and major enhancements in-house. To satisfy this demand there are a number of companies that now specialize in software maintenance under contract. Some of these are located in the United States, and others are located offshore in countries such as India, China, Russia, and the Ukraine. From visits to both these companies and their clients, maintenance outsourcing seems to be fairly effective and less prone to failure than development outsourcing.

While it might seem logical to have the original development personnel also handle maintenance and defect repairs, this can lead to a number of serious logistical problems that are hard to solve. Following are two small case studies. In one case developers handle maintenance, and in the second case defect repairs go to maintenance specialists.

Case Study 1: Development Personnel Tasked with Maintenance Defect Repairs

Assume that a software engineer has been tasked with developing an enhancement to a Java application of 5,000 function points or 250,000 Java statements that is already deployed. The requirements and specifications are complete, and the enhancement is slated to be about 2,500 new Java statements or 50 function points in size.

The software engineer and his manager agree that the work can be accomplished in two calendar months, after which the enhancement will be turned over to the quality assurance and test groups. Assume that the software engineer starts work on March 1, 2011, and is scheduled to deliver the software on May 1, 2011.

Now assume that the application's major customer reports a severity 2 defect on March 10, 2011, and the defect is known to be located in the same code segment that the software engineer is updating. This marks the start of logistical problems. Defects are reported at random intervals and tend to interrupt planned activities.

High-severity defects from major clients take precedence over enhancements and new development work, so the software engineer has to put aside the enhancement and spends two days on finding and repairing the defect. This is a comparatively small loss, but it is a loss.

Now assume that due to rushing to fix the severity 2 defect, the programmer accidentally made a mistake that escaped testing without being detected, so the repair was a bad fix with a new defect in it.

The bad fix, of course, upsets the client, so the software engineer needs to spend another day eliminating the secondary defect and carefully unit testing and regression testing the second repair. A static analysis tool is used as well. Now the software engineer has lost three days from the planned schedule.

To compensate for the days lost due to defect repairs, the software engineer now has to work several hours in the evening and also works part of the weekend to get back on track. But because he is now rushed and perhaps tiring, there is a tendency to be somewhat careless, so the enhancement ends up with perhaps ten more defects than might have occurred had the software engineer been fully available. These ten defects require another three days to repair, so now the software engineer has lost a total of six days, or about 10% of the original schedule.

The enhancement is finished and turned over to testing more or less on schedule, but its quality is suboptimal, so additional days to repair defects in the enhancement cause a delay of one week in finishing testing and achieving a final build. Instead of being delivered on May 1, the application is delivered on May 6. This slippage is not major, but it is a slippage.

The essential problem with interleaving development and maintenance defect repairs is that the two kinds of work are antagonistic. Each one subtracts time from the schedules allotted to the other, and the combination can lead to schedule overruns for both activities, to frustration on the part of software engineers, to higher than expected defect rates, and to more bad fixes than normal. This assumes a constant stock of resources; adding to this stock is likely to introduce further problems of communication and coordination (as documented by Frederick Brooks in his seminal book, *The Mythical Man Month*).

Case Study 2: Maintenance Specialists Handle Defect Repairs

In Case Study 2, the original application and the enhancement are the same sizes. The only difference is that now a maintenance specialist is available to handle defect repairs, and the software engineer is only concerned with the planned enhancement.

We can assume that the same severity 2 defect was reported on March 10, 2011, and was assigned to the maintenance specialist. Because it is known that the defect is in the same area of the system that is being enhanced, the maintenance specialist and the software engineer have to coordinate their work, but this is really a standard practice.

The maintenance specialist makes the repairs in two days but is very careful to use a static analysis tool prior to testing and is also careful with unit testing and regression testing. The repair is successfully integrated with no problems. The client is pleased with the repair.

Because the software engineer is concentrating full-time on the enhancement, he is able to do an excellent job and has ten fewer defects than might occur. He also uses static analysis and asks colleagues to perform a peer review on the new code.

As a result, the enhancement finishes testing two days early with few defects found. The combination of the enhancement and the defect repair are delivered to the client two days ahead of schedule.

In many fields, specialists tend to be more effective than generalists. The maintenance of software applications seems to be one of these fields.

Comparing the Case Studies

Both of the case studies make a number of simplifying assumptions, but they both also illustrate a key point. Concurrent maintenance and development by the same person degrade performance on both tasks.

If these two case studies are scaled up to entire portfolios that might consist of 500 applications that total 1,000,000 function points, it is easy to see why maintenance specialists and maintenance outsourcing are generally cost effective.

For a portfolio of 500 applications and 1,000,000 function points there will probably be in the range of 10,000 latent defects. If these latent defects are allowed to interfere with planned development and enhancement tasks, schedules will be essentially unpredictable. Worse, rushing to finish defect repairs or rushing development because of defect repairs will add unexpected new defects that probably would not occur if development and maintenance were handled by two different teams.

Litigation Due to Poor Quality

Many internal projects are released with poor quality, but these do not end up in court. As a rule, litigation for poor quality is restricted to either software developed under contract or to commercial software acquired under license. Of these two, litigation for software developed under contract is far more common.

Litigation against commercial software vendors, even if their software causes serious harm, is made difficult by the fact that their end-user license agreements exclude damages, consequential damages, and all other harmful consequences. It is still possible to sue commercial vendors, but it is not easy.

One unusual case dealing with poor quality was filed several years ago against a major software vendor by the vendors' own shareholders. The allegation was that the quality of the application was so poor that shareholder value was being degraded. Among the claims enumerated in the initial complaint was the fact that the vendor was unable to use its own application internally for the same purpose that it was being sold to clients. This case settled out of court without a decision, but the fact that such a case was filed against a major vendor by its own shareholders is a sign that software quality needs to be improved.

One of the authors frequently works as an expert witness in such cases. While poor quality is not the only reason for litigation, charges of poor quality always seem to be part of the plaintiff's charges.

The four most common charges by plaintiffs in the breach of contract cases where one of the authors has been an expert witness are

1. **Poor quality control**: Quality control was deficient in terms of both defect prevention and defect removal. After deployment the software had so many serious bugs that production use was either delayed or not possible. In the cases where poor quality was a major cause for litigation, it is interesting and significant that the defendants did not use pretest inspections or static analysis. Also testing was sometimes cut short due to schedule commitments. There may be other legal cases where inspections and static analysis were used, but in the most recent 12 cases for which the author was an expert witness, none of the defendants used either inspections or static analysis.

2. **Poor change control**: Change control was deficient in every case. The plaintiff and defendant did not have effective change control processes in place or included in the contract.

   In one case there was language in the contract covering out of scope changes, but the company refused to pay the vendor. The claim by the company was that the changes were only elaborations of requirements and not actual out of scope changes. There were more than 80 substantial changes cited in this case. (The case was decided in favor of the vendor.)

   It is interesting that usually both the plaintiffs and the defendants charge each other with poor control of changes. The plaintiffs or customers charge that the defendants did not make the changes with effective quality control. The defendants or outsourcers countercharge that there were excessive numbers of changes and that the plaintiffs were ineffective in reviewing the plans and documentation for the changes.

3. **Poor estimates or rejection of estimates:** For most lawsuits for breach of contract, accurate estimates were either not prepared or were rejected by the client. This is an interesting problem. In about half of the cases, the estimates prepared by the vendor and approved by the customer turned out to be excessively optimistic in terms of both schedules and quality levels. In the other half of the cases, accurate estimates were prepared by the vendor but were arbitrarily rejected by the client. In place of the vendor-prepared estimate, the client imposed arbitrary delivery dates that were not based on team capabilities.

   However, there were also problems on the part of the vendors. In one case the client demanded that the software be delivered with zero defects. Because the application was fairly large (more than 5,000 function points), fairly novel, and fairly complex, it was beyond the state of the art to deliver zero-defect software for such an application. However, instead of challenging this clause and including a mutually agreeable defect rate in the contract, the vendor actually agreed to the clause and was contractually obligated to produce zero-defect software.

   When the software was finally delivered, the quality was not too bad, but it did not meet the zero-defect contractual obligation, so the client sued. In fact, the plaintiff won this case, which was decided by a jury trial. Both parties should have known that zero-defect software is close to impossible for all applications and certainly impossible for large and complex applications. The defendant and the defendant's attorneys can be faulted for agreeing to such an impossible demand in a legal contract.

4. **Inaccurate status tracking:** The fourth problem is that progress reports by managers to the client concealed rather than revealed serious technical problems that caused schedule delays or cost over-runs. Instead of admitting to problems and asking for extensions, the progress reports did not even discuss them. Apparently the managers hoped to be able to solve the problems before the client found out about them, but this is not a realistic scenario.

   What is interesting about this issue is that during the discovery and depositions in the cases, it turned out that dozens of technical people knew about the problems and, in fact, had reported them almost every week to their management. It was the project managers who concealed the issues rather than the software engineers and technical workers.

   The obvious solution to this problem is to start every status report with an explicit discussion of problems that had been reported by technical personnel and a discussion of their potential impact. Managers might still bury problems or not discuss them, but if they sign a progress report whose initial section discusses known issues, then the case might escalate from breach of contract to fraud, which is a much more serious issue.

The authors are, of course, not attorneys, so no legal advice is intended in this section. But the authors do recommend that both vendors and clients discuss outsource contracts with their own attorneys. Both parties should ensure that the contracts include formal estimates and approval of estimates; formal change control and approval of changes; formal quality control and approval of quality results; and formal progress tracking and approval of progress with special emphasis on problems that might impact schedules, costs, or quality levels.

Incidentally, the new agile method of having embedded users and frequent scrum sessions seems to be effective in eliminating concealment of technical problems. If the embedded users are present during the stand-up meetings, they will know as much about problems as anyone else. Concealment by managers is not impossible but seldom occurs.

If litigation does occur, it can be extremely costly for both the plaintiff and the defendant. Some litigation attorneys may have billable fees in excess of $450 per hour; some experts may bill in excess of $600 per hour, and even paralegal support may be billed at $150 per hour.

A full-scale lawsuit that goes to court can easily accumulate more than 1,000 hours of billable attorney time; perhaps 200 hours of expert witness time; and over 2,500 hours of paralegal support time for each side, resulting in more than $1,000,000 in billable costs for both the plaintiff and the defendant. In addition, there will be probably 500 hours of time required for executives and technical personnel to produce discovery documents, participate in depositions, and appear in court for the actual trial.

It is far better to use state-of-the-art quality control methods and to have well-prepared contracts than it is to enter into a lawsuit; they are very costly for both parties, and often the results satisfy neither.

Cost Patterns of Post-Release Defect Repairs

The topic of post-release defect repairs is a very complex subject with many factors that need to be considered. These factors are significant independently and also combine to form patterns. The factors that have an influence on software maintenance and defect repair costs include

- The nature of the software and whether it is mission-critical
- The installation of the software either at a client site or in a cloud

- The issue of customer modifications to commercial applications

- The nature of the latent defects and the amount of consequential damages

- The various kinds of personnel involved in defect reporting and repairs

- The communication channels established for defect reporting

- The existence or absence of service-level agreements

- The existence or absence of explicit warranties for released software

- The existence or absence of contractual clauses dealing with defects

- The numbers of defects in released software

- The severity levels of defects in released software

- The numbers of defects in applications that interface with released software

- The numbers of defects in hardware platforms for the released software

- The numbers of defects in operating systems used by the released software

- The numbers of customers who use the released software

- The size of the released application measured in function points or lines of code

- The complexity of the code, normally measured using cyclomatic complexity

As is evident here, there are a great many variables involved, and these variables can form very complicated patterns. There are formal methods for analyzing the maintainability of software. For example, the Dutch company Software Improvement Group (SIG) offers a maintainability analysis service in Europe that rates maintainability using a method that awards up to five stars for the most maintainable applications.

Software Occupation Groups Involved with Defect Repairs

The major occupation groups associated with post-release defects include but are not limited to the following:

1. The clients or customers who initially discover a defect in released software.

2. A customer support or help desk worker at the client site if the company is large enough to have such. Defects are normally reported to the help desk first and then to the vendor through the help desk.

3. Commercial software sales personnel who may be contacted by clients or client support personnel to report defects for large commercial applications.

4. Onsite vendor personnel who are colocated with major clients for large applications such as enterprise resource planning (ERP) packages.

5. Remote vendor personnel who are located in their own offices but who provide support for specific clients often within specific industries such as banking or insurance.

6. Specialists in embedded equipment such as medical devices, navigation packages, aircraft flight controls, and other physical products controlled by software.

7. Dedicated customer maintenance support personnel whose jobs involve keeping major applications updated and running smoothly. For major commercial packages these personnel install new releases from vendors and integrate defect repairs.

8. Telephone customer support personnel who receive initial defect reports from actual clients.

9. Email customer support personnel who receive initial defect reports from actual clients. Both telephone and email support can be combined or handled by the same person, although often they are separate groups.

10. Second- and third-line customer support personnel, who handle more complicated issues, primarily for large applications with many customers.

11. Dedicated maintenance programmers, who actually analyze and repair valid defects.

12. Development programmers, who actually analyze and repair valid defects in organizations that lack dedicated maintenance programmers.

13. Build and test personnel who integrate defect repairs into applications and perform regression testing.

14. Administrative personnel who keep track of defect status, numbers of defects, duplicates, and other logistical topics.

15. Maintenance managers, who supervise teams of maintenance personnel.

16. Software Quality Assurance (SQA) personnel employed by the vendor, who may be notified for specific situations such as reports of high-severity defects by major clients. SQA personnel also keep records of issues such as defects against specific applications.

17. Corporate executives employed by the client organization, who may be involved in special situations such as high-severity defects that damage or slow down business operations or cause major errors in financial reports.

18. Corporate attorneys employed by the client organization or outside counsel, who may be involved in special situations such as high-severity defects that cause problems that might include legal liabilities.

19. Corporate executives at the vendor company, who may be involved in special situations such as major defects reported by major clients.

20. Corporate attorneys employed by the vendor organization or outside counsel, who may be involved in special situations such as major defects that might cause legal liabilities.

21. Independent experts who may be hired by either the client organization or the vendor organization in special situations such as major defects that caused serious problems that resulted in litigation.

It will probably never happen that all of these occupation groups are involved at the same time for the same defects. But for large software applications released by and used by large enterprises, it often happens that perhaps 10 to 12 occupations may be involved.

The ranges of occupations involved with defect repairs can be examined by looking at the smallest combination, the largest combination, and a typical combination and are discussed in the next few sections. A severity 2 defect is noted and reported in all three cases. For simplicity, assume everyone involved in the defect reporting and repair process is compensated at a fixed rate of $60 per hour.

Smallest Combination

For small software applications released by small companies to only a few customers, defects are normally reported directly back to the development team. In other words, individual customers report defects directly to the source.

A colleague of one of the authors owns a one-person software company with several hundred clients. He does not have many defect reports, but when one is initiated, he answers the phone and handles the entire reporting and repair sequence personally. It is interesting that he receives more suggestions for new features than he does defect reports.

If you assume that the personnel involved in defect reporting and repairs are compensated at a rate of $60 per hour, then this simplest combination will probably cost the client about $60 to report the defect. It will cost the vendor perhaps $120 for defect analysis and $120 to repair and test the defect; $240 in total. Thus for a small company with few clients, this severity 2 example costs $360 in total, with one-third of the costs being user costs and two-thirds being vendor costs.

Typical Combinations

For software developed for internal use by a medium-sized enterprise, any defects discovered by users are reported to a help desk, which then completes a formal defect report. The defect report is routed to the appropriate maintenance group or to the maintenance manager. Next, the defect report is routed to the appropriate maintenance programmer or to a developer if there are no dedicated maintenance programmers. After analysis the defect is repaired. Then the repair is regression tested and added to a new build. It is integrated into a specific release, possibly together with other defects or with new features. In this typical case between four and seven occupation groups are involved.

In this pattern, the defect reporting process will probably cost about $180. The administrative costs of routing the defect and entering it into a tracking system will cost about $60. The defect repairs themselves might cost $150 for analysis and $150 for repair—$300 so far. Repair integration and testing of the repairs might cost another $240. If the company is sophisticated and performs root-cause analysis, that will add another $60 to the cost.

The total cost for the severity 2 defect might be $840. The cost breakdown would be about $180 for the logistics of getting the defect reported and entered into the tracking system, $150 for defect analysis, $150 for the actual repair, $240 for test and integration, and $60 for root-cause analysis.

Logistical costs for tracking defects should be included in overall defect repair costs for economic purpose. For a single defect logistical expenses may be small, but for a large corporation that has to deal with thousands of duplicate defects and hundreds of invalid defects as well as hundreds of valid defects, logistics costs mount up quickly.

Note that in this example the same company employs both the user and the software maintenance personnel. This fact is significant for studying defect repair economics because the costs for external clients (including cost to the brand or the reputation of the company) are usually unknown, while the costs for internal clients are often recorded.

Largest Combination

For a very large system such as an enterprise resource planning (ERP) application installed in a major corporation, the defect repair chain can be quite lengthy. Here, too, a severity 2 defect is assumed.

When a user or customer notes a defect, the next step is to report it to the dedicated support team for the ERP package. This team is normally located at the client site. The support team will help to prepare a formal defect report for the vendor.

The channel of submission to the vendor is either through the vendor's sales organization or through a support group inside the vendor corporation that is linked to specific clients. After the vendor receives the defect report, it is logged by an administrative group and entered into a defect tracking system.

A support specialist analyzes the defect report to ascertain whether it is new or a duplicate, or perhaps invalid. Valid unique defect reports are then routed to the appropriate maintenance team and assigned to a specific programmer or programming team. From time to time a defect is misrouted to the wrong team. If this happens it is returned to the central defect routing site for reanalysis and rerouting.

When the defect has been analyzed and repaired, the fix is turned over to the integration and test organization for regression testing and for addition to the next planned release. Configuration control records are also updated after the bug is repaired and the fix is integrated.

For high-severity defects there may also be a patch or quick repair that is dispatched to specific clients who are known to have the same defect. The symptoms and availability of the fix are added to the corporate support website for the application so that other groups who may want to report the same defect will know that it has already been reported and whether or not a fix is available.

At this point, we can assume that reporting the defect costs the client organization about $240. The logistics of entering the defects into the vendor tracking system and routing it cost about $120. The defect repairs cost about $180 for analysis and $180 for the repair itself; $360 in total.

Post-repair testing and integrating the repair into the ERP application plus configuration control cost about $420. This is due to the huge size of the ERP application. If root-cause analysis is performed (which it should be), that will cost another $120.

When the repaired version reaches the client, then installation and final testing might cost another $420. The total cost to this point would be $1,680 for this example of a severity 2 defect. Of these costs, about $660 were spent by the client and $1020 by the vendor.

It is interesting that the actual analysis and repair of this defect only cost $360 out of the total cost of $1,680, or 21%. Logistics costs, integration costs, configuration control costs, and testing costs totaled to $1,320 out of $1,680.

For commercial software usually the vendor will not know the defect cost breakdown for the client. The client will not know the defect cost breakdown for the vendor. This disconnect in cost data makes it difficult to study the true economics of post-release defect repairs because there is no single source that actually includes all cost elements.

To assemble the total cost structure of defect repairs it is necessary to interview both client and vendor personnel. If both the clients and the users are employed by the same company it is easier to study defect removal economics. But even within one company it seldom happens that clients, developers, and maintenance personnel all record their costs or effort using the same tracking system.

Note that if the application discussed in this third example were operating from a cloud or from the vendor's server, then no installation at the client site would be needed. Therefore, defect repair costs for the client would be lower by about $420 considering installation would not be necessary.

It should be noted that installing a new release of a large mainframe application such as an ERP package or a mainframe operating system is not a trivial task. These applications can take more than a week to install, tune, and regression test. The work can involve up to a dozen specialists.

A survey by IBM of client preferences for MVS operating system releases showed that the costs were so high that the clients preferred no more than quarterly releases. They also wanted the releases on fixed schedules so they could plan for them, instead of having the releases appear at random intervals.

These short examples illustrate some of the variables that impact post-release defect repairs. In general, larger software applications developed by and used by larger companies have significant logistical costs tacked on to the basic costs of fixing bugs. Also for large applications, integration and test costs go up due to the overhead of ensuring that the defect repairs don't cause regression defects or introduce new problems into the bulk of the application.

If the defect happens to have been extremely serious, then there may be contacts between executives at the client enterprise and executives at the vendor company. For example, the presidents of several major companies once called Thomas J. Watson, the chairman of IBM, about the poor quality of a specific IBM software application. (Watson immediately commissioned a task force to improve the application's quality.)

If actual damages occur or the defect causes a significant business problem or loss of money, then attorneys for both sides will no doubt become involved, and a lawsuit may be filed.

If litigation does occur, then lawyers for both sides, expert witnesses for both sides, the judge, court officials, possible jury members, and a host of paralegals and support personnel will probably become involved for a period that may last more than four years if the case goes all the way to trial (about 90% are settled out of court).

Not only will legal teams on both sides be involved, many executives and some technical workers will be subject to discovery and deposition proceedings. A typical breach of contract lawsuit will probably require about a month of extra work for the defendant executives and several weeks for the plaintiff executives. Depositions may be taken for some of the software engineers who worked on the application or on the defect repair.

For this maximum combination, around 20 occupation groups will be involved with the defect in question. About five of the occupation groups will be employed by the client, ten employed by the vendor, and five by the court or outside legal counsel. Needless to say defects that end up in court and go all the way to trial are very expensive problems for both sides.

Without detailing the specifics of the costs, a software defect that triggers a lawsuit might cost both the plaintiff and the defendant at least $1,000,000 each; $2,000,000 in total. It is much better to improve quality control than to risk litigation.

One of the authors once worked as an expert witness in a lawsuit where a single severity 2 defect in a financial package cost the client more than $3,000,000 in consequential damages due to having to restate prior year earnings and thereby losing a favorable banking relationship.

The litigation itself ran on for almost five years and cost the client (who was the plaintiff) about $2,000,000 in legal and witness fees. The costs for the defendant were not made available but probably were somewhat lower due to using internal corporate counsel for many of the day-to-day proceedings. We can assume the defendant's legal costs might have been about $1,500,000.

Because it took the vendor five attempts to repair the defect before it was finally fixed (and four of the five attempts included new defects), the total cost for defect repairs for this single severity 2 defect amounted to about five months of effort on the part of vendor maintenance personnel, or about $37,500.

Thus the total cost for this single severity 2 defect included $3,000,000 in business losses for the client; $2,000,000 in legal fees for the client; $1,500,000 in legal fees for the vendor, and $37,500 in defect repair expenses: $6,537,500 in all. This example is a fairly unusual situation, but the fact that it occurs at all indicates that better quality control would be beneficial to all parties.

These examples show that the observed costs for a severity 2 latent defect can range from a low of about $360 to a high of more than $6,500,000. The costs include logistical expenses for tracking and keeping tabs of defects;

analysis costs to pin down the specifics of the defect; repair costs to change the offending code; and integration and test costs to put the revision into the original application. There may also be costs associated with business losses or consequential damages on the part of the client and, of course, litigation costs if the defects cause serious harm.

The bulk of the literature on the cost-per-defect metric does not include information on logistics costs, analysis costs, repair costs, configuration control costs, and integration costs. Undifferentiated statements that "it costs 100 times as much to fix a bug after release as during requirements" do more harm than good because they do not show where the costs were expended.

The actual defect repair costs after release are not greatly different from those during testing, but the logistics costs are higher. Worse, because some of the logistics costs tend to be fixed costs, the overall effect is that cost per defect goes up as defect volumes come down.

Examining the Independent Variables of Post-Release Defect Repairs

The major independent variables that have an impact of post-release defect repairs include the following:

- The size of the application in function points

- The size of the application in logical coded statements

- The complexity level of the source code

- The size of the company that produces the application

- The number of users of the application

- The number of latent defects in the application

- The presence or absence of error-prone modules in the application

- The use of maintenance specialists rather than developers for repairs

So what are some of the impacts of these independent variables on post-release defect repairs? One purpose of this book is to provide guidelines for estimating software defects, so whenever possible the variables are expressed in such a manner that readers can use the information to predict aspects of applications they might be building or maintaining.

Although some guidelines are provided, the interaction of variables is so complex that automated estimation tools are preferred rather than attempting hand calculations.

The Size of the Application in Function Points

Because software defects originate in requirements, architecture, design, and user documents as well as in source code, the function point metric is the best overall metric for dealing with all defect origins. The major defect origins that can quickly be predicted by means of function points include these five:

1. Requirements

2. Design

3. Source code

4. User documents

5. Bad fixes or secondary defects

These five defect origins occur for essentially 100% of software applications.

For large applications, architecture defects can also be predicted using function points. Architecture defects, however, seldom occur for applications below 1,000 function points due to the fact that smaller applications do not create or use architectural specifications. For massive applications in the 100,000 function point size range, architectural defects can be serious, but such applications are quite rare.

There are, of course, other defect origins such as defects in data, defects in web content, defects in test cases, and several others. However, this section of the book deals primarily with software defects, so the five here comprise the main origin points. There is very little empirical data as of 2011 on defects in test cases. For defects in databases, there is even less data due to the fact that there is no effective "data point" metric for quantifying the size of a database, repository, or data warehouse.

A useful rule of thumb for predicting the overall defect potentials, or the combined total number of defects from the five origin points just shown is this:

Raise the size of the application in function points to the 1.25 power. The result will approximate total defects between applications whose sizes range from a low of 100 function points to a high of 10,000 function points.

This rule is not precise, but it does give a useful approximation of how many defects might be encountered. Readers are urged to experiment with their own data because the observed powers can vary from less than 1.2 for sophisticated projects using methods such as TSP to perhaps 1.26 for projects with no discernable development formality and careless quality control.

It is useful to show the aggregated results of more than 13,000 projects examined between about 1975 and 2011 and rounded to illustrate key trends. The data includes some extrapolation, given there are no applications of

1,000,000 function points. Neither are there applications of 1 function point, although that size is common for small enhancements. The purpose of Tables 6.9 through 6.11 is to show trends and variations.

Because the tables represent averages, it should be noted that many results can be either better or worse than the tables indicate. The highest observed level of defect removal efficiency, for example, approaches 99%. The lowest level of observed defect removal efficiency can be below 70%.

Table 6.9 shows approximate average defect potentials for seven types of software and seven size plateaus.

As can be seen, defect potentials or total defects increase in number as application size increases. This problem seems to be universal for software and has very few observed exceptions.

Table 6.10 shows the actual numbers of defects rather than defect potentials normalized using function points and is merely a mathematical extension of table 6.9.

Table 6.11 shows the approximate defect removal efficiency, or percentages of defects that will be eliminated prior to releasing the software to customers.

Note the unfortunate combination of events: Defect potentials go up with increasing application size, but defect removal efficiency goes down with increasing application size. Both of these observations are common enough so that they might perhaps be viewed as *laws* of software.

Table 6.12 gets to the heart of the matter and shows approximate numbers of latent defects that are delivered to customers with the initial releases of software applications.

Although there are many latent defects delivered, not all of them are of high severity levels. Only about 20% to 30% of delivered defects are of severity 1 or severity 2 levels.

In any case, Table 6.12 shows why major applications such as ERP packages and large operating systems need full-time maintenance teams for many years after deployment.

Table 6.13 shows the same results as Table 6.12 but normalized to illustrate delivered defects per function point.

As discussed earlier, clients will not find all delivered defects in the first year of usage. In general, defect discovery goes up with numbers of users. However, if software is delivered with an excessive number of defects (more than 1.0 per function point), users become distrustful and discouraged and attempt to avoid using the software if possible. This reaction slows down defect discovery rates.

Table 6.14 illustrates the approximate percentages of delivered latent defects that are likely to be discovered in the initial year of customer usage.

Table 6.15 uses the same data as Table 6.14 but shows actual numbers of reported defects. Here, too, only about 20% to 30% of reported defects are of severity level 1 or severity level 2.

Table 6.9 *Average Defect Potential per Function Point by Type and Size of Software Projects*

Size in FP	MIS Projects	Web Projects	Outsource Projects	Systems & Embedded Projects	Commercial Projects	Civilian Government Projects	Military Projects	Average
1	1.50	1.50	1.50	1.50	1.50	1.50	1.50	1.50
10	2.25	2.00	2.00	2.50	2.00	2.70	2.90	2.34
100	2.80	2.50	2.50	3.00	3.15	3.30	4.00	3.04
1,000	4.30	4.25	4.00	4.30	4.75	5.25	5.50	4.62
10,000	5.50	5.75	5.25	6.25	6.60	6.80	7.00	6.16
100,000	7.50	8.00	7.00	7.75	7.90	8.00	8.25	7.77
1,000,000	8.50	8.50	8.00	8.25	8.75	8.90	9.00	8.56
AVERAGE	4.62	4.64	4.32	4.79	4.95	5.21	5.45	4.86

Note: Defect potential includes requirements, design, code, document, and bad-fix defect categories.

Table 6.10 *Total Potential Defects by Type and Size of Software Projects*

Size in FP	MIS Projects	Web Projects	Outsource Projects	Systems & Embedded Projects	Commercial Projects	Civilian Government Projects	Military Projects	Average
1	2	2	2	2	2	2	2	2
10	23	20	20	25	20	27	29	23
100	280	250	250	300	315	330	400	304
1,000	4,300	4,250	4,000	4,300	4,750	5,250	5,500	4,621
10,000	55,000	57,500	52,500	62,500	66,000	68,000	70,000	61,643
100,000	750,000	800,000	700,000	775,000	790,000	800,000	825,000	777,143
1,000,000	8,500,000	8,500,000	8,000,000	8,250,000	8,750,000	8,900,000	9,000,000	8,557,143
AVERAGE	1,329,943	1,337,432	1,250,967	1,298,875	1,373,012	1,396,230	1,414,419	1,342,983

Note: Defect potential includes requirements, design, code, document, and bad-fix defect categories.

Table 6.11   *Defect Removal Efficiency by Type and Size of Software Projects*

Size in FP	MIS Projects	Web Projects	Outsource Projects	Systems & Embedded Projects	Commercial Projects	Civilian Government Projects	Military Projects	Average
1	98.00%	94.00%	99.00%	99.50%	97.00%	93.00%	98.00%	96.93%
10	97.50%	90.00%	98.00%	99.00%	95.00%	89.00%	96.00%	94.93%
100	94.00%	86.00%	96.00%	98.00%	93.00%	87.00%	95.00%	92.71%
1,000	86.00%	82.00%	90.00%	96.00%	91.00%	84.00%	93.00%	88.86%
10,000	82.00%	74.00%	86.00%	93.00%	89.00%	80.00%	91.00%	85.00%
100,000	74.00%	70.00%	82.00%	89.00%	86.00%	76.00%	90.00%	81.00%
1,000,000	70.00%	68.00%	77.00%	86.00%	82.00%	73.00%	88.00%	77.71%
AVERAGE	85.93%	80.57%	89.71%	94.36%	90.43%	83.14%	93.00%	88.16%

Note: Defect removal activities include inspections, static analysis, and testing.

Table 6.12 *Delivered Defects by Type and Size of Software Projects*

Size in FP	MIS Projects	Web Projects	Outsource Projects	Systems & Embedded Projects	Commercial Projects	Civilian Government Projects	Military Projects	Average
1	0	0	0	0	0	0	0	0
10	1	2	0	0	1	3	1	1
100	17	35	10	6	22	43	20	22
1,000	602	765	400	172	428	840	385	513
10,000	9,900	14,950	7,350	4,375	7,260	13,600	6,300	9,105
100,000	195,000	240,000	126,000	85,250	110,600	192,000	82,500	147,336
1,000,000	2,550,000	2,720,000	1,840,000	1,155,000	1,575,000	2,403,000	1,080,000	1,903,286
AVERAGE	393,646	425,107	281,966	177,829	241,902	372,784	167,029	294,323

Note: About 20% to 30% of delivered defects are of high severity levels.

Table 6.13 *Delivered Defects per Function Point by Type and Size of Software Projects*

Size in FP	MIS Projects	Web Projects	Outsource Projects	Systems & Embedded Projects	Commercial Projects	Civilian Government Projects	Military Projects	Average
1	0.03	0.09	0.02	0.01	0.05	0.11	0.03	0.05
10	0.06	0.20	0.04	0.03	0.10	0.30	0.12	0.12
100	0.17	0.35	0.10	0.06	0.22	0.43	0.20	0.22
1,000	0.60	0.77	0.40	0.17	0.43	0.84	0.39	0.51
10,000	0.99	1.50	0.74	0.44	0.73	1.36	0.63	0.91
100,000	1.95	2.40	1.26	0.85	1.11	1.92	0.83	1.47
1,000,000	2.55	2.72	1.84	1.16	1.58	2.40	1.08	1.90
AVERAGE	0.91	1.15	0.63	0.39	0.60	1.05	0.47	0.74

Note: Most delivered defects will not be found for a number of years.

Table 6.14 *Percentage of Delivered Defects Found and Reported in the First Year of Application Usage*

Size in FP	MIS Projects	Web Projects	Outsource Projects	Systems & Embedded Projects	Commercial Projects	Civilian Government Projects	Military Projects	Average
1	95.00%	97.00%	96.00%	99.00%	95.00%	90.00%	99.00%	95.86%
10	92.00%	95.00%	94.00%	96.00%	92.00%	85.00%	96.00%	92.86%
100	80.00%	90.00%	85.00%	90.00%	75.00%	75.00%	92.00%	83.86%
1,000	55.00%	80.00%	70.00%	85.00%	70.00%	68.00%	82.00%	72.86%
10,000	35.00%	60.00%	52.00%	72.00%	55.00%	57.00%	75.00%	58.00%
100,000	20.00%	40.00%	35.00%	64.00%	40.00%	33.00%	70.00%	43.14%
1,000,000	17.00%	33.00%	27.00%	60.00%	35.00%	18.00%	65.00%	36.43%
AVERAGE	56.29%	70.71%	65.57%	80.86%	66.00%	60.86%	82.71%	69.00%

Note: First-year defect reports rise with numbers of users.

The values of Table 6.15 are sensitive to the number of users. Obviously, a software application with a million users will have a higher percentage of defects found than a software application with only ten users.

There is a hidden variable in Table 6.15 that needs a word of explanation. Reported defects go up with numbers of applications users, which is an obvious correlation. The hidden variable is the fact that numbers of users tend to go up with application size. The reason for this is that large applications are so expensive to construct that it would not be economical to build them unless they were needed by thousands of customers.

To be cost effective, commercial software applications need to be used by one company for every two function points and to have about five individual users per function point. In other words, a software application of 1,000 function points needs to be used by around 500 companies and have 5,000 users to be cost effective.

Internal software produced for a single company does not follow the same pattern as commercial software but still needs at least one user per function point to be cost effective. Therefore, an in-house application of 1,000 function points will probably have 1,000 users.

A related topic, which is outside the scope of this book, is how many function points are needed by knowledge workers to perform their tasks effectively? As it happens, both project managers and software engineers in leading companies tend to use between 15 and 20 tools, which total to about 30,000 function points in performing their jobs.

Table 6.16 uses the same data as Table 6.15 and shows the approximate numbers of defects per function point reported by clients in the first year of usage.

Tables 6.8 through 6.16 are not precise, but they illustrate important trends. Large applications tend to have many defects, and these are difficult to eliminate prior to release of the software to customers. As a result, both customers and software development and maintenance groups need to prepare for dealing with software defects as a normal part of doing business. While unfortunate, until software quality control improves far beyond average levels of performance in 2011, released defects will continue to be numerous for large applications.

Two final tables in this section show the approximate numbers of high-severity defects released to customers. To recap severity levels, they have the following definitions:

Severity 1: Application failure

Severity 2: Major problem

Severity 3: Minor problem

Severity 4: Cosmetic problem that does not affect execution

Table 6.15 *Probable Number of Defects Found and Reported in the First Year of Application Usage*

Size in FP	MIS Projects	Web Projects	Outsource Projects	Systems & Embedded Projects	Commercial Projects	Civilian Government Projects	Military Projects	Average
1	0	0	0	0	0	0	0	0
10	1	2	0	0	1	3	1	1
100	13	32	9	5	17	32	18	18
1,000	331	612	280	146	299	571	316	365
10,000	3,465	8,970	3,822	3,150	3,993	7,752	4,725	5,125
100,000	39,000	96,000	44,100	54,560	44,240	63,360	57,750	57,001
1,000,000	433,500	897,600	496,800	693,000	551,250	432,540	702,000	600,956
AVERAGE	68,044	143,316	77,859	107,266	85,686	72,037	109,259	94,781

Note: First-year defect reports rise with numbers of users, but excessive defects will slow usage growth.

Table 6.16 *Probable Number of Defects per Function Point in the First Year of Application Usage*

Size in FP	MIS Projects	Web Projects	Outsource Projects	Systems & Embedded Projects	Commercial Projects	Civilian Government Projects	Military Projects	Average
1	0.03	0.09	0.01	0.01	0.04	0.09	0.03	0.04
10	0.05	0.19	0.04	0.02	0.09	0.25	0.11	0.11
100	0.13	0.32	0.09	0.05	0.17	0.32	0.18	0.18
1,000	0.33	0.61	0.28	0.15	0.30	0.57	0.32	0.37
10,000	0.35	0.90	0.38	0.32	0.40	0.78	0.47	0.51
100,000	0.39	0.96	0.44	0.55	0.44	0.63	0.58	0.57
1,000,000	0.43	0.90	0.50	0.69	0.55	0.43	0.70	0.60
AVERAGE	0.25	0.57	0.25	0.26	0.28	0.44	0.34	0.34

Table 6.17 shows the approximate number of high-severity defects for each of the seven types and size ranges.

As can be seen, below 1,000 function points, high-severity defects are fairly low in number. But for larger applications, high-severity defects become progressively more numerous.

Table 6.18 shows the approximate number of high-severity defects per function point.

The overall purpose of Tables 6.8 through 6.18 is to illustrate some basic trends for software applications. Defect volumes tend to go up with size. Defect removal efficiency tends to drop down with size. Discovered defects after release correlate with numbers of users. However, software with excessive defects present at release discourages users and therefore slows down defect discovery rates.

In extreme cases such as a severity 1 defect in an install procedure, there may only be one bug report for the first month because none of the features of the application can be used until it is installed and operational.

Tables 6.8 through 6.18 show approximate averages, but there are ranges of performance for every table. Table 6.19 shows the distribution of defect repair hours for customer-reported defects at IBM for various operating system components and several large applications.

The table shows that the overall average in terms of the mode would be close to perhaps five hours, although the range is quite wide. In fact, the range is wide enough that averages in terms of arithmetic means don't show the whole picture.

A few defects such as abeyant defects can take more than a week to analyze and repair. At the other end of the spectrum, other defects can be analyzed and repaired in a few minutes.

Severity 2 defects seem to be the most subtle and difficult to repair. If an application stops totally due to a severity 1 defect, usually there is a fairly obvious overt problem. But for severity 2 defects, the causes may be subtle and involve interactions of many modules and even interactions of multiple applications. For these reasons, severity 2 defects are often somewhat larger than severity 1 when measured using lines of code or function points. Severity 1 defects are often triggered by a single erroneous code statement, but severity 2 defects usually involve a number of code statements, sometimes scattered widely through the application.

Error-Prone Modules in Software Applications

In the 1970s when software applications and systems software began to balloon in size, IBM began to perform distribution analyses of customer defect

Table 6.17 Probable Number of Severity 1 and 2 Defects in First Year of Application Usage

Size in FP	MIS Projects	Web Projects	Outsource Projects	Systems & Embedded Projects	Commercial Projects	Civilian Government Projects	Military Projects	Average
1	0	0	0	0	0	0	0	0
10	0	0	0	0	0	1	0	0
100	3	8	2	1	4	8	4	4
1,000	73	147	62	29	81	137	63	85
10,000	762	2,153	841	630	1,198	1,860	945	1,198
100,000	8,580	23,040	9,702	10,912	13,714	15,206	11,550	13,244
1,000,000	95,370	215,424	109,296	138,600	176,400	103,810	140,400	139,900
AVERAGE	14,970	34,396	17,129	21,453	27,343	17,289	21,852	22,062

Note: Severity 1 = application failure; Severity 2 = major problem.

Table 6.18 *Probable Number of Severity 1 and 2 Defects per Function Point in First Year of Usage*

Size in FP	MIS Projects	Web Projects	Outsource Projects	Systems & Embedded Projects	Commercial Projects	Civilian Government Projects	Military Projects	Average
1	0.00	0.00	0.00	0.00	0.00	0.00	0.00	0.00
10	0.01	0.05	0.01	0.00	0.02	0.06	0.02	0.03
100	0.03	0.08	0.02	0.01	0.04	0.08	0.04	0.04
1,000	0.07	0.15	0.06	0.03	0.08	0.14	0.06	0.08
10,000	0.08	0.22	0.08	0.06	0.12	0.19	0.09	0.12
100,000	0.09	0.23	0.10	0.11	0.14	0.15	0.12	0.13
1,000,000	0.10	0.22	0.11	0.14	0.18	0.10	0.14	0.14
AVERAGE	0.06	0.15	0.06	0.06	0.10	0.12	0.08	0.09

Note: Severity 1 = application failure; Severity 2 = major problem.

Table 6.19 *Defect Repair Hours by Severity Levels for Field Defects*

	Severity 1	Severity 2	Severity 3	Severity 4	Invalid	Average
> 40 hours	1.00%	3.00%	0.00%	0.00%	0.00%	0.80%
30–39 hours	3.00%	12.00%	1.00%	0.00%	1.00%	3.40%
20–29 hours	12.00%	20.00%	8.00%	0.00%	4.00%	8.80%
10–19 hours	22.00%	32.00%	10.00%	0.00%	12.00%	15.20%
1–9 hours	48.00%	22.00%	56.00%	40.00%	25.00%	38.20%
> 1 hour	14.00%	11.00%	25.00%	60.00%	58.00%	33.60%
TOTAL	100.00%	100.00%	100.00%	100.00%	100.00%	100.00%

reports. They wanted to know if defects were randomly distributed through the modules of large systems or if defects followed identifiable patterns.

The initial results were somewhat surprising. Defects did not seem to be random, but rather clumped in a small number of modules that contained far more bugs than average. For example, for IBM's MVS operating system, about 4% of modules contained almost 50% of customer-reported bugs.

The most extreme skew was that of the Information Management System (IMS). This was a large database application. The reliability of IMS was poor at the time, and customer-reported defects were numerous.

In the mid-1970s when the distribution study was done, IMS had about 425 modules in total. About 300 modules had zero defects or never received any customer-reported defects at all. About 57% of all customer-reported defects were found in only 35 modules out of 425. These were dubbed error-prone modules, and that term continues to be used in 2011.

When these error-prone modules were identified IBM decided to remove them and develop replacements. IBM also decided to use inspections on the replacements (which had not been used on the originals). When the error-prone modules were eliminated, customer-reported defects declined by more than 50%, and customer satisfaction increased by more than 50% based on surveys of customer opinions.

The removal of error-prone modules and the use of inspections also paid unexpected dividends by improving development schedules and costs by about 15%.. The main savings in time and costs were in the area of reduced testing schedules. IMS testing went from three months of three-shift testing to one month of single-shift testing.

The results were interesting enough that IBM shared some of the findings with clients and with other companies, some of whom were motivated to carry out distribution studies on their own software.

Within a few years it had become clear that error-prone modules were an endemic problem for the software industry. Many companies that carried out distribution studies of software defects noted the same pattern as IBM: Defects tend to clump in specific modules.

Many of these error-prone modules were high in cyclomatic complexity and hence difficult to maintain or modify. Not only did error-prone modules receive at least three times as many bug reports as average modules, but the bad-fix injection percent was at least three times higher. In other words, instead of about 7% bad fixes happening when fixing bugs or making updates, error-prone modules topped 20%.

Error-prone modules are the most expensive and troublesome modules ever developed. Within five years of release, error-prone modules accumulate maintenance costs that are five times higher than average.

If error-prone modules are so troublesome, what can be done to eliminate them? This question is important but not easy to answer. The answer is also unpalatable.

Error-prone modules tend to come into existence due to poor quality control, which skimps on defect prevention and bypasses pretest inspections and static analysis. Testing is also poor for error-prone modules. Worse, quality measurement practices are so bad that many companies do not even know that they have error-prone modules in a majority of their larger applications!

To identify error-prone modules, defect tracking has to be sophisticated enough to identify the specific modules that contain the most defects. Less than 10% of the author's clients have quality measurement systems good enough to identify error-prone modules.

Of course, even without precise measurements, the maintenance programmers know that some modules are much tougher to deal with than others. But unfortunately, complaints by maintenance programmers are usually not sufficient to correct the problems.

Most error-prone modules are so complex and so difficult to understand that they cannot be repaired once they are created. What is necessary is to surgically remove the error-prone modules and replace them with new modules, which are built using state-of-the-art quality practices.

Removing and replacing error-prone modules costs twice as much as developing an average module. As a result, it is hard to get funding or approval for error-prone module elimination.

Because error-prone modules are complex and difficult to understand, they tend to act like black holes and draw in maintenance programmers and keep them there permanently. Because error-prone modules are difficult to understand, the programmers who work on them tend to be locked into the same positions for years with no opportunity to handle other work. In case of illness or job changes by these maintenance programmers, the new replacements have a very difficult time getting up to speed. Therefore, bad-fix injections go up for several months if new maintenance programmers take over.

There is also a social problem with error-prone modules. If a software development team admits to the presence of error-prone modules in applications they built and delivered, then clients and senior managers might justifiably question their competence. The combined results of the high costs of replacement plus the potential embarrassment of admitting to creating error-prone modules leads to ignoring them and continuing to maintain them for perhaps many years. This dilemma could be solved if companies had sophisticated quality measures that included economic costs, but very few companies measure software quality well enough for error-prone modules to be identified.

As a caution to readers, if your company builds or maintains large applications bigger than 10,000 function points in size, the odds of these applications containing error-prone modules is about 80%. This statement is based on the results of companies that have carried out defect distribution studies. If you do not have a quality measurement system that is capable of identifying error-prone modules, then you probably have them.

The authors recommend a distribution analysis of reported defects to identify probable error-prone modules. If such modules are found, the authors recommend formal inspections plus static analysis to ascertain if the modules can be repaired in place or need to be redeveloped.

If an application with error-prone modules processes critical data or is important to the business, the authors recommend immediate repairs or total replacement based on the specifics of the situation. Money goes into these error-prone modules and nothing useful comes back out. Measurement practices are so bad in the software industry that many error-prone modules either escape detection or are deliberately concealed to keep the software organization from looking as bad as it probably is.

User and Industry Costs from Post-Release Defects

A number of websites and blogs have lists and citations that discuss famous and expensive software defects. One website, the Consumerist, cites daily problems that customers experience with retail stores, cell phones, websites, and other current issues. Many of these involve software errors. This site is updated daily and therefore is useful for current information. For example, on November 17, 2010, this site had a discussion of confidential customer data from Chili's restaurant being accidentally compromised. Almost every day there are software problems reported on this site.

Other websites contain lists such as the "20 most expensive bugs" and go back in time to show older bugs. Some of these classic bugs may be urban legends, but many actually did occur. For example, only a few months ago the MacAfee antivirus program had a bug that caused part of Microsoft Windows to be misidentified as malware. This stopped Windows from loading. This bug was cited in the *Providence Journal* and other local news sources. Among the local problems noted was that of having to suspend surgical procedures at several Rhode Island hospitals due to the fact that operating room schedules could not be accessed.

Only a few days ago, one of the authors received a notice from Hewlett-Packard about the settlement of a class-action lawsuit. The plaintiffs alleged that the algorithm embedded in many HP printers that notified consumers to change ink cartridges was miscalculating, leading to replacement of cartridges that still contained substantial amounts of ink.

Because HP makes a great deal of money from expensive ink, this could be a valuable windfall. (It could also be costly for consumers, given that printer ink can cost up to $50 per cartridge.)

As it happens, one of the HP printers used during the writing of this book did in fact issue a change-ink message even though a high-capacity ink cartridge was installed. At least another 35 pages were printed after the message with no degradation of print quality. In fact, that same cartridge was still working more than two weeks after the change-ink message occurred.

HP has denied any wrong doing in this class-action case (such as deliberately miscalculating ink supplies). But the case illustrates how pervasive both computers and embedded devices have become in the modern world.

Another recent and expensive defect involves errors in the billing algorithms for Verizon cell phones. According to various reports in local papers and on the Web, in October of 2010 the Federal Communications Commission (FCC) fined Verizon a record $25,000,000 for this error, and Verizon has agreed to refund $53,000,000 in fees to affected customers.

According to an FCC news release, about 15,000,000 customers with "pay as you go" plans had been over charged for data usage for three years between 2007 and 2010. These overcharges included some "mystery charges" that no one could explain. For example, charges were being levied for accessing "free" sites such as Verizon Mobile Web home pages. Several customers who had content filters that blocked data transfer were charged anyway, and some charges apparently occurred for cell phones that were not only turned off, but had their batteries removed!

Here, too, the situation shows how pervasive computerized devices have become. In this case, the situation also shows how complicated billing statements have become. A typical cell phone bill contains dozens of entries, and some of these seem to be inexplicable even to customer support personnel.

Incidentally, in both the HP ink case and the Verizon billing case, it is not actually clear if the problems are due to accidental bugs or to deliberate actions on the part of the vendors. In the modern world the difference between a software bug and consumer fraud is sometimes hard to distinguish. Because both individuals and companies should be viewed as innocent until proven guilty, both of these software problems can be assigned to the "bug" category unless further evidence is brought forth.

From scanning a variety of websites that contain information on major software defects, some of these defects in embedded and systems software include the following in no particular order:

- Class-action suit against HP inkjet cartridge sensors

- Toyota brake problems

- AT&T long-distance shutdown

- NASA Mariner 1 failure

- NASA Polar Lander failure

- NASA Mars survey failure

- Therac-25 radiation poisoning

- Smartphone banking failures

- FAA air traffic control delays

- Denver Airport luggage handling problems

- Voting machine malfunctions

- Microsoft Xbox errors

- Sony PlayStation clock errors

- LA Airport grounding of 800 flights

Defects in military software include

- Ariane-5 launch failure and crash

- Patriot Missile targeting error

- Chinook helicopter engine failure

- F-22 Raptor flight control errors

- Shutdown of shipboard software on the Yorktown

- Possible failure to identify incoming Exocet missile

- Possible mistargeting of drone-fired missiles

Defects found in web and information systems have included the following:

- Verizon refunding $50,000,000 for data charge billing errors

- Mortgage documents lost in cyberspace

- Error in Moody's valuations of securities

- Errors in property foreclosure calculations

- Attorneys General for all 50 states investigating mortgage errors

- Errors in property tax valuation assessments

- Errors in dependent child payments

- MacAfee antivirus defect impacting Windows

- Errors in reporting political candidate contributions

- Google misidentification of harmful websites

- Health insurance billing errors

- Health insurance cancelled by mistake

- Health insurance records released by mistake

- Student loan privacy breaches

- A-380 Airbus wiring design problems

- Double debits of the same charge due to SQL errors

- 1987 Black Monday stock crash

Software problems that are serious enough to make news on television and in newspapers are not common, but they do occur fairly often. The big and expensive problems are the ones that are obviously newsworthy, so they get a great deal of coverage.

What seems to be happening is a range of business losses and some technical shut downs that can top a billion dollars at the high end of the scale and approach zero dollars at the low end of the scale.

From examining a number of websites and from keeping rough tabs on news reports, Table 6.20 shows what might be the approximate pattern of the impact of software defects on customers and clients. Both the amounts and the numbers of incidents are based on extrapolation from a small number of samples, so the results have a large margin of error. The point of Table 6.20 is that really expensive defects do occur but not in very large numbers.

Table 6.20 is speculative, but from observations within several hundred companies, serious defects are rare; less serious defects are common. The table illustrates defects that might cause business interruptions or shut down some business operations.

Bugs or defects have caused death or serious injury. Perhaps the best known is the Therac-25 radiation therapy device. This device had low-power and high-power beams, each with different purposes and different kinds of shielding devices. A software bug allowed the high-energy beam to be turned on by mistake instead of the low-energy beam. This condition was not sensed by the

Table 6.20 *Approximate U.S. Annual Costs for Software Defects to Clients*

Cost per Incident	MIS/Web Software	Systems & Embedded Software	Total Annual Incidents	Annual Cost of Incidents
> $1,000,000,000	5	2	7	$7,000,000,000
> $100,000,000	50	15	65	$6,500,000,000
> $10,000,000	100	50	150	$1,500,000,000
> $1,000,000	200	75	275	$275,000,000
> $100,000	1,000	250	1,250	$125,000,000
> $10,000	2,000	1,000	3,000	$30,000,000
> $1,000	6,000	5,000	11,000	$16,000,000
> $100	20,000	10,000	30,000	$3,000,000
TOTAL	29,355	16,392	45,747	$15,449,000,000

embedded Therac-25 software, nor were any warnings given to operators. The high-power beam delivered about 100 times the amount of X-rays as the low-power beam. Six patients were injured, and three died according to a web report on Wikipedia on the Therac-25 problems.

From looking at the root causes of 20 major software defects that either caused injuries or major expenses, it appears that about 12 of them might have been prevented or detected via quality function deployment (QFD), formal inspections, static analysis, and careful testing.

The other eight problems were subtle and difficult to detect using normal quality control method. For example, a problem with the Airbus A380 wiring harness was apparently caused by two design groups, one of which used version 4 of a CAD program, while the other used version 5.

The CAD vendor asserted the two versions would be compatible, but apparently they were not. The result included some erroneous dimensions in the wiring harness, which is a highly complicated set of cables and connectors. Even a small dimensional error in an airplane wiring harness is a costly situation given that neither the airframe nor the wiring harness can be modified easily after they are assembled.

If the wiring harness does not fit into the airframe, there is no easy or inexpensive solution, considering manual repairs are sometimes impossible. Only redesign and remanufacture of the wiring harness is a viable option, and a very costly one that will introduce significant delays in assembly of the aircraft.

Another aspect of the wiring problem was the use of aluminum wire rather than copper for most of the A380 cables. Aluminum wire is thicker than copper wire and not as flexible. Here the differences between the two kinds of wires were apparently not included in the harness design. Apparently the design software was set up to assume copper wiring, but this may have been a human error.

In retrospect, the claims of compatibility by the vendor of the CAD package might have been tested or examined. But almost all of us use different version levels of applications on a daily basis, so this factor is not something that is immediately obvious as a source of major problems. For example, Microsoft Office 2003, Office 2007, and Office 2010 are frequently used interchangeably. So many applications have so many working versions that most of us would disregard this as a potential source of serious errors.

It should obvious that if software controls hazardous physical devices, controls devices that have medical implications, or deals with high-security data such as personal identities and bank information, then the software needs a formal risk analysis and a full suite of pretest defect removal activities followed by a full set of test stages. It was surprising that these obvious safeguards were not always utilized.

Because of the wide range of possible damages to customers and the difficulty in predicting such damages, vendors are urged to be very thorough in quality control of devices and software that have the potential for causing serious harm.

Impact of Security Flaws on Corporations and Government Agencies

Table 6.20 only showed defects that affected software operations. There are also security flaws in software. These are defects, too, but what makes them important is the fact that hackers, viruses, worms, and other forms of malware are constantly aimed at computer systems and firewalls and waiting to take advantage of security vulnerabilities.

In other words, classic quality flaws simply cause problems and usually don't propagate themselves from location to location. Security flaws invite serious problems into a computer from outside sources. Worse, when these pieces of malware gain a foothold, they immediately attempt to transmit themselves to other sites and other computers.

To make a medical analogy, traditional quality problems are like an impacted wisdom tooth. They may be painful, but they are not contagious. Malware is like cholera or a highly contagious form of pneumonia; if a computer is infected, there is a good chance that other computers may also come down with the same condition.

The cost of quality (COQ) concept has no explicit rules for dealing with security flaws, denial of service attacks, or theft of customer data. In fact, the essential topic of whether security is a subset of quality remains ambiguous. If a security attack is due to an explicit flaw in software, then the costs of dealing with the attack should probably be included in COQ calculations.

On the other hand, denial of service attacks from hundreds of slave computers or botnets should probably not be included in COQ calculations because such attacks are not usually based on specific security flaws. However, this topic needs additional study.

If hackers gain access to client data such as Social Security numbers or account numbers, the potential damages to the clients are enormous. Large potential losses may occur to the company based on liabilities if their security protection was substandard. No clear consensus has been reached as to whether or not theft of client data should be included or excluded from cost of quality calculations.

What might be worth doing is to create a new *cost of security* (COS) form of measurement that uses logic similar to cost of quality, but encompasses prevention, removal, and recovery for viruses, worms, botnets, denial of service attacks, and other problems such as hacking and theft of data.

The effort and costs for recovering from security attacks are highly variable for both companies and consumers. However, the recovery also tends to be expensive for both companies and consumers. Recovering from identity theft can take several months in dealing with law enforcement agencies, credit card companies, banks, and other service providers.

In today's world the most sophisticated companies have an in-house *Computer Security Incident Response Team* (CSIRT) that is trained and ready to deal with security problems. Because these groups are new, there is no fixed place in corporate hierarchies for locating them. Some report to CIOs, some report to CTOs, some report to VPs of quality, while some report to telecommunications groups or data center management; a few report to CEOs.

The sizes of these groups have no solid empirical data as of 2011. From informal discussions with colleagues who do security work, it would seem that a trained security person may be needed for about every 500,000 function points in a corporate portfolio that is linked to other computers and the outside world.

Assuming a bank or insurance company has perhaps 500 software personnel and a portfolio of 3,000,000 function points, about 6 trained people are likely in a CSIRT response team. Some of these people will be needed on every shift, assuming computers run around the clock. Of course, the CSIRT team does not spend all of their time on security issues, so it might not be necessary to bring in new personnel. But it will be necessary to make sure that the CSIRT responders are well trained and capable.

Customer Logistics for Defect Reports and Repair Installation

As it happens, one of the authors had to report the loss of Internet connectivity to Verizon as this chapter was being written. Because Internet service was down, the report had to be done by telephone. Reaching an automated service location took only about 1 minute but required several voice responses to get to the correct repair service for Internet failures.

Automated remote tests took about 12 minutes but did not resolve the problem. The next step was speaking to a live customer support person, and that took more than 20 minutes of wait time on the phone.

The live support person took about 3 minutes to gather information already provided such as phone numbers, address, and client name. Another remote set of tests were run, which took about 10 minutes to complete. The author also was requested to reset the modem, which took only about 1 minute. Thus far, the remote tests had been for the modem, router, and internal equipment. After these were done, some additional remote tests were done on outside equipment.

Some kind of remote diagnostic tests were run, and apparently remote repairs were made, too. After about 15 more minutes, service was restored for one of the three computers in use at the time of failure. The other two computers had to be shut down and restarted, although perhaps running an Internet repair utility might have worked, too.

From the moment of failure until service was restored took about an hour. It is interesting and fairly common that the longest block of time, 20 minutes, was spent on hold waiting to speak to a live service representative. The other two longest blocks of time, 12 minutes and 15 minutes, were spent waiting for remote diagnostic tests to be completed.

Overall, the experience was fairly typical. The long hold times for live personnel are common and are due to understaffing. It was a pleasant surprise to find that the remote diagnostic tests eventually did find the problem and that service could be restored without an onsite visit, which no doubt would have left the author with no Internet service for most of the day if not longer.

Defect reports for conventional software bugs are similar, in that long wait times are the norm rather than an exception. Indeed, a 20-minute wait is probably shorter than average. What would probably not occur for most software bug reports would be remote diagnostics and remote repairs, although these can occur for some applications.

Table 6.21 illustrates how application size and number of application customers interact when dealing with reporting bugs by phone, getting an email response from a vendor, getting a temporary repair (if any), and getting a permanent repair in a new release. Table 6.20 deals with commercial software. In-house software would probably have much shorter wait times for reporting a defect and probably shorter intervals across the board.

Table 6.21 *Customer Defect Report and Repair Experiences for Severity 2 Defects*

Size in FP Function Points	Number of Users or Customers	Telephone Wait (minutes)	Email Response (days)	Work Around (days)	Temp Repair (days)	New Release (months)
1,000	100	10	1	1	2	1
1,000	1,000	20	2	3	5	3
1,000	10,000	40	3	4	7	4
10,000	1,000	20	3	3	3	4
10,000	10,000	40	5	5	7	4
10,000	100,000	75	None	None	9	6
100,000	10,000	30	3	4	5	6
100,000	100,000	60	5	7	9	6
100,000	1,000,000	90	None	None	None	6

Table 6.21 illustrates a typical severity 2 defect. A severity 1 defect would not take less time to report, but the repair intervals would be shorter. Three sizes of 1,000 function points, 10,000 function points, and 100,000 function points are shown.

The essential message of Table 6.21 is that defect repair wait times go up with application size and number of customers and for that matter with numbers of defects.

Because many variables operate concurrently and form complex patterns, the most effective way of predicting post-release defect repairs is probably to use one of the commercial estimation tools that include maintenance estimation. Application size, number of customers, number of defects, severity levels of defects, invalid defects, and duplicates all need to be handled simultaneously.

To provide some sense of the costs of post-release defect repairs, two case studies are discussed next. One case study represents a small application of 1,000 function points with 1,000 customers and 500 defects in the first years. The second case study is a large system of 10,000 function points, 10,000 customers, and 5,000 defects in the first year.

Case Study 1: A Small Application by a Small Company

Case Study 1 assumes a commercial application of 1,000 function points that is used by 1,000 customers. In the course of a year, 500 valid unique defects are reported against the application. (Having 500 defect reports in one year is higher than average, but this is merely an example, and round numbers were used for simplicity.)

Assume the company that produced the software has 10 software engineers and technical personnel. For maintenance purposes in this example, the maintenance team consists of two maintenance programmers (who also do development), one professional tester, one person who handles integration and configuration control, and one administrative staff member who handles customer calls and defect logging: five personnel in all. There is a manager for the entire group.

In the course of a year, assume the total numbers of reported defects by severity level and category were the following:

Severity 1	=	5
Severity 2	=	125
Severity 3	=	170
Severity 4	=	200
Total	=	500
Invalid	=	25
Duplicate	=	1,000
Improvements	=	10

Table 6.22 shows the approximate distribution of effort between tasks for defects of all four severity levels, plus invalid and duplicate defects, and also suggested enhancements. The effort is expressed in terms of minutes per reported defect.

Management effort is excluded from Table 6.21 but would amount to about 12% of the total for each task, assuming a normal span of control.

On an individual basis, severity 2 defects accumulate 610 minutes of effort or just over 10 hours each. Severity 2 defects are usually the most troublesome. Actual repairs for severity 2 defects average 360 minutes or 6 hours each.

The range is not shown in Table 6.22, but for severity 2 defects the probable range would be from less than 1 hour to more than 40 hours if there were abeyant defects. Abeyant defects are excluded from Table 6.22 because they are too complex and so costly that they skew normal repairs.

Suggested improvements are in the number three spot, at about 435 minutes or 7.25 hours each. This time is more than most actual defects require. In real life, deciding whether a specific report should be classed as a defect report or a suggested improvement is not a trivial issue. Note that when a defect report is converted into a suggested improvement, it should not be counted as a defect.

Table 6.22 *Defect Repair Effort for 1,000 Function Points, 1,000 Customers, and 500 Defects*

(Data expressed in terms of minutes per reported defect)

	Call Logging	Routing	Tracking Projects	Analysis	Repair	Test	Integ. & Config.	TOTAL
Severity 1	15	10	5	90	180	120	30	450
Severity 2	20	15	5	120	240	180	30	610
Severity 3	5	10	3	60	90	90	30	288
Severity 4	5	5	3	30	30	30	10	113
Invalid	10	20	5	60	0	0	0	95
Duplicate	5	3	3	15	0	0	0	26
Improve	15	30	30	360	0	0	0	435
AVERAGE	11	13	8	105	77	60	14	288

Note also that invalid defects and duplicates do not require actual repairs, but they do accumulate logistical costs, and they also require analysis to ascertain that the defect reports are in fact invalid or duplicates of prior reports.

Because minutes are not normally used for economic studies, if we convert minutes into months of effort, the entire technical staff accumulated 17.31 months of effort. Looking at effort by severity level, the results are

Technical Staff Months

Severity 1	=	0.21
Severity 2	=	7.22
Severity 3	=	4.64
Severity 4	=	2.14
Subtotal	=	14.21
Invalid	=	0.22
Duplicate	=	2.46
Improvements	=	0.41
Subtotal	=	3.10
TOTAL	=	17.31

Because full-time effort for a team of 5 technical personnel would total to 60 months, the example shows that maintenance activities were not the only kinds of work performed by the maintenance personnel. This situation is common for small companies that tend to use generalists rather than specialists and where most technical employees perform multiple tasks.

Case Study 2: A Large Application by a Large Company

For Case Study 2 a commercial application of 10,000 function points that is used by 10,000 customers is assumed. In the course of a year, 5,000 valid unique defects are reported against the application. (Having 5,000 valid defect reports in one year is not uncommon for applications for 10,000 function points.)

Assume the company that produced the software has 500 software engineers and technical personnel. For maintenance purposes in this example, the maintenance team for the application consists of 15 dedicated maintenance programmers, 5 professional testers, and 3 people who handle integration and configuration control. Assume there is an offshore call center with 6 personnel assigned to the application: 2 on every shift for around-the-clock support. Thus the domestic staff totals 23 maintenance personnel plus 6 offshore personnel in the call center. Assume the domestic staff only work one shift but no doubt contribute some unpaid overtime if needed.

Two U.S. managers are assigned for maintenance activities, and there's a supervisor in place over the call center. Managers are not included in Table 6.23. Also an application of this size would be important enough for Software Quality Assurance (SQA) to monitor defect reports and include them in monthly quality reports for executives. The SQA effort is also excluded from Table 6.23. The SQA effort would not be full-time and would probably only involve perhaps two hours per month by one person.

In the course of a year, assume the total number of reported defects by severity level and category was

Severity 1	=	25
Severity 2	=	1,275
Severity 3	=	1,700
Severity 4	=	2,000
Total	=	5,000
Invalid	=	300
Duplicate	=	15,000
Improvements	=	150

Note that when numbers of customers go up, duplicate defects go up. For that matter, suggested improvements go up. In real life, valid defect reports would go up, too, but in this example valid defects were artificially limited to 10 times those shown in Case Study 1 in order to highlight what happens to duplicates and invalid defect reports and to show what happens to defect repair effort for big systems.

Table 6.23 shows the approximate distribution of effort between tasks for defects of all four severity levels, invalid and duplicate defects, and suggested enhancements.

When you compare Tables 6.22 and 6.23, the most striking difference is that every form of defect repair goes up for large systems. This increase is because large systems are more difficult to analyze, defects are harder to fix, and integration and testing are much more difficult. In fact, many more test cases are needed per function point or per KLOC for big systems than for small applications.

Table 6.23 *Defect Repair Effort for 10,000 Function Points, 10,000 Customers, and 5,000 Defects*

(Data expressed in terms of minutes per reported defect)

	Call Logging	Routing	Tracking Projects	Analysis	Repair	Test	Integ. & Config.	TOTAL
Severity 1	20	15	10	120	180	180	75	600
Severity 2	30	20	20	180	360	240	75	925
Severity 3	10	15	10	90	120	180	75	500
Severity 4	10	15	5	60	60	60	30	240
Invalid	20	30	5	75	0	0	0	130
Duplicate	7	10	5	20	0	0	0	42
Improve	15	60	30	480	0	0	0	585
AVERAGE	16	24	12	146	103	94	36	432

Management effort is excluded from Table 6.23 but would amount to about 12% of the U.S total for each task assuming a normal span of control and 14% for the offshore total.

On an individual basis, severity 2 defects accumulate 925 minutes of effort, or about 15.4 hours each. Severity 2 defects are usually the most troublesome for every application size and especially for large systems. Actual repairs for severity 2 defects average 540 minutes or 9 hours each. The range is not shown in Table 6.23, but for severity 2 defects the probable range would be from less than 2 hours to more than 60 hours if there were abeyant defects. Abeyant defects are excluded from Table 6.23 because they are too complex and so costly that they skew normal repairs. For an application of this size with 10,000 customers, it is possible that 3 abeyant defects might be reported in the course of one calendar year.

For large systems, severity 1 defects tend to be in second place in terms of effort at 600 minutes, or 10 hours each. Suggested improvements are not far behind and are in the number three spot, at about 585 minutes, or 9.75 hours each. This time is more than some actual defects require. In real life, deciding whether a specific report should be classed as a defect report or a suggested improvement is not a trivial issue. Note that once a defect report is converted into a suggested improvement, it should not be counted as a defect.

Note also that invalid defects and duplicates do not require actual repairs, but they do accumulate logistical costs, and they also require analysis to ascertain that the defect reports are in fact invalid or duplicates of prior reports.

Here, too, if we convert minutes into months of effort, the entire technical staff accumulated 310.71 months of effort. Looking at effort by severity level, the results are

Technical Staff Months

Severity 1	=	1.42
Severity 2	=	111.68
Severity 3	=	80.49
Severity 4	=	45.45
Subtotal	=	239.05
Invalid	=	3.69
Duplicate	=	59.66
Improvements	=	8.31
Subtotal	=	71.66
TOTAL	=	310.71

Because full-time effort for a team of 23 domestic technical personnel would total to 276 months, it can be seen that in this example maintenance activities were almost the only kinds of work performed by the dedicated maintenance personnel. This situation is common for large companies that tend to use specialists rather than generalists.

Cyclomatic complexity levels are usually higher for large systems than for small applications, but complexity was excluded from the two case studies because having too many variables dilutes the basic message that maintenance for large systems is much tougher than for small applications.

Management effort is excluded from Table 6.23 but would amount to about 12% of the total for each domestic task assuming a normal span of control. The management effort for the off-shore work would probably be about 14% and is excluded as well.

Tables 6.22 and 6.23 illustrate a few key issues in post-release defect repairs and maintenance:

- Defect reports increase with application size.

- Defect reports increase with numbers of application users.

- Duplicate defect reports increase with numbers of application users.

- Defect repair effort increases with application size.

- Invalid defects increase with number of users.

- Invalid defects increase with number of valid defects.

- Invalid defects require effort and accumulate costs.

- Suggested improvements require effort and accumulate costs.

Unfortunately, there are many other variables that affect post-release defect repairs and maintenance costs that are not shown in Table 6.22 or 6.23:

- The impact of cyclomatic complexity on defect repairs

- The impact of abeyant defects on maintenance costs

- The actual value of maintenance specialists

- The impact of programming languages on maintenance costs

- The impact of certified reused code on maintenance costs

- The impact of maintenance workbenches on maintenance costs

- The impact of refactoring on maintenance costs

- The impact of training of maintenance personnel

- The impact of maintenance manuals and schematic diagrams on maintenance

- The impact of comments and comment clarity on maintenance costs

- The impact of concurrent enhancements and defect repairs

- The impact of ITIL on post-release defect repairs

- The impact of CMMI levels on post-release defect repairs

Because all of these variables interact in intricate and complex fashions, there are no really effective static methods for predicting maintenance costs or post-release defect repairs. Some of the commercial software cost-estimating tools do include algorithms that can handle all of these variables.

It is possible to use manual methods to get a fair approximation of post-release defect repair effort and costs, but due to the wide range of results and to the very different results by severity level, automation is both easier and more accurate.

Measurement Issues in Maintenance and Post-Release Defect Repairs

Measuring software maintenance in the form of defect repairs and measuring enhancements have some special problems that make the work more difficult than measuring development.

Both defects themselves and the repairs to those defects are too small for conventional counting by means of function points. Normal function point analysis does not work below about 15 function points. Most defects range from a fraction of a function point up to perhaps 2 function points, although there are a few larger ones.

Also defects clearly are not "user benefits," and hence they are outside of the ground rules for counting function points. Backfiring and pattern matching are the two methods that can provide approximate sizes for defect and repairs in function point form, although neither technique is reliable. Automated tools can provide function points for legacy applications by means of code analysis but not for specific defects or defect repairs.

For example, the 500 defects noted in Case Study 1 probably totaled only about 250 function points. For the 5,000 defects noted in Case Study 2, they probably totaled about 3,000 function points. Individually each defect is small, but the sum total can add up to a significant quantity of work.

Another issue with maintenance measurement is the fact that the word "maintenance" actually includes 30 different kinds of work, and each kind has its own deliverables and its own productivity rates. Many of the 30 kinds of maintenance are outside the scope of this book, but the following list illustrates the many kinds of work that are all found under the term "maintenance."

1. Major enhancements (new features of > 20 function points)

2. Minor enhancements (new features of < 5 function points)

3. Null function point enhancements (new features of 0 function points)

4. Maintenance (repairing defects for goodwill)

5. Warranty repairs (repairing defects under formal contract)

6. Logistics (logging, tracking, and measuring defects)

7. Integration and configuration control after updates

8. Conversion of defect reports into potential enhancements

9. Customer support (responding to client phone calls or problem reports)

10. Email support (responding to client emails or problem reports)

11. Error-prone module removal (eliminating very troublesome code segments)

12. Mandatory changes (required or statutory changes)

13. Complexity analysis (quantifying control flow using complexity metrics)

14. Code restructuring (reducing cyclomatic and essential complexity)

15. Optimization (increasing performance or throughput)

16. Software migration (moving software from one platform to another)

17. Hardware migration (moving software from one computer to another)

18. Cloud migration (moving software to the cloud)

19. Conversion (changing the interface or command structure)

20. Data conversion (changing databases or file structures)

21. Data migration (moving data to a new database)

22. Reverse engineering (extracting latent design information from code)

23. Re-engineering (transforming legacy application to modern forms)

24. Dead code removal (removing segments no longer utilized)

25. Dormant application elimination (archiving unused software)

26. Language conversion (converting languages such as COBOL to new languages such as Java)

27. Nationalization (modifying software for international use)

28. Mass updates to multiple applications (i.e., Y2K and Euro changes)

29. Retirement (withdrawing an application from active service)

30. Field service (sending maintenance members to client locations)

For the purposes of this book, the measurement issues are those that concern post-release defect repairs. Some of the measures and metrics used to monitor post-release defect repair performance include the following:

- **Maintenance assignment scope:** When a software application is released, how many programmers will it take to keep it up and running? The answer to this basic question is the *maintenance assignment scope*. This value is calculated by dividing application size by number of programmers. As noted earlier, the range is between about 300 and 3,000 function points, with an average value of about 1,000 function points.

  The LOC metric is sometimes used for assignment scope. If so, the assignment scopes vary for specific languages, complexity levels, and defect volumes. Ranges might be between 1,000 and 100,000 logical code statements.

- **Call center performance:** Call centers are brutal places to work, being generally understaffed and demanding very long hours with few breaks for employees. Normally, performance is measured by calls answered per day. Ranges are between 24 and 48 per day. Other metrics would include wait times per client (from 10 to 60 minutes) and successful outcomes in terms or resolving issues (about 30%); and escalations to level 2 or level 3 service experts (about 25%).

- **Incoming defect reports per month:** One of the more complex issues of maintenance operations is predicting the number of defect reports that will arrive from clients each month. An initial rule of thumb is to expect 1 defect report per month for every 1,000 function points. You can also expect 1 defect report per month for every 100 users. This assumes average values of delivered defects of about 0.75 per function point. Because of other factors such as financial software defects spiking at the end of fiscal years, every company needs to derive its own values for its own custom software. This kind of information is needed to handle maintenance and support staffing levels.

- **Incoming defect reports per client:** Defect reports should also be recorded for specific applications and also for specific clients. Surprisingly, for both Beta test defects and post-release defects, less than 15% of clients usually report more than 50% of all defects. Defect reports should also be recorded by country for international applications and by geographic regions for domestic applications. Obviously, this applies to commercial software with many companies or government groups as clients. Even for internal software within a single company, 15% of users will tend to report more than 50% of defects.

- **Defect repairs per month:** Measuring how many defects are fixed per calendar month is used as an organizational metric and sometimes as a personnel metric, too. The problem with this metric is that if there are months with zero defects coming in, productivity will seem to be low for artificial reasons.

  For buggy applications with a large supply of defects, expect between 10 and 25 defect repairs per programmer per month. However, defects can be reduced faster than personnel can be reassigned. As quality improves, staffing reductions can eventually occur, but several months are needed to ascertain whether the quality improvements are real or only a statistical anomaly. Thus if reported defects per programmer drop below 5 per month, then apparent productivity will decline merely because of the reduction in defect reports.

- **Defect repair schedule ranges:** A topic of great importance to customers and executives is that of how long it takes to fix defects from the initial report to a temporary repair and then to a final repair in a new release. Small companies and small applications are much quicker in turning around defects than are large companies and large applications. Abeyant defects that are hard to diagnose also need to be included. For high-severity defects of severity level 1, about 24 hours for a workaround might be expected. For severity 2 defects, which often are more complex, 24 hours would be good, but usually 48 hours is more normal. For abeyant defects that are hard to diagnose more than 5 to 10 days may be needed, and perhaps onsite visits will be required.

- **Defect repair effort by activity**: Dealing with software defects requires logistical support for logging and tracking defects; programming support; and often the support of test personnel and integration/configuration control personnel. Call center personnel and help desk personnel may be needed. Quality assurance personnel may also be involved. For defects reported against user manuals or training materials, technical writers or even artists may be involved. These issues affect large companies with specialists more than they do small companies that use generalists.

- **Defect root-cause analysis**: IBM and other sophisticated companies don't just fix defects, they also investigate what caused them. For example, the well-known IBM APAR defect reporting form includes origin codes that identify whether the defect originated in requirements, design, code; is a bad fix; was caused by poor testing; or by other reasons.

   This kind of root-cause analysis takes some extra time but is worthwhile for severity 1and severity 2 defects because it leads to long-range improvements. In fact, the IBM data on defect origins is a primary source for information on defects that originated in requirements, architecture, design, and other noncode activities used in this book.

It is an unfortunate fact that maintenance operations are not quantified as well as they should be. Part of this problem is due to the very large number of activities that are included in the word "maintenance." Another part of the problem is the endemic situation that software measurements are neither common nor effective. For complicated work such as maintenance, this situation is the norm.

The traditional method of calculating cost per defect by merely dividing total defects by total effort has serious economic issues. For one thing, due to fixed costs and overhead, the cost per defect goes up as defect reports come down, and the metric cannot be used for zero-defect software. For another, the real value of software quality is not found in defect repairs, per se, but in the cost and schedule reductions that high quality levels will yield.

The traditional LOC metric also has economic problems. LOC metrics penalize high-level languages and therefore conceal the value of modern languages. LOC metrics cannot be used to measure defects in requirements, architecture, and design, and therefore more than 60% of all defects tend to be invisible.

A caution is needed for readers. If your enterprise is embarking on a quality improvement program, when it becomes effective your cost per defect will go up, and the number of defects fixed per month will go down. This paradox is not because your team is slacking but because of intrinsic economic flaws in both cost-per-defect and defects-per-time-period metrics. Both of these metrics penalize quality. Your executives may not understand this, but they should not depend upon either metric to show the economic gains from better quality.

Looking to the future, annual maintenance costs per function point can be used as an aggregate metric for all maintenance activities. For example, Case Study 1 indicated total annual maintenance effort of 17.1 staff months for 1,000 function points. If you assume a burdened rate of $7,500 per month, then the total cost was $128,250, which is $128.25 per function point per year.

For Case Study 2, the annual maintenance effort totaled 310.71 staff months for 10,000 function points. Assuming the same cost structure of $7,500 per staff month, the costs were $2,330,325. This is equivalent to $233.03 per function point per year.

The advantage of function point metrics for maintenance activities is that they encompass all forms of defects and all forms of maintenance activities. Even better, as quality improves and defect volumes are reduced, the annual cost per function point will be reduced, too. Thus measuring maintenance costs with function point metrics permits economic analysis, which cannot be done using either lines of code, defects per staff month, or cost-per-defect metrics.

Even more useful, as defect repair maintenance costs per function point decline, development costs per function point will decline as well. Thus function points can show the correlation between high quality and software total costs of ownership, which cannot be shown by other metrics.

This book uses function points as defined by the International Function Point User's Group (version 4.3). The same comments would be true for other forms of function point metrics such as COSMIC, NESMA, FISMA, unadjusted, and several others. Conversion from one form of function point to another would be necessary for large-scale studies across the various forms of functional metrics, but all forms of function point metrics are effective for economic analysis.

Unfortunately, neither story points nor use-case points have equal value for economic studies. The problem with these metrics is that they can only be used for projects that utilize user stories or use cases. It is not feasible to perform large-scale economic studies or comparisons between use-case projects and story-point projects.

Function point metrics can easily be applied to projects that utilize use cases or user stories and also to projects that use conventional text-based requirements and many forms of design such as decision tables, flowcharts, or any other representation. For economic analysis of software, function points are the most effective metric yet developed.

Summary and Conclusions on Post-Release Defects

Finding and fixing bugs after release has been a common activity since the software industry began and shows no real sign of diminishing in the future. But using observations from almost 600 companies, day-to-day quality control is much less effective than the actual state of the art.

If state-of-the-art combinations of defect prevention, pretest defect removal, and formal testing were utilized on every major software project, delivered defects would go down by perhaps 60% compared to 2011 averages. This improvement in quality would simultaneously improve development speed and costs and, of course, make major improvements on post-release maintenance costs.

If the industry should reach a level of sophistication where certified reusable components are utilized instead of custom design and custom coding, then delivered defects might drop down by more than 90% compared to 2011 averages. Should this occur, software development would become a true engineering field rather than an art form or craft as it is today in 2011.

If readers want to reduce post-release defects and lower maintenance costs, the work needs to start at the beginning of software development with better methods for requirements and design (such as quality function deployment, or QFD) with formal inspections of requirements and design, with static analysis, and with test cases designed using effective mathematical methods. Code rigor is important, too. Testing alone at the end of development is not sufficient to make major improvements in quality.

The economic motive for using state-of-the-art quality control methods is discussed and illustrated in Chapter 7. High quality leads to shorter schedules, lower costs, lower maintenance costs, lower total cost of ownership, and higher levels of customer satisfaction than the norms of 2011.

Chapter 7

Analyzing the Economics of Software Quality

Introduction

Many readers of this book and one of its authors are older than the software industry, in the sense that "software" consists of stored programs that operate on digital computers.

The phrase "software industry" implies more than just methods for creating computer programs. To be considered a software industry, these criteria should be present:

1. The industry produces marketable products.

2. The industry contains companies that produce those marketable products.

3. The people who create the marketable products are compensated for their work.

4. There are sufficient clients for the marketable products to generate profits.

5. There are sufficient clients for open-source products to be sustained.

Note that although open source applications are nominally free, they do accept voluntary donations from users. Also many open source applications have revenue-generating training and consulting work associated with them.

Ideas that resemble software can be traced back to mechanical devices from the thirteenth century or perhaps earlier that used cams or pegs to control physical devices.

Notes written in 1842 and 1843 by Ada King, the countess of Lovelace, are viewed by many researchers as probably the first recognizable description of stored programs. Her notes discussed translating a sequence of Bernoulli numbers as might be done using the analytical engine designed by Charles Babbage. Her work may well be the first clearly identifiable description of a computer program. Later, the Ada programming language was named in her honor.

The primary motive of Charles Babbage in designing both his difference engine and the uncompleted analytical engine was to reduce the burdensome effort of performing tedious mathematical calculations.

Prior to and during World War II many researchers began to construct devices that would evolve into modern computers. Some of these were created at universities and others by military groups. They were not "marketed" in the conventional meaning of the word. Here, too, a key motive was to speed up and reduce the errors in complex mathematical calculations.

The factors that began to coalesce to form the modern computer and software industries seemed to occur in the 1950s when mainframe computers were applied to business problems and therefore needed software to address those problems.

Existing companies such as IBM, General Electric, RCA, Honeywell, Burroughs, and many others began to add new business units that built computers and software for sale or lease to clients.

At first most software was not marketed separately from the computers themselves, which gave the computer manufacturers a competitive edge. There were some contract software groups, but they sold software to computer companies rather than to end users.

In 1969 IBM "unbundled" many software applications and began to lease or sell them as separate products. (The unbundling was triggered by an antitrust investigation.) However, it was unbundling that made the modern software industry economically feasible. For the first time, small companies could develop and market software applications directly to clients rather than to the restricted markets of computer manufacturers.

As a result of unbundling, the 1970s witnessed the birth of a large number of software companies. Apparently the first software company to go public with stock offerings was Cullinane in 1978.

While mainframe computers had already formed a significant industry by the end of the 1970s, the power and usage of computers were about to expand by several orders of magnitude with the advent of personal computers.

The history of the personal computer industry is outside the scope of this book, but the widespread deployment of personal computers led to an ever-increasing demand for software and hence a rapid increase in companies that built such software. Microsoft, through a combination of luck and technical skills, became the dominant company in the growing personal computer software business.

The Economic Value of Software

As a prelude to discussing the economic value of software quality, it is useful to consider the economic value of software itself. The word "value" is ambiguous in both daily use and also in economic texts.

There are obviously many kinds of value in addition to economic value. For example, medical software that can aid physicians in diagnosing illness has enormous value for health care, but this is kind of value is not exactly "economic" value. Software that improves national security or military effectiveness is also extremely valuable, but this kind of value is in addition to its economic value.

In this book economic value centers on two areas that can be analyzed in terms of normal accounting and finance: 1) revenue generation and 2) cost reduction. Of course, other software metrics also matter, and this chapter and the book as a whole are replete with them. The study of software economics leads us to trace the connections between software metrics, like structural quality violations (just to pick one example), and the economic metrics of revenue and cost.

Methods of Measuring Value

Prior to spending any serious amount of money for building a major new software application, the stakeholders and the software managers should convene a formal risk/value analysis study to determine if the application is good enough to be fast-tracked, of moderate value but fundable, or potentially so risky that finding is unwise.

It is obvious that new applications need a formal analysis prior to funding. But major enhancements and significant updates should also be reviewed for risks and potential value.

The best time for such a study would be at about the time that requirements are known, but unfortunately this may not be for six to nine months after project initiation, so quite a bit of money might already be spent. Risk and value need to be identified and quantified as early as possible.

If a proposed new application resembles existing applications whose costs, schedules, and quality levels are known, then the study can be done prior to full requirements by using historical results as the basis for analysis. Internal data is best, but external historical data from groups such as the International Software

Benchmark Standards Group (ISBSG) are useful surrogates for internal data. Indeed, acquisition of information about the costs, schedules, quality, and successes or failures of similar applications should be a standard part of risk and value studies. Because historical data on project failures and overruns is available, one important aspect of a funding decision is to consider the track records of similar applications.

Also the projected costs for the application can be predicted with reasonable accuracy by means of one or more commercial estimation tools such as COCOMO, KnowledgePlan, SEER, SLIM, and others. Formal manual estimates are also useful although more difficult to construct than automated estimates. (A study of manual and automated cost estimates by one of the authors found that below 1,000 function point accuracy was about equal. Above 10,000 function points, automated estimates were more accurate, and manual estimates tended to be significantly optimistic for both costs and schedules.)

As of 2011 a combination of historical data from industry and internal sources combined with commercial tools that handle software risks, cost estimates, and quality estimates can provide a good business case for determining whether or not projects should be funded and go forward. For applications that resemble prior applications, this risk and value analysis can occur early, near the start of requirements.

There are more than a dozen financial and accounting methods for measuring value. For example, the accounting rate of return (ARR), internal rate of return (IRR), and net present value (NPR) all use different calculations for value.

As another example, return on investment (ROI) is narrow in scope and can be applied to specific applications.

If an application might be a gateway to additional future applications, a technique called "real options valuation" (ROV) can be used to include future developments as well as the current application.

Without continuing through a list of available valuation methods, it is perhaps more useful to consider the specific topics that need to be included for determining software values. There are different topics to consider for software that is going to be developed than for commercial software that is going to be acquired. However, this book is concerned primarily with software development rather than software acquisition from commercial vendors.

In general the potential future value of a software application needs to be balanced against the potential risks of failure, poor quality, or other expensive problems. Most companies have internal rules of thumb that require between $3.00 and $5.00 in positive value for every $1.00 expended, with about a five-year return period. Venture capitalists, on the other hand, may ask for a $10.00 return in positive value for every $1.00 invested with perhaps a three-year return period.

Table 7.1 shows the major risk and value topics that are part of software value and risk analysis calculations, whichever specific financial or accounting method is used.

Table 7.1 *Risk and Value Factors for Major Software Development Projects*

	Application Risk Factors
1	The odds that the software application might be terminated and not completed
2	The odds that the software application will be successfully completed on time
3	The odds that the software application will be successfully completed within budget
4	The odds that the application will operate effectively if it is completed
5	The odds that the application will operate with adequate transaction rates
6	The odds of cost overruns from time and material contracts
7	The odds of cost overruns from fixed-price contracts with out-of-scope adjustment
8	The odds that the application might violate Sarbanes-Oxley regulations
9	The odds that the application might violate international standards
10	The odds that the application might violate Federal safety regulations
11	The odds that the application might violate international safety regulations
12	The odds of security attacks against the application
13	The odds of attempted data theft from the application
14	The odds of contract award litigation from rejected contractors
15	The odds of litigation occurring with contractors or subcontractors
16	The odds of litigation occurring with disgruntled clients
17	The odds of litigation occurring about patent violations or intellectual property
18	The odds of hardware platform changes that will require rework
19	The odds of changes in related software that will require rework
20	The odds of uncoordinated changes by supply chain applications
21	The number of competitive applications in the same space
22	The odds of competitive applications reducing the value of the planned application
23	The odds of "fast followers" bringing out similar applications
24	The odds of equity dilution from multiple rounds of venture funding
25	The odds of major disagreements among stakeholders
	Benchmark Factors
1	The probable size of the initial release in function points
2	The probable size of the initial release in terms of logical code statements

(Continued)

Table 7.1   *(Continued)*

	Benchmark Factors
3	The probable monthly growth rate of unplanned new requirements
4	The probable percentage of certified reusable components
5	The probable percentage of uncertified reusable components
6	The international standards that are known to affect the application
7	The government regulations and mandates that are known to affect the application
8	The quantitative results from similar internal application benchmarks
9	The quantitative results from similar external application benchmarks
10	The quantitative results from formal automated estimation tools and methods
11	The market successes and market shares of competitive applications
12	The percentage of similar applications that were cancelled due to overruns
13	The percentage of similar applications that were ineffective after deployment
14	The percentage of similar applications on time, within budget, and effective
15	The success-to-failure ratio from similar applications
	Application Cost Factors
1	The purchase or lease costs of special hardware to support the application
2	The annual lease costs of COTS packages to be acquired or included
3	The anticipated costs and schedule for COTS modifications or customization
4	The costs of acquiring patent and intellectual property licenses for the application
5	The costs of filing patent applications for intellectual property in the application
6	The costs of extracting algorithms and business rules from legacy applications
7	The costs of external consulting studies prior to development
8	The costs of external consulting studies during development
9	The costs of external consulting studies after deployment
10	The costs of nationalization and translation for global markets
11	The costs of travel for coordinating offshore and domestic subcontract work
12	The initial investment in constructing the first release of a software application
13	The anticipated schedule from start until deployment of the first release
14	The anticipated cost and schedule for installation, tuning, and training
15	The cost of capital for constructing the first release of a software application
16	The life expectancy of the software application after initial release
17	The frequency of future release intervals after the initial release
18	The costs of migrating data to the new application from legacy applications
19	The costs of acquiring and maintaining data to be stored in the application
20	The costs of poor data quality over the life of the application

	Application Cost Factors
21	The inflation rate over the life expectancy of the software application
22	The anticipated currency exchange rates for international applications
23	The costs of enhancing the application over its expected life cycle
24	The cost of fixing defects in the application prior to release
25	The cost of fixing defects in the application over its expected life cycle
26	The cost of customer support per year and in total for the application
27	The total cost of ownership (TCO) of the application over its expected life cycle
28	The monthly and annual costs for application funding
29	The monthly and annual tangible value if the application is funded
30	The probable number of venture funding rounds to achieve the initial release
31	The probable amount of equity dilution for acquiring venture capital
	Tangible Cost Reduction Factors
1	The tangible value of the application in terms of operational cost reduction
2	The tangible value of the application in terms of operational speed increase
3	The tangible value of the application in terms of transaction volume increase
4	The tangiblue value of the application in terms of supporting more clients
5	The tangible value of the application in terms of reduced human error
6	The tangible value of the application as a gateway to future applications
7	The tangible value of the application as a supply-chain link
	Tangible Revenue Generation Factors
1	The tangible value of the application in terms of direct revenue
2	The tangible value of the application in terms of indirect revenue
3	The tangible value of patents and intellectual property in the application
4	The tangible value of the application in terms of bringing in new customers
5	The tangible value of the application in terms of additional sales to current customers
6	The tangible value of the application in terms of reduced warranty costs
7	The tangible value of the application in getting external grants or funds
8	The tangible value of the application in getting government grants or funds
9	The probable number of users or clients in first year of usage
10	The probable revenue per client and total revenue for first year of usage
11	The distribution of new licenses versus maintenance for five years
	Intangible Value Factors
1	The value of the application as a gateway to future applications
2	The value of the application as a competitive advantage

(Continued)

Table 7.1   *(Continued)*

Intangible Value Factors
3   The value of the application to overall systems architecture
4   The value of the application to enterprise prestige
5   The value of the application to employee morale
6   The value of the application to human life or safety
7   The value of the application to national defense

Tangible Negative Factors or Potential Losses
1   The negative tangible cost if the application is cancelled and not completed
2   The negative value to stocks and equities from a major project failure
3   The negative tangible cost for significant schedule delays
4   The negative tangible cost for significant cost overruns
5   The negative tangible costs of business interruptions during installation
6   The negative tangible costs of performance losses due to learning curves
7   The negative tangible costs of poor quality causing business interruptions
8   The negative tangible costs of security attacks to the application
9   The negative tangible costs of inadequate performance or transaction rates
10   The negative tangible costs of correcting erroneous transactions
11   The negative tangible costs of any litigation that might occur
12   The negative tangible costs of exhausting venture funding prior to completion

Intangible Negative Factors
1   The damages to enterprise prestige from outright failure
2   The damages to enterprise prestige from major delays and overruns
3   The damages to enterprise prestige from poor quality and recalls
4   The damages from negative press coverage
5   The damages from reduced competitive position
6   The damages to board of director confidence in senior management
7   The damages to executive futures from lack of confidence at the board level
8   The damages to employee morale from cancelled projects
9   The increased odds of switching from in-house to outsource development
10   The loss of executive and employee time if litigation should occur due to failure

Financial Analysis Methods Used and Quantitative Results
1   Total Cost of Ownership (TCO)
2   Cost of Quality (COQ)
3   Return on Investment (ROI)

Financial Analysis Methods Used and Quantitative Results
4   Internal Rate of Return (IRR)
5   Accounting Rate of Return (ARR)
6   Economic Value Added (EVA)
7   Real Options Valuation (ROV)
8   Return on Assets (ROA)
9   Return on Infrastructure Employed (ROIE)
10   Earned-value analysis (EVA)
11   Other:

Combined Risk and Value Results
1   Excellent project that should be funded and given high priority
2   Good project that should be funded
3   Acceptable project that should be added to funding queue
4   Acceptable project that should be revised prior to funding
5   Risky project that needs major revised planning prior to funding approval
6   Hazardous project that should not be funded

Although Table 7.1 is large, commercial software cost and quality estimation tools can provide fairly good answers for most of the cost questions. By using such tools early during risk and value studies, only unpredictable cost questions need to be dealt with. An example of an unpredictable cost question is that of the cost of COTS licenses, if needed for the application. Even here it is theoretically possible for a software estimation tool to contain COTS licensing data, although none actually contain such data today.

Not every question in Table 7.1 is relevant to every software project. However, the sum total of questions should probably be at least thought about prior to committing major funds for major software projects. Unfortunately, part of the length and complexity of Table 7.1 is due to the fact that a single table combines information relevant to internal civilian projects, government projects, commercial software, and venture capital-backed start-up projects.

The questions in Table 7.1 were not originally designed for publication in a book, but rather to be used as part of a software project evaluation tool. In the automated tool, the questions are divided into subsets based on application size, type, and other differentiating factors. Also the tool includes estimating capabilities that can provide answers to many of the cost questions, which allows users to focus on value. Some cost questions, such as fees for patent licenses, are unpredictable because they are based on private negotiations between patent holders and patent users.

Using Table 7.1 as a guide, a proposed software application with a high probability of successful completion combined with a low risk of failure and quality problems would pass the first decision point to funding. Having tangible life-cycle value exceed tangible life-cycle costs by more than 5 to 1 would be a second decision point for funding. Having minimal business interruptions during installation and a short learning curve would be a third decision point. Such applications would probably meet corporate funding criteria and should receive funding if so.

A proposed software application with a low probability of successful completion, severe odds of schedule and cost overruns, and potential quality problems or litigation, however, should raise serious questions during funding discussions. If this same proposed application were only going to return about 2 to 1 in terms of financial value, that is too low a margin for safety.

If the application is complex enough to require a long installation period and a slow learning curve, that also counts against funding. Such applications would probably not meet corporate funding criteria, although a surprisingly large number are funded anyway.

At the very least, the application should be rethought and replanned if there are cogent reasons for wanting to resubmit the project for funding after an initial rejection.

Even in its complexity, Table 7.1 provides a checklist of topics that need to be considered carefully in order to make rational funding decisions for large applications. Software applications that top $1,000,000 in potential development costs should always have formal risk and value studies.

Many applications that cost $1,000,000 or more are required to pass a series of phase reviews, which theoretically must be successfully passed to get funding for the next phase. However, from participating in many such phase reviews, they are often ineffective in stopping questionable projects. A key reason for this is that project management tends to downplay risks and exaggerate benefits. Unless higher management sees through this charade, many hazardous applications slip through several phase reviews and are not detected until it is too late for a successful recovery.

For massive software projects that might top $100,000,000 in development costs, failure to perform a formal risk and value analysis prior to funding can lead to potential legal liabilities for executives if the application is terminated without being completed, or if the clients sue, such as for breach of contract, fraud, or negligence. At the very least, termination for cause might occur for executives who funded a large project without performing effective due diligence.

Funding Approval and Application Size

The level in an enterprise that actually approves software project funding will vary with the size of the project, the size of the enterprise, whether the enterprise is a corporation or a government unit, a nonprofit organization, or an open source group, and several other factors.

Because costs and risks go up with size, the probable approval level for funding would often resemble the following pattern:

- **10 function points:** Small projects of this size are usually enhancements to existing applications, although some smart phone applets are this small. Development costs are between $5,000 and $10,000, so funding approval is normally made by operating unit management. Risks are low, failures rare, and success is the norm.

- **100 function points:** This is the size of significant enhancements to existing applications and a common size for smart phone applications. Development costs are usually above $75,000, which is enough to require approval by divisional executives. Risks are still low and successes common in this size range.

- **1,000 function points:** This is the size of many stand-alone commercial software applications and also of major enhancements to large systems. Development costs can top $1,000,000 (although many are below that), so approval normally requires an operational VP plus at least as review by a CIO, CTO, or CFO. This size is also one where venture capital may be used for start-up companies that plan to produce new software applications.

  Due diligence studies by a venture capitalist would no doubt consider most of the factors shown in Table 7.1. The VC community tends to favor projects that might give a large return on investment in a short time period of perhaps three years. This is a partial explanation for why so many venture-funded start-up companies fail. The normal problems and delays associated with software development cause the companies to run out of funds before revenue is substantial.

- **10,000 function points:** This is the size where failures and cancellations can exceed 30% of the projects that are started. Delays and cost overruns are rampant. It is interesting that every breach-of-contract lawsuit except one in which one of the authors has been an expert witness involved applications of 10,000 function points or larger. Because development costs can approach $25,000,000 and total cost of ownership can top $50,000,000, approval for such systems normally involves both divisional and corporate executives, including the CEO, CIO, CTO, and CFO. A majority of the questions in Table 7.1 should be considered.

- **100,000 function points:** In this size range failures outnumber successes. Of the surviving projects, the great majority will exceed planned budgets and are more than a year late when delivered. Software applications of this size present probably the greatest business risks of any commercial product.

  Development costs for this size can top $250,000,000, and TCO for the projects that actually make it through development can top $1,000,000,000. These projects are too big to replace easily, so once they are deployed expect them to last for 20 years or more.

For corporations, funding approval for such large projects involves all of the top executives, including the CEO and sometimes the board of directors as well. For government projects at the state level, the CIO, the assembly, and the governor's staff will be involved.

For federal projects, a cabinet secretary at the level of the secretary of defense or the secretary of the treasury will be involved. Even the president will be informed and might have a say, and Congress can get involved at least to lobby for having some of the development money spent in their districts. No matter who gives approval, these projects are extremely risky and hazardous. There are hundreds of paths that lead to failure for big systems and only a few paths that lead to success.

Incidentally, the largest known software projects as of 2011 are in the range of 300,000 function points. Such large projects include military and defense applications and some large civilian projects such as enterprise resource planning (ERP) applications.

As this discussion shows, the value of software quality is a major component of the value of the software itself. However, the value of software also includes innovation, useful features, and many other topics in addition to quality.

Because large projects with poor quality fail in alarming numbers, the economic value of quality is directly proportional to applications size. The larger the project, the more valuable quality becomes.

The Impact of Software Construction Difficulties on Software Quality

Software has exploded into the modern world as one of the most significant technological advances in all history in terms of the impact software has on business, government, military operations, social interactions, and medicine.

Yet in spite of the enormous value of software applications, they remain difficult to construct and often contain alarming numbers of defects when software is deployed. It is necessary to consider why this is so.

First, in part due to the comparatively young age of the software industry, development of software applications is largely a manual activity. As discussed in the past few pages, the original impetus for building computers and software was to speed up manual activities. But to a surprising degree, software has not been recursively applied to software itself.

Even in 2011 most software applications are custom-designed and custom-coded on a line-by-line basis. It is true that objects and other forms of reusable materials are available, but even so custom code remains the dominant construction method for software applications.

Another problem with software construction is that of intellectual difficulty and complexity. Software is complex at many levels, including requirements, architecture, design, and above all, code.

For large applications with thousands of instructions and hundreds of paths, no human mind can keep track of all the possible combinations of events that will occur when the software executes. As a result, error-free coding is almost impossible, testing is difficult, and 100% test coverage of all executable instructions is close to being impossible for applications larger than about 1,000 logical code statements or roughly 20 function points. As it happens, code coverage of 100% is less difficult than testing 100% of requirements or 100% of potential risks. In fact the term "coverage" is ambiguous and needs to consider code, risks, requirements, architecture, and design attributes.

The high error content in all software deliverables is why a combination of defect prevention, pretest defect removal, and testing stages are needed to achieve acceptable quality levels after deployment.

A number of methods such as object-oriented class libraries for code, design patterns, and development of a taxonomy of common software application functions have the potential to change the situation but to date have not fully succeeded. Also reuse of test plans and test cases is part of the overall spectrum of reuse and tends to lag most other forms of reusability.

What might occur in the future if technology trends continue is the inclusion of standard libraries not only of code objects, but also of standard reusable requirements, standard architectural structures, standard data structures, and standard reusable design elements.

The central idea is to replace labor-intensive and error-prone custom designs and custom code with certified reusable materials that approach or achieve zero-defect levels.

To accomplish this goal, some of the precursor steps include the development of an effective taxonomy of software application types that is organized by industry. A low-level taxonomy of specific application features is also needed.

For example, all software applications have some kind of input validation routines.

The reason for needing these taxonomies is to identify the specific kinds of software features used within an industry such as banking, insurance, or general manufacturing. As it happens, most companies within an industry use software that performs the same general functions.

Consider the software industry itself. All companies that produce software use compilers, test tools, static analysis tools, software defect tracking tools, debugging tools, and a number of other generic tools aimed at software design, development, and management.

The fact that multiple companies within an industry use software that has similar features is why large-scale reuse could be economically valuable. In fact, this situation is why today vendors can market packaged applications within specific industries. True, the applications may need customization, but that is still much more cost-effective than complete custom development.

The enterprise resource planning (ERP) packages have taken this idea to a higher level by including dozens of application types within a single massive application that can be tailored to match the needs of multiple operating units within many industries. Although customizing ERP packages within specific companies is far from trivial, it is still much less expensive than custom development.

Let us leave software for a moment and consider automobiles. If the automotive industry were at the same level of technology as the software industry, when a reader of this book wanted a new car, it would not be possible to visit a dealer and buy one. Instead, a team of automotive designers and mechanics would be assembled, and the reader's requirements would be recorded and analyzed. Then the car would be custom-designed to match the user's needs.

After the design was finished, construction would commence. However, instead of assembling the automobile from standard components, many of the parts would have to be hand-turned on metal lathes and other machine tools. Thus instead of buying an automobile within a day or two, the customer would have to wait a period of months for construction.

Instead of spending perhaps $30,000 for a new automobile, custom design and custom construction would make the car about as expensive as a Formula 1 race car, or in the range of $750,000.

Although no doubt the automobile would have been tested prior to delivery, it probably would contain more than 100 defects, with 20 of them serious, that would need to be removed prior to safe long-distance driving by the owner.

If the automobile were built under the same legal conditions as software end-user license agreements, there would be no warranty, expressed or implied. Also ownership of the automobile would not be transferred but would remain with the company that built the automobile. There would also be restrictions on the number of other drivers who could operate the automobile, and if there were more than three drivers, additional costs would be charged.

Worse, if something breaks or goes seriously wrong after the car is delivered, there would probably not be neighborhood mechanics who could fix it. Due to the custom handmade parts, a repair center with a great deal of machinery would be needed. Something as basic as replacing the brakes might cost more than $5,000 instead of $300.

It might be asserted that forcing everyone to use standard features would reduce originality. This might be true, but in fact this has turned out to be more valuable than harmful. Every personal computer user acquires essential packages such as virus protection, spyware protection, office suites, photo-editing suites, and dozens more. These packages range in cost from open source applications up to perhaps $500 for a PC accounting package or the professional version of an office suite. The basic idea is to expand the concept of large-scale reuse of standard features to a wider and wider range of applications.

So the economic value of software centers basically on four major themes:

1. Reducing the harmful consequences that defects have on software development and maintenance—in other words, comparing the costs, staffing, and schedules of building and maintaining high-quality software versus low-quality software.

2. Evaluating the different results of high-quality software and low-quality software on the revenue and market shares of organizations that build software under contract or market software as commercial products.

3. Evaluating the different results of high-quality software and low-quality software on innovative new kinds of products and services that cannot be performed with software.

4. Evaluating the different results of high quality and low quality on day-to-day use of software by its intended customers. In other words, does high-quality software improve the performance of physicians, airline reservation clerks, insurance claims representatives, or millions of other occupations that use software every day as part of their jobs? How common and expensive are the business damages from low-quality software?

It has long been obvious to those who work in the software field that large software projects are troublesome and prone to fail. Dozens of methods and hundreds of tools have been developed. Some are aimed at increasing development speed, others at improving development quality, and some at both topics simultaneously.

In general, the methods and tools that aim at improving quality have demonstrated more long-range success than those aiming at speed. The methods dealing with both quality and speed concurrently also have staying power.

Table 7.2 lists a short collection of well-known software development methods, tool categories, and practices. Based on the authors' discussions with practitioners, the list attempts to show whether the primary focus of the method is improving development speed, improving quality, or improving both at the same time.

The placement of specific methods is subjective and not definitive. The idea of Table 7.2 is that many methods have been created due to the endemic problems of software development.

Table 7.2   *Primary Focus of Selected Development Methods*

Both Quality and Speed are joint focus
Agile unified process
Certified reusable libraries
Essential unified process
Extreme Programming (XP)
Flow-based programming
Object-oriented development
Iterative development
Microsoft solutions framework (MSF)
Pattern-based development
Spiral development
Lean software development
Quality is primary focus
Automated static analysis
Automated testing
Clean room development
CMMI
Inspections
Joint Application Design (JAD)
Personal Software Process (PSP)
Pair programming
Quality Function Deployment (QFD)

Quality is primary focus
Rational Unified Process (RUP)
Six Sigma
Structured development
Team Software Process (TSP)
Unified modeling language (UML)
Use cases
V model development
Speed is primary focus
Agile
CASE
Crystal Development
Enterprise Resource Planning (ERP)
I-Case
Rapid Application Development (RAD)
SCRUM

From the large number of entries in Table 7.2, it is apparent that none of these methods have become dominant or universal, in the sense that they consistently demonstrate better results than all or some of the other methods.

Another reason for such a long list, not shown in Table 7.2 itself, is the fact that various sizes and types of software tend to need different solutions. None of the methods are "one-size-fits-all" techniques that are equally effective for applications that range from 10 function points and 100,000 function points.

In general, the "speed-based" methods tend to work well for small applications below 1,000 function points. The "quality-based" methods tend to work well for large systems above 10,000 function points. The methods for both together have been used for a broad range of sizes and types. Given that high quality leads to high speed, in the long run the quality-based methods tend to be the most valuable.

Because the term value in this book considers software revenue generation and cost reduction as well as development and maintenance costs, at this point it is interesting to consider all of the various ways that software applications generate revenue (cost reductions are also discussed).

Revenue Generation from Software

Software generates revenue from 12 primary channels, as the following sections discuss.

Direct Revenue from New Clients

Innovation opens up new markets, brings in new clients, and may create entirely new kinds of businesses. Software has been a stellar performer in innovation and developing new kinds of products. Look at the market created by the first spreadsheet. Some of the newer products such as the iPad and Amazon Kindle are hardware devices with embedded software; others such as the software operating eBay, Craigslist, the Google search engine, and Twitter are pure software applications. At a larger scale, the computer gaming industry has become a multicompany, multibillion dollar industry that has profoundly changed the concept of "home entertainment." Few if any industries have created so many innovations in such a short time span as the software industry.

Innovation has been the primary source of wealth creation for the software industry and has led to the creation of dozens of large software companies, including a number of multibillion dollar companies such as Apple, Microsoft, Facebook, Google, Oracle, and the like. As all readers know, software innovation has also created a number of the wealthiest individuals of any industry.

Direct Revenue from Existing Clients

Software that is leased or sold as a product generates direct revenue from the clients that acquire it. Repeat business and recurring revenues are an integral part of revenue generation from existing clients. This is why all software applications add new features at least on an annual basis and charge for updates. The costs of marketed software applications range from less than one dollar for smart phone applications to more than one million dollars for large mainframe applications. Post-release maintenance is another form of direct revenue. In any case recurring revenue from software is a critical factor for corporate profitability and survival.

Contract Revenue

In today's world about half of the software used internally by major corporations is not produced by the employees of the corporation, but rather by contractors or outsource vendors. Contract software has been in existence since the 1950s and is probably the oldest form of direct revenue generation from pure software, considering software was included originally in the cost of computers. Software contractors develop applications for specific clients and not for marketing to the general public. Of course, some contractors may also sell commercial applications, such as Computer Associates (CA) and Computer Aid Inc. (CAI).

Indirect Revenue

This is revenue that accrues from software clients that purchase related goods or services. For example, training, consulting, and fee-based customer support are examples of indirect revenue. The revenue is related to specific software applications but marketed separately. There are sometimes multiple vendors supporting the same primary software application, such as providing instructions on how to use Excel, Word, or other common applications.

Hardware Revenue

For embedded software inside physical devices, the software per se is not sold but rather the devices themselves. Examples of hardware revenue include cell phones, medical devices, robotic manufacturing tools, GPS systems, digital cameras, and smart appliances.

Hardware Drag-Along Revenue

When software is acquired, there may also be markets for peripheral devices that make using the software easier and more convenient. Examples of hardware drag-along revenue includes computer mice, USB storage devices, larger and faster disk drives, sophisticated or specialized gaming keyboards, external web cameras, and hundreds of other products.

Software Drag-Along Revenue

For many kinds of software there are additional useful features that are not included in the software packages themselves. As a result, clients who acquire these packages usually acquire other kinds of software with value-added features. A primary example for many years has been that of anti-virus packages that are marketed to protect operating systems and other software applications from virus attacks.

Some of these separate applications were at one time part of larger applications but were forced to be marketed separately due to antitrust litigation. This is one of the reasons why web browsers are now separate from operating systems. Almost every personal computer owner acquires specialized software packages for topics such as enhanced security, editing photographs, communication, games, music, and many other topics.

Patents and Intellectual Property

Although the future of software patents is uncertain as this book is written, there are thousands of existing software patents already filed. For some kinds of valuable software features, patents themselves generate revenue via licensing. Patents also generate revenues via litigation for patent violations.

Teaching Software Skills

Although many software professionals learn their skills in colleges and universities, there is a substantial sub-industry of companies that teach various software topics. Among the more common subjects taught commercially are those of Agile development, function point analysis, Six Sigma for software, using automated test tools, using static analysis tools, cost estimating, software testing, and software quality assurance. Computer game design is also a popular topic, as is building applets for smart phones. Nonprofit associations also teach courses about various software topics.

Books and Journals about Software

Software is a major genre for book publishers and also has a number of print journals. More recently hundreds of blogs about software topics have appeared on the Web. Software topics are also widely published in ebook format.

Software Personnel Agencies

The large number of software personnel employed brings with it many sub-industries. One of these consists of personnel agencies that specialize in software engineering jobs and ancillary positions such as testing and quality assurance.

Illegal Revenue Generation

The topic of illegal revenue generation is outside the primary scope of this book but seems to be growing rapidly and generating billions of dollars on a global basis. Perhaps the most striking form of illegal revenue is piracy, or selling illegal copies of software applications.

Another growing form of illegal revenue generation is "phishing," or sending bogus email that purports to be about lottery winnings or transferring funds from other countries. In fact, they are seeking private information such as bank accounts. Phishing is older than the software industry, but the ease of using email has increased the frequency more than a thousand fold.

Among the other fast-growing forms of illegal revenue generation are those of theft of vital records from computerized storage, using software to conceal embezzlement, and using software to support or conceal Ponzi schemes. One alarming trend associated with theft of vital records is attempts by the thieves to sell the data back to the companies from which the records were stolen.

Other forms of possibly illegal revenue generation center on patent violations and theft of intellectual property. This topic is not clear-cut because sometimes patents are voided by courts or deemed to have been improperly granted. As this book is written, there are dozens of patent lawsuits in progress, some of which may have significant implications based on how they are decided.

Difference Between Software and Other Industries

There are a few areas where software revenue channels differ in significant ways from the revenue channels of other kinds of products and services. Perhaps the most striking difference is the fact that there is almost no commercial market for used software applications other than computer games.

The market for used automobiles actually has more retail outlets than those selling new cars. For many products such as furniture and appliances, channels such as local stores, websites such as craigslist.com, and swap meets provide ready markets for thousands of secondhand products. There is a market for second-hand computer games, but, in general, software resale items are much less common than for many other commodities.

End User License Agreements (EULA) by vendors do not actually transfer ownership of software to customers. As a result, when customers stop using older versions of software, there is no viable method for transferring them to other companies. Some used software is sold, but the volume of secondhand software is rather sparse compared to many other kinds of products. Of course, every day, people give personal computers as gifts to friends and relatives, and quite a bit of software is preloaded on these computers.

The emerging and expanding open source software market is also unique. There are very few products of any kind that are offered for free or for a voluntary donation.

Another interesting difference between software and other products is distribution. For many years software was distributed via tapes or disks, but today in 2011 directly downloading from vendors is the dominant method or at least approaching a parity for delivery on a physical disk. As a result, software distribution costs are fairly inexpensive compared to physical products that require shipping and warehousing prior to sale. Of course, disks are still marketed for those who want them for back-up and recovery purposes, but software distribution from the Web is more cost-effective.

The 11 legal revenue channels have triggered the creation of enormously profitable companies such as Microsoft, Google, Computer Associates (CA), and Oracle. They have also triggered the growth of the modern software industry, which now has thousands of companies and millions of employees.

Software has even more millions of clients, customers, and users. It is fair to say that computers and software have had an impact on our daily lives that is at least as profound as the invention of printing, the invention of the automobile, and the invention of the airplane.

In today's world a majority of complex machines are controlled by software. The bulk of all vital and financial records is stored in computers and accessed via software. Our military services are dependent upon software not only for large-scale purposes such as radar and intelligence gathering, but for operating many kinds of weapons systems. Indeed, some modern fighter aircraft cannot be flown without computers and software because human pilots cannot react quickly enough. Even our social lives have been transformed via social networks such as Facebook and Twitter.

In a period of roughly 60 years from 1950 to 2011, computers and software have formed one of the largest industries in history and transformed many business and government activities from manual to automated operations. They have also transformed the way we gather information and the way we communicate with friends and colleagues.

However, the fact that software is largely custom-designed and hand-coded means that software applications are routinely delivered with hundreds and sometimes thousands of latent defects. These defects lower the profits of software vendors and their customers and degrade the operational performance of software applications. Some defects are serious enough to cause catastrophic harm.

Unfortunately, the growth of the software industry has also triggered a corollary growth in illegal activities. In fact, perhaps 15% of the readers of this book will experience identity theft over the next few years.

As a prelude to the discussion of the economic value of software quality, a majority of readers have probably already experienced problems caused by software errors, such as billing errors, real estate assessment errors, tax errors, and the like. A common problem associated with the recession is the loss or misplacement of paper mortgage records because mortgages are transferred electronically and the original paper documents may not reach the owner. There are also numerous problems with mechanical devices such as automobiles that are really caused by software errors in fuel injection systems, braking systems, or other systems now controlled by embedded computers.

Cost Reduction from Software

It is an interesting historical fact that the primary motive for developing both mechanical calculating devices and also early electro-mechanical computers before software was to save time and speed up difficult and complex manual operations. Charles Babbage himself was motivated to design his difference engine and his analytical engine by the tiresome work of astronomical calculations.

Herman Hollerith, another pioneer in computing design, was approached by the Census Bureau because of the enormous labor required to tabulate census records manually. Saving human labor was a major incentive for the development of both computers and software applications.

Computers and software reduce costs via ten methods, as the following sections discuss.

Faster Results and Lower Costs for High-Frequency Recurring Calculations

Every day, millions of customers book airline flights, hotel rooms, and rental cars. Millions more deposit or withdraw funds in banks, buy or sell stocks, purchase insurance, make insurance claims, or return merchandise to stores. All of these transactions require records, and many of these records, such as bank records, have legal requirements for storage durations, accuracy, audit trails, and privacy.

In the days before computers and software, thousands of clerks spent their entire careers creating and maintaining paper documents about business and financial transactions. Computers and software have radically changed record keeping, and for the most part made it faster and easier. (Although correcting errors in computerized records actually seems more troublesome than older manual methods.) Scientific analysis and performing mathematical calculations associated with astronomy, physics, chemistry, and other disciplines are also quicker using computers.

Fewer Errors in High-Frequency Recurring Calculations

Human performance that involves complex arithmetic or combining a number of complicated rules is naturally error-prone. One of the advantages of using computers and software for such work is the fact that in spite of computer and software bugs, automated calculations tend to have many fewer errors than manual calculations. Also for situations where many different people might have slightly different interpretations of rules, computerized transactions lower the variations in expected results.

Reduction in Manual Effort and Costs for Operating Complex Equipment

Some modern manufacturing operations have substantially replaced human operators with robots or computer-controlled manufacturing devices. Although the initial costs are often high for computer-controlled equipment, the recurring costs are greatly reduced. Some fairly large factories that turn out hundreds of products per day now only have staffs of only about a dozen people, when a few years ago producing the same number of the same products might have required several hundred assembly line workers.

Reduction in Errors While Operating Complex Equipment

Whenever humans are involved in operating complex machines, fatigue or inattention can cause errors and sometimes cause injuries as well. Modern manufacturing equipment, medical devices, and some forms of transportation such as commercial aircraft now use computers and software to assist human operators and hopefully lower errors. Of course, there are errors caused by computers and software, but in general human beings tend to make more errors than software for complex activities and complicated devices.

Faster Collection and Analysis of Data on Business Issues

Prior to the advent of computers and web browsers such as Internet Explorer, Google, Chrome, and a number of others, collecting information for business decisions required weeks or months and required many phone calls and perhaps some actual visits to libraries or consulting companies. In today's world information on almost any topic is available quickly. In fact, an issue with computer and software data collection is the fact that too much data is available rather than too little. Whether or not high-speed data collection has led to more business successes or reduced bankruptcies is uncertain.

From many discussions and interviews with CIOs, CTOs, CFOs, and other executives in software groups, the availability of vast amounts of data and information from web sources does not yet seem to be an integral part of how business decisions are planned and made. Instead, gut feels, using data from colleagues and competitors, and personal experience of the executives themselves still seem to be the main sources of information. Even major business decisions such as funding projects that are very likely to fail because they are too large and complicated are based on partial data, even though much more information is available.

Faster Collection and Analysis of Data on Scientific Issues

Science has benefitted from computers and software as well as business. Many kinds of scientific data can now be gathered easily in a few hours, many fewer than 25 years ago, that data gathering might have required weeks or months of effort by librarians and research assistants.

Faster Collection and Analysis of Data on Legal Issues

One of the earliest and most successful computerized collections of data was that of information for legal purposes. The famous Lexis/Nexis legal search methods were first developed in 1966, although under a different name, and pioneered full-text retrieval in 1973. The Lexis portion contains U.S. legal records from the 1700s through today; the Nexis portion contains from about 20,000 sources of legal and business information. Other companies also do legal research, but Reed Elsevier publishing has acquired some of these in addition to Lexis/Nexis. The essential point is that law produces and consumes vast quantities of printed information. Computerized searching and analysis of legal documents are natural targets of computers and software.

Faster Training and Learning of Some but Not All Skills

Until fairly recently in the twentieth century, education was primarily a teacher-to-student relationship. Technologies such as voice recordings, television, animated films, tapes, CDs, and DVDs began to augment live instruction.

More recently, online webinars and podcasts have been added to the sources of educational channels. Soon virtual reality learning environments may begin to enter the mainstream. Ebooks have also been added to the sources of educational information.

As can be determined from interviews with students, live instruction is still the preferred channel. However, there is no question that computerized learning is a great deal cheaper than live instruction. It is possible that hybrid methods that utilize webinar tools combined with conference calls using tools such as Skype may add enough human contact to raise the effectiveness of automated methods.

Faster Communication Between Businesses

In recent years the phrase "business to business," or B2B, has become popular in the software press to describe new methods of connecting clients and vendors. The B2B concept has become fairly common in supply chains in which a number of companies produce parts or components that must be delivered to other companies for assembly. There are related concepts for "business to government" (B2G) and "business to client" (B2C). However, B2B connections are the most common because they are usually created among companies that do business together fairly often.

Faster Communication Between Businesses and Clients

Part of this chapter is written during December of 2010. The Monday before this segment was drafted was heavily advertized locally as being "Cyber Monday." The meaning of the phrase was that local vendors with websites were offering discounts and sale prices for products ordered via the Web or Internet. Web purchases are now a standard part of doing business and will continue to grow in volume.

Fairly recently, between about 1995 and 2000, the idea of selling products over the Web exploded in popularity. Hundreds of new companies were formed, and many were funded by venture capitalists. These were called *dot-com companies* because of the standard Internet address protocol.

However, it turned out that many products are not easily salable via the Web, and especially so if ordering is complex and customer support is spotty. For a variety of reasons, the explosion of dot-com startup companies was followed by the dot-com crash, which started in March of 2000.

Between 2000 and about 2002 the dot-com crash saw the failure of hundreds of ecommerce companies and a loss of several trillion dollars of equity. However, ecommerce was not wiped out, and many of the stronger companies such as Amazon and eBay have done well since. The survivors also tried to improve websites, security, and raise customer satisfaction.

There is one feature of B2C communication that no one likes. That feature is the use of automated telephone voice responses instead of live personnel. Such applications are no doubt cost-effective for the companies, but they tend to waste significant time on the part of clients. Also they cannot be used by the deaf and are hard to use by those with significant hearing losses.

Another feature is so unpopular that several states are preparing legislation to curb it. This is the use of "robo calls" that dial both land lines and cell phones with recorded messages either about politics or products.

Faster Communication Between Government Agencies

One of the troubling discoveries in the wake of the 9/11 terrorist attacks was the discovery that quite a bit of information had been put forth by individual security agencies that might have prevented the attacks, but the information was not shared between the security agencies. As a result, at least the security portions of the U.S. government moved to speed up and broaden communication channels. However, as seen in the recent flap in December of 2010 over the leaks of classified information on the Wikileaks website, as many as 600,000 people had access to confidential data. It is clear that a better balance is needed between communication and confidentiality.

On the whole, government communication at both the federal and state levels is not as rapid or effective as might be wished. There are also gaps in communication that are troubling. For example, as this book is being written, the state of Rhode Island spent more than $65,000,000 on a new school for the deaf. Yet reimbursements for cochlear implants in Rhode Island are among the lowest in the country.

Increasing the availability of cochlear implants for young children would have substantially reduced the student population for the school for the deaf, and therefore a much smaller facility would have been needed. The money spent on the Rhode Island school for the deaf would have paid for about 1,300 cochlear implants for deaf children. Because of the low insurance reimbursements, only one or two cochlear implants per year for children are performed in Rhode Island. In other words, the state spent millions of dollars to build a structure that might not have been needed had the money been directed toward eliminating childhood deafness using cochlear implants.

Faster Communication Between People

Today in 2011 children start using smart phones and personal computers as early as age three. By the time they enter school, many are computer literate. By the time they enter high school, some are skilled enough to be hackers.

Computers and software are making major changes in human communications. Some children and high-school students spend more hours per day sending text messages than they do speaking. Millions of users now follow friends and celebrities using Twitter, and more millions use Facebook or other social networks as an expanded way of reaching out to friends and colleagues.

Email is so popular that the U.S. Post Office is operating at a loss. Less than 25 years ago, personal and business contacts were limited to face-to-face meetings augmented by phone calls, which were expensive enough that local calls were the norm. In today's world almost every email user gets at least 25 emails per day, and many are from other states or other countries. Computers with video cameras and services such as Skype make face-to-face calls inexpensive or even free across many international boundaries.

Scores of special interest groups have sprung up. Services such as Plaxo and LinkedIn that allow colleagues with similar interests to communicate are now so common that it is difficult to participate in all of the ones that might be relevant for people who work in the software industry.

Yet as profound as the changes have been, it is certain that even more changes will unfold within a few years. It should soon be possible to have virtual reality conferences where speakers are seen either in holographic form or at least in high definition.

People with medical disabilities have also benefitted from improved communication methods assisted by software. For example, automated translation from voice to text is now common; automatic creation of closed captions is common; and of course cochlear implants restore hearing to many profoundly deaf patients.

Other kinds of medical disabilities are also supported, such as computers that can be operated by puffs of breath or by other nonstandard means for those who are paralyzed or have no limbs. One of the most impressive examples of the kinds of assistance software can give is shown daily use by Representative James Langevin of the Second Congressional District of Rhode Island. Representative Langevin was injured and became a quadriplegic. He now uses an automated wheelchair produced using the same software and engineering as the Segway personal transportation device.

This wheelchair is powered by electricity and includes a gyroscope for stability. The chair can climb stairs and therefore makes entry possible into many buildings that lack wheelchair ramps.

As a rule of thumb, the combination of emails and social networks has probably doubled the daily contact among individuals compared to 25 years ago. Of course, that does not mean that the increased numbers of contacts add social or intellectual value to our daily lives, but every citizen who uses a cell phone and a computer has almost no limits on connecting to friends or colleagues anywhere in the world.

It is interesting that, as this book is being completed, Egypt has been having daily riots and civil unrest. One of the proofs that computerized communications are now major channels is the fact that the Egyptian government attempted to shut down both cell phones and most Internet connections shortly after the riots started. However, hackers and those with high levels of technical understanding were able to get around these shutdowns within a few days. While full Internet service is still not available in Egypt, many individuals are in contact by email with news services and colleagues in other countries by means of clever work-arounds.

Somewhat distressing is a fact broadcast on talk radio about the U.S. Embassy in Cairo. When U.S. citizens who were stuck in Egypt due to airport closures attempted to get help from the Embassy, they were referred to a website. Apparently the Embassy was slow to react to the Internet shutdown, considering the Embassy still had the website information on their telephone system for more than a week after Internet service was shut down. This situation caused so many U.S. citizens to try dialing the emergency phone number that it was almost always busy.

Economic Impact of Low-Quality and High-Quality Software

As discussed earlier in this chapter, software is one of the most valuable goods of the modern world. Software is also troublesome and expensive to build. Between the many problems of software construction and the business purposes of software, there are four primary areas where software quality has an impact:

1. The effort and costs of software construction and maintenance

2. The profitability of commercial software applications

3. The impact on human performance when using software

4. The role of software in novel and innovative new products

In examining the impact of quality on these four economic topics, it is useful to consider polar opposites, or the impact of very high quality compared to very low quality.

In many kinds of research, the most useful insights often come from studies of polar opposites. For example, it is instructive to compare highly profitable companies against those companies in the same industry that go bankrupt; it is instructive to compare people with high levels of natural immunity to certain diseases against those with low immunity; it is instructive to compare the best primary educational institutions against those that have the highest rates of failure and dropouts. Averages are of course useful too, but polar opposites tend to highlight key differences that lead to success or failure.

For software, that raises a question of how to identify polar opposites. Applications that have very bad quality levels often end up in litigation. (In fact, the same week this chapter was being written, a jury trial decision in Tennessee awarded $61,000,000 to a software client who sued a vendor about poor software quality.) One of the authors has been an expert witness in a number of such trials, and from observing the depositions and discovery documents, it is apparent that effective quality practices are not widely understood, even among major companies.

Applications that have very good quality are somewhat more difficult to identify. Among the methods used to identify high quality are interviews with users, reports by user forums or associations (many commercial packages have web forums or user associations), and technical reviews by software editors. Interviews with software quality assurance (SQA) personnel and professional test personnel who have worked on applications also provide useful information.

Quantitative methods such as comparing defect volumes, defect removal efficiency levels, and warranty costs are also useful in separating high-quality applications from low-quality applications.

While these methods of distinguishing high quality from low are somewhat subjective, they are probably about as effective as any others.

The following sections summarize the main distinctions between very high quality and very low quality on the key business topics associated with software.

Software Development and Maintenance

Low Quality

1. Low quality stretches out testing and makes delivery dates unpredictable.

2. Low quality makes repairs and rework the major software cost driver.

3. Low quality leads to overtime and/or major cost overruns.

4. Low quality after release leads to expensive customer support.

5. Low quality after release leads to expensive postrelease maintenance.

6. Low quality after release can lead to litigation for contract projects.

High Quality

1. High quality shortens testing schedules and improves delivery schedules.

2. High quality reduces repairs and rework by more than 50%.

3. High quality reduces unplanned overtime and reduces cost overruns.

4. High quality after release leads to inexpensive customer support.

5. High quality after release leads to lower maintenance and support costs.

6. High quality lowers the odds of litigation for contract projects.

Software as a Marketed Commodity

Low Quality

1. Low quality necessitates repairs and recalls and lowers profit levels.

2. Low quality reduces customer satisfaction.

3. Low quality can reduce market share.

4. Low quality can give advantages to higher-quality competitors.

5. Low quality raises the odds of litigation with software contractors.

6. Low quality can lead to criminal charges in some situations.

High Quality

1. High quality reduces repairs and raises profit levels.

2. High quality raises customer satisfaction and repeat business.

3. High quality can expand market share.

4. High quality can give advantages over low-quality competitors.

5. High quality reduces the odds of litigation with software contractors.

6. High quality reduces the odds of software causing life-threatening problems.

Software as a Method of Human Effort Reduction

Low Quality

1. Low quality increases down time when equipment cannot be used.

2. Low quality can slow transaction speed and degrade worker performance.

3. Low quality can lead to accidents or transaction errors.

4. Low quality causes errors that require worker effort to correct.

5. Low quality leads to increases in invalid defect reports.

6. Low quality leads to consequential damages and expensive business problems.

High Quality

1. High quality leads to few outages and little down time.

2. High quality optimizes human worker performance.

3. High quality reduces the odds of accidents and transaction errors.

4. High quality and low error rates mean low user effort for repairs.

5. High-quality software has fewer invalid defect reports.

6. High quality reduces consequential damages and business problems.

Software and Innovative New Kinds of Products

Low Quality

1. Low quality can keep new users from trying novel products.

2. Low quality can cause novel products to fail in use.

3. Low-quality software with excessive defects discourages users when learning new products.

4. Low quality and numerous defects can lead to user mistakes and human problems.

5. Low quality and numerous defects can lead to recalls from vendors.

High Quality

1. High quality tends to attract new users.

2. High quality minimizes operational failures.

3. High quality keeps users interested and focused when learning new products.

4. High quality correlates to fewer user mistakes and human problems.

5. High quality minimizes recalls and disruptions.

For cancelled projects and those ending up in litigation, one of the authors has been an expert witness in a dozen of these cases and is in daily contact with many other expert witnesses. In addition, a number of companies have commissioned studies on significant project failures, although most are content to write off the failures and move on without any careful analysis.

It should be noted that because cancelled projects are not completed, their final exact size is unknown except for a few that were installed prior to cancellation. Size was estimated for many of the cancelled projects by means of pattern matching against similar completed projects.

This chapter illustrates some of the major differences between high-quality and low-quality software based on observations from clients. To facilitate the comparisons, information is presented based on application size an order of magnitude apart, ranging from 10 function points to 100,000 function points. Very few applications are exactly round numbers of function points, so mathematical conversion of results is used.

The value of this approach lies in the ease of illustrating trends and differences rather than absolute precision of results. Readers are cautioned that the data has a significant margin of error. Formal estimates should be used for actual projects, and the results in this book should be compared to accurate local historical data.

Note also that although actual costs of development ranged from a low of about $5,000 per staff month to a high or more than $12,500 per staff month, the figures shown in this chapter use a constant value of $10,000 per staff month. This cost includes compensation for workers plus the burden or overhead for health care, Social Security, office space, and so on.

Special costs such as patent licenses, legal fees, and COTS acquisition costs are not shown in this chapter because they are too variable for comparisons to be meaningful. Domestic and international travel for coordinating multicompany, multicountry projects is excluded.

Note also that for large applications with multiyear development cycles, inflation is a significant factor that needs to be included in formal cost estimates. However, in this book constant dollars are used. This simplifies construction of the tables and graphs and also makes it easier to see the true differences between small projects and large systems.

In general, the data on low-quality software comes from a combination of litigation results plus client observations. The data on high-quality software comes from onsite client studies augmented by discussions with clients and user associations. The data on average-quality software comes from the same sources as high-quality software.

As we get into greater depth on the value of high quality and the damages of low quality, it is useful to explain the sources of information cited.

Over the years about 13,000 software projects that were completed have been examined. For some, the examination included onsite interviews with developers and managers. For others, the examination consisted of reading reports produced by others, such as consulting studies or post-mortems by developers.

The company where one of the authors is employed, CAST, has performed a large-scale international study of software quality. Data from this study has been cited in previous chapters and presented in some detail in Chapter 6. CAST's database of projects (called *Appmarq*) contains structural quality data. A number of structural attributes of software product quality are defined, analyzed, and measured in Appmarq.

As we saw in Chapter 2, these quality attributes are the key drivers of software costs and risks. In the next two sections we sketch frameworks for quantifying the costs and business value (or lack thereof) of software quality. These frameworks are grounded in the Appmarq data on software quality obtained from 296 applications from 75 organizations worldwide.

Technical Debt—A Measure of the Effect of Software Quality on Software Costs

Technical debt is defined as the cost of fixing the structural quality problems in an application that, if left unfixed, puts the business at serious risk. Technical debt includes only those problems that are highly likely to cause business disruption (due to operational problems and/or product/service launch delays) and hence put the business at risk; it does not include all problems, just the serious ones.

If we define technical debt this way, measuring it requires us to quantify the structural quality problems that put the business at risk. This is where Appmarq comes in. Appmarq contains data on the *structural quality of the software applications* (as opposed to data on the *process* by which these applications are built). Structural quality measures how well an application is *designed* and how well it is *implemented* (the quality of the coding practices and the degree of compliance with the best practices of software engineering that promote security, reliability, and maintainability).

The basic measure of structural quality in Appmarq is the *number of violations per thousands of lines of code (KLOC)*. Violations are instances in which an application fails to accord with one or more rules of software engineering. Violations can be grouped according to their potential customer impact in terms of the problems or the defects they can create if left unresolved. The higher the potential customer impact, the higher the severity of the violation. The most severe violations are categorized as *critical violations*.

The number of violations per KLOC for each application is not obtained from surveys of project/program managers; rather, it is measured using the repeatable, automated CAST Application Intelligence Platform. Our approach therefore rests on the foundation of objective, repeatably measured quantities. Moreover, the size of the data set is large enough to make robust estimates of the number of low-, medium-, and high-severity violations per KLOC in the universe of applications.

We have independently verified the strong correlation between violations and business disruption events in a number of field tests of mission-critical systems used by our customers. By focusing solely on violations, the calculation takes into account only the problems that we know will cause serious business disruption. We apply this conservative approach to the cost and time it takes to fix violations.

In defining and calculating technical debt as we do, we err on the side of a conservative estimate of the scale of technical debt. To calculate it, we first examine the number of violations per KLOC in the data set. Violations come in three levels of severity—low, medium, and high—depending on the weight the violation is assigned in the automated measurement system.

The large size and diverse composition of the Appmarq data set makes it possible to go beyond simply describing the data in our sample to making inferences about the population as a whole. In particular, we use such an inference to estimate the value of the mean number of low-, medium-, and high-severity-violations per KLOC.

From the data we can infer that with 95% certainty, the *mean number of high-severity violations lies somewhere between 107 and 123 per KLOC.* Although not as satisfying as a point estimate, it is more useful to have this range because it leads to a more accurate estimate. Point estimates are easy to use in calculations, but a lot of information is lost when they are used, leading to results that are often far from the target.

The data also tell us that the 20th, 50th, and 80th percentile values for the number of high-severity violations per KLOC are 70, 102, and 151, respectively. We use these percentile values and some additional ones as parameters in the Technical Debt Model.

How the Technical Debt Model Works

The Technical Debt Model contains two types of parameters. The first type, the one we saw in the previous section, is those values that can be inferred from the Appmarq data (Appmarq-Derived Parameters). The model also requires a second type of parameter—values that have to be set independently of the data set

(Non-Appmarq Parameters). So now that we have them all in one place, the following are lists of both the Appmarq-Derived and the Non-Appmarq parameters of the model.

Appmarq-Derived Parameters and Their Values

The following parameters of the model come from the statistical analysis of the Appmarq data set. For the calculation of technical debt, all the Appmarq-derived parameters are assumed to be uniformly distributed within their ranges. In other words, there is an equal probability of getting any of the values in the specified range.

A. Range of Mean Values of Number of High-Severity Violations per KLOC at the 95% Confidence Level (Uniformly distributed values from 107 to 123)

B. Range of Mean Values of Number of Medium-Severity Violations per KLOC at the 95% Confidence Level (Uniformly distributed values from 120 to 159)

C. Range of Mean Values of Number of Low-Severity Violations at the 95% Confidence Level (Uniformly distributed values from 191 to 228)

D. Range of Mean Values of Application Size in KLOCs at the 95% Confidence Level (Uniformly distributed values from 308 KLOCs to 563KLOCs)

Non-Appmarq Parameters and Their Values

The values chosen for these parameters do not come from the Appmarq data set. They are chosen to result in conservative estimates but can be readily adjusted to suit any desired IT or business scenario. These values can be estimated from other data sets, but we have not done so here.

E. Percentage of High-Severity Violations That Require Fixing to Avoid Business Disruption (Value = 50%)

F. Percentage of Medium-Severity Violations That Require Fixing To Avoid Business Disruption (Value = 25%)

G. Percentage of Low-Severity Violations That Require Fixing To Avoid Business Disruption (Value = 10%)

H. Time to Fix a Violation (Poisson distributed with mean value of 60 minutes per fix)

I. Cost per Hour to Fix a Violation (normally distributed with a mean value of $30 per hour and a standard deviation of $5)

Steps to Calculate Technical Debt

After the parameters are set, the technical debt of the typical application is calculated in four steps:

Step 1: Total Number of Violations That Require Fixing per KLOC:

$[(A * E) + (B * F) + (C * G)]$

Step 2: Total Time to Fix the Violations That Require Fixing per KLOC:

$H * [(A * E) + (B * F) + (C * G)]$

Step 3: Total Cost to Fix the Violations That Require Fixing per KLOC:

$I * H * [(A * E) + (B * F) + (C * G)]$

Step 4: Total Cost to Fix the Violations That Require Fixing per Application:

$D * I * H * [(A * E) + (B * F) + (C * G)]$ = Technical Debt per Application

Many of the values in these calculations are ranges of numbers, not point estimates. To calculate the mean technical debt per application, the model runs a 1,000-trial Monte Carlo simulation over these ranges. For example, the number of high-severity violations per KLOC is modeled as a series of 1,000 independent trials, each trial resulting in a single value between the range of 107 and 123. Every integer in this range has an equal probability of occurring.

Multiplying over such ranges and averaging is hard for humans but very easy for computers. And doing so gives a much better estimate of technical debt than simply taking single-point estimates. The Monte Carlo simulation approach incorporates the natural variation of the number of violations in applications across technologies, business objectives, and industry sectors.

Technical Debt Results

Figure 7.1 shows the results of the 1,000-trial Monte Carlo simulation. Technical debt per application is centered around $1.5 million. It is rarely greater than $2.5 million or less than $500,000 per application.

Further analysis of the distribution in Figure 7.1 shows that the mean technical debt per application is $1.49 million, and we can be 95% certain that the mean technical debt per application for the population as a whole lies somewhere between $1.46 and $1.51 million.

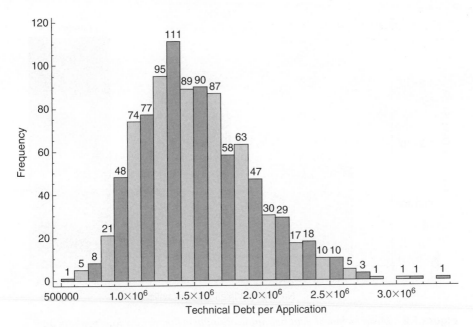

Figure 7.1 *Distribution of technical debt per application resulting from the monte carlo simulation*

The Appmarq data also enables us to establish benchmarks for scenarios of low, medium, and high levels of technical debt. Using the values derived from Appmarq, we build three benchmarks for the best, median, and worst technical debt per application.

We define the best applications to have counts of low-, medium-, and high-severity violations that are at the 20th percentile for these counts in the Appmarq data set. Similarly, we define median applications to have violation counts in the 50th percentile and the worst applications to have violation counts in the 80th percentile for low-, medium-, and high-severity violations. Figure 7.2 displays the benchmarks for the best, median, and worst applications.

The 80th percentile scenario value is more than twice that of the 20th percentile scenario value, indicating that large improvements can be made in reducing technical debt.

The first step to getting a handle on the systemic risks in your portfolio is to measure the scale of technical debt in your applications. Measurement is the first step but it is an important step. To ensure objective, cost-effective measurement, use an automated system to evaluate the structural quality of your

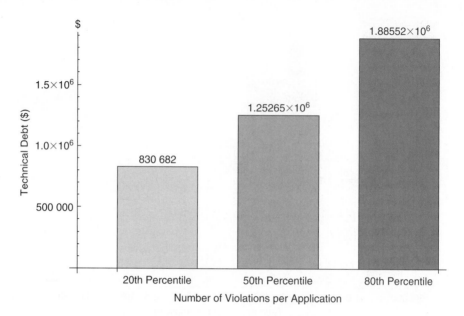

Figure 7.2   *Mean technical debt per application: benchmarks for low, median, and high scenarios*

business-critical applications. Make sure that your assessment of technical debt is grounded on a key driver of software structural quality.

The analysis used here is grounded in objective counts of violations that have been proven in numerous field tests to be the key drivers of application costs and risks in organizations worldwide. The power of this Technical Debt Model is not in its mechanics but in the fundamental bits of data on which it is based and the independent confirmation that these fundamental elements (structural quality lapses measured as number of low-, medium-, and high-severity violations) play a significant role in the business productivity of companies worldwide.

When technical debt is measured it can be juxtaposed with the business value of applications and with business plans to create a concrete technical debt reduction plan. Software quality is not an end in itself; indeed, the economics of software quality is about being able to determine the appropriate level of quality that balances costs on the one hand with business value delivered on the other. We next turn to a framework for quantifying business value.

A Framework for Quantifying Business Value

Here a framework is created for quantifying business value created by Dr. Bill Curtis. Because software animates business objectives, the structural quality of business applications is critical for achieving important business outcomes. There are four primary business objectives against which the business value of an application can be assessed. These business objectives are

- Reducing business risks

- Increasing business agility

- Improving business productivity

- Improving customer experience

The next five sections present equations to express the business value of the structural quality of applications. These equations are not presented as formal ROI analyses because the cost of money, investment recovery periods, and other components of formal ROI models are not included. Rather they represent loss functions attached to each business objective that indicate how poor internal quality is translated into lost revenue and increased costs.

Reducing Business Risks

Business risks often present the easiest case for quantifying quality benefits. The cost of quality problems can be expressed as the loss of known current or future revenue, the cost of underutilized workers, liquidated damages, and other costs based on historical business data. Different types of risks experience different types of losses.

- **Outages that terminate business transactions**: Consider a simplified evaluation of the loss due to an outage in a commercial application, such as a reservation or customer order system. The costs involve lost revenue, effort for the business to recover and reactivate transactions, spikes in help desk and related costs for managing customer interactions, liquidated damages, and other costs that may be unique to the specific area of business. Although not all costs are triggered in each outage, they should be considered to ensure they do not remain hidden in ongoing business activities.

  Loss = ((avg. revenue per minute) × (number of minutes unavailable)) +

  cost to reactivate business +

  ((Additional customer service minutes) × ($ per minute) +

  future revenue lost from defecting customers +

  liquidated damages if applicable +

  other related costs)

- **Corrupted data**: The costs associated with corrupted data include re-creating accurate data, redeveloping or correcting inaccurate outputs and reports, and any liabilities resulting from the use or reporting of inaccurate data. The cost of data corruption is compounded by the length of time before the inaccurate data is detected, considering in many cases this makes the cleanup more extensive. The business bears many of the costs of data corruption either through having to correct the data or for unproductive downtime while IT restores accurate data.

Loss = cost of data reconstruction +

cost of recreating accurate reports +

liabilities created from inaccurate data +

other related costs

- **Violated security**: Defects in an application's architecture or code often create vulnerabilities that hackers and cyber-criminals exploit to penetrate the system. These costs can include those related to theft of business or customer information, repairing malicious damage, informing customers of possible compromised information, security improvements to systems and business processes, liquidated damages, and lost future revenue from defecting customers. Although expensive, the identifiable costs of these breaches are often less than the lost revenue from customers who either no longer use the application or who defect to competitors they perceive to be more secure.

Loss = cost of stolen resources +

cost of rectifying data, records, or accounts +

cost of informing customers +

cost of security improvements +

future revenue lost from defecting customers +

liquidated damages if applicable

- **Regulatory noncompliance**: Weaknesses in an application's code can place the enterprise in noncompliance with industry standards or government regulations. Noncompliance can result in financial penalties, and violations of regulations such as Sarbanes-Oxley can have criminal implications.

Loss = cost of penalties for noncompliance +

cost of bringing the system into compliance

Increasing Business Agility

Modern communication technology (cellular grids, the Internet, and so on) has multiplied the pace of business. Consequently, competition has shrunk the time available for responding to customer demands and market conditions. The agility of a business to respond quickly is strictly limited by the structural quality of its applications. The more needlessly complex the architecture or coding of an application, the longer it takes to add or modify functionality, verify its correctness, and deliver it into operation. Worse, unnecessary complexity induces more mistakes and rework, lengthening the time to develop and transfer new functionality into operation.

Loss = revenue lost from missing the customer's buying window +

revenue lost to faster moving competitors +

future revenue lost from defecting customers +

diminished profit from dilution of first mover advantage +

diminished economy of scale from loss of market share

The value of structural software quality to business agility is in terms of lost opportunity cost. It represents the lost revenue or market share experienced when competitors can respond more quickly or when the response misses the customer's buying window. The importance of business agility cannot be overstated for long-term business viability and growth. Both improving agility and reducing business risk produce immediate business benefits. However, improvements in business agility also affect a company's ability to execute its business strategy and optimize long-term results.

Improving Business Productivity

Given that a primary purpose of many applications is to improve business productivity, defects that cause outages or performance degradation rob the organization of the full benefit from its investment in both the application and the workforce using it. Business losses caused by outages are covered as business risks. The productivity impact on employees and revenue generation is treated separately here. The costs of lost productivity are usually calculated in terms of additional person hours to complete work or of lost opportunity for revenue generation. Even if the additional hours were performed as unpaid overtime, there is an impact on staff morale that can further reduce productivity or induce voluntary turnover. In addition, reduced productivity can inject delays into the completion of tasks that have other costs such as penalties for late delivery.

Loss = [(1 − (reduced output under degraded performance ÷

avg. output at normal performance)) ×

number of workers affected ×

avg. hourly cost ×

hours of degraded performance] +

[(1 − (reduced output or revenue under degraded performance ÷

avg. output or revenue at normal performance)) ×

performance ×

avg. revenue per hour] +

costs of delayed work

Improving Customer Experience

As more customer transactions move online, business applications increasingly become the face of the business. The customer's experience with the company becomes his or her experience with the application's usability and performance.

Confusing user interfaces, labyrinthine websites, and glacially slow system responses frustrate customers. At a minimum, these problems reduce the amount of business a customer may transact, and in the worst case they drive customers to competitors.

To compound the customer loyalty problem, confused customers create even more costs per transaction. When customers have difficulty using a company's automated business systems, they call customer support to conduct transactions that could have been performed online. The more confusing the interface, the more customer support personnel must be available to assist customers in completing transactions. For instance, when system response is slow, customers often begin pushing buttons that may be interpreted as commands to pages that have yet to display. Many of these incorrect entries require staff time to undo and return to the original state in a customer's account. Usability and responsiveness contribute to revenue growth and lower customer interaction costs.

Loss = future revenue lost from departing customers +

future revenue lost from reduced transactions with loyal customers +

cost of conducting transactions shifted from online to customer service +

cost of customer service calls related to online difficulties

An Example of Business Loss Due to Poor Quality

Using the formula for application outages that terminate business transactions, consider the business costs of a one-hour outage for an application that yields $120 in revenue per minute ($7,200 per hour). In addition to lost revenue, the business will spend $1,000 in employee time to verify, correct, or regenerate partially completed transactions and to verify the system is working correctly when brought back online. The help desk experienced a surge of 250 additional minutes of customer service calls at $2 per minute. Business intelligence analyses discovered that 20 existing customers made no further contact with the company after the outage, with annual revenue from those customers being $150 per year. Fortunately, this application did not involve any liquidated damages. The total cost of this outage is estimated to be

Loss = ((60 minutes) × ($120 per minute)) + $1,000 reactivation cost +

$500 customer service costs + $3,000 lost customer revenue this year

= $11,700

If the company experienced a one-hour outage with this application once per quarter, the total annual business revenue loss just from outages would be $46,800, not including IT costs for repairing the cause of failure, retesting the application, and similar IT costs.

Next, consider that in addition to outages this application's performance degrades by 10% due to poor database access procedures that reduce its ability to handle an increasing load of business transactions. Also consider that this application supports 100 knowledge workers whose fully burdened cost is $25 per hour. This loss of productivity is calculated both as lost revenue and as loss in the productive value of knowledge worker compensation. The cost of this application's structural quality problems per quarter is estimated to be

Loss = ((0.1 output) × (100 workers) × ($25 per hour)

× (500 hours per quarter)) ×

((0.1 output) × ($7,200 revenue per hour) × (500 hours per quarter))

= $485,000 per quarter

The loss from the risk of business outages, lack of business agility, lost business productivity, and suboptimal customer experience is surprisingly large. Based on the sizes of these losses, improvements in the quality of applications offer substantial benefits to the business. When the value of software quality is computed only against development or maintenance costs fully contained within IT, the full impact of loss due to poor quality remains invisible to the business. However, when computed against business costs and lost opportunities, it is much easier to make a strong case for investing in quality.

Moving Beyond Functional Quality

Improving the quality of applications has two components; external, functional quality and internal, structural quality. Most defect detection and related quality activities built into standard application development and maintenance processes focus on external or functional quality. These are the defects that represent deviations from the specified requirements for the application. Advances in testing, peer review, and requirements management processes and technology have improved the ability of application development teams to detect and remove the majority of these defects before placing the application into operation.

Because structural quality problems are harder to detect, hidden as they are in the architecture and engineering of the application, they are frequently the causes of outages, degraded performance, security breaches, corrupted data, and similar problems. These quality problems come in a wide range of manifestations, from bad coding techniques, to needlessly complex designs, to violations of coding standards. By detecting these structural quality problems and correcting those with the most critical priorities, application developers can dramatically increase the value of an application to the business.

The objective of the Technical Debt and the Business Value Models is to create an objective, repeatable framework for quantifying software costs and value. The specific values used in the models are chosen to be conservative and can be modified to suit a wide range of IT and business conditions.

The Impact of Software Structure on Quality

A number of structural topics exist that have an impact on software quality. Observations on the relationship between structure and quality date back to early analysis of "go-to" statements in the 1960s and the later development of the cyclomatic complexity measure by Tom McCabe in 1978. In addition to these measures, please refer to Chapters 1 and 2 for information about the full set of attributes for measuring structural quality.

Table 7.3 shows observations on the structural aspects of software projects.

The "star" system for evaluating maintainability is used in Germany, the Netherlands, and other European countries. A number of consulting groups analyze software maintainability and provide reviews for clients.

Many years of historical data that contrast development and maintenance costs between well-structured applications and chaotic or poorly structured applications clearly favors structures that are formally planned and low in accidental complexity.

Table 7.3 *Application Structure Assumptions*

Low Quality	Average Quality	High Quality
Complex structure does not allow effective decomposition	Partial decomposition but many structural problems	Effective decomposition into discrete, buildable components
Maximum Cyclomatic Complexity > 50	Maximum Cyclomatic Complexity < 20	Maximum Cyclomatic Complexity < 10
Unreliable reusable materials	Uncertified reusable materials	Certified reusable materials
Unplanned requirements > 1.5% per month	Unplanned requirements > 0.8% per month	Unplanned requirements < 0.25% per month
Many security vulnerabilities > 0.3 per function point	Some security vulnerabilities > 0.15 per function point	Very few security vulnerabilities < 0.01 per function point
Multiple error-prone modules	At least one error-prone module	Zero error-prone modules
Poor maintainability (1 star)	Fair maintainability (3 stars)	Good maintainability (5 stars)
No static analysis of legacy code	Partial static analysis of legacy code	Static analysis of legacy code
No renovation of legacy code before enhancements	Partial renovation of legacy code before enhancements	Full renovation of legacy code before enhancements

The Impact of Staff Training on Quality

Table 7.4 shows a topic that may surprise many readers. Software quality and productivity tend to correlate with the amount of training provided to technical workers and managers.

A very surprising finding made in 1978 in an internal IBM study, but noted by other companies since then, is that even though five days a year might be subtracted from working time, training benefits productivity and also quality. With training, the software projects, employees, and companies tend to have higher annual productivity rates than groups that provide no training at all. In several companies, as many as ten days of annual training yielded productivity rates higher than zero days of training.

Because software technologies are changing rapidly, continuous education is as important for software as it is for the older professions of law, medicine, electrical engineering, and other engineering fields.

The sources of the training include internal courses, external courses, and university extension courses. The courses can be provided by live instructors or in the form of webinars, podcasts, DVDs, or self-study materials.

The Impact of Professional Certification on Quality

Table 7.5 deals with the controversial topic of professional certification. As all readers know, software development is not currently a licensed profession, nor does it have board-certified specialties as does the medical profession, for example. Indeed, the Bureau of Commerce does not yet define software as a profession, but rather as a skilled craft.

However, there are both nonprofit organizations and for-profit organizations that do certify skill-based software occupations such as quality assurance, testing, and project management. Although the data is not conclusive as of 2011, certified personnel tend to be found on high-quality projects more than on low-quality projects. Table 7.5 shows current results from client observations.

Table 7.4   *Annual Training Assumptions for Managers and Technical Staff*

(Courses or self-study courses)		
Low Quality	**Average Quality**	**High Quality**
No curriculum planning	Marginal curriculum planning	Effective curriculum planning
Managers = < 2 days	Managers = +/– 3 days	Managers = > 5 days
Developers = < 2 days	Developers = +/– 3 days	Developers = > 5 days
Maintainers = < 2 days	Maintainers = +/– 3 days	Maintainers = > 5 days
Testers = < 2 days	Testers =+/– 3 days	Testers = > 5 days
SQA = < 2 days	SQA =+/– 3 days	SQA = > 5 days
Webinars = < 2 per year	Webinars = +/– 4 per year	Webinars = > 8 per year

Table 7.5   *Professional Certification Assumptions for Managers and Technical Staff*

(Percent of full-time employees attaining professional certification)		
Low Quality	**Average Quality**	**High Quality**
Managers = < 10%	Managers = +/– 15%	Managers = > 30%
Developers = < 10	Developers = +/– 15%	Developers = > 20%
Maintainers = < 10%	Maintainers = +/– 12%	Maintainers = 15%
Testers = < 15%	Testers = +/– 20%	Testers = > 50%
SQA = < 10%	SQA = +/– 15%	SQA = > 25%

Certification is an ambiguous topic in 2011. At some point in the future, no doubt professional licensing and formal certification, as is in place for medicine and law, will arrive for software engineering. Until then there are many forms of certification, and some of these seem to be in competition with others.

Certification for test and quality assurance personnel, however, does show up more frequently on high-quality projects than on either average or low-quality projects.

The Impact of Technology Investment on Quality

Table 7.6 also deals with an ambiguous and somewhat controversial topic. This table delineates the amount of money per capita spent each year to provide new tools, methods, and training for software engineers, testers, quality assurance, and managers.

Some small companies spend close to $0.00 for technology improvements on an annual basis. At the other end, some sophisticated companies spend more than $10,000 per capita per year, although not every year.

Per capita costs are difficult to calculate. For example, a commercial software cost-estimating tool might be acquired for a cost of $5,000 per seat. But for an overall software population of 1,000 people, only five to ten copies may be needed.

The companies in the right, or high-quality, column usually have some kind of process improvement program at work and are making planned changes to their development and maintenance practices.

Examples of some of the technology investments would include static analysis tools, automated test tools, maintenance workbenches, automated project office support tools, external benchmark data, commercial software estimating tools, defect tracking tools, new languages and new compilers, and perhaps acquiring libraries of certified reusable materials.

Table 7.6 *Annual Technology Investments for Management and Technical Staff*

(Training, tools, and methodologies)		
Low Quality	Average Quality	High Quality
Managers < $1,000	Managers +/− $2,500	Managers > $3,000
Developers < $1,500	Developers +/− $2,000	Developers > $3,500
Maintainers < $1,000	Maintainers +/− $1,500	Maintainers > $3,000
Testers < $1,500	Testers +/− $2,500	Testers > $3,000
SQA < $500	SQA +/− $1,000	SQA > $1,500
TOTAL < $6,000	TOTAL +/− $9,000	TOTAL > $14,000
AVERAGE < $1,100	AVERAGE +/− $1,900	AVERAGE > $2,800
PERCENT < 58%	PERCENT 100%	PERCENT > 147%

The Impact of Project Management on Quality

Table 7.7 deals with one of the more important factors that distinguish high quality from low quality—project management performance. In many of the lawsuits for cancelled projects or poor quality, the managers were more at fault than the software engineers and testers. It was management decisions to bypass inspections, not to acquire static analysis tools, to truncate testing, and to conceal problems that contributed to the litigation.

Poor management decisions can cause serious quality problems and also cause major schedule delays, cost overruns, outright cancellation of projects, and sometimes litigation in the wake of disasters.

In all of the breach-of-contract litigation for which one of the authors has been an expert witness, management problems far outnumbered software engineering problems. Among the common management issues were inaccurate

Table 7.7 *Software Project Management Assumptions*

Low Quality	Average Quality	High Quality
No risk analysis	Late risk analysis	Early risk analysis
No effective risk solutions	Late risk solutions	Early risk solutions
No risk monitoring	Intermittent risk monitoring	Continuous risk monitoring
Inadequate project corrections	Slow project corrections	Rapid project corrections
Informal manual cost estimates	Formal manual cost estimates	Automated cost estimates
Inaccurate manual schedule estimates	Manual schedule estimates	Automated schedule estimates
Grossly inaccurate progress tracking	Inaccurate progress tracking	Formal, accurate progress tracking
Grossly inaccurate cost tracking	Inaccurate cost tracking	Formal, accurate cost tracking
Ineffective or erroneous status monitoring	Marginally effective status monitoring	Effective "dashboard" status monitoring
No internal benchmark data available	Partial benchmark comparisons	Formal benchmark comparisons: Internal
No external benchmark data utilized	Partial benchmark data from unknown sources	Formal benchmark comparisons: External (ISBSG or others)
Casual change control	Informal change control	Formal change control
Inadequate governance	Partial governance	Effective governance

estimates of schedules and costs; inadequate status tracking; failure to alert clients and higher management to problems; understating the magnitude of future schedule slips; and truncating quality-control methods in failed attempts to speed up delivery.

Another aspect of poor management was noted when reviewing the exit interviews for software engineers who were leaving voluntarily to take new jobs. This study showed two alarming phenomena: The software engineers with the highest appraisal scores left in the largest numbers, and the most common reason given by top software engineers for changing jobs was "I don't like working for bad management."

Because management problems are endemic in the software field, some companies have introduced "reverse appraisals" so that employees appraise managers as well as being appraised themselves.

Many years ago IBM introduced an open-door policy, which allowed any employee who felt mistreated by management to appeal to any higher-level executive. There were guarantees that the claim would be investigated carefully. There were also guarantees that no reprisals would occur, and the employee's job security and future appraisals would not be in danger.

The Impact of Quality-Control Methodologies and Tools on Quality

Table 7.8 combines all of the major quality factors that distinguish high quality, from average quality, from low quality. Needless to say, the factors in Table 7.8 are significant.

Successful projects tend to stay with the methods shown in the right or High Quality column. Drifting to the left is a recipe for serious quality problems and perhaps for cancelled projects and major cost and schedule overruns.

Table 7.8 *Quality Method and Practice Assumptions*

(Low, Average, and High Quality)		
Quality Estimation and Measurement Assumptions		
Low Quality	**Average Quality**	**High Quality**
No quality estimates	Manual quality estimates	Automated quality estimates
Defect tracking: post-release	Defect tracking: from testing on	Defect tracking: from project start
No test coverage measurements	Partial test coverage measurements	Automated test coverage measurements
No cyclomatic complexity measures	Cyclomatic complexity measures	Cyclomatic complexity measures

(Continued)

Table 7.8   *(Continued)*

Quality Estimation and Measurement Assumptions

Low Quality	Average Quality	High Quality
LOC measures	Function point measures	Function point measures
		Defect potentials
		Defect detection
		Defect removal
		Defect severity
		Duplicate defects
		Bad-fix injection
		Invalid defects
		Defects by origin
		False positives
		Defect repair cost
		Defect repair time
		Root causes
No standards used	Partial adherence to ISO 9126	Adherence to ISO 9126 quality standards
	Partial adherence to ISO 14764	Adherence to ISO 14764 maintainability standards
	No adherence to ISO 14143	Adherence to ISO 14143 functional sizing
	Partial adherence to ISO 12207	Adherence to ISO 12207 software lifecycle

Defect Prevention Method and Practice Assumptions

Low Quality	Average Quality	High Quality
None	Joint Application Design (JAD)	Joint Application Design (JAD)
		Quality Function Deployment (QFD)
		Six Sigma

Development Method and Practice Assumptions

Low Quality	Average Quality	High Quality
Methods chosen by popularity and not by evaluation of results	Methods chosen by popularity with partial evaluation of results	Methods chosen based technical evaluation and empirical data
CMMI 0 or 1	CMMI 1 or 2	CMMI 3, 4, 5
Waterfall	Agile	PSP/TSP
Uncertified reuse	XP	RUP

	Hybrid	XP
	Uncertified reuse	Hybrid
		Certified reuse

Pretest Defect Removal Methods and Practice Assumptions

Low Quality	Average Quality	High Quality
No SQA	Informal SQA	Certified SQA
None	Static analysis	Static analysis
		Requirements inspections
		Design inspections
		Architecture inspections
		Code inspections
		Test inspections

Testing Method and Practice Assumptions

Low Quality	Average Quality	High Quality
Uncertified Test teams	Uncertified Test teams	Certified Test teams

Testing Method and Practice Assumptions

Low Quality	Average Quality	High Quality
Informal test case design	Informal test case design	Formal test case design using mathematical models
Informal, ineffective test	Informal test	Formal, effective test
Library control	Library control	Library control
> 50 builds during test	> 20 builds during test	< 10 builds during test
No risk-based tests	Partial-risk based tests	Risk-based tests
No reusable tests	Some reusable tests	Many reusable tests
Unit test	Unit test	Unit test
Function test	Function test	Function test
Regression test	Regression test	Regression test
System test	Performance test	Performance test
Beta test	System test	Security test
	Beta test	Usability test
		System test
		Beta test
No test coverage analysis	Partial test coverage analysis (Percent of code executed during testing)	Test coverage analysis (Percent of requirements, code, and risks tested)

Table 7.8 might be segmented into a number of smaller tables, but it seemed a better approach to consolidate all of the quality-control methods in one large table because they need to be planned concurrently.

As is shown in figures later in the chapter, the projects whose quality methods come from the High Quality column tend to have shorter schedules and lower costs than similar applications of the same size and type that used methods from the Low Quality and Average Quality columns.

The Impact of High and Low Quality on Software Schedules

One of the earliest and most surprising kinds of quantitative data about quality is the finding that high-quality applications have shorter development schedules than low-quality applications. The main area for schedule reduction due to high quality is that of testing. This phenomenon was noted by IBM in the 1970s for both applications and systems software.

For software projects that start testing with thousands of latent defects, test schedules will always be longer than anticipated and sometimes longer by many months. They will also be unpredictable because as long as defects are being found in large volumes, testing cannot be stopped or reduced.

Unfortunately, applications "learn" their test libraries. This means that when a given number of test cases stop finding bugs, it does not mean all bugs have been found. It merely means that the existing set of test cases have run out of steam and will not find any more bugs because the remaining latent bugs are outside of the control flow being tested.

(As noted earlier in the book, pretest inspections shortened the test duration of a major IBM application from three months of three-shift testing to one month of one-shift testing.)

A combination of defect prevention, pretest inspections, and pretest static analysis will normally pay off with greatly reduced testing schedules. Inspections will stretch out the time for requirements and design, but the savings from shorter testing are greater. Static analysis is a high-speed method that normally has no negative impact on schedules but rather speeds up downstream testing.

As Figure 7.3 shows, the difference in schedules between high-quality and low-quality projects becomes larger as application size increases. This variance is because large systems have more bugs and hence more kinds of testing and longer test schedules than small projects.

The Impact of High and Low Quality on Software Staffing

It is also surprising that high-quality software projects require fewer staff numberss than low-quality applications of the same size and type. The staffing

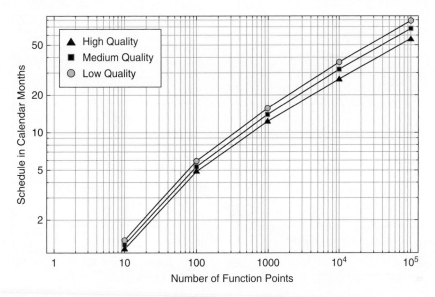

Figure 7.3 *Software development schedules by size and quality level*

reductions are concentrated primarily in the areas of programming and testing.

Low-quality projects have enormous amounts of repair and rework during development and also after release. Low-quality projects have lengthy test schedules that require both test and programming personnel to work full-time and often to spend many hours of overtime work as well.

By contrast, high-quality projects have reduced amounts of repair and rework. They also have much shorter testing schedules. Even better, the improved structure and reduced complexity of high-quality software also makes it easier and faster to design and construct test cases.

Large software projects can have hundreds of development personnel. Perhaps surprising to some readers, as many as 75 different occupation groups may be involved. Among the many occupations can be found architects, business analysts, data base analysts, software quality assurance, software engineering, systems analysis, testing, technical writing, graphics artists, metrics specialists, project office specialists, and many more.

For many of these specialized groups the main impact of high quality will be shorter schedules, which reduce overall costs. But for software engineers, testers, and quality assurance personnel, high quality can reduce the total number of employees needed, as seen in Figure 7.4. The reason for this is that with low-quality large software projects, almost 50% of the effort is devoted to finding and repairing bugs and performing rework. As quality goes up, repair and rework effort comes down, and in turn this reduces staffing needs.

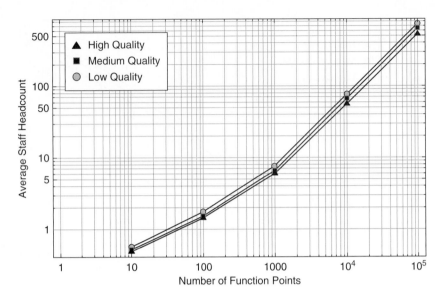

Figure 7.4   *Software development staffing by size and quality level*

The Impact of High and Low Quality on Software Development Effort

High quality levels shorten schedules and reduce staffing needs, so it is also obvious that software development effort will be improved. The reason is the same as already noted: High quality reduces repair and rework, which traditionally have been the major cost drivers of large software projects. Figure 7.5 shows effort by size and quality level.

Readers might wonder why Figure 7.5 uses a decimal place when such precision is clearly impossible to achieve for large software projects. The reason is that for very small projects of ten function points or fewer, the normal rounding used by spreadsheets might result in zero months of effort. At least one decimal place is needed to drop below ten function points.

Here, too, reduction in the effort devoted to repairs and rework is the reason why high-quality projects require less effort.

The Impact of High and Low Quality on Development Productivity Rates

To show productivity trends, it is useful to normalize the data using function point metrics. Due to the existence of about 2,500 programming languages of various levels and the frequent use of multiple languages in the same application, it is not useful to normalize data using lines of code.

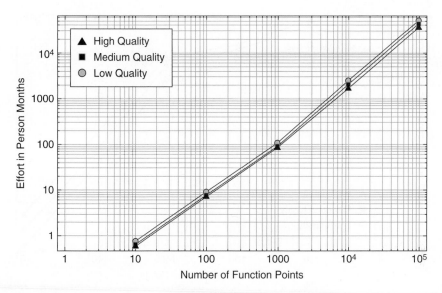

Figure 7.5   *Software development effort by size and quality level*

Figure 7.6 shows comparative productivity rates. Readers will note that even for high-quality software projects, productivity declines, and projects increase in size. There are a number of reasons for this, but the dominant reason is that large projects require many more kinds of work than small projects.

Think outside of software at the kinds of work needed to build a 100,000-ton cruise ship compared to the kinds of work needed to build a small rowboat.

As with other measures of schedules, staffing, and effort, the differences between high-quality projects and low-quality projects gets bigger as application size increases.

The Impact of High and Low Quality on Software Development Costs

Because software costs are derived from the combination of schedules, staffing, effort, and productivity, Figure 7.7 is based on the aggregate results of the previous four figures.

Figure 7.7 assumes all work from the start of requirements until deployment. The cost structures in Figure 7.13 will probably seem much higher than those available to readers from their own local data.

The reason for this is that most local data "leaks," or omits, many of the true costs associated with software. The most common forms of leakage are

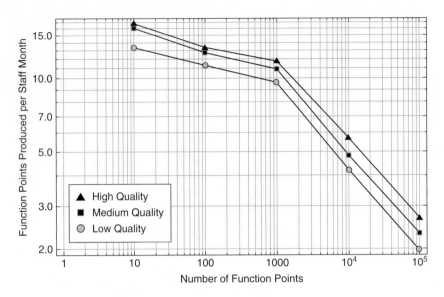

Figure 7.6   *Software productivity rates by size and quality level*

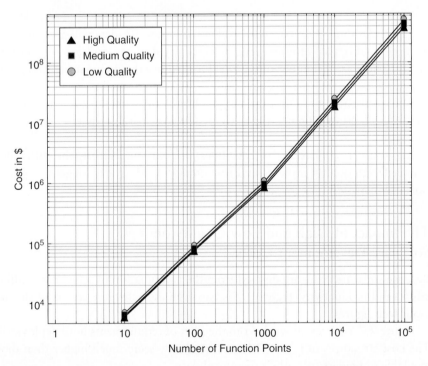

Figure 7.7   *Software development costs by size and quality level (burdened cost =
$10,000 per staff month)*

those of unpaid overtime, the work of part-time specialists such as quality assurance, and the work of project managers and administrative staff.

Though development costs clearly favor high-quality software applications, they are only part of the story. High quality generates even larger savings for maintenance, enhancements, and total cost of ownership (TCO), which is depicted in later figures.

Note that Figure 7.7 uses a constant arbitrary value of $10,000 per staff month. This rate includes both staff compensation and also burden or overhead costs for Social Security, health insurance, office space, and other overhead items.

The Impact of High and Low Quality on Development Cost per Function Point

Normalization to a metric such as function points is useful to illustrate how software costs vary by size and quality level. Figure 7.8 shows data taken from Figure 7.7, but normalized.

Here, too, costs are based on an arbitrary value of $10,000 per staff month, which includes compensation and overhead costs.

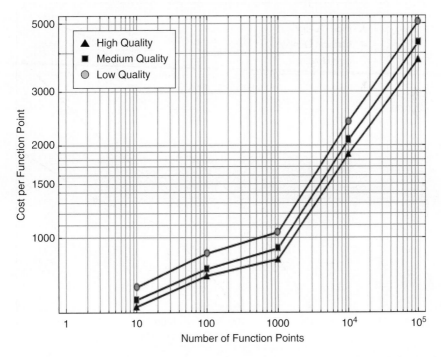

Figure 7.8 *Software development costs per function point by size and quality level*

When data is normalized it is easy to see that rather than offering economies of scale, large software projects cost much more per function point than small projects. Low-quality projects also cost much more per function point than high-quality projects due primarily to excessive repair and rework costs for low-quality projects.

The Impact of High and Low Quality on Project Cancellation Rates

One of the major differences between high-quality software projects and low-quality software projects is their cancellation rate. Indeed, much of the economic value of high quality for large projects resides in the greatly reduced odds of cancellation due to schedule and cost overruns. Of course, cancellations for business reasons can still occur.

As applications grow in size, low-quality projects tend to be cancelled in alarming numbers. The reason for this is that schedule slips and cost overruns

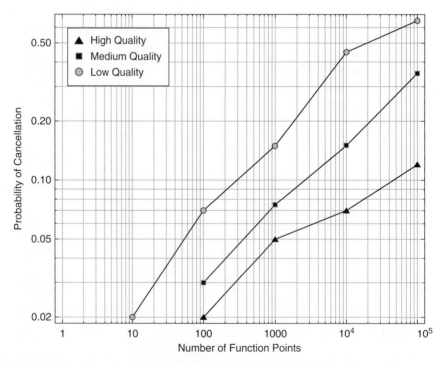

Figure 7.9   *Odds of cancellation by size and quality level (includes negative ROI, poor quality, and change in business need)*

prior to cancellation erode the value of the application and turn a planned positive ROI into a strongly negative ROI.

From lawsuits dealing with cancelled projects for which one of the authors has worked as an expert witness, an average cancelled project is already months late and well over budget at the time the plug is pulled. As a result, projects cancelled for cause cost a great deal more than successful projects of the same size and type.

The Impact of High and Low Quality on the Timing of Cancelled Projects

Even very high-quality software projects can be cancelled for business reasons. For example, both IBM and ITT had an internal method of beginning several similar projects using varying architectures and technologies and then selecting one of these for eventual completion. This technique was used in developing relational databases, for example.

As another example of a business-driven cancellation, a company in the midst of a major software development project acquired another company that happened to already own an identical application to the one then under construction. It was decided by top management to use the application in the acquired company rather than continuing development.

Figure 7.10 shows the approximate schedule month for cancelling software projects. There are very important differences between the cancellation points of high-quality projects and low-quality projects. The month of cancellation represents calendar months from the start of requirements until termination.

Low-quality projects are usually in serious trouble and already late when cancelled. High-quality projects are often in no trouble at all.

The low-quality projects are usually cancelled after they are already late and over budget. The high-quality projects are usually cancelled for business reasons, and therefore the point of time for cancellation is much earlier than for low-quality projects.

Of course, unpredictable business events such as a change in tax laws, acquisition or merger with another company, or the unexpected release of commercial software that negates a need for internal development can occur at any time. These external events are outside the control of software organizations.

For low-quality projects that are cancelled, desperate project managers keep trying to get the project back on track by pleading for schedule extensions in small dribbles of time, but never succeed in actual recovery.

For high-quality projects that are cancelled, there is no question that they would work and be finished on time, but business needs have changed, for reasons just noted.

The Impact of High and Low Quality on Cancelled Project Effort

Because low-quality cancelled software projects are normally late and over budget when stopped, they expend a great deal of effort.

By contrast, high-quality projects cancelled for business reasons are usually terminated early in development, prior to accumulating major amounts of effort.

Average-quality projects are cancelled for both business and quality issues. Because large average projects routinely run late and are over budget, sometimes they morph toward a negative ROI, which leads to termination as noted in Figure 7.11.

The fact that low-quality projects are costly and late when cancelled is one of the major economic factors that show the value of high quality and the negative economic value of low quality.

The Impact of High and Low Quality on Effort Compared to Average Projects

When cancelled project data is expressed in terms of percentages of the costs of average projects, it can be seen that the late termination of unhealthy

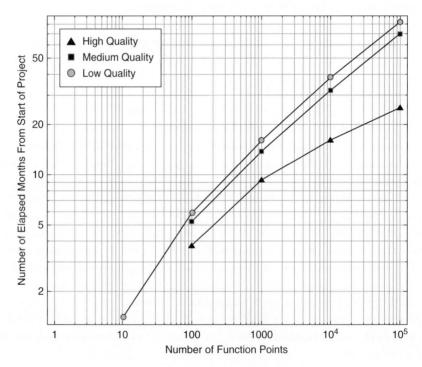

Figure 7.10 *Probable month of cancellation from start of project*

low-quality projects results in a huge balloon of effort compared to either average projects or high-quality projects. Figure 7.12 shows the results of Figure 7.11 in percentage form.

The reasons low-quality projects are cancelled is self-evident. They are late and over budget and have a negative ROI. High-quality projects are usually cancelled for external business reasons.

It is not so clear why average projects are cancelled. Some of them are cancelled for business reasons and not for quality reasons. However, because "average" large projects in the 10,000 and 100,000 function point ranges usually run late and are over budget, some average projects are terminated because the initial positive ROI turned negative. This may be due to excessive volumes of creeping requirements, or it may be due to marginal quality control, or both.

It is difficult to study cancelled projects because being unfinished, their final size is not known with accuracy. Also their final schedules and costs are not known either. For example, a project that is cancelled for being 12 months late and $1,000,000 over budget might well have continued for another year and spent another million had the cancellation not occurred.

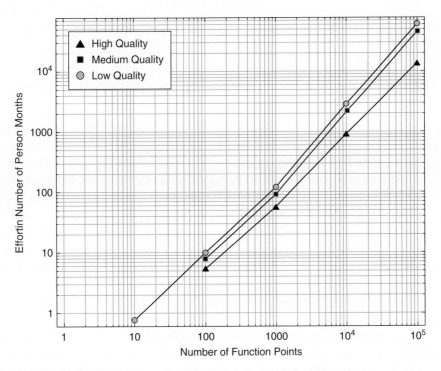

Figure 7.11 *Probable effort from project start to point of cancellation*

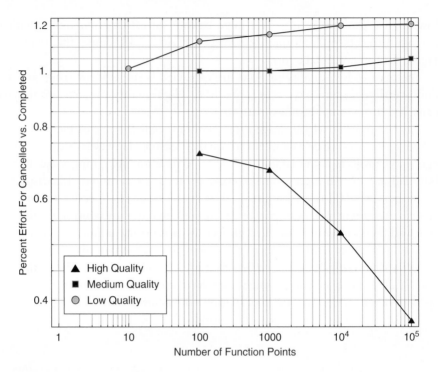

Figure 7.12 *Percent of effort on cancelled projects compared to completed projects (includes negative ROI, poor quality, and change in business need)*

The Impact of High and Low Quality on Software Test Stages

Some of the information about testing in the context of low- and high-quality projects is counterintuitive. Figure 7.13 shows a topic that may be surprising and counterintuitive to some readers. Low-quality projects use fewer kinds of testing than do high-quality projects.

It might be expected that due to the problems and defect rates of low-quality projects they would do more kinds of testing. Low-quality projects do require more time and effort on testing, as is shown in future figures, but they tend to use only a sparse set of basic kinds of testing such as unit testing, function testing, regression testing, and system testing. Sophisticated forms of testing such as usability testing, performance testing, and security testing are often bypassed on low-quality projects.

Figure 7.13 shows the numbers of test stages by application size and application quality level.

Most readers who have worked on large applications know that they require extensive testing, and those who have worked in leading-edge organizations that build large software projects know that many different kinds of testing are needed.

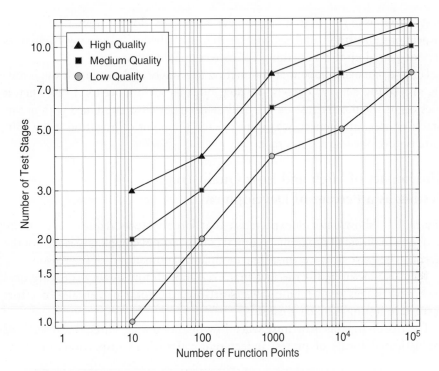

Figure 7.13 *Probable number of test stages by application size and quality level (test stages include unit, function, regression, Beta, system, etc.)*

The primary reason that low-quality projects use fewer forms of testing is that each form of testing takes much more time and effort than expected, so managers eliminate or bypass specialized kinds of testing in a vain hope to regain lost schedule time.

As testing schedules begin to slip and discovered defect counts begin to rise to alarming volumes, there are no effective methods of project recovery. One project within IBM was able to recover by suspending testing and performing code inspection. However, testing had only been going on for two weeks when this decision was made. The inspections added several weeks before testing resumed, but the final test schedule and application delivery dates were met.

In today's world it might be possible to suspend testing briefly and perform static analysis on the application. This would take only a few days, assuming the company can move quickly to bring in static analysis tools. Of course, the time is dependent on the volume of the code base being testing. Also static analysis tools only cover a few dozen out of about 2,500 known languages. Applications written in unusual languages such as Bliss, Chill, Coral, or Mumps may not be able to use static analysis tools.

A larger issue is that most project managers don't know that pretest inspections and static analysis will shorten test schedules, so many companies are not geared up to do anything but conventional testing.

Unwise managers hope that eliminating test stages and rushing through testing may allow delivery dates to be met, but this seldom occurs. Even when it does occur, the post-release defects will incur major costs combined with unsatisfactory user satisfaction, which may reach the point of litigation if the software is developed under contract.

The Impact of High and Low Quality on Testing as a Percent of Development

Figure 7.14 shows, not unexpectedly, that large systems require much more testing than do small programs. Normal combinatorial complexity is part of the reason. The existence of error-prone modules is another part of the reason.

What is unexpected is the fact that even though low-quality software uses fewer test stages than high-quality software, the total percentage of effort devoted to testing is much greater.

The reason for this is because when low-quality testing starts, the absence of sophisticated forms of pretest defect removal such as inspections or static

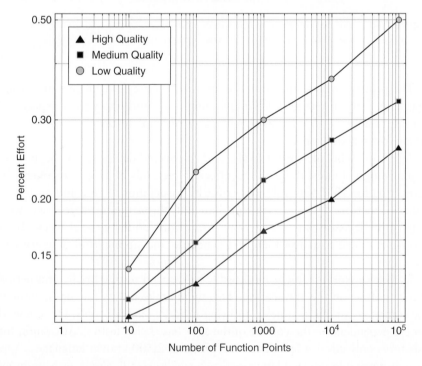

Figure 7.14   *Percentage of development effort for testing (testing without prior inspections or static analysis is unpredictable)*

analysis means that the software being tested might have thousands of latent defects. What stretches out the test schedules and elevates testing costs for low-quality software is not merely designing, creating, and running test cases; it is the enormous amount of effort associated with repairing the huge numbers of defects that raises testing effort and pushes out testing schedules.

Some low-quality applications enter a nightmare cycle of build, test, and repair that can include more than 50 builds. High-quality software, on the other hand, may need only 10 or fewer builds.

Counting builds and number of times the same test cases are run can provide useful data. Note also that it is significant to record information on defect test cases, which can be numerous and troublesome.

The Impact of High and Low Quality on Test Cases per Function Point

Another unexpected phenomenon when comparing high quality and low-quality software is the fact that high-quality software creates many more test cases than low-quality software. This fact by itself is not surprising, but the fact that high-quality testing costs are lower is surprising. Figure 7.15 shows the

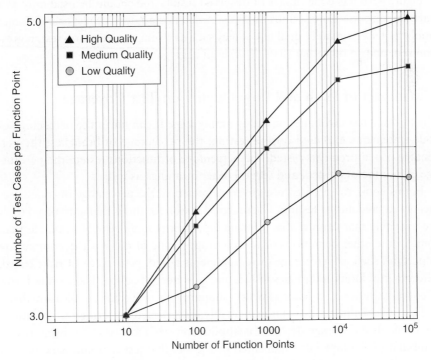

Figure 7.15   *Probable number of test cases per function point by application size and quality level (test stages include unit, function, regression, performance, system, etc.)*

number of test cases per function point typically created for all test stages in aggregate.

With high-quality software, formal mathematical methods can be used to create an optimal number of test cases that result in fairly high test coverage.

With low-quality software that is typically high in cyclomatic complexity and difficult to navigate, the structure prevents formal mathematical test case design from being fully deployed. Therefore, test case design uses ad hoc, informal methods.

Because it soon becomes obvious that effective testing of low-quality software might require an infinite number of test cases, the developers and testers tend to write test cases primarily for the major avenues of control flow and ignore the thousands of minor avenues. This kind of informal method of test case design usually results in a smaller number of test cases, but they tend to have low test coverage and are low in defect detection efficiency levels.

The Impact of High and Low Quality on Numbers of Test Cases Created

Figure 7.16 extends the data shown in Figure 7.15 and illustrates typical volumes of test cases for the sum of all test stages.

Figure 7.16 has wide ranges of observed results and should be used only as a starting point for more serious analysis. A detailed analysis of test case volumes would be based on individual test stages such as a unit test, function test, regression test, and so on rather than the overall aggregate.

The Impact of High and Low Quality on Test Coverage

The phrase "test coverage" is highly ambiguous. It can mean the percentage of code statements executed during testing; the percentage of branches; the percentage of requirements tested; the percentage of functions tested; the percentage of risk factors tested, and several other meanings as well.

In this book, the phrase "test coverage" refers to the percentage of code statements executed during testing. The practical reason for this is that automated tools are available that capture this information, so it is more readily available than some of the other definitions of test coverage. Some of the other definitions are important, such as percentage of requirements tested, percentage of risks tested, percentage of limits and ranges tested, and a number of others. These other forms of coverage, however, are not as widely supported by tools that can measure them.

Figure 7.17 illustrates what is probably an expected pattern by this point in the book. Test coverage declines as application size increases, due primarily to combinatorial complexity augmented by the fact that test case numbers rise at a steeper slope than code volume.

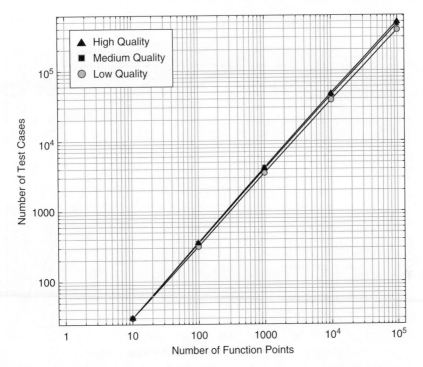

Figure 7.16   *Probable number of test cases by application size and quality level (tests are for unit test through system test)*

An interesting question would be: What combination of application size and cyclomatic complexity would permit 100% coverage? There is no definitive upper boundary to this question, but empirical observations indicate that 100% coverage has not been observed for applications larger than about 100 function points or 5,000 logical code statements where cyclomatic complexity rises above 5. The main issue that deals with coverage is not size per se, but size combined with cyclomatic complexity. For a cyclomatic complexity level of 1, applications of 10,000,000 source code statements could achieve 100% code coverage. However, as complexity rises, branches and paths increase rapidly. These branches tend to reduce code coverage.

An IBM group built a mathematical model that could predict the number of tests cases needed for 100% coverage. Above 10,000 function points the number of test cases approached infinity.

It may be that readers have noted different and hopefully better results. But such information is not readily accessible from either books or web sources.

Test coverage also declines for low-quality software, due primarily to poor code structure, high levels of cyclomatic complexity, and the probable presence of error-prone modules that are close to impossible to test thoroughly.

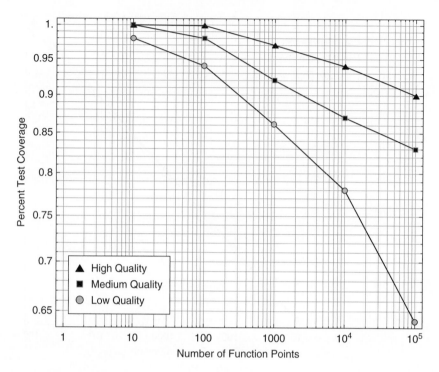

Figure 7.17 *Probable test coverage by application size and quality level (coverage = percent code executed during all test stages)*

The Impact of Professional Testers on High and Low Quality

Software testing can be performed by software developers, by trained software testers, or by both with developers handling unit testing and professional testers handling function tests, regression tests, and the other forms of testing that are based on multiple modules or components being tested concurrently.

Figure 7.18 shows the typical results noted among the authors' clients, but the figure is probably controversial. There are some companies where 100% of the testing is carried out by development (or maintenance) personnel and where professional test personnel are not even employed.

There are other companies in which almost 100% of testing is carried out by professional testers. These companies tend to build very large and very complex applications such as systems software, weapons systems, medical instruments, and the like. Even with professional testers, developers should still be thorough during unit testing and should also utilize static analysis tools and perhaps code inspections for mission-critical code modules.

The high percentage of testing noted for large applications in the 100,000 function point size range is due to the fact that only a very few companies and government agencies can even attempt projects in this size range.

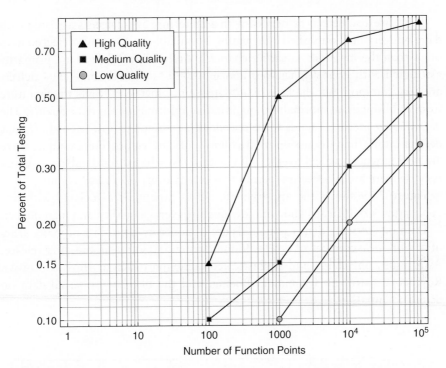

Figure 7.18 *Percent of total testing performed by professional testers (remainder of testing performed by developers or maintainers)*

Unless pretest inspections, static analysis, and multi-stage testing by professional testers are all employed, the odds of failure would be alarmingly close to 100%. In other words, untrained developers cannot successfully test large software applications, although they might do a creditable job for small applications up to perhaps 1,000 function points in size.

Among the authors' clients, the test groups staffed by trained professional test personnel average perhaps 3% to 5% higher for each testing stage than testing performed by developers, other than for unit testing.

Certified test personnel also seem to outperform uncertified test personnel, although poor measurement practices make this finding somewhat controversial. Much of the published data on testing does not distinguish between testing by certified or uncertified personnel.

The Impact of High and Low Quality on Software Defect Potentials

Readers may recall from earlier chapters that the term "defect potentials" refers to the sum total of defects found in requirements, design, source code, user documents, and bad fixes.

There are also defects associated with architecture and defects associated with data, but very little published information is available on these two defect sources other than the materials in earlier chapters. Architectural defects are primarily associated with large applications above 10,000 function points. Data defects are very common, but the lack of a "data point" metric prevents the literature from publishing any normalized quantitative information on data quality. The data quality literature tends to be anecdotal and emphasizes extremely serious defects rather than discussion total volumes of data errors. For example, there are no known statistical averages for data defects based on database volumes because there are no effective metrics that can quantify database "volumes."

Figure 7.19 shows the approximate defect potentials associated with five application size plateaus and with low quality, average quality, and high quality.

Data on software defect potentials are of necessity a product of many years of careful measurement of defects found during development and after release. As a result, only large and sophisticated companies such as IBM, Motorola, Raytheon, Northrup Grumman, Boeing, and the like have internal data on defect potentials.

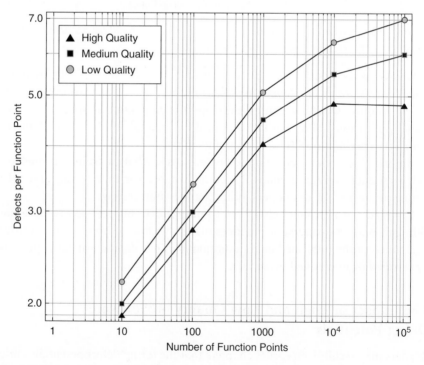

Figure 7.19   *Software defect potentials per function point*

As with many other factors, defect potentials increase as application sizes grow larger. Defect potentials are also much higher for projects in the low-quality column than for projects in the high-quality column.

For companies that create primarily small applications below 1,000 function points in size, it is important to note that individual human variances are a major contributor to defect potentials. Top-gun designers and programmers will create many fewer defects than novices.

For large systems in the 10,000 function point size range with teams of 100 people or more, the law of large numbers comes into play, and individual performance diminishes as a factor because the performance of large groups tends to hover around "average" even though there may be significant ranges within the group.

The Impact of High and Low Quality on Total Software Defects

Figure 7.20 extends the data in Figure 7.19 and shows the total volume of defects that might be encountered in requirements, design, source code, user documents, and bad fixes. The numbers will seem alarmingly big to some readers.

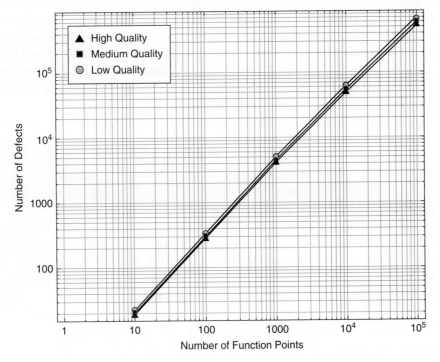

Figure 7.20 *Software defect potentials by application size and quality level (defects: requirements, design, code, documents, bad fixes)*

Figure 7.20 deals with defects that range from severity 1 through severity 4. Figure 7.20 also deals with defects in multiple work products such as design as well as code.

If only high-severity coding defects were included, then the defect potential for a high-quality application of 10,000 function points would be only about 5,000 defects instead of 45,100. Because 10,000 function points are equal to around 500,000 logical code statements in a language such as Java, a total of 5,000 code defects is equivalent to about 1 serious code defect for every 100 code statements.

Readers should note that the defect potential refers to the total defects encountered. Prior to delivery, more than 90% will probably be found and removed. Data on defect detection efficiency (DDE) and defect removal efficiency (DRE) are discussed in the next two figures.

The Impact of High and Low Quality on Defect Detection Efficiency (DDE)

Figure 7.21 deals with one of the more important quality factors: defect detection efficiency. During inspections, static analysis, and testing there will, of course, be many defects discovered. After all of the defect removal activities are complete and the software is delivered, users will also find and report defects.

Defect detection efficiency is measured by accumulating all defects found internally, adding the defects reported by users in the first 90 days, and then calculating the percentage of defects detected prior to delivery. If developers and testers found 900 defects and users reported 100 in the first three months, then defect detection efficiency would be 90%.

As might be expected, DDE goes down as application size goes up. There are also very significant differences between low-quality and high-quality projects.

Note that DDE is not the same as defect removal efficiency (DRE). Some detected defects will not be repaired until after software applications are delivered. This is due in part to wanting to speed up delivery and in part to letting users work as a surrogate for repairing defects.

The range between DDE and DRE seems to be broadening. In the 1970s software was seldom released with more than perhaps a dozen detected defects that had not been repaired, and these were detected during the final week prior to shipment. Today in 2011 some large applications are delivered with hundreds of known defects that have not been repaired.

The Impact of High Quality and Low Quality on Defect Removal Efficiency (DRE)

Defect removal efficiency (DRE) is probably the single most important quality metric. Its importance is due to the fact that DRE has strong correlations to

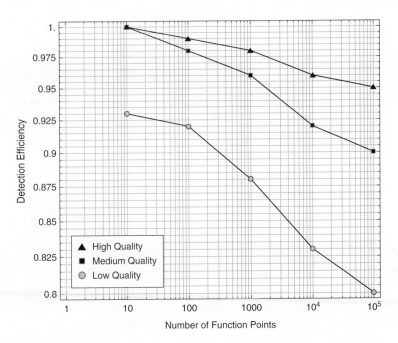

Figure 7.21 *Software Defect Detection Efficiency (DDE) (defects: requirements, design, code, document, bad fixes)*

reliability, to user satisfaction, and to the odds of litigation occurring for contract projects. Figure 7.22 shows ranges of DRE by application size and by high-, average-, and low-quality ranges.

Observant readers will note that defect removal efficiency is always lower than defect detection efficiency. Toward the end of a final test cycle, defects will be discovered, but project managers make a business decision to delay fixing some of them until after delivery.

Delays in fixing known defects are a hazardous practice. But, unfortunately, the gap between detected defects and removed defects is probably larger today than it was in 1980 before personal computers emerged as a major market.

Mainframe companies such as IBM tended to be very careful in fixing known defects prior to release. The personal computer software makers are not so careful. For that matter, large mainframe vendors such as ERP companies also ship software with thousands of latent defects, although only a small percentage of those were known prior to release.

The Impact of High and Low Quality on Total Defect Removal

Figure 7.23 extends the data from Figure 7.22 and shows the total probable number of defects removed prior to delivery of the software to customers.

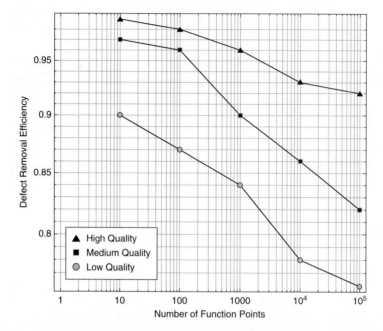

Figure 7.22 *Software Defect Removal Efficiency (DRE) (defects: requirements, design, code, documents, bad fixes)*

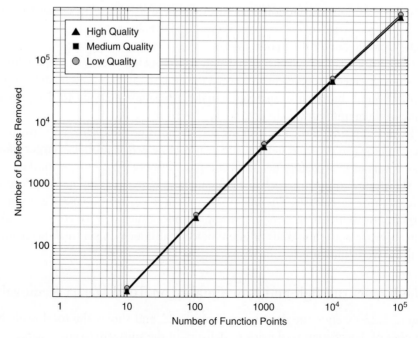

Figure 7.23 *Defects removed before release by application size and quality level*

It should be apparent from Figure 7.23 why finding and fixing defects is such a major cost driver for large software applications for projects with greater than 10,000 function points.

The Impact of High and Low Quality on Defects Delivered to Customers

Figure 7.24 illustrates one of the central issues of software quality: the large numbers of latent defects that are still present in the software when it is delivered to customers or users.

For really large applications of greater than 10,000 function points in size, even high-quality software still contains significant volumes of latent defects at delivery.

The Impact of High and Low Quality on Delivered Defects per Function Point

Figure 7.25 converts the data from Figure 7.24 into normalized form and shows the numbers of latent defects per function point upon delivery to customers.

Currently in 2011 based on data collected by the authors, the approximate average number of latent defects per function point is about 0.75. As can be

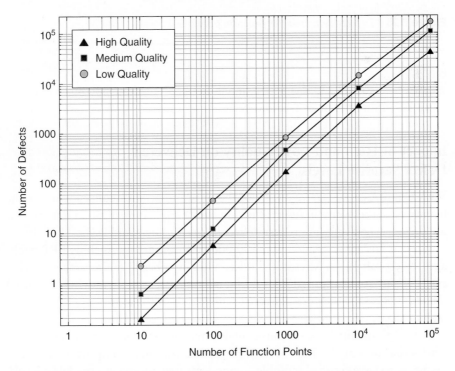

Figure 7.24 *Defects delivered by application size and quality level*

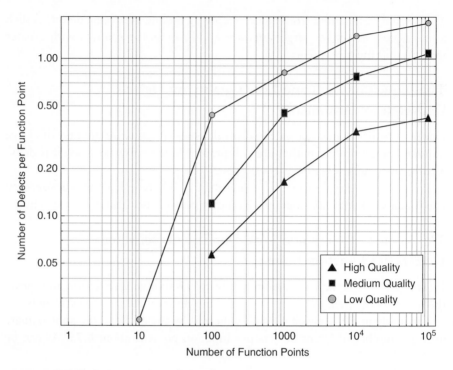

Figure 7.25   *Defects delivered per function point*

seen from Figure 7.25, the best is much better than that, but the worst is a much larger number of delivered defects.

Impact of High and Low Quality on Delivered Defect Severity Levels

With Figure 7.26 we arrive at one of the most important quality factors in the history of the software industry: the number of high-severity latent defects that are present when software is first delivered to customers and users.

Quite a few large systems top 100,000 function points, such as ERP packages, Microsoft Vista, Microsoft Office, and a number of mainframe operating systems and applications. It should be no surprise to readers who have used those systems that they are delivered with significant numbers of high-severity latent defects.

Even high-quality large systems contain latent defects that can be troublesome. This situation can be improved slightly, but for major improvements it is necessary to have certified reusable components that approach zero defect levels.

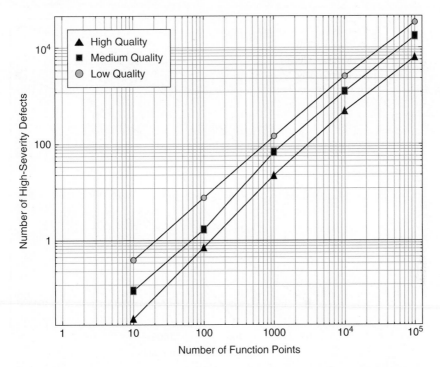

Figure 7.26   *High-severity defects delivered (severity 1 and severity 2 on the IBM severity scale)*

Note that low-quality software has about 5.8 times more high-severity defects than high-quality software and almost twice as many high-severity defects as average software. Today's state-of-the-art software quality-control techniques are very good, but even they have trouble with large systems greater than 10,000 function points.

The Impact of High and Low Quality on Severe Defects per Function Point

When delivered high-severity defects are normalized to "defects per function point," it is necessary to use several decimal places to show the results for small applications. Indeed, the International Software Benchmark Standards Group (ISBSG) normalizes to a base of 100 function points. They report delivered defects after only one month instead of the 90-day interval used in this book. Therefore, the volume of defects reported by ISBSG is only about one-third (or less) than the volumes shown in this book.

Because Figure 7.27 includes defects that are in documents and HELP screens as well as code defects, normalization to defects per KLOC or code volumes would not be suitable.

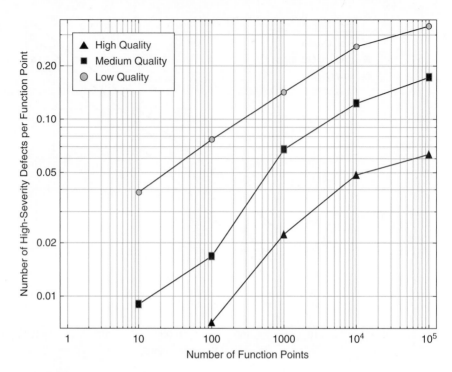

Figure 7.27   *High-severity defects delivered per function point (severity 1 and severity 2 on the IBM severity scale)*

The Impact of High and Low Quality on Software Reliability

Those who have measured software reliability know that it is a complicated and ambiguous topic. In this book, "reliability" is defined as the mean time to failure (MTTF) on the first day of production, that is, after installation and tuning are complete.

Obviously, many defects will be encountered for large systems when they are first installed and especially if they require modifications or tuning. Therefore, Figure 7.28 bypasses installation and uses the first day of actual customer usage.

It would probably be best to use average results over a longer time period, but such data is not readily available.

Note that small applications can sometimes operate around the clock directly after being installed, but large systems typically encounter defects in fewer than 24 hours of continuous usage. The majority will be severity 3 and 4 defects, but, of course, high-severity defects do occur.

Already cited were defects in the installation procedure of an office suite that triggered more than 10,000 defect reports on the first day of the release. This defect was only one bug, but it was a severity-1 bug found by all clients more or less simultaneously.

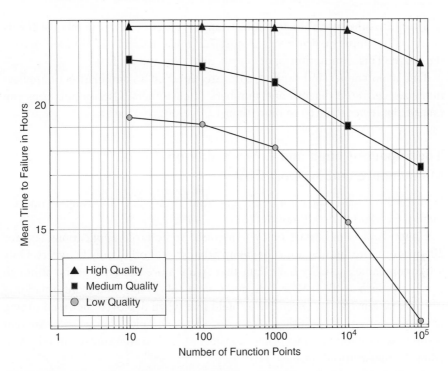

Figure 7.28 *Reliability in Mean Time to Failure (MTTF) at deployment of release (24 hours = maximum time to failure)*

The Impact of High and Low Quality on Maintenance and Support

In this book, the terms "maintenance," "support," and "enhancement" are not the same. Due to a custom that originated in IBM, the word maintenance is restricted to defect repairs. The word support is defined as responding to telephone and email requests for assistance, and the term enhancement is defined as adding new features, either due to explicit customer requests or due to changes in hardware platforms or some external event such as changes in federal laws.

In the software literature the term maintenance is often used as an umbrella that combines all three activities. This is not really a good idea for economic studies because the funding for defect repairs, the funding for support, and the funding for enhancements can be quite different.

Defect repairs are normally charged to the software development and maintenance organizations. Enhancements are normally paid for by clients. Support can either be free of charge or based on a cost-per-incident, which occurs with some commercial applications.

Figure 7.29 shows the approximate combined effort for maintenance and support for five years.

There are other variables that affect support costs, such as numbers of clients or users. To simplify calculations, Figure 7.29 assumes a flat 1,000 users across, the board. This assumption is, of course, arbitrary and artificial.

True maintenance and support costs are based on a combination of application size, delivered defects, and numbers of customers. User populations can range from fewer than 10 to more than 1,000,000.

The Impact of High and Low Quality on Maintenance and Support Costs

Figure 7.30 extends the effort numbers from Figure 7.29 by using a constant total of $10,000 per staff month.

Figure 7.30 is only part of the equation. Some large applications last for 20 years or more, and Figure 7.30 has an arbitrary cut off of only five years. Only a few companies actually have data that spans more than five years, although companies such as IBM, Microsoft, and Oracle collect this kind of information.

Large systems are so expensive to build that when deployed they tend to stay in service many years past their prime. As a few examples of large software that is still in service long past its prime, consider U.S. air traffic control and the Veterans Administration's medical records.

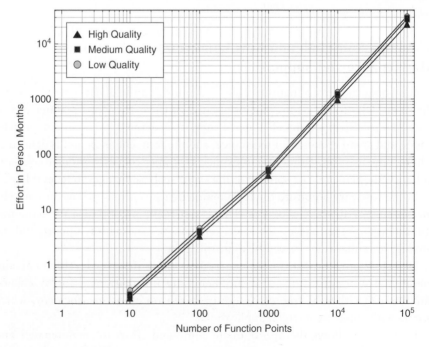

Figure 7.29   *Maintenance and support effort for five years of usage*

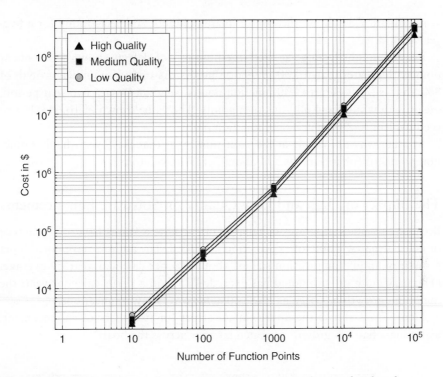

Figure 7.30   *Maintenance and support costs for five years of usage (burdened cost = $10,000 per staff month; 1,000 users)*

The Impact of High and Low Quality on Maintenance Defect Volumes

When software is initially released, that is not the end of the story. There will be a continuous stream of enhancements for as long as the software remains in use. Among the authors' clients, enhancements average about 8% per calendar year, using the number of function points as the basis of comparison.

For example, an application of 1,000 function points at delivery will grow by about 80 function points per calendar. (Application growth does not match the assumptions of compound interest. Usually every year adds roughly the same amount of new features, although there can be exceptions to this rule such as a "mid-life kicker" for commercial packages to attract new users.)

The reasons for continuous growth vary widely. Some are due to changes in external business factors, some are due to new technologies that need to be included, and some are due to competitors adding new features to their own software.

These functional additions will, of course, add new defects. Also some of the original latent defects from the first release may not be discovered for several years. Figure 7.31 shows the approximate numbers of defects found for a five-year period.

Readers might wonder at the large numbers of defects shown for applications with greater than 10,000 function points. Assuming an annual growth of 8%, that is equivalent to 800 function points per year. Over a five-year period, the growth would be 4,000 function points. The value shown of 10,643 defects is equivalent to 2.62 defects per function point.

Another way of looking at the same number is that every year the 800 function points of enhancements add about 2,129 new defects.

The Impact of High and Low Quality on Software Enhancements

Because this book separates enhancements or new features from maintenance or defect repairs, a note of explanation is needed. The authors have noted a net growth in annual application size of about 8% per calendar year on average. (The maximum growth noted has exceeded 15% in a single calendar year; the minimum growth has been as low as 0% for a very few applications.)

Figure 7.32 shows the approximate effort for five years of enhancement, assuming a flat 8% growth per calendar year across the board.

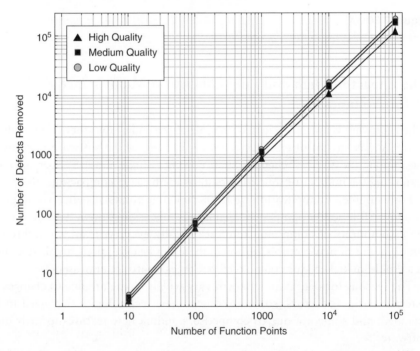

Figure 7.31 *Defects removed during five years of usage (assumes 1,000 users of the software for five years)*

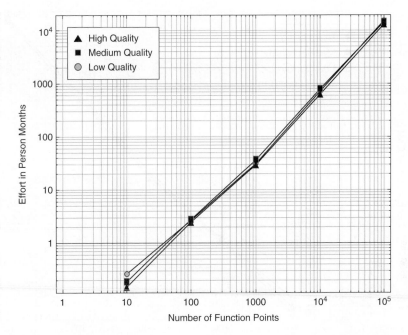

Figure 7.32 *Enhancement effort during five years of usage (assumes 8% growth per year in effort)*

Note that productivity rates for these enhancements are similar to those shown earlier in Figure 7.6 for new development. In other words, it is easier to enhance high-quality software applications than low-quality, assuming the same volume of enhancements.

The actual costs of enhancements are determined by the size of the enhancements themselves, the size and complexity of the applications being enhanced, the methods and processes used, as well as a number of other factors.

A somewhat surprising finding is that productivity rates tend to peak for software updates that are about 3% of the size of the original application. For larger updates the changes tend to cause many internal modifications to the legacy application, which slows things down. For smaller updates, the reason for low productivity lies in the overhead costs of having to regression test the entire package to be sure that even very small changes have not caused harm. Possibly by chance updates in the range of 3% often add specific new features that do not require a great deal of internal modification to the underlying legacy code.

The Impact of High and Low Quality on Enhancement Costs

Figure 7.33 extends the information shown in Figure 7.32 using a flat rate of $10,000 per staff month, using constant dollars that excludes inflation.

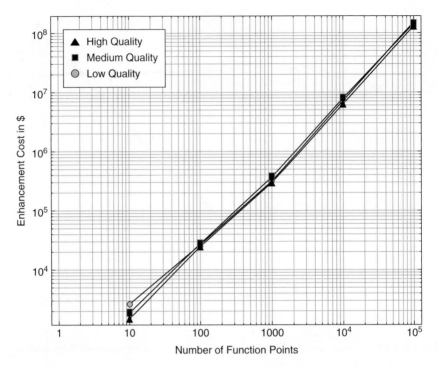

Figure 7.33   *Enhancement costs for five years of usage (burdened cost = $10,000 per staff month; 1,000 users)*

Over long periods of time, numerous small changes to software applications degrade their original structures and raise cyclomatic complexity levels. For example, if an application is released with an average cyclomatic complexity level of 10, within a five-year period assuming normal bug repairs and functional updates, average cyclomatic complexity might rise to 13.

It is interesting that the rate of entropy increase, or the increase in cyclomatic complexity, seems to be proportional to the starting value. Applications that are high in complexity when released will experience much faster rates of entropy or structural decay than applications put into production with low complexity levels.

The Impact of High and Low Software Quality on Maintenance and Enhancement Staffing

In many companies and government groups, maintenance (defect repairs) and enhancements (new features) are carried out by the same groups. In other companies, maintenance is performed by separate teams, and enhancements are performed by development teams.

Because both maintenance and enhancements are concerned with modifying the same existing legacy applications, it is convenient to aggregate the staffing for both forms of work.

Figure 7.34 shows the approximate staffing needed for five years of continuous updates for both maintenance and enhancements.

As a general rule, maintenance and enhancements are performed by smaller teams than original development. This is due to the fact that some occupation groups such as architects may not be involved. While business analysts, software engineers, and test personnel will obviously be involved, sometimes ancillary personnel such as quality assurance do not participate in maintenance and perhaps not in enhancements, other than really major changes with external business significance.

The Impact of High and Low Quality on Total Effort for Five Years

At this point the structures of the figures change. Figure 7.35(a–e) shows the combined effort for original development, maintenance (bug repairs), and enhancements (new features) for a five-year period.

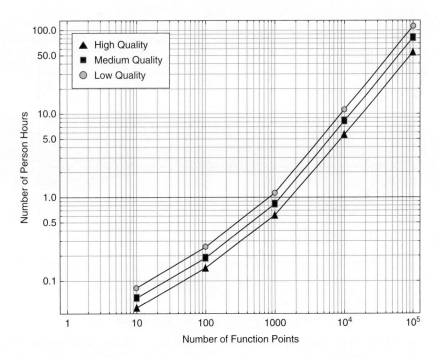

Figure 7.34 *Maintenance and enhancement staffing for five years usage (maintenance, test, integration, documents, and management)*

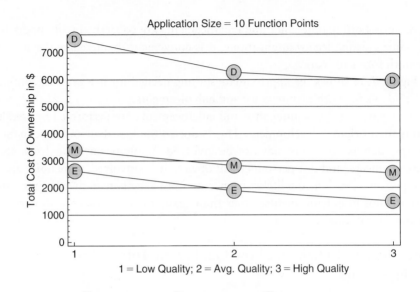

Figure 7.35a   *Total effort for development and five years of usage for application size of 10 function points*

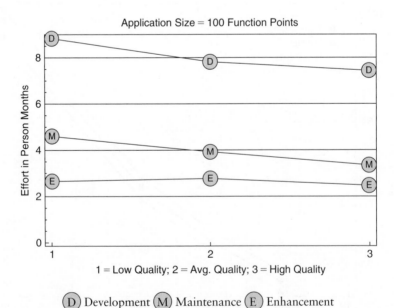

Figure 7.35b   *Total effort for development and five years of usage for application size of 100 function points*

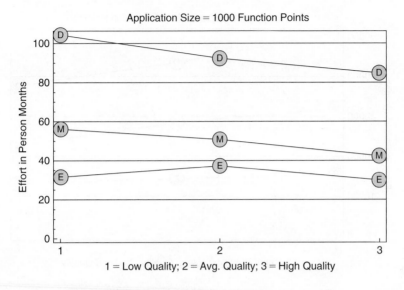

Figure 7.35c   *Total effort for development and five years of usage for application size of 1,000 function points*

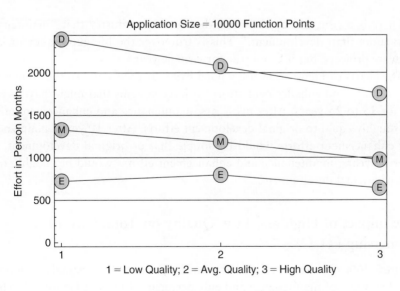

Figure 7.35d   *Total effort for development and five years of usage for application size of 10,000 function points*

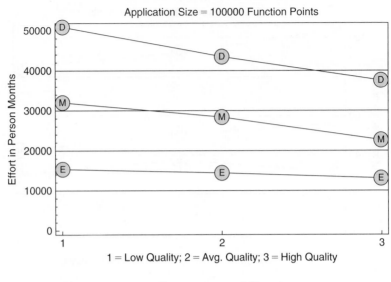

Figure 7.35e   *Total effort for development and five years of usage for application size of 100,000 function points*

There is a common aphorism in the software industry that "maintenance costs more than development." This is true over the life expectancy of large software projects, but it is not true for a single year.

The charts of Figure 7.35 use a fixed five-year time span, so they understate maintenance and enhancement effort for large systems that might have been in use for 15 to 25 years. After five years, maintenance and enhancement efforts are roughly equal to original development efforts. After 10 years, maintenance and enhancement efforts would be double that of original development, and after 15 years, maintenance and enhancement efforts would be roughly triple that of original development.

The Impact of High and Low Quality on Total Cost of Ownership (TCO)

Figure 7.36(a–e) shows total cost of ownership (TCO) for original development plus five years of maintenance and enhancement. Note that Figure 7.36 charts show only software costs and do not include factors such as hardware acquisitions or the leases for COTS packages. Figure 7.36 depictions are an extension of the data shown in the graphs of Figure 7.35, using a flat $10,000 per staff month and constant dollars without inflation.

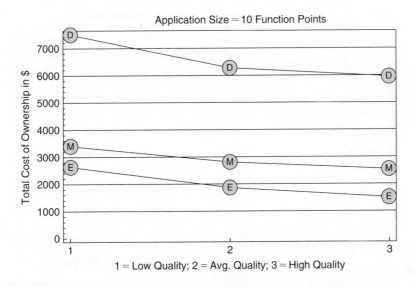

Figure 7.36a   *Total Cost of Ownership (TCO) for development and five years of usage and application size of 10 function points (burdened cost = $10,000 per staff month; 1,000 users)*

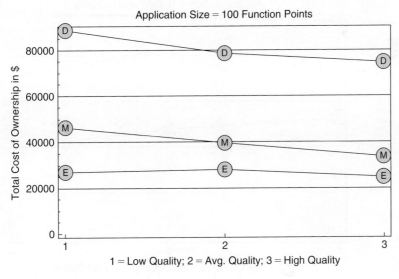

Figure 7.36b   *Total Cost of Ownership (TCO) for development and five years of usage and application size of 100 function points (burdened cost = $10,000 per staff month; 1,000 users)*

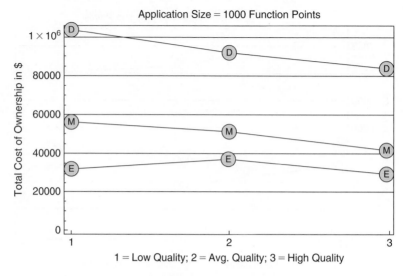

Figure 7.36c   *Total Cost of Ownership (TCO) for development and five years of usage and application size of 1,000 function points (burdened cost = $10,000 per staff month; 1,000 users)*

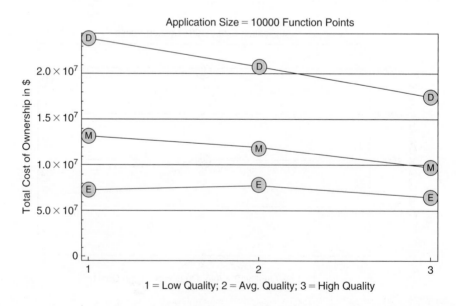

Figure 7.36d   *Total Cost of Ownership (TCO) for development and five years of usage and application size of 10,000 function points (burdened cost = $10,000 per staff month; 1,000 users)*

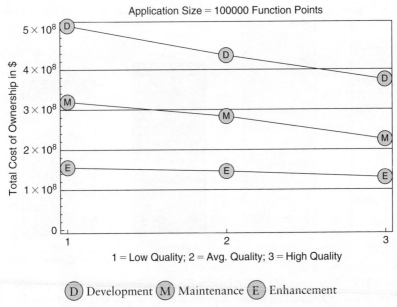

Figure 7.36e *Total Cost of Ownership (TCO) for development and five years of usage and application size of 100,000 function points (burdened cost = $10,000 per staff month; 1,000 users)*

Even though the charts of Figures 7.36 are limited to a five-year period, it is alarming that the TCO of poor-quality software applications in the 100,000 function point size range tops a billion dollars. It is no wonder that the CEOs of major corporations do not have a high regard for their software organizations. We have too many failures, too many delays, too many cost overruns, and software quality levels that are embarrassingly poor.

The Impact of High and Low Quality on Cost of Quality (COQ)

Figure 7.37(a–j) extracts information from earlier figures and attempts to show the cost of quality (COQ) as a percentage of total cost of ownership (TCO). The COQ information in the Figure 7.37 bar charts combine pretest inspections, static analysis, all forms of testing, and post-release defect repairs.

There are wide ranges in the results shown in Figures 7.37. Some large systems have COQ costs that top 50% of total costs of ownership. Even the high-quality applications average about $.15 spent out of every dollar for finding and fixing bugs.

High COQ costs are endemic in the software industry and will stay higher than desirable for the indefinite future as long as software applications are

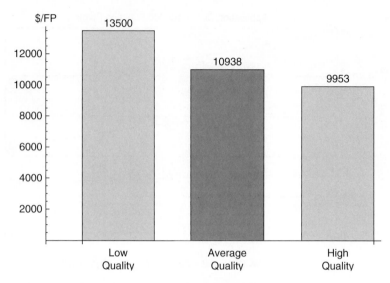

Figure 7.37a *Total Cost of Ownership for development and five years of usage for application size of 10 function points (burdened cost = $10,000 per staff month; 1,000 users)*

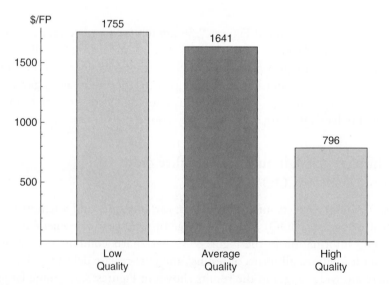

Figure 7.37b *Cost of Quality for development and five years of usage for application size of 10 function points (burdened cost = $10,000 per staff month; 1,000 users)*

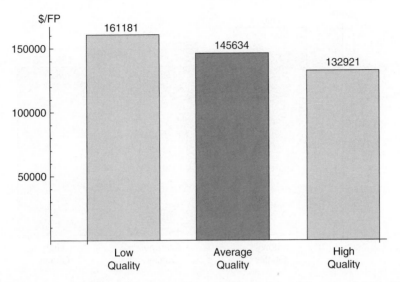

Figure 7.37c *Total Cost of Ownership for development and five years of usage for application size of 100 function points (burdened cost = $10,000 per staff month; 1,000 users)*

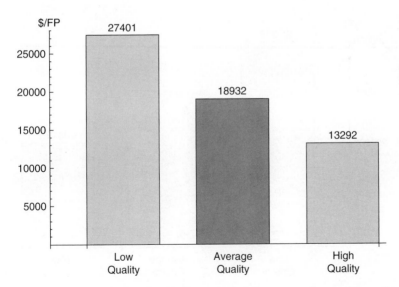

Figure 7.37d *Cost of Quality for development and five years of usage for application size of 100 function points (burdened cost = $10,000 per staff month; 1,000 users)*

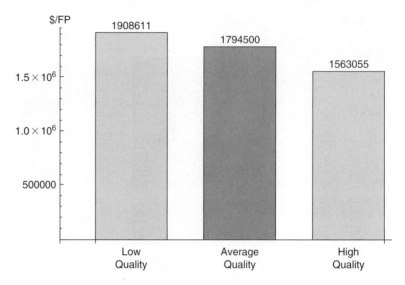

Figure 7.37e   *Total Cost of Ownership for development and five years of usage for application size of 1,000 function points (burdened cost = $10,000 per staff month; 1,000 users)*

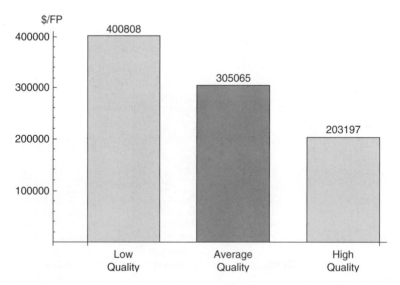

Figure 7.37f   *Cost of Quality for development and five years of usage for application size of 1,000 function points (burdened cost = $10,000 per staff month; 1,000 users)*

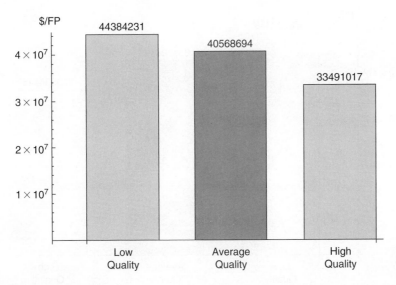

Figure 7.37g *Total Cost of Ownership for development and five years of usage for application size of 10,000 function points (burdened cost = $10,000 per staff month; 1,000 users)*

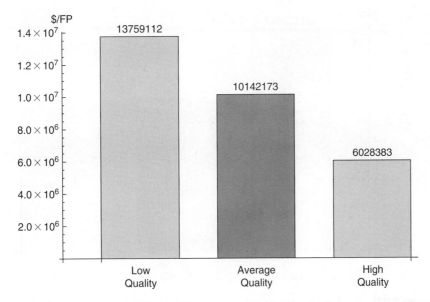

Figure 7.37h *Cost of Quality for development and five years of usage for application size of 10,000 function points (burdened cost = $10,000 per staff month; 1,000 users)*

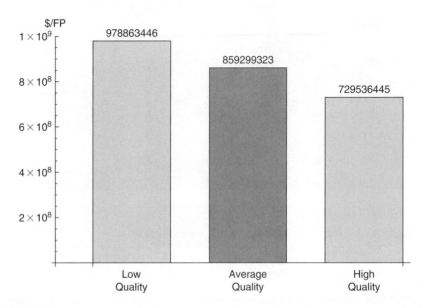

Figure 7.37i   *Total Cost of Ownership for development and five years of usage for application size of 100,000 function points (burdened cost = $10,000 per staff month; 1,000 users)*

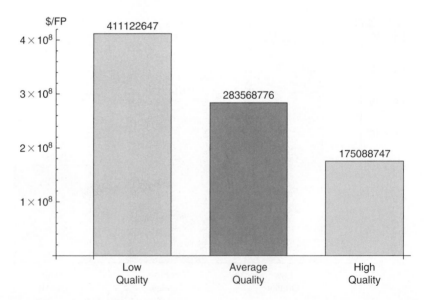

Figure 7.37j   *Cost of Quality for development and five years of usage for application size of 100,000 function points (burdened cost = $10,000 per staff month; 1,000 users)*

custom-designed and hand-coded. Only the large-scale deployment of certified reusable materials that approach zero defects can bring COQ costs down to a 5% level, which should probably be the goal for the software industry between 2011 and 2025.

The Impact of High and Low Quality on TCO and COQ per Function Point

Figure 7.38(a–j) extends the results of the graphs of Figure 7.37 and expresses the results in terms of cost per function point.

The charts of Figure 7.37 use a flat rate of $10,000 per staff month and exclude inflation. They also normalize the data to the size of the application at delivery, rather than including the size growth due to five years of enhancements.

The Impact of High and Low Quality on the Useful Life of Applications

Figure 7.39 attempts to show troublesome areas of the software industry: How long is the useful life of a software application after it is deployed?

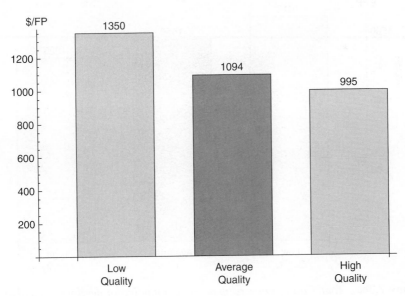

Figure 7.38a *Total Cost of Ownership per function point for development and five years of usage for application size of 10 function points (function point size at initial delivery is assumed)*

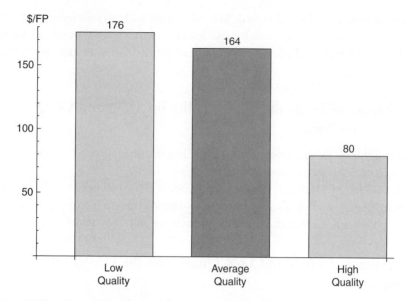

Figure 7.38b   *Cost of Quality per function point for development and five years of usage for application size of 10 function points (function point size at initial delivery is assumed)*

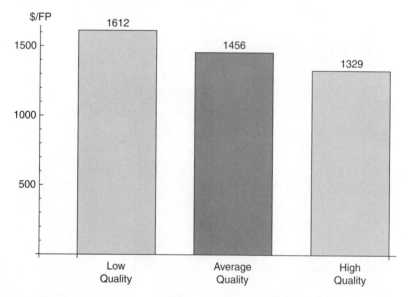

Figure 7.38c   *Total Cost of Ownership per function point for development and five years of usage for application size of 100 function points (function point size at initial delivery is assumed)*

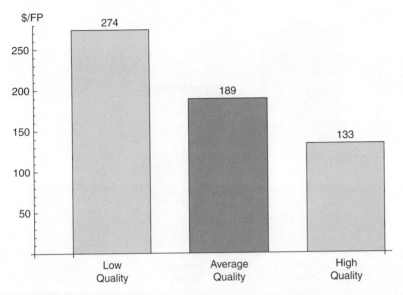

Figure 7.38d   *Cost of Quality per function point for development and five years of usage for application size of 100 function points (function point size at initial delivery is assumed)*

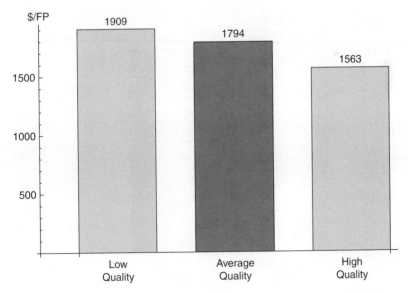

Figure 7.38e   *Total Cost of Ownership per function point for development and five years of usage for application size of 1,000 function points (function point size at initial delivery is assumed)*

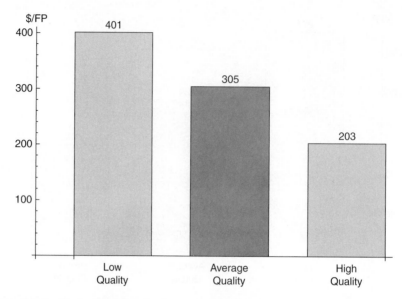

Figure 7.38f   *Cost of Quality per function point for development and five years of usage for application size of 1,000 function points (function point size at initial delivery is assumed)*

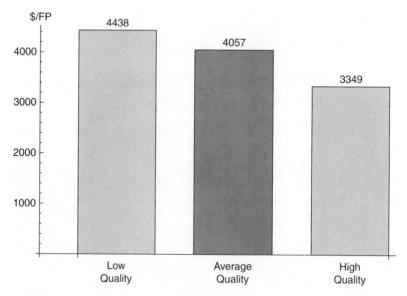

Figure 7.38g   *Total Cost of Ownership per function point for development and five years of usage for application size of 10,000 function points (function point size at initial delivery is assumed)*

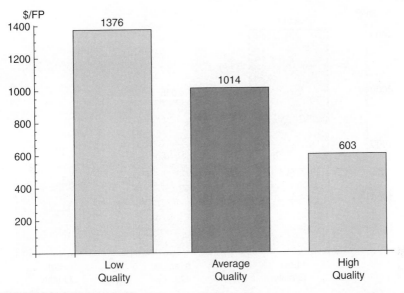

Figure 7.38h   *Cost of Quality per function point for development and five years of usage for application size of 10,000 function points (function point size at initial delivery is assumed)*

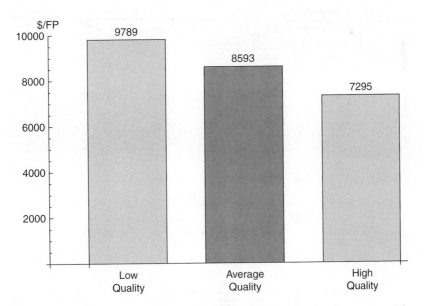

Figure 7.38i   *Total Cost of Ownership per function point for development and five years of usage for application size of 100,000 function points (function point size at initial delivery is assumed)*

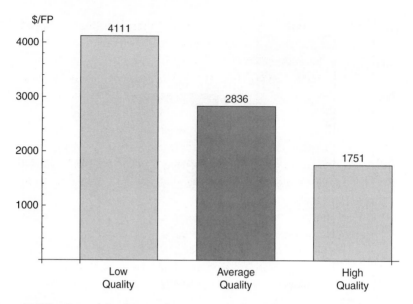

Figure 7.38j   *Cost of Quality per function point for development and five years of usage for application size of 100,000 function points (function point size at initial delivery is assumed)*

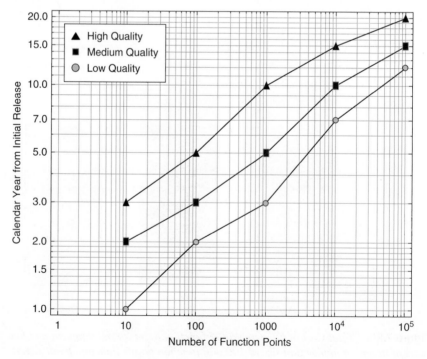

Figure 7.39   *Approximate useful life before replacement or major renovation*

Small applications are easily replaceable and therefore often are phased out after a year or two. Consider how often personal applications such as antivirus packages or personal financial packages are replaced by new versions.

Large systems, on the other hand, are so expensive and take so many years to develop that they are very difficult to replace. As a result, many large applications are kept in service well past their period of optimum value.

Because entropy or structural decay is proportional to initial levels of cyclomatic complexity and initial quality, annual effort devoted to maintenance and enhancements for low-quality applications will be very costly initially, and the costs will increase every year. Unfortunately, the high cost of replacing large applications tends to keep them in use longer than desirable.

To make an analogy, a large poor-quality application is like a house built with substandard components. As time passes the furnace might fail, the roof might leak, and the walls might crack due to settling. But there is little choice for the homeowner but to continue with repairs because the cost of replacing the house with a new one would be untenable.

The Impact of High and Low Quality on Software Application Tangible Value

Figure 7.40 deals with a highly complex issue with many variables: the initial tangible value of software when it is first being considered for funding. The funding might be for in-house development, for outsource development, or perhaps for funding by a venture capitalist to create a commercial application.

Figure 7.40 depicts applications that are planned for internal use rather than for commercial sale. The reason for this is that a $10,000 smart phone applet might perhaps generate more than $1,000,000 in revenue.

Internal applications have value primarily because they reduce operating costs or because they raise revenue expectations.

From observations of funding decisions in large companies, there is a tendency to understate probable development costs by perhaps 50% and to overstate anticipated value by perhaps 30%.

What Figure 7.40 illustrates is the probable minimum value to meet normal ROI expectations of more than $3.00 in savings or revenue for every $1.00 expended. Because most companies naively assume best-case development costs, Figure 7.40 is based on a high-quality scenario. Figure 7.40 also uses total cost of ownership as the value target, not just development.

Note that Figure 7.40 uses high-quality results throughout because most companies naively expect such results. Even if companies attempt worst-case scenarios, they tend toward optimism rather than toward actual historical results.

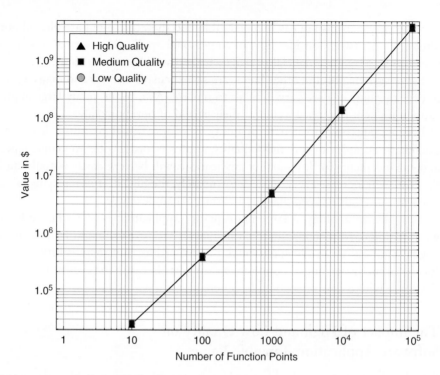

Figure 7.40 *Probable financial value of application to receive initial funding (value assumes five years of usage; 1,000 users)*

The Impact of High and Low Quality on Return on Investment (ROI)

Figure 7.41 compares the probable value data from Figure 7.40 against the TCO data from the charts of Figure 7.37. What Figure 7.41 shows is that high-quality software returns greater value than either average-quality or low-quality software.

Note that Figure 7.41 shows only software that is completed, deployed, and actually put to use. If cancelled projects were included, the ROI of the entire software organization might switch from positive to negative if they had attempted to build large applications that failed.

Figure 7.41 concentrates on operational cost reductions and internal value such as greater speed and higher capacity. Commercial software that is marketed or leased could return enormous values, as shown by applications such as Microsoft Windows, the Google browser, and hundreds of successful applications for personal computers, smart phones, and other devices.

Although software that is completed and put to use tends to generate positive return on investment, cancelled projects do not. They generate losses and

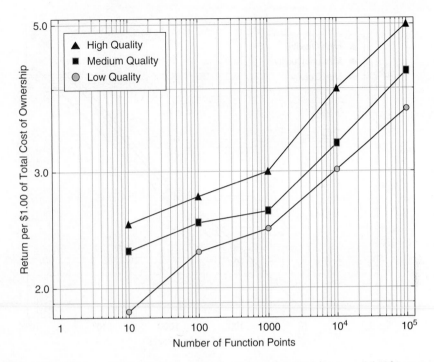

Figure 7.41   *Return on Investment (ROI) for released applications used for five years (Note: High-volume commercial software exceeds these values.)*

negative return on investment. A single cancelled project of 100,000 function points can negate the efforts of more than 1,000 people who worked for more than five years!

The Impact of High and Low Quality on the Costs of Cancelled Projects

Figure 7.42 shows the probable financial losses associated with cancelled projects of various sizes. Recall that low-quality large applications with greater than 10,000 function points are normally late and at the point of cancellation, so they cost more than completed applications.

High-quality projects, on the other hand, are normally cancelled due to external business reasons and therefore are usually cancelled much earlier than low-quality projects.

The costs and stigma of major projects cancelled for cause erode the value of entire software organizations. Indeed, a major impetus for switching over from internal development to outsource development is having too many cancelled projects by the internal software teams.

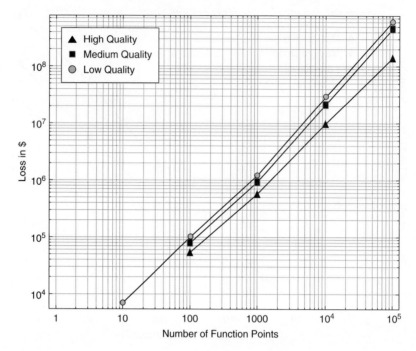

Figure 7.42   *Financial losses on cancelled software projects (assumes total expenses from project start to point of cancellation; low-quality cancellations cost more than high-quality completions)*

The Impact of High and Low Quality on Cancellation Cost Differentials

Figure 7.43 compares the cost of cancelled projects for low-quality, average-quality, and high-quality projects.

This figure shows one of the more significant economic differences between the polar opposites of high quality and low quality. Low-quality software cancellations for large applications rank among the most costly forms of business failures in the twenty-first century.

Large poor-quality projects are usually cancelled for cause due to schedule overruns, cost overruns, or the prognosis of excessive defects after deployment. High-quality projects are usually cancelled for business reasons and therefore are not late and over budget at the point of cancellation.

The Distribution of High-, Average-, and Low-Quality Software Projects

Figure 7.44 shows the approximate distribution of about 13,000 software projects examined between 1973 and 2010 in terms of quality levels. It is

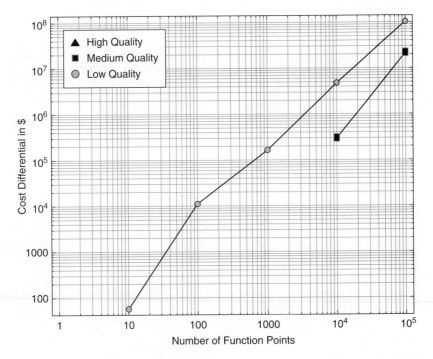

Figure 7.43 *Cost differential between cancelled and completed projects of the same size (cost of completed projects subtracted from cost of cancelled projects; low-quality cancellations cost more than high-quality completions)*

interesting that overall quality levels have not changed much, although the best results are higher in 2010 due to static analysis and mathematical test case design methods.

For small applications below 100 function points, the results approximate a normal bell-shaped curve with about as many high-quality projects as low-quality projects. But as applications grow larger, the distribution changes ominously. There are very few high-quality software projects in the size ranges larger than 10,000 function points.

For small projects in which coding is the major form of work, there are many different quality methods available that are widely known and used, such as debugging tools, static analysis tools, and test tools.

As applications grow in size, coding diminishes in terms of the overall cost of development. Defects begin to increase in requirements, architecture, and design. Bad-fix injections or secondary defects increase; error-prone modules begin to occur, and higher levels of cyclomatic complexity tend to drive up coding defects and make them harder to eliminate.

There is comparatively poor understanding of effective quality measures that work well for large applications. The net result is that quality results shift from

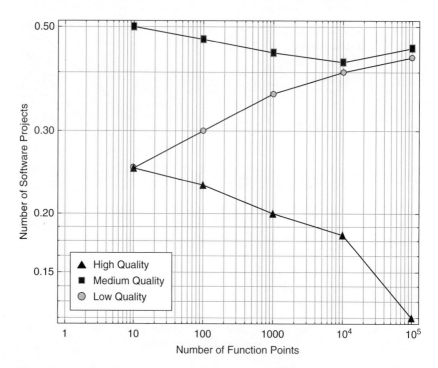

Figure 7.44   *Distribution of software projects by quality levels (n = approximately 13,000 software projects)*

the high-quality column to the low-quality column. Instead of a bell-shaped curve, large applications above 10,000 function points in size are strongly skewed toward poor quality.

Overall, there are about twice as many low-quality projects as high-quality projects. Even worse, for applications with greater than 10,000 function points in size, there are more than three times as many low-quality projects as high-quality.

For the software industry to achieve a professional status equal to that of electrical engineering, mechanical engineering, aeronautical engineering, and other older forms of engineering, we need to achieve higher quality levels at all size plateaus and especially so for massive applications (> 10,000 function points).

The best available quality results in 2011 are very good, but they are not well understood nor widely deployed because of, for one reason, the incorrect belief that high quality is expensive. High-quality software is not expensive. High-quality software is faster and cheaper to build and maintain than low-quality software, from initial development all the way through total cost of ownership.

Summary and Conclusions on the Economics of Software Quality

Because of the usefulness of considering polar opposites, consider the probable outcomes of a high-quality software application and a low-quality application. Because 10,000 function points is the size where troubles tend to become very serious, that is a good plateau to consider. Also assume 1,000 users of the software, and to complete the economic picture, assume that 1,000 companies are clients of the organization that build the software. We also assume a flat $10,000 per month for costs. This is equal to $454.54 per day for 22 work days per month at $56.81 per hour.

High-Quality Results for 10,000 Function Points

Using data from the figures in Chapter 7 plus some additional assumptions on usage patterns, the high-quality version of the application would have resembled the following pattern:

Development schedule	27 calendar months
Development staffing	57 personnel
Development effort	1,748 staff months
Development productivity	5.72 function points per staff month
Total Cost of Ownership (TCO)	$33,491,017

After the high-quality software is deployed and 1,000 people begin to use it, the following results are anticipated:

Hours application is used per day	4 hours per day
Labor savings from application use	1 hour per day compared to prior methods
Savings per day from application use	$56.81 per user per day
Savings per day for 1,000 users	$56,810
Cost savings per year	$12,498,200
Cost savings for five years	$62,491,000

Clients previously served per day	12
Clients served due to the software	14
Daily revenue per client	$1,000
Increase in revenue per day per worker	$100
Increase in revenue per year	$22,000,000
Increase in revenue for five years	$110,000,000
Total value for five years	$172,491,000
Total Cost of Ownership for five years	– $33,491,017
Net Value	$138,999,983
Return on Investment	$5.15

Although the example is largely hypothetical, it shows that high-quality software can combine low total costs of ownership with reduced operating costs and also with revenue increases.

Low-Quality Results for 10,000 Function Points

Using identical assumptions for numbers of users and clients and costs, consider what the results might be for low-quality software that serves the same business purposes as the previous high-quality example:

Development schedule	36 calendar months
Development staffing	75 personnel
Development effort	2,393 staff months
Development productivity	4.18 function points per staff month
Total Cost of Ownership (TCO)	$47,255,247

When the low-quality software is deployed and 1,000 people begin to use it, the following results are anticipated:

Hours application is used per day	4 hours per day
Labor losses from application use	– 0.5 hours per day vs. prior method

Losses per day from application use	– $28.41 per user per day
Losses per day for 1,000 users	– $28,410
Losses per year	$6,250,200
Losses for five years of usage	$31,250,000
Clients previously served per day	12
Clients served due to the software	11
Daily revenue per client	$1,000
Decrease in revenue per day	– $50
Decrease in revenue per year	
Decrease in revenue for five years	– $55,000,000
Total value	– $86,250,000
Total Cost of Ownership	– $47,255,247
Net Value	– $133,505,247
Return on Investment	– $2.85

In this extreme example of the negative impacts of poor quality, a higher total cost of ownership is compounded by a reduction in daily operational efficiency and a loss in revenue due to a reduction in clients served. In other words, the entire project returns a severely negative ROI.

Some readers might think that such grotesquely negative situations might never occur, but unfortunately they do. One of the authors worked as an expert witness in a lawsuit involving software for a state government where monthly transaction rates declined by about 12% as a result of new software, and errors in the transactions increased by more than 30% per month. Even worse, some of the errors involved updating the wrong accounts, which led to incorrect penalties for citizens that should never have been incurred.

A smaller example occurred in the home town of one of the authors, where new software was installed to calculate property taxes. There were so many errors in the software that tax bills were late and a substantial number of bills had errors. Not only were the errors difficult to correct, but the town council was unable to get a clear picture of property tax revenues. Finally, after about a year of frustration, the software was replaced, along with the town financial manager.

The bottom line is that poor-quality software costs more to build and to maintain than high-quality software, and it can also degrade operational performance, increase user error rates, and reduce revenue by decreasing the ability of employees to handle customer transactions or attract additional clients.

For the software industry, not only is quality free as stated by Phil Crosby, but it benefits the entire economic situations of both developers and clients.

References and Readings

CHAPTER 1

Websites

Bureau of Labor Statistics
  www.bls.com
  This is the main source of data on U.S. employment, wages, and trends over time for software as well as for other industries.
Manta
  www.manta.com
  The Manta company is a business intelligence company that provides data and information on 63,778.867 companies around the world. Some of the data is sparse but the volume of useful information is large.
Hoovers Guides to Business
  www.hoovers.com
  The well-known Hoovers Guides provide fairly detailed information about industries and thousands of specific companies. Some of the data included are employment statistics, earnings for public companies, stock exchanges where stocks are traded, and considerably more. Some Hoovers data is available for free, but much more detailed information requires fee-based subscription.

Books and Publications

Boehm, Barry. *Software Engineering Economics*, Prentice Hall, Englewood Cliffs, NJ, 1981.

Brooks, Fred. *The Mythical Man-Month*, Addison-Wesley, Reading, MA, 1974, rev. 1995.

Bundschuh, Manfred and Carol Dekkers. *The IT Measurement Compendium*, Springer-Verlag, Berlin, DE, 2008.

Charette, Bob. *Software Engineering Risk Analysis and Management*, McGraw-Hill, New York, NY, 1989.

Crosby, Philip B. *Quality Is Free*, New American Library, Mentor Books, New York, NY, 1979.

Curtis, Bill, et al. *The People CMM: A Framework for Human Capital Management, Second Edition*, Addison-Wesley, Boston, MA, 2009.

DeMarco, Tom. *Controlling Software Projects*, Yourdon Press, New York, 1982.

Galorath, Dan and Michael W. Evans. *Software Sizing, Estimation, and Risk Management: When Performance Is Measured, Performance Improves*, Auerbach Publishers, Philadelphia, PA, 2006.

Garmus, David and David Herron. *Function Point Analysis—Measurement Practices for Successful Software Projects*, Addison-Wesley, Boston, MA, 2001.

DeMarco, Tom. *Peopleware: Productive Projects and Teams*, Dorset House, New York, NY, 1999.

Gack, Gary. *Managing the Black Hole, The Executive's Guide to Software Project Risk*, Business Expert Publishing, 2010.

Gilb, Tom and Dorothy Graham. *Software Inspections*, Addison-Wesley, Reading, MA, 1993.

Glass, R.L. *Software Runaways: Lessons Learned from Massive Software Project Failures*, Prentice Hall, Englewood Cliffs, NJ, 1998.

Glass, Robert L. *Software Creativity, Second Edition*, developer.*books, Atlanta, GA, 2006.

Humphrey, Watts. *Winning with Software: An Executive Strategy*, Addison-Wesley, Boston, MA, 2002.

——. *Managing the Software Process*, Addison-Wesley, Reading, MA, 1989.

——. *TSP—Leading a Development Team*, Addison-Wesley, Boston, MA, 2006.

——. *PSP: A Self-Improvement Process for Software Engineers*, Addison-Wesley, Boston, MA, 2005.

Jones, Capers. *Applied Software Measurement, Third Edition*, McGraw-Hill, New York, NY, 2008.

——. *Estimating Software Costs*, McGraw-Hill, New York, NY, 2007.

——. *Software Assessments, Benchmarks, and Best Practices*, Addison-Wesley, Boston, MA, 2000.

Kan, Stephen H. *Metrics and Models in Software Quality Engineering, Second Edition*, Addison-Wesley, Boston, MA, 2003.

Kappelman, Leon A. (editor). *The SIM Guide to Enterprise Architecture*, CRC Press, 2009.

Kuhn, Thomas. *The Structure of Scientific Revolutions*, University of Chicago Press, Chicago, IL, 1996.

Levy, Leon S. *Taming the Tiger, Software Engineering and Software Economics*, Springer, 1987.

Love, Tom. *Object Lessons*, SIGS Books, New York, 1993.

McConnell, Steve. *Code Complete*, Microsoft Press, Redmond, WA, 1993.

Myers, Glenford. *The Art of Software Testing*, John Wiley & Sons, New York, NY, 1979.

Pirsig, Robert M. *Zen and the Art of Motorcycle Maintenance*, Harper Collins, New York, NY, 1974.

Pressman, Roger. *Software Engineering—A Practitioner's Approach, Sixth Edition*, McGraw-Hill, New York, NY, 2005.

Starr, Paul. *The Social Transformation of American Medicine*, Basic Books, Perseus Group, 1982.

Strassmann, Paul. *The Squandered Computer*, Information Economics Press, Stamford, CT, 1997.

Weinberg, Gerald M. *The Psychology of Computer Programming*, Van Nostrand Reinhold, New York, NY, 1971.

——. *Becoming a Technical Leader*, Dorset House, New York, NY, 1986.

Yourdon, Ed. *Death March—The Complete Software Developer's Guide to Surviving "Mission Impossible" Projects*, Prentice Hall, Upper Saddle River, NJ, 1997.

——. *Outsource: Competing in the Global Productivity Race*, Prentice Hall, Upper Saddle River, NJ, 2005.

CHAPTER 2

Boehm, Barry. *Software Engineering Economics*, Prentice Hall, Englewood Cliffs, NJ, 1981.

Booch, Grady. *Object Solutions: Managing the Object-Oriented Project*, Addison-Wesley, Reading, MA, 1995.

Capability Maturity Model Integration, Version 1.1, Software Engineering Institute, Carnegie-Mellon Univ., Pittsburgh, PA, Mar. 2003, http://www.sei.cmu.edu/cmmi/.

Brooks, Fred. *The Mythical Man-Month*, Addison-Wesley, Reading, MA, 1974, rev. 1995.

Charette, Bob. *Software Engineering Risk Analysis and Management*, McGraw-Hill, New York, NY, 1989.

——. *Application Strategies for Risk Management*, McGraw-Hill, New York, NY, 1990.

Cohn, Mike. *Agile Estimating and Planning*, Prentice Hall, Upper Saddle River, NJ, 2005.

DeMarco, Tom. *Controlling Software Projects*, Yourdon Press, New York, NY, 1982.

Ewusi-Mensah, Kweku. *Software Development Failures*, MIT Press, Cambridge, MA, 2003.

Galorath, Dan and Michael W. Evans. *Software Sizing, Estimation, and Risk Management: When Performance Is Measured, Performance Improves*, Auerbach Publishing, Philadelphia, PA, 2006.

Glass, R.L. *Software Runaways: Lessons Learned from Massive Software Project Failures*, Prentice Hall, Englewood Cliffs, NJ, 1998.

Harris, Michael, David Herron, and Stacia Iwanicki. *The Business Value of IT: Managing Risks, Optimizing Performance, and Measuring Results*, CRC Press (Auerbach), Boca Raton, FL: 2008.

Humphrey, Watts. *Managing the Software Process*, Addison-Wesley, Reading, MA, 1989.

Johnson, James, et al. The Chaos Report, The Standish Group, West Yarmouth, MA, 2000.

Jones, Capers. *Software Engineering Best Practices*, McGraw-Hill, New York, NY, 2010.

——. *Estimating Software Costs*, McGraw-Hill, New York, NY, 2007.

——. *Assessment and Control of Software Risks*, Prentice Hall, Englewood Cliffs, NJ, 1994.

——. *Patterns of Software System Failure and Success*, International Thomson Computer Press, Boston, MA, 1995.

——. *Software Assessments, Benchmarks, and Best Practices*, Addison-Wesley, Boston, MA, 2000.

——. *Program Quality and Programmer Productivity*, IBM Technical Report TR 02.764, IBM, San Jose, CA, Jan. 1977.

——. *Programming Productivity*, McGraw-Hill, New York, NY, 1986.

——. "Estimating and Measuring Object-Oriented Software," *American Programmer*, 1994.

——. "Why Flawed Software Projects Are Not Cancelled in Time," *Cutter IT Journal*, Vol. 10, No. 12, Dec. 2003, pp. 12-17.

——. "Software Project Management Practices: Failure Versus Success," *Crosstalk*, Vol. 19, No. 6, June 2006, pp. 4-8.

Laird, Linda M. and Carol M. Brennan, *Software Measurement and Estimation: A Practical Approach*, John Wiley & Sons, Hoboken, NJ, 2006.

Park, Robert E., et al. *Software Cost and Schedule Estimating—A Process Improvement Initiative*, Technical Report CMU/SEI 94-SR-03, Software Engineering Institute, Pittsburgh, PA, May 1994.

——. *Checklists and Criteria for Evaluating the Costs and Schedule Estimating Capabilities of Software Organizations*, Technical Report CMU/SEI 95-SR-005, Software Engineering Institute, Pittsburgh, PA, Jan. 1995.

McConnell, Steve. *Software Estimating: Demystifying the Black Art*, Microsoft Press, Redmond, WA, 2006.

Roetzheim, William H. and Reyna A. Beasley. *Best Practices in Software Cost and Schedule Estimation*, Prentice Hall, Saddle River, NJ, 1998.

Strassmann, Paul. *Information Productivity*, Information Economics Press, Stamford, CT, 1999.

——. *Information Payoff*, Information Economics Press, Stamford, CT, 1985.

——. *Governance of Information Management: The Concept of an Information Constitution, Second Edition* (eBook), Information Economics Press, Stamford, CT, 2004.

——. *The Squandered Computer*, Information Economics Press, Stamford, CT, 1997.

Stukes, Sherry, et al. *Air Force Cost Analysis Agency Software Estimating Model Analysis*, TR-9545/008-2, Contract F04701-95-D-0003, Task 008, Management Consulting & Research, Inc., Thousand Oaks, CA 91362, Sept. 30, 1996.

Symons, Charles R. *Software Sizing and Estimating—Mk II FPA (Function Point Analysis)*, John Wiley & Sons, Chichester, UK, 1991.

Wellman, Frank. *Software Costing: An Objective Approach to Estimating and Controlling the Cost of Computer Software*, Prentice Hall, Englewood Cliffs, NJ, 1992.

Whitehead, Richard. *Leading a Development Team*, Addison-Wesley, Boston, MA, 2001.

Yourdon, Ed. *Death March—The Complete Software Developer's Guide to Surviving "Mission Impossible" Projects*, Prentice Hall, Upper Saddle River, NJ, 1997.

——. *Outsource: Competing in the Global Productivity Race*, Prentice Hall, Upper Saddle River, NJ, 2005.

Books and Readings on Measurements and Metrics

Abran, Alain and Reiner R. Dumke. *Innovations in Software Measurement*, Springer Verlag, Aachen, DE, 2005.

Abran, Alain, et al. *Software Measurement News*, Vol. 13, No. 2, Oct. 2008 (periodical).

Bundschuh, Manfred and Carol Dekkers. *The IT Measurement Compendium*, Springer-Verlag, Berlin, DE, 2008.

Chidamber, S.R. and C.F. Kemerer. "A Metrics Suite for Object-Oriented Design," *IEEE Trans. on Software Engineering*, Vol. SE20, No. 6, June 1994, pp. 476-493.

Dumke, Reiner, et al. (editors). *Software Process and Product Measurement*, Springer-Verlag, Berlin, 2008.

Ebert, Christof and Reiner Dumke. *Software Measurement: Establish, Extract, Evaluate, Execute*, Springer-Verlag, Berlin, DE, 2007.

Garmus, David and David Herron. *Measuring the Software Process: A Practical Guide to Functional Measurement*, Prentice Hall, Englewood Cliffs, NJ, 1995.

——. *Function Point Analysis—Measurement Practices for Successful Software Projects*, Addison-Wesley, Boston, MA, 2001.

IFPUG Counting Practices Manual, Release 4, International Function Point Users Group, Westerville, OH, Apr. 1995.

International Function Point Users Group (IFPUG). *IT Measurement—Practical Advice from the Experts*, Addison-Wesley, Boston, MA, 2002.

Jones, Capers. *Applied Software Measurement, Third Edition*, McGraw-Hill, New York, NY, 2008.

——. "Sizing Up Software," *Scientific American Magazine*, Vol. 279, No. 6, Dec. 1998.

——. "A Short History of the Lines of Code Metric", Version 4.0, May 2008, Capers Jones & Associates LLC, Narragansett, RI, 15 pages (monograph).

Kemerer, C.F. "Reliability of Function Point Measurement—A Field Experiment," *Communications of the ACM*, Vol. 36, 1993, pp. 85-97.

Parthasarathy, M.A. *Practical Software Estimation—Function Point Metrics for Insourced and Outsourced Projects*, Infosys Press, Addison-Wesley, Upper Saddle River, NJ, 2007.

Putnam, Lawrence H. *Measures for Excellence—Reliable Software on Time, Within Budget*, Yourdon Press, Prentice Hall, Englewood Cliffs, NJ, 1992.

Putnam, Lawrence H. and Ware Myers. *Industrial Strength Software—Effective Management Using Measurement*, IEEE Press, Los Alamitos, CA, 1997.

Stein, Timothy R. *The Computer System Risk Management Book and Validation Life Cycle*, Paton Press, Chico, CA, 2006.

Stutzke, Richard D. *Estimating Software-Intensive Systems*, Addison-Wesley, Upper Saddle River, NJ, 2005.

Books and Readings on Architecture, Requirements, and Design

Ambler, S. *Process Patterns—Building Large-Scale Systems Using Object Technology*, Cambridge University Press, SIGS Books, 1998.

Arlow, J. and I. Neustadt. *UML and the Unified Process*, Addison-Wesley, Boston, MA, 2000.

Bass, Len, et al. *Software Architecture in Practice*, Addison-Wesley, Boston, MA, 1997.

Berger, Arnold S. *Embedded Systems Design: An Introduction to Processes, Tools, and Techniques*, CMP Books, 2001.

Booch, Grady, et al. *The Unified Modeling Language User Guide, Second Edition*, Addison-Wesley, Boston, MA, 2005.

Cohn, Mike. *User Stories Applied: For Agile Software Development*, Addison-Wesley, Boston, MA, 2004.

Curtis, B., et al. "Third time charm: Stronger prediction of programmer performance by software complexity metrics," *Proceedings of the Fourth International Conference on Software Engineering*, Washington, DC: IEEE Computer Society, pp. 356-360, 1979.

Fernandini, Patricial L. *A Requirements Pattern, Succeeding in the Internet Economy*, Addison-Wesley, Boston, MA, 2002.

Gamma, Erich, et al. *Design Patterns: Elements of Reusable Object-Oriented Design*, Addison-Wesley, Boston MA, 1995.

Inmon, William, et al. *Data Stores, Data Warehousing, and the Zachman Framework*, McGraw-Hill, New York, NY, 1997.

Marks, Eric and Michael Bell. *Service-Oriented Architecture (SOA): A Planning and Implementation Guide for Business and Technology*, John Wiley & Sons, New York, 2006.

Martin, James and Carma McClure. *Diagramming Techniques for Analysts and Programmers*, Prentice Hall, Englewood Cliffs, NJ, 1985.

Nygard, M.T. *Release It! Design and Deploy Production-Ready Software*, Pragmatic Bookshelf, 2007.

Orr, Ken. *Structured Requirements Definition*, Ken Orr and Associates, Inc., Topeka, KS, 1981.

Robertson, Suzanne and James Robertson. *Mastering the Requirements Process, Second Edition*, Addison-Wesley, Boston, MA, 2006.

Spinellis, Diomidis. *Code Quality: The Open Source Perspective*, Addison-Wesley, Boston, MA, 2006.

Warnier, Jean-Dominique. *Logical Construction of Systems*, Van Nostrand Reinhold, London, UK.

Wiegers, Karl E. *Software Requirements, Second Edition*, Microsoft Press, Bellevue, WA, 2003.

Books and Readings on Software Quality Control

Albrecht, A.J. "Measuring Application Development Productivity," *Proceedings of the Joint SHARE/GUIDE IBM Applications Development Symposium*, pp. 83-92, IBM, 1979.

Beck, Kent. *Test-Driven Development*, Addison-Wesley, Boston, MA, 2002.

Boehm, Barry. *Characteristics of Software Quality*, Elsevier Science Ltd., 1978.

Chelf, Ben and Raoul Jetley. "Diagnosing Medical Device Software Defects Using Static Analysis," *Coverity Technical Report*, San Francisco, CA, 2008.

Chess, Brian and Jacob West. *Secure Programming with Static Analysis*, Addison-Wesley, Boston, MA, 2007.

Cohen, Lou. *Quality Function Deployment—How to Make QFD Work for You*, Prentice Hall, Upper Saddle River, NJ, 1995.

Crosby, Philip B. *Quality Is Free*, New American Library, Mentor Books, New York, NY, 1979.

Everett, Gerald D. and Raymond McLeod. *Software Testing*, John Wiley & Sons, Hoboken, NJ, 2007.

Gack, Gary. *Applying Six Sigma to Software Implementation Projects*, http:// software.isixsigma.com/library/content/c040915b.asp.

Gilb, Tom and Dorothy Graham. *Software Inspections*, Addison-Wesley, Reading, MA, 1993.

Hamill, M. and K. Goseva-Popstojanova. "Common faults in software fault and failure data." *IEEE Transactions of Software Engineering*, 35 (4), pp. 484-496, 2009.

Hallowell, David L. *Six Sigma Software Metrics, Part 1.*, http://software. isixsigma.com/library/content/03910a.asp.

International Organization for Standards. ISO 9000 / ISO 14000, http://www. iso.org/iso/en/iso9000-14000/index.html.

Jones, Capers. *Software Quality—Analysis and Guidelines for Success*, International Thomson Computer Press, Boston, MA, 1997.

Jackson, D.J. "A direct path to dependable software," *Communications of the ACM*, 52 (4), 2009.

Kan, Stephen H. *Metrics and Models in Software Quality Engineering, Second Edition*, Addison-Wesley, Boston, MA, 2003.

Land, Susan K, et al. *Practical Support for Lean Six Sigma Software Process Definition: Using IEEE Software Engineering Standards*, Wiley-Blackwell, 2008.

Mosley, Daniel J. *The Handbook of MIS Application Software Testing*, Yourdon Press, Prentice Hall, Englewood Cliffs, NJ, 1993.

Myers, Glenford. *The Art of Software Testing*, John Wiley & Sons, New York, NY, 1979.

Nandyal, Raghav. *Making Sense of Software Quality Assurance*, Tata McGraw-Hill Publishing, New Delhi, India, 2007.

Radice, Ronald A. *High Quality, Low Cost Software Inspections*, Paradoxicon Publishing, Andover, MA, 2002.

Wiegers, Karl E. *Peer Reviews in Software—A Practical Guide*, Addison-Wesley, Boston, MA, 2002.

CHAPTER 3

Beck, Kent. *Test-Driven Development*, Addison-Wesley, Boston, MA, 2002.

Chelf, Ben and Raoul Jetley. "Diagnosing Medical Device Software Defects Using Static Analysis," *Coverity Technical Report*, San Francisco, CA, 2008.

Chess, Brian and Jacob West. *Secure Programming with Static Analysis*, Addison-Wesley, Boston, MA, 2007.

Cohen, Lou. *Quality Function Deployment—How to Make QFD Work for You*, Prentice Hall, Upper Saddle River, NJ, 1995.

Crosby, Philip B. *Quality Is Free*, New American Library, Mentor Books, New York, NY, 1979.

Curtis, Bill, et al. *The People CMM: A Guide for Human Capital Management* (Kindle Edition), Addison-Wesley, Boston, MA, 2009.

Everett, Gerald D. and Raymond McLeod. *Software Testing*, John Wiley & Sons, Hoboken, NJ, 2007.

Gack, Gary. *Managing the Black Hole: An Executive Guide to Software Risks*, Business Expert Publishing, New York, NY.

——. *Applying Six Sigma to Software Implementation Projects*, http://software.isixsigma.com/library/content/c040915b.asp.

Gilb, Tom and Dorothy Graham. *Software Inspections*, Addison-Wesley, Reading, MA, 1993.

Hallowell, David L. *Six Sigma Software Metrics, Part 1*, http://software.isixsigma.com/library/content/03910a.asp.

International Organization for Standards. ISO 9000 / ISO 14000, http://www.iso.org/iso/en/iso9000-14000/index.html.

Jones, Capers. *Software Engineering Best Practices*, McGraw-Hill, New York, NY, 2010.

——. *Assessment and Control of Software Risks*, Prentice Hall, Englewood Cliffs, NJ, 1994.

——. *Software Quality—Analysis and Guidelines for Success*, International Thomson Computer Press, Boston, MA, 1997.

Kan, Stephen H. *Metrics and Models in Software Quality Engineering, Second Edition*, Addison-Wesley, Boston, MA, 2003.

Land, Susan K., et al. *Practical Support for Lean Six Sigma Software Process Definition: Using IEEE Software Engineering Standards*, Wiley-Blackwell, 2008.

Mosley, Daniel J. *The Handbook of MIS Application Software Testing*, Yourdon Press, Prentice Hall, Englewood Cliffs, NJ, 1993.

Myers, Glenford. *The Art of Software Testing*, John Wiley & Sons, New York, NY, 1979.

Nandyal, Raghav. *Making Sense of Software Quality Assurance*, Tata McGraw-Hill Publishing, New Delhi, India, 2007.

Radice, Ronald A. *High Quality, Low Cost Software Inspections*, Paradoxicon Publishing, Andover, MA, 2002.

Wiegers, Karl E. *Peer Reviews in Software—A Practical Guide*, Addison-Wesley, Boston, MA, 2002.

CHAPTER 4

Albrecht, A.J. *"Measuring Application Development Productivity,"* Proceedings of the Joint SHARE/GUIDE IBM Applications Development Symposium, pp. 83-92, IBM, 1979.

Beck, Kent. *Test-Driven Development*, Addison-Wesley, Boston, MA, 2002.

Ben-Menachem, M. and G.S. Marliss. *Software Quality, Producing Practical and Consistent Software*, International Thomson Computer Press, 1997.

Chelf, Ben and Raoul Jetley. "Diagnosing Medical Device Software Defects Using Static Analysis," *Coverity Technical Report*, San Francisco, CA, 2008.

Chess, Brian and Jacob West. *Secure Programming with Static Analysis*, Addison-Wesley, Boston, MA, 2007.

Chidamber, S. and C. Kemerer. "A Metrics Suite for Object Oriented Design," *IEEE Transactions on Software Engineering*, 20 (6), pp. 476-493, 1994.

Cohen, Lou. *Quality Function Deployment——How to Make QFD Work for You*, Prentice Hall, Upper Saddle River, NJ, 1995.

Crosby, Philip B. *Quality Is Free*, New American Library, Mentor Books, New York, NY, 1979.

Curtis, Bill, et al. *The People CMM: A Guide for Human Capital Management* (Kindle Edition), Addison-Wesley, Boston, MA, 2009.

Everett, Gerald D. and Raymond McLeod. *Software Testing*, John Wiley & Sons, Hoboken, NJ, 2007.

Gack, Gary. *Managing the Black Hole: An Executive Guide to Software Risks*, Business Expert Publishing, New York, NY, 2010.

——. *Applying Six Sigma to Software Implementation Projects*, http://software.isixsigma.com/library/content/c040915b.asp.

Gilb, Tom and Dorothy Graham. *Software Inspections*, Addison-Wesley, Reading, MA, 1993.

Hallowell, David L. *Six Sigma Software Metrics, Part 1*, http://software.isixsigma.com/library/content/03910a.asp.

Halstead, M.E. *Elements of Software Science*, Elsevier, North-Holland, NY, 1977.

International Organization for Standards. ISO 9000 / ISO 14000, http://www. iso.org/iso/en/iso9000-14000/index.html.

Jones, Capers. *Software Engineering Best Practices*, McGraw-Hill, New York, NY, 2010.

——. *Assessment and Control of Software Risks*, Prentice Hall, Englewood Cliffs, NJ, 1994.

——. *Software Quality—Analysis and Guidelines for Success*, International Thomson Computer Press, Boston, MA, 1997.

Kan, Stephen H. *Metrics and Models in Software Quality Engineering, Second Edition*, Addison-Wesley, Boston, MA, 2003.

Land, Susan K., et al. *Practical Support for Lean Six Sigma Software Process Definition: Using IEEE Software Engineering Standards*, Wiley-Blackwell, 2008.

Martin, R. "Managing vulnerabilities in networked systems," *IEEE Computer*, 2001.

McCabe, T. "A complexity measure," *IEEE Transactions on Software Engineering*, Dec. 1976.

Mosley, Daniel J. *The Handbook of MIS Application Software Testing*, Yourdon Press, Prentice Hall, Englewood Cliffs, NJ, 1993.

Myers, Glenford. *The Art of Software Testing*, John Wiley & Sons, New York, 1979.

Nandyal, Raghav. *Making Sense of Software Quality Assurance*, Tata McGraw-Hill Publishing, New Delhi, India, 2007.

Nygard, M.T. *Release It! Design and Deploy Production-Ready Software*, Pragmatic Bookshelf, 2007.

Park, R.E. "Software Size Measurement: A Framework for Counting Source Statements," CMU/SEI-92-TR-020, Software Engineering Institute, Carnegie Mellon University, 1992.

Poppendieck, Mary and Tom Poppendieck. *Leading Lean Software Development: Results Are Not the Point*, Addison-Wesley, Boston, MA, 2009.

Radice, Ronald A. *High Quality Low Cost Software Inspections*, Paradoxicon Publishing, Andover, MA, 2002.

Wiegers, Karl E. *Peer Reviews in Software—A Practical Guide*, Addison-Wesley, Boston, MA, 2002.

CHAPTER 5

Beck, Kent. *Test-Driven Development*, Addison-Wesley, Boston, MA, 2002.

Black, Rex. *Critical Testing Processes: Plan, Prepare, Perform, Perfect*, Addison-Wesley, Boston, MA, 2003.

——. *Pragmatic Software Testing: Becoming an Effective and Efficient Test Professional*, Wiley, 2007.

——. *Managing the Testing Process: Practical Tools and Techniques for Managing Hardware and Software Testing*, Wiley, 2009.

——. *Advanced Software Testing Volumes 1, 2, and 3*: Rocky Nook (volume 1).

Chelf, Ben and Raoul Jetley. "Diagnosing Medical Device Software Defects Using Static Analysis," *Coverity Technical Report*, San Francisco, CA, 2008.

Chess, Brian and Jacob West. *Secure Programming with Static Analysis*, Addison-Wesley, Boston, MA, 2007.

Cohen, Lou. *Quality Function Deployment—How to Make QFD Work for You*, Prentice Hall, Upper Saddle River, NJ, 1995.

Crispin, Lisa and Janet Gregory. *Agile Testing: A Practical Guide for Testers and Agile Teams*, Addison-Wesley, Boston, MA, 2009.

Crosby, Philip B. *Quality Is Free*, New American Library, Mentor Books, New York, NY, 1979.

Everett, Gerald D. and Raymond McLeod. *Software Testing*, John Wiley & Sons, Hoboken, NJ, 2007.

Gack, Gary. *Managing the Black Hole: The Executive's Guide to Software Project Risk*, Business Expert Publishing, Thomason, GA, 2010.

——. *Applying Six Sigma to Software Implementation Projects*, http://software.isixsigma.com/library/content/c040915b.asp.

Gilb, Tom and Dorothy Graham. *Software Inspections*, Addison-Wesley, Reading, MA, 1993.

Hallowell, David L. *Six Sigma Software Metrics, Part 1*, http://software.isixsigma.com/library/content/03910a.asp.

International Organization for Standards. ISO 9000 / ISO 14000, http://www.iso.org/iso/en/iso9000-14000/index.html.

Jones, Capers. *Software Engineering Best Practices*, McGraw-Hill, New York, NY, 2010.

——. *Software Quality—Analysis and Guidelines for Success*, International Thomson Computer Press, Boston, MA, 1997.

Kan, Stephen H. *Metrics and Models in Software Quality Engineering, Second Edition*, Addison-Wesley, Boston, MA, 2003.

Land, Susan K., et al. *Practical Support for Lean Six Sigma Software Process Definition: Using IEEE Software Engineering Standards*, Wiley-Blackwell, 2008.

Mosley, Daniel J. *The Handbook of MIS Application Software Testing*, Yourdon Press, Prentice Hall, Englewood Cliffs, NJ, 1993.

Myers, Glenford. *The Art of Software Testing*, John Wiley & Sons, New York, NY, 1979.

Nandyal, Raghav. *Making Sense of Software Quality Assurance*, Tata McGraw-Hill Publishing, New Delhi, India, 2007.

Radice, Ronald A. *High Quality, Low Cost Software Inspections*, Paradoxicon Publishing, Andover, MA, 2002.

Japanese Union of Scientists and Engineers. *SQuBOK Guide—Guide to the Software Quality Body of Knowledge*, Omsha Publishing, Tokyo, Japan, 2007.

Poppendieck, Mary and Tom Poppendieck. *Leading Lean Software Development: Results Are Not the Point*, Addison-Wesley, Boston, MA, 2009.

Wiegers, Karl E. *Peer Reviews in Software—A Practical Guide*, Addison-Wesley, Boston, MA, 2002.

CHAPTER 6

Arnold, Robert S. *Software Reengineering*, IEEE Computer Society Press, Los Alamitos, CA, 1993.

Arthur, Lowell Jay. *Software Evolution—The Software Maintenance Challenge*, John Wiley & Sons, New York, NY, 1988.

Gallagher, R.S. *Effective Customer Support*, International Thomson Computer Press, Boston, MA, 1997.

Parikh, Girish. *Handbook of Software Maintenance*, John Wiley & Sons, New York, NY, 1986.

Pigoski, Thomas M. *Practical Software Maintenance—Best Practices for Managing Your Software Investment*, IEEE Computer Society Press, Los Alamitos, CA, 1997.

Sharon, David. *Managing Systems in Transition—A Pragmatic View of Reengineering Methods*, International Thomson Computer Press, Boston, MA, 1996.

Takang, Armstrong and Penny Grubh. *Software Maintenance Concepts and Practice*, International Thomson Computer Press, Boston, MA, 1997.

Ulrich, William M. *Legacy Systems: Transformation Strategies*, Prentice Hall, Upper Saddle River, NJ, 2002.

CHAPTER 7

Black, Rex. *Critical Testing Processes*, Addison-Wesley, Reading, MA, 2003.

——. *Foundations of Software Testing*, International Thomson, Boston, MA, 2008.

——. *Managing the Testing Process*, Wiley, New York, NY, 2009.

Charette, Bob. *Software Engineering Risk Analysis and Management*, McGraw-Hill, New York, NY, 1989.

——. *Application Strategies for Risk Management*, McGraw-Hill, New York, NY, 1990.

DeMarco, Tom. *Controlling Software Projects*, Yourdon Press, New York, NY, 1982.

Everett, Gerald D. and Raymond McLeod. *Software Testing—Testing Across the Entire Software Development Life Cycle*, IEEE Press, 2007.

Ewusi-Mensah, Kweku. *Software Development Failures*, MIT Press, Cambridge, MA, 2003.

Flowers, Stephen. *Software Failures: Management Failures, Amazing Stories and Cautionary Tales*, John Wiley & Sons, New York, NY, 1996.

Gack, Gary. *Managing the Black Hole: The Executive's Guide to Managing Risk*, Business Expert Publishing, Thomson, GA, 2010.

Galorath, Dan and Michael Evans. *Software Sizing, Estimation, and Risk Management: When Performance Is Measured Performance Improves*, Auerbach, Philadelphia, PA, 2006.

Garmus, David and David Herron. *Function Point Analysis—Measurement Practices for Successful Software Projects*, Addison-Wesley, Boston, MA, 2001.

Gibbs, T. Wayt. "Trends in Computing: Software's Chronic Crisis," Scientific American Magazine, 271(3), Intl. Edition, pp. 72-81, Sept. 1994.

Gilb, Tom and Dorothy Graham. *Software Inspections*, Addison-Wesley, Reading, MA, 1993.

Glass, R.L. *Software Runaways: Lessons Learned from Massive Software Project Failures*, Prentice Hall, Englewood Cliffs, NJ, 1998.

Harris, Michael, et al. *The Business Value of IT: Managing Risks, Optimizing Performance, and Measuring Results*, CRC Press, Boca Raton, FL, 2008.

Hill, Peter (editor). *Practical Software Project Estimation*, McGraw-Hill, New York, NY, 2011.

International Function Point Users Group (IFPUG). *IT Measurement—Practical Advice from the Experts*, Addison-Wesley, Boston, MA, 2002.

Johnson, James, et al. The Chaos Report, The Standish Group, West Yarmouth, MA, 2000.

Jones, Capers. *Software Engineering Best Practices: Lessons from Successful Projects in Top Companies*, McGraw-Hill, New York, NY, 2010.

——. *Applied Software Measurement, Third Edition*, McGraw-Hill, New York, NY, 2008.

——. *Assessment and Control of Software Risks*, Prentice Hall, Upper Saddle River, NJ, 1994.

——. *Patterns of Software System Failure and Success*, International Thomson Computer Press, Boston, MA, Dec. 1995.

——. *Software Quality—Analysis and Guidelines for Success*, International Thomson Computer Press, Boston, MA, 1997.

——. *Estimating Software Costs*, McGraw-Hill, New York, NY, 2007.

——. *Software Assessments, Benchmarks, and Best Practices*, Addison-Wesley, Boston, MA, 2000.

——. "Sizing Up Software," Scientific American Magazine, Volume 279, No. 6, pp. 104-111, Dec. 1998.

——. *Conflict and Litigation Between Software Clients and Developers*, Software Productivity Research technical report, Narragansett, RI, 2007.

Kan, Stephen H. *Metrics and Models in Software Quality Engineering, Second Edition*, Addison-Wesley, Boston, MA, 2003.

Pressman, Roger. *Software Engineering—A Practitioner's Approach, Sixth Edition*, McGraw-Hill, New York, NY, 2005.

Radice, Ronald A. *High Quality, Low Cost Software Inspections*, Paradoxicon Publishing, Andover, MA, 2002.

Wiegers, Karl E. *Peer Reviews in Software—A Practical Guide*, Addison-Wesley, Boston, MA, 2002.

Yourdon, Ed. *Death March—The Complete Software Developer's Guide to Surviving "Mission Impossible" Projects*, Prentice Hall, Upper Saddle River, NJ, 1997.

——. *Outsource: Competing in the Global Productivity Race*, Prentice Hall, Upper Saddle River, NJ, 2005.

Index

Addison Wesley

REGISTER

THIS PRODUCT

informit.com/register

Register the Addison-Wesley, Exam Cram, Prentice Hall, Que, and Sams products you own to unlock great benefits.

To begin the registration process, simply go to **informit.com/register** to sign in or create an account. You will then be prompted to enter the 10- or 13-digit ISBN that appears on the back cover of your product.

Registering your products can unlock the following benefits:

- Access to supplemental content, including bonus chapters, source code, or project files.
- A coupon to be used on your next purchase.

Registration benefits vary by product. Benefits will be listed on your Account page under Registered Products.

About InformIT — THE TRUSTED TECHNOLOGY LEARNING SOURCE

INFORMIT IS HOME TO THE LEADING TECHNOLOGY PUBLISHING IMPRINTS Addison-Wesley Professional, Cisco Press, Exam Cram, IBM Press, Prentice Hall Professional, Que, and Sams. Here you will gain access to quality and trusted content and resources from the authors, creators, innovators, and leaders of technology. Whether you're looking for a book on a new technology, a helpful article, timely newsletters, or access to the Safari Books Online digital library, InformIT has a solution for you.

THE TRUSTED TECHNOLOGY LEARNING SOURCE

Addison-Wesley | Cisco Press | Exam Cram
IBM Press | Que | Prentice Hall | Sams

SAFARI BOOKS ONLINE

informIT.com
THE TRUSTED TECHNOLOGY LEARNING SOURCE

PEARSON

InformIT is a brand of Pearson and the online presence for the world's leading technology publishers. It's your source for reliable and qualified content and knowledge, providing access to the top brands, authors, and contributors from the tech community.

Addison-Wesley · Cisco Press · EXAM/CRAM · IBM Press. · QUE · PRENTICE HALL · SAMS · Safari Books Online

---

LearnIT at InformIT

Looking for a book, eBook, or training video on a new technology? Seeking timely and relevant information and tutorials? Looking for expert opinions, advice, and tips? **InformIT has the solution.**

- Learn about new releases and special promotions by subscribing to a wide variety of newsletters.
  Visit **informit.com/newsletters**.

- Access FREE podcasts from experts at **informit.com/podcasts**.

- Read the latest author articles and sample chapters at **informit.com/articles**.

- Access thousands of books and videos in the Safari Books Online digital library at **safari.informit.com**.

- Get tips from expert blogs at **informit.com/blogs**.

Visit **informit.com/learn** to discover all the ways you can access the hottest technology content.

Are You Part of the IT Crowd?

Connect with Pearson authors and editors via RSS feeds, Facebook, Twitter, YouTube, and more! Visit **informit.com/socialconnect**.

informIT.com THE TRUSTED TECHNOLOGY LEARNING SOURCE

PEARSON

Addison-Wesley · Cisco Press · EXAM/CRAM · IBM Press. · QUE · PRENTICE HALL · SAMS · Safari Books Online

Try Safari Books Online FREE

Get online access to 5,000+ Books and Videos

FREE TRIAL—GET STARTED TODAY!
www.informit.com/safaritrial

Find trusted answers, fast

Only Safari lets you search across thousands of best-selling books from the top technology publishers, including Addison-Wesley Professional, Cisco Press, O'Reilly, Prentice Hall, Que, and Sams.

Master the latest tools and techniques

In addition to gaining access to an incredible inventory of technical books, Safari's extensive collection of video tutorials lets you learn from the leading video training experts.

WAIT, THERE'S MORE!

Keep your competitive edge

With Rough Cuts, get access to the developing manuscript and be among the first to learn the newest technologies.

Stay current with emerging technologies

Short Cuts and Quick Reference Sheets are short, concise, focused content created to get you up-to-speed quickly on new and cutting-edge technologies.

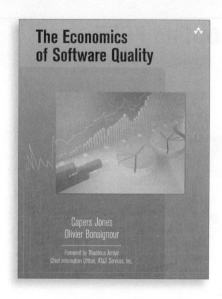

FREE Online
Edition

Your purchase of *The Economics of Software Quality* includes access to a free online edition for 45 days through the Safari Books Online subscription service. Nearly every Addison-Wesley Professional book is available online through Safari Books Online, along with more than 5,000 other technical books and videos from publishers such as Cisco Press, Exam Cram, IBM Press, O'Reilly, Prentice Hall, Que, and Sams.

SAFARI BOOKS ONLINE allows you to search for a specific answer, cut and paste code, download chapters, and stay current with emerging technologies.

Activate your FREE Online Edition at
www.informit.com/safarifree

> **STEP 1:** Enter the coupon code: FLMOZBI.

> **STEP 2:** New Safari users, complete the brief registration form.
> Safari subscribers, just log in.

If you have difficulty registering on Safari or accessing the online edition,
please e-mail customer-service@safaribooksonline.com